THE PAPERS OF ULYSSES S. GRANT

THE PAPERS OF

ULYSSES S. GRANT

Volume 25: 1874

Edited by John Y. Simon

ASSISTANT EDITORS

William M. Ferraro

Aaron M. Lisec

TEXTUAL EDITOR

Dawn Vogel

━━

SOUTHERN ILLINOIS UNIVERSITY PRESS

CARBONDALE AND EDWARDSVILLE

Library of Congress Cataloging in Publication Data (Revised)

Grant, Ulysses Simpson, Pres. U.S., 1822–1885.
   The papers of Ulysses S. Grant.

   Prepared under the auspices of the Ulysses S. Grant Association.
   Bibliographical footnotes.
      CONTENTS: v. 1. 1837–1861.—v. 2. April–September 1861.—
   v. 3. October 1, 1861–January 7, 1862.—v. 4. January 8–March 31,
   1862.—v. 5. April 1–August 31, 1862.—v. 6. September 1–December 8, 1862.—v. 7. December 9, 1862–March 31, 1863.—v. 8.
   April 1–July 6, 1863.—v. 9. July 7–December 31, 1863.—v. 10. January 1–May 31, 1864.—v. 11. June 1–August 15, 1864.—v. 12.
   August 16–November 15, 1864.—v. 13. November 16, 1864–February 20, 1865.—v. 14. February 21–April 30, 1865.—v. 15. May 1–
   December 31, 1865.—v. 16. 1866.—v. 17. January 1–September 30,
   1867.—v. 18. October 1, 1867–June 30, 1868.—v. 19. July 1, 1868–
   October 31, 1869.—v. 20. November 1, 1869–October 31, 1870.—
   v. 21. November 1, 1870–May 31, 1871.—v. 22. June 1, 1871–January 31, 1872.—v. 23. February 1–December 31, 1872.—v. 24. 1873.
   —v. 25. 1874.

      1. Grant, Ulysses Simpson, Pres. U.S., 1822–1885. 2. United
   States—History—Civil War, 1861–1865—Campaigns and battles—
   Sources. 3. United States—Politics and government—1869–1877—
   Sources. 4. Presidents—United States—Biography. 5. Generals—
   United States—Biography. I. Simon, John Y., ed. II. Ulysses S. Grant
   Association.
   E660.G756   1967   973.8'2'0924   67-10725
   ISBN 0-8093-2498-9 (v. 25)

The paper used in this publication meets the minimum requirements
of American National Standard for Information Sciences—Permanence of Paper for Printed Library Materials, ANSI Z39.48-1992. ∞

Published with the assistance of a grant from the National Historical
Publications and Records Commission.

Contents

———

Introduction

———

ULYSSES S. GRANT BEGAN 1874 with a diplomatic suc-
cess as he announced to Congress that Spain had agreed to settle the
Virginius affair on terms "moderate and just, and calculated to cement
the good relations which have so long existed between Spain and the
United States." The country's brief bout of war fever, precipitated
after Spain seized the *Virginius* off Cuba and executed part of the
crew and passengers as insurgents, faded away when Spain surrendered both ship and survivors and promised to pay limited claims.

Other developments at the start of the year were less gratifying.
Grant nominated Caleb Cushing, a veteran lawyer and diplomat, as
chief justice. A letter then surfaced showing that Cushing had cor-
responded with Jefferson Davis in early 1861 on behalf of a friend
seeking appointment in the Confederate government, compelling
Grant to withdraw Cushing's name in favor of an obscure Ohio lawyer, Morrison R. Waite.

An election dispute in Texas foreshadowed the end of Reconstruction. The Republican governor challenged his recent defeat and
asked for troops to back his claims. Grant refused. "The act of the
legislature of Texas providing for the recent election having received your approval and both political parties having made nominations and having conducted a political campaign under its provisions, would it not be prudent as well as right to yield to the verdict
of the people as expressed by their ballots." Without federal support,
the Republican party in Texas essentially collapsed.

The recent financial panic had hampered fund-raising for the Centennial and threatened to delay the construction of exhibition buildings in Philadelphia. Grant challenged Congress—in vain—to appropriate enough money to match the efforts of previous European hosts. "Let us have a complete success in our centennial exposition, or suppress it in its infancy, acknowledging our inability to give it the international character to which our self-esteem aspires."

In March, South Carolina whites chafing under Republican rule gathered at a taxpayers' convention and then sent a delegation to Grant. Maligned by a speaker at the convention, an angry Grant told the delegates he could do nothing. "But what is the cause of the evils in your State may be a question worth considering. Whether a part of that cause is not due to yourselves, whether it is not due to the extreme views which you have held, whether your own action has not consolidated the non-tax-paying portion of your community against you, are questions which I leave for your own consideration."

In April, the "Brooks-Baxter War" between Arkansas gubernatorial contestants Joseph Brooks and Elisha Baxter again tested Grant. Baxter, the Republican, had legislative backing, while Brooks, the Democrat, found support in the courts. Grant tried to remain neutral, but as armed bands opposed each other across the state, he became involved. "I urgently request that all armed forces on both sides be disbanded, so that the General Assembly may act free from any military pressure or influence. The United States will give all necessary protection to the legislature and prevent, as far as practicable, all violence and disturbance of the public peace." Attorney General George H. Williams affirmed the state legislature's jurisdiction, and on May 15 Grant proclaimed Baxter governor.

Grant continued to hope that the nation could move to a politics rooted in principles rather than race. "Treat the Negro as a citizen and a voter—as he is, and must remain—and soon parties will be divided, *not on the color line*, but on principle. Then we will have a Union not calling for interference in one section that would not be exercised under like circumstances in any other." In a passage he later omitted from his 1874 annual message, Grant envisioned the reconciliation of north and south. "Public opinion will have more to do with the settlement of all questions of feeling that unsettle us sectionally. Let the North see the good and not always the bad in south-ern state affairs; and let the better class of society South condemn, and aid in bring to justice, the violaters of the law, good order & good morals, and of the public peace, and there will be but a short dura-tion of existing trouble."

In reality, a sharp increase in violence throughout the south pre-ceded the midterm elections as Democrats struggled to regain power. Newspaper accounts of atrocities and letters from victims troubled Grant at his seaside retreat in Long Branch. He advised Secretary of War William W. Belknap to consult with the attorney general on the best course to curb violence. "The recent atrocities in the South, particularly in Louisiana, Alabama and South Carolina, show a dis-regard for law, civil rights and personal protection that ought not to be tolerated in any civilized government. It looks as if, unless speed-ily checked, matters must become worse, and life and property there will receive no protection from the local authorities until such au-thority becomes powerless."

Grant favored moving Indians to the Indian Territory, a place he visited in the fall and called "that truly beautiful garden." Some tribes thought differently about their allotted lands. Roving Cheyennes, Kiowas, Comanches, and Arapahoes crossed into Kansas and Texas and clashed with settlers. Troops retaliated in a campaign that lasted until October, when most of the Indians surrendered. Elsewhere, Grant's peace policy held. In Dakota Territory, however, Lieutenant Colonel George A. Custer led an expedition to scout the Black Hills, and the news he brought back of gold discoveries launched a pros-pectors' rush that angered the Sioux.

The issue of specie resumption dominated politics in the first half of 1874. Set amid economic depression, the debate pitted "soft money" interests, chiefly small merchants and farmers from the midwest and west, against "hard money" advocates, led by eastern financiers. The latter strove to return the country to the gold standard and retire the greenbacks—paper money issued to help pay for the Civil War. Such a course favored lenders over borrowers. Early in the debate, Grant favored this approach, advocating "immediate, permanent, un-repealable steps" to end the system of "irredeemable" currency.

Still, when Congress passed a bill that some judged inflationary,

Grant prepared to sign it and penned a message justifying his approval. "It cannot be claimed that the legislation has been hasty, for it has been discussed by Congress almost from its earlyest meeting in December last, and by the press of the Country, and writers on finance even before that. I have nowhere heard it claimed that the law is unconstitutional. Under these circumstances an executive should feel very sure of his ground before defeating the will of the Majority by his Veto." Then, apparently unconvinced by his own rationale, Grant discarded this message and drafted a veto instead. Capitalists greeted Grant's veto with resounding praise. Congress resumed debate and passed a compromise bill that Grant signed in June. Angry opponents, including farmers beset by grasshoppers and floods and desperate for relief from debt and low commodity prices, flocked to the new Greenback party and the Grange.

In a year when Mark Twain and Charles Dudley Warner published *The Gilded Age*, Grant cast his lot with the captains of industry. He scolded the attorney general for overzealous prosecution of a suit for penalties against Western Union Telegraph and ordered the acting postmaster general to speed up inspection of two new steamships slated for service with the Pacific Mail Company. American interests in the Pacific were again highlighted in December, when Grant entertained King Kalakaua of Hawaii at the White House and reported to Congress on Samoa, where a State Department agent had made commercial overtures to local chiefs.

Grant's farm near St. Louis continued to lose money. In June, he wrote his new manager. "As I have not heard from you recently I write to make some enquiries and to make one or two conditional suggestions. First, I would like to know how you have the farm planted this season? the condition of crops, fruit &c. Next, I would ask the condition of the stock, how the mares have been bred, whether they are supposed to be in foal &c." The operation remained unprofitable, and Grant eyed possible returns from a Chicago real estate venture. "I have got to sell mine right along from the 4th of March /77 to get something to live upon. That land and my farm are the bulk of my estate and must be put in a condition to produce something when my salary seases."

In October, when Grant attended the St. Louis fair, judges awarded first prize to one of his horses. Even the friendly local press complained. John McDonald, appointed revenue supervisor by Grant, later described his role in fixing the contest. McDonald also alleged that he paid Grant's hotel bills on this visit and gave the president a valuable team of horses and a buggy, masking this gift as a transaction. True or not, Grant's choice of friends later came back to haunt him. On the same trip west, Grant stopped in Springfield, Illinois, for the dedication of a monument to Abraham Lincoln. His short speech, centered on the personal attacks Lincoln endured, reflected as much on the speaker as on his subject.

Grant retained his sense of humor. Julia C. Conkling, wife of Senator Roscoe Conkling of New York, saw this side of the president in a letter of invitation. "Mrs. Grant & I will be pleased if we can have you & Miss Bessie spend next week with us at the Branch, where we will try to make your time pass pleasantly. Bring the Senator too, *just for company while traveling*, and to look after the baggage." He also poked fun at his wealthy Philadelphia friends when he invited Adolph E. Borie to stay at the White House. "I would like to have Childs or Drexel with you. But they are poor men and must work,—without loss of time—for their living."

Two of Grant's four children were married in 1874. In May, Grant gave away daughter Ellen (Nellie) at a White House ceremony. In October, eldest son Frederick Dent married a Chicago socialite. Grant praised his new daughter-in-law, the former Ida M. Honoré. "Fred's wife is beautiful and is spoken of by all her acquaintances, male & female, young & old, as being quite as charming for her manners, amiability, good sense & education as she is for her beauty." Ulysses, Jr., continued at Harvard, and Jesse entered Cornell. Grant was proud of his children. "As my children are all leaving me it is gratifying to know that, so far, they give good promise. They are all of good habits and are very popular with their acquaintances and associates."

A happy family life balanced ups and downs Grant experienced as president, but challenges loomed. Black Hills gold augured confrontation with the Sioux. Postelection violence in Mississippi and

Louisiana forced him to send more troops. Republican losses in November meant that Democrats would control the next House of Representatives. Yet Grant remained resolute and optimistic. "I think the republican party will grow stronger as the days lengthen and the nights shorten. I feel very confident for the future of our country and party."

We are indebted to J. Dane Hartgrove and Michael T. Meier for assistance in searching the National Archives; to Harriet F. Simon for proofreading; and to Dana McDonald and Matt Olsen, graduate students at Southern Illinois University, for research assistance.

Financial support for the period during which this volume was prepared came from Southern Illinois University, the National Endowment for the Humanities, and the National Historical Publications and Records Commission.

JOHN Y. SIMON

August 17, 2001

Editorial Procedure

1. Editorial Insertions

A.   Words or letters in roman type within brackets represent editorial reconstruction of parts of manuscripts torn, mutilated, or illegible.

B.   [. . .] or [— — —] within brackets represent lost material which cannot be reconstructed. The number of dots represents the approximate number of lost letters; dashes represent lost words.

C.   Words in *italic* type within brackets represent material such as dates which were not part of the original manuscript.

D.   Other material crossed out is indicated by ~~cancelled type~~.

E.   Material raised in manuscript, as "4th," has been brought in line, as "4th."

2. Symbols Used to Describe Manuscripts

AD	Autograph Document
ADS	Autograph Document Signed
ADf	Autograph Draft
ADfS	Autograph Draft Signed
AES	Autograph Endorsement Signed
AL	Autograph Letter
ALS	Autograph Letter Signed
ANS	Autograph Note Signed
D	Document
DS	Document Signed

Df	Draft
DfS	Draft Signed
ES	Endorsement Signed
LS	Letter Signed

3. *Military Terms and Abbreviations*

Act.	Acting
Adjt.	Adjutant
AG	Adjutant General
AGO	Adjutant General's Office
Art.	Artillery
Asst.	Assistant
Bvt.	Brevet
Brig.	Brigadier
Capt.	Captain
Cav.	Cavalry
Col.	Colonel
Co.	Company
C.S.A.	Confederate States of America
Dept.	Department
Div.	Division
Gen.	General
Hd. Qrs.	Headquarters
Inf.	Infantry
Lt.	Lieutenant
Maj.	Major
Q. M.	Quartermaster
Regt.	Regiment or regimental
Sgt.	Sergeant
USMA	United States Military Academy, West Point, N.Y.
Vols.	Volunteers

4. *Short Titles and Abbreviations*

ABPC	*American Book Prices Current* (New York, 1895–)
Badeau	Adam Badeau, *Grant in Peace. From Appomattox to Mount McGregor* (Hartford, Conn., 1887)
CG	*Congressional Globe.* Numbers following represent the Congress, session, and page.

J. G. Cramer	Jesse Grant Cramer, ed., *Letters of Ulysses S. Grant to his Father and his Youngest Sister, 1857–78* (New York and London, 1912)
DAB	*Dictionary of American Biography* (New York, 1928–36)
Foreign Relations	*Papers Relating to the Foreign Relations of the United States* (Washington, 1869–)
Garland	Hamlin Garland, *Ulysses S. Grant: His Life and Character* (New York, 1898)
Julia Grant	John Y. Simon, ed., *The Personal Memoirs of Julia Dent Grant* (New York, 1975)
HED	*House Executive Documents*
HMD	*House Miscellaneous Documents*
HRC	*House Reports of Committees.* Numbers following *HED, HMD,* or *HRC* represent the number of the Congress, the session, and the document.
Ill. AG Report	J. N. Reece, ed., *Report of the Adjutant General of the State of Illinois* (Springfield, 1900)
Johnson, Papers	LeRoy P. Graf and Ralph W. Haskins, eds., *The Papers of Andrew Johnson* (Knoxville, 1967–)
Lewis	Lloyd Lewis, *Captain Sam Grant* (Boston, 1950)
Lincoln, Works	Roy P. Basler, Marion Dolores Pratt, and Lloyd A. Dunlap, eds., *The Collected Works of Abraham Lincoln* (New Brunswick, 1953–55)
Memoirs	*Personal Memoirs of U. S. Grant* (New York, 1885–86)
Nevins, Fish	Allan Nevins, *Hamilton Fish: The Inner History of the Grant Administration* (New York, 1936)
O.R.	*The War of the Rebellion: A Compilation of the Official Records of the Union and Confederate Armies* (Washington, 1880–1901)
O.R. (Navy)	*Official Records of the Union and Confederate Navies in the War of the Rebellion* (Washington, 1894–1927). Roman numerals following *O.R.* or *O.R.* (Navy) represent the series and the volume.
PUSG	John Y. Simon, ed., *The Papers of Ulysses S. Grant* (Carbondale and Edwardsville, 1967–)
Richardson	Albert D. Richardson, *A Personal History of Ulysses S. Grant* (Hartford, Conn., 1868)
SED	*Senate Executive Documents*
SMD	*Senate Miscellaneous Documents*

SRC	*Senate Reports of Committees.* Numbers following *SED*, *SMD*, or *SRC* represent the number of the Congress, the session, and the document.
USGA Newsletter	*Ulysses S. Grant Association Newsletter*
Young	John Russell Young, *Around the World with General Grant* (New York, 1879)

5. *Location Symbols*

CLU	University of California at Los Angeles, Los Angeles, Calif.
CoHi	Colorado State Historical Society, Denver, Colo.
CSmH	Henry E. Huntington Library, San Marino, Calif.
CSt	Stanford University, Stanford, Calif.
CtY	Yale University, New Haven, Conn.
CU-B	Bancroft Library, University of California, Berkeley, Calif.
DLC	Library of Congress, Washington, D.C. Numbers following DLC-USG represent the series and volume of military records in the USG papers.
DNA	National Archives, Washington, D.C. Additional numbers identify record groups.
IaHA	Iowa State Department of History and Archives, Des Moines, Iowa.
I-ar	Illinois State Archives, Springfield, Ill.
IC	Chicago Public Library, Chicago, Ill.
ICarbS	Southern Illinois University, Carbondale, Ill.
ICHi	Chicago Historical Society, Chicago, Ill.
ICN	Newberry Library, Chicago, Ill.
ICU	University of Chicago, Chicago, Ill.
IHi	Illinois State Historical Library, Springfield, Ill.
In	Indiana State Library, Indianapolis, Ind.
InFtwL	Lincoln National Life Foundation, Fort Wayne, Ind.
InHi	Indiana Historical Society, Indianapolis, Ind.
InNd	University of Notre Dame, Notre Dame, Ind.
InU	Indiana University, Bloomington, Ind.
KHi	Kansas State Historical Society, Topeka, Kan.
MdAN	United States Naval Academy Museum, Annapolis, Md.
MeB	Bowdoin College, Brunswick, Me.
MH	Harvard University, Cambridge, Mass.

MHi	Massachusetts Historical Society, Boston, Mass.
MiD	Detroit Public Library, Detroit, Mich.
MiU-C	William L. Clements Library, University of Michigan, Ann Arbor, Mich.
MoSHi	Missouri Historical Society, St. Louis, Mo.
NHi	New-York Historical Society, New York, N.Y.
NIC	Cornell University, Ithaca, N.Y.
NjP	Princeton University, Princeton, N.J.
NjR	Rutgers University, New Brunswick, N.J.
NN	New York Public Library, New York, N.Y.
NNP	Pierpont Morgan Library, New York, N.Y.
NRU	University of Rochester, Rochester, N.Y.
OClWHi	Western Reserve Historical Society, Cleveland, Ohio.
OFH	Rutherford B. Hayes Library, Fremont, Ohio.
OHi	Ohio Historical Society, Columbus, Ohio.
OrHi	Oregon Historical Society, Portland, Ore.
PCarlA	U.S. Army Military History Institute, Carlisle Barracks, Pa.
PHi	Historical Society of Pennsylvania, Philadelphia, Pa.
PPRF	Rosenbach Foundation, Philadelphia, Pa.
RPB	Brown University, Providence, R.I.
TxHR	Rice University, Houston, Tex.
USG 3	Maj. Gen. Ulysses S. Grant 3rd, Clinton, N.Y.
USMA	United States Military Academy Library, West Point, N.Y.
ViHi	Virginia Historical Society, Richmond, Va.
ViU	University of Virginia, Charlottesville, Va.
WHi	State Historical Society of Wisconsin, Madison, Wis.
Wy-Ar	Wyoming State Archives and Historical Department, Cheyenne, Wyo.
WyU	University of Wyoming, Laramie, Wyo.

Chronology
1874

———

JAN. 12. USG refused to send troops to Tex., where defeated Republicans balked at conceding power.

JAN. 13. USG withdrew the nomination of Caleb Cushing as chief justice, U.S. Supreme Court.

JAN. 19. USG nominated Morrison R. Waite as chief justice.

JAN. 29. USG met delegates from the National Education Association.

FEB. 13. USG purchased a lot in Washington, D.C., reportedly to build a house for his retirement.

FEB. 25. USG challenged Congress to either fund the Centennial celebration in Philadelphia or "suppress it in its infancy."

FEB. 27. USG read to his cabinet a draft veto of pending legislation to expand the currency.

MAR. 3. USG pardoned three Buffalo men convicted of registering Susan B. Anthony and other women to vote in 1872.

MAR. 13. USG attended the funeral of Charles Sumner, who had died two days earlier.

MAR. 24. USG attended the funeral of his brother-in-law Lewis Dent, who died March 22 in Washington, D.C.

MAR. 27. An Osage delegation met USG at the White House. USG rebuked visitors from an S.C. taxpayers' convention, where a speaker had attacked him. "I have never seen a speech equal to it in malignity, vileness, falsity, and slander. When I think of it, I can scarcely restrain myself."

APRIL 3. USG traveled to New York City.

APRIL 18. USG recommended that Congress continue funding the Civil Service Commission and ordered U.S. troops in Ark. to protect telegraph lines in a dispute between two gubernatorial contenders.

APRIL 22.   Overcoming his own qualms and a divided cabinet, USG vetoed the controversial Legal Tender Act to expand paper currency, citing fears of inflation. USG instead advocated specie resumption, or the redemption of greenbacks in coin.

APRIL 23.   USG signed legislation to aid victims of spring flooding along the Mississippi River.

MAY 7.   Elihu B. Washburne, minister to France, declined consideration for secretary of the treasury.

MAY 15.   USG proclaimed Elisha Baxter as Ark. governor, over Joseph Brooks.

MAY 21.   Ellen Grant married Algernon Sartoris at the White House.

MAY 22–23.   USG and family visited New York City, where the newlyweds embarked for England.

JUNE 1.   USG nominated Benjamin H. Bristow as secretary of the treasury, replacing William A. Richardson.

JUNE 2.   USG laid the cornerstone for the Museum of Natural History in New York City.

JUNE 3.   Mandan and Arikara chiefs visited the White House.

JUNE 13–15.   USG and party spent the weekend at Cape May, N.J.

JUNE 18.   USG sent a treaty regulating trade with Canada to the Senate, which declined to act.

JUNE 20.   USG signed a compromise currency bill intended to better distribute the nation's money supply.

JUNE 22.   USG approved legislation creating a commission to study levees and flood protection on the lower Mississippi River.

JUNE 23.   Congress adjourned.

JUNE 24.   Postmaster Gen. John A. J. Creswell resigned, the last member of USG's original cabinet.

JUNE 25–30.   USG and Julia Dent Grant toured West Va., stopping in White Sulphur Springs and Charleston.

JULY 1.   The first typewriter went on sale in the U.S., priced at $125.

JULY 2.   USG designated Marshall Jewell, minister to Russia, to succeed Creswell as postmaster gen.

JULY 3.   USG selected a commission to study navigation at the mouth of the Mississippi River.

JULY 4.   USG and family arrived at their Long Branch summer home.

JULY 4.   The Eads Bridge opened at St. Louis.

JULY 12. William S. Hillyer, USG's friend and wartime aide, died in Washington, D.C.

JULY 13. USG interceded on behalf of the Western Union Telegraph Co. in a dispute with the Justice Dept. USG and party traveled to Saratoga Springs, N.Y., to attend weeklong regatta festivities.

JULY 14. USG and Orville E. Babcock watched a Yale-Harvard baseball game at Saratoga Springs.

JULY 15. USG and Julia Grant attended a camp meeting at Round Lake, N.Y.

JULY 22. USG attended a Grand Army of the Republic reunion at Paterson, N.J.

JULY 25–27. USG and party visited Atlantic City, N.J.

AUG. 26. USG and party left New York City for Newport, R.I., aboard the *City of Peking*.

AUG. 27–31. USG and party attended a Methodist camp meeting at Martha's Vineyard, Mass., and visited Cape Cod and Nantucket.

SEPT. 2. USG wrote that "recent atrocities" in southern states showed a disregard for law "that ought not to be tolerated in any civilized government." On Sept. 3, Attorney Gen. George H. Williams ordered federal officials in southern states to protect lives and civil rights.

SEPT. 5. Blacks in La., citing persecution, petitioned USG for resettlement in a new territory or in Africa.

SEPT. 12. USG returned to Washington, D.C.

SEPT. 14. USG entertained fellow members of the Aztec Club, composed of officers from the Mexican War. In New Orleans, armed "White Leaguers," challenging Governor William P. Kellogg, battled state and city militia.

SEPT. 15. Forgoing plans to return to Long Branch, USG issued a proclamation ordering lawless elements in La. to disperse.

SEPT. 17. USG ordered U.S. troops and naval vessels to New Orleans.

SEPT. 22. Secretary of State Hamilton Fish submitted his resignation, which he later withdrew upon USG's urging.

SEPT. 25. USG and Julia Grant moved back into the White House, which had undergone summer repairs.

SEPT. 27–30. USG and Julia Grant visited New York City.

OCT. 1. USG and Julia Grant attended the Washington wedding of Minnie Sherman (daughter of Gen. William T. Sherman) and Thomas W. Fitch, a navy engineering officer.

Oct. 3.   USG and Julia Grant, Adolph E. and Elizabeth M. Borie, and Babcock left the capital for the west.

Oct. 5–10.   At St. Louis, USG and party attended an agricultural fair. A local paper protested that a blue ribbon awarded to USG's horse "was given as a compliment to the President and not to the animal."

Oct. 11–12.   Touring the Indian Territory by train, USG greeted gatherings of Cherokees, Choctaws, and Creeks.

Oct. 14–15.   USG attended an Army of the Tennessee reunion at Springfield, Ill. On Oct. 15, at the dedication of a monument to Abraham Lincoln, USG praised Lincoln's magnanimity in the face of "obloquy, personal abuse and hate undisguised," and his tendency "to find excuses for his adversaries."

Oct. 20.   At Chicago, USG attended the wedding of Frederick Dent Grant and Ida M. Honoré.

Oct. 24.   USG returned to Washington, D.C.

Nov. 3.   Republicans lost control of the House of Representatives at midterm elections.

Nov. 18.   The Women's Christian Temperance Union organized in Cleveland.

Nov. 21.   USG attended a Baltimore lecture on George Washington.

Nov. 25.   The Greenback party formed in Indianapolis.

Dec. 7.   In his annual message to Congress, USG reiterated his support for specie resumption. John McDonald, St. Louis revenue supervisor, accompanied USG on a carriage ride.

Dec. 9.   USG declined a request for U.S. troops to intervene in La.

Dec. 10.   A Navajo delegation visited the White House.

Dec. 13.   Under the pseudonym "Sylph," Babcock telegraphed to McDonald concerning a plan to send treasury agents to investigate St. Louis whiskey frauds. "I succeeded. They will not go."

Dec. 18.   USG welcomed King Kalakaua of Hawaii to the White House.

Dec. 21.   Responding to violence at Vicksburg, USG ordered lawless elements to disperse.

Dec. 22.   USG hosted a state dinner for King Kalakaua.

Dec. 24.   USG ordered Lt. Gen. Philip H. Sheridan to New Orleans to investigate unrest in La. and Miss.

The Papers of Ulysses S. Grant
1874

To Congress

To the Senate and House of Representatives:

In my annual message of December last I gave reason to expect that when the full and accurate text of the correspondence relating to the steamer Virginius, which had been telegraphed in cipher, should be received, the papers concerning the capture of the vessel, the execution of a part of its passengers and crew, and the restoration of the ship and the survivors would be transmitted to Congress.

In compliance with the expectations then held out, I now transmit the papers and correspondence on that subject.

On the 26th day of September, 1870, the Virginius was registered in the custom-house at New York as the property of a citizen of the United States, he having first made oath, as required by law, that he was "the true and only owner of the said vessel, and that there was no subject or citizen of any foreign prince or state directly or indirectly, by way of trust, confidence, or otherwise, interested therein."

Having complied with the requisites of the statute in that behalf, she cleared in the usual way for the port of Curaçoa, and on or about the 4th day of October, 1870, sailed for that port. It is not disputed that she made the voyage according to her clearance, nor that, from that day to this, she has not returned within the territorial jurisdiction of the United States. It is also understood that she preserved her American papers, and that when within foreign ports she made the practice of putting forth a claim to American nationality, which was recognized by the authorities at such ports.

When, therefore, she left the port of Kingston, in October last, under the flag of the United States, she would appear to have had, as against all powers except the United States, the right to fly that flag, and to claim its protection, as enjoyed by all regularly documented vessels registered as part of our commercial marine.

No state of war existed, conferring upon a maritime power the right to molest and detain upon the high seas a documented vessel; and it cannot be pretended that the Virginius had placed herself without the pale of all law by acts of piracy against the human race.

If her papers were irregular or fraudulent, the offense was one against the laws of the United States, justiciable only in their tribunals.

When, therefore, it became known that the Virginius had been captured on the high seas by a Spanish man-of-war; that the American flag had been hauled down by the captors; that the vessel had been carried to a Spanish port; and that Spanish tribunals were taking jurisdiction over the persons of those found on her, and exercising that jurisdiction upon American citizens, not only in violation of the rules of international law, but in contravention of the provisions of the treaty of 1795, I directed a demand to be made upon Spain for the restoration of the vessel, and for the return of the survivors to the protection of the United States, for a salute to the flag, and for the punishment of the offending parties.

The principles upon which these demands rested could not be seriously questioned, but it was suggested by the Spanish government that there were grave doubts whether the Virginius was entitled to the character given her by her papers; and that therefore it might be proper for the United States, after the surrender of the vessel and the survivors, to dispense with the salute to the flag, should such fact be established to their satisfaction.

This seemed to be reasonable and just. I therefore assented to it, on the assurance that Spain would then declare that no insult to the flag of the United States had been intended.

I also authorized an agreement to be made that, should it be shown to the satisfaction of this Government that the Virginius was improperly bearing the flag, proceedings should be instituted in our courts for the punishment of the offense committed against the United States. On her part Spain undertook to proceed against those who had offended the sovereignty of the United States, or who had violated their treaty rights.

The surrender of the vessel and the survivors to the jurisdiction of the tribunals of the United States was an admission of the principles upon which our demands had been founded. I therefore had no hesitation in agreeing to the arrangement finally made between the two Governments—an arrangement which was moderate and just, and calculated to cement the good relations which have so long existed between Spain and the United States.

Under this agreement the Virginius, with the American flag flying, was delivered to the Navy of the United States at Bahia Honda, in the island of Cuba, on the 16th ultimo. She was in an unseaworthy condition. In the passage to New York she encountered one of the most tempestuous of our winter storms. At the risk of their lives the officers and crew placed in charge of her attempted to keep her afloat. Their efforts were unavailing and she sank off Cape Fear. The prisoners who survived the massacres were surrendered at Santiago de Cuba on the 18th ultimo, and reached the port of New York in safety.

The evidence submitted on the part of Spain to establish the fact that the Virginius at the time of her capture was improperly bearing the flag of the United States is transmitted herewith, together with the opinion of the Attorney-General thereon, and a copy of the note of the Spanish minister, expressing, on behalf of his government, a disclaimer of an intent of indignity to the flag of the United States.

U. S. GRANT.

WASHINGTON, *January* 5, 1874.

HED, 43-1-30. See *PUSG*, 24, 244–53.

On Nov. 20, 1874, Secretary of State Hamilton Fish wrote to USG. "I have the honor to lay before you a copy of a correspondence between the British Chargé d'Affaires at Madrid and the Spanish Minister of Foreign Affairs in relation to the indemnity claimed by Great Britian for British subjects who were captured on board to Virginius and were slain at Santiago de Cuba. This correspondence comes into my possession confidentially, but through a well informed and trustworthy channel, and may, be relied upon as substantially, although probably not a literally, accurate, translation of the originals. I shall transmit a copy to Gen. Cushing, for his information as well as for the purpose of accurate verification of the text of the letters, if this be practicable. I am very credibly assured, through other sources that the payment of the sum promised to be paid to Great Britian in August last had not been made up to the seventh instant." Copy, DNA, RG 59, Reports to the President and Congress. *Foreign Relations, 1875*, p. 1228. For correspondence mentioned in this letter and related items, see *ibid.*, pp. 1228–34; Hamilton Fish diary, Nov. 19, 1874, DLC-

Hamilton Fish. On Nov. 20, Fish recorded in his diary. "I bring up 'Virginius' matter, . . . & state fully the substance of interview whichith Mantilla as recorded yesterday—Call attention to the confidential nature of the communication & read the notes passing between British Chargé at Madrid & Minister of State, which he left with me & asks instructions from President whether to make a proposal similar to that made by Great Britain—Subject considered generally by Cabinet & President authorizes a proposal to receive $2500 for each American citizen shot—Robeson thinks a larger sum might be claimed in order to receive more than Great Britain has received—I replied that $2500 is more than £500 & that Great Britain accepted £300 for 9 out of 19 of her subjects   I further object to offering a premium for filibustering by claiming too large an indemnity for those who may suffer from its consequences—In case of arbitration, it is understood the specific questions to be submitted be defined—" *Ibid.* Indemnity negotiations continued. See Hamilton Fish diary, Nov. 25, 28, Dec. 3, 5, 11, 1874, *ibid.*; *Foreign Relations, 1875*, pp. 1235–46.

On Feb. 24, 1875, Fish recorded in his diary. "Having received from Cushing by telegraph the text of the notes which passed between him and Castro of the 11th & 15th insts and the proposed text of the final agreement for settlement of the Virginius claim I carry them to the President and read them to him   He expresses a most cordial and earnest approval and authorizes my telegraphing to Cushing to sign the final agreement." DLC-Hamilton Fish. On March 15, USG wrote to the Senate. "In answer to the resolution of the Senate of the 12th of March instant, I herewith transmit a report from the Secretary of State, with accompanying correspondence." Copies, DNA, RG 59, Reports to the President and Congress; *ibid.*, RG 130, Messages to Congress. On the same day, Fish had written to USG "that the question of the indemnity demanded from Spain for such of the Ship's Company of the Virginius as were executed or detained by the Spanish authorities, and for such of the passengers executed as were citizens of the U. S., has been disposed of by an agreement entered into between Mr. Cushing the Minister of the U. S. at Madrid and the Minister of Foreign Affairs, as will appear from the correspondence on the subject herewith transmitted." Copy, *ibid.* A list of the enclosures is *ibid.* On May 4, Fish recorded in his diary. "Mr Mantillia the Spanish Minister presented his new credentials from King Alfonso making what was unusual on such occasions a formal speech from a written memorandum I had told the President before the presentation that he would so do but had prepared no reply for him not wishing him to make a formal speech but suggested that he should express his satisfaction at the anticipation on the part of the Spanish Government of the payment on the Virginius indemnity. After Mantillia read his speech the President made a very admirable reply expressing his satisfaction that the new King had continued a Minister so acceptable as himself, that he was glad to hear of the prospect of restoring peace to Spain and expressed feelings of friendship for the Sovereign and the people of Spain and of satisfaction in contemplating the relations between the two Governments. That he especially was gratified at the course of Spain in anticipating the payments due under the late convention which he accepted not only as evidence of their good faith but of their determination to meet all their convention obligations and that it gave him an assurance of the early & satisfactory settlement of all questions between the two Governments & concluded by saying that he hoped for a long time the Minister of Spain might find it pleasant to continue in his present position." DLC-Hamilton Fish. At a cabinet meeting on May 7, Fish recorded in his diary that he "read Cushings telegram of May 5th announcing the payment of the balance of the Virginius Indemnity: also his dispatch #349 of April 16th on the subject of the payment at that time of a sum of money on account of the indemnity." *Ibid.* On July 21, USG issued an order regulating distribution of the $80,000 indemnity.

Copy, DNA, RG 59, Miscellaneous Letters. See *Foreign Relations, 1875*, pp. 1247–56; *HED*, 45-1-15.

On May 7, John G. Ryan, Chicago, had written to USG. "Your humble servant would most respectfully inquire what is the *modus operandi* to be proceeded with to recover the portion of the *Virginius indemnity* to which his family is entitled. He would state that he is the brother of the (Gen.) W. A. C. Ryan who was among the *murdered* at Santiago de Cuba, Nov. 4, '73. He would further most respectfully state that his reason for this intrusion upon your excellency is the fact that he is under the impression that it is to your excellency direct that application has to be made in the premises before mentioned. Hoping this will be received favorably by your excellency." ALS, DNA, RG 59, Miscellaneous Letters. See *SRC*, 47-1-485.

On Nov. 15, Alejandro Calvo, Richmond, petitioned USG "that he was captured while on the 'Virginius' by the Spanish Man of War 'Tornado.' That he was born at Havana Cuba on the 24th April 1835 & is now forty years old—that he is a Cigar Maker by trade. He served from 17th May 1861 till July 23rd 1862 in Co: I 39th New York Vols & was honorably discharged. He was imprisoned by the Spanish brutally treated & sentenced to be shot & except for the intervention of the U. S. Consul would have been executed—He was a Citizen of New York City at the time he took passage & engaged passage for Costa Rica —He further represents that he has always claimed this country as his home—Your petitioner prays that your Excellency will make such an award to him as will to your excellency appear right & just" DS, DNA, RG 59, Miscellaneous Letters. No award followed.

On Nov. 22, Ramon R. De Armas, New York City, wrote to USG. "The undersigned, American citizen and one of the passengers of the ill-fated Steamer 'Virginnius,' before Y. E. appears and says, that sometime in August last, and through the Agency of Mess. Casanova's & Cotterill, his statement and papers of his case, were duly filled with the Department of State at Washington; That said statement and papers were done up according to the circular which the State Department sent to the undersigned for him to apply for a distributive share of the 'Virginnius' indemnity fund; That some time in October last the undersigned received from the State Department a paper purporting to be a final settlement for his full share in the indemnity fund aforesaid; That the undersigned declined to accept the paltry sum of $250. as a payment in full offor his claim and respectfully returned said paper to the party it came from, . . . " ALS, *ibid.* Alleging fraud in the distribution of the indemnity fund, De Armas claimed higher compensation for property seized and "an incurable heart disease, brought about by long imprisonment in damp dungeons, bad food and ill treatment, and which incapacitate him for all active work as long as his life last." *Ibid.* A related letter is *ibid.* De Armas received $250 in March, 1876. See *SED*, 49-2-82, 8.

On July 10, Philip Meitzler, former *Virginius* passenger, Charleston, S. C., wrote to USG. "If you have the kindness and give me some information about the claims of the S. S. Virginius I really must say I think it is wrong for me to receive no more than $250 00 out of $80.000 in g[*old*] and besides I am the only one who has defended the American flag and I am a young man that has lost my good health . . . " ALS, DNA, RG 59, Miscellaneous Letters.

To Samuel M. Shoemaker

Washington, D. C. Jany. 6. 1874

DEAR SIR:

I am in receipt of your very kind invitation to be present at a dinner to be given by the Baltimore Shoe & Leather Board of Trade on the 8th inst. and regret that my official duties will not permit me to be present.

I trust that the occasion may be a very happy one, and that the great commercial interest represented by the Board may very soon be entirely relieved from the effects which, in common with all interests and industries of the country, it has suffered from the late financial embarrassments.

Again thanking you
I am very truly
U. S. GRANT

MR. S. M. SHOEMAKER BALTO. MD.

Copy, DLC-USG, II, 2. Samuel M. Shoemaker was a founder of the Adams Express Co. On Jan. 2, 1874, Orville E. Babcock wrote to Shoemaker, Baltimore. "The President requests me to acknowledge the receipt of your favor containing the complimentary Frank over the Adams Express Co's. lines for the year 1874, and to thank you for the continued courtesy." Copy, *ibid.*

On May 20, 1873, Tuesday, Shoemaker had telegraphed to USG. "The General Assembly, Presbyterian Church now in session here, desire to call upon you on Thursday, between two and three o'clock. Will you receive them at that hour?" Telegram received, *ibid.*, IB. On May 26, Babcock wrote to Secretary of State Hamilton Fish to arrange such a visit on May 28. LS, DNA, RG 59, Miscellaneous Letters. See Fish diary, May 28, 1873, DLC-Hamilton Fish.

To Secretary, Philomathean Society

Washington, D. C. Jany 10th 1874

MY DEAR MISS:

Your letter of the 11th of December was duly received, and would have been answered earlier but for sickness in my house, and death shortly after. I now however take pleasure in answering your enquiry as to the date of my birth—the 27th of April 1822—a very long time ago you will say; and to forward you a book for the society of which you are Secretary. But you do not give your name so that I can only direct this to your title.

Hoping that your Society may prosper, and prove of great benefit in developing the literary tastes and attainments of its members,

I subscribe myself
Very truly yours,
U S GRANT.

Copy, DLC-USG, II, 2. A note was added to this letter: "The following written in the book (E B Browning's Poems) & letter & book sent by Express Jan. 12. 'Contributed to the Philomathean Society, St. Mary's, Columbus, Ohio. U. S. Grant.'" Copy, *ibid.* St. Mary's Catholic Church, Columbus, Ohio, organized in 1863, probably housed the Philomathean Society.

To Edmund J. Davis

Washington D. C. Jany 12th *1874*

GOVR DAVIS,
AUSTIN TEXAS.

Your dispatches and letters reciting the action of the Supreme Court of Texas in declaring the late election unconstitutional and ~~predicting trouble~~ asking the use of troops to prevent apprehended violence, are received. The call is not made in accordance with the Constitution of the United States, and Acts of Congress under it, and Cannot therefore be granted. The act of the legislature of Texas providing for the recent election having received your approval and both political parties having made nominations and having conducted a political campaign under its provisions, would it not be prudent as well as right to yield to the verdict of the people as expressed by their ballots.

U. S. GRANT

ADf, DLC-USG, IB. On Jan. 6, 1874, Governor Edmund J. Davis of Tex. wrote to USG. "Governor A. J. Hamilton will take with him a copy of the decision of the Supreme Court of this State rendered yesterday touching our recent State election. Though personally I would have preferred that this question should not have been brought into the Court, and had myself, taken a different view of the law, yet it is sufficient to say that the decision was rendered in a case properly within the jurisdiction of the Court and I suppose must be taken by the State authorities as settling the construction to be given the election provision of our State Constitution. I am in no way interested in this question excepting as a citizen desirous that there shall be no confusion of authority or public disturbance My term ends on the 28th of April next, and though our Constitution looks to the holding of the office till my 'successor shall be duly qualified,' it would not be agreeable to me to give that clause such construction as would continue my possession of the office beyond the reasonable delay necessary in turning over to my legitimate successor. If another election were had I would not again be a candidate (and believe the other Republican candidates for State offices would take the same course) because while there were, undoubtedly, great wrongs and frauds perpetrated by our opponents who controlled the registry and the ballot boxes, in much the most of the counties, yet I am inclined to think they might have beaten all of the State ticket even had they acted with perfect fairness and honesty. Probably then the result of another election would be about the same for State officers, but with an election fairly conducted it would by no means be so in regard to many local officers and members of the Legislature. There were also certain amendments of the State Constitution submitted and voted on at this election. One of these amendments is *now* said to provide for the *abolition* of the present Supreme Court. Its terms are so vague that it might be so construed by a political party trying to get rid of them. These amendments are believed to have received a majority of the votes cast, and they add especially to the difficulties of the situation. If another election is to be had there is no way clear to that end unless by an Enabling Act of Congress. The old election law has been repealed and the Governor has no express authority given him anywhere to order one. Should he under his general authority to see that the laws are enforced, assume to do this, there is no guarantee that his action would be accepted as binding. I refer to to these facts so as to give you a more complete understanding of the situation and because the disentanglement of the embroglio may have to come from Washington. I do not see how otherwise an issue can be avoided. The new Legislature will I suppose try to meet on the 13th inst., (the regular day of meeting.) It will attempt to legislate and to elect a U. S. Senator in place of Mr Flanagan. A distinct expression of opinion as to the course to be pursued, coming from the National Administration and leading men of the majority in Congress, in default of an Enabling act, might, I think, be accepted and followed by all parties here and prevent trouble." LS, DNA, RG 60, Letters Received, Tex. On Jan. 11 and 12, Davis telegraphed to USG. "The Supreme Court of Texas having decided the late Election for legislature &c of state a nullity this may cause here a conflict of authority   those claiming to be the newly elected legislature will attempt to organize and legislate on tuesday next whilst many of the old or thirteenth legislature also propose at the same time assume legislative functions   the authority of neither is recognized   a display of U. S troops will be most likely to keep the peace till the trouble is settled   I therefore request that assistance   on *sixth* inst I wrote you fully about situation" "There is no such domestic Violence Existing as defined in Constitution and act of Congress consequently I cannot call for assistance under that authority. My request was made to secure peace and as preventative of such violence threatened here as result of foolish Counsels and inflamed public feeling. I do not propose personally as I wrote you to make any objections to late election but do not perceive how I can with propriety disregard the decision of the Supreme Court and recognize the body to assemble tomorrow as legal but if Congress and yourself accept it as such I suppose everybody here will finally acquiese," Telegrams received (at 10:35 P.M. and on Jan. 13), *ibid*. On Jan. 5, Davis had written to Adolph Zadek, secretary, Republican Executive Committee, Washington, D. C. "The Supreme Court as I telegraphed you to day decided that the recent election was unconstitutional and null and void. Their decision was very full and covered all questions. This of course necessitates another election. The Democrats however are threatning that the members of the Legislature elected at that election will meet next week (13th inst) and inaugurate Coke without regard to the decision   There is reason to anticipate that some rash act may be attempted unless demonstrations are made that will show those amongst them who are disposed to be violent that such schemes cannot be successful. Perhaps even before that time there may be some attempts to create a disturbance so I think you had better see the President and represent these facts to him to the end that he may be prepared to assist me in maintaining order pending the new election and installation of my successor. Please show this letter to the president when you have your interview and telegraph me conclusions" LS, *ibid.*

On Jan. 16, Davis telegraphed to USG. "According to the Constitution of our state I am the Governor until the twenty eighth of April next, other state and County officers hold their terms for the same time but today the persons composing what is called the fourteenth legislature have inaugurated Messers Hoke and Hubbard as Gov and Lieut Govr They will attempt to seize the Governor's office and buildings. Have made preparations to defend the offices but I call upon you for military assistance to aid in defending the Govt offices and keeping the peace" Telegram received (at 2:00 P.M.), *ibid.* On the same day, Richard Coke, Austin, telegraphed to U.S. Representative John Hancock of Tex. and the five other U.S. Representatives from Tex. "I was inaugurated as Gov and R B Hubbard as Lt. Gov. on yesterday   Transpiring events make it proper for me to advise you of the situation of affairs and so ask you to lay the matter before President Grant for his information and consideration that he may not be deceived by false representations and that he may be enabled in accordance with law to speak peace to a deeply anxious people. The inauguration was peacefully conducted in the representatives hall   During the day Gov Davis called around him in the basement of the capitol a squad of armed men for what reason I do not know as we had envoked no force and had assured him none would be used, and had understood the same was his wish & intention. Later in the day he caused an armed volunteer company of this city to be called out. It was afterwards turned over to the sheriff of this county to assist him if necessary in preserving the peace. . . . Please see the President at once & say to him that the public peace is menaced but that I will do everything which prudence can seggest & the performance of my constitutional duties as Gov will premit to preserve the peace   Please say to him that if he will at once assure Gov Davis that he will not sustain him in his extraordinary pretensions all cause of disturbance will be at an end and that he will speak peace & joy to our whole people and receive my & their heartfelt thanks   Call upon Senators Hamlton & Flanagan & ask their cooperation" Telegram received, *ibid.* On Jan. 19, Davis resigned as governor, conceding office to Coke. In 1874, Coke wrote to USG criticizing Davis and commending USG's course. William Evarts Benjamin, Catalogue No. 42, March, 1892, p. 7. See *HMD*, 43-1-175; *New York Times*, Jan. 13–14, 16–18, 1874; Carl H. Moneyhon, *Republicanism in Reconstruction Texas* (Austin, 1980), pp. 191–94.

On Feb. 25, Mijamin Priest, Rusk, Tex., wrote to USG. "though an humble individual, I presume to address you, in regard to our situation in Texas, which none can fully appreciate who do not live here—The Republican party of Texas has become a hiss & a by word, & we have no rights here that Democrats seem bound to respect—Even our vested rights are disregarded—Your letter to Govr Davis is considered a license for unrestrained action by the present Coke administration—The Decisions of the supreme Court are set at nought, & it is now proposed to authorize, by law, a rehearing of all Cases for the last two years, especially the Decision against the late election, by the newly made Court— The old Supreme Judges, under Gov. Davis have been displaced—& now fourteen District Judges, myself among the number are moved against, to be removed . . . Are we to be left to the tender mercies of this spirit of proscription? In 1870, I was made Judge of this, the 4th Judl Dist. for eight years, & other Judges were for the same Term—& it is not only now proposed to remove every one of us, who will not do the bidding of the Dominant party of Texas, but the large amounts due us for services already rendered and in arrears, it is proposed to withhold, for an indefinite Term—amounting almost to repudiation— These are only a few of our grievances—Justice & toleration seem to have fled—We are Citizens of this great nation, this great Republic, & friends to the Government, because it guarantees equal rights, & a Republican form of Government—not simply the form, but the substance of a Republican Government—The form may exist, & still rights may be trampled under foot—We want our rights enforced—One hundred thousand Dollars will not pay the expenses now being incurred by the present Legislature, in turning out Republican Judges that Democrats may get their places—Excuse me sir, for addressing you, as I feel it duty to lay facts before you, for to you & Congress only Can we look to protect us in our rights as freemen—" ALS, DNA, RG 60, Letters Received, Tex.

On Nov. 2, John C. Montgomery, Denison, wrote to USG. "I have been in Texas four years and have never voted for Greely, either, was born and educated in Iowa have tried and in vain to make my living in the practice of my profession (the law) now I want a position with a salary sufficient to keep me until I can do better it is strange to me how you appoint and reappoint old Greely Texans who hate the sound of a Northern mans voice there are a few in the state good republicans too who have never sought office yet you place men in power over us who are as out an out unreconstructed rebels as you will find any where. why I tried to get up a reception for you here but couldnt get men enough to make even a decent crowd so strong is the feeling, and unless some thing is done sooner or later I tremble for the party here in the next campaign. . . ." ALS, *ibid.*, RG 56, Collector of Customs Applications. No appointment followed.

On Nov. 9, Anonymous, Galveston, wrote to USG. "The recent removals of Federal officials in Texas is simply an outrage, they are all the most popular and efficient set of officers that could have been selected in any community, You have appointed men who are your personal enemies & publicly denounce your administration. We fear you have been grossly imposed upon, We must suffer—this hungry set will make changes in the already well organized Departments by the removal of the present efficient incumbents —& filling their places with inexperienced & incompetent men, and we the citizens, and public generally, will be the sufferers of all this *disorganization* If in your judgement you deemed that changes were neccessary, we expected that you would have appointed gentlemen endorsed by our citizens. We doubt that you can find in the U. S. a more *Competent efficient* & *popular* set of officials than the gentlemen just suspended, our postmaster, US. Marshall and Collector, their offices are well organized & give satisfaction to this community. They each have able assistants, and if a change was neccessary we feel that you could have selected gentlemen who have had experience and are competent of running the offices with credit to the Government" L, *ibid.*, RG 60, Letters from the President. Clippings recommending retention of Thomas P. Ochiltree as marshal, Eastern District, Tex., are *ibid.* On Nov. 6, Ochiltree, Galveston, had written to USG. "I have the honor to enclose You, herewith a petition, signed by over *two thirds* of the Bar of this city, respectfully urging that

Your Excellency will revoke the order suspending me from office. Most of these Gentlemen have been in the past, and are now, distinguished citizens of Texas, and are well known to Messrs Justices Bradley & Miller, & Judge Woods & Morrill of the Circuit & Dist Courts for this State. Another petition goes with this, the signatures to which are almost exclusively of a business Character, nearly all being Bankers, Merchants, Insurance, Rail Road Presidents, Superintendants &c &c—*but which represents nearly the whole taxable wealth of this the leading City of the Gulf of Mexico! . . .*" ALS, *ibid.* See *PUSG,* 23, 169–72.

On Feb. 20, 1875, L. F. Pannell, Houston, wrote to USG. "For God's sake Send your Bayonets to Texas—and break up the assemblage of Maniacs—Ruffians—and Thieves At Austin—Texas—They are Stealing every thing—breaking—and riding over every Law —that protects colored men and Republicans. They would not hesitate to make a constitution—That would place the colored man in a peonage worse than Slavery—But they fear the mighty Ulysses might Break up there Goverment—They may Delay it, the making of a Constitution untill *you* are Deprived of the Executive functions. Then farewell to the rights of the colored man forever. *You* are the hope of the nation—Let *your* strong powers protect the down Trodden Republicans at the mercy of the vindictive Goverments and Rigemes Existing in this State   I will aid *You* in any way *Your* Excellency may desire" ALS, DNA, RG 60, Letters Received, Tex. On April 3, Bolivar J. Pridgen, Galveston, wrote to USG. "I beg to call your attention to the anomilous conduct of the United States Marshal for the Eastern Disct of the State of Texas, in delaying the arrest of parties indicted for violations of the act Commonly known as 'The enforcment act of Congress'   The facts of the case are simply these: viz: In the months of June and July last about thirty five persons confederated in De Witt County in this State, and disguised with masks and other devices to conceal their identity, proceeded to the homes of good and loyal citizens of the United States and tearing them from the bosom of their families despite the remonstrating cries and shreeks of women and children perpitrated deeds of barbarous cruelty, shocking to human sensibilities and revoling to Christian civilization. A large number of loyal citizens both white and colored have at the dead hour of midnight, been foully murdered by this conclave of lawless characters. Four persons that had been unthoughtedly draged into their ranks, became dissatisfied with their unparalelled cruelty, and turned States evidence against them. The witnesses had then to flee the country for their own safety. . . . No effort has ever been made to arrest the parties and their appearance before the court, is in my judgment as remote as the marshal will be able to make it. He has fed me on promises until he has starved myself and the witnesses out, and I appeal to you and the Atty Gen'l Williams to have the matter promptly investigated and such action in the premises as your Honors may deem proper for speedy and effectual relief." ALS, *ibid.*

On April 6, Asa C. Hill, Gonzales, Tex., wrote to USG. "As humble and obscure as I feel to approach you, yet please permit me to appeal to you for help. For union sentiments and refusing to fight against the flag of my Country during the rebellion, I was not only robbed of all my property, but imprisoned Six months, and had it not been for my wounds and sore afflictions during that time, execution, or imprisonment at least, would have been my fate. Since that time while Commanding Rangers on our Frontier, because I would obey orders and have them executed with Strict discipline, and Cooperate with the Federal Forces Commanding at San Antonio Forts Griffin & Richardson, also while Captain of Police because I did arrest, Desperadoes, Horsethieves, Ku Klux and mobs, and prevented them from breaking up the U. S. Commissioners Court in Tarrant County June 10th 1872 from which time I acted as Special Dept. U. S. M. until April 25th 1873 when I was Commissioned as Dept. U. S. Marshal for the Western District of Texas, and continue as such trying to do my duty faithfully. Also because I obeyed orders strictly, as Col. of Millitia, at the Capital of our State, in January 74, I am hunted down and forced to travel about eighteen hundred miles each year since June 10th 1872, to attend the District Courts of Tarrant County, during which time several attempts was made to assassinate me. They did murder and run off all the witnesses I had gathered against them. In every petty case they hatch up against me I am compelled to give bond, and travel this great distance at a great expense which has drained me to the bottom. All that; I can endure, but to day, these preju-diced set of madmen, whose motto is, rule or ruin, has thrust me into the inner prison of our County Jail, and treated me worse than a dog, because, I refused to pay a fine of fifty dollars for Carrying arms while in the discharge of my duty as Deputy U. S. Marshal of the Western District of Texas. My appeals to the U. S. Marshal seem to avail nothing. They would not even respect the Seal of the U. S. Court. Unless speedy relief is given, Republi-cans must seek a better country for safety than Texas. There does prevail to day, a worse spirit than in Sixty one. As an evidence of this I enclose a small clip from one of our Town Papers. All proof required to the foregoing Statements will be ready when demanded." ALS, *ibid.* The enclosed clipping, advocating USG's impeachment for his La. policy, is *ibid.*

On July 24, George Peoples *et al.,* "Rosebeck" [*Groesbeck*], Tex., wrote to USG. "We the colored Citizens of of Lime-Stone co. Texas. and of the State We do honorably ask you permission of presenting you this Petition. To inform you of the condition of the colored people in the State of Texas, but it is almost impossibly Mr President for us to tell you all. but We will try to tell you a few things. But we have now runned a way from home. and have to be this Distance from home to get up this petition for we will leave this County and State to post this petition or it will never be seen by you   For we have have Sent Several petitions from this county and never have been heard of Since but will try to go to Louisiana and Mail it there   Now Mr President We will estate to you what have been done to us right here in our county. We here estate the property of colored people destroyed by the white people   Twelve houses burnt up. belonging to colored men. . . . In this Lime Stone county in this State May 1875. four hundred armed white men through the country runing colored men of from their crops and killing Some of us. and whipping Some of us. and hanging Some and burnig Some. and Said every one (col man) that did Issue a Republican ticket in that State Should leave or Die and running large numbers of us from our wives and chil-dren and compeling our wives to give up our Land Deeds. and abandon their homes and flee to the rugh woods, to Save thier lives   they have been taken the majority of our crops from us. every Sine 1865, up to the Present moment, they have taken our wives, and Sis-ters, and Mothers and Daughters, and the white men of the Southern States have Spoiled the majority of our daughters, and if we test against them about our ladies, they kills us. Mr President, let us tell you the truth   When ever we or any of us even ʜ ask the leave of walking or riding with a white Lady we are took and ether Shot or hung or Burnt. or whipped nearly to death. or be compeled to leave the State. and in this county. Mr P. We are not allowed to Sit on grand Jury. or a very few of us on Petd Jury. and mighty few coun-ties in this State that a a colored man is allowed to be on Jury. and if we look at white lady very hard as we wish to Say Somthing to them We are Shot.   there is been a large num-ber of col people Sent to Huntsville penitentiary with out Judge or Jury. and Some of them has been Sent from this county for Stealing fifteen cts (15) worth and in Said Co. of Lime Stone we will Send you a few names of our race that have been murdered by ~~our~~ white men here of late. and a few in Marion county that we know are facts. . . . have been So much dev-ilment done by these outragious Slave holding Masters in the county of Lime-Stone. and other county in this State until it is almost impossiby for us to explain to you Mr Presi-

dent what have been done in this State. Mr President We ask you and congress of the
United States. In the name of the almighty God. to Send us protection in this State. and
also give us our citizenShip. give us Justice at Law. give us what we work for. let us
enjoys the rights that any other white man in the South. Stop the revels from Killing of us,
and Stop them from whipping us. Stop them from taken our crops. Stop then from runig
us from our crops. prepare a law to make them let our women alone. or let us alone about
their women. let us have a right to Set on the Jury Seat give us Justice by the laws. or
give us a Territory to our selves. Mr President We col. people is in a terrible fix. We hope
that you and Congress will prepare Some Meins by the congress of the U. S. States to
Strike a line betwen the white & the black of the Southern States. Our race have ask you
before and asked Congress before. to Send us to Liberia. We are willing to go and will go
at any moment We would try to move our Selves, but we will never be able to to move
our seles. as long as we live here in the South. among our old Slave-holding masters. because they have got int in their resolutions to not let us be able. to move our selves. When
ever they find out that we are getting able to hire our own race. they Kills us or make us
leave the country or puts us in prison and Swear that we have done Soming that we never
thought of. and they Swear here in this county that a every col. man that Issue a Republican Ticket. or act like a Republican. that they intend to kill him this year or the next year.
all these white men that committed these murders of Texas. never has ben punished, and
the Office holders of this State is the leading men of the murdering, and Robing and plun-
dering. Mr President. how in the name of God can we Stand that must we raise arms and
go to war, or must we die like dogs as we have been. or must we have a territory to our
Selves. or must we take all the abuse that we have been for the last past Ten yrs. Mr P. and
congress of the U. S. We call your attention to this petition We hope that you and congress will take Action on this and release us from this great Struggle. Mr President if
Congress do Set and adjourn again and do not take no action upon this or our Desolation
and Suffrage. we will apply to farther nation to help us out of our Struggle. and We. and
all of us. are willing to pay any Government if it takes us fifty years, to pay it to releave us
of this terrible Struggle. if it take us fifty yrs. And Mr President. We intend next Winter if you will allow us. we will Send men from our country here. to State the Conditions
of the Southern States. We shall not Send no man that ever held an Office in the South,
We are going to take our hard laboring men who clears the land. and Sews the Seed. and
cultivates the land and reaps the grain. and gathers the Crop, and who Supports the whole
entire Southern States. Now Mr President please answer in the News paper to let us know
if you recieved this. for Some of the whites of this State has taken our children for debt and
[ma]king slaves of us. Mr President we will close our petition In name of God And you
have done your duty by us once, and Know you will do it again We look at you as we did
Abraham Lincoln and We looked at Abraham L. as the children did Jashua and they looked
at him as a Second god and We look to you as a god on earth Your Petitioners will forever pray, and they wait for the Voice of you as the christian did wait for the Voice of God.
This the Voice of the whole colored people State of Texas . . . " D, *ibid.* On Sept. 24, Allie
Huston, Austin, telegraphed and wrote to USG. "Can nothing be done to stop wrongs
which republicans suffer from lawless men in Limestone County Tex about which petition
was sent you. state authorities will not act & troubles continue. I ask on behalf of my father who is in their hands his life may be taken we have no hope here please answer"
"I Teligraphed you to day asking you for poteckton for my father whom they have confined
in Groesbeck. Limestone Co in Jail, they say they mean to mob him, & my poor old mother
has to lie on the Jail steps ever night & now they have ordered her to leave in so many days,

so they, can get to mob my father, & it is all becase he is a Republican, nothing else for he never troubles any one, & I have ask all the Offercers hear to help us but none of them wont do it so I thought I would ask you to proteck, us, if you remember thire was a Patistion sent you some time ago by the Negroes of Limestone County, I saw that it is correck ever word &c. can be proven, & General Pierapoint sent it to A J Evens & told him to investigate the matter, & Evens told some one from the County, & as soon as they heard it they said my Father was at the head of it & they put him in Jail & have got him their now, & we are looking all the time for him to be killed, & one John W Love deputy Sherif, as soon as he heard of the Patesion commenc riding over the County & telling the Negroes to come in to Groesbeck, & sighn a paper saying they never sighn the Patesion & that their had not been any one killed & kno Housen birnt telling them if they did not sighn it that he would, have all killed that did not sighn it some are leaving to keep from sighning it & some say they will not sighn it & of corse they will be killed, all the white men in the County will sighn it for they are all guilty alike, their has been at least fifty men killed & I cant tell the Number of houses that has been birnt, & all their crops destroyed & the women & Children left to to starve, or be put back in to slavery agen they say that they mean to kill & run all the men off & put the women & Childre back into slavery agen, & the Negroes are not allowed to vote in facked kno Republican is, in that County, that Patision told fackes & nothing else, & I have been trying for a month to try to get A J Evens & Purnell the Marshel, to Act & help us but they wont . . . I feel confident you will help us, & not see us all killed up like dogs, & left hanging in the woods for the varments to eat, like ove fifty have already been done, I am almost Crazy, . . . Woman as I am they say if I ever come back to Limestone County agen they will kill me, . . ." Telegram received (at 12:10 A.M.) and ALS, *ibid.*, Letters from the President.

On Sept. 1, William V. Tunstall, Creswell, Tex., wrote to USG. "Enclosed I have the honor to Send you a note I received this morning from one Jno. W. Satterwhite who two years ago was convicted to the Penitentiary in this county and who broke loose from the Sheriff and has been runing at large ever Since. For months past he has been back here and no effort being made to capture him. I am U. S. Commissioner and Post Master and have made myself obnoxious to the good people hereabouts by a hearty support of the Republican cause. It is out of the question for me to sell out for any thing and leave as I have a large family to support. I have sent a copy also to Governor Coke at Austin. If your Excellency has any remedy for such cases I respectfully petition your Excellency to afford such aid as the exigency requires." ALS, *ibid.*, Letters Received, Tex. The enclosed letter dated Aug. 1 ordered Tunstall to leave his home by Jan. 1, 1876. Copy, *ibid.*

On Sept. 13, 1875, Jasper Starr, postmaster, Plenitude, Tex., and many others, petitioned USG and Congress. "Whereas we, Citizens of Anderson County and State of Texas, feel ourselves laboring under grievances too heavy to be borne by loyal citizens of this Government, we deem that duty to ourselves and our Country requires us to make this appeal to you as the trusted guardians of the best interests of this nation. If fidelity to the Constitution and laws make us citizens worthy of your protection, we claim that protection of the Government due us at your hands, and ask for speedy and effective redress of our wrongs. In this, Anderson County, and we believe it an average County of the state, including those who approvingly attended murdering mobs, there are at least a thousand murderers, besides those of individuals and mobs perpetrating crimes of less magnitude. These are not only unpunished and at large, but manufacture and control public opinion. These in a mass, as well as separately inculcate Treason to the Federal Government in as many ways as the ingenuity of man can invent. Among which we will enumerate as follows:—1st Almost the entire Press of the State either outspokenly or tacitly endorse the

above characters—extol and build up the leaders of the late rebellion—traduce and ca-
lumniate all loyal men, denying them a hearing, and presenting a general false face to facts
as they exist; aiding and abetting all rebel criminals in their murders and robberies, and
obtaining persecuting prosecutions against all who do not co-operate with them in their
treasonable crimes; and are filled with falsehoods and false issues as deadly vehement to the
vitals of Constitutional liberty as in the palmiest days of the Confederacy. 2nd The courts
instead of being administrators of justice are transformed into engines of oppression for
the weak and powerless law-abiding citizen. Rebel grand juries find bills of indictment
against loyal men without any foundation of fact, while murderers, robbers, and such as are
guilty of arson and other great crimes, are winked at by the courts as faithful adherents to
the cause 'that Radicals have 'no rights that Democrats are bound to respect.' While the colored citizens are 'sytematically intimidated, brow-beaten, personally maltreated, cheated
of their earnings, often prevented from exercising their rights of suffrage, driven from
their houses in penury to endure the inclemencies of the weather, and dispossessed of their
rights to vindicate themselves before the courts'—while the Ku Klux rule everything their
own way. No white man, not in sympathy with the Rebellion, has any show in Courts—in
the social circle, or in any business in the practical departments of life where rebels can
hinder him. 3d The Amendments of the Federal Constitution are ignored; no colored man
is allowed to sit on the jury even where colored citizens are only interested, and no jury
empaneled that has not rebels enough to control it; while colored men are made to suffer
the severest penalties of the law for the most trifling offenses, especially when they are too
well informed to willingly act as rebel tools to aid them in exterminating their most sacred rights. 4th The entire property forfeited in the late rebellion and too generously surrendered to those who had forfeited their lives by treason, is turned into an engine of oppression to crush us, while all the donations of Congress for educational or other purposes
are perverted to treasonable uses in denying to all loyal citizens their rights to life, liberty,
and the pursuit of happiness. 5th Life and property, outside of the rebel ranks has no security; and robbed of all redress, loyal men stand in jeopardy every hour of their lives, of
their meagre livings and their sacred honors, from rebel powers and perjuries, all of which
we have the statistical data to show. We ask you, we entreat you, we implore you in the
name of humanity to relieve us and that speedily of our wrongs, and grant us that security
and protection which is the inherent right of every loyal citizen of this government: All of
which we respectfully submit." DS (most by mark), *ibid.*, Letters from the President. On
May 21, 1876, Starr wrote to USG. "When Editor of the 'Bosque Beacon' at Meridian, this
state, I was the first Editor, South of Mason's & Dixon's line to hoist your name for the
Presidency. This was in the year 1867. And if I am not mistaken, I was about the third in
the United States. I have not been, neither am I now an applicant for any appointment at
your hands to office. I, with others, last year, sent an application for protection, which you
have not deigned to notice. I do not claim that my advocacy of you for President, cut any
big figure in the election, for Texas did not vote in your first election, & the last she went
against you; but this I do claim, that for that advocacy, and my identification with the Republican party; I have suffered more than death, and am now hedged in by Rebel persecution and unlawful tyranny till death is preferable a hundred fold, and but for my family's
sake, I should not hesitate a moment to fill a suicide's grave. For my own sake, I have suffered, till I care but little; for I cannot now foresee any worse pangs in store for me than I
now endure: but for the sake of my helpless children, I do claim that protection of the Government due to the humblest loyal citizen. Is it possible that it is your intention to still suffer the loyal element of the South to be tortured, in face of their rights as American citizens, by those guilty of Treason at first; & who now, by every principle of law and justice,

have forfeited their pardon for Treason; being not only guilty of perjury in their amnesty oath & to support the Constitution; but constantly make Treason of the past and present, the passport to office, emoluments and honors; and the stripping of loyal men of their lives, fortunes and sacred honors; till it is a shame to be classed with loyal men—death itself preferable, and the last spark of patriotism blotted from the face of this Sunny South? Do you need more aggressive acts, or further delay for the enemies of the Government to show their hand, when hourly acts of violence fill the whole land, & scare an officer, either Federal or State, but rides down the law? When shall Treason cease to be a virtue, as well as a passport to office, emoluments and honors? When shall the Federal laws be respected, & the protection due to every loyal citizen in his life, person & property, be enforced? When shall those guilty of murder, perjury, Treason & every crime known to the law, receive the just reward for their deeds? When shall Ku-Klux, no longer armed with the semblance of law, cease to make courts engines of oppression, in indicting loyal men for malfeasance with parties, with whom they never had any dealings even privately, much less officially? —For embezzlement when holding the Treasurer's Receipts &c. &c?—Robbing them of their dues for their hard earned labors, both privately & officially, & throwing net works of complicated difficulties, too difficult to overcome, in preventing from making an appropriately legal showing in their behalf? When shall the murderers of prisoners in jail, & the lawless oppression of others, cease to be sustained by Rebel Courts, & rebel votes; & the contempt thrown around prisoners unjustly incarcerated, tauntingly threatening to feed them on 'Bull Cod,' when thrown in jail, hungry, & needing the necessaries of life, &c.? When shall the visits of Ku Klux officers, cease to drag helpless children by the hair of the head while sick with raging fever, in order to ascertain their father's whereabouts who fled the vindictiveness of rebel wrath? When shall Ku Klux cease to visit houses of citizens, shoot, whip, & maltreat them—& then with threats of intimidation to all in the house, to kill them if they dare speak of it; rendering a state of fear so great that they feel like giving their lives into the keeping of their friends to whom they might dare to breathe out their grievous sufferings, or their fearful condition? When shall these and others of the same nature too many and too fearful to tell, cease to hang over this people, as a deadening pall, crushing out hope, and all that is near and dear to the human heart? Tell, not me alone, but the people of this great Nation, when shall these things cease? Shall the breathings & deeds of such men as Toombs & those who support his course, receive the executive sanction of this nation? Why is the negro tantalized with the names of freedom ~~of freedom~~ & citizenship; while his condition as a whole is made far worse than when he was a slave? Why is he suffered to be driven from the polls—cheated of his earnings—Ku-Kluxed in his home —driven from the jury; while his merciless persecutors, incarcerate him for the slightest offenses—starve him in jail—intimidate him so he dare not complain of his wrongs, lest his penalty is death?—Why is the condition of the loyal white man, made even worse than that of the negro? Why must he be persecuted, murdered, incarcerated unjustly, robbed of his property, insulted on every hand—his family pointed at with scorn, treated with every contumely; while the Traitor is upheld, eulogized for his Treason? Elected Governor, as Coke was with over 100000 majority—& thence to the Senate, for the faithfulness of his rebel record? The press teems with falsehoods—false issues—false representations, and if a man must be robbed, murdered, or set down upon, the finger of scorn, the poison of the press, must point him out tauntingly as 'a nigger equality man.' Shall the same spirit—the same people—the same treason always rule us, that disgraced the Andersonville prison pen? It may be said, you are to a certain extent powerless? Why powerless? Is treason more palatable now than under the martyred Lincoln's Administration? Because it is more cunning—more secret—more destructive in its workings, must it still be tolerated, and nurtured as a bantling of the slave power's pet idea of State rights—making the State law higher than the Federal law? Why is Texas filled with Federal officers either too timid or too corrupt, to execute the Federal laws? And it is even too late now, for here in Texas; they cannot be executed unless backed by the military; and even then resistance is sure, and the want of confidence in sustaining permanently the citizen in his rights, will fail to develop the most horrid crimes known to law or humanity?—Personally, I am unjustly stripped of my hard earnings—unjustly persecuted by under the state laws, and made to suffer in every way tyrants regardless of law can invent?! Why, because I, in my folly believed this a free government—believed that loyalty should be rewarded, by protection; and that Treason, though forgiven, should not be placed at a premium as it has. I ask, not only for myself, but for the loyal people of the South, to be protected in our rights of citizens, and though you may still continue to pardon Treason, we demand, as our inalienable right, that it be shorn of its power to harm us—and that a way be provided for an ample, speedy and efficacious redress for all our wrongs. If this government fails to protect its citizens, it is unworthy of support? If our jails and penitentiaries must be filled with loyal men, because they are obnoxious for their devotion for the Union, and murderers, in their retinue of every grade of crime, let go free; I say, if this is to continue; let us know it, that we may seek protection where it may be found. These are fearfully momentous questions with us now; and I hope you may see proper to speak at large, through the press, on these subjects at an early day. I do not ask that my name be blazoned forth, but let us know, and that speedily, if the prospect is that the present regime of things must continue." ALS, *ibid.*

On Feb. 5, Elizabeth Schobey, Austin, had written to USG. "I take the liberty to inform you that my husband G W Schobey was killed by two desperados on the 29 of Jan that was last Saturday Evening   about 7 P M the Ruffins rode up to his home called him to the door   he invited them to come in   they said they could not stop that they only wanted to see him a few minutes   he walked about twelve steps from the door when they both shot him through the heart   they fired three times   either shot would have killed him   Mr Schobey was a Republican a firm frind of Governor Davies and the Republicans were runing him as Candidate for the Legislature   it is said that he had secured the Magority of the vots in Fayitte and Bastrop Countys   he has been Teaching Colored school for several years along with my self and has also been a very successful lawer and was considred a very smart inteligent man   he was peaceble temprate and religous and perlectly honest and never had a personal difficulty with any one that i know of. He had made several speches that did not pleas the opposit party and was shot shot down like a dog in his own yard whitout one word of warning . . ." ALS, *ibid.* HED, 44-2-30, 134–35.

To John F. Long

Washington, D. C. Jan. 12, 1874.

DEAR JUDGE:

Enclosed I send my check for $220^{00}/$_{100}$ with which—with some money which you inform me you have of mine—please pay the enclosed bills.

I received your letter touching the appointment of Mr. Drake to a Consulate, and delayed answering until I could tell you what consulates were vacant, or could be made so. I have neglected in the press of public business to do so; but say to you that I will gladly do what you ask in the matter: that is, I will give Mr. D. a consulate if he wishes it, and will have expressed to Judge Dillon my views as to your eminent qualifications for his place.

My kindest regards to your family,

In haste, your obt. svt.

U. S. GRANT

JUDGE JOHN F. LONG (LANGHAM[1] & LONG)
ST. LOUIS, MO.

Copy, DLC-USG, II, 2.

    1. Philip S. Lanham, John F. Long's partner in a real estate business.

To Senate

To THE SENATE;

~~Circumstances~~ Information having come to my knowledge since making the nomination for Chief Justice of the Supreme Court of the United States effecting the usefulness of an officer in ~~that high~~ so controling a position, ~~though not necessarily effecting his honor or usefulness in other spheres,~~[1] I hereby withdraw the said nomination of Caleb Cushing Chief Justice.

Information of circumstances having come to my knowledge since sending to the Senate the name of Hon. Caleb Cushing for the controlling office of Chief Justice of the Supreme Court of the United States ~~effecting his fitness~~ impairing his usefulness, in my opinion, for that office, I hereby withdraw the same.

U. S. GRANT

JAN.Y 13TH /74

ADfS, Babcock Papers, ICN. Drafts of this message in the handwriting of Orville E. Babcock and Levi P. Luckey are *ibid.* On Jan. 13, 1874, USG wrote to the Senate. "Since nominating the Hon: Caleb Cushing for Chief Justice of the Supreme Court of the United States, information has reached me which induces me to withdraw him from nomination as the highest judicial officer of the Government, and I do therefore hereby withdraw said nomination" Copy, DNA, RG 130, Messages to Congress. On Jan. 14, Secretary of State Hamilton Fish recorded in his diary. "The President read a communication to the Senate which he had prepared yesterday withdrawing the nomination of General Cushing as Chief Justice. The communication was modified in some of its expressions, and subsequently a letter was received from General Cushing suggesting the withdrawal of his name—brought to the President, it was understood by General Butler—another communication to the Senate was prepared to accompany the former and transmitting a copy of Cushing's letter. The question of another nomination was discussed—it was deemed not advisable to make a nomination to-day, but that the President should see and converse with some Senators. The names of persons for the position were considered. I again pressed Judge Hoar but the President mentioned that Hoar had yesterday told him that he was preparing a speech to be delivered soon, denying the power of Congress to emit legal tenders. The names which eventually seemed to be the most acceptable were those of Woodruff, M. R. Waite, and Dillon." DLC-Hamilton Fish. In 1874, U.S. Representative Joseph R. Hawley of Conn. wrote to USG concerning the nomination for chief justice. "The influence of Benj. F. Butler is already too great in the Republican party. His influence is a great popular objection to the party. He is a bad man. I believe him a dangerous man to the country, and therefore I am his enemy without concealment or compromise." William Evarts Benjamin, Catalogue No. 42, March, 1892, p. 12.

On Jan. 14, USG wrote to the Senate. "After signing the above withdrawal, I have received from the Hon: Caleb Cushing, whose nomination it is proper to say was made without his knowledge, a letter requesting the withdrawal of his name, a copy of which letter is herewith attached." Copy, DNA, RG 130, Messages to Congress. On the same day, Caleb Cushing, Washington, D. C., wrote to USG. "Animated by the sense of profound gratitude for the honor you have done me in nominating me to the high office of Chief Justice of the Supreme Court of the United States, and perceiving that the Continuance of my name before the Senate may be the cause or occasion of inconvenience to yourself or your political friends there, I respectfully request you to withdraw the nomination. Permit me to add, that the charges of disloyalty to the Union and the Constitution, which have been brought against me in this Connection, are utterly destitute of foundation in truth or in fact. I indignantly repel the imputation. In all the time anterior to the commencement of hostilities in the Southern States, every act of my political life in whatever relation to parties was governed by the single dominant purpose of aiming to preserve the threatened integrity of the Union, and to avert from my country the calamity of its disruption and of consequent fratricidal carnage. How could such a purpose be promoted, otherwise than by political association or personal intercourse with citizens of different States, including those of States professedly disaffected to the Union? Should the only possible means of laboring to prevent civil war be Stigmatised as disloyalty to the Constitution? But, immediately on occurrence of the first act of hostility to the Union being struck in the State of South Carolina, I took my stand with the Union and its Government; I publicly announced my adhesion to them in the most unequivocal terms; I tendered my services to the Government in the field, or in any other way which might testify my fidelity to it; and I have continued, from that day to this, as well in official as unofficial action, to tread in the path of unswerving devotion to the Union, whether during the actual progress of hostilities against it, or in the subsequent events of its reconstruction, and of the successive amendments of the Constitution rendered necessary by the changed conditions and relations of the several states of the United States and of their respective inhabitants. The recent amendments of the Constitution each and all of them, as they were in turn adopted, and the legislative acts for their enforcement and for accomplishing reconstruction had my cooperation and adhesion; and I have supported them constantly—if not in political debate, for which my comparatively reserved habits of life afforded neither occasion nor opportunity,—yet in legal opinion or in the Courts, and in counsel or discussion with officers of the Government, Members of Congress and private persons: I entertaining the same general respect for these amendments as for the other provisions of the Constitution, and also rendering the special observance due to them as the first and necessary incidents of the reconstruction of the Union. While my nomination was undergoing consideration in the Senate, it would have been unbeseeming for me to speak in explanation of my acts or opinions, but now, with relative indifference to whatever else may have been said either honestly or maliciously to my prejudice, it belongs to my sense of public duty, and it is my right, to reaffirm and declare that I have never, in the long course of a not inactive life, done an act, uttered a word, or conceived a thought, of disloyalty to the Constitution or the Union." LS, USG 3; ADfS, DLC-Caleb Cushing. A letter of March 20, 1861, from Cushing to Jefferson Davis in the C.S.A. archives cast doubts on Cushing's loyalty. "Mr Archibald Roane, for the last six or seven years a clerk in the Attorney General's Office, desires from me a letter of introduction to you; and he desires it, not in the view of anticipating administrative favors, but that he have the honor of your personal intercourse. . . . He now resigns his present office, from sentiments of devotion to that which alone he can feel to be his country namely, the *Confederate* States, from one of which (Texas) he was appointed. I most heartily commend him as a gentleman and a man to your confidence and esteem . . . " ALS, DNA, RG 109, Papers Relating to Citizens and Business Firms. Senate consideration of this letter and widespread newspaper publication of a fraudulent version doomed Cushing's nomination. See Hamilton Fish diary, Jan. 13, 1874, DLC-Hamilton Fish; Claude M. Fuess, *The Life of Caleb Cushing* (1923; reprinted, Hamden, Conn., 1965), II, 364–76; David Donald, *Charles Sumner and the Rights of Man* (New York, 1970), pp. 580–81.

On Jan. 9, USG had nominated Cushing as chief justice. On the same day, Fish recorded in his diary. "The President brought up the question of an appointment of a Chief Justice, and suggested the name of General Cushing—some hesitation was expressed on the part of one or two members. I suggested the name of Judge Hoar which was not sustained by any member of the Cabinet, but the President spoke very cordially of him, but was convinced from what he had heard that his nomination could not be confirmed. Cushing's nomination was signed and sent in, all assenting. Attorney General Williams made a statement with reference to the charges preferred against him before the Committee; leaving the impression that although he may have been indiscreet he had not been intentionally wrong." DLC-Hamilton Fish. See *PUSG*, 24, 285–87.

On Jan. 14, U.S. Representative Stephen A. Hurlbut of Ill. wrote to Orville E. Babcock. "The Cushing affair has about done its worst—the point is to make the best of what is left. Nobody supposes that suspicion even of his correspondence with Davis was entertained at the White House. But the whole matter has badly involved the Republican party & is another & a dangerous attack upon its vitality. If I was asked what is best to be done, more than has been, I would say at once, nominate Hoar of Mass or Miller of Iowa for Chief Justice—& would greatly prefer Miller as a man of equal ability with any, progressive yet steady & above all from the West & in sympathy with the West. The promotion of Miller would leave a vacancy that could be filled by an acceptable man, say Drummond from Illinois—or Bristow from the South if Bristow is up to the stature I believe him to be. It will be at once the most graceful acknowledgment and reparation. Something ought to be conceded by the President to the sentiment of the Republican party—for after all he is not only President of the Nation but head of the Republican party & can do both duties—& it is hardly fair to shock our sense of propriety by such a nomination as Cushings and yet expect us to stand firmly as we want to do by our chief. We are going to have all we can do to hold any thing like our ground next fall & we cannot bear much extra load. I scarcely know personally either Judge Miller or Hoar & have not seen Bristow since Shiloh, where he was nearly killed under my eye. I want nothing from them & no one knows of this writing. But I hear many men, representative men of the country, talk & talk more freely than you hear up there and I know we are on tender ground, and so I assume to suggest these things for consideration—if you choose to call the matter up in your intercourse with the President. I think he knows enough of me to believe that I do it for the highest purposes and with no possible personal object" ALS, USG 3. On the same day, U.S. Senators Powell Clayton and Stephen W. Dorsey of Ark. wrote to USG. "In obedience to what we feel convinced is the general sentiment of our constituents, we beg the privilege of joining some of our colleagues in suggesting the name of *John. F. Dillion.* of Iowa, for the position of Chief Justice of the United States." LS, PHi. In 1873, William Claflin had written to USG recommending Ebenezer R. Hoar as chief justice. William Evarts Benjamin, Catalogue No. 42, March, 1892, p. 7.

On Jan. 18, Benjamin H. Bristow, Louisville, wrote to USG. "As ~~your~~ an earnest friend of yr adm. I trust I may be pardoned for suggesting that ~~in my~~ the bench, bar and country would, in my opinion be gratified by the appt of Chf Justice from the present Justices. I do not believe it possible to make any other appt that would give such general satisfaction & besides it is certain that several of the Justices are eminently qualified for the position. I beg you to believe me sincere in saying that the mention of my name in connection with judicial position has been without my procurement or knowledge and that in making this suggestion I am actuated solely by regard for the high character of the Supreme Court and desire for the continued success of your administration" ADf (initialed), DLC-Benjamin H. Bristow. See telegram to Morrison R. Waite, Jan. 22, 1874.

    1. See *PUSG*, 24, 294–95.

To Senate

To THE SENATE OF THE UNITED STATES:

    In reply to the resolution of the Senate of the 8th instant, requesting information "relative to any unauthorized occupation or invasion of, or encroachment upon, the Indian Territory, so-called, by individuals, or bodies of men, in violation of treaty stipulations," I have the honor to submit herewith the reply of the Secretary of the Interior, to whom the resolution was referred.

U. S. GRANT.

EXECUTIVE MANSION, JANUARY 19, 1874.

SED, 43-1-21. On Jan. 16, 1874, Secretary of the Interior Columbus Delano had written to USG that although there was no current encroachment on Indian Territory, "occasions have not been infrequent when portions of said Territory have been invaded and occupied by unauthorized persons, who have been treated as trespassers, and for whose removal from said Territory the aid and co-operation of the military have been required." *Ibid.*

On June 6, Delano wrote to Secretary of War William W. Belknap transmitting papers "relating to outlaws, thieves, robbers and others who violate law and disturb the peace in the Indian territory and recommending that troops be sent to the locality named for the purpose of recovering stolen property; preventing the violation of the Intercourse laws and preserving order, and arresting the thieves and all others who violate law, and turning them over to the civil authorities at Fort Smith or some other suitable place, to be dealt with, as may be deemed necessary. The recommendations of the Commissioner and Superintendent have the approval of this Department. In the absence of the Honorable, the Secretary of War, the papers have been presented to the President, who, verbally, expressed his concurrence in the measures proposed and authorized the application, by this Department, for the requisite number of troops to be detailed in accordance with the request of the Officers of the Indian Department, . . ." LS, DNA, RG 94, Letters Received, 1938 1874. Related papers are *ibid.* On June 15, Lt. Gen. Philip H. Sheridan, Chicago, endorsed these papers. "I coincide with the views of the Interior Department on the subject presented in these papers, and as soon as I receive the requisite orders will instruct General Pope to act accordingly. But I would like to have some specific authority for the action necessary to be taken, to cover suits that may be instituted, by these desperadoes or their friends, against the officers and soldiers that may be employed on this duty. I have a personal knowledge of the difficulties in the way of discharging duties of this nature, from having myself been arrested and prosecuted for attempting to break up organizations of the kind referred to, which cost me much time and money. If we only had the proper authority, I would only be too happy to rid the country of this class of persons." ES, *ibid.* On June 22, Belknap wrote to Delano outlining restrictions preventing the army from arresting persons not on military reservations. LS (press), *ibid.* On June 25, Delano wrote to Belknap that he had requested an opinion from Attorney Gen. George H. Williams on removing intruders from the Cheyenne and Arapahoe reservation, but he believed "that a Presidential Order to remove all unauthorized persons from the Indian Territory, would be a sufficient vindication of the action of the Military Officers and soldiers who may be directed to perform the service." LS, *ibid.* On Sept. 1, Williams wrote to Delano supporting his view. ". . . But I do not think it essential, in this case, that the order should be issued by the President by his own hand. If one were issued by the Hon Secretary of War, it would, as I conceive, be sufficient—the general rule being that the direction of the President is to be presumed in orders or instructions emanating from the appropriate Executive Department." Copy, *ibid.* See *HED*, 43-2-1, part 5, I, 542, 544.

On Dec. 6, 1871, Delano had written to Belknap concerning plans to remove intruders from Indian Territory. ". . . Referring to the interview with the President on yesterday, at which yourself and Superintendent Hoag were present, in relation to this subject, I now have the honor to modify my letter of the 9th ultimo so far as to request that the order of removal shall be carried into effect except as to those persons only who shall have the written authority of the Superintendent to remain, and respectfully request that the proper officers of the War Department be advised accordingly." LS, DNA, RG 94, Letters Received, 3971 1871. On Dec. 21, Brig. Gen. John Pope, Fort Leavenworth, wrote to AG Edward D. Townsend. ". . . The removal of Settlers on the Osage lands will be the occasion of much suffering at this season of the year and will bring upon those actually engaged in the removal an immense deal of ill feeling—It does not seem fair that the whole of this odium should fall on the military forces, who are not in the least responsible for a condition of things on this Indian Reservation which has made the use of force necessary—It is certain that if the Military authorities had had the charge of these reservations no intrusion of White Settlers would have been permitted in the first instance, and it seems hard now that the Army should be saddled with ill will and unpopularity arising from the neglect of bad management of others. I therefore respectfully ask in Justice to the Commander and Military forces of this Department that the Superintendent of Indian Affairs here be ordered to his post and directed to execute the order for the expulsion of white intruders from the

Osage Reservation, aided by the Military force some time since detailed for that service and now awaiting the presence of a duly authorised Officer of the Indian Department—. . ." LS, *ibid.*

On March 9 and 15, 1872, Sheridan, Chicago, telegraphed to Townsend. "The indian agent in South eastern Kansas has notified the Commanding officer that he is ready to accompany the troops to remove intruders on the Cherokee lands,   is it the desire of the War Dept that this shall be done,   this information is asked for, in view of a telegram from the Adjutant General to Genl Pope of the date of January eighteenth, which informs him that nothing need be done in the matter until further instructions which have not since been received" "Gen Pope telegraphs that Superintendent of Indian Affairs is anxious for removal of intruders on Cherokee lands—I do not feel at liberty to act in view of your dispatch of January eighteenth" Telegrams received, *ibid.* On March 16, Belknap wrote to Sheridan. "Your despatch received. The President directs that notice be given to the settlers on Indian lands that they can make no preparation for spring crops, and they must be compelled—by force, if necessary, to vacate in time for the Indians to plant." ADf (initialed), *ibid.* On March 22, Townsend telegraphed to Sheridan. "The President now directs that all persons found within the Indian Territory south of Kansas and west of Arkansas and Missouri except such as have authority of the Superintendent to remain, be at once removed. For this purpose you will please cause to be detailed a sufficient military force. Acknowledge receipt." Copy, *ibid.*, Letters Sent. On March 23, Sheridan telegraphed to Townsend. "Your telegram of yesterday received. Is the President aware that his directions cover all the Indian territory, and that there is now a railroad being built throughout it, or did he simply expect his directions to cover the neutral lands about which I telegraphed on March ninth and on March fifteenth." Telegram received, *ibid.*, Letters Received, 3971 1871. On March 26, Townsend telegraphed to Sheridan. ". . . the following are the Presidents orders—All persons actually, in good faith, engaged in building and operating the two (2) railroads now being constructed through the creek and choctaw country, may be reorganized as having authority for their presence in that territory—The Indian agents have been notified not to interfere with their legitimate operations. Acknowledge receipt." Copy, *ibid.*, Letters Sent. On May 6, Sheridan telegraphed to Townsend. "Have the pleasure of reporting that all intruders on netral lands immediately south of Kansas have been removed without difficulty by Captain Upham   sixth (6) Cavalry and troops have returned to Fort Scott. General Grierson is performing same duty further south without trouble" Telegram received (on May 7), *ibid.*, Letters Received, 3971 1871. Related papers are *ibid.* See *HED*, 42-3-1, part 5, I, 617–18.

On Feb. 8, Louis Rough, Indian Territory, had written to USG. "pleas give me a litle infermation, what the dark popution is to doo a bout thos schoul funs to have our Children edicatd   are we to stay here and rais them up like hethens . . . if it is lefte to the Chery kees we never will have nothing done   there are six darkeys   the Shery kees has in Counsel denied them ahome or privalig what ever and you mr grant promest to make a step for us and now i want you to doo some thing for us pore degraded set . . . the Chery kees says they ante in favour of the black man havin eny clam that they had rather eny body else have a rite than us pour blacks and what are we to doo when there only three that speks in our behalf and the reste of the nation are all a ganst us Coulerd foke   downing is for us Chelater and mas six killer   them three is in our favour and what Can they doo with so meny . . . doo you think it rite for us to mocked of like dogs and not no nothing so we Can go up and talk and in Joy our selves like we we was human men . . ." ALS, DNA, RG 75, Letters Received, Cherokee Agency. Also in Feb., William S. Madden *et al.*, Saline District, Indian Territory, petitioned USG and Congress. "We the Undersigned freedmen living in the Cherokee Nation, very respectfully beg leave to represent. That in the Ninth article of the Cherokee Treaty of 1866, it is provided that 'all freedmen who have been liberated by voluntary act of their former owners or by law, as well as all free colored persons who were in the country at the commencement of the rebellion, and are now residents therein, or who may return within six months, and their descendants, shall have all the rights of native Cherokees:' Now many of us, were so circumstanced at the time, that we did not know that we were required by the Treaty to be back in the Cherokee Nation within six months from its date, in order to secure the privileges conferred. We knew nothing about the Treaty and had no means of gaining the information Some of us had fled North to get away from slavery, or to take our families away from the horrors and sufferings of the War, While we ourselves enlisted in the Union army. Some of us, had been dragged by our owners, to the south to keep us from being freed by the Union army, so that we were a long way off from the Cherokee Country when the Treaty was made. We were so poor, that we had no way of getting back to our old homes, so that we could not possibly have reached there in time, even if we had known what provision was made for us in the Treaty. Some of us, who were not so far off, started to come back, in the fall of 1866, and we got a few miles into the Cherokee Nation, when we were attacked by reputed rebel desperados who infested the road, when several of our people were killed; others were wounded, and soon died; others who still live, are now suffering from their Wounds. Those of the party who were not killed, fled back to Kansas. The news of this massacre spread among the Cherokee colored people every where and they became afraid to come into the Cherokee Country for fear of being killed, and robbed by the returning southern men. For these, and other causes, many of us have not been able to comply with the strickt letter of the requirements of the 9th article of the treaty, although our being here at all, is strong proof that we would gladly have complied if we had had the ability, yet for this inability *We are to be driven out of the nation, as intruders.* Some of us, who were in the nation, before the six months had expired, owing to fortuitous circumstances, and in some instances, our ignorance, have not been able to prove the fact to the satisfaction of the supreme court of the cherokee nation, sitting as commissioners. *And for this, we are to be driven out of the nation, as intruders.* . . . Col Downing, the Principal Cheif, who marched out at the head of the loyal Cherokees to fight for the Union, has recommended our adoption as citizens, in his last two annual messages to the National Council. Col W. P. Ross, who is the leader of the political party opposed to Cheif Downing, sustained the cheif in this measure, and spoke in our favor, both in the senate, and out of it. Yet the disloyal part of the Cherokees have succeeded in working upon the prejudices of some of the councillors and have defeated the cheifs kind recommendation of measures for our releif. And we are *in consequence to be driven out as intruders.* We have sent humble and respectful petitions to the national council, praying for releif, and a liberal construction of the 9th article of the treaty of 1866. But it was in vain. Our enemies drowned the voice of our Prayer, and some times our petitions were not even read in the council. These very men, who are now the hardest upon us are those for whom we have in past years toiled unpaid, as slaves. Their education, which gives them their present power was paid for by the toil of slaves, and now that we are free, they are about to drive us from the land of our birth, homeless, and houseless, and to rob us of the little we have saved by these years of labor, and suffering In obediance to these demands of our enemies, the United States Indian Agent for the Cherokees, has issued a public notice to all intruders, to leave this Nation immediately; and we are told that *we are intruders.* Thus we are to be driven out by the United States military, on the demand of those, against whom we have fought in defence of Your Government, and ruthlessly deprived of the benefits intended for us by the United States, and the mass of the Cherokees . . ." DS (111 signatures, undated), *ibid.,* RG 233, 42A-D1. On Feb. 21, John B. Jones, agent, Tahlequah, Indian Territory, wrote to Brig. Gen. Oliver O. Howard. ". . . The petition of these colored people sets forth quite correctly their situation. Their case calls for some action, & they certainly are objects of commiseration I hardly know what to suggest as the Cherokee National Council (Legislature) has refused for two successive years to adopt these people as citizens, which measure was recommended by Col Lewis Downing Principal Chief, in his messages of 1870 & 1871. In case the Delegation of this Nation, now in Washington, will not, for any reason, make an arrangement to have these people become citizens, on an equality with those of their brethren who were adopted under the 9th Art. of the Treaty of 1866, I see but one other course open. It is this. Under the same treaty the Cherokees agree that all of their territory west of the 96th meridian be held in trust by the U. S. upon which to settle various Indians. Now it may be that the Government can obtain for these non-citizen colored people, a tract of country west of 96th meridian, & make some arrangement by which they may be permitted to sell their improvements here or have the Nation buy the improvements & dispose of them to its own citizens   At any rate a home ought to be secured for them & they ought not to lose all the labor they have bestowed on their farms in this Nation. Perhaps this course is impracticable. If you can devise any other measures for their relief I shall be most happy to give you any aid in my power to carry them out. I sympathize deeply with these people, but it became my duty to rid the Cherokee Nation of all intruders, & in the performance of that duty these people were thus notified to leave. Hoping that you will interest yourself in behalf of these people, & that some measures may be taken for their relief. . . ." ALS, *ibid.* On July 16, Jones testified before a visiting House subcommittee on Indian Affairs that he had been ordered "not to press the removal against those colored persons, but to go on and put out all other intruders." *HRC,* 42-3-98, 471. On Oct. 30, 1872, and March 3, 1873, John McDonald, Upper Sandusky, Ohio, wrote to USG. "with pleasure I a vail my self the preasant oppertunity to in form you of the Cherochee Nation   the Cherochees the talk of turnen the poor Col people out of the Nation Mr preasadent Grant accorden to the treatia in the year of 1867 When the treaia the Cherochees wer to take them in and give them the same rigtes as the had   Mr Preasadent is this right to turnn the poor people out of hauses when the have the same rightes and prievliges as the Cherochees have   you know that is not fare   the poor people have never asked you for any money and the indians have asked you fore money time and agan but thes poor people have neve asked you   the made the money by the seet of the brow   the whit people the say the Wont take them in   the say the never have bin slaves under them and thare fore the wont have them   I think it hard to turn them out What whar the are over 200 000 of acres of land lays vacant and then turn ~~out of homes~~ then turn Thes poor people out of homes and Mr Preasadent the ask you fore protections   you know it is hard When the have the same rightes as the Cherochees have accorden to the treatia in the year of 1867 and I know you are a friend to the poor Colard people wich mad me ask you   please anseer this not if you please mr Preasadent" "I im brace the oppertunity to in form you on the most im portant queston Mr preasiden as hear be fore I writen to you and received no aseer from you as I thought it wer my dutey to address you once more agane a pon the mose im portan queston as I asked you a bout maken provison fore those poor blakes in the Cherochee Nation   Mr Preident the asked me to see to this buisness and so I thought it was my buisness to represent those poor coullar people wich is in sad condition   the want some provison made fore the own a bout public money fore schools fore them   Mr Preident pleas make a provison fore them so the may educate ther posterity   the claim the have bin slaves all of there lives and now and the claim there giten old and not longe fore this wirld but the are well wisher fore ther posterity   well now Mr Preident if you pleas helpe those blackes with public funds if you please   the claim the had orto have public funds as well as the cherochees have   Mr Preident I think the have the same rite and priveliges to the public funds as the cherochee indians have   I hant any more to say a pon the queston   hopen to receive a favor & reply from you Mr President" ALS, DNA, RG 75, Letters Received, Cherokee Agency. On Feb. 10, McDonald also wrote to USG "a bout the poor blackes Wich have bin slaves under the Cherochees" ALS, *ibid.*, RG 48, Miscellaneous Div., Letters Received. See Daniel F. Littlefield, Jr., *The Cherokee Freedmen: From Emancipation to American Citizenship* (Westport, Conn., 1978), pp. 75–79.

On March 3, William Stephens, Russell Creek, Indian Territory, wrote to USG. "Being a citizen of the Cherokee Nation by Birth I beg permission to submit to your notice the following fact namely, That the council convened at Tahlequah lately have passed a law refusing to grant permits to us to employ proper help to enable us to carry on our legitimate business which is that of farming,   Now said law is oppressive and detrimental to the interests of the Nation in every way and in my humble opinion ought to be abolished for if carried out to the letter we are no better than slaves for it deprives us of our only means of support and confines us to the whims of a class of people who have always been and still are opposed to improvement of any kind I mean the full Bloods. I have the laws and treaties in my house and I have carefully read them and the inference I draw from them is this, that whenever any law is found to be oppressive to us it is in the power of the President of the U S A to suspend or abolish said law. I have never seen your Excellency since the surrender of Vicksburg but I think if I could see you now I could convince you that the enacting of such laws is both unjust and oppressive and tend to degrade instead of enlighten the inhabitants of the Nation   I served faithfully as did many others of my race four years in the war and now upon coming home to my own country I am trying to live by cultivating the soil. Heretofore we have been allowed to employ white men to assist us and everything appeared to pass of pleasently and agreeably to both parties. We are not in favor of allowing white families to squat on our lands and open farms for themselves but we are in favor of being allowed to hire single men work for us by the day or month and for which we are willing to pay. . . . Now Mr President I do not mean to dictate in this matter but only express my opinion when I say that if the land in the Nation were allotted to us equally according to our families and we were allowed to open our farms to be cultivated by the whites it would be much better for each family would own enough land to start a small neighborhood and establish schools, our children would grow up and be educated together and in time to come the race would be extinct, or if you thought better to give each citizen his own part or portion of land to keep or sell as he pleased it would only be fair and just for why not let the red man have the same right to sell his land for $1.25 per acre or retain it as best suits himself. It is too true that our lands are lying idle and we are not to blame in the least for if we are not to be allowed to improve our farms of what use is the land to us, . . ." ALS, DNA, RG 75, Letters Received, Cherokee Agency. See William G. McLoughlin, *After the Trail of Tears: The Cherokees' Struggle for Sovereignty, 1839–1880* (Chapel Hill, 1993), pp. 294–97.

On Jan. 23, 1872, the House of Representatives had referred to committee an undated petition from "freedmen of the Choctaw Nation" complaining of discrimination under Choctaw laws. *HMD*, 42-2-46. On March 18, William Bryant, principal chief, Choctaw Nation, transmitted to USG resolutions approved on March 4. "Where as there is now with in the limits of this Choctaw Nation a large number of Freedmen whose relations to the Choctaw Nation are novel and unsatisfactory both to the Freedmen and to the Choctaw Nation. And where as the proper relations of the said Freedmen has become a question of great and growing interest both to them and us. And where as the Principal Chief of this Nation has earnestly urged upon the National Council to adopt such measures as may seem best calculated to releave this great question of its embarrassments. And where as also a very large number of the Freedmen afore said have petitioned the Government of the

United States, by their single petition presented to the House of Congress and referred to the Committee on Freedmen affairs in said House, setting up many pretended grievances suffered by them at the Hands of this Nation, and praying the Government of the United States to take such steps as may seem necessary to relieve them from their pretended grievances at our Hands and to enable them to find homes beyond the limits of this Nation. Therefore Sect 1st Be it enacted by the General Council of the Choctaw Nation Assembled; That it Shall be and it is hereby made the duty of the Principal Chief of this Nation and all other executive Officers thereof to aid all necessary continuance and support to the United States in any measures it may adopt in the removal of the said Freedmen petitioners as aforesaid and all others desiring in like manner to be removed beyond the limits of this Nation to such place as may be agreed upon between said Freedmen and the United States. . . ." Copy, DNA, RG 75, Letters Received, Choctaw Agency. On March 28, Charles Anderson, Boggy Depot, Choctaw Nation, wrote to USG. "we or the collord poplation of the Choctow and Chicksaw nation have found out, that a men by the nem of finn have Slipt in down blow us and taking in So. meny nems and Repoted to the Government it the want to be removed, and fiend it out and We have com togearther to triy to cove our Selfts   the majarrity of the Choctow and Sicksaw nation ar the Sam oppinon is was we agread com Under the potection of the Government, of, US, therefor I pray to my God, in your bhave for you onebel president of US, to keep Back our Rights in Washington   We or doing So will and we dont want to be out of hom.   thes peopl what these mens the dont Know what the or doing So Stope them for Gods Sake And S cire our Rights   So here is nams of the responcbel mans Watch gotogearther wrot this letter to See if you could do Somthing for uS . . . this is mens is com togreather to triy to Stope this. and, if this 300—will Go, give them thrir rights Keep ours Back, So god helpe you   Writ and let Us know as Soon as posbel" ALS, *ibid.* See *HED*, 42-3-1, part 5, I, 622; 43-1-212; *SMD*, 43-1-118; Angie Debo, *The Rise and Fall of the Choctaw Republic* (2nd ed., Norman, 1961), pp. 89–90, 99–109.

To Morrison R. Waite

———

Dated at Washn D C Jan 22 *187*[4]

Your Commission is signed   Shall it be held here for delivery or mailed to you

U. S. GRANT

Telegram received (at 8:00 P.M.), DLC-Morrison R. Waite. On Jan. 23, 1874, Morrison R. Waite, Cincinnati, telegraphed to USG. "Please retain Commission   it will be two weeks before I can get to Washn unless my presence there is required earlier" Telegram received, DLC-USG, IB. On Jan. 19, USG had nominated Waite as chief justice. A graduate of Yale (1837) and lawyer in Toledo, Waite lost congressional elections as a Whig (1849) and an independent Republican (1862). He served as U.S. counsel before the Geneva tribunal. See *PUSG*, 22, 122; C. Peter Magrath, *Morrison R. Waite: The Triumph of Character* (New York, 1963); Waite to Secretary of the Interior Columbus Delano, Nov. 18, 1871, DNA, RG 59, Letters of Application and Recommendation; letters to Waite from Orville E. Babcock and Gen. William T. Sherman, May 1 and 11, 1874, DLC-Morrison R. Waite.

On Nov. 19, 1869, Luther Day, Ravenna, Ohio, had written to USG. "I am informed that the friends of Mr. M. R. Waite, of Toledo, Ohio, will request his appointment to the judgeship for the circuit of Michigan, Ohio, Kentucky and Tennessee. He is a man of unquestioned integrity, possessed of the first order of abilities thoroughly educated and diciplined. He is an experienced and able Lawyer, ranking with the best in the state, and we have as good lawyes in this state as there are in the west. He is eminently fitted for the position; and, if he receives the appointment, the office will be worthily filled, and its duties faithfully and ably discharged. His reputation is such, ~~that~~ I doubt not that his appointment would be generally approved by the Bar and people." ALS, OFH.

To Otis Keilholtz et al.

————

Washington D. C. Jan. 28, 1874

GENTLEMEN:

I have the honor to acknowledge the receipt of your polite invitation to be present at the meeting to be held on the 29th inst. in behalf of the Centennial celebration of 1876, and regret that I shall be unable to be present and participate with you. I wish you, however, the greatest success.

The object of your meeting is one which appeals to every earnest lover of his country, and in the success of which we all must feel a personal interest.

I trust your meeting will result in much good to the Centennial.

Very respectfully yours

U. S. GRANT

To MESSRS. OTIS KEILHOLTZ [1] GEO. S. BROWN [2]
S. M. SHOEMAKER [3] & OTHERS, COM. BALTO. MD.

Copy, DLC-USG, II, 2. See *Baltimore Sun,* Jan. 24, 28–30, 1874.

1. Otis Keilholtz served as chairman, committee on invitation and reception.
2. George S. Brown, born in 1834, directed an influential banking house in Baltimore.
3. See letter to Samuel M. Shoemaker, Jan. 6, 1874. On Feb. 26, 1874, Governor William P. Whyte of Md. wrote to USG. "Hon John W. Davis, who was heretofore, appointed by your Excellency, an Alternate Commissioner from the State of Maryland to the American Centennial Exposition of 1876. has resigned that Position, and I beg leave to nominate as his successor, Samuel M. Shoemaker Esq of Baltimore City." LS, DNA, RG 59, Letters of Application and Recommendation.

To Nathaniel Carlin

———

Washington D. C. Feb.y 12th *1874*

DEAR SIR:

Your letter of the 3d inst. was duly received. I think it not advisable to hire Dunham and his team. In regard to the purchase of a pair of mules it may be advisable to do so. But in that event you might sell the two horses that you speak of as unsafe and useless.—Elrod wrote me that one of the men in the stable kicked the mare Beauty until he caused the loss of her colt. If that is the case it may be well to try her again as a breeder. She is of fine blood and ought to bring fast colts.

I sent Mr. Long $500 00 recently for Elrod. That makes $1000 00 since he left the place. I will send him the balance along as I can, though I do not agree that his account is correct. It is wrong in the amount he was to received for the first and second year particularly. With these exceptions I will settle his accounts as he presents them.[1]

Yours Truly
U. S. GRANT

N. CARLIN, ESQ.

ALS, OClWHi.

1. See *PUSG*, 24, 233–34.

To John F. Long

———

Strictly Confidential

Washington D. C. Feb.y 16th *1874*

DEAR JUDGE:

Mr. Fox was here last week, or the week before, and asked to know if he would probably be re-appointed at the expiration of his term, about two months hence. I frankly told him that I proposed a change at that time, but that no complaints had reached me of his management of the office.—Your name was not mentioned.

Yours Truly

U. S. GRANT

ALS, MoSHi. On Feb. 16, 1874, William H. Benton, St. Louis, wrote to USG. "Very many of your friends here are anxious to have Judge *John F. Long* Occupy the Office of Surveyor of this Port 'Tis not necessary for us to tell you of his integrity, capacity & fitness—you know him well, but we do wish to say that if you can find it convenient to place him in the position suggested it will be very gratifying to very many of your personal & political friends" ALS, DNA, RG 56, Collector of Customs Applications. William McKee and Constantine Maguire, collector of Internal Revenue, favorably endorsed this letter. AES, *ibid.* On June 8, USG nominated John F. Long as surveyor of customs, St. Louis. A St. Louis newspaper editorialized. "The nomination of Judge John F. Long for Surveyor of the Port of St. Louis, vice Mr. E. W. Fox, resigned, will give general satisfaction to the people of this city, to whom the new appointee is well and favorably known. Judge Long is an old personal friend of the President's, and, although he has not been known as a Republican in politics, we believe his appointment will be indorsed by the staunchest adherents of the Administration." *St. Louis Globe*, June 9, 1874. See letter to Elias W. Fox, June 5, 1874.

To Congress

———

[*Feb. 21, 1874*]

To THE SENATE & HOUSE OF REPRESENTAT[IVES]

While feeling an unwillingness to press my views on subjects of legislation,—further than recommendations in Annual Messages— there is one subject which seems to me now of parimount interest, and which justifies a special message.

Out of the war to preserve the perpetuity of the Union grew up a financial system which gave us an irredeemable currency—justified at the time by the necessities—but now—so long after those events —I feel ~~that~~ there is an obligation upon the Govt to take immediate, permanent, unrepealable steps towards ~~that end~~ resumption. The end is all that I recommend specifically but throw in [volunteer] one or two suggestions [as to the manner in which] of ~~reaching it~~ how it may be reached.—First; there is a necessity of increasing the revenues of the Country—both in currency and Gold—to give the power to ~~increase the reserves of~~ the Treasury to ~~a specie basis~~ aid in the accomplishment of the end. ‡ To secure the former I would recommend an increase of the tax on whisky to One dollar per gallon; an increase which I believe could be faithfully collected; and an increase of four cents pr. pound on tobacco; Aa restoration of the tax on Legacies & successions is one that might be advisable. For the gold increase of receipts I suggest first a repeal of the 10 pr. ct. horizontal reduction of the tariff. I am clear in my own mind also that the duty on tea & coffee should never have been taken off. It has not reduced the price of the article but has increased the receipts of the treasuries of the Countries producing these articles, at our expense. A restoration of the duties on Tea & Coffee now would no doubt, temporarily, chance the price of those articles: but the price ultimately would be independent of our tariff. There is a competition in the article of coffee which will bring to the country the cheapest supply when we collect a duty. While an export duty is collected, in the the country most favorable for its production, just in the proportion that we diminish the tariff. The same reasoning is applicable to the importation of tea, except that middle men reap, a portion of the advantages of a reduction, of or abolishment, of tariff on that commodity.—I suggest therefore for your consideration the propriety of restoring those duties, and of taking in the whole field where revenue may be increased without embarrassing public interests and industries.

Without receipts in the Treasury, beyond expenditures, there is no possibility of Government being able to assume its pledge of redeeming the currency issued by it in coin. By having increased, means and increasing, means the power will approach, day by day, without giving any sudden shock to business and industries such as must come, periodically, from the use of a currency perfectly valuless out of the country where issued—

I recommend a repeal of the 10 pr. ct. horizontal reduction of the tariff; a renewel of the tariff on tea & coffee; an increase of the tax on whiskey & tobacco—say to $1.00 pr. gallon on the latter former; and an increase of 4 cts. pr. pound on the latter, and a restoration of the legacy and succession tax.—There may be other items that which will meet your approval; but my desire is to call up the general subject so that it may receive the best solution.

ADf (bracketed material not in USG's hand), NRU. See following letter; message to Congress, Feb. 27, 1874.

To William A. Richardson

Washington D. C. Feb.y 21st *1874*

DEAR SIR:

Enclosed I send you rough draft of a message hastily drawn off in pencil, which I propose to send to Congress; but wish to submit to you first. After the first paragraph I propose to recite the different Acts of Congress pledging the faith of the Govt. against expansion, particularly the pledge given when U. S. bonds were first put on the market; and the first bill signed by me, in March 1869,[1] and the pledges in the different republican conventions since, as further reasons for sending this message. I wish you would draw off for me this paragraph.

I will also add a recommendation for free banking with such restrictions as to prohibit an increase of legal tenders; demanding compulsory retention of gold interest received by National banks, and forced redemption.

Yours &c.

U. S. GRANT

HON. WM A. RICHARDSON,
SEC. OF THE TREAS.

ALS, MH. See preceding message; message to Congress, [*Feb. 27, 1874*].

1. On March 18, 1869, USG had signed an *"Act to strengthen the public Credit."* *U.S. Statutes at Large*, XVI, 1.

To Congress

TO THE SENATE AND HOUSE OF REPRESENTATIVES:

I have the honor, herewith, to submit the report of the Centennial Commissioners, and to add a word in the way of recommendation.

There have now been international expositions held by three of the great powers of Europe. It seems fitting that the one-hundredth anniversary of our independence should be marked by an event that will display to the world the growth and progress of a nation devoted to freedom, and to the pursuit of fame, fortune, and honors by the lowest citizen as well as the highest. A failure in this enterprise would be deplorable. Success can be assured by arousing public opinion to the importance of the occasion. To secure this end, in my judgment, congressional legislation is necessary to make the exposition both national and international.

The benefits to be derived from a successful international exposition are manifold. It will necessarily be accompanied by expenses beyond the receipts from the exposition itself; but they will be compensated for, many fold, by the commingling of people from all sections of our own country; by bringing together the people of different nationalities; by bringing into juxtaposition, for ready examination, our own and foreign skill and progress in manufactures, agriculture, art, science, and civilization.

The selection of the site for the exposition seems to me appropriate from the fact that one hundred years before the date fixed for the exposition, the Declaration of Independence—which launched us into the galaxy of nations as an independent people—emanated from the same spot.

We have much in our varied climate, soil, mineral products, and skill, of which advantage can be taken by other nationalities to their profit. In return they will bring to our shores works of their skill, and familiarize our people with them, to the mutual advantage of all parties.

Let us have a complete success in our centennial exposition, or suppress it in its infancy, acknowledging our inability to give it the international character to which our self-esteem aspires.

U. S. GRANT.

FEBRUARY 25, 1874.

SED, 43-1-30. On Feb. 23, 1874, U.S. Representative Joseph R. Hawley of Conn., president, Centennial Commission, Philadelphia, wrote to USG reviewing preparations for the Centennial exhibition and requesting a government appropriation. "... The recent almost unprecedented depression in manufactures, trade, and finance has interfered with the progress of subscriptions to the stock of the Centennial Board of Finance, and with the payment of installments due on those already made. This state of affairs affords another imperative reason for such action by Congress as will provide sufficient and timely appropriations to guarantee the success of the national undertaking. . . . The commission has information that preparations are in progress throughout the country to make the most creditable exhibits of the products and industries of the nation, and that this feature of the exhibition is assured beyond any doubt; but as the enterprise is regarded as a national one, there is an unwillingness to contribute money for the preparation and installation of the exhibition, which it is regarded as specially incumbent on the National Government to provide for. While many of the States of the Union are not in a financial condition to contribute money for this purpose, the citizens thereof express the warmest sympathy in the success of the enterprise, and will give it their cordial support so far as it is in their power. . . . The time has now arrived when it is imperatively necessary to proceed with the erection of the buildings; but it is an indispensable prerequisite to know whether the money which Congress thought would be raised by the act of June 1, 1872, will be furnished in part by Congress. There is time enough for the work, but not a month to spare. The commission, therefore, respectfully and earnestly urges submitting this report to Congress as speedily as practicable, with such recommendations as, to the President, the exigency of the case may seem to require." *Ibid.*, pp. 2–7. Congress did not appropriate funds. *CR*, 43–1, 3600–13, 3635–60, 3670–82; *ibid.*, Appendix, 253–63. On June 5, USG signed a bill authorizing invitations to other nations but also providing that "the United States shall not be liable, directly or indirectly, for any expenses attending such exposition, or by reason of the same." *U.S. Statutes at Large*, XVIII, part 3, p. 53. See also *CR*, 43–1, 809–16, 4256–64; *SMD*, 43-1-110; James D. McCabe, *The Illustrated History of the Centennial Exhibition*, . . . (Philadelphia, 1876), pp. 215–16.

On Feb. 27, Secretary of State Hamilton Fish had recorded in his diary. "I then referred to a report made by the Centennial Exhibition directly to the President, which he had communicated on the 25th instant to Congress, and stated that it was a gross irregularity and insubordination, and that I should have no further charge of the Commission, and requested the President to transfer it to some other Department. He begged me to retain it, and said that the Report had come to him without his knowing whence it came, and he had transmitted it without thought, because of his interest in the success of the Exhibition; that he did not think any disrespect had been intended to the Department of State. I insisted that the act was so insubordinate and irregular, that it showed either incapacity of administration of the interest committed to the Commission or ignorance of the proprieties of official intercourse with the Commission. It was decided that the business of the Commission should be transferred to the Department of the Interior." DLC-Hamilton Fish.

On June 5, George W. Childs, Philadelphia, wrote to USG. "I find myself obliged to trespass upon your [a]ttention with an unusually long letter, through a desire to lessen the anxiety just now imposed on my good and valued friend Mr John Welsh. His position as President of the Centennial Board of Finance has brought upon him a load of heavy but almost unseen labor, and he fears that the full success of the undertaking cannot be assured unless the [i]ntercourse between the Government and the Centennial Commission [(o]f which General Hawley is the President) shall be conducted through the medium of the of the Department of State. From words dropped in the Congressional debates and from allusions in published letters, he fears that the change from the State Department to the Interior Department must have been the result of a misapprehension that the Commission had purposely interfered between the Department and the President at the time when the Report of the Commission was made to the President, and when the President's special message was sent into Congress last February . . ." LS, DNA, RG 59, Miscellaneous Letters.

To Congress

[*Feb. 27, 1874*]

TO THE SENATE AND HOUSE OF REPRESENTATIVES:

While feeling an unwillingness to press my views on subjects of legislation—further than recommendations in Annual messages—there is one subject which seems to me now of paramount interest, and which justifies a special message.

Out of the war (conflict?) to preserve the perpetuity of the Union grew up a financial system which gave us an irredeemable currency —justified at the time by the necessities—but now—so long after those events—I feel there is an obligation upon the Government to take immediate, permanent irrepealable steps towards resumption. The end is all that I recommend specifically, but ~~volunteer~~ will make one or two suggestions as to the manner in which it may be reached. First;—there is a necessity of increasing the revenues of the country, both in currency and gold, to give the power to the Treasury to aid in the accomplishment of the end. To secure the former, I would recommend an increase of the tax on whisky to one dollar per gallon; an increase which I believe could be faithfully collected; and an increase of four cents per pound on tobacco. A restoration of the tax on Legacies and Successions is one that might be advisable. For the gold increase of receipts I suggest first, a repeal of the ten per. cent. horizontal reduction of the tariff. I am clear in my own mind also that the duty on tea and coffee should never have been taken off. It has not reduced the price of the articles but has increased the receipts of the treasuries of the countries producing those articles, at our expense. A restoration of the duties on tea and coffee now, would no doubt temporarily advance the price of those articles, but the price ultimately would be independent of our tariff. There is a competition in the article of coffee which will bring to the country the cheapest supply when we collect a duty. An export duty is collected in the country most favorable for its production, just in the proportion that we diminish the tariff. The same reasoning is applicable to the importation of tea, except that middle men reap a portion of the advantages of a reduction, or abolishment, of tariff on that commodity. I suggest, therefore, for your consideration the propriety of restoring these duties, and of taking in the whole field where revenue may be increased without embarrassing public interests and industries.

Without receipts in the Treasury beyond Expenditures, and the amount required for the sinking fund, which in order to keep faith with the public creditors and support the credit of the country must be maintained and provided for, there is no possibility of Government being able to ~~assume~~ keep its pledge of redeeming the currency issued by it in coin. By having increased, and increasing, means the power will approach, day by day, without giving any sudden shock to business and industries such as must come periodically, from the use of a currency perfectly valueless out of the country where issued.

And I recommend that whatever surplus may arise from increased taxation be applied, first to reduce the legal tender circulation down to the minimum fixed by law, and the balance to the accumulation of coin in the Treasury until the amount so held will be sufficient to enable the Secretary of the Treasury to redeem United States notes in coin whenever demanded. While the process of accumulation is going on it would no doubt be necessary to sell some coin to meet the demands on the Treasury which will continue to be larger than the currency receipts, the surplus revenue being from coin receipts alone.

These measures should not interfere with any of those which are undertaken with a view to reduce the expenses of the Government to the lowest point of economy at which it is practicable to carry on the public business in a proper manner. The greater the economy the greater will be the surplus to be used for the purpose of hastening a return of specie payments. The necessity of an early resumption of specie payments has heretofore been recognized by the Executive and Legislative branches of the Government, as well as by the people in their several national political conventions. As early as December 4. 1865. the House of Representatives passed a Resolution by a vote of 144 yeas to 6 nays cordially concurring "in the views of the Secretary of the Treasury in relation to the necessity of a contraction of the currency, with a view to as early a resumption of specie payments as the business interests of the country will permit", and pledging "co-operative action to this end as speedily as possible."

The first act passed by the 41st Congress on the 18th day of March 1869, was as follows:

"An Act to strengthen the public credit of the United States. Be it enacted &c. That in order to remove any doubt as to the purpose of the Government to discharge all its obligations to the public creditors, and to settle conflicting questions and interpretations of the law, by virtue of which such obligations have been contracted, it is hereby provided and declared that the faith of the United States is solemnly pledged to the payment in coin, or its equivalent, of all the obligations of the United States, and of all the interest bearing obligations, except in cases where the law authorizing the issue of any such obligations has expressly provided that the same may be paid in lawful money, or in other currency than gold and silver, but none of the said interest bearing obligations, not already due, shall be redeemed or paid before maturity, unless at such times as the United States notes shall be convertible into coin at the option of the holder, or unless at such time bonds of the United States, bearing a lower rate of interest than the bonds to be redeemed, can be sold at *par* in coin. And the United States also solemnly pledges its faith to make provision at the earliest practicable period for the redemption of the United States notes in coin."

This act still remains as a continuing pledge of the faith of the United States "to make provision at the earliest practicable period for the redemption of the United States notes in coin".

In my first annual message to Congress in December, 1869, I called the attention of that body to the subject in the following words:

"Among the evils growing out of the rebellion, and not yet referred to, is that of an irredeemable currency. It is an evil which I hope will receive your most earnest attention. It is a duty, and one of the highest duties of Government, to secure to the citizen a medium of exchange of fixed, unvarying value. This implies a return to a specie basis, and no substitute for it can be devised. It should be commenced now and reached at the earliest praciticable moment consistent with a fair regard to the interests of the debtor class. Immediate resumption, if practicable, would not be desirable. It would compel the debtor class to pay, beyond their contracts, the premium on gold at the date of their purchase, and would bring bankruptcy and ruin to thousands. Fluctuations, however, in the paper value of the measure of all values (gold) is detrimental to the interests of trade. It makes the man of business an involuntary gambler, for, in all sales where future payment is to be made, both parties speculate as to what will be the value of the currency to be paid and received. I earnestly recommend to you then, such legislation as will insure a gradual return to specie payments and put an immediate stop to fluctuations in the value of currency". I still adhere to the views then expressed.

A declaration contained in the Act of June 30th 1864. created an obligation that the total amount of United States notes issued or to be issued should never exceed four hundred millions of dollars, ~~and of this sum~~ [it has been assumed that 44 Millions was] ~~there should be at least forty-four millions kept in reserve in the Treasury to meet emergencies such as have heretofore happened and are likely in the future to occur again when the revenues suddenly fall below the expenditures~~. [The amount in actual circulation was actually reduced to 356 Million of dollars at which point Congress passed the Act of Feb. 4 1868 suspending the further reduction of the currency. The 44 Millions have ever been regarded as a reserve to be used only in case of emergency such as has occured on several occasions and must occur when from any cause revenues suddenly fall below expenditures   And Such a reserve is ~~actually~~ further necessary because the fractional currency, amounting to 50 Millions is redeemable in legal tender, on call. It may be said that such a return of fractional currency for redemption is improbable. But let ~~there be~~ steps be taken for a return to a specie basis and it will be found that silver will take the place of fractional currency as rapidly as it can be supplied, when

the premium on gold gets ~~below the~~ to ~~premium on silver~~ a sufficiently low point.]

With the amount of United States notes to be issued permanently
fixed within proper limits, and the Treasury so strengthened as to
be able to redeem them in coin on demand, it will then be safe to inaugurate a system of free banking with such provisions as to make
compulsory redemption of the circulating notes of the banks in coin
or in United States notes themselves redeemable and made equivalent to coin.

As a measure for strengthening the banks to enable them to prepare for the redemption of their own notes in coin I believe it would
be advisable to require them to retain part or all of the coin received
by them as interest on the bonds deposited to secure their circulation.

Df (bracketed material in USG's hand), DLC-USG, III. For an earlier draft, see message
to Congress, Feb. 21, 1874. On Feb. 27, 1874, Secretary of State Hamilton Fish recorded
in his diary. "The President reads a draft of a proposed Message to Congress, which he said
he had prepared some days since under apprehension that a measure might pass Congress
relative to the financial condition of the country in the form which seemed to be indicated
by the debates of that day in the Senate and which would require his veto. That he was not
certain whether it was expedient to send the message, but he wished to submit his views
to the Cabinet, and to ask their opinion as to the expediency of sending the message. The
paper which he read was very strong and positive in favor of an early resumption of specie
payments and opposed to any inflation or expansion of the currency—recommended increased taxation on whiskey, and the restoration of the impost on tea and coffee: and a repeal of the horizontal reduction of ten % in the legislation of 1872. Doubts were expressed
as to the propriety of specific recommendations—all seemed to agree in the general policy
and views of the paper, as far as there was any expression of opinion—but there seemed
to be a general doubt as to the expediency or necessity of a message at the present time—
it was eventually decided to await the action of Congress, and that if legislation assumed
an objectionable form a veto might be interposed and an opportunity would be presented
for the presentation of the general views set forth in the paper." DLC-Hamilton Fish. A
Senate bill to redistribute banknote circulation, introduced Feb. 3, had provoked extensive
debate. See *CR*, 43–1, 1511–23, 1545–59, 1584–98, 1626–39, 1667–81.

On Jan. 3, William Radde, New York City, had written to USG. "It is a feeling of deep
interest for the welfare and prosperity of our beloved country that prompts me to offer the
enclosed simple plan, under which we can safely and at once return to Specie payment, and
otherwise improve the financial condition of the country. Will you be pleased to look it
over and, if it meets your approval, be kind enough to see it carried into effect. Perhaps you
remember that I have been introduced to you by Genl F. Sigel and Hon. Fr. Kuehne, when
you were in New York on the occasion of the departure of your daughter for Europe. I have
been nominated by the Committee of Seventy and was elected one of the Reform Alder-
man of this City in 1872. May I ask the kindness of you to let me know whether this communication has come into your possession, . . . P. S. New York February 4, 1874. I intended
to hand this to you personally but as pressing business prevents me from doing so I have

to send it by mail. This the reason of the delay." ALS, DNA, RG 56, Letters Received from the President. The enclosure is *ibid.*

On Jan. 13, William Thorpe, New York City, wrote to USG. "This country presents the unfortunate spectacle of plenty of currency for every legitimate purpose, yet so disposed that an insufficient amount is available. We have three classes of currency or money, each of different value; viz. 1. Gold, which is par; 2. Silver, which is about 6% discount; & 3. Govt. notes and National Bank Notes, which vary from 10 to 15% discount. Why not equalize the three? I[.] Gold is the standard money all over the world, and never varies. It is now par, and therefore all right. II. The silver dollar is worth about 94 cents, and rarely ever changes. Put a little more silver in the Silver Dollar, when coined, and it becomes par, and will remain so for 50 years to come. III. The currency issued by the Treasury is simply the Govt promise to pay ~~coin~~ money (*coin money*) on demand. It is below par simply and solely because the Govt. fails to redeem it, as per agreement, and also refuses to receive it for debts (viz. duties on imports.) Let the Treasury provide itself with sufficient money to keep its credit good by redeeming these demand notes, and also receive these notes for all kinds of dues. These simple things will bring about the following beneficial results: I. Establish the credit of the Government on a sound basis; because the Govt. keeps faith; II. Give the country a sound currency to do its business, and protect all classes from the demoralizing effects, losses, panics and bankruptcies of the present vicious system; III. Increase the currency to the extent of all gold and silver now horded up or used to speculate upon   IV. Do away with the necessity of all expansion or contraction, and give us a few years of peace and prosperity. Do not say this is an impossibility—that the Treasy has not the gold and can't get it. The *Gold* can be got to do this. Do not listen to theories about the *shrinkage of values.* Values don't shrink when measured by a gold standard. We have had enough of experiments. McCulloch tried *contraction*; Richardson has been trying to liquidate the bonded debt. Both are failures. Gold is about where it was at your first inauguration, and you can't change it *except by redeeming matured obligations,* (viz Treasy Notes) in gold. The bonded debt is not due and is at par because people believe it will be redeemed." LS, *ibid.*

On Feb. 11, A. B. Hicks, Topeka, wrote to USG. "In view of the present financial condition of the country, permit me to offer the following proposition; hoping that you will give it careful concideration. Get congress to amend the present banking Law so that parties desiring to do so can buy Gov't Bonds, by depositing in their Stead, Mortgages are unencumbered, Improved Farms, said Mortgages to bear the same rate of Interest, as the Bonds. Then make Banking free to all who can fullfill the requirements of the Law, thereby leaving our Currency subject to the Laws of supply & demand. Let the Bonds issued be a special Series issued for the purpose, Then let the Gov't return to Specie payment imediately. One of the benefits to be derived from the above is, that the increase in the volume of the currency will in a great measure compensate for the decreace in values arising from a return to a Specie basis. I think I can answer; and shall be happy to do so; any and all objections to the above plan." ALS, *ibid.*

On Feb. 24, Edward J. Nieuwland, Brooklyn, wrote at length to USG concerning alleged European origins of the recent financial panic, asking for $1,200 in return for sharing his "secret ideas" to restore the U.S. economy. ALS, *ibid.*

Pardon

———

To all to whom these Presents shall, come, Greeting:

Whereas, at the June Term, 1873, of the United States Circuit Court for the Northern District of New York, one Beverly W. Jones, one Edwin T. Marsh and one William B. Hall were convicted of illegally registering certain persons as voters, and receiving their votes, and were sentenced, each, to pay a fine of twenty-five dollars;—

And whereas, the Honorable A. A. Sargent[1] asks that they be pardoned, in view of the peculiar circumstances of their offence:—

Now, therefore, be it known, that I, Ulysses S. Grant, President of the United States of America, in consideration of the premises, divers other good and sufficient reasons me thereunto moving, do hereby grant to the said Beverly W. Jones, Edwin T. Marsh and William B. Hall, a full and unconditional pardon.

In testimony whereof, I have hereunto signed my name and caused the seal of the United States to be affixed.

Done at the City of Washington, this Third day of March, A. D. 1874, and of the Independence of the United States the Ninety-eighth.

U. S. GRANT.

Copy, DNA, RG 59, General Records. On Feb. 25 and 26, 1874, Susan B. Anthony, Rochester, N. Y., telegraphed and wrote to U.S. Representative Benjamin F. Butler of Mass. "The inspectors are in Jail tonight   get the president to remit their fine soon as possible" "I telegraphed to you last night asking President to send on remittal of fines of the 8th Ward Inspectors—that they were in our Monroe County jail—have, to day, sent you our City papers—now the *two* who are in jail propose to *stand* by their denial to pay—a friend paid fine of the other—Beverly W. Jones—and he is, therefore, out of jail—but I want the President to order *his* money returned—. . ." Telegram received and ALS, DLC-Benjamin F. Butler. A related letter of March 5 from Anthony to Butler is *ibid.*

On March 25, William B. Hall, Rochester, wrote to USG. "On the 5th day of November 1872 I was acting as Inspector of Election 1st dist. 8th Ward in this City at which time and place Miss Susan B. Anthony and other Ladies Voted, and which caused so much trouble in the U. S. Courts. I wish to make a statement in regard to the part I took in the matter also as to how I was subsequently used by the U. S. Officers. On the last day of registry (in the afternoon) prior to the Election Miss Anthony and others presented themselves for registry claiming as such right the provision made in the 14th amendment. Daniel Warner Esq, then a Supervisor of Election and a Gentleman whom I had known from Boyhood and one whom I had the utmost confidence in advised, and said we would have to register their names   after some discussion I consented and they were registered. After they were registered I consulted three of our eminent Lawyers who said no harm had been done in registering but thought it would not be safe to receive their Ballots. Accordingly upon Election day when they offered their Ballots I protested and refused to receive them   the other two Inspectors Messrs. Jones & Marsh after consultation concluded to receive them,   Complaint was then made to Commr. Ely before whom we had an examination when Jones and Marsh were held and I discharged. At the sitting of the U. S. Court at Albany the following January I was indicted with the other two, and while they were Subpoenaed as witnesses and drawing fees [*for*] such I was obliged to pay my own Expences during all the trials amounting to nearly One hundred and Seventy five dollars ($175.—) I therefore write you as the matter is now settled and most respectfully ask that the Expense to which I have been be remitted as I am unable to lose it having to work hard for a livelihood and having a mother to support. The amount I received for the five (5) days services was Twenty three ($23) dollars thus leaving me about $150.—expense over and above amt recd for service.   hoping my re[*quest may be*] granted . . ." ALS, DNA, RG 60, Letters from the President. See *SMD*, 43-1-39; *SRC*, 43-1-472; *HRC*, 43-1-608, 43-1-648; Elizabeth Cady Stanton, Susan B. Anthony, and Matilda Joslyn Gage, eds., *History of Woman Suffrage* (1882; reprinted New York, 1969), II, 627–715.

1. Born in 1827 in Mass., Aaron A. Sargent moved to Calif. in 1849, worked as a journalist and lawyer, and served as U.S. Representative (1861–63, 1869–73) before he was elected to the Senate in 1873.

To Nathaniel Carlin

———

Washington D. C. March 8th *1874.*

DEAR SIR:

In my last letter I forgot to say anything in answer to your questions in regard to the two stallions on the farm. So far as Peacemaker's pedigree is concerned I can get it reniewed from the gentleman —Mr Sanford—who raised him. Young Hambletonian was sired by Iron Duke—now owned, and always owned, in Orange Co. N. Y. and almost on the adjoining farm to his sire, Old Hambletonian. The full pedigree of Iron Duke can be got—if you have not got it—from the Turf Register. Hambletonian's dam was a very fast and stylish mare —Addie—that I got in 1865. She was the full sister of one of the best stallions in Massachusetts—where both were raised—but I do not know the name of the stallion nor do I recollect his owner's name. If I knew either, the pedigree of the dam would be easily obtained. Addie was a dark bay—not a white spot on her—of great speed and high carriage. Her full brother is a sorrel with white face and two or

three white legs. This accounts for the color of Hambletonian, he being from a bay sire as well as dam.

Now that the "fence law" has gone into effect, and the Spring
promises to be an early one, might you not have Dr. Sharp's place put
in oats & clover? If it can be done, even by a few days hire of extra
teams, I think I would do it.

Yours &c,
U. S. GRANT

N. CARLIN, ESQ.

ALS, CSmH.

To William B. Washburn

M[*arch*] 21 *1874*

By Telegraph from Washn
To Gov Washburn
No insinuation of the kind Contained in the Dispatch from Wilson
Claflin and yourSelf against Judge Russell[1] has been made to me
U. S. GRANT

Telegram received, Duke University, Durham, N. C. A Yale graduate (1844) and Mass.
banker, William B. Washburn served as Republican U.S. Representative (1863–71) until
elected governor. William Claflin, Washburn's predecessor as Mass. governor, was on the
Republican National Executive Committee. On March 2, 1874, Claflin, Boston, wrote to
USG. "It is generally understood that Judge Russell's name is before you for the Venezeu-
lain Mission. His appointment, it seems to me, would be a graceful recognition of his faithful services to the Republican cause, from the formation of the party and, also, a testimony
of his success as a public officer. No one for a quarter of a century has filled the position
of Collector, with such satisfaction to the public   He has always discharged public trusts
with signal ability and fidelity.—Should the desires of his friends here and else where be
acceded to, in this matter, I have no doubt that the Government will be honored in his selection." ALS, DLC-Benjamin F. Butler. Related papers are *ibid.* On April 10, Secretary
of State Hamilton Fish recorded in his diary. "The President suggested that Mr Pile be removed, and on my suggestion modified his proposal to, that he be asked to resign, and
if not done that he be removed—" DLC-Hamilton Fish. On April 14, USG nominated
Thomas Russell as minister to Venezuela, to replace William A. Pile. See *New York Times*,
Feb. 17, 1874.
    On March 17, Thomas J. Owen and Son *et al.*, New York City, had written to USG.
"We, the undersigned merchants of the city of New York, would respectfully recommend
to your consideration the nomination of Mr. Richard Gibbs of this city as Resident Minister to the Republic of Venezuela, for the duties of which we believe him to be fully compe-

tent. Mr. Gibbs has been a merchant of good standing and Consular Agent of the United States at Nuevitas, Cuba, for over Twenty years; is thoroughly acquainted with the Spanish language, and versed in the laws and customs of Venezuela." DS (24 signatures), DNA, RG 59, Letters of Application and Recommendation. Related papers are *ibid.*

On Jan. 26 and 29, 1875, Fish recorded conversations with USG. "He wants to appoint a man by the name of Gibbs, a brother in law of Thos Murphey, to Peru, the only qualifications known is that he is a brotherinlaw of Murphey's, has lived in Cuba, and lost his property and Murphey has to support him   I remonstrate against the appointment: no decission is reached" "He states that Richd Gibbs (Tom Murphey's brotherinlaw) has been to see him and wishes the mission to Peru and has left with him a copy of a paper which he says is on file in the State Department containing his recommendations, and that Sen Conkling is very anxious for the appointment   I tell him that I doubt whether the appointment is advisable or would be popular   He then says that Conkling has not spoken to him on the subject but he is told that he is anxious for it" DLC-Hamilton Fish. See Fish diary, Feb. 5, March 8, 26, and April 6, 1875. *Ibid.* On April 9, USG appointed Richard Gibbs as minister to Peru. Copy, DNA, RG 59, General Records.

1. Russell graduated from Harvard (1845), practiced law, and was elected Boston municipal judge (1853). Elevated to the Mass. Superior Court (1859), he served until nominated as collector of customs, Boston and Charlestown (1867). On Feb. 16, 1874, USG nominated William A. Simmons to replace Russell. On Feb. 17, John M. Forbes *et al.*, Boston, petitioned USG. "The undersigned citizens of Massachusetts beg leave to offer their remonstrances against the appointment of W. A. Simmons to the office of Collector of the Port of Boston, as in every respect unsuitable and repugnant to the sentiments and wishes of the community; While men of all parties subscribe to these views those of us who belong to the Republican party would represent to you that this appointment is peculiarly adverse to the interests of our party, in the State and in the Nation—" DS (36 signatures), *ibid.*, RG 56, Collector of Customs Applications. On the same day, U.S. Representative Ebenezer R. Hoar of Mass. telegraphed to USG. "I am authorized by Messrs Buffinton, Dawes, Gooch, Harris, and Hooper of the delegation from Massachusetts to say that they have not given their consent or approbation to the appointment of Mr Simmons." Telegram received, *ibid.* On Feb. 18, Washburn wrote to USG. "May I beg you for the sake of the harmony and purity of the Republican party of this state to withdraw the nomination of Simmons as Collector of this Port." ALS, *ibid.* On the same day, Vice President Henry Wilson, Boston, telegraphed to USG. "If you accept the withdrawal of Collector Russell resignation You will gratify the business men of Boston—" Telegram received, *ibid.* Also on Feb. 18, Alexander H. Rice and Eugene H. Sampson, Boston, telegraphed to USG. "At an informal meeting of merchants and members of the Board of Trade it was unanimously voted that Hon Thomas Russell be requested to withdraw his resignation as Collector of the Port of Boston and that the President of the United States be respectfully & earnestly requested to concur in such withdrawal. We are authorized to state that Collector Russell accedes to this request." Telegram received (at 12:47 P.M.), *ibid.* On the same day, U.S. Representative Alvah Crocker of Mass. wrote to USG. "I signed the request for the withdrawal of Mr W. A. Simmons for the reason that I did not feel that Boston & my delegation had been sufficiently consulted all of whom are strong Supporters of your Administration— So far as Mr Simmons is concerned in the Administration of his present Office; it has met my approbation" ALS, *ibid.* On Feb. 19, Forbes and Nathaniel Thayer, Boston, telegraphed to USG. "The Simmonds nomination is utterly objectionable to the whole community Except a few proffessional politicians. If persisted in it will break the republican

party here" Telegram received, *ibid.* Related papers are *ibid.* On Feb. 5, 1870, E. H. Lovering, Boston, had written to USG. "It is hoped that you will *not* reappoint Thomas Russell Collector of this Port   He is a *Johnson Appointment* and is all things to all men—Can I say more" ALS, *ibid.*

On Feb. 17 and 18, 1874, U.S. Representative Benjamin F. Butler of Mass. telegraphed to Orville E. Babcock. "Boston Custom House has always been held a New England and not a local office. Collectors have been appointed from Maine & New Hampshire,   I trust that the President will not be moved by the action of a minority of the Massachusetts delegation as against the majority who are satisfied. The only republican senator from Mass will move the Confirmation" "Vice President Wilson will telegraph the President that better withdraw Simmonds name   President knows Willsons good nature. I have a pocket full of telegrams from leading Senators & leading Merchants in Simmons favor" Telegrams received, *ibid.*, RG 107, Telegrams Collected (Bound). On Feb. 18, George B. Harriman, Boston, wrote to USG. "Mr Simmons who you have nominated fo collector of Boston is an honest and truthful man, and has done more for the republicans of this city than any other man. He does not belong to the *Advertiser clique* nor has he graduated from College but he is as good a man for the place as Rice or any body else.   *stick to him*" ALS, *ibid.*, RG 56, Collector of Customs Applications. On Feb. 19, John L. Swift, Boston, telegraphed to USG. "Mr Simmons was a private soldier in the war & commander G A R post fifteen   the soldiers here are all enthusiastically in favor of his appointment as collector of customs" Telegram received, *ibid.* On the same day, Austin Bigelow, Brighton, Mass., telegraphed to USG. "Collector Russell has never enforced your order in regard to holding two offices & after having been informed of the facts still allows a person holding a position in the Custom House to hold a Civil office in this town" Telegram received (at 4:10 P.M.), *ibid.* On Feb. 20, G. A. Somerby, Boston, telegraphed to USG. "Do not fail to support Simmons   the public feeling underneath is strong in his favor & the only safe course is to have him confirmed & all will be quiet" Telegram received, *ibid.* On Feb. 25, Asa Bartlett, Woonsocket, R. I., wrote to USG. "without having any Self interest Whatever, I think the whole tirade against Simmons is a Sumner trick against all apointments of Soldiers to Civil offices," ALS, *ibid.* Other papers supporting Simmons are *ibid.*

On Feb. 21, E. B. Stoddard, Worcester, Mass., wrote to USG. "I desire most respectfully to give you my views in regard to the appointment of a Collector for the port of Boston—. . . It is needless to say, that if the nomination of Mr. Simmons is confirmed it will cause bitter feeling in the party and make a decided split—Some say let it come—but for one I should prefer to avoid it and not let either party of our Congressmen feel that they had triumphed—It was very difficult at our last State Convention to decide upon a chairman: but finally both wings yielded to the Selection of Hon. Alexander H. Bullock our Ex Governor and it was satisfactory to Gen. Butler and his opponents—Now I presume each congressman would like to have his personal friend appointed collector, and it will be very difficult for them to agree on any one man—They probably could not agree upon Gen. Banks   His defection from the party would not be the only reason—I was formerly on his Staff when Governor and have faith to believe that his prospects for political preferment are brightening—But there is one man, whose nomination would meet a universal approval & would not be objectional to Gen Butler, if Mr Simmons is to be withdrawn —That name is Alexander H. Bullock—. . ." ALS, *ibid.* On Feb. 24, George H. Stuart, Philadelphia, wrote to USG. "Mr Tobey having telegraphed me to get a letter from his friend Mr Borie I have just seen him & he is quite willing to add his personal endorsement as below to my previous commendation of Mr T— for the office of Collector of the port of Boston,   He would fill the office with Credit to your Administration." ALS, *ibid.*

Adolph E. Borie favorably endorsed this letter. AES (undated), *ibid.* On Feb. 27, DeWitt C. Butler, Boston, wrote to USG. "A few days since I sent a telegram to you suggesting the name of ex Gov Frederick Smyth of Manchester New Hampshire for Collector of this Port in case of the possible withdrawal of the nomination of Mr Simmons. . . . When I telegraphed to you the name of Gov Smyth I had consulted no person, but have since informed him by letter. He endeavored to see me yesterday as he passed through Boston on his way to an Agricultural meeting in this state, but failed to do it. I write this in explanation of my telegram. I write it *annoyed* by persons on business. . . . P. S. I will add that I am not a relative of Gen Butler's, although born in the same town, and am personally friendly. Also that J M Fiske has been a popular Deputy Collector with the merchants. He is in no way a politician if he even votes." ALS, *ibid.* DeWitt Butler's telegram of Feb. 23 to USG is *ibid.* An undated telegram from George W. Clark, Warren, Mass., to USG recommending George M. Newton as collector of customs, Boston and Charlestown, is *ibid.*

On Feb. 26, Thursday, Babcock wrote to Secretary of the Treasury William A. Richardson, U.S. Senator George S. Boutwell and U.S. Representatives Samuel Hooper and Butler of Mass. "The President will be pleased to have you call at his office at Eleven (11) o'clock tomorrow morning." LS, DLC-Benjamin F. Butler. On the same day, Boutwell reported adversely to the Senate on Simmons's nomination. Also on Feb. 26, Forbes, Washington, D. C., wrote to USG denouncing B. F. Butler's alleged misrepresentations in favor of Simmons. "Since we have waited upon you we have ascertained beyond a doubt that the representations upon which, as we understood from you, the nomination of Mr. Simmons was based were totally unfounded in fact. We have called upon every member of our delegation now in the city for the purpose of getting authentic information upon this subject and of seeking a way out of this difficulty. . . . We are thus enabled to assure you that the statement made to you of the nomination having the approval of the majority of the delegation, and which was used to induce you to make the nomination, is untrue. It is a recognized rule in all business and legal proceedings that a promise or even a contract made under misrepresentation of important facts is null and void. Surely a political appointment made under such circumstances, and upon which the harmony of the Republican party in Massachusetts depends, is fully open to review. . . . Following your suggestion made to us on Tuesday, trying to find a way out of this difficulty, a majority of our whole delegation in the Senate and House have now agreed upon three names which they have presented to you for the position; we beg leave to support their recommendation. . . ." *Boston Evening Transcript,* Feb. 28, 1874. On Feb. 27, "Kappa," reported from Washington, D. C. "Secretary Richardson, Senator Boutwell and Representatives Butler, Hooper and Buffinton were at the White House this forenoon, and had an interview with the President. . . . The President said he had come to the conclusion to do just as Simmons's friends advised. If they saw proper to withdraw him he would do so, and if not he would allow him to take his chance in the Senate. Butler said he and other friends of Simmons did not desire to have his nomination withdrawn. . . . The President said if the parties could agree upon any compromise, he would be glad to carry it out. For the present, he would not withdraw Simmons's name. . . ." *Ibid.,* Feb. 27, 1874. On the same day, the Senate confirmed Simmons. Also on Feb. 27, Anonymous, Boston, telegraphed to USG. "In the name of ninety thousand 90000 true administration Republicans of Massachusetts I thank you for the stand you have taken in favor of Confirmation of Simmons the gallant young soldier" Telegram received, DLC-USG, IB. On Feb. 28, "Kappa," reported an interview involving USG, Simmons, and U.S. Senator Roscoe Conkling of N. Y. "It is understood that the President talked very freely to Simmons as to the course he ought to pursue towards those in Boston who were so bitterly opposed to his confirmation. He advised him to pursue a line of policy that would not needlessly offend those who are inimical to Butler; and in the administration of his office not to allow partizan feeling to control his judgment, but use his best efforts to harmonize all conflicting interests in the Republican party." *Boston Evening Transcript,* Feb. 28, 1874. B. F. Butler's support for Simmons, which aroused fears that Butler exerted improper influence over USG, divided Mass. Republicans. See *ibid.,* Feb. 20, 1874; Blanche Butler Ames, comp., *Chronicles From the Nineteenth Century: Family Letters of Blanche Butler and Adelbert Ames . . .* (1957), I, 653–56, 658; George F. Hoar, *Autobiography of Seventy Years* (New York, 1903), I, 210–11; William D. Mallam, "The Grant-Butler Relationship," *Mississippi Valley Historical Review,* XLI, 2 (Sept., 1954), 259–76; Margaret Susan Thompson, *The "Spider Web:" Congress and Lobbying in the Age of Grant* (Ithaca, 1985), pp. 230–48; Mark Wahlgren Summers, *The Era of Good Stealings* (New York, 1993), pp. 246–49.

On July 26, 1876, B. F. Butler, Boston, wrote to USG. "*Personal.* . . . Upon looking over the political condition of this state I find that certain men who made themselves very conspicuous as representatives of 'Bristow and Reform,' are now so arranging the campaign that they may appear as special representatives of the party in the support of Hayes and Wheeler. They and their newspapers entirely ignore the present administration, and desire also that Hayes and Wheeler in fact shall wholly ignore its friends, in which latter enterprise I do not think they will succeed. While I look upon Massachusetts as safe for Hayes and Wheeler, by a very considerable, but not an old fashioned majority, owing to the action of those of whom I have spoken, yet I do wish that the administration would take such course in its appointments as would put somebody from our state in close relations with it in Washington, who, not being burdened with the care of the Secretary of the Treasury, would be able to look carefully at this condition of things here. The election of Hayes and Wheeler will be a vindication of the administration. That, its opponents in the republican party here know; but they propose that that vindication shall be turned into a criticism upon it through the men whom they propose to have it elevate to office as its representatives from this state. If the President has seen at all the outpourings of our so called republican newspapers, which are supported in part by the advertising given them by the Government, he will fully understand what I mean. Is it not possible that some staunch and tried friend of the President, loyal to him and his administration can be put in position to see to it that the administration is properly represented in this state, and in New England, so as to meet the machinations of those who ought to be, but are not, friends of the administration? If that can be done, I think not only good may be done to the party, but the good judgment and the efficiency of the present administration be brought before the people during the campaign in a way to commend it to them in a very different manner from what it has been portrayed. Asking no other consideration for these views but that which their good intentions deserve, . . ." LS, USG 3. On Sept. 27, Forbes, Boston, wrote to USG, Long Branch. "When I called upon you in regard to the appointment of Simmons to the collectorship of Boston, I ventured to say that sooner or later you would find that Butler was the worst enemy of the Republican party. The enclosed telegrams, which some of the Democratic papers have dug out, prove conclusively that at that very time Butler was in close affiliation with the leaders of the Democratic party and was using the alliance to get Simmons confirmed, their motive being to split the Republican party, which he gladly availed himself of for his selfish ends. The split came and left him entirely out of sight until Ben Hill has again brought him to the surface, and now with the help of the federal officers whom he then got appointed, he has turned up a threatening nuisance and is now doing more harm to the party than any man alive. We shall keep Massachusetts right side up in spite of him and Mr Adams both, but the mischief he is doing outside of the state is incalculable. I cannot believe that he and the rebels will triumph but he is doing all that one man can for them, and if they succeed there will be one consolation,—we shall get rid of him and see him go back to them, where he belongs." Typed copy, OFH.

On March 4, 1877, Simmons, Boston Highlands, wrote to USG. "It is just three years since, thanks to your kindness of heart and firmness of purpose, I was appointed and confirmed as Collector of the Port of Boston. From the day I assumed the duties of the position until this hour I have endeavored to discharge the responsibilities of the trust in such a manner as to merit your approbation and win the esteem and confidence of the people of this community. I am glad to be able to say to you that the merchants of this city would not only endorse my administration but would contend for my retention in office with greater unanimity than they before opposed me. I have ever felt my deep indebtedness to you for your determined support and your kind words of encouragement to me a comparative stranger, in those anxious hours of my great life struggle. For all your kindness to me and mine I thank you and in your retirement from the cares of public life I sincerely hope you will find peace, comfort, and all of God's choicest blessings abiding in your household" ALS, USG 3.

To John C. Dent

Dated Wash'n D C [*March*] 24 18734

To JOHN C. DENT

CR JUDGE JOHN F LONG StL

The remains of Judge Dent leave here this afternoon for StLouis will reach EastStLouis thursday[1] one thirty pm   please make arrangements for burial in the lot with your father on arrival   funeral services will be held here so there need be no detention in StLouis Dr Sharp & Col Grant will accompany the remains   acknowledge receipt

U S GRANT

Telegram received (at 10:56 A.M.), MoSHi. Lewis Dent, brother of Julia Dent Grant and John C. Dent, died on March 22, 1874, in Washington, D. C. On the same day, USG telegraphed to Helen L. Dent, wife of Frederick T. Dent. "Louis Dent Died this morning at six surrounded By his friends" Telegram received (undated), USGA. On March 24, Levi P. Luckey wrote to Gen. William T. Sherman. "The President directs me to ask you if you will be kind enough to act as Pall bearer at the funeral of Judge Dent, at the residence No. 1532 I Street this afternoon at three o'clock." LS, DLC-William T. Sherman.

On [*March 14*], Saturday, USG had written. "Ask sec. of Navy to telegraph authority for Baine Dent to come to Washington to-day to remain until Monday to see his father who is not expected to live many days," AN, Wayde Chrismer, Bel Air, Md. On the same day, Orville E. Babcock wrote to Secretary of the Navy George M. Robeson on this subject. LS, DNA, RG 45, Letters Received from the President. Baine C. Dent graduated from the U.S. Naval Academy in 1880.

On April 15, 1874, USG wrote a note. "Will the Sec. of the Treas. please see the bearer Warren in whos behalf I handed the Sec. a note from Mrs. Dent some week or ten days since. Mrs D. is anxious that he should have a place and board with her for protection." ANS, *ibid.*,

RG 56, Applications. In a letter docketed April 10, Lewis Dent's widow, Anna E., had written to USG. "Warren will hand this request to you. I would like to get a place for him in the Treasury Department, so I can have his services after he is through work and before going to work in the morning. This is asking a great favor of you, but will be a help to me as I cannnot afford to keep a servant any other way.   besids he is a protection in the house at night. This is not at all out of the way as have several friends keeping servants the same way." ALS (undated), *ibid.* Related papers are *ibid.* Warren Dent, identified as "colored," received an appointment as laborer for one month.

    1. March 26. See *St. Louis Globe*, March 27, 1874.

Endorsement

———

Applies to be mustered in to the general service. Served as a soldier through the war and has two honorable discharges. Was some time in charge of the inlisted men at my Hd Qrs. after the close of the war. Is I think an entirely reliable man.

U. S. GRANT

MARCH 25TH /74

AES, DLC-Nathaniel P. Banks. Written on a letter of Feb. 3, 1873, from E. L. Norton, Charlestown, Mass., to U.S. Representative-elect Daniel W. Gooch of Mass. "I have to ask you to give Mr. M. B. Buckley an introduction to some one in Washington who will secure for him an interview with the President. . . ." ALS, *ibid.* On March 28, 1874, Secretary of War William W. Belknap wrote to AG Edward D. Townsend concerning a position for Michael B. Buckley. Copy, DNA, RG 107, Letters Sent, Military Affairs. As of Sept. 30, 1875, Buckley served as watchman, War Dept.

    On March 9, 1867, Bvt. Capt. Alfred B. Taylor and five others, "Commissioned Officers of the 5th U. S. Cavalry," had recommended Buckley, "formerly Sergeant Company "C," 5th U. S. Cavalry, for any position that he may be capable of filling." DS, DLC-Nathaniel P. Banks. On March 13, USG endorsed this petition. "The bearer, a faithful soldier, is re[spect]fully recommended to the Sgt. at Arms of the U. S. Senate for employment." AES, *ibid.*

Speech

———

[March 27, 1874]

GENTLEMEN: After listening to what has been said, I do not see that there is anything that can be done, either by the executive or by the legislative branch of the National Government, to better the condition of things which you have described. South Carolina has now a complete existence as a sovereign State, and must make her own laws. If those laws are oppressive to her people, it is very much to be deplored. But what is the cause of the evils in your State may be a question worth considering. Whether a part of that cause is not due to yourselves, whether it is not due to the extreme views which you have held, whether your own action has not consolidated the non-tax-paying portion of your community against you, are questions which I leave for your own consideration. I feel great sympathy with any people who are badly governed and overtaxed, as is the case in Louisiana, and as also seems to be the condition of South Carolina. But I will say to you candidly that while I have watched the proceedings of your Tax-payers' Convention with no little interest, a portion of my sympathy has been abstracted by the perusal of a certain speech delivered during its deliberations, viler and more slanderous than anything I have ever experienced before, even among my worst enemies in the North—a speech more bitter in its personality and falsehood than anything I have ever seen, even in *The New-York Sun. . . .* I have never seen a speech equal to it in malignity, vileness, falsity, and slander. When I think of it, I can scarcely restrain myself.

New York Tribune, March 31, 1874. On March 26 and 27, 1874, Secretary of State Hamilton Fish recorded in his diary. "Governor Alcorn, Gov. Manning, Gen'l Simmons, and Mr. Richd. Lathers all of South Carolina called at my house I being detained at home by indisposition and stated that two Committees one representing the Tax payers Association of South Carolina, the other representing the Chamber of Commerce of Charleston, had arrived in this wishing an opportunity of an interview with the President, to lay before him the statement of the grievances under which they were laboring and to solicit such relief as either the Executive or Congress might afford them. I addressed a note to the President asking if he would receive them and he named eleven o-clock to-morrow—. . ." "At eleven o-clock these Committees were at the Executive Mansion and were introduced to the President. The chairmen of the two Committees severally made statements to him; in reply the President stated generally that their difficulties seemed to arise from their own internal legislation and he was at a loss to see how Congress or the Executive could relieve them. Mr. Potter, Chairman of the Committee of Tax Payers, and Colonel Lathers, of the Chamber of Commerce, severally made addresses. The President with much feeling referred to the proceedings of the Tax Payers Convention and stated that in the whole course of his life he had never encountered such vile abuse and calumny as was reported to have been heaped upon him at that meeting. Several gentlemen attempted to explain that a speech denunciatory of him had been made, but had been suppressed in their official proceedings.—The President inquired whether there had been any public condemnation thereof. Some of the gentlemen said they had thought the best mode was to treat it with silent contempt. The President finally said that, not doubting that they were suffering, he hoped that they might find relief, but that they had been among the advocates of State Sovereignty which had brought on the war, and he did not see how they could appeal to Congress or the Executive to interpose between them and their State legislature, that after the war the North had been disposed to treat them with great kindness, but that their attitude of resistance had forced Congress and the Government and the North into legislation and Amendments to the Constitution which they had been very reluctant to adopt, but that he hoped that they might soon find the relief they desired." DLC-Hamilton Fish.

On April 3, Robert K. Scott, Columbia, wrote at length to USG and Congress. "I hold that individuals have the same right to present their grievances to those in authority that a community of individuals have; and that his wrongs complained of should be as carefully considered as though they involved the interests of hundreds of persons. I therefore feel myself compelled in self defense, as well as to vindicate the public service with which I have been entrusted, both as asst. Commissioner of the 'Freedmen's Bureau,' and as the governor of South Carolina, to protest against the unwarranted charges made against me in the recent 'tax payers' Convention held in this city, and afterwards reiterated before His Excellency, the President, and your honorable bodies. . . . Permit me briefly to recur to the difficulties attending the attempt to organize the government of the State upon the basis of the 'Reconstruction Acts.' Without a system of taxation that could be made available; without credit in the money markets, her bonds selling at 25¢ on the dollar, with a large floating debt to provide for; with inexperienced men in every department of the government, in which a whole year passed without the collection of a cent from the levy of taxes, and even when the tax levy was made, and the tax Collected in June 1869, it was found far inadequate to meet the expenses of a government of two years administration . . . Perhaps it might have been policy to have permitted the State to fall into complete anarchy, but I assumed that few persons placed in so responsible a position would have allowed a commonwealth to fail simply because it became difficult and expensive to sustain it. In addition to all these difficulties, I had two antagonistic races to reconcile to their new relations to each other, both believing themselves right, one holding on to the power they had just acquired, and the other strugling by every means within their reach to wrest that power from their hands. No one need be surprised that I was held up to public condemnation for every act of the State government that did not meet the approbation of those who felt that they were successfully being deprived of their 'natural right to govern' Notwithstanding all the difficulties I had to encounter, the credit of the State gradually increased until 1870, when our securities attained a value in the money markets of the country but little below that of those States whose credit had never been impaired. . . . I scarcely deem it proper for me to recount the causes that led to the destruction of the credit of the State, and the sacrifice of a large amount of her bonds for a mere nominal price, as I regarded it the duty of the committee who were seeking redress at the hands of the Federal government to have presented the acts that led to this result as a part of their legitimate cause for complaint, namely; the violence of the Ku Klux organization, and the extravagant expenditures of money by the Legislature of the session commencing Nov. 26th 1870 in retaliation for the violence that had been perpetrated during that year. . . ." ADf, OHi. See *HMD*, 43-1-233, 43-1-234; Alvan F. Sanborn, ed., *Reminiscences of Richard Lathers: Sixty Years of a Busy Life in South Carolina, Massachusetts and New York* (New York, 1907), pp. 319–24.

On Aug. 19, John H. Furman, "Scottsboro near Milledgeville," Ga., wrote to USG concerning S. C. politics. ". . . The ignorant or *non property holders* desire to become *the property owners* and they are fully persuaded that it is in their power to oppress the wealthy to such an extent that the State will become possessed of the lands—in which event they can easily acquire possession of the whole, thinking because they control the State it will not be difficult for them to 'share and share alike.' This to the ignorant is such a fancy that there can none seem more charming, it is the hidden life of their organization and is most particularly idolized by the female portion of that population. Here then Mr President we have worse than Agrarianism lurking as a venomous serpent *determined to succeed by overwhelming gradually.* When in a guarded manner I approached an individual on the subject *not one* failed to proclaim his *agrarian expectation* and they exult over the hope. It is not in my power to state positively how or *whence* these ideas have originated but it is certain they have this allurement held out to them and to such a people it is as a matter of course bright and dazzling. These people I noticed are as a general rule respectful to their superiors and the most civil are the most determined beleivers in their dogma be it one who is chairman of a precinct or the greatest tatterdemalion among them; however, I have had one to parade his expectancy before me in no instance until it was lead out of him—then the acknowledgement was at once fairly and squarely made. I may be mistaken but to me it is chimerical for any one to suppose those people will heed any home appeal that may be made to their patriotism and good sense, one may as well indulge in flights of rhetoric or read Tyndall on radiation for their benefit. They beleive in the 'rapacity and dishonesty of their trusted leaders' they do not desire a change, their hopes and their principles are fixed. The question then simply resolves itself into an attack made by one portion of the population upon the capital of the other and if allowed and encouraged to progress must surely succeed in bringing about a little fight to say the least of it. The evil to grow out of this idea of robbery might be incalculable, and if it be not already lying in wait in some Northern body, even! from the negroes of So Carolina may emanate the conception that will in the future revolutionize this government. One accustomed to the negro knows that there are but two ways of bringing the ill to rights. First he has transferred his peculiar ideas of dependence from his old master to the U S Government and especially the Executive,   Secondly He is influenced by his fear of the White Man's might, and it is my humble opinion that either one authority or the other will be exercised in that unfortunate State. Need I say Mr President that the eye of the intelligent white man ~~rests~~ of the South rests upon you and each heart welcomes the hope that you will frown down villainy of such a nature." Copy, DLC-Alexander H. Stephens.

To Adolph E. Borie

———

Washington D. C. Mch 29th *1874*

My Dear Mr. Borie:

  Mrs. Borie says in a letter to Mrs. Grant that you have been quite unwell for a week back. Come down to-morrow and stay with me until Friday[1] and get entirely well. Mrs. Grant & Nellie go to New York on tuesday to do some shopping. On friday, by the noon train, I follow them and will return with them on the following Monday. You and I can have a grand time entertaining our bachelor friends. I shall expect a dispatch from you to-morrow announcing the train you will leave on. I would like to have Childs or Drexel with you. But they are poor men and must work,—without loss of time—for their living.

Mrs Grant & Nellie send a greatdeal of love to Mrs Borie. My kindest regards also.

Very Truly Yours
U. S. GRANT

ALS, Strouse Collection, Free Library of Philadelphia, Philadelphia, Pa. Adolph E. Borie noted on this document his reply of March 30, 1874. "Would like it much but not quite well enough" AE (initialed), *ibid.*

On Feb. 19, James Pollock, superintendent, U.S. mint, Philadelphia, had written to Borie recommending his son-in-law, Henry T. Harvey, as attorney, Western District, Pa. LS, Morristown National Historical Park, Morristown, N. J. On Feb. 20, Borie endorsed this letter to USG. "I hasten to transmit the above: no one rendered greater service in our late election than Gov Pollock, and on that account as well as his other constant merits, I should like to see him gratified" AES, *ibid.* No appointment followed.

1. April 3.

To Col. Stewart Van Vliet

Washington, D. C. Mch 30, '74

DEAR GENL.

The head of the Rocky Mountain Sheep has arrived. It is very fine and must have belonged to a noble specimen. It came safely, and after being duly admired by all the family I had it re-packed and shipped to Long Branch to be placed in the cottage, where it will many times, I hope, remind me of your kind remembrance.

Please accept many thanks.

Very truly yours
U. S. GRANT

GENL STEWART VAN VLIET
FT LEAVENWORTH, KAS.

Copy, DLC-USG, II, 2. See *PUSG*, 12, 161.

On Dec. 4, 1873, Robert Campbell, St. Louis, wrote to USG. "I have received a letter from Genl S. Van Vleit, informing me that he that he had made application to you to have his son R. C. Van Vleit appointed to a cadetship at West Point, and he requested me to write to you, and solicit the appointment. . . ." ALS, DNA, RG 94, Correspondence, USMA. On Jan. 26, 1874, Col. Stewart Van Vliet, Fort Leavenworth, Kan., telegraphed to Orville E. Babcock. "Has my son been appointed to West Point? Please answer" Telegram received, DLC-USG, IB. On Sept. 4, 1876, Van Vliet, Washington, D. C., wrote to USG, Long Branch. "I want you to do me a favor—I want you to appoint my son Robt. Campbell Van Vliet a Lt. in the Army—I think he will make a good soldier—He has now, no bad habits thanks to one of the best of mothers—He passed a good examination at West Point, but got frightened & *resigned* before the Jany. examination—As he was not found *deficient* he is eligiable for an appointment   If you cannot appoint him on my account, I hope you may do so on account of the services of his Grandfather Major Jacob Brown, who was killed while defending Fort Brown Texas—There is not a single person of Major Browns family who holds any position under the Govt. either civil or military   I wanted my son to go to college & study a profession but his heart is set on going into the Army, & I think there is no use in thwarting him—. . . I shall go to Shrewsby on Friday, & will call to see you on Saturday or Sunday." ALS, DNA, RG 94, ACP, 6403 1876. On Dec. 7, USG nominated Robert C. Van Vliet as 2nd lt., 10th Inf.

To Nathaniel Carlin

—————

Washington D. C. Apl. 14th *1874.*

DEAR SIR:

Your letter announcing the arrival of Richard with the six mares is received. Of the four that went from here one is an old thoroughbred race mare; raised in Virginia not far from here; whos pedigree and performance can, no doubt, be easily obtained. The two mares taken on at Pittsburg are mother and colt. The mother is supposed to be thoroughbred; but her pedigree cannot be obtained. She was raised in the South. Her colt was sired by a Yellow Mexican saddle horse I had, of great beauty, but not blooded of course.—Enclosed I send you all I know of the largest of the three black mares!   The other two are Black Hawk Morgan's, no doubt sire & dam ~~side~~. They are too small to breed from to get anything extra; but if they have colts they should make good durable roadsters. I would breed them to the bay stallion. I presume you will breed Topsey's three year old colt? If there is any promise in Jennie's three year old I would develope it, otherwise breed her too. You are aware that she was sired by ~~y~~Young Hambletonian when but two years old.

Your statement for Feb.y & March was received. I would like expense account to be given with the same detail that you give receipts

—same as given in your previous statements.—Soon you will have pasture for all but the work horses so that most of the expense of purchasing feed will be cut off. I hope that hereafter we will be able to raise enough.

Yours Truly
U. S. Grant

Nat. Carlin, Esq.

ALS, CSmH. On April 2, [*1874*], Thursday, USG telegraphed to William W. Smith. "Richard leaves today with horses for the farm   will take yours in at Pittsburg and if necessary remain over a train to get them   will probably be there on Saturday" Telegram received, Washington County Historical Society, Washington, Pa.

A ledger recording purchases for USG's farm, March 3–Nov. 24, 1874, is in MoSHi.

To Domingo F. Sarmiento

Washington, 15 April 1874.

To His Excellency D. F. Sarmiento,
President of the Argentine Republic.
Dear Sir:

I have received the letter which you did me the honor to address to me under date the 12th. of February last, expressing a wish that some of the distinguished pupils of a school which has been established in your Republic, may be admitted into the Military Academy at West Point.

Your Excellency does me no more than justice in supposing that I entertain the utmost good will towards your country and would do any thing which might be in my power towards contributing towards its progress. In governments, however, of a form like that of the Argentine Republic and of the United States you are aware that the Chief Magistrate can exercise no authority which has not been conferred by the Constitution and the Laws. The Statutes which prescribe who shall be admitted into the Military Academy at West Point do not allow foreigners to be received there. This, however, in my opinion, is an unwise restriction and might without contravening the public interest, be so far relaxed as to allow the reception of a fair proportion of young men from abroad specially recommended by their governments. Your application and my regret that I cannot at once grant it, will therefore move me to request of Congress the necessary authority. If it shall be bestowed, I shall be happy to exercise it without delay by complying with your request.

I have the honor to be,

> Your Excellency's
> Most obedient servant,
> U. S. GRANT.

Copy, DNA, RG 84, Argentina, Instructions. On Feb. 12, 1874, Domingo F. Sarmiento, Argentine president, wrote to USG. "I again address myself to you, confiding in your benevolence, and hoping that the good will manifested by you towards everything concerning the greater advancement of the Argentine Republic, will move you to assent to my request. Being desirous of giving full development to the institutions of my country, and as its military organization demands our special attention, we have established a school which has already given very satisfactory results, and which I hope will serve as a basis for the realization of projects of greater magnitude. To ensure the success of this work, so favourably commenced, we must needs give a complete education to those pupils who have most distinguished themselves, and I believe that the desired end would be obtained, if some of them could be admitted into the Military School at Westpoint. My object is, therefore, to ask you to acquiesce to our sending four or six of of our most advanced pupils to the aforementioned establishment,—the expenses arising therefrom, being of course on account of the Argentine Government.—The instruction and the knowledge acquired by these young men in the United States would be a guarantee that our purposes would be carried out. Having thus expressed my just desires, I await your answer,—begging of you to accept my anticipated thanks, as well as the assurances of consideration and respect . . ." LS, *ibid.*, RG 94, Correspondence, USMA. *HED*, 43-1-224. On April 14, Secretary of War William W. Belknap wrote to the House of Representatives indicating USG's support for the proposal outlined in this letter. *Ibid.*; DS (press), DNA, RG 94, Correspondence, USMA. On April 21, the House received these communications without debate or subsequent action. *CR*, 43–1, 3248.

To William P. Kellogg

WASHINGTON, April 17. [*1874*]

To GOVERNOR W. P. KELLOGG, NEW ORLEANS, LA.—Your despatch of this date asking aid for the sufferers by the disastrous overflow of the lower Mississippi is received. Congress being in session at this time, I do not feel authorized to order Government aid, as I did in the case of suffering from yellow fever in Shreveport and Memphis last summer,[1] and in the case of the burning of Chicago, two years ago, without the authority of Congress. I will, however, send your despatch to the Louisiana delegation, and, if a resolution is passed by Congress authorizing it, I will exert every authorized means to avert suffering from the disaster which has overtaken the citizens of Louisiana.

U. S. GRANT.

Boston Evening Transcript, April 18, 1874. On April 17, 1874, Governor William P. Kellogg of La. telegraphed to USG. "The unprecedented rise in the Mississippi River by violent local storms has caused a most destructive overflow. Six or seven of the largest parishes of the State are already under water and thousands of people, white and black, are without food or shelter, and in danger of starvation. The emergency is so great that I feel constrained to appeal to you directly, asking the General Government, if possible, to extend to these poor people the same relief that was given in the scarcely more disastrous calamity at Chicago." *Ibid.* On April 18, U.S. Representative John Coburn of Ind. telegraphed to USG. "The Committee on Military Affairs desire to know the extent of suffering from floods on the lower Mississippi so far as you are informed" Copy, DNA, RG 107, Telegrams Collected (Bound). On the same day, Orville E. Babcock telegraphed to Coburn. "The President has received nothing relating to the floods on the lower Miss River except one telegram from Gov. Kellogg which he answered and sent the telegram to Mr Sheldon of La. retaining no copy." Copy, *ibid.* On April 23, May 13, and June 23, USG signed legislation to relieve flood victims. See *CR*, 43–1, 3171–72; *U.S. Statutes at Large*, XVIII, part 3, pp. 34, 45–46, 230; *PUSG*, 24, 227–29.

1. See *ibid.*, p. 458.

To Congress

TO THE SENATE AND HOUSE OF REPRESENTATIVES:

Herewith I transmit the report of the Civil Service Commission authorized by the act of Congress of March 3. 1871, and invite your special attention thereto. If sustained by Congress, I have no doubt the rules can, after the experience gained, be so improved and enforced as to still more materially benefit the public service, and relieve the Executive, members of Congress and the heads of departments from influences prejudicial to good administration. The rules, as they have heretofore been enforced, have resulted beneficially, as is shown by the opinions of the members of the Cabinet and their subordinates in the departments; and in that opinion I concur. But rules applicable to officers who are to be appointed by and with the advice and consent of the Senate are in great measure impracticable, except in so far as they may be sustained by the action of that body. These must necessarily remain so, unless the direct sanction of the Senate is given to the rules. I advise, for the present, only such appropriation as may be adequate to continue the work in its present form, and would leave to the future to determine whether the direct sanction of Congress should be given to rules that may perhaps be devised for regulating the method of selection of appointees, or a portion of them, who need to be appointed by the Senate. The same amount appropriated last year would be adequate for the coming year, but I think the public interest would be promoted by authority in the Executive for allowing a small compensation for special service performed beyond usual office hours, under the act of 1871, to persons already in the service of the Government.

U. S. GRANT

EXECUTIVE MANSION
APRIL 18. 1874

Copy, DNA, RG 130, Messages to Congress. *SED*, 43-1-53; *HED*, 43-1-221. On April 1, 1874, Levi P. Luckey wrote to Dorman B. Eaton, chairman, Civil Service Commission. "The President directs me to say that he has read the report of the 'Civil Service Board' with interest and has no comments to make or changes to suggest. Also that the Board may have the number of copies printed they desire." Copy, DLC-USG, II, 2. On April 15, Eaton *et al.*, Civil Service Commission, reported to USG: ". . . The first and more important questions, then, are, whether the principles of civil service reform, as sanctioned by the President under the act referred to, are consistent with the Constitution and the national character; and, if they are, whether the essential methods of administration they require are best adapted to promote the welfare of the people. . . . We hardly need say that it is not this Commission, but the party in power, the disinterested members of all parties, and honest and intelligent people in every part of the Union, who have the responsibility and the defense of civil service reform on their hands. Aided by the more patriotic members of all parties, the President and the Congress, elected by the dominant party, inaugurated the reform in its present shape; and, while it was in full force, the resolutions of that party commended itself and its President to the people, and he secured a triumphant reëlection, in some degree at least, on the pledge and basis of that reform. Though we regard these facts as no reasons why the methods adopted for redeeming this pledge should be continued, if not found beneficial, they do seem to be reasons why we should not be regarded as alone responsible, or as having mistaken the wishes of the people. . . ." *SED*, 43-1-53, 7–9; *HED*, 43-1-221, 7–9. See *PUSG*, 22, 297–302; message to Senate, May 25, 1874; Ari Hoogenboom, *Outlawing the Spoils: A History of the Civil Service Reform Movement 1865–1883* (Urbana, 1961), pp. 128–30.

On April 28, USG issued an order modifying a Civil Service category in the General Appraiser's office. DS, DLC-Executive Orders.

To Capt. Thomas E. Rose

Washington DC. April 18th 1874

CAPTAIN ROSE, COMMANDING U. S. TROOPS, LITTLE ROCK, ARK—
I have a despatch from the acting president of the W. U. Telegraph
Company, saying that Baxters Officers, now inspect all the Messages
at Little Rock before transmission, and will allow no messenger to
pass out with any message for the Brooks party, whether from the
United States Officials or otherwise,   under these circumstances it
will be seen that the Company is unable at present to maintain the
sanctity of Telegraphic correspondence. While the government takes
no part in the unhappy state of affairs existing in Arkansas at this
time, you will see that all official despatches of the government,
whether from the Military or Civil Departments, are transmitted
without molestation by either of the contestants for the Gubernatorial chair.[1] Report to the Secretary of War the situation of affairs.

U. S. GRANT

Copy (embedded in Capt. Thomas E. Rose's report, May 20, 1874, DS), DNA, RG 94, Letters Received, 1491 1874. *HED*, 43-1-229, 18; *SD*, 57-2-209, 309. On April 19, 1874,
Sunday, a correspondent reported from Washington, D. C., that USG telegraphed Capt.
Thomas E. Rose, 16th Inf., "at a late hour on Saturday night." *New York Times*, April 20,
1874. Rose, bvt. brig. gen. for service that included a tunnel escape from Libby Prison,
commanded the detachment at Little Rock because of court-martial proceedings against
his superior. On April 19, 20, and 21, Rose, Little Rock, telegraphed to Secretary of War
William W. Belknap. "Received the Presidents instructions   they are carried out   there is
some excitement   it will soon subside   force sSmall on Each side" "It will not do to trust
despatches sent from here   I send this by Memphis   Since I sent my report this morning
a disturbance Occurred again by a mob marching in front of Baxters quarters   I rode near
to them alone on horseback to observe them as they were violating a truce   when I got
near them the leader fired a pistol at me & several of the mob fired also   I then formed the
troops to resist an attack   the mob fired in all directions and stampeded without making
further attack   one of the wounded is since dead   the troops nor myself did not fire a shot
I was unarmed & therefore could not   the Soldiers were too far off   I think the strife is
ended   I do not need any more troops than I have" "In compliance with yours of yesterday I have to report that the situation here is about the same except that both parties continue to be reinforced . . . negotiations are pending which I think will end the strife"
Telegrams received (the second on April 22), DNA, RG 94, Letters Received, 1491 1874.
HED, 43-1-229, 18, 20–22; *SED*, 43-1-51, 139–40. Joseph Brooks, a Methodist minister
who had edited an antislavery newspaper and served as chaplain, 1st Mo. Art. and 33rd
Mo., later entered Ark. politics and ran for governor in 1872 as the Liberal Republican and
Democrat coalition candidate against Republican Elisha Baxter. In 1873, Baxter assumed

office amid allegations of fraudulent voting returns and alienated his Republican supporters by pursuing policies favorable to the Democrats. In April, 1874, Brooks secured a
court decision upholding his claim to office; with Republican support and armed backers
he seized the Ark. state house. Armed adherents and Democrats rallied behind Baxter,
confronting USG with the constitutional and political challenge of recognizing Brooks or
Baxter as legal governor. See *PUSG*, 24, 57–58; telegram to Elisha Baxter, April 22, 1874;
letter to George H. Williams, May 11, 1874; Proclamation, May 15, 1874; *New York Times*,
April 16, 17, 1874; Earl F. Woodward, "The Brooks and Baxter War in Arkansas, 1872–
1874," *Arkansas Historical Quarterly*, XXX, 4 (Winter, 1971), 315–36; George H. Thompson, *Arkansas and Reconstruction: The Influence of Geography, Economics, and Personality* (Port
Washington, N. Y., 1976), pp. 95–158.

On Sept. 4, 1873, Baxter, Little Rock, had written to USG denouncing efforts to dis-
place him as governor. "I have so far refrained from presenting to you the State of affairs
in Arkansas, but now at the hazard of annoying you, I deem it necessary that this should
be done, and such are the circumstances surrounding me, that I beg your indulgence for
the length of this communication, which in justice to myself and the party in Arkansas that
elected me, it might be difficult to abbreviate. I was the regular nominee of the republican
party, as it sat in Convention here in August last, for the office of Governor of the State,
and was elected on the 5th day of November 1872. If frauds were committed in that election, I know nothing of them. They were charged and still are by either side, and it is quite
reasonable to suppose, that the supporters of Mr Greeley were as obnoxious to this objection, as those who advocated the election of yourself. . . . For myself I am heartily in sympathy with the National administration and would not willingly incur its displeasure. I am
desirous also to see that the Republican party maintains its ascendency in Arkansas, but
to do this it must have accessions. Otherwise it will suffer continuous defeat, as disfran-
chisement for causes growing out of the late war no longer exists, and thousands will hereafter vote, who have not done so since the close of the war. The old Democratic party is
disintegrated. Its elements will not heartily re-unite, and by the exercise of good sense,
much of its most valuable material can be drawn to our ranks. I am aiming to be Governor of the whole State; to vitalize its material interests as best I may, and while my appointments to office have not been made exclusively from a partisan stand point, I have
given position to no democrats who are not now in accord with the republican party, and
who will not maintain its principles and policies. Virginia is progressing rapidly in this direction and Arkansas cannot too soon follow her most commendable example In conclusion, permit me again to express the desire to be fully in accord with you, and the hope that
you will think proper to make some suggestions to me that will be of service in the present exigency, as in their absence, the course of events may compel me to resort to the extreme remedy of martial law, as the only means by which an effectual stop can be put to the
proceedings of those men who are now disturbing the peace and good order of the State.
Would it be too much also to suggest that in asmuch as there is but one company now at
the Little Rock Barracks—a Co. of the 16th Inft'y U. S. A.—~~that~~ it would have an excellent effect, if it can be done without detriment to the service to send one or more additional
companies here, without explanation, before the first of October, or as soon thereafter as
it can be done." LS, DNA, RG 60, Letters from the President. *HED*, 43-1-229, 10–13. On
Sept. 15, Attorney Gen. George H. Williams wrote to USG. "I have the honor to enclose
copy of my answer to Governor Baxter's letter of the 4th inst, referred by you to me. Please
advise me whether or not it is satisfactory. I shall be at court at Hartford for most of the
time this week." Copy, DNA, RG 60, Letters Sent to Executive Officers. On the same day,
Williams wrote to Baxter. ". . . Interference by the Executive of the General Government
in controversies between those who claim the offices of a state, is never desirable, . . . As-

suming what you say to be correct, that the Constitution and Laws of Arkansas, confer upon the general assembly of the State exclusive jurisdiction to hear and determine contested elections as to the office of Governor, that the Supreme Court of the State, has in a proper case, affirmed that jurisdiction, and that the general assembly has decided the question as between you and your competitor in your favor there would seem to be little room for controversy about your right to the office. You say that notwithstanding these decisions, your competitor has brought suit in one of the inferior courts of the State to oust you from the office of governor, and you seem to apprehend that a judgment will be rendered in that Court in his favor and that he will be installed in office before you can appeal the case to the Supreme Court, and you add that it may become necessary to stop such proceedings by a prompt declaration of Martial Law. . . . I am not at liberty of course to anticipate the President's decision upon any question that may hereafter arise; but I am quite sure that he will not interfere in your state affairs, before his intervention is invoked in the manner prescribed by the Constitution of the United States; and if it shall then appear that the general assembly and the Supreme Court of the State have decided, that you are its lawful governor, I presume that he will recognize those decisions in so far as it may be necessary to prevent the overthrow of your official authority by illegal and disorderly proceedings." Copy, *ibid.*, Letters from the President. *HED*, 43-1-229, 14.

On April 15, 1874, Baxter telegraphed to USG. "I have been advised by public rumor that in the state circuit court for this county in a long pending case brought by Jos Brooks for the office of Governor of this state a demurrer to the complainant was overruled & immediately Judgment of Ouster against me given   this was done in the absence of counsel for me and without notice and immediately thereafter the circuit Judge adjourned his court   The claimant has taken possession of the state buildings & ejected me by force   I propose to take measures immediately to resume possession of the state property & to maintain my authority as the rightful Governor of the state   Armed men acting under this revolutionary movement are now in charge of the Government Armory & Capitol buildings   I deem it my duty to Communicate this state of affairs to the President   I trust these revolutionary acts may be settled without bloodshed and respectfully ask the support of the General government in my efforts to maintain rightful Government of the state of Arkansas & that the Commander of the *US* arsenal at this post be directed to sustain me in that direction. I respectfully request a reply to this Communication at an early moment" Telegram received (at 5:00 P.M.), DNA, RG 60, Letters from the President. *HED*, 43-1-229, 2; *SD*, 57-2-209, 166. On the same day, Brooks, Little Rock, telegraphed to USG. "Having been duly installed as governor of the state of Arkansas by the judgment of a court I respectfully ask that the commanding officer at the arsenal be instruct[ed] to deliver the arms belonging [to] the state now in his custo[dy] or hold the same subject t[o] my order." Telegram received, DNA, RG 60, Letters from the President. *HED*, 43-1-229, 2; *SD*, 57-2-209, 165. A memorandum dated April 16 reported that the army held "no arms or other stores" at the arsenal in Little Rock. D, DNA, RG 94, Letters Received, 1491 1874.

On April 16, 1:10 P.M., Orville E. Babcock wrote to Belknap. "The President directs me to request that you will please instruct the Commanding Officer at Little Rock, Arkansas to take no part in the political controversy in that State unless it should be necessary to prevent bloodshed or collision of armed bodies." LS, *ibid.*; copy, DLC-USG, II, 2. *HED*, 43-1-229, 14–15; *SD*, 57-2-209, 308.

Also on April 16, U.S. Representative William W. Wilshire of Ark. transmitted to USG "a statement of the Baxter-Brooks case." ALS, DNA, RG 60, Letters from the President. This statement is dated April. "It was with feelings of the most profound regret that I learned last night, by private dispatches, that the slumbering insurrectionary feeling of the defeated reform element in Arkansas has again broken loose to disturb the peace, quiet

and good order that has prevailed there for the past six or eight months, . . ." LS, *ibid. HED*,
43-1-229, 3–4.

1. On April 18, Alonzo B. Cornell, act. president, Western Union Telegraph Co., New
York City, telegraphed to USG. "I deem it my duty to Communicate to you the following
information which I have received from the General Superintendent of the Southern Division of this Company—under date of Seventeenth—He Says—'Baxter has Control of that
portion of Little Rock, in which our office is located. He placed an armed guard at our office
door at eight (8) pm yesterday who denied admission to persons having no permits—
Our Manager Called on Baxter this morning & urged him to withdraw the guard & all restrictions—The guard was removed at nine (9) am to day probably on account of the Managers request'—Today he Says, 'Baxters officers now inspect all Messages at Little Rock
before transmission & will allow no Messenger to pass out with any messages for the
Brooks party whether from the united States officials or otherwise'   under these Circumstances it Will be Seen that this Company is unable at present to Maintain the Sanctity of
telegraphic Correspondence at Little Rock" Telegram received (at 3:00 P.M.), DNA, RG 94,
Letters Received, 1491 1874. *HED*, 43-1-229, 17–18. On April 19, Maj. George Gibson,
5th Inf., Little Rock, telegraphed to Townsend. "Your telegraphic order to Col Rose was
delivered in Person   I did not telegraph yesterday owing to the occupancy of the office of
(by?) Baxter party—up to this time Col Rose has succeeded in maintaining perfect order
He has directed Gov Baxter & Gov Brooks to have the streets cleared of armed men by
four oclock tomorrow Monday pm this length of time being given them to communicate
with the Prest if they so desire   telegraph messenger delivered to (the?) Presdts message
to Col Rose this am remarking He has (had?) to secrete it about his person   both contending parties have recd numerous forces the Baxter party the largest it is thought   It is estimated that Each party has about six hundred effective men   I will return to Memphis
tonight unless otherwise directed by you. Fuller particulars by mail" Telegram received
(at 1:15 P.M.), DNA, RG 94, Letters Received, 1491 1874. *HED*, 43-1-229, 18–19.

On April 17, William S. Oliver, sheriff, Little Rock, had telegraphed to U.S. Senator Powell Clayton of Ark. "Armed men are now in possession of a part of City. Baxter has
issued martial law proclamation   they are arresting peaceable Citizens   I can serve no
civil process without trouble as Baxter orders are to allow none to be served   the Telegraph office in possession of an armed mob   I cannot enforce the law unless I use force &
the Commanding officer at arsenal requests me not to attempt this   am forced to send this
Smuggled through U S Marshall Mills. Brooks has peaceable possession of state house
& desires peace   none of his force will molest any one but will hold state house. I hope that
the commanding officer will be ordered to aid me in keeping peace & dispersing all armed
men from the streets who are now molesting & arresting peacable citizens   the commanding officer was halted last night & taken to Baxter the U S Marshal Stopped twice   the
courts cannot sit so that this matter may be settled unless this armed mob be dispersed.
The supreme court will not meet till June   this thing cannot continue long without bloodshed & then it will be too late for U. S. troops to interfere. All can now be peaceably settled
by having their troops clear the streets & this can be done without bloodshed—I hope you
will see the President at once. I cannot even telegraph any official business except in the
way I do this" Telegram received (at 12:50 P.M.), DNA, RG 60, Letters from the President.
On the same day, Clayton endorsed this telegram to USG. AES, *ibid.* Also on April 17, John
McClure, Ark. chief justice, Devalls Bluff, telegraphed to Clayton or U.S. Senator Stephen
W. Dorsey of Ark. "Cannot send dispatches from Little Rock as the telegraph office is in
the possession of Baxters Militia   Baxter has placed the county under Martial law   we are

likely to have trouble   the officer here is not disposed to do his duty   have him instructed definitely   none of the State officers recognize Baxter" Telegram received, DLC-USG, IB. On the same day, Belknap may have referred this telegram to USG. "This telegram has just been received. Unle[ss] instructed to the contrary, I propose to give no further orders until we hear from Gibson, as we probably will, tomorrow—" ANS, OFH. Also on April 17, Secretary of State Hamilton Fish recorded a cabinet exchange in his diary. "The two Senators from Arkansas were present to represent the political situation in that state and are desirous that orders should be issued to the military at Little Rock to interfere to preserve the peace representing that Baxter had seized the telegraph; the orders already issued were deemed to be quite sufficient and there is every indication that the Government telegrams had passed without interruption." DLC-Hamilton Fish.

To Senate

[*April 22, 1874*]

To The Senate of the United States

In approving Senate Bill No 617, entitled a bill "To fix the amount of United States notes and the circulation of National Banks and for other purposes" I adopt the unusual, and almost unprecedented method of communicating my reasons for this course to the House in which the bill originated. I deem this course due to myself and to the public also. Due to me because no opponent of the measure has been more unreserved in expressing views against the expansion of irredeemable currency than I have, or advocated more earnestly than me the duty and obligation of Congress to legislate in such manner as to best carry out their repeated pledges ~~pledges~~ to return to a specie bases at the earliest practicable day. Due to the public because there seems to be a general feeling that if the measure under con- cideration becomes law it is a triumph of industry over Capital: if it fails, a triumph of Capital. In reality the measure is a compromise be- tween the two, and in my judgement is the best compromize for all ~~classes~~ occupations and sections likely to be attained.

My reasons for approving senate bill No 617 are: that, in my judgement, the country at large have been expecting Congressional action upon the question of finance by this Congress, at this ses- sion: that Capital is withheld from legitimate purposes of trade and commerce until the character of this legislation is known, that if this measure should be returned, without approval nothing more favorable could be expected, and that during the discussion trade and commerce would remain paralized; that the second section of said bill gives a much better banking law,—looking to carrying out the pledges of Congress and of both political parties of the Country to return to a specie bases at the earlyest practicable day—than the existing lay, and it is fairer to all sections of the Country. Much of the trouble through the panic of last fall was no doubt due to the fact that three fifths of the reserve of country banks were locked up in the city banks when they suspended. The country banks had to follow their example because they were not in possession of their own reserves. Interest ~~was~~ is allowed on these deposites, hence they cease to have the character of reserves because they must be loaned to earn this interest and a proffit. Being subject to "call," all loans from this reserve must necessarily be "call" loans. Legitimate business cannot be transacted with Capital borrowed on these terms. Hence under the existing banking law we have a large percentage of the Capital belonging to the country concintrated in the large cities, and used almost exclusively in stock and other speculations prejudicial to the general industries of the country. The measure under discussion cures this by requiring three fourts of the reserves to be kept at home; and takes away the incentive to send the other fourth to designated City banks, by prohibiting interest to be paid on it. The new law requires one fourth the gold interest received upon bonds held as security for the circulation and deposites of National banks to be held as a portion of their reserve. This is a step towards preparing for resumption, but it would have been more effective had the requirement been to hold this in addition to the Legal Tender reserve.—The present measure may be looked upon as a compromise between the advocates of the two financial extremes, and as a final settlement of the question. It has been agreed upon by the representatives of the people chosen by them to make laws for the goverment of the whole. It cannot be claimed that the legislation has been hasty, for it has been discussed by Congress almost from its earlyest meeting in December last, and by the press of the Country, and writers on finance even before that. I have nowhere heard it claimed that the law is unconstitutional. Under these circumstances an executive should feel very sure of his ground before defeating the will of the Majority by his Veto.—The present measure is not expansive as claimed, but is more properly a bill to keep currency where it is owned, for legitimate purposes. Until banks actually go into operations under it it is actually contractive to the extent of at least twenty Millions of dollars—and may be much more—by ~~compeling~~ taking that amount of reserves from where it is now being loand, to the controll of the banks banks owning it. The authorization of the use of what has been know as the Forty-four Million reserve is in reality no expansion because it has already been used, and as I have claimed under legal advice, by authority of law. That part of the measure receiving my approval has no practical effect whatever unless it may be to legalize what has already been frequently done not only by this administration, but by the one preceeding it.

With legislation now to increase the revenues of the country: thereby enabling the National Treasury to come to the aid of the National Banks in accumulating coin, with which to reduce circulation I believe all the pledges so frequently refered to in opposition to expansion may be carried out. I am no believer in patent methods of making currency equal to coin except by having coin enough on hand to inspire confidence in the holder of the currency that he can convert one into the other at pleasure. There is not coin enough in the country at this time to give this confidence. So long as it is not used as a ciculating medium—or the basis of such circulation—it remains an article of commerce. The fact that duties on imports have to be paid in coin creates a demand for a limited amount of gold. Enough to supply that demand stays in the country and all the surplus seeks investment where it is used as a medium of exchange precisely as the surplus of any one article of farm products seek foreign markets. This is entirely independent of how the balance of trade may be. The new banking law will accumulate an additional five & a half Millions annually. If the govt. can come to their relief by ~~purchasing~~ redeeming annually the amount of bonds required by law, and add fifteen millions to the gold reserve every pledge heretofore given will be in the process of being rapidly carried out.

ADf, DLC-USG, III. On April 10 and 15, 1874, Secretary of State Hamilton Fish recorded
in his diary. "The Bill (now pending in Congress) for regulating the currency &c was discussed. Richardson thought it would not have the effect of expansion—that it only legal-
izes the issue of the 44 million greenback reserve which the Government has claimed to be
already authorized and has upon; that while the provisions as to the National Banking currency seem to contemplate expansion the requirement that they should hold one fourth of
the gold received on their bonds deposited as security for their circulation and the prohi-
bition of their leaving on deposit in New York or other redeeming depositaries more than
¼ of their reserve & that no interest will be paid thereon will compel them to keep ¾ of
their own reserve in their own vaults and will practically operate in the line of contraction." "A conversation took place relative to the financial bill passed yesterday. He says he
has examined the bill as printed in the papers with some care, that the main objection is
the animus or intent of the bill which in itself is comparatively harmless and is rather one
of contraction than of expansion. Unfortunately it had passed by almost a geographical division and that a veto would tend to array one section of the country against the other. His
present idea is not to be in a hurry to sign the bill and not to sign it without assigning his
reasons. His present intention is to prepare a message reviewing the bill and pointing out
such conservative features as it may possess and forestalling any measures of expansion
which may be in contemplation." DLC-Hamilton Fish.

On March 22, U.S. Senator Oliver P. Morton of Ind. had written to USG. "It would
be much more satisfactory to see you and talk the subject over about which I shall write,
but I am not able to do so. The importance of doing something in regard to the currency
is becoming more apparent every day. The stagnation of business is increasing. There is
an apparent abundance of money in New York and other financial centres simply because
there is not a demand for it; but the conviction prevails outside of banking and financial
circles that should business revive there is not enough currency in the country with which
to carry it on; and this conviction stands in the way of enterprise everywhere, especially in
the West. Men who would engage in building houses, manufactories, railroads, or other
large enterprises, do not hesitate because they think there will be more money, but because
they think there will not be more, and may be even less. The memorial sent to Congress
by the bankers merchants and brokers of New York calling for the return to the Treasury
of the Twenty seven millions, out of the Forty Four Million Reserve, that have been issued,
and much talk in the same direction in Congress in regard to the return to specie payments,
have alarmed the country in every part, and business will not start forward while this threat
hangs over it. An increase of the currency, which simply keeps pace with the increase of
population and wealth, is no inflation. The currency is the instrument with which the business of the country is carried on, and the volume of it should be increased with the volume
of business. To me it seems absurd that the volume of currency can be fixed at a particular point unless you can also fix the volume of business. You stated truly in your late message that there was not more than enough currency in the country for the dullest season
of the year; consequently there is too little for the busy season, when money is in the greatest demand. You also said that the currency had been contracted sixty-three millions since
1870; and referred to other causes in operation which had produced the consequences of
contraction. If the volume of currency was not too large in 1870 it must be too small now.
Population has increased rapidly since that time, and the amount of business and wealth
in a still greater ratio. After all that has been said about an irredeemable currency, how
trifling are the evils we have suffered from it in the last ten years compared with the advantages we have enjoyed? However desirable it may be to return to specie payments, the

simple fact is that the gold is not in the country with which to do it. The first step, in my opinion, to the return to specie payments, is the restoration of good times, and the creation of a surplus revenue. There are but two ways of getting the gold into the Treasury; one is, through the revenue, and the other, by sending our bonds to Europe, buying gold and bringing it here: which latter, I am perfectly certain, Congress will not consent to do. The advantages of a speedy return to specie payments are too theoretical for that. But whether we return to specie payments or whether we increase the currency or not, the advantages of the national banking system must be equally distributed throughout the United States, or the system will become so odious that no party can carry it. It is now regarded as a monopoly, and that certain States have a great deal more than their share of the monopoly. Its monopoly character should be destroyed, and the growing States of the West should have the opportunity of supplying their local demands for banking. When the United States took possession of the whole field of banking and taxed the State banks out of existence, the act carried with it an imperative obligation to divide the benefits of the system equitably among all the States and make it co-extensive with their wants. The difficulty in the way to a return to specie payments is not in our system but in the condition of the country. The facts are, that we owe about 1300 millions abroad in government and railroad bonds, on which we have to pay the interest: that the balance of trade runs largely against us from year to year: that there is less than 150 millions of gold in the country, and that we export an amount every year fully equal to the product of the mines. If there were 500 millions of gold coin brought into the country tomorrow we could not keep it. The trouble is in the situation, and we must accept it. Any legislation now to contract the greenback circulation, would outside of small circles, meet with a storm of execration throughout the country. The benefits of the national banking system should be equalized in all the States without being hampered with new conditions, or made dependant upon a speedy return to specie payments. For the longer continuance of the inequality of the national banking system no excuses or explanations can be offered that will be accepted by the country. The injustice is susceptible of mathematical demonstration, is attested by wide-spread and general discontent, and the responsibility for it will be permanently settled upon the Republican party. The government pledged its faith in the Act of 1869 'to make provision at the earliest practicable period for the redemption of the United States notes in coin.' The word 'practicable' in this act is not synonymous with 'possible.' It does not mean, at every sacrafice, or at all hazards; but when the government is in a condition to do it and it can be done without injury to the general prosperity and the business of the country. And in the case of *The Bank vs. the* Supervisors, 7th Wallace, the Supreme Court defined the nature and character of the greenback circulation in these words: 'The law therefore directed that they should be made payable to bearer at the Treasury of the United States, but did not provide for payment on demand. The period of payment was left to be determined by the public exigencies.' People who take the greenbacks do not expect to get the gold for them; not one in ten thousand thinks of such a thing; they take them as money, in which they have perfect confidence, in the transaction of business, and not with a view to their ultimate redemption; unless it be here and there a hoarding capitalist to whom specie payments would be a speculation, like a venture in cotton or stocks. The pretences therefore that the people are disappointed and complain because the greenbacks are not redeemed in coin are gross exaggerations and wild extravagances of speech. To the man whose wealth consists in money the resumption of specie payments is a business transaction of a profitable character. If it should be brought about in one year, it would be equal to a profit of ten per cent, free from all taxes and without labor or risk. If money be already yielding ten per cent, resumption within a year would make it twenty per cent. It need not therefore excite surprise that there is a strong pressure from many quarters for speedy resumption." LS, USG 3. See *CR*, 43–1, 2353–58; William Dudley Foulke, *Life of Oliver P. Morton* (1899; reprinted, New York, 1974), II, 321–35.

On April 15, Martin B. Anderson, Rochester, N. Y., wrote to USG. "My apology for writing this note must be found in my ~~earnest~~ sincere ~~regard for~~ admiration for your personal qualities and ~~my ear~~ an earnest desire for the highest success of your administration ~~I tak The~~ From present appearances ~~the~~ measures looking toward the further inflation of our currency and by consequence an in definite delay in the resumption of specie payments, are likely to pass Congress (1) You are aware that these measures are taken in total disregard of the ~~f~~Financial experience of the world and in opposition to the judgment of all scientific Political Economists ~~the~~ in our own ~~and~~ country and Europe. In my intercourse with scholars and business men for several months past I have not met a single man who ~~was intelligent~~ had an opinion at all who did in the strongest terms deprecate the measures likely to be adopted by Congress (2) We believe that those who urge these measure on are either ignorant of the laws of finance or ~~actuated by unworthy motives~~ are willing to sacrafice the honor of the govt and the financial future of the county to a few months of unhealthy ~~ae~~ activity of business to be followed by a depression more disastrous than any which we have suffered in the past 3 The relief which the South and West expect from inflation is clearly impossible to be realized. ~~All trade is a bottom barter and~~ 4 ~~when~~ If ~~weithght~~ weight of opinion instead of numbers could be reached the preponderance of judgment against the inflation measures would be found enormously in the ascendancy ~~These If mere numbers were to hones~~ We believe also that a clear majority of the voters taking the whole country together is against these measures We believe that no party could go before the people on an inflation platform without meeting a disastrous defeat. In view of these considerations permit me to say that in case of these ~~disastrous~~ measures passing Congress ~~there will occur~~ the occasion will justify and demand the exercise on the part of the President the ~~exercise~~ of the constitutional power of *veto* We believe that in excersing this power you will render a service to your county which will pass into history among the most honorable acts of your entire public life We believe that such an act would give tone and vigor to the republican party and by founding its policy in sound moral and financial doctrines make it the party of progress in the future ~~and make for it an history in time to come more as honorable~~ as it has been in the past We believe that such an ~~course will be~~ an exersise of the veto power will be the crowning act of your administration of the" ADf, NRU.

Also on April 15, L. Montgomery Bond, president, United States Banking Co., Philadelphia, wrote to USG. "It is currently reported that your Excellency will veto the Free Banking Law Bill, as it has been reported from the House Committee of the National Legislature. I trust you will not do so. The inspiration of the National Banks, and the great private Bankers, does not express the wishes of the people; neither do they understand the wants of the people. I know from information received from all parts of the country west of the Alleghenies, that the people are starving for money—for currency—! There is absolutely no money *among the masses* in the far west. A gentleman in this Bank to day from Wisconsin told me that currency was hardly ever seen at all in his section; and he was coming to the East to get into business as he would starve there. The Country Banks send their reserves east because the New York Banks allow interest on these reserves, and the people there can get nothing. A statement of a New York Bank is before me, which shows an *individual* deposit of one million, and of Banks *Five millions and over.* This money is loaned again by the N York Banks to stock jobbers and the country is suffering for the want of it. What do the great Bankers who hold immense meetings, and get up monster petitions know of the wants of the people who are out of their range. They have a grand monopoly and it is their interest to make money scarce. Pardon this intrusion, for I know how you are beset with letters but I feel it to be a duty to say to your Excellency what my impressions are from my daily experience." ALS, DNA, RG 56, Letters Received from the President.

On April 16, William Gray presented to USG a petition from Boston citizens who opposed the Senate bill. "I read the paper through without interruption from the President. When I had finished he said, 'There are two things in that paper which I do not like. The resolutions say the legal-tender acts were first declared unconstitutional, and afterwards constitutional by a majority of one vote. That is not exactly so. The resolutions attack my administration in saying that the legal-tender notes should have been paid with the reserves, instead of using them to buy up long bonds. This was the policy of my administration, and such a resolution is an attack upon it which I do not like. I think that policy right, and they call it wrong. That policy reduced the premium on gold from thirty-four per cent. to thirteen per cent.' I replied that it was the general understanding that the citizens of the United States were at full liberty to assemble in public meetings and pass any resolutions which they saw fit, and present them to the President, observing proper courtesy; that I did not write the resolutions, but was the official organ deputed by the citizens to present them to him. He then remarked that in the memorial we deplored the passage of the original legal-tender acts, and he did not like that; that the war could not have been successfully carried on without them, that the country had approved them, and he did not think it right that we should come to ask a favor of him, and at the same time censure his administration. . . . He remarked that we were now coming toward an accord; that he was not in favor of expansion, and he wished to add that he did not intend to tell me what he should do with the bill. I replied that I had not asked him that question, nor did I intend to do so; that if I had done so I should have expected a reply which would have deterred me from asking another question. . . ." *Boston Evening Transcript,* April 22, 1874. See editorial, *ibid.*

Also on April 16, Edward S. Jaffray, New York City, wrote to USG. "I beg most respectfully to urge upon you the propriety of vetoing the Senate Currency bill just passed by both Houses of Congress. This bill is a violation of the faith of the United States, and if it should become a law would be a lasting disgrace to the nation. It will very much impair the credit of the United States all over the world, and will prevent future investments in our securities, and will cause a large proportion of those now held abroad to be returned to us for payment. It is the first step in a fatal downward course that can but end in disgrace and repudiation. Let this first step be taken and the subsequent course will be easy and rapid. It violates the sanctity of contracts, enabling debtors to pay off their obligations in a depreciated currency, and thus to defraud their creditors of a portion of their just demands. The argument of the inflationists is that as the majority of the people are debtors, the issue of fresh irredeemable paper would facilitate the payment of their debts, and that thus the majority of the nation would be benefited by the proposed bill. This argument is entirely fallacious as well as unprincipled. If the debtors are really in the majority, surely that is no reason for passing a law to enable them to cheat the minority of the nation. But the statement that the debtors are the majority is utterly untrue. The creditors are in an immense majority, in proof of which I need only state that the depositors in the savings banks of this State alone number more than 800,000, a number exceeding that of all the voters in the State. You surely cannot sanction the defrauding these poor people out of a part of their hard earnings! The freedmen of the South belong almost entirely to the creditor class. They have not the power to run into debt, but they have to work on a credit, waiting for their pay either to the end of each month, or the gathering of the crop. You cannot surely concur in forcing these people to receive a diminished amount of money when their pay-day comes. . . ." *New York Tribune,* April 17, 1874. Jaffray's letter was presented to USG by Cyrus W. Field, member of a delegation to deliver a petition to USG signed by "over 2,500 leading business men." "The undersigned, citizens of New York, viewing with alarm the recent action of the Congress of the United States, and the imminent danger that, in a time of profound peace, laws will be enacted which, a few years since, were held to be constitutional only as 'war measures,' and in the enactment of such laws as are now pending in both Houses, all the limitations, promises, and pledges of the last ten years will be rendered nugatory, respectfully solicit the intervention of your veto, should there be need thereof, in order that the honor of the country may not suffer in the estimation of our own people, and in the estimation of all the civilized nations of the world; and the undersigned appeal from their own judgment to the language of the most eminent of our statesmen in the Senate and House of Representatives in 1862, in justification of their plea that a further issue of greenbacks, under existing circumstances, without the warrant of necessity, will inflict a stain on the honor of the Republic, and impair confidence in every future pledge and promise given in its name." *New York Times*, April 16, 1874. On April 16, U.S. Senator Roscoe Conkling of N. Y. telegraphed to USG. "Committee of New York business men telegraph that they will be here tomorrow morning to present memorial to you and ask me to arrange that they may call as early as you will receive them   What hour may I say?" Copy, DNA, RG 107, Telegrams Collected (Bound). On the same day, Orville E. Babcock telegraphed to Conkling. "The President says he will receive the committee any time between ten and twelve tomorrow morning" Copy, *ibid.* Also on April 16, Thursday, Simeon B. Chittenden, New York City, telegraphed to USG. "If you can give me fifteen minutes at half past eight Friday morning Please indicate at Arlington tonight." Telegram received, DLC-USG, IB. On April 17, Field, Chittenden, and others presented the petition to USG. "The President, in reply, said he had watched the progress of this bill through Congress with more interest than he had any other measure before that body since he had been President. He had at all times been entirely free in the expression of his views, and was always opposed to expansion without redemption, and in favor of free banking accompanied with such legislation as would carry out the pledges of Congress and the party in the direction of a resumption of specie payments. But he had to look at this matter a little differently from the views of this Committee. They show very well what they want, and may imagine, as he might were he a citizen of New-York, that the whole country want what they do. The Chairman of a similar committee from Boston called on him yesterday. If he ever could be in favor of inflation, it would be from the effects of such arguments as that gentleman advanced against it. . . . In conclusion, the President repeated that his views on this question were already known as against inflation, and as opposed to breaking away from the redemption of pledges." *New York Tribune*, April 18, 1874. See *ibid.*, April 20, 1874. On April 17, Fish recorded in his diary. "The President had been visited this morning by Committees from Boston and New York urging a veto of the recently passed financial measure. He had evidently been very much irritated by the conduct of the Boston Committee. The general line of policy to be adopted with regard to this Bill (Senate Bill 617) was discussed but no conclusion reached; some of the features of the bill were considered and Richardson and Delano were of the opinion that the practical effect of the bill tended to contraction rather than expansion. The sectional character of the vote on the bill, and the importance of having some policy determined were urged in favour of approval. On the other hand the general Animus of the bill and the apprehension of further legislation and the fact of an authorization of increased circulation were urged in favour of withholding an approval. The subject was held under advisement." DLC-Hamilton Fish.

On [April 18], Albert E. Redstone, president, National Labor Council, criticized the N. Y. delegation. ". . . Who are these men who dare to approach the Executive and make such demands? How do they come? They come representing three hundred and fifty millions of money, and demand the enactment shall not become a law, because it increases the paper currency, and shamelessly pretending it will prevent a return to specie payments. What would they do, could they induce Congress to authorize the purchase of gold to pay United States notes on demand? They would present all the notes they could obtain, take the specie to Europe, buy goods, bring them here, induce the people to buy them instead of buying goods of American manufacture, thereby depriving the American laborer of the employment requisite to the production of the goods bought with the gold, and thus continuing the process of depleting the country of gold which these same men have practiced for years, and have caused to be paid away to foreigners of specie the enormous sum of over nine hundred millions of dollars since 1861—more than enough to pay for every United States note and every bank note extant, and relieve the country from the 'stain of dishonor of unredeemed pledges,' so loudly sounded in the President's ears. . . . And I hope the Executive, as I have no doubt he will, in the fulfillment of this duty of his office, do it in the letter and spirit of the Constitution made to guide him, obey the will of the people, and do his duty in this instance, as he has in times past. When the enemies of the Republic have presented themselves to the front he has always been equal to the occasion, and will show that the people did not make him President to prevent their will and prevent their prosperity." *Washington National Republican*, April 18, 1874. See following Veto.

Veto

[*April 22, 1874*]

TO THE SENATE OF THE UNITED STATES:

Herewith I return Senate Bill No 617 [entitled . . .] without my approval.

In doing so I must express my regret at not being able to give my assent to a measure which has received the sanction of so large a majority of the legislators, chosen by the people to make laws for their guidance, and I have studiously sought to find [sufficient] arguments to justify such assent. But I fail to see them [but unsuccessfully].

Practically it is a question whether the measure under discussion would give an additional dollar to the irredeemable paper currency of the country or not, and whether by requiring three fourths of the reserves to be retained by the banks, and prohibiting interest to be retained received on the balance, whether it might not prove a contraction. But the fact can not be concealed that theoretically the bill increases the paper circulation One Hundred Millions of dollars, less only the amount of reserves restrained from circulation by the provision of the second section. The measure has been supported on the theory that it would give increased circulation. It is a fair inference therefore that if in practice the measure should fail to create the abundence of circulation expected of it the friends of the measure,—particularly [those] out of Congress—would clamor for such inflation—as would give the expected relief.

The theory in my belief is a departure from true principles of finance, national interest, national ~~hon~~ obligations to creditors, Congressional promises, party pledges—both political parties—and of personal views and promises made by me, ~~if not~~ in every Annual Message sent ~~by~~ to Congress, ~~at least in the first one sent, and no views on the subject have been expressed or entertained by me since inconsistent with those then expressed~~ and in each inaugural address. In my Annual Message to Congress in December 1869 the following passages appear (1)...

As early as December 4, 1865 the House of Representatives passed a Resolution by a vote of 144 yeas to 6 nays concurring "in the views of the Sec. of the Treas. (2)...

The first act passed by the 41st Congress on the 18th day of March 1869, was as follows: (3)... This act still remains as a continuing pledge of the faith of the United States, "to make provision at the earlyest practicable moment for the redemption of the United States notes in coin" (4)...

As a measure preparitory to free banking, and for placing the govt. in a condition to redeem its notes in coin "at the earliest practicable moment" the revenues of the country should be increased so as to pay current expenses, provide for the sinking fund required by law and also a surplus to be retained in the Treasury in gold.

I am not a believer in any patent method of making paper money equal equal to coin when the coin is not owned or held ready to redeem the promises to pay—for paper money is nothing more than promises to pay,—and is valuable exactly in proportion to the amount of coin that it can be converted into. While coin is not used as a circulating medium, or the currency of the country is not convertable into it, at par, it becomes an article of commerce as much as any other product. The surplus will seek a foreign market as will any other surplus. The balance of trade has nothing to do with the question. Duties on imports being required, in coin, creates a limited demand for gold. About enough to satisfied that demand remains in the country. To increase this supply I see no way open but by the goverment horeding, through the means above ~~just~~ given, and possibly by requiring the National Banks to aid.

It is claimed by the advocates of the measure here with returned that there is an unequal distribution of the Banking Capital of the country: I was disposed to give great weight to this view of the question at first. But on reflection it will be remembered that there still remains Four Millions of dollars of authorized banking Capital not yet taken, any portion of which could have been taken at any time since the passage of the law authorizing it,—and can be taken yet— by any of the states having less than their quota. In addition to this the states having less than their quota of Bank circulation have the option of Twenty ~~six~~ five Millions more to be taken from those states having more than their proportion. When this is all taken up, or when specie payments are fully restored ~~will be~~ or are in rapid process of restoration, will be the time, to consider the question of "more currency"

ADf (bracketed material not in USG's hand; ellipses in original), DLC-USG, III. *SED*, 43-1-44; *SMD*, 49-2-53, 386–89. See preceding message. On April 27, Orville E. Babcock wrote to George C. Gorham, secretary, U.S. Senate. "The President directs me to request you to have two clerical errors in his message of the 22d inst., returning Senate bill No. 617, corrected. The first occurs near the beginning in the following sentence, 'But the fact cannot be concealed that, theoretically the bill increases the paper circulation one hundred millions of dollars &c.' This should read ninety millions of dollars. Again in the paragraph commencing 'As early as December 4, 1865, the House of Representatives passed a resolution by a vote of 144 yeas to 6 nays concurring in the views of the Secretary of the Treasury &c.' The date December 4th is incorrect, and the President desires the '4' stricken out, that it may read simply 'as early as December 1865, &c.' You will be kind enough to make these corrections and this letter will be your sufficient authority for so doing." Copy, DLC-USG, II, 2.

On April 21, Secretary of State Hamilton Fish had recorded in his diary. ". . . the President stated that he wished to dispose of the currency bill this day; that he had given it most careful consideration with an earnest desire to give it his approval, that he had written a message assigning the best arguments he had heard or could think of in that direction, but the more he wrote the more he thought the more he was convinced that the bill should not become a law, and having written the draft of a message in that direction he felt that it was fallacious and untenable and had come to the conclusion to return it without his signature and had written another message which he proceeded to read, placing his objection mainly on the animus of the Bill and on the pledged faith of the Government—several amendments were suggested and adopted. Delano fought it from the jump. Williams decidedly objected. Robeson expressed the wish that the President had reached a different conclusion   Belknap thought it would array the entire West in opposition. Richardson acquiescently approved. Creswell considerately discussed it and gave it a cordial approval, on the President's saying that he had come to this conclusion the Post Master General (Creswell) applauded and said 'You are right.' Delano after various suggestions in opposition cautioned the President that the exercise of the veto power was not popular except when exercised on the ground of the unconstitutionality of the law; I interposed saying the good faith of the nation was above the Constitution. The President remarking that is so and I shall stand by it. He was desirous of sending the message in to-day but Mr. Robeson suggested that it was wise to lay a paper aside after writing to think it over and in view of the hour the President concluded to have it copied and convened the Cabinet for eleven to-morrow for consideration of the subject. Robeson raised the question of the political effect of a veto. Williams, Delano, and Belknap all thought it would be injurious. I dissented utterly and said that the whole honest sentiment of the country irrespective of party would sustain it: that an approval of the bill would rally the democratic party throughout the whole country on their old doctrine and cry of 'hard money' and would drive to it the whole capital now in the Republican party. The President thought the first effect would be one of denunciation of him—but he had confidence that the judgment of the country would approve. . . . It has for a long time been my intention to resign at some period before the next winter, probably soon after the adjournment of Congress. My last interview with the President left me seriously apprehensive that he would be led to sign the Currency Bill now before him—my disapproval of the bill and of his signing it is unqualified and I had expressed it to him most decidedly. I went to the Cabinet fearing his decision in favour of the Bill, and this with the matter previously stated determined me to announce to him my withdrawal. But his decision on the Currency Bill and the fact that a majority of the Cabinet were opposed to him on that point: that Richardson could give him no moral support and must shortly leave the Cabinet and was, in fact as much on one side as on the other, determined me to withhold my resignation and to stand by the President in support of his veto. I may therefore have to encounter the efforts of the Cuban bondholders—but my expectation of withdrawing from the Cabinet during the coming summer or Autumn remains unchanged." DLC-Hamilton Fish. See Nevins, *Fish,* 705–14; Irwin Unger, *The Greenback Era: A Social and Political History of American Finance, 1865–1879* (Princeton, 1964), pp. 233–45; Memorandum, [*June 1, 1874*].

On April 22, U.S. Representative Joseph R. Hawley of Conn. wrote to USG. "I only anticipate the unanimous voice of my constituents in offering you in their name our most grateful thanks for this days glorious work. So long as we have a history you will be remembered as having saved the nation's life, but in the coming centuries there will be historians who will claim that in saving our national honor you have done the cause of republican government even a greater service.—The bill in question was a step toward indefinite expansion: every succeeding step would have been easier, and the end must have been repudiation." ALS, USG 3; copy, CtY. On "Wednesday Eve," [*April 22*], U.S. Senator Roscoe Conkling of N. Y. wrote to USG. "Bessie says you are going out this Eve., so I do not come as I would do to express my admiration for your latest proof that you are as great as any duty ever set before you. I send a telegram, the first to come, from President Andrew White. I go in the morning on an errand to New York to be back however in season to give my mite to the vindication of your position and your fame." ALS, USG 3; copy, DLC-Roscoe Conkling. Also on April 22, Will Byrnes and Bill Jackson, Pittsburgh, telegraphed to

USG. "You have Vetoed the Inflation bill.   bully." Telegram received (at 6:04 P.M.), USG 3.
On the same day, Zachary Eddy, "Pastor of First Cong. Church," Detroit, wrote to USG.
"Believing that I represent the feeling of ninety nine clergymen out of any hundred in this
country, I wish to thank you for your Veto of the so called Inflation Bill. Had you signed
it, I doubt not the outraged moral sense of the body to which I belong would have, at once
and with emphasis, pronounced against your administration. I thank God that our trust in
you is so splendidly justified." ALS, *ibid.* Also on April 22, U.S. Senator William B. Washburn of Mass., Boston, wrote to USG. "I want to thank you for your veto of the Expansion
bill. It is right and I believe three fourths of the legitimate business men of the Country
will most heartily sustain you in this action. I hope to be able to reach Washington the last
of next week and if the matter is not disposed of in the Senate before I reach there, I shall
most willingly and heartily sustain your action by my word and vote." ALS, *ibid.* Washburn had resigned as Mass. governor to fill the seat of Charles Sumner, who died March 11.

On April 22, Edwards Pierrepont, New York City, telegraphed to USG. "GOD AL-
MIGHTY BLESS YOU. THE BRAVEST BATTLE AND THE GREATEST VICTORY
OF YOUR LIFE." Telegram received, *ibid.* On April 23 and 30, Pierrepont wrote to USG.
"My Telegram of last evening expresses the real sentiment of this region, and I am sure
that the West will before long share in the same sentiment. It is madness to suppose that
the interests of the East & the West are adverse—they are the same on this question—
Whatever deranges the finances here is forthwith felt in every city of the West. We fail or
prosper together—this will certainly become apparent to every intelligent mind—yesterday was the greatest day in your history—" "Sometimes one can make suggestions to another which may be of service, even if the same things have occurred to the person to whom
the suggestions are made. Never have you done an act so important as the veto—Now to
reap the advantage of that brave act you need to follow it up by affiramative action—The
effort will be to have nothing done & so go to the country next fall upon the currency question while the industries are all depressed.—If a good financial plan is adopted the industries *will not be depressed*; but if there is *no plan*, then there is danger & the inflationists will
hurt us—There should be an *administration plan of finance*, and duly advocated, it would
surely pass & save us much trouble, and possible defeat next fall   I cannot too earnestly
urge this.—" ALS, *ibid.*

On April 23, Benjamin H. Brewster, Philadelphia, wrote to USG. "You have done as
General Jackson did and put an end to fraud. Your veto will stand the test of time as his
acts have been justified   Those of us who have lived through those dark days of the Bank
War and paper delusions understand that there is a scriptural curse on those who deal with
false weights & measures and know that 'men can not gather grapes of thorns or figs of
thistles'   Before this I would have written to you but that I feared to intrude my personal
views—now I write because I can not help thanking you & applauding your wise brave act."
ALS, *ibid.* On the same day, John F. Long, St. Louis, wrote to USG. "Without claiming
more than ordinary inteligence or foresight, I *did predict* the consequence of passing the
Senates 'Finance Bill.—Hence you will allow me to congratulate you upon the handsome
manner and the able style, in which you *disposed of it.* In this instance, long to be remembered, and soon to be realized as beneficial, the Executive power of a *Veto*, has been wielded
with a master hand.—Upon its reception last night many of your friends including myself,
were at the Globe Office, and the enclosed Editorial, was the result of our conferences
Your time is too precious to be taken up longer with *my* ideas of the matter, and I close
with renewed assurances of my high regard." ALS, *ibid.* Also on April 23, Julie R. Seavey,
New York City, wrote to USG. "Permit me, Honored Sir, to add my *mite* to the general congratulation which ought to follow the *veto*, you pronounced, against inflation of the currency. It was just *splendid.* And, although I am 'only a woman' I feel some slight interest in

the affairs and *honor* of my Country, and will not resist the temptation of adding my little word of approbation at your course, and to say I am proud of the manner in which all foreign journals will comment today, upon 'America' and our *Commander-in-Chief*! Every one, whom I have heard express an opinion, heartily approves your action. What a pity women can not vote(!) that I might have the pleasure of depositing mine, at the proper time, in favor of the *third term* for our noble President. With sincerest best wishes, . . ." ALS, *ibid.* On the same day, "Your Friend," Kalamazoo, wrote to USG. "I have just read your Vetoe Message. *God bless* you for one, and many good acts of your life. Your Vetoe Message has the sanction of two thirds of the business men of this City, and the South West part of this State. Our Senator Ferry, his grosly misrepresented our State. I am a man of Sixty four years of age, have seen most fifty years of active business life, while our *Boy* in the U. S Senate, has not probley seen more than 20 years of business life. Ancient or Moderen history dose not furnish a Record of a nation—who has made a paper Currency a legal tender that has every redeemed its pledge,   let the pupies bark at your heals: they will do you no harm, and I feel confident two thirds of the business men throught the nation will sustain you in your Vetoe. May God bless and sustain you in all ~~and~~ good acts of this kind and retire from your Offical Office with honour." L, *ibid.* Also on April 23, Manning F. Force, Cincinnati, wrote to USG. "It is Vicksburg over again. The veto is as glorious, and as vital to the honor and safety of the country, as was the capture of Vicksburg. It stirs my blood, like the bugles sounding a charge." ALS, *ibid.* On the same day, David Fairbanks, Charlestown, N. H., wrote to USG. "Our people are going wild on the subject of business. There are two men ready to go in debt, where one is willing or ready to pay. A large class of our younger people despise work. They are crazy to go in business on borrowed capital. We are eaten with pride and consumed by extravagance. More money is not what is needed. Elasticity in the money market is what is needed, which can be secured only by a uniformity from day to day in the value of our currency, together with a free banking law *whereby each state* may charter its own banks securing the bill holder by means of low rate bonds, perhaps three per cents, deposited in U S Treasury. When government pays specie on its notes the banks shall pay specie or U. S. notes on their bills, which, shall be at their option. Every community will correctly judge of its needs as regards a circulating medium as soon as that medium has an *established value.* . . . Congress as a class (and they are a class as much as individuals of any other pursuit) are irresponsible. Congresses and parliaments always were irresponsible. Cabinets are irresponsible. But the *President* is responsible. . . ." ALS, *ibid.* Also on April 23, James Thomson, Mendota, Ill., wrote to USG. "As a working man, I tacke the liberty of thanking your Exclency for your veto message to the U. S. Senate of Senate bill No 617. I also tacke the liberty of saying that my opinion is that you have at the same time efectualy 'bottled up' at least two espirants to the pressidential succession viz. Messrs Morton & Logan   If your Excelency will hold on, the cours you have tacken as well as being honorabl & just ~~it~~ will very lickely lead to a further residence of four years in the Executive Mansion of the nation. May you recive many & hartfelt thanks from thousands of citizens, & may God Protect you" ALS, *ibid.*

On April 24, James F. Wilson, president, First National Bank of Fairfield, Iowa, wrote to USG. "I have just read your veto of the currency bill, and approve it heartily. Speaking advisedly of the community in which I reside it is safe for me to say that a large proportion of its members will approve the position you have taken on the currency question. The representations which have been so persistently made that the West is practically a unit in favor of expansion are very far from being true. Every thoughtful man ought to know that the amount of currency now authorized by law is greater than the country can use under present existing circumstances. Our trouble does not arise from too little money but from the obstructions which at present close to a greater or less degree the channels through which it is accustomed to flow. More paper money will not open them up, but rather tend to greater obstruction. If Congress would let our monetary system severely alone for a reasonable time it would be in the high road of assuring some relief to the country." ALS, *ibid.* Also on April 24, Elias H. Derby, Boston, wrote to USG. "Allow me to congratulate you on the tone and effect of your veto message. I do not forget either Vicksburg or Richmond but think this one of the best things you have ever done—It gives us courage and prevents the return of our Bonds from England and Germany which private advices assure us were coming if the Finance Bill had become a law. The late depression seems to me due to no want of currency but to the check the *West* has given to the Railway system. By reducing the yearly growth four thousand miles it has prevented the diffusion of one or two hundred millions of dollars among artisans iron-men and traders. This check may reduce our imports but must, as it seems to me accumulate gold, the sure basis of a prosperous trade—I have strong hopes that a gradual recovery will give us the coming year a handsome surplus for the sinking fund." LS, *ibid.*

On April 25, Robert P. Lane, president, Second National Bank of Rockford, Ill., wrote to USG. "Permit me to congratulate you on your wise course in vetoing the Senate currency bill;—and to say, that in this section of the country your course is approved and applauded by nearly all. In my judgment free banking coupled with provisions for retiring or funding, say 50% of greenbacks for all increase of bank circulation over $400.000.000. will establish public confidence and bring us safely to specie basis." ALS, *ibid.* On the same day, Edward R. Wiswell, New York City, wrote to USG. "On the 7th April I had the honor of writing you a brief note in which I urged you to veto the Senate Bill increasing the irreedemable paper currency 90 millions dollars; and predicted that if you did so you would have the support of a very large portion of the country as well as of Congress itself. Allow me to congratulate you on the great act which you did by that Veto last Wednesday for the credit and honor of America. You never did a greater service to your country. Had you signed that Bill an act of national dishonor would have been consumated which a thousand battles could not overcome. It strikes me that if this veto is followed up by the appointment of an able Secretary of the Treasury, (like John J. Cisco of New York for instance,) the paper money swindle must come to an end in perhaps two years; and the credit and honor of America be as high in the markets of the world as it should be. The French Minister at Washington can give you the details of the manner in which specie payments are being restored in France at this time. Certainly what France can do after her great disasters America can. We have delayed too long already, and every interest in the country suffers. Now is a good time to make the greenback something better than a promise to pay." ALS, *ibid.*

On April 26, J. P. Southard, Omaha, wrote to USG. "Permit me although perhaps unknown to you now, to congratulate you on your Veto of the repudiation bill just passed, as I consider it one of the best acts of your official life,   it will tend to strenghten confidence in our Financial affairs both in this Country and Europe—Here let me suggest that to rid yourself of Richardson would add additional luster to your administration   this is the sentiment of the people out here—You and I were boys together in Georgetown Ohio. I was intimately acquainted with your father, was frequently advised by him and once prevented from going off down the river by his timely interference—I shall never forget his kindly advice and admonitions—" ALS, *ibid.*

On April 27, Henry C. Guffin, Indianapolis, wrote to USG. "In obedience to the instructions of a meeting of the business men of the city of Indianapolis held on Saturday evening the 25th inst I send you the inclosed report of their proceedings clipped from the Indianapolis Journal of today." ALS, *ibid.* The meeting produced several resolutions critical of USG's veto, and decried the influence of Wall Street financiers. ". . . It is an insult to the virtue, intelligence, honor and patriotism of the people of this nation, to have a few of those, whose god is the dollar, to go with brazen impudence and flaunt in the face of the people's Chief Executive officer the fact of their great wealth, and it is utterly shameful that that Chief Executive should bow at their behests and do their bidding. . . ." Clipping, *ibid.* On the same day, W. J. Tanner, Atlanta, wrote to USG. ". . . I cannot after reading your message upon the *vetoe* of the currency bill refrain my hearty congratulation for the wisdom displayed in its logical & incontrovertable reasoning & to this end allow me as an humble yet as I hope honest Plebian present you with the kindest wishes & hearty support of all those who not unlike myself desire the restoration of harmony & the happy return of the day when Commerce—Agriculture—Mechanism & all the atributes of vocation reveling in freedom & Brotherly affection—hail with rapturous enthusiasm the prosperity of the Nation . . ." ALS, *ibid.*

On April 29, Joseph Cooke, postmaster, Waynesburg, Pa., wrote to USG. "Suffer one of your old Soldiers to congratulate you on your Veto. One word more from your old friend. Advise Congress to pass a usury law for the money changers that will operate in every State alike, with the loss of property to money changers if they violate it." ALS, *ibid.*

On April 30, Samuel Bard, postmaster, Atlanta, wrote to USG. "At the first blush your veto of the 'Inflation Bill' was not well received by the business community here; but the 'second' sober thought of the people *sustains* you *fully.* A prominent merchant, of more than ordinary business capacity, advised me, yesterday, that the arguments in your veto message were practical and unanswerable. I am also informed by a wealthy and influential business house in Savannah, that your course is fully sustained there." LS, *ibid.*

On May 1, John H. Gilmer, Richmond, wrote to USG. "The papers having published the declaration of Senator Johnson—that the people of Virginia—would not sustain your veto—allow me to assure you—that in my opinion—the veto has done more to strengthen you and your future policy—then all other acts. *Virginia* will sustain the veto—and the *policy* on which it is based. I am as sure of this—as I was, when in 72, I assured you V.a would vote for your re election—and you dobted it. In my opinion—but one other step is necessary—to place you and your administration on firm and immovable ground—A thorough change in your cabinet. Consider the wise policy of *Washington* and *Jackson?*" ALS, *ibid.*

On May 4, James McCosh, president, Princeton College, wrote to USG. "You have done *your* duty nobly in vetoing the inflation bill, and it is now *our* duty to support you. We have little direct political influence in Colleges but we have some moral weight to throw in, and this we mean to give. It is my earnest hope that during your administration we may have two measures past to make your name as famous in peace as in war—a specie basis— and Civil reform" ALS, *ibid.*

On May 6, Benjamin F. Weems, cashier, City Bank of Houston, wrote to USG. "It is likely that when you felt yourself constrained to veto the recent currency bill of Congress you were prepared for the various expressions of approval and disapproval evoked, and content to rest upon your conviction of conscientious discharge of duty. Nevertheless I cannot refrain from testifying, as an ex:confederate who voted for your re:election, to the gratification it gave me that in the face of so much popular clamor, and the action of a congressional majority you should have stood firm in the protection of the national honor, and of the true best interests of the country as well, as the future will prove." ALS, *ibid.*

On May 9, Anthony J. Drexel, Philadelphia, wrote to USG. "I have not written in regard to your late Veto as I felt assured you knew I appreciated the noble stand you took in the matter. I have just received letters by the last mail from London & Paris and they are most just & complimentary in regard to yourself in relation to the financial question, and I may say they express the views of the ablest and best men, not only throughout Europe, but of our own Country as I have yet to hear an adverse opinion from a really sound or solvent man from *any section.* Mr Borie has been quite poorly but is improving. Mr Childs unites in sending kindest regards to Mrs Grant, Miss Nellie & yourself" ALS, *ibid.* In all, USG received more than one hundred letters and telegrams in support of his veto, including messages from commercial and banking associations in Chicago, Cincinnati, Detroit, Duluth, Milwaukee, New York City, and San Francisco. Correspondents included Smith D. Atkins, John J. Cisco, John A. Dix, George F. Edmunds, James W. Flanagan, William W. Holden, Ben Holladay, Marshall Jewell, Horatio King, Edwin D. Morgan, Levi P. Morton, John M. Palmer, Daniel E. Sickles, Alexander T. Stewart, and others. USG 3.

To Gen. William T. Sherman

Washington, D. C. Apl. 22, '74

GENERAL:

When the Court of Inquiry, provided for by joint resolution of Congress of 13th of Feby. last, and convened by Special Order No. 35 from the War Department, of which court you are President, report their opinion to me, I will be pleased to have stated fully the facts on which the opinion is rested.

Very truly yours
U. S. GRANT

GENL. WM T. SHERMAN U. S. A.

Copy, DLC-USG, II, 2. *Proceedings, Findings, and Opinion of the Court of Inquiry Convened under the Act of Congress of February 13, 1874, . . . in the Case of Brig. Gen. Oliver O. Howard, United States Army* (Washington, 1874), p. 368. The court, which began to hear testimony on March 16, 1874, arose from allegations that Brig. Gen. Oliver O. Howard had mismanaged the Freedmen's Bureau by approving inaccurate accounts submitted by his agents. See *CR*, 43–1, 168–70, 347–48, 1035–36. On Feb. 14 and 16, Orville E. Babcock had written to Secretary of War William W. Belknap. "The President will be pleased to have the following named officers detailed under the provisions of the Joint Resolution of the House of Representatives, authorizing a special court of inquiry concerning General O. O. Howard—Approved Feby. 13th 1874: Lieut. Genl. Philip H. Sheridan Major Genl. Irvin McDowell Brig. Genl. John Pope Brig. Genl. M. C. Meigs Brig. Genl. Joseph Holt Major Asa B. Gardner, Judge Advocate. The Court will meet in Washington on Tuesday March 3d 1874." "The President directs me to say that you may place Col. J. J. Reynolds on the Howard, Ccourt of inquiry Board in the stead of Judge Advocate General Holt." LS, DNA, RG 94, Letters Received, 640 1874. On Feb. 16, Belknap endorsed the docket. "The President directs that Gen'l. Sherman be substituted for Gen'l. Sheridan—" AE (initialed), *ibid.* On March 9, Babcock again wrote to Belknap. "The President requests me to say that he will be pleased to have Colonel Nelson A. Miles and Colonel George W. Getty, added to the Howard Court of Inquiry." LS, *ibid.* Related papers are *ibid.*

On Nov. 27, 1873, Howard, Washington, D. C., twice wrote to USG. "After I conversed with you the other day, I began carefully to review my own past, and, after consideration I feel that I must withhold my application for retirement, and ask to be assigned to duty anywhere the interest of the service may demand it. If I should state my case as it appears to me, it would be this;—I had as good standing as any officer at the close of the war; —I was called from the command of an Army to take a difficult Bureau and one, of necessity, not popular from the beginning;—I have worried through seven years of unusual labor and anxiety, and discharged my duty to the best of my ability. In the main important results have been secured. On my recommendation the Bureau has been closed by law. The great majority of the officers connected with me were honorable men, and have left a good record. Indeed, with few exceptions, the Bureau officials have been honest men, and have sustained you and your administration; certainly *I* have done it with constancy and enthusiasm. Now I cannot disguise it from myself nor my friends, that circumstances are so arranging themselves as to leave a serious blur upon my reputation and upon the administration of my late office. If I retire I render myself comparatively helpless. This putting the whole responsibility upon me of certain Bureau officers, and holding me accountable for alleged failures on their part must be met by me with firmness and steadiness. If I retire the impression will be that I do it to escape investigation and legal censure. I am therefore ready for duty. Again if there should be war with Spain or Cuba I would much prefer to be on the active list. Further, I feel that I have sufficient health and vigor, notwithstanding the loss of my arm, to do any duty however severe and exacting that you may put upon me." "I have the honor, through the Honorable Secretary of War, to request to be returned to Army duty. My special reasons are; 1st, that I am unwilling to leave the service while suspicions and accusations are rife in the country against me; I must face them: and 2nd, that if active service should come I do not wish to be counted out." ALS, *ibid.*, ACP, 638 1872; (press), MeB.

On May 9, 1874, the court of inquiry exonerated Howard. *Proceedings, Findings, and Opinion of the Court of Inquiry . . .* , pp. 593–602. On May 25, Babcock wrote to Judge Advocate Gen. Joseph Holt. "By direction of the President, I herewith transmit the proceedings of the Court of Inquiry, investigating charges against Brig. Gen. O. O. Howard, for review and report to the President." Copy, DLC-USG, II, 2. On June 20, Holt wrote to USG "that with whatever indulgence or commendation the prevailing spirit which characterized General Howard's performance of his arduous and responsible duties may be regarded, it is believed that in the expression of such indulgence or commendation care should be taken to give no sanction, express or implied, to the manifest violations of law which this investigation has brought to light, . . ." *Court of Inquiry in the Case of Brig. Gen. O. O. Howard. Review of the Judge-Advocate-General, . . .* (Washington, 1874), p. 32. On July 2, USG approved the finding of the court. D, DNA, RG 94, Letters Received, 2605 1874. *Proceedings, Findings, and Opinion of the Court of Inquiry . . .* , p. 602.

On July 3, USG assigned Howard to command the Dept. of the Columbia and to "proceed to the Headquarters, Portland, Oregon, with as little delay as practicable." D, DNA, RG 94, Letters Received, 2605 1874. Perhaps shortly after this date, Howard wrote to USG. "As you have always been kind to me, even when the waves of trial rolled in upon me, so have I ever been at heart appreciative and grateful to you. I know that you are too strong to need or ask sympathy, but you know also in your rugged career how the dark hours are the best test of real friends. . . ." Laura C. Holloway, *Howard: The Christian Hero* (New York, 1885), p. 216. On July 11, Howard wrote to his brother. ". . . It will be hard for me to serve under W. W. Belknap, even in Oregon. . . . I regard the Sec. as the moving spirit against me all the time. He has bad associates—foul-mouthed men—Kentucky democrats meets them at night. He is not really a republican, not in favor of the Peace policy with the Indians—He deceives Gen. Grant. Crook is promoted & I am sought to be disgraced—Mc-Kenzie raids into Mexico & shoots Indians—to him my place is promised. I risk everything for the President's policy and am rewarded by Belknap & others with charges. I say this without bitterness, but yet think it is true. The President is represented by Belknap, Babcock &c. His vigorous independent self does not appear much. Sherman says often to me I dont wish to crowd myself upon him—others have his ear and such like expressions, then that Gen. Sherman & Grant are not as intimate [as they] once were. . . ." ALS (press), MeB.

Allegations against Howard persisted despite his exoneration by the court of inquiry and by USG. On Feb. 21, 1876, Howard wrote to USG. "Two suits at law, have already been commenced against me, in the U. S. District Court of Oregon. Three others are threatened by the Second Auditor of the Treasury in case I do not pay into the Treasury of the U. S. what the Officials, in settling the accounts of the different disbursing Officers of the Freedmens Bureau, have seen fit to suspend or disallow. Now I wish to make a proposition to yourself, with a view to a speedy and equitable settlement of all these accounts that appertain indirectly to me. It is this: That you yourself designate a United States Judge, and that I be permitted to designate another, and that the two shall be empowered in case of disagreement to choose a third, to sit as a board of arbitration for the adjustment of all questions of law and equity between myself and the Government officials involved, and for the complete and final settlement, so far as I am concerned, of all these indirect accounts. . . ." LS (press), *ibid.* On March 22, Howard wrote to his brother. ". . . I wrote a fuller letter to his Excellency the the President of the United States proposing a method of complete settlement in law and equity on all accounts that do not ~~nor~~ & never did belong to me. Even this letter was written more to bring the subject clearly before the President than with expectancy of relief. Now that I am sued in the Courts I suppose there is no relief for me except in a decision by the Courts. 'The Conspiracy' undoubtedly ~~lay~~ laid a trap for me that a Kind Providence enabled me to avoid. The trap was 'walk into my parlor' &c' i. e. come to Washington with your suit, where you will find true friends and small expense, friends like Belknap Babcock Vincent Schriver backed up by Bristow & Bluford Wilson who are eager in pursuit of any real or supposed cases of wrong. I do not think Gen. Grant unfriendly to me certainly not more so the atmosphere close arround him might has induced. . . ." ALS (press), *ibid.* See Oliver Otis Howard, *Autobiography* (New York, 1907), II, 447–55; Paul Skeels Peirce, *The Freedmen's Bureau: A Chapter in the History of Reconstruction* (Iowa City, 1904), pp. 118–28; George R. Bentley, *A History of the Freedmen's Bureau* (Philadelphia, 1955), pp. 212–14; John A. Carpenter, *Sword and Olive Branch: Oliver Otis Howard* (Pittsburgh, 1964), pp. 220–35.

To Elisha Baxter

———

Washington, April 22, 1874.

Hon. Elisha Baxter,
Little Rock, Ark.:

I heartily approve any adjustment peaceably of the pending difficulties in Arkansas by means of the legislative assembly, the courts, or otherwise.

I will give all the assistance and protection I can under the Constitution and laws of the United States to such modes of adjustment. I hope that the military on both sides will now be disbanded.

U. S. GRANT.

HED, 43-1-229, 10; *SED*, 43-2-25, 46; *SD*, 57-2-209, 173. On April 22, 1874, Elisha Baxter telegraphed to USG. "As I cannot move with my troops to assert my claims to the office of Governor without a collission with the u. S. troops which I will not do under any circumstances I propose to call the legislature together at an Early day and leave them to settle the question as they alone have the power   but to do this, the members of the legislature must have assurances of protection from you and a guarantee that they may meet in safety   this will be a peaceable solution of the difficulty and I will readily abide by the decision of the legislature." Telegram received, DNA, RG 60, Letters from the President. *HED*, 43-1-229, 9; *SED*, 43-2-25, 46; *SD*, 57-2-209, 172. On the same day, Capt. Thomas E. Rose, Little Rock, telegraphed to Secretary of War William W. Belknap. "It is now proposed by Gov Baxter to evacuate the City of Little Rock and encamp on the north side of the river with the understanding that no hostilities shall be carried on from that side of the river nor any movements made with a view to the Commencement of hostilities without due notification thereof made to the Commandant of Little Rock Barracks   I think such a movement would result in the disintegration of Baxter's force,   There is no change in the situation since last report except that one Company of Baxter's men went home this morning,   Company D, sixteenth (16th) U. S. Infantry reported here this morning for temporary duty." Telegram received, DNA, RG 94, Letters Received, 1491 1874. *SED*, 43-1-51, 140; *HED*, 43-1-229, 22. Also on April 22, Belknap, perhaps referring to Rose's telegram, wrote to USG. "This telegram was received since the other papers were sent over to you —" ANS, MiU-C. On April 23, AG Edward D. Townsend telegraphed to Rose. "You may retire to the Arsenal with your command as soon as danger to life is no longer threatened, and leave the question to be settled by the contestants by the courts or other peaceable methods." Copy, DNA, RG 94, Letters Received, 1491 1874. Belknap endorsed this telegram. "By direction of the President the above telegram will be sent—" AES, *ibid. SED*, 43-1-51, 142; *HED*, 43-1-229, 23. On the same day, Rose telegraphed to Townsend. "your dispatch of the twenty third is received   I will gladly retire to the Barracks as soon as I find the armed bodies disbanding in good faith. I removed my barricades & attempted to retire last evening   the effect was not satisfactory & the troops were ordered back   there is danger of general riot but neither party I think contemplates a collision . . ." Telegram received, DNA, RG 94, Letters Received, 1491 1874. *SED*, 43-1-51, 142. On April 24 and 26, Baxter telegraphed to USG. "In accordance with my correspondence with you by Telegraph I have convened the legislature for the eleventh May   I have sent home part of my forces & would willingly send the balance except a small body guard but Brooks retains his whole force & receives reinforcements   all the people desire is that the peace be restored and the legislature prompted in the performance of their legitimate business." "It is not true that I have declared martial law outside of Pulaski Co   nothing has been done on my part to prevent a peaceable settlement by the Legislature   I only want to protect myself until that is done" Telegrams received (at 5:10 P.M. and 7:15 P.M.), DNA, RG 60, Letters from the President. *HED*, 43-1-229, part 2, p. 36. On April 27, Baxter again telegraphed to USG. "On the nineteenth day of this month as Governor of this State I telegraphed you there was an armed Insurrection against the Legal Government of this State and made requisition upon you for aid to Suppress it & to prevent domestic violence I have just now been advised you never received that requisition   I now take occasion to say that an armed Insurrection exists in this State against the lawfully constituted authority thereof & as the Legislature cannot meet until the eleventh day of may I call upon you for aid to protect the State against domestic violence" Telegram received, DNA, RG 60, Letters from the President. *HED*, 43-1-229, part 2, p. 43. On April 28, Baxter wrote to USG "that divers evil disposed persons conspiring the overthrow of the goverment of the state of Arkansas have unlawfully and by force of arms taken possession of the capitol building and Archives of goverment; that the legislature is not now in session; that the insurrection aforesaid has grown into such magnitude as to seriously interfere with, if not prevent the assembling of the legislature which I have called to convene at the seat of Goverment on the eleventh day of May next, and cannot be suppressed by the state Militia under my command without great bloodshed and loss of life. Now therefore pursuant to the provision of the constitution of the United States in that behalf I respectfully call on your Excellency for the necessary Military force to suppress such insurrection, and to protect the state against the domestic violence aforesaid . . ." DS, DNA, RG 60, Letters from the President. *SED*, 43-1-51, 6, 8–9; *SD*, 57-2-209, 173–74. On May 2, Albert Pike and Robert W. Johnson, "Counsel & Representatives of *Govr Elisha Baxter*," Washington, D. C., wrote to USG. "We present respectfully to you the duly authenticated 'CALL' upon you by the Governor of the State of Ark, Elisha Baxter, made in due form, and in accordance with the Constitution of the United States, . . ." L, DNA, RG 60, Letters from the President. *SED*, 43-1-51, 8. On April 30, Rose had telegraphed to Townsend. "Nothing of importance has transpired here for several days   forces on both sides considerably reduced," Telegram received, DNA, RG 94, Letters Received, 1491 1874. See telegram to Capt. Thomas E. Rose, April 18, 1874; telegram to Elisha Baxter, May 11, 1874; *New York Times*, April 22, 1874.

On April 19 and 21, Baxter had telegraphed to USG. "A few days since in the absence of my counsel and at a time wholly unexpected the circuit Judge of this county a court of inferior jurisdiction rendered judgement in favor of Brooks against me for the office of Governor of this state & without notice to me or my Counsel I was at once forcibly put out of the Office and that without any pretence of a writ being served on me   all this was done too after the supreme court of this state had twice decided that no court in the state had jurisdiction of the case at all & the Legislature alone had the Jurisdiction   at once on being ejected from the office I took steps to restore myself and to get possession of the office and to carry on the Government   the People are coming to my aid and are ready to restore me at once   in making this organization I am obstructed by the interference of the U. S. Troops in Displacing my guards from the Telegraph Office and now is apprehended that there will be further interference   such interference breaks mMe down & prevents any effort on my part to restore the state Government & to protect the People in their rights   I beg of you to modify any order to the extent of such interference and leave me free to act in this way to restore law and peace as the legitimate Governor of the State such interference does not leave me any chance to assert my claim to the office of Governor   in the interests of peace and of those people who are flocking here to my support by the hundred I beg of you to remove the U. S troops back to the arsenal and permit me to restore the legitimate Government by my own forces which I will do promptly if the U. S. will not interfere   there is an armed insurrection against the legal state Government here and I call upon you to aid in suppressing it but if you will not then leave me free to act and order the U S troops without an hours delay to their own Ground & keep them out of my way. I have been thwarted & delayed thus long and in fact ejected from my office because of the fact that I had heretofore disbanded the Militia of the state   I make this earnest demand to repress insurrection & prevent domestic violence under my sense of duty to the constitution & laws of the U. S. as well as of the state of Arkansas and I rely confidently as I have all the time upon the assurances Contained in your letter of september fifteenth Eighteen Seventy three to prevent the overturn of my official authority by illegal & Disorderly proceedings   an immediate answer is requested otherwise bloodshed may be the result" "I have no reply to my dispatch of the nineteenth   it is of the utmost importance for me to have a reply, and I now earnestly request one," Telegrams received (the first at 5:04 P.M.), DNA, RG 60, Letters from the President. *HED,* 43-1-229, 6–7, 9; *SD,* 57-2-209, 171.

On April 20, U.S. Representative William J. Hynes of Ark. had telegraphed to USG from the capitol. "Sergeant at Arms of the House of Reps has just received the following dispatch from the Assistant Sergeant at Arms now at Little Rock, Arkansas viz: 'Little Rock Ark. Apr. 20th /74   Battle expected every minute   U. S. troops have possession of telegraph office.   signed A. BRADSHAW.'" Telegram received, DLC-USG, IB. On the same day, Belknap wrote to Townsend. "The President directs that the Comd'g. Officer U. S. Troops at Little Rock be telegraphed as follows: 'No call having been made upon the President as provided by the Constitution & Laws of the United States as was anticipated, by either of the contestants for the Governorship of the State, you are instructed, until otherwise ordered, to take no official actions as to the pending difficulties, excepting to carry out the President's order concerning the telegraph and to protect the property of the United States—" ALS, DNA, RG 94, Letters Received, 1491 1874. A copy of this proposed telegram was endorsed. "This dispatch was not sent the Sec'y of War having recalled it . . ." E, *ibid.*

Also on April 20, Joseph Brooks, Little Rock, telegraphed to USG. "I hereby inform you that one Elisha Baxter a private citizen pretending to be governor of Arkansas without warrant or authority of law assumed to declare martial law in the capital county of the state and to appoint a pretended military governor of the city of Little Rock the seat of government   that he called out armed bodies of men for the avowed purpose of attacking and capturing the capitol of the state by military force and forcibly installing himself as governor of such state   That large bodies of armed men have assembled and are continually assembling under said Baxters proclamation of matial law and are in close proximity to the state house and have this day actually advanced on the state House and confronted a body of Federal troops stationed in front of the State House under orders from their commanding officer acting under your command to preserve the peace and were only prevented from making the attack by the presence of Federal troops   That those armed bodies have seized and appropriated private property and are hourly seizing and appropriating private property without compensation have conscripted and are continually conscripting private citizens and compelling them to aid and abet them in their insurrectionary purposes and have seized and are daily seizing railroads in the state and appropriated them to the same illegal and insurectory purposes   That these are armed bodies at this moment are assembled within a few hundred yards of the state House and threaten an immediate attack upon it   That the legislature adjourned sine die in April last has not since been convened is not now in session and cannot be convened in time to prevent the threatened attack   That domestic violence now actually exists in this state and at the seat of government which the civil and military authorities under my control are powerless to prevent or supress   Therefore I Joseph Brooks Governor of the state of Arkansas in pursuance of the constitution and laws of the United States hereby make application to your Excellency to protect the State Capital and the State of Arkansas against domestic violence and insurrection . . ." Telegram received (on April 21, at 4:00 A.M.), DNA, RG 60, Letters from the President; LS, *ibid. SED,* 43-1-51, 2–3; *HED,* 43-1-229, 7–8; *SD,* 57-2-209, 309–10. On the same day, John McClure, Ark. chief justice, and others, Little Rock, telegraphed to USG. "We the undersigned being state officers of the state of Arkansas since the Pulaski Circuit Court rendered the judgment of ouster against Elisha Baxter for the office of governor and awarded the said office of Governor to Joseph Brooks and he qualified as governor and entered upon the discharge of his duties as such we have and do now recognize said Brooks as governor of said state in all official intercourse with the executive of the state" Telegram received (on April 21, at 4:15 A.M.), DNA, RG 60, Letters from the President; LS, *ibid.* *SED*, 43-1-51, 1–2; *HED*, 43-1-229, 8–9.

On April 21, W. Hines Furbush, sheriff, Lee County, Marianna, telegraphed to USG. "For the sake of law and order take some steps to suppress the riot in Arkansas,   every good citizen will abide your command,   speak and will obey,   the general impression is that you will not interfere thus they keep up the fight, . . ." Telegram received, DNA, RG 60, Letters from the President. *HED*, 43-1-229, 9, 21; *SD*, 57-2-209, 313–14. On the same day, Rose, Little Rock, telegraphed to Belknap. "The situation is about the same except that there is an uncontrollable armed mob constantly parading on the streets. All parties agreed to a truce until tomorrow at nine o'clock, but at about five o'clock this afternoon the usual armed mob commenced parading on the streets in front of Mr Baxters quarters. I immediately went near to observe them and inquire of their leaders what their object was, about which time an indiscriminate firing took place resulting in the wounding of two men,   the leaders will now probably disperse their own mobs and the strife cease." Copy (received at 11:35 P.M.), DNA, RG 60, Letters from the President. *HED*, 43-1-229, 21. Also on April 21, Secretary of State Hamilton Fish recorded a cabinet exchange in his diary. "A large deputation from Arkansas was in attendance with the two Senators urging the President's intervention to preserve peace: President thought all necessary measures had been taken, within the proper limits of the power of the Government and was not disposed to issue any further orders; before they left a despatch was received by the Secretary of War indicating a probability of an agreement about to be reached between the parties." DLC-Hamilton Fish.

To House of Representatives

To The House of Representatives:

I transmit herewith the papers called for by the Resolution of the House of Representatives of the 20th instant requesting all correspondence by telegraph or otherwise between the persons claiming to be Governor of Arkansas and myself, relating to the troubles in that State, together with copies of any order or directions given by me or under my directions to the military officer in charge of the garrison, or in command of the U. S. troops at Little Rock.

U. S. Grant

Executive Mansion
April 23d 1874

Copy, DNA, RG 130, Messages to Congress. *HED*, 43-1-229. On April 22, 1874, Secretary of War William W. Belknap wrote to USG. "I have the honor to enclose, herewith, copies of all correspondence on file in this Department relative to the present political controversy in the State of Arkansas, the same being furnished in compliance with House Resolution of the 20th instant." LS (press), DNA, RG 94, Letters Received, 1491 1874. *HED*,

43-1-229. On April 23, Attorney Gen. George H. Williams wrote a similar letter to USG. Copy, DNA, RG 60, Letters Sent to Executive Officers. *HED*, 43-1-229.

On April 28, USG wrote to the House of Representatives. "I have the honor to transmit herewith additional correspondence received since my communication of the 23d instant in reply to the resolution of the House of Representatives of the 20th instant requesting copies of correspondence between persons claiming to be Governor of Arkansas and myself, relating to troubles in that State." Copy, DNA, RG 130, Messages to Congress. *HED*, 43-1-229, part 2.

To House of Representatives

To THE HOUSE OF REPRESENTATIVES:

In pursuance of the resolution of the House of Representatives of the 15th instant, requesting to be informed "what geographical and geological surveys under different departments and branches of the government are operating in the same and contiguous areas of territory west of the Mississippi river and whether it be not practicable to consolidate them under one department or to define the geographical limits to be embraced by each," I have the honor to transmit herewith the views of the officers of the War and Interior Departments on the subjects named in the said resolution and invite attention thereto.

Where surveys are made with the view of sectionizing the public lands, preparatory to opening them for settlement or entry, there is no question but such surveys, and all work connected therewith, should be made under the direct control of the Interior Department, or the Commissioner of the General Land Office subject to the supervision of the Secretary of the Interior. But, where the object is to complete the map of the country; to determine the geographical, astronomical, geodetic, topographic, hydrographic, meteorological, geological and mineralogical features of the country;—in other words to collect full information of the unexplored, or but partially known portions of the country, it seems to me a matter of no importance as to which department of the government should have control of the work.

The conditions which should control this subject are in my judgment, first: which department is prepared to do the work best; second: which can do it the most expeditiously and economically.

As the country to be explored is occupied in great part by unciv-
ilized indians, all parties engaged in the work at hand must be supplied with escorts from the Army—thus placing a large portion of
the expense upon the War Department—and as the Engineer Corps
of the Army is composed of scientific gentlemen, educated and practiced for just the kind of work to be done, and as they are under pay,
whether employed in this work or not, it would seem that the second
condition named would be more fully complied with by employing
them to do the work.

There is but little doubt but that they will accomplish it as
promptly and as well, and much more economically.

U S. GRANT

EXECUTIVE MANSION
APRIL 30. 1874

Copy, DNA, RG 130, Messages to Congress. *HED,* 43-1-240; *HRC,* 43-1-612. Ongoing
surveying expeditions in 1874 included teams led by 1st Lt. George M. Wheeler, Ferdi-
nand V. Hayden, and John Wesley Powell. Conflict between the Wheeler and Hayden parties concerning overlapping assignments helped to spark congressional inquiry. See *ibid.;*
William H. Goetzmann, *Exploration and Empire: The Explorer and the Scientist in the Winning
of the American West* (New York, 1966), pp. 478–81, 578–80; *PUSG,* 17, 406–7.
  On April 10, 1873, George M. Robeson, act. secretary of war, had written to USG.
"I herewith enclose application on behalf of Lieut. Wheeler, U. S. Engr. Corps, for escort.
It is a matter about which Gen. Sherman and Gen. Humphries seem to differ. Gen. Sher-
man's recommendation strikes me as most proper, though the expense of transportation—
a memorandum of which is enclosed—may be an unanswerable argument against it. It is
a question, however, which I did not like to decide without referring to you, and I now enclose it for such suggestion as you may think proper." LS, DNA, RG 108, Letters Received.
On March 28, Gen. William T. Sherman had endorsed a request for troop escorts from
Wheeler, supervising geographical surveys west of the 100th meridian. "Respectfully returned to the Hon Sec of War—The only objection is the utter breaking up of organization, and the Special Equipmt herein suggested.—Soldiers thus detached are lost to their
companies, & leave the remnant of companies too small for any good. Why not take their
own Engineer troops from Willets Point? They can far better be spared than our over
taxed Small Garrisons of the Frontier!" AES, *ibid.* Related papers are *ibid.* On April 15,
Henry T. Crosby, chief clerk, War Dept., endorsed these papers. "By direction of the President the detail for escort as requested by the Chief of Engineers will be made as soon as
practicable" AES, *ibid.* See *ibid.,* RG 94, Letters Received, 5161 1873.
  On April 10, Secretary of the Interior Columbus Delano wrote to USG. "I have the
honor to enclose, herewith, a copy of a letter of the Commissioner of Indian Affairs, of the
8th instant, in which he invites my attention to the accompanying copy of a telegram from
T. H. Barrett, Esqr., U. S. Surveyor, dated the 4th instant, reporting the murder in the Indian Territory of a surveying party of four men &c., by Cheyenne Indians, and asking protection. You will observe that, in view of the circumstances alluded to, the Commissioner
recommends that the President be requested to direct that two companies of United States
troops be sent to the locality bounded by the South line of the State of Kansas, and the North

fork of the Canadian River, and the 98th and 100th degrees of west Longitude for the purpose of affording the necessary protection to the U. S. surveyors operating in that region
of country under the direction of this Department, and that the necessary instructions be
communicated to the proper military commanders by telegraph. Concurring as I do in the
recommendation of the Commissioner, before referred to, I have respectfully to call your
attention to the subject and request that the necessary orders be given, provided you see no
reasons why this should not be done." LS, *ibid.*, 1300 1873. Related papers are *ibid.*

On April 23, Robeson wrote to Delano. "Referring to your request of the 14th instant, for an escort for a party to be sent to survey the northern boundary of the State of
Nebraska, I have the honor to say that it appears by the report of the Lieutenant General
that the complete protection of this party will require an escort of at least three companies
of infantry, and the General of the Army reports that such an expedition at this time will
be likely to cause an Indian outbreak and perhaps lead to a war along the route of the survey. Under these circumstances I am directed by the President to ask whether you think
it absolutely necessary that the survey should proceed this year? Please answer at your
earliest convenience." LS (press), *ibid.*, 1075 1873. Related papers are *ibid.*

On March 20, 1875, Edward F. Beale, Washington, D. C., wrote to USG. "In a conversation with you, some time since, in relation to the Colorado River, I suggested that instead of turning it into the Desert at '*New River*' it should be taken out, by a canal, above
the cañon which, to distinguish it from many others on the same river, is called the '*Great
Cañon*,' and below the junction of Green and Grand rivers its principal tributaries. This
point would be several hundred miles above the other, and would bring within the benefit
of water thousands of square miles which 'New River' would not reach. My first idea was
that a system of Lakes could be thus formed along the Southern and South Eastern flank
of the Sierra Nevada, and that the wonderful basin of 'Deaths Valley,' some four hundred
feet below the Sea level, could be converted into one of them, but on talking over the matter with Leiut Wheeler, I find that barriers of elevation exist which would render that impossible. My view of the subject was, that with such a system of lakes the entire climatic
condition of Southern California would be beneficially changed, and even, although compelled to abandon the hope of the transformation of that remarkable desert basin into a
great lake, I still think the same object might be accomplished by using the water in reclaiming to cultivation the soil of the country through which such a canal would pass, and
converting into lakes such other basins as it would reach on its line. At present the Colorado is a worthless stream, running through chasms of precipitous rock sometimes a mile
in depth, and, in places, forty or fifty miles in length, and with but a few valuable vallies
for several hundred miles. If it should prove possible to take this splendid river from its
present bed, and by a canal carry it out on the Desert, and thence to a point below Fort
Yuma, an amount of land large enough to make a great State would be restored to cultivation—I say *restored*, because it is evident that portions of the country through which it
would pass have once sustained a population who had made considerable advances in the
arts of civilized life. Whether this is practicable or not I do not know, but it is surely worth
the test of Sientific and instrumental examination, which, even if it proved what I suggest
to be impossible, could not fail to be worth all it would cost, in the information we should
obtain of the country traversed and examined. I would suggest that such a corps as could
be spared for the duty should be directed to begin a line of survey below the mouths of
Grand and Green rivers, and carry a line of level, at as great an altitude as possible, along
the base of the mountains to the westward, observing and estimating closely the cost of
a canal,—The amount of water at all seasons to be furnished,—The vallies and basins, if
any, which could be converted into Lakes,—The amount of land which could be brought
into cultivation by using the water for irrigation,—The probable climatic changes to be

effected,—The absolute amount and distance of artificial canal to be constructed, as well as that which could be used by reason of natural ducts, such as narrow vallies, gorges, cañons &c,—and, finally, the farthest point Westward to which the river could be thus carried within our our own territory, and, if the scheme should prove feasible, how much of the Peninsular of Lower California would be necessary to enable us to carry it into the Gulf of California. Should this turn out to be practicable, and this noble but at present idle river be made to do what is herein conceived and suggested as being within the possible, I cannot imagine a more patriotic work, or one better calculated to add to the many illustrious acts of your life and administration." ALS, *ibid.*, RG 77, Letters Received. On April 8, Henry T. Crosby, chief clerk, War Dept., endorsed this letter to Brig. Gen. Andrew A. Humphreys, chief of engineers. "The President desires this subject to be sent to Lt. Wheeler for Consideration" AES, *ibid.* On April 27, Wheeler, Washington, D. C., reported to Humphreys that existing surveys "lead to the belief that it will prove impracticable to divert the Colorado River of the West at any point above its lower Grand Cañon for the purpose of transferring its waters to areas of marked depression known to exist in its western basin. . . ." LS, *ibid.*

In [*1876*], USG wrote a note. "Glover Alcorn,—son of the Senator—asks to go, and be useful, with one of the explorations to the Rockey Mountains. I wish the Sec. of War would have Lt. Wheeler, Eng. Corps, spoken to in behalf of this young man." AN (initialed, docketed 1876), *ibid.*, RG 107, Appointment Papers.

To Brig. Gen. John Pope

Washington. D. C.
May 9th 1874

MY DEAR GENERAL,

Your letter of the 18th of April in regard to your position in the matter of a re-hearing of the Fitz John Porter Court Martial was duly received. You are under the apprehension that I had not fully examined the case or rather that the public so thought and that you had used means to prevent me from giving the subject fair consideration —In reply I will make two emphatic statement: First, to the best of my recollection I have never had but one letter from you on this subject, prior to the one I am now answering & that simply contained the request that if I contemplated re-opening the case that I examine both sides—I read during the trial the evidence, & the final findings of the Court; looking upon the whole trial as one of great importance and particularly so to the army & navy—

When Genl Porter's subsequent defence was published I received a copy of it & read it with care and attention, determined if he had been wronged & I could wright him, I would do so—My conclusion was that no new facts were developed that could be fairly considered and that it was of doubtful legality whether by the mere authority of the Executive, a re-hearing could be given—

Yours truly
U. S. GRANT.

GENERAL JOHN POPE—U. S. A.

Copy, DLC-Joseph Holt. *SED*, 46-1-37, part 3, p. 1094. On April 18, 1874, Brig. Gen. John Pope, Washington, D. C., wrote to USG. "It is no doubt known to you that General Fitz John Porter claims to have procured evidence since his trial, not attainable at the time, which would either acquit him of the crime of which he stands convicted or greatly modify the findings and sentence of the Court Martial before which he was tried and that he has embodied in a printed pamphlet the kind and character of this evidence and what he expects to establish by it, together with an appeal for a re-hearing of his case—It is widely asserted by those who sympathise with him and probably believed by many who have no personal interest in his case, that influences hostile to him have restrained you from examining this statement of his case and have thus worked great injustice by preventing the Executive from considering statements or evidence which might vindicate his character. It is needless to say to you that *I* have never used any influence with you, personal or other, to prevent the investigation of his statements nor even intimated to you in any manner, that I objected to any action you might think proper to take in the matter—Nevertheless as I do not wish even to seem to consent to any additional misconceptions concerning me or my action in this case, I beg (if you have not already done so) that you will yourself, Mr. President, examine as fully into the question as you think justice or mercy demands: or that you will order a Board of competent officers of high rank, unconnected with the Armies or transactions involved, to investigate fully the statements of this new evidence made by Genl Porter & report to you, what, if any, bearing it would have upon the findings & sentence of his Court Martial, even if it could be fully established—" Copy, DLC-Joseph Holt. *SED*, 46-1-37, part 3, pp. 1093–94. On Jan. 29, 1875, Pope, Fort Leavenworth, Kan., wrote to Judge Advocate Gen. Joseph Holt. "I have to apologize to you for my remissness in not sending you the copies of the letters referred to in your note just received—I enclose them herewith—The President's letter he put off writing until just as I was leaving the city & wrote it while I was waiting in his house to take leave of him and his family. It is not so full as I would wish nor so strongly expressed as he expressed himself in conversation, but it answers the purpose—Garfield's resolution is in substance (indeed almost verbatim) the same as the request I made in my letter to the President & relates wholly & solely to *new testimony* not *attainable at the time* on which the President is asked to appoint a Board to report—It seems better that this should be done now and finally closed—I presume Garfield has spoken to you about it.—If not I would suggest that you talk with him on the subject—" ALS, DLC-Joseph Holt. On Jan. 18, U.S. Representative James A. Garfield of Ohio had introduced a resolution "in regard to alleged new evidence in the case of Fitz John Porter." *CR*, 43–2, 555. No action followed.

On Jan. 26, 1874, Montgomery Blair had written to Fitz John Porter, Morristown, N. J. "You ask me what can be done to get your case reviewed by this Administration. Nothing that I know of. They probably see some trouble, and no political advantage in it, and will let it alone. . . . I fear that neither the party as a whole, nor the administration will take trouble to do you justice, although you have the testimony of a personal and political friend of President Lincoln that at the time of his death he purposed a re-hearing of your case, . . ." *SED*, 46-1-37, part 1, pp. 531–33; *Honorable Montgomery Blair, Postmaster-General During President Lincoln's Administration, to Maj.-Gen. Fitz John Porter* (Morristown, N. J., 1874). On Feb. 9, the Pa. legislature passed a resolution requesting USG to appoint a court-martial to reexamine Porter's case. Copy, DLC-Fitz John Porter. See *PUSG*, 19, 524–26; letter to Fitz John Porter, [*Feb., 1875*].

To George H. Williams

Washington, D. C. May 11th 18674.

HON. GEO. H. WILLIAMS;

I send herewith two dispatches just received from Little Rock, Ark. one from Govr Baxter and the other from a portion of the Members of the legislature of the state. Baxter's proposition seems to me reasonable and if not accepted by the Brooks party by to-morning I think we had better put an end to the controversy by publishing a proclamation recognizing Baxter as Governor. Please send such dispatches to both Baxter & Brooks as will indicate to them this determination.

Very Truly
U. S. GRANT

ALS, PHi. On May 10, 1874, John B. Burton and twenty-nine others, Little Rock, telegraphed to USG. "We the undersigned members of the Legislature of this state have come here to meet under the call of Governor Baxter on tomorrow & we wish to meet under the call of Governor Baxter on tomorrow & we wish to meet and settle the troubles now existing here as the country requires it and we respectfully ask protection of the general government while we meet and deliberate   we hold the matter should not be postponed and all that we can do to have a fair and honorable adjustment shall be done and unless we are protected there may be bloodshed here in a very short time & the consequence no one can tell   we are well satisfied there will be a quorum of the legislature present tomorrow under the call of Gov Baxter and we are satisfied a quorum would be here now were it not for the unwarranted seisure & suppression of the trains on the Little Rock and Fort Smith railroad necessarily delaying the members of the Legislature from the North western portion of the State" Telegram received, DNA, RG 60, Letters from the President. *SED*, 43-1-51, 18; *SD*, 57-2-209, 311. On May 11, Elisha Baxter, Little Rock, telegraphed to USG. "THERE IS ALMOST A QUORUM OF BOTH HOUSES OF THE LEGISLATURE PRESENT AND THEY HAVE POWER UNDER THE CONSTITUTION TO ADJOURN FROM DAY TO DAY UNTIL THEY HAVE A QUORUM AND THEY CAN ADJOURN NO LONGER UNTIL THEY HAVE A QUORUM   I AM IN FAVOR OF

THEIR ADJOURNING AS LONG AS THEY PLEASE UNTIL EVERY SUPPOSED BROOKS ADHERENT IS PRESENT WITH THIS UNDERSTANDING I WILL DISBAND MY TROOPS IN PROPORTION AS BROOKS DIS[BANDS HIS] BUT FOR THE MEETING OF THE LEGISLATURE AT THE USUAL PLACE MR. BROOKS MUST GET AS FAR FROM IT WEST AS I AM EAST AND DEPOSIT THE STATE ARMS IN THE STATE ARMORY AND LET THE STATE HOUSE AND PUBLIC BUILDINGS BE TURNED OVER AT ONCE TO J. M. JOHNSON THE SEC-RETARY OF STATE TO WHOM UNDER THE LAW THEY BELONG." Telegram re-ceived, DNA, RG 60, Letters from the President. *SED*, 43-1-51, 25–26. See telegram to Elisha Baxter, April 22, 1874; *New York Times*, May 6, 9–12, 1874.

On April 25, John M. Johnson, Little Rock, had written to USG recounting his "sum-mary ejectment" as Ark. secretary of state and other actions by armed forces answering to Joseph Brooks. LS, DNA, RG 60, Letters from the President. *SED*, 43-1-51, 3–5. On April 27, Creed Taylor, Taylor Plain, Ark., wrote to USG. "as an old citizen of Arkansas I presume to address you upon the present troubles in our State . . . The Country is now full of Morauding parties recruiting soldiers, and unless soon checked and sent home will ~~soon~~ degenerate into a bandit of robers, to sustain their Lawless idle vagabondism they offer their dupes 22$ twenty two dollars a month and board to enlist on their side Where Sir is the money to come from to pay and support these betrayed poor negros who leave their crops and families to the mercies of an indignant & injured people. . . ." ALS, DNA, RG 60, Letters from the President. *SED*, 43-1-51, 5. On April 30, William T. Brown, Bolesville, Ark., wrote to USG. "*Private* . . . I hope you will pardon me for presuming to address you But I suppose you would like to get a history of the *Ark* muddle from some unpredjudiced source, And I am sure I can give an impartial history of the affair as I have no confidence in, nor *use* for either of the contestants. . . ." ALS, DNA, RG 60, Letters from the President. *SED*, 43-1-51, 6–7.

On May 1, Brooks, Little Rock, telegraphed to USG. "H. King White, who fired on the Commander of the U. S. troops at Little Rock has been ordered to Pine Bluff by Bax-ter and is pillaging and murdering. The state is perfectly peaceful except in Jefferson Co, the scene of White's robberies and murders. I have refrained from sending out forces in order to avoid conflict." Telegram received, DNA, RG 60, Letters from the President. *SED*, 43-1-51, 8. On the same day, U.S. Senator Powell Clayton of Ark. wrote to USG transmit-ting telegrams on the Brooks-Baxter dispute. LS, DNA, RG 60, Letters from the President. The enclosures are *ibid. SED*, 43-1-51, 7–8.

On May 4, Brooks, Baring Cross, Ark., telegraphed to USG. "LAST EVENING JUDGES BENNETT AND SEARLE OF THE SUPREME COURT WERE AR-RESTED AND HAVE BEEN SPIRITED AWAY. THEY COME TO THE CITY T[O] ATTEND A REGULAR SITTING OF THE COURT THE OFFICER MAKING THE ARREST WHEN INTERROGATED BY JUDGE BE[NNE]TT BY WHAT AU-THORITY HE WAS ARRESTED REPLIED BY AUTHORITY OF GOV. BAXTER. WHEN ASKED WHAT FOR. THE OFFICER REPLIED THAT BAXTER HAD REASON TO FEAR THAT THE SUPREME COURT IF ALLOWED TO MEET MIGHT POSSIBLY PASS UPON SOME QUESTION THAT MIGHT PREJUDICE HIS CASE NOW PENDING BEFORE T[H]E ATTORNEY GENERAL OF THE UNITED STATES AND THAT THE COURT SHOULD NOT MEET UNTIL THE QUESTION OF [W]HO IS GOVERNOR SHOULD BE DECIDED AT WASHING-TON. I RESPECTFULLY ASK THAT YOU DIRECT THE OFFICER COMMAND-ING TO DEMAND A SURRENDER OF THE ARRESTED PARTIES. THE ARREST OF THESE PARTIES HAS CAUSED MUCH EXCITEMENT AND INDIGNATION." Telegrams received (at 2:18 P.M.), DNA, RG 60, Letters from the President; (at 5:00 P.M.), *ibid. SED*, 43-1-51, 9–11. On the same day, William S. Oliver, sheriff, Little Rock, had telegraphed to Secretary of War William W. Belknap, via Clayton. "I have asked the commander of U. S troops here for aid to serve writs of habeas corpus for Judges Searle & Bennett who were arrested at Argenta last night by Capt Williams Commanding Company from Hempstead Co of Baxters Militia   Williams says He arrested the Judges by order of Baxter stating it was to prevent meeting of supreme court today which is the adjourned term. I fear if writs are not served at once the Judges will be assassinated   I am powerless without the Cooperation of the US force here. See Secty of war at once   have now waited twelve hours for the reply of Col Rose to my application made in writing   Judges of U. S authorities being american citizens & are now held without warrant or shadow of law" Telegram received (at 1:12 P.M.), DNA, RG 60, Letters from the President. *SED*, 43-1-51, 12. On the same day, Thomas Allen, president, St. Louis, Iron Mountain & Southern Railway, Little Rock, telegraphed to USG. "Both sides here are arming & recruiting   your decision either way will be conclusive & beneficial" Telegram received (at 5:45 P.M.), DNA, RG 60, Letters from the President. *SED*, 43-1-51, 11. On May 6 and 7, Capt. Thomas E. Rose, Little Rock, telegraphed to AG Edward D. Townsend that U.S. troops had liberated the Ark. judges. Telegrams received (the first at 6:00 P.M.), DNA, RG 94, Letters Received, 1491 1874. *SED*, 43-1-51, 143–44.

On May 6, 7, and 8, Brooks telegraphed to USG. "Associat justice searle has been recaptured from the insurgents   judge Bennett is in the woods & expected in soon   the supreme court met this morning at its regular adjourned term   the suit of Joseph Brooks against Henry Page treasurer which is an application for mandamus to compel the state treasurer to pay a requision made by governor Brooks involving the question of the jurisdiction of the pulaski circuit court on the case of Brooks against Baxter the validity of the judgement in that court & the whole gubernatorial controversy the decision of which will settle the question as to who is the legal gov of Arkansas and give us peace which ever way it may be decided has been commenced in the supreme court and submitted this morning a decision is expected tomorrow morning" "Supreme Court decided today that the pulaski Circuit Court has jurisdiction of the subject matter of the case of Brooks vs Baxter & the Judgement is regular & valid & that I am Governor of Arkansas   a certified copy of the opinion has been telegraphed attorney Genl williams" "The court convened on the first Monday in Dec eighteen hundred & twenty three under the provisions of an act fixing the time of holding the supreme Court of this state approved Dec fifth eighteen hundred & sixty eight and under it has been in session in contemplation of law ever since being adjourned by its own order from one day to another   the present setting of the Court is but a continuation of the December term" Telegrams received (at 3:56 P.M., 4:30 P.M., and 4:10 P.M.), DNA, RG 60, Letters from the President. *SED*, 43-1-51, 12–13, 15.

On May 5 and 9, Secretary of State Hamilton Fish recorded cabinet discussions in his diary. "The Arkansas difficulties were discussed at some length. The Attorney General says there can be no possible doubt that Baxter is legally entitled to the office; his right having been decided by the legislature which by the Constitution of the State is made the exclusive judge of the returns of the elections: both he and the President express the opinion that Brooks had received an actual majority of the votes, but that the President could not go behind the count and decision of the Legislature." "Arkansas troubles are discussed at length. The Attorney General reads a long and very able opinion in support of the legal right of Baxter; also a decision of the Supreme Court of the State, which he has just received, overruling their former decisions and now sustaining the right of Brooks and the jurisdiction of the Court to pass upon the question of the conflict between the claimants: it was decided that the Attorney General should consult with the judiciary Committee of the Senate on the subject." DLC-Hamilton Fish.

On May 9, Brooks telegraphed to USG. "I was elected to the office of governor of Arkansas by a large majority of voters   this I have established by proof in the courts   I have been adjudged entitled to the office by the circuit court the only court of general jurisdiction in this state   the force & effect of this judgement was submitted to the supreme court in a proceeding which called into question the jurisdiction of the circuit court & the forces and effect of its judgement & my right to execise the duties & office of governor & now the supreme court has adjudicated me to be the lawful governor of the state & directed the treasurer to honor my warrant on the treasury to suppress violence & disorder an act that can be performed only by the governor   I in in actual possession & exercising the unctions of the office   a formidab[le] insurrection & armed rebellion against the right & lawful authoritys exists actual conflict wages & several lives have been lost   it is my duty to defend the government I have sworn to administer   I have appealed & do now appeal to your excellency as chief magistrate of the united states for assistance to quell insurrection & domestic violence   two days have the insurgents project a desperate struggle to gain possesion of the state house & public property   I am able to hold the situation against all the force that the insurgents can rally but prompt recognition & interposition on your part would prevent the effusion of much blood—" Telegram received (at 4:20 P.M.), DNA, RG 60, Letters from the President. *SED*, 43-1-51, 16–17; *SD*, 57-2-209, 174–75.

On May 7, P. Lynch Lee, sheriff, Ouachita County, Camden, had telegraphed to USG. "Both Baxter and Brooks Claim to be Governor of our state and have officers organizing troops   the citizens of this county are law abiding and do not know which to recognise, Can I organize and sustain neutrality till the question is settled," Telegram received, DNA, RG 60, Letters from the President. *SED*, 43-1-51, 13. On May 8, J. A. Conrad, Little Rock, "Representing many Farmers in the State of Ark County of Pulaski," wrote to USG. "Please condecene to Listen to the Working men & peacable Citizens of the state of Ark. . . . Both men are to blame   Baxter has called upon the White people to help him   they have in a measure responded but such a responce there are a few men it is true that might be called respectable Citizens but the most of his army consists of Gamblers Murders & Robers & bush Whackers of the Last war. Brooks has Called upon the Blacks to assist him   he has not a singel regment of white troops   the offices are in a measur white but office seekers . . ." ALS, DNA, RG 60, Letters from the President. *HED*, 43-2-25, 21–22. On May 9, Tobias Kelly *et al.*, Fort Smith, Ark., petitioned USG. "We the undersigned Citizens, irrespective of political party would most earnestly ask that something be done and that immediately to relieve the law abiding Citizens from the annoyance of steamboats being stopped on the Arkansas River by the two political factions in our state. We would further ask that the mails on Railroad and Stage be attended to and these political factions be punished in accordance with law for stopping the same. All this we ask for as Citizens of the U S. of America." DS (65 signatures), DNA, RG 60, Letters from the President. *SED*, 43-1-51, 15–16. On May 10, Allen, St. Louis, telegraphed to USG. "Belligerants thrown troops to North Bank of Arkansas. Brook's men hold our bridge   skirmishing between pickets active. We cannot long carry mails or run trains" Telegram received, DNA, RG 60, Letters from the President. *SED*, 43-1-51, 25. On the same day, Rose telegraphed to Townsend. "Everything quiet here thus far today. Considerable disorder yesterday morning—One colored man was Killed within fifty feet of my troops by parties firing from the direction of Baxters guards—the frequent firing of these men greatly endangers the lives of the United States troops . . ." Telegram received (at 7:30 P.M.), DNA, RG 94, Letters Received, 1491 1874. *SED*, 43-1-51, 145.

Probably in early May, U.S. Representative William W. Wilshire of Ark. and Ralph P. Lowe wrote to USG. "In relation to the Baxter-Brooks controversy, as to the rightful governorship of the state of Arkansas, the undersigned, authorised agents and attys of the party first named, in the present strange and complicated attitude of the controversy, growing out of the irregular and conflicting dicisions of the question at issue, by the courts of said state, and the unhappy division of sentiment on the subject among the people, do make the following proposition, to the end that a peaceful and early adjustment of the difficulty may be secured, namely, That the legislature of the state now being convened, shall be recognised as the general assembly of the same—that its session shall be held in the state house, without interruption or molestation from any quarter—that it shall entertain a petition from Mr Brooks, setting forth specifically the grounds of his claim to the office of governor as well as his reasons for contesting Baxters right thereto that the investigation of the facts of the petition shall be conducted in the manner prescribed by the constitution and statute laws of said state, giving to both parties a full hearing upon the competent & relavent testimony which either may be offered—that the legislature shall determine by joint ballot which of the contestants had received a majority of the legal votes at said election; this done, such party which-ever it may be shall be recognised by the Government at Washington as the rightful Governor—And untill such determination is made and announced, Baxter will be recognised and treated by the Federal Authorities here as the ad interim Governor of the State—this under the circumstances is considered reasonable and proper, in as much as heretofore he has been recognised as such by the legislature and the people of the state and all the departments of the Federal government—The forgoing suggestion derives much emphasis from the fact that it never could have been in contemplation that two tribunals of equal dignity and from neither of which there is any appeal, should have concurrent jurisdiction over the same controverted question   The evils resulting from such a construction must be patent to every thinking mind—" LS (docketed May 11), DNA, RG 60, Letters from the President. Wilshire and Lowe presented this document to USG on May 9. *New York Herald*, May 10, 1874. On May 10, Wilshire and Lowe, Washington, D. C., wrote to USG. ". . . we, the agents and attorneys of Gov. Baxter, in order that the conflicting claims of Baxter and Brooks may be speedily and finally settled by competent authority and thus relieve the national authorityies of any further trouble on that account, respectfully urge your Excellency, in the name and on behalf of Gov. Baxter, to recognize and protect the meeting of the general assembly to-morrow at the capitol of the state, and, pending the investigation by it of the contest between Baxter and Brooks, to recognize Gov. Baxter as the lawful governor, subject to the disposition of the question by the general assembly. . . . As to the conflicting decisions of the courts of the state in regard to the power of the courts to determine the question between Baxter and Brooks, we shall content ourselves by calling attention to the fact that the supreme court has twice held that *no court* of the state had jurisdiction to try and determine a contest for the office of governor or any other Executive office named in section 19 of article 6 of the constitution of Arkansas. It will be borne in mind that both of these decisions were rendered by the supreme court, consisting of five judges, in a time of peace, when all could attend and assert their rights or claims without let or hindrance from any one, while the last and only decision adverse to that was made by four judges only, called together evidently for the purpose and held within the military barricade or fortifications of Joseph Brooks, amid the wildest excitement, and where neither Baxter nor any of his friends could go with safety. The apparent cause that brought these four judges together, and the circumstances under which they assumed to hold court, and the indecent haste with which their pretended decision was made, can serve no other purpose than to stand as a monument of their judicial partisanship, and a disgrace to the name of the Judiciary. And this decision is what is claimed as the cause of confusing the speedy determination of the question pending before your Excellency. . . ." DS (misdated April 10), DNA, RG 60, Letters from the President. *SED*, 43-1-51, 19–21. See *New York Herald*, May 11–13, 1874.

To Elisha Baxter

May 11. 1874.

HON. ELISHA BAXTER,
LITTLE ROCK, ARK.

I recommend that the members of the General Assembly now at
Little Rock adjourn for a reasonable time, say for ten days, to enable
Brooks to call in to the body his supposed adherents, so that there
may be a full legislature. Any hasty action by a part of the Assembly
will not be satisfactory to the people. Brooks friends here agree that
if this course is pursued, no opposition will be made to the meeting
of the Assembly in the State House as usual, and that he will at once
dismiss his forces if you will do the same. I urgently request that
all armed forces on both sides be disbanded, so that the General Assembly may act free from any military pressure or influence. The
United States will give all necessary protection to the legislature
and prevent, as far as practicable, all violence and disturbance of the
public peace. Answer.

U. S. GRANT.

Copy (telegram sent), DNA, RG 60, Letters Sent. *HED*, 43-1-51, 22–23; *SD*, 57-2-209,
312. On May 11, 1874, Elisha Baxter, Little Rock, telegraphed to USG. "YOURS RE-
CEIVED AND UNDER CONSIDERATION. WILL ANSWER IN THE COURSE OF
THE EVENING." Telegram received, DNA, RG 60, Letters from the President. *SED*, 43-
1-51, 25. On the same day, Ark. Senator B. F. Askew and eight other senators and Ark.
Speaker of the House X. J. Pindall and thirty-six other representatives telegraphed to
USG. "WE THE UNDERSIGNED MEMBERS OF THE GENERAL ASSEMBLY OF
ARKANSAS PRESENT HERE TO MEET UNDER THE CALL OF GOVERNOR
BAXTER HAVE READ HIS . . . BAXTERS . . . RESPONSE TO YOUR TELEGRAM
TODAY AND WE MOST HEARTILY APPROVE AND [EN]DORSE IT." Telegram re-
ceived, DNA, RG 60, Letters from the President. *SED*, 43-1-51, 26. See preceding letter.
      On May 12, Baxter telegraphed to USG. "I am informed Mr Brooks is now removing
all of the records of State from the Public Buildings   I respectfully ask that the Public records be returned to the Public Buildings and placed in charge of the U. S. troops here, until the return of the Secretary of State who is the proper Custodian under the law,   Answer" Telegram received, DNA, RG 60, Letters from the President. *SED*, 43-1-51, 29. On
the same day, USG endorsed this telegram to Attorney Gen. George H. Williams. "Would
it not be proper to advise Brooks that if he is removing the State records, as reported, that
he should desist from such a course?" AES, DNA, RG 60, Letters from the President. On
May 12 and 13, Baxter again telegraphed to USG. "Want three in the Senate & One in the
house for a quorum   Would have full attendance but for the interference by Brooks with

the trains" "The assertion of Brooks that assassination will follow the disbandment of his troops in my opinion is utterly unfounded   in the event of such disbandment I will use every possible means to preserve perfect peace & would ask the cooperation of the federal troops to assist in preserving order" Telegrams received (at 7:00 P.M. and 8:50 P.M.), *ibid.* *SED*, 43-1-51, 29, 30.

On May 13, John Thompson, Philadelphia, had written to USG supporting Baxter. ALS, DNA, RG 60, Letters from the President. *SED*, 43-1-51, 30. On the same day, J. W. Keep, New York City, telegraphed to USG. "A party wish to visit Hot Springs Arkansas, to do so must pass through Little Rock. Can that be done with safety,   Please reply" Telegram received, DLC-USG, IB. Also on May 13, Capt. Thomas E. Rose, Little Rock, telegraphed to AG Edward D. Townsend. "Both sides here considerably reinforced,   Baxter has two additional brass guns for two days,   there has been some strict fighting though of a very low grade . . ." Telegram received, DNA, RG 94, Letters Received, 1491 1874. *SED*, 43-1-51, 146. On May 14, Secretary of War William W. Belknap noted that a copy of Rose's telegram had been read to USG. E, DNA, RG 60, Letters to the President.

To Joseph Brooks

May 11. 1874.

HON. JOSEPH BROOKS,
LITTLE ROCK. ARK.

I have suggested to Mr. Baxter that the members of the General Assembly now in Little Rock adjourn for a reasonable time, say ten days, to give you an opportunity to call in those members who may not respond to his call; so that there may be a full legislature. The United States will give all necessary protection to the legislature in meeting and transacting its business as usual at the State House, and prevent as far as practicable, all violence and disturbances of the public peace. I urgently request that the military of both parties be at once disbanded, which is the first step towards a peaceable settlement.

U. S. GRANT.

Copy (telegram sent), DNA, RG 60, Letters Sent. *HED*, 43-1-51, 22; *SD*, 57-2-209, 312. On May 11, 1874, Joseph Brooks, Little Rock, telegraphed to USG. "On the ninth of May the Attorney General submitted to me a proposition that he said had your approval   on the tenth I accepted the same out of deference to ~~def~~ your wishes feeling that in doing so I was humeleting myself and the courts of the State   This I did solely in the interest of peace supposing that Baxter ~~will~~ould be required to assent to your proposed plan of settlement   In accordance with the proposition of the attorney general I issued a proclamation convening the legislature on the fourth Monday of the present month   To my surprise Baxter has declined to submit the question of his election to the legislature   In conversation with members thereof he boldly proclaims that he does not and will not permit an investigation of his right to the office yet you ask me to recognize call of the legislature at the instance of one who declare the question at issue and for which you insists on its being assembled Shall not be settled by the tribunal you desire convened   In the attempted organization made today which failed although persons were sworn in as members from districts in which no vacancies had been declared Both Houses of the legislature now have a quorum in existence   this quorum should pass upon the election return and qualifications of the newly elected members instead of the newly elected members themselves   This action I cannot not and will not willingly submit to   Section on[e] article four of the constitution of the United States declares that full faith and credit shall be given to the judicial proceedings of every state and if in the face of the decision of the Supreme and circuit courts of the states deciding that I am and recognizing me as the legal governor you can recognize Baxter as governor it is your duty to respond to his application for Federal help If you cannot it is your duty to assist me to suppress the present domestic violence   To disband my troops at this time under no other assurances than is contained in your telegram of today would result not only in the assassination of the judges of the Supreme court but of many of my friends and especially the colored men who have been guilty of no crime save fidelity to law and order   I shall hold my troops together for the purpose of protecting the citizens of the state who believe the expression of the will of the people at the ballot box should be enforced and for the protection of those who stand by the constitution laws and the adjudications of the courts of the country   Federal bayonets can put Baxters legislature in the State House but I am ignorant of the clause of the Constitution under which the President has this power   nothing else will and when there I doubt if you can compel them to determine who is governor   It is time this agony doubt and uncertainty was over   The interests of humanity demands it shall be settled and if you have the power under the constitution and laws of the United States to settle the question of who is governor of Arkansas adverse to the decision of the courts of the state settle it and settle it at once   I shall not resist what you may order US Troops to do but shall with all the power at my command repel any and all attempts by Baxters forces to take possession of the state House   I am confident that a legal quorum of the legislature will not respond to Baxters call and I shall not assent nor be a party to convening the legislature under any other agreement than that submitted by yourself through the attorney General on the ninth instant" Telegram received (on May 12, at 2:45 A.M.), DNA, RG 60, Letters from the President. *SED*, 43-1-51, 24−25. On the same day, Brooks, Baring Cross, Ark., also telegraphed to USG. "I am just informed that the way Baxter got a pretended quorum in the Senate was by arresting Mr Good a senator from white Co & baxters adjutant Genl Keeps him under guard all the time & makes him vote as he dictates   Senator Good is an old & feeble man & in great fear of his life   they allow none of his friends to see him unless they are present without him they have no quorum although they swore in six without authority of law" Telegram received (at 11:00 P.M.), DNA, RG 60, Letters from the President. *SED*, 43-1-51, 26. Also on May 11, 4:15 P.M., Brooks, Baring Cross, telegraphed to Secretary of War William W. Belknap. "Last evening I crossed a company of Infantry to the North side of the river to protect a squad of State troops engaged in transporting arms and ammunition from the State University at Fayetteville. The insurgents crossed a force of Cavalry and Infantry and pursued my men with the avowed purpose of attacking and capturing them and the boat with our arms. At daylight this morning we crossed our additional forces under Colonel Clayton to support the first force supposed to be falling back; the boat and arms having arrived in safety. Learning of this the insurgents have been engaged all morning crossing in force at the ferry. They have formed in line of battle advancing on the state troops, and skirmishing has been progressing for two hours. General Togin [*Fagan*] chief in command of state forces has been instructed by me to act strictly upon the defensive and advance only so far as is absolutely necessary to protect our position and cover bridge and approaches upon which Capt Gibbon and his forces first sent out are supposed to be returning, having refused the terms of peaceful adjustments submitted by the U. S. Atty Genl. with the sanction of the President. Baxter and his adherents seem resolved to precipitate a conflict at (of ?) arms today. We shall maintain our position & defend our friends." Copy, DNA, RG 60, Letters from the President. On May 12, Secretary of State Hamilton Fish recorded in his diary. "Nothing done except discussion of the Arkansas question. Mr. Williams read a telegram received last evening or this morning from Brooks declining the proposition for adjustment, but seemingly intended to invite the President's intervention. Williams states that Baxter's friends are still asking for delay   he thinks there is a bare possibility of an adjustment. The President thinks the Proclamation should not be delayed, but tacitly assents to await the decision now under consideration. Williams says the Proclamation is drafted and can be issued on short notice but that the legislature was convened to meet to-day at noon and possibly may adopt Resolutions calling upon the President to aid in suppressing insurrection   if such Resolutions are adopted it will require a change in the form of the Proclamation. The President consents to await the result of the meeting of the Legislature." DLC-Hamilton Fish. See *SED*, 43-1-51, 21–22; *New York Times*, May 13, 1874.

Also on May 12, William S. Oliver, sheriff, Baring Cross, telegraphed to USG. "More U. S. force will be needed here to prevent bloodshed   the only question now is shall loyal men white and black be allowed to live here   if Baxter is sustained by your old comrades in arms and the colored men must have protection and help to leave the state   if courts are not sustained by the general government we can not enforce the laws the State will be turned over to the enemies of the government all leading men will be assassinated who sustain Gov Brooks and the courts   I am powerless to protect if not aided by you" Telegram received (at 4:00 P.M.), DNA, RG 60, Letters from the President. *SED*, 43-1-51, 29. On the same day, Brooks, Baring Cross, telegraphed to USG. "I have acted upon your suggestion as to the assembling of the legislature on the twenty fifth inst   before that time it will be impossible to have all the members of that body present   I understand the question is likely to be presented to Congress   I feel so confident of the justness of my cause that I am content that either the latter body or a full legislature investigate the facts regarding the election in conformity with terms of your adjustment of may ninth   if it is to be done by the Legislature I insist upon time for all the members to assemble which cannot be earlier than the twenty fifth inst the time designated by you" Telegram received (at 6:10 P.M.), DNA, RG 60, Letters from the President. *SED*, 43-1-51, 29. Also on May 12, Brooks telegraphed to Attorney Gen. George H. Williams. "The members of the general assembly here, even if there were a quorum, & there is not do not constitute a legislature unless convened by the Governor   if you recognize this assemblage as a legislature you recognize Baxter as Governor for no one but the Governor can convene the Legislature on extraordinary session   if it is not a legislature called by proper authority its adjournment is a matter of no consequence   so far as the Secry of State is concerned if any of his prerogatives are interfered with the courts of the State & not the President is the proper tribunal before which to redress his grievances   I have answered the presidents despatch at length & I shall not disband any troops under my Command until the question of who is Governor of Arkansas is settled unless required so to do by the direct command of the President   I have no proposition to submit & will not entertain any on the subject other than that proposed by yourself sanctioned by the President & agreed to by the agents & attorneys of Baxter & myself   The case made on the paper requires the president to recognize either Baxter or myself as Governor of Ark   the settlement of the question either before the Courts or the legislature is one that in my opinion does not require the intercession of the

President on Baxters behalf he must act on the papers before him & not upon what a legislature may or may not do in the future upon a majority of the votes of the legal voters of this State & upon the Judgements of the Supreme & Circuit Courts. I am willing to stand or fall but if those are to be held for naught by the President until such time as he can ascertain the opinion of the legislature to guide him in determining who is Govr & during the pendency of the question to allow the State & citizens to be plundered & Robbed by an armed Mob which has already fired upon federal troops & commenced an indiscriminate slaughter of Colored men to avoid a further Sacrifice of life & loss of property I am impelled by a sense of duty to Submit my case as it now stands & abide the presidents determination" Telegram received, DNA, RG 60, Letters from the President.

On the same day, J. M. Murphy and thirty-two others, Baring Cross, telegraphed to U.S. Representative William J. Hynes of Ark. to present to USG a petition from "citizens of the State of Arkansas, who shared with you the privations & dangers of the battlefield in the suppression of the great rebellion" stating that "should your excellency see fit to reinstate what is known as the Baxter government the greatest possible injustice will be done to the entire union element of this state and a triumph achieved by the unreconstructed element over the loyal which KuKlux appliances failed to accomplish and every Union man and that portion of the late confederate soldiers who have manfully and boldly in this movement cut loose from the Bourbon will have to abandon their homes and take refuge in some loyal state The imminency of this danger is well known here and among the colored people who compose so large a proportion of the population of the state the alarm is indescribable . . ." Telegram received (at 1:30 A.M.), *ibid. SED*, 43-1-51, 27–28. On May 13, Dr. L. W. Wilcox, "Late of Galena Ill," Baring Cross, telegraphed to USG. "any recognition of Baxter at present would result in general assassination of many citizens especially the colored men a number of unarmed colored men belonging to neither side have already been killed by Baxters forces humanity demands that you should keep the peace, until Congress or an agreed legislature can investigate any partizan legislature on either side would make matters worse" Telegram received (at 5:15 P.M.), DNA, RG 60, Letters from the President. *SED*, 43-1-51, 30.

On May 14, Brooks twice telegraphed to USG. "In my despatch to you of the eleventh inst I stated that a quorum of both houses existed & that this quorum should pass upon the election returns & qualifications of the new members there are now fourteen pretented members of the Senate here six of this number were admitted to seats without any evidence of election & pretend to represent districts where no vacancies had been declared in the House there are forty five pretended members present twenty three of this number were admitted to seats without any evidence of election and to represent districts where no vacancies had been declared instead of there being a legal quorum in either branch of the Legislature there is in point of fact but eight Senators in the Senate & twenty two representatives in the House when there should be fourteen Senators and forty two representatives to constitute a quorum in both houses of the legislature you will readily see why I could not consent to recognize his call I was willing and am now willing to make a joint call of the Legislature to meet at the State House & let the quorum now in existence pass upon the question as to whether there any vacancies in the districts these few members claim to represent and whether they are entitled to seats but I cannot consent to recognize a body organized as this has been within the lines of Baxter where no man can enter it without a pass from himself or one of his subordinate Officers as to whether the present pretended legislature it being called by Baxter after the Judgement of ouster and after I was in full possession of the Office has any authority depends upon the fact as to whether it was convened by the Governor of Arkansas this is a question that can only be determined by the courts of this state and the moment it takes any affirmative action I shall bring the matter before the Supreme court which is now in session and test the question that tribunal having lately compelled the Treasurer of state to pay a warrant drawn upon a fund that no one one but the Governor can use has recognized me as Governor and it is not unreasonable to assume under this state of facts that the courts will not recognize any act passed by a legislature called together by one who is not authorized to convene it." "First I was elected by the vote of the people   this is universally admitted by all parties Is not denied by Baxter & has been clearly proven by the testimony on file in the Circuit Court —Second I have a Judgment of the Circuit Court our only Court of General and original Jurisdiction awarding me the office to which the people elected me   3d under that Judgment I am in possession of the office & exercising its functions & have been for thirty days —Fourth the Supreme Court has passed upon my claims collaterally in which it is clearly decided that the Circuit Court has Jurisdiction of the subject matter that the proceedings are regular & the Judgment authorative and binding that as Govr I am authorized to draw warrants upon the treasurer of state according to law   fifth I have with the sole exception of the secretary of state the recognition & cooperation of every branch and member of the state Government   sixth the actual case decided by the Circuit Court has gon[e] up by appeal and will doubtless be decided in a few days   seventh In the interest of peace I promptly acceeded to your proposition of may ninth to submit the question as therein proposed to a full legislature convened under a mutual call of Baxter & myself which among other things provided that all the votes cast at the November election eighteen hundred & seventy two should be counted and the ~~Governor~~ result declared   this is all I have Ever asked for either from legislature or courts   this having been rejected by Baxter & Congress appearantly disposed to inquire into the case I now propose cheerfully to submit to and ask an investigation as to who received the majority of votes to be conducted upon the Ground by a congressional Committee & consent to abide their decision   I am reliably informed that Baxter refused your proposition of May ninth for the reason that it required all the votes to be counted & the result declared   he has uniformly ever since the election made every effort to prevent an investigating into the result of the election has never raised any question but those of Jurisdiction and now openly declares that he will not submit to any such investigation   all I ask is a full & fair investigation   if I do not establish unequivocally that I was elected & am both in law & equity entitled to exercise the functions of governor of Arkansas I will promptly and without a murmur retire" Telegrams received (at 6:10 P.M. and on May 15, at 1:25 A.M.), DNA, RG 60, Letters from the President. *SED*, 43-1-51, 32–34.

Also on May 14, Volney V. Smith and thirty-seven others, Baring Cross, telegraphed to USG. "The pretended legislature have passed some kind of a resolution recognizing Baxter as governor . . . We Therefore protest against said proceedings being made the basis of any action on the part of your Excellency and we further protest against any recognition of Baxter until a decision is had in the case of Brooks vs Baxter now pending in the Supreme Court which will be heard on the first monday in June   Should you recognize Baxter and the Supreme Court should declare Brooks Governor in June which we feel confident it will do your recognition of Baxter at this time instead of quieting the public would only create more confusion   as Republican officials that have ever supported your administration and as citizens of the state we implore you to withhold your decision until the Supreme court determines the question which will not be more than two or three weeks at the outside" Telegram received (at 2:00 A.M.), DNA, RG 60, Letters from the President. *SED*, 43-1-51, 31–32. On May 15, U.S. Representatives John Coburn of Ind. and Horace Maynard of Tenn. telegraphed to USG transmitting a dispatch dated May 14 from Sydney M. Barnes, Baring Cross, "now of Arkansas formerly of Kentucky and a prominent republican," calling for USG to recognize Brooks as governor. Telegram received, DNA, RG 60, Letters from the President. *SED*, 43-1-51, 34–35.

Order

———

May 12th 1874.

Whereas, it is provided in the 7th article of the treaty concluded with the Cherokee Indians, July 19, 1866, [U. S. Stats. at Large, Vol. 14, p. 799] "That any or all of the provisions of this treaty, which makes distinction in rights and remedies between the citizens of any district, and the citizens of the rest of the nation, shall be abrogated whenever the President shall have ascertained, by an election duly ordered by him, that a majority of the voters of such district desire them to be abrogated, and he shall have declared such abrogation," and

Whereas satisfactory evidence has been presented to me that it is the desire of the Cherokees that such election should take place.

Therefore, it is ordered that an election be held on the 1st day of July next, for the purpose of ascertaining, whether the people of the Canadian district desire the abrogation of the distinction in the rights and remedies between the citizens of said district and the citizens of the rest of the nation, which election shall be conducted under the laws of the Cherokees relative to the manner of conducting elections, and the return thereof shall be submitted to the Secretary of the Interior through the Agent for said Cherokee Indians.

U. S. GRANT

DS (brackets in original), DNA, RG 75, Orders.

To Otis H. Tiffany

———

Washington D. C. May 14th 1874

DEAR DOCTOR:

Mrs Grant and I will be obliged if you will be so kind as to perform the marriage ceremony of our daughter Nellie to Mr Sartoris on Wednesday the 21st of this month at Eleven A. M. at the Execu-

tive Mansion. If you will do so may I ask you to have the necessary
certificates &c. procured and oblige

Yours truly

U. S. GRANT

DR O. H. TIFFANY WASHINGTON, D. C.

Copy, DLC-USG, II, 2. On May 19, 1874, John Russell Young, New York City, twice telegraphed to Orville E. Babcock. "Present my compliments to the President and say that as
there will inevitably be publications in reference to approaching ceremony, I feel personally anxious that so far as can be controlled here, there should be nothing that would not be
pleasant to him and that with his consent, will gladly go on and write the account myself.
Please send answer to my Brother at Senate" "My Brother sends me your message to him,
much obliged for your trouble. It will of course be impossible to keep some kind of an account of an event national in its character and interesting every home in America, from the
newspapers and as other affairs happen to call me to Washington I immediately thought I
might do what I could to make any narrative that came under my supervision as pleasant
as possible. Much obliged, all the same, will be at Ebbitt House in the morning" Telegrams
received, *ibid.*, IB. On May 21, Young reported that "when Mr. Sartoris first sought permission to address Miss Nellie that President Grant made it a condition that he should become an American and a resident here. Sartoris senior was also informed by the President
of this *sine qua non*, and in fitting terms expressed his appreciation of the high honor accorded to his son, admiration for this country, and his entire approbation of the course
proposed. Mr. Sartoris was then a member of the British Parliament, but at the last election was beaten by the liberal candidate. Young Sartoris immediately made preparations
for obtaining citizenship and residence, and purchased property in Michigan, but his elder
brother being killed, he, as the only living son, became heir to the entailed estates, which
are of large extent and situated in the south of England, just opposite to the Isle of Wight.
This changed the situation, and, the affection of the parties having ripened into genuine
old fashioned love, the President and Mrs. Grant felt that it was not best to interfere, and
the ceremony of to-day has followed." *New York Herald*, May 22, 1874. On May 14, Babcock
had written a letter marked "*Personal*" to Charles Griswold, Fifth Avenue Hotel, New York
City, requesting that "Mr Sartoris and wife" be "as nicely cared for as you can." ALS, USGA.
See *PUSG*, 24, 59–60, 163–64; *Washington National Republican*, May 21, 1874; *New York
Herald*, May 23–24, 1874; *New York Times*, May 22, 24, 1874; *New York Daily Graphic*,
May 24, 1874.

   Also on May 14, Secretary of State Hamilton Fish wrote to USG. "The Minister from
Turkey informs me that he is directed by his Government to present its sincere congratulations, on the occasion of the approaching marriage of Miss Grant, and asks for an answer to enable him to comply with the instructions. If agreeable to you, I will inform him
that you will receive him tomorrow at twelve, (at which time you have an appointment
with the Russian Minister,) and that I will meet him at the Executive Mansion for the purpose. I enclose a translation of the speech which he will make, and a form for a reply." Copy,
DNA, RG 59, Reports to the President and Congress. On the same day, Culver C. Sniffen
wrote to Fish. "The President directs me to reply to your note of inquiry and to say that
it will be entirely agreeable to him to receive the Minister from Turkey tomorrow at 12. M.
The President retains the two enclosures to your note." ALS, *ibid.*, Miscellaneous Letters.

   On May 20, USG wrote to Postmaster Gen. John A. J. Creswell. "In directing invitations for the Cabinet to attend the marriage of our daughter to-morrow, Mrs. Grant is not

certain whether one was sent to Mrs. McIntyre or not. If none was sent it was an oversight which we hope she will excuse, and that she will attend all the same. When the clerks come in to the office in the morning I will direct a formal invitation to be sent if none has been sent." Typescript, USGA. On the same day, Babcock telegraphed to George H. Stuart. "Your invitation was sent with others to Philad'a.   the presd't regrets that you did not receive it." Telegram received, DLC-George H. Stuart.

On Aug. 7, Marshall Jewell, Liverpool, wrote to Elihu B. Washburne after spending "part of three days with Nellie Grant." ". . . I have never seen her look so well or so happy. She is happy too. Her husband is a tolerably fine specimen of a young English Country Gentleman   He spent two years at Rugby 2 in Germany & three in France so he is a pretty well educated boy of 23. . . . He is not her equal in position of course but *is* in all else. He will have I guess two or three thousand pounds per year when his father dies—He now has whatever his father allows. . . ." ALS, DLC-Elihu B. Washburne. On Oct. 3, John Jay, U.S. minister, Vienna, wrote to Julia Dent Grant. "You said to me one evening when I had the pleasure of calling upon the President & yourself at Washington with General von Schweinitz, during our recent visit, that you had not chanced to see any of the writings of Mrs Sartoris; and I take the liberty of sending you one of them—'A Week at a French Country House.'   With the title of the volume you are no doubt familiar, as it has acquired a wide reputation for its singularly graceful style, and picturesque descriptions. I did myself the honour of paying a visit at 'Warsash,' as I passed thro' England, in the hope of seeing your daughter, but unfortunately for me she had gone with her husband, I think to attend a ball at some country seat the Evening before, & they were not expected until the Afternoon. While I missed the pleasure of seeing them to my great regret, I passed a delightful hour with Mr Sartoris, who notwithstanding a slight rain shewed me over the gardens rich in vines shrubbery flowers & fruit, & through the grounds with their magnificent trees & pleasant views of the Hamble River & Southampton water Embracing in clear weather the Isle of Wight. On returning from our walk I looked with interest at the tapestries & works of art that fill with beauty the principal room. Mr Sartoris said that your daughter of whom he spoke affectionately as 'Nellie' was looking better than Ever, & had acquired quite an English appetite—It struck me as I came away from 'Warsash' that you must find some consolation for her absence, in the thought that your daughter occupies one of the loveliest homes of England. Pray present my best Compliments & regards to the President, . . ." ALS, USG 3.

Proclamation

Whereas, certain turbulent and disorderly persons, pretending that Elisha Baxter, the present executive of Arkansas was not elected, have combined together with force and arms to resist his authority as such executive, and other authorities of said State; and

Whereas, said Elisha Baxter has been declared duly elected by the general assembly of said State, as provided in the constitution thereof and has for a long period been exercising the functions of said office, into which he was inducted according to the constitution and laws of said State, and ought by its citizens to be considered as the lawful executive thereof; and

Whereas, it is provided in the Constitution of the United States that the United States shall protect every State in the Union, on application of the legislature or of the executive when the legislature cannot be convened, against domestic violence; and

Whereas, said Elisha Baxter under section 4 of Article IV of the Constitution of the United States and the laws passed in pursuance thereof, has heretofore made application to me to protect said State and the citizens thereof against domestic violence; and

Whereas, the general Assembly of said State was convened in extra session at the capital thereof on the 11th instant pursuant to a call made by said Elisha Baxter and both houses thereof have passed a joint resolution also applying to me to protect the State against domestic violence; and

Whereas, it is provided in the laws of the United States that in all cases of insurrection in any State or of obstruction to the laws thereof, it shall be lawful for the President of the United States on application of the legislature of such State, or of the executive when the legislature cannot be convened, to employ such part of the land and naval forces as shall be judged necessary for the purpose of suppressing such insurrection or causing the laws to be duly executed; and

Whereas, it is required that whenever it may be necessary in the judgment of the President to use the military force for the purpose aforesaid, he shall forthwith by proclamation command such insurgents to disperse and retire peaceably to their respective homes within a limited time.

Now, therefore, I, Ulysses S. Grant, President of the United States, do hereby make proclamation and command all turbulent and disorderly persons to disperse and retire peaceably to their respective abodes within ten days from this date, and hereafter to submit themselves to the lawful authority of said executive and the other constituted authorities of said State; and I invoke the aid and cooperation of all good citizens thereof to uphold law and preserve public peace.

In witness whereof I have hereunto set my hand and caused the
seal of the United States to be affixed.

Done at the City of Washington, this fifteenth day of May, in the
year of our Lord eighteen hundred and seventy-four and of the Independence of the United States the ninety-eighth.

U. S. GRANT

DS, DNA, RG 130, Presidential Proclamations. *SED*, 43-1-51, 136; *HRC*, 43-2-2, 565; *SD*,
57-2-209, 176–77, 314. On May 15, 1874, Attorney Gen. George H. Williams submitted
an opinion to USG. ". . . According to the Constitution and laws of the State, the votes for
Governor were counted and Baxter was declared elected, and at once was duly inaugurated
as Governor of the State. There is great difficulty in holding that he usurped the office into
which he was inducted under these circumstances. . . . Looking at the subject in the light
of the Constitution alone, it appears perfectly clear to my mind that the Courts of the State
have no right to try a contest about the office of Governor, but that exclusive jurisdiction
over that question is vested in the General Assembly. . . . The General Assembly has decided that Baxter was elected. The Circuit Court of Pulaski County has decided that Brooks
was elected. Taking the provision of the Constitution which declares that *contested elections*
about certain State officers, including the Governor, *shall be determined* by the General Assembly and that provision of the law heretofore cited which says that *all contested elections*
of Governor shall be decided by the Legislature, and the two decisions of the Supreme Court
affirming the exclusive jurisdiction of that body over the subject, and the conclusion irre-
sistibly follows that said judgment of the Circuit Court is void. . . . Respecting the claim
that Brooks received a majority of the votes at the election, it must be said that the President has no way to verify that claim. If he had it would not, in my opinion, under the circumstances of this case, be a proper subject for his consideration. Perhaps if everything
about the election was in confusion and there had been no legal count of the votes, the question of majorities might form an element of the discussion, but where, as in this case, there
has been a legal count of the votes and the tribunal organized by the Constitution of the
State for that purpose has declared the election, the President, in my judgment, ought not
to go behind that action to look into the state of the vote. Frauds may have been committed
to the prejudice of Brooks: but; unhappily, there are few elections where partisan zeal runs
high, in which the victorious party with more or less of truth is not charged with acts of
fraud. There must, however, be an end to controversy upon the subject. Somebody must
be trusted to count votes and declare elections. Unconstitutional methods of filling offices
cannot be resorted to because there is some real or imagined unfairness about the election.
Ambitious and selfish aspirants for office generally create the disturbance about this matter for people are more interested in the preservation of peace than in the political fortunes
of any man. Either of the contestants with law and order is better than the other with discord and violence. I think it would be disastrous to allow the proceedings by which Brooks
obtained possession of the office to be drawn into precedent. There is not a State in the
Union in which they would not produce conflict and, probably, bloodshed. They cannot
be upheld or justified upon any ground, and, in my opinion, Elisha Baxter should be recognized as the lawful executive of the State of Arkansas. . . ." Copy, DNA, RG 60, Opinions. *SED*, 43-1-51, 130–36, 43-2-25, 9–13; *HRC*, 43-2-2, 432–36; *Official Opinions of the*
Attorneys-General, XIV, 391–400. On May 14, Ark. Senator J. G. Frierson and three others
had telegraphed to USG. "The General aAssembly of the State of Arkansas passed the fol-

lowing resolution today by unanimous Vote in the Senate & forty Six to one in the House. 'To wit. whereas The legislature of the State of Arkansas has convened a quorum of each house being present & whereas the Capitol of our State is occupied by armed & contending forces, & whereas the State house is now in the possession of armed troops therefore be it resolved by the General assembly of the State of Arkansas that the President of the U S be & is hereby requested to put this legislature in possession of the legislative Hall & that the public property on the State House square be placed under the supervision & control of this body the legal Custodians thereof while in session & that he be make such order for the disposition of Said armed & contending forces as will more perfectly protect the State against domestic Violence & insure this body due protection & it is further resolved that a duly certified copy of this resolution be at once transmitted to the Pres't of the U S." Telegram received (at 4:20 P.M.), DNA, RG 60, Letters from the President. *SED*, 43-1-51, 31. On May 15, P. H. Carnes and thirty-three others, Little Rock, telegraphed to USG. "We the undersigned citizens of Little Rock ark return you profound thanks for your proclamation of the fifteenth inst in regard to the political trouble we have been passing through during the past four weeks   we regard your proclamation as on the side of right & merits the respect of all men of all political parties of honest proclivities." Telegram received (at 9:15 P.M.), DLC-USG, IB. See letter to George H. Williams, May 11, 1874; *New York Times*, May 16, 1874.

On May 16, Secretary of War William W. Belknap wrote a memorandum, presumably to AG Edward D. Townsend, to telegraph Capt. Thomas E. Rose, commanding officer, Little Rock. "The President directs that as his proclamation recognizing Baxter as lawful Governor has been issued, he is to be protected in that position by the U. S. forces, if necessary—" ANS, DNA, RG 94, Letters Received, 1491 1874. On the same day, Rose telegraphed to Townsend. ". . . not much change in Situation here except less danger of Collision of organized bodies & More Marauders through the city.   have mounted detachment looking after them to prevent bloodshed" Telegram received (at 2:20 P.M.), *ibid.* This telegram was endorsed: "Copy made and sent to the President, May 16 /74 3 15 *PM*" E, *ibid.* On May 17, Rose telegraphed to Townsend. "Yesterday both sides entered into a written agreement to disband all their forces as quickly as possible   the disbandment is now going on & the city orderly & quiet . . ." Telegram received (at 7:55 P.M.), *ibid.*; copy, *ibid.*, RG 60, Letters from the President. On May 19, Col. William H. Emory, New Orleans, telegraphed to Townsend. "Capt Rose telegraphs Baxter is in the state house & the us troops are with drawn to the garrison & asks that the command be turned over to capt Bartholemew. . . ." Telegram received (at 11:20 P.M.), *ibid.*, RG 94, Letters Received, 1491 1874; copy, *ibid.*, RG 60, Letters from the President. On May 20, Rose telegraphed to Townsend. "Brooks forces all disbanded quietly yesterday, all troops withdrawn to the garrison, temporary service of Company D, Sixteenth Infty no longer needed," Telegram received (at 2:00 P.M.), *ibid.*, RG 94, Letters Received, 1491 1874. On the same day, Belknap referred a communication to USG. "Orders have been given for the return of Co. D. to its post—" ANS, OFH.

On May 25, Baxter wrote to USG. "I desire to thank you in my own name, and in the name of the poeple of Arkansas, for your action in regard to the disturbance of the peace in our State. I never for a moment doubted what your action and that of the federal government would be, when you understood the real facts in the case. Although I greatly feared that by some accidental collision between subbordinates, the bold and unscrupulous men, whose deep laid design was to put me in collision with the United States, would appear to have accomplished their end, the delay painful as it was at the time was not prejudicial. You have gained a great many friends here, both personal and to the government. It has always been my object here to free the party which elected me from the influence of the unscrupulous and corrupt men who have in the past almost entierly controled its organization, and to so administer the State Government as to make the Republican party the party of the really good poeple of the State. The great majority of our poeple are as tired and sick of old party organizations as they are of corruption and fraud. In accordance with the avowed principles on which I was elected, and in which I at least was sincere, the poeple of the State had been enfranchised, and everything was in train to restore free government to our poeple under Republican auspices and pledges, when the coup d'etat of Brooks, promoted and supported by Clayton, Dorsey, McClure and so many other mere political adventurers and robbers, threw the State into a convulsion, from which your action has done so much to rescue it: and now I hope and desire, in pursuance of the same line of policy indicated above, and supported by yourself and the real Republican party of the Country, to re-establish civil liberty on sure foundations in this State. I desire to act in harmony and confidence with you. I beleive that you are not without a some what similal experience with my own with regard to a powerful and unscrupulous clique of corruptionists and can appreciate my possition here. The poeple of this State as well as other Southern States have suffered severely for their past folly, and in the main are very ready to reccognise as their friends any person or party that will treat them fairly and honestly. They are too much impoverished to longer afford very good pasturage for mere adventurers whose only industry is stealing. There are numerous Northern men in our community including many who have served in the federal army, whose possition is in all respects as favorable in our community, as that of those of Southern birth, notwithstanding the despairing howls of disappointed political aspirants to the contrary. I beleive that under the auspices of your administration a new era will be inaugurated in this and other Southern States. Your course is meeting with general approval and strengthening the hands of your true freinds. So great is the poverty to which this State has been reduced by bad and dishonest administration, that the State government has not the power to maintain its authority so vigorously as would be desirable but relying on the support of the federal arm in case of any attempt to renew civil discord extending beyond the resources at my own command, I shall endeavor to effect the objects I have proposed to myself from the begginning, i. e.; free the Republican party in the State from corruption, and supply the places of theives with honest men, and thus strengthen the party and restore good government and prosperity to our unfortunate poeple." ALS, DNA, RG 60, Letters from the President. *SED*, 43-2-25, 22–23. On May 17, Ark. Senator T. J. Ratcliffe had telegraphed to USG. "Let the large portraits hang in the room and puzzle Mr Grant no more about it for Arkansas is for inflation of third term" Telegram received (at 11:13 A.M.), DLC-USG, IB.

On May 25, USG wrote to the Senate. "In response to the Resolution of the Senate of the 15th instant, I have the honor to transmit herewith 'all papers and correspondence relating to the troubles in the State of Arkansas, not heretofore communicated to either House of Congress.'" Copy, DNA, RG 130, Messages to Congress. *SED*, 43-1-51. See message to House of Representatives, April 23, 1874.

On May 28, W. Hines Furbush, sheriff, Lee County, Ark., Marianna, wrote to USG alleging political corruption and recriminations. "In brief let me State a few facts in regard to Matters in this state. In the first place there is not a man in the state that has as much political sense as an Oyster . . . I have never seen such bitterness in the state sense I have been here   Now to settle the difficulties let Congress investigate and put in the proper men the men that were elected and the truble will end   I have had to be a political slave ever sense I have been in the state either to Clayton or Dorsey   I know of all the truble in the state and how it came about   I hope you will pardon me for trubling you with this letter but I am anxious to know our future" ALS, DNA, RG 60, Letters from the President. *SED*, 43-2-25, 23–24. On Nov. 7, U.S. Senator Stephen W. Dorsey of Ark. wrote to USG. "At

the earnest request of the writer who I know to be a person of intelligence and high character and the wife of one of the leading Union men of our state, I beg to hand you herewith a letter which she has thought best to address to you, in regard to the condition of
political affairs in the remote part of the state in which she lives" ALS, DNA, RG 60, Letters from the President. On Oct. 29, Loucinda Grayson, Arkadelphia, had written to USG.
"I have been thinking of writing to you for some time but have never had the courage
to do so until now. This portion of Arkansas is in a very bad condition. The loyal people
and republicans are in great danger and neither their lives or property are safe. The present state officers afford us no relief and the civil law is powerless to protect us. My husband George W Grayson is the ex Sheriff of Clark County. He was a Republican before the
war and loyal during the war and still worships the old stars and stripes. His father John
Grayson of Arkansas is a noted loyal man and Republican of considerable property. My
husband was born and raised in the South and it has always been our home. We have property here and cant well leave. My husband is in great trouble and danger. His political enemies say that he shall not live in this country. Several prominent Republicans in this part
of the state have already been notified to leave the state. Thus far they have been restrained
from some cause from warning my husband to leave. I do most humbly hope and pray that
you will assist in some way to relieve us of our danger as we have no protection as matters
now stand. It is useless to call on Gov Baxter for protection for he has betrayed the Republicans into the hands of their worst enemies who are determined to run them all out
of the country, or if they dare to stay murder and assassinate them as they have been doing in Tennessee and Louisana. . . ." ALS, *ibid.* See message to Senate, Feb. 8, 1875; *HRC,*
43-2-2.

To Jeremiah M. Rusk

Washington, May 19, 1874

SIR:

Late Capt. James W. Shirk served in command of a Gun Boat on
the Mississippi River while I was in command of the forces operating against Vicksburg and vicinity. He was among the first in running the blockade of Vicksburg and Port Hudson; was always attentive, active, willing and efficient; never faltering from any duty.
If relief can properly be given his family it will be bestowed upon a
worthy widow and children and will be an expression of appreciation
of the valuable services of a very efficient officer of the Government.

Very truly yours
U. S. GRANT

HON. JEREMIAH M. RUSK
CHAIRMAN COMMITTEE ON INVALID PENSIONS
HOUSE OF REPRESENTATIVES.

Copy, DLC-USG, II, 2. *HRC*, 43-1-604; *SRC*, 43-2-500. Commander James W. Shirk died
on Feb. 10, 1873. On May 22, 1874, the Committee on Invalid Pensions, U.S. House of Representatives, recommended a bill increasing the monthly pension of Mary W. Shirk and her
three minor children from thirty-six to fifty dollars. *HRC*, 43-1-604. On Jan. 7, 1875, the
Committee on Pensions, U.S. Senate, recommended indefinite postponement of this measure. ". . . Her present pension is as high as the widow of any naval officer now on the roll is
drawing, with the single exception of Mrs. Farragut; she gets all that was promised by the
law when her husband entered the naval service, and when she became his wife. She gets
what other widows of military and naval officers have got and were content with, until they
became apprised that discriminations are made by special legislation. She gets what the
cool judgment of Congress established as a just rule of compensation, when undisturbed
by solicitation . . ." *SRC*, 43-2-500, 3–4. The bill did not pass.

To Senate

———

To the Senate of the United States:

I have the honor to transmit, in response to the resolution of the
Senate of the 18th instant, requesting "the answers in full received
by the Civil Service Commission in reply to their circular addressed
to the various Heads of Departments and Bureaux requesting a report as to the operation and effect of the Civil Service Rules in their
several departments and offices", a copy of a letter received from the
Chairmain of the Civil Service Commission, to whom the resolution
was referred.

U. S. Grant

Executive Mansion
May 25. 1874

Copy, DNA, RG 130, Messages to Congress. *SED*, 43-1-53. On May 21, 1874, Dorman
B. Eaton, chairman, Civil Service Commission, wrote to USG transmitting a copy of the
report of the Civil Service Commission. *Ibid.* Born in 1823 in Hardwick, Vt., Eaton graduated from the University of Vermont (1848) and Harvard Law School (1850), joined the
N. Y. bar, and served as counsel for the Erie Railroad. He left the law in 1870 to advocate
civil service and municipal government reform. See *PUSG*, 24, 93–100; Eaton, *Civil Service in Great Britain: A History of Abuses and Reforms and Their Bearing Upon American Politics* (New York, 1880) and *The "Spoils" System and Civil Service Reform in the Custom-House
and Post-Office at New York* (New York, 1881).

On May 29 and Aug. 31, 1874, USG issued orders. "The Civil Service Commission,
at its sessions at Washington, having recommended certain rules to be prescribed by the
President for the government of the Light House Service of the United States, these rules,
as herewith published, are approved, and their provisions will be enforced by the proper

officers." "It appearing to me from their trial at Washington and at the City of New York that the further extension of the Civil Service Rules will promote the efficiency of the public Service it is ordered that such Rules be & they are hereby extended to the several Federal Offices at the City and in the Customs District of Boston and that the proper measures be taken for carrying this order into effect." DS, DLC-Executive Orders. Related papers are *ibid.*

To Congress

———

Washington, May 26th 1874.

To THE SENATE AND HOUSE OF REPRESENTATIVES.

I transmit to the Senate and House of Representatives a communication from the Secretary of State and a copy of the Report of the Commissioners to inquire into depredations on the frontiers of Texas, by which it is accompanied.

U. S. GRANT.

Copies, DNA, RG 59, Reports to the President and Congress; *ibid.*, RG 130, Messages to Congress. *HED*, 43-1-257. See *PUSG*, 23, 123–30.

On Dec. 12, 1873, H. W. Berry, Corpus Christi, wrote to USG. "I write you to inform you that the indians have been down in the Settlements between here and Lorado in the Last few days have Killed and Scalped 17 of our nabors that we know off. And perhaps a great many more that we have not herd of yet   now as an old citzen have been on this frontier as you are well aware off, that I have for the last 25 years. I ask it as a favor to the Settlers of this county to allow us to form a company for the Express porpose of defending our Selves against the redman of the forrest and the bad and outlawed mexicans in varible raid on our Stock men and defenceless citisens who are trying to make an honest living. I have tried to get the citisens to organize but they Say it is a gainst the law of the U. S. and there fore we must depend on the general goverment. I admit this true but cant you in trust and permit Such a company to the good citisens of this county for there own protection. I think it is in your power if you will.   we want nothing but the Sanction of you.   we have all else that is necessary men and arms. Hopeing to hear from you at your earliest conenience . . . P. S they come every new moon" ALS, DNA, RG 75, Letters Received, Central Superintendency.

On Dec. 15, N. Gussett, Corpus Christi, wrote to USG. "I have this placher to write you afew lines and inclose you Some letters receved from my correspondence Giving facts inrelation to the Indians and Desperredoes. I Enclose you these letters to show you that it is not Indians alone that are Robbing and murdring the Sheppards and Sheep Rasers.   you have no Idea of the murdders commited between the Rio Grande and Nueaces Rivers and it is Gitting worse every day   it is now not Safe for a man to Go out ten miles from Town the Cattle men are at worr with the Sheep men and the Mexican and Indians are at worr with boath—and the Custom House officers must have ther r[o]de clean or the can not Get Smugling anough don to pay them Good wages. I hope you will Give this your attention and Give our People Protection" ALS, *ibid.* Related papers in Spanish are *ibid.* On Dec. 17, Gussett again wrote to USG. "you will please pardon me for asking you for So much of your valluble time. but at the Same time alow me to ashore you that we are in need of your Protectin. I here Enclose to you a letter from Mr N. G. Collins of SanDiego one of the best men of the county   I have other letters but one from Such a man as N. G. Collins is Quite Sufacint to Show you how the Whites are murders.   we want troops not under the controle of Capt R King but under Good officer that will bring men to Justices.   during these murders the hase been and is yet a company of Troops at the Rancho of Capt R. King interly under his controle and I have been told that he Capt. R. King hase this company to Gard him alone.   we want also Good Custom House officers that will do ther duty   thes men are paid to keep a lookout for Partys crossing the Rio Grande and the Should be mad do ther duty." ALS, *ibid.*, RG 94, Letters Received, 36 1874. The enclosure and related papers are *ibid.*

On June 3, 1874, USG signed a bill "for the better protection of the frontier settlements of Texas against Indian and Mexican depredations." *U.S. Statutes at Large*, XVIII, part 3, pp. 51–52. This bill authorized $100,000 to construct a telegraph line connecting army posts in Tex. and Indian Territory. See *CR*, 43–1, 3204–5; *HED*, 42-3-179, 43-1-166.

Memorandum

Washington D. C. [June 1,] 187[4]

DEAR SIR:

Having been consulted by you and ~~also~~ the Hon. H. Maynard,[1] also of the Conference Committee on the *Senate* Finance bill, as to my views upon that question, and for the purpose as stated of ascertaining if it might not be possible to suggest a *measure* which might ~~be~~ enable the Committee to recommend a measure acceptable both to the legislative & Executive branches of the govt. ~~and~~ ~~a~~As my views are being constantly asked on this subject, both by the friends of "expansion" and "contraction"—as usually designated, I have thought it advisable to express to you in writing my general views in order that there may be no misunderstanding ~~of~~ them.

I believe it to be the duty of [the] Government to return to a specie basis ~~of finance~~ at the earlyest practicable day not only to carry out ~~Con~~ legislative ~~pledges~~ and party pledges, but also as a necessary step to secure permanent national prosperity. I believe further that the time has come when this can be accomplished with less embarass-

ment to every branch of industry, the *country over*, than at any future
time if ~~any~~ patchwork is resorted to to stimulate apparent prosperity and speculation on other basis than that of coin—the recognized
medium of exchange the world over. The method to accomplish this
return to a specie basis of exchange is not so important as that a plan
~~should~~ shall be devised, the day fixed when currency shall be convertable into coin, at par, and the plan adopted adhered to. There is
probably no plan which I could suggest that would meet the approval
of both branches of Congress, asnd further it might be ~~further~~ that a
full discussion of any such plan would shake my faith in it. I will venture to state however about what legislation seems to me advisable
—or the financial platform I would stand upon—and all departure
from the principle of it would be in a spirit of compromise for the
sake of peace and harmony. First I would like to see the legal tender
clause of the Act. of _____ repealed to take effect [say] on the
1st day of July 1875. This would cause all contracts after that date,
all sales made, wages paid &c. to be estimated in coin. ~~or its equiva-
lent~~. It would change the current of reasoning as to values. The specie
dollar would be the only dollar known in estimating values. Where
debts, whether for wages, material or anything else, (contracted after
that date) were paid in currency instead of calling the paper dollar a
dollar and quoting gold at so much premium, we would see the paper at so much discount. This alone would aid materially in bringing
the two currencies near to a par, with each other. Second, I would like
to see a provision that on the 1st day of July 1876 the currency issued by the United States should be redeemable in coin, on presentation at the office of any Asst. Treas. of the United States,—and that
all ~~coin~~ currency so redeemed should be canseled and never reissued.
To provide for this it would be necessary to authorize the issue of sufficient gold bonds, bearing an interest that would make them command par in gold, to be held by the Sec. of the Treasury and only
disposed of in such quantities as might prove necessary from time
to time to carry out this redemption. This would secure a return to
sound financial principles in two years and would not, in my judgement, work as much injustice to the debtor class as they are likely to

be subjected to by a delay of the day of final settlement. It may be rec-
ollected too that this class had its *day*, in ~~a fair p~~ a larger degree, on
the adoption of our present financial system,—~~perfectly justifiable at
the time~~ by reason of the great necessities of the Nation at the time
of its adoption—

   The next step that I would propose would be that from and after the date fixed for redemption ~~that~~ no bills—whether of National
banks or of govt. issue—returned to the Treasury to ~~get~~ be exchanged for new bills ~~in their place~~ should be replaced by bills of less
denomination than Ten dollars, and that in one year after resumption all bills of less denomination than Five dollars should be withdrawn from circulation, and that within two years from the same
date all bills of less than Ten dollars should be so withdrawn.

   The benefit of this would be to [give] ~~strengthen~~ [to] the country
in time of depression, whether caused by war, failure of crops or any
other cause, by retaining in the hands of the people a large amount of
the precious metals. All ~~the~~ smaller transactions ~~of the people~~ would
be conducted in coin. This would give employment to many Millions
of it and thereby retain it in the country. There is no question in my
mind *as to the fact* that the poorer currency always will drive the better out of ~~the market~~ [circulation]. With paper as a legal tender, and
at a discount, gold and silver become articles of Merchandise as much
as wheat or [cotton]. The surplus will find the best market it can.
The balance of trade has nothing to do with the question. With small
notes in circulation there ceases to be use for coin except in the vaults
of banks with which to redeem their circulation. In times of great
speculation and apparent prosperity there will be but few calls for
~~the~~ coin, hence its outflow to a market where it can be made to earn
something which it ~~is~~ [can] not ~~doing~~ while [lying] idle. ~~in the vaults~~.
It becomes a surplus seeking a market. By giving active employ-
ment to it, it seems to me, this evil may be remidied in a great measure, and the periodical panics and depressions which [occured] ~~the
country was subjected to~~ in the days of nominal specie payments,
be wholly avoided or materially mitigated. In deed I very much question whether it would have been necessary to depart far from a specie basis during the trying times which begat the legal tender act if

the country had *have* adopted the theory of "no small bills" as early as 1850.

Next, I would ~~increase the~~ [provide a] surplus of ~~the~~ revenue over expenditures, ~~to~~ by economy and increas~~ed~~ [of] receipts where [that] can be best borne, [so] that there should be a constant reduction of the public debt, and an ~~increase~~ [accumulation] of coin to meet the demands upon the Treasury for the redemption of its notes, ~~without~~ diminishing thereby the amount of bonds necessary ~~to sell~~ to acquire gold. All taxes, after redemption, should be paid in gold or National currency. This would force redemption on the National banks. With measures like th~~is~~[ese], or which would accomplish the same purpose[s]—I do not see that there could be the least danger in authorizing unlimited free banking.

ADf (bracketed material not in USG's hand), DLC-USG, IB. On June 1, 1874, Secretary of State Hamilton Fish recorded in his diary. "The President stated that . . . Senator Sherman and Mr. Maynard respectively Chairmen of the Conference Committee of the two Houses on the Currency bill had been to see him with reference thereto; that Carpenter had also been to see him, in behalf, as he said, of Morton who *'felt that he could not come.'* That he (the President) found much difficulty in being correctly understood by those who had different views from him and so much misrepresentation of his views that he had put them [his own views] in writing, in the form of a letter to be addressed to Sherman and Maynard: which he proceeds to read. He take the highest ground in favour of resumption and against inflation, going somewhat into detail as to his policy. The question is raised as to the expediency or propriety of his addressing a letter to members of the Committee; with the exception of Robeson, all concur that it would not be advisable for him to send a letter as proposed. Delano dissented to some extent from the purport of the letter arguing that the concluding part of it which recommended the strengthening of the Treasury by economy of expenditures and judicious taxation was correct, and, as he said, was the essence of the whole thing. I dissented from that view saying that the best point in the letter was the unqualified position taken, in favour of resumption, against inflation, and for the repeal of the legal tender acts; and I also approved the recommendation to abolish small notes. Robeson, Creswell, and Williams concurred with me, but the conclusion was that the letter should not be sent. It had better be placed in the form of a memorandum which the President might read to Sherman or Maynard. As the President is going away tonight it is left in this condition until his return; but he expresses much anxiety to have his views put on paper so as to avoid further misrepresentation" Brackets in original, DLC-Hamilton Fish. See following letter.

1. Born in 1814 in Mass., Horace Maynard graduated from Amherst College (1838) and moved to Tenn., where he served as U.S. Representative (1857–63) and state attorney gen. (1863–65) before returning to Congress in 1866. On Jan. 29, 1874, Maynard, chairman, Committee on Banking and Currency, had introduced House Bill 1572 to regulate the national currency and establish free banking. Maynard's bill later supplanted Senate Bill 617, vetoed April 22.

To John P. Jones

Washington, D. C. June 4, 1874.

DEAR SIR:

Your note of this date requesting a copy of a memorandum which I had prepared expressive of my views upon the *financial question,* and which you, with others, had heard read is received, but at too late an hour to comply to-night. I will however take great pleasure in furnishing you a copy in the morning as soon as I can have it copied

It is proper that I should state that these views were reduced to writing because I had been consulted on this question not only by some members of the Conference Committee upon it, but by many other Members of Congress. To avoid any and all possibility of misunderstanding I deemed this course both justifiable and proper.

With this explanation I enclose you herewith the memorandum referred to.

Very respectfully
U. S. GRANT

HON. J. P. JONES, U. S. SENATE.

Copy, DLC-USG, II, 2. See preceding Memorandum. Born in 1829 in England, John P. Jones grew up in Ohio and engaged in mining in Calif. and Nev., which elected him to the U.S. Senate in 1873. On June 4, 1874, Jones wrote to USG. "I was so deeply impressed by the clearness and wisdom of the financial views (some of which you had fortunately reduced to writing) recently expressed by you in a conversation in which I had the honor, with a few others, to be a participant, that I can not dismiss them from my mind. The great diversity of ideas throughout the country upon this subject, and the fact that public opinion concerning the same is still in process of formation, lead me to believe that the publication of these views would be productive of great good. I venture, therefore, to request of you that I may have a copy of the written memorandum to which I have alluded, with your permission that it may be made public." *Washington Chronicle,* June 6, 1874.

On June 3 and 4, Secretary of State Hamilton Fish recorded in his diary. "I received a note from Gen'l. Babcock stating that the President desired me to call there at 8½. P. M. I accordingly did so and met at the White House Senators Conkling, Morrill (Me.) & Jones (Nevada) together with Secretary Bristow. The President desired consultation on the subject of the currency bill now pending in Congress; it was carefully discussed by sections; the President making notes on each section; after completing the consideration of the bill, the President alluded to conversations he had had with several Senators and Members of the House; and stated that owing to the liability to misapprehension of such conversations he had reduced his views to writing and had read the paper to several members of the Houses of Congress. The wish being expressed by the gentlemen present to hear it he produced the paper which he had read in Cabinet Monday and handed it to Senator Jones who read it aloud. All present expressed most cordial concurrence in its views and a desire that it should be brought before the public. Conkling thought he could induce Sherman as Chairman on the part of the Senate Managers of the Conference to ask for it in the name of his Committee—And with that conclusion at about 12½ we retired. Senator Conkling followed me home and expressed a doubt whether Sherman would address the letter he had suggested and said it would be much better for it to come out through Jones. He asked whether I would not arrange with the President in the morning to have it appear thus." "I called upon the President in the morning and stated what Conkling had said: he readily assented, adding that he cared more about getting it before the public than about the mode of getting it before the public." DLC-Hamilton Fish.

On June 6, James R. Snowden, clerk, Pa. Supreme Court, Philadelphia, wrote to USG. "I venture upon your valuable time to express my admiration of your views upon the questions of Currency and Finance as evinced in your Veto of the Inflation Bill (so called) and especially in your 'memorandum of views,' upon those subjects published in the papers of to-day. Having been for some years Treasurer of the State of Penna during which I was instrumental in restoring the credit of the Commth; and having subsequently held the Offices of Asst Treas U. S. and Treasurer of the Mint, and for many years Director of the Mint, I have given the subject much consideration, and have published some works, some of which I had the honor to present to you a few years ago. I merely state this to show that the subject has received my careful attention. You state the true policy of the government when you say that 'it is a high and plain duty to return to a specie basis at the earliest practicable day.' And, that any currency based upon temporary expedients and not upon Coin—the recognized medium of exchange throughout the Commercial world—must be injurious to the National prosperity, and ought to be withdrawn as soon as practicable. I venture to suggest that this is an opportune time, in connexion with the anticipated measures for a resumption of specie payments at no very distant day, to renew the subject of some practicable and useful unification of the Coinage of all nations; or at least the introduction of uniformity in the *fineness* of gold used in coinage and thus accomplish a Common Standard of Comparison as to values; for then each ounce would be of like intrinsic or mint value. I wrote a paper on this subject some years ago which was published in Lippencotts Magazine. Happening to have a separate copy at hand of that paper I herewith send it to you: and if you have time to read it I will be honored and obliged—At page 86 (Mag. page) you will see two or three sentences corroborative of your veiws on the subject of currency. This country owes you thanks, which posterity also will recognize for your able and patriotic stand on those subjects." ALS, USG 3. Also on June 6, Cook & Brother, "Importers of Hosiery Goods," Philadelphia, wrote to USG. "We cannot deny ourselves the pleasure of assuring you of the great satisfaction with which we have read your views on financial matters, as published in to days papers. Our business experience demonstrates the wisdom of placing our financial policy upon a gold basis, and, while we are personally only a small portion of your 40 millions of Constituents, we cannot deny our applause to that firm sense of right & duty which are so evident in your Action upon financial matters. We can scarcely hope that this letter may reach your eye; but, we believe ourselves to have only fulfilled a duty in (however humbly it may be) endeavoring to strengthen your hands in this matter." L, *ibid.*

On June 7 and 12, David B. Sickels, New York City, wrote to USG. "I trust you will excuse the liberty which I have taken in addressing you; but having made the subject of *Finance* a life-long study, I have been so much impressed with the soundness and wisdom of the method which you have so modestly suggested intended to relieve our present monetary exigencies, that I could not refrain from expressing my cordial endorsement of your views. The provision suggested for the return to specie payments—the repeal of the legal tender act and the early withdrawal of small notes from circulation are the best and safest remedies which can be applied to cure our diseased financial system. Those who are in favor of *inflation* surely should not object to these propositions, because the repeal of the legal tender clause necessarily involves the abolishment of *all the reserves* held by the National Banks, thereby adding to the circulation over one hundred of millions of dollars. The adoption of the measures proposed and the authorization of Free Banking by Congress could not fail in supplying the country with all the money required for business purposes, and it is quite surprising that the gentlemen who compose the Conference Committee should fail to discover that fact. . . ." "For Heaven's sake & for the sake of the Country 'stand by your colors' in the great contest between the advocates of a sound and an unsound financial policy. 'Fight it out on that line' if it takes the balance of the session. Free Banking —unlimited, with the restrictions and provisions proposed in your Memoranda, is all the Country needs. The Gould Panic of September ruined me; but I can see no hope of recovery if the *possibility* of such events recurring is to be increased by Congressional enactment. Enforce the repeal of the Legal Tender act and then *all* will be well." ALS, *ibid.*

On June 8, Monday, Alexander T. Stewart, New York City, wrote to USG. "On the 23d of April last I had the pleasure to state to you the gratification entertained by all business men, as well as myself, at your Veto message of the Senate bill—That firm and just act certainly led your friends to look forward to a hopeful and healthy future, and yet there seemed doubt and uncertainty as to the manner in which that condition was to be arrived at. Your views upon the Financial questions of the day, as published in the newspapers of Saturday last, puts all those doubts at rest, and clearly and forcibly define the true course to be followed, to enable our country to resume her former prosperity, freed from the incubus of an irredeemable currency. They come too, at an appropriate time, when the mercantile community is looking to you with hope, confidence, and reliance justified by the noble words contained in your Veto message, which first gave them encouragement As one feeling a deep interest in the result you indicate being attained, and as your personal and warm friend, accept my sincere thanks" ALS, *ibid.* On the same day, Duncan S. Walker, secretary, Washington City and Point Lookout Railroad Co., Washington, D. C., wrote to USG. "Enclosed I hand you a copy of a letter of the late Robert J. Walker, dated November 30th 1867 on the subject of our National Finances, which I have concluded to republish at this time, hoping that the suggestions therein contained may assist in reaching a correct solution of the financial problem. This letter was written at a time when repudiation seemed popular. The then Secretary of the Treasury was draining the life-blood of the Country by excessive taxation, and at the same time diminishing the volume of paper currency without any equivalent. As a natural consequence many went to the opposite extreme, and practical repudiation, by the payment of all our bonds in Greenbacks and the substitution of Greenbacks for National Bank Currency, was advocated strongly by the debtor class, speculators, and demagogues. Without contraction the discount upon greenbacks has been gradually reduced below 10 per cent, and our 5 pr. ct. bonds have advanced above par on Gold. Another crisis has come upon us. Trade is dull. The debtor class are oppressed. Labor is restless. Want of confidence is everywhere. As a cure for all our evils more currency is proposed. At first they propose a compromise, by which a small amount of expansion may be secured. But who doubts that the policy once sanctioned, in time of peace,—not as a necessity, but as a good principle in itself,—it will end in constantly augmenting expansion, and finally in repudiation? At this time it is the duty of every American to lay aside the prejudice of party and support you in that fearless action which has

saved our Country from disgrace and our people from ruin. It is to be hoped that your letter will arouse the people, and produce immediate action by their Representatives. Let us
have specie payments by bringing the specie here from abroad, together with Free Banking thus improving whilst increasing our circulating medium: a Tariff for Revenue, with
incidental protection: a judicious reduction of Government Expenditures, whilst encouraging to the extent of our ability much needed Internal Improvements, and we will soon
have both peace and prosperity." ALS, *ibid.* The enclosure is *ibid.* Also on June 8, William
Thorpe, New York City, wrote to USG. "I have read with the most profound satisfaction
your letter to Senator Jones relative to the financial condition of the Government. Let me
say that, while I have differed with you on nearly every subject since your first inauguration, here I can use my every effort in your support. The Legal-tender act is the main obstacle in the way of resumption. Repeal that and immediately Gold becomes by law, the
standard of value, and is necessarily brought again into circulation, thereby increasing the
currency of the country. Besides that, we are brought into harmony with the monetary
systems of the great nations of the world—England, France and Germany. At present we
are in danger of falling into the condition of Mexico, Spain & Turkey. Stop the purchase of
bonds. They are far from due. If you have any surplus coin, after providing for interest, &c,
lock it up in the Treasury till you have ~~enough~~ almost enough to call in the demand notes.
Then provide for the possibility of requiring more and notify the holders of demand notes
to call for their money if they want it. It is a mistaken notion that the resumption of specie
payments will seriously hurt a single citizen. The country is not divided into *two* classes—
debtor & creditor. Nearly every man owes something, but at the same time he is also a creditor to others. I am both a debtor and a creditor. So it is with a majority everywhere, and
the whole matter is more evenly balanced than some suppose. Wishing you continued
health and prosperity and satisfactory results to all your undertakings, . . ." ALS, *ibid.*

On June 9, William E. Cramer, *Evening Wisconsin,* Milwaukee, wrote to USG. "You
will perhaps recollect me. ~~when~~ I called upon you with my wife at the White House in February last. We then had some conversation on the question of specie payment. Your views
were so in accord with my own, that since my return I have been one of the most pronounced
supporters of the veto message and of your financial views as expressed to Senator Jones,
in the Northwest. I was always a disciple of Jefferson and Wright and therefore have regarded finance as the supreme question of the day. I enclose you two articles since the publication of the Jones memoranda. You will perceive that there is no quailing on my part,
though your views are more advanced than even the specie payment men are now willing
to accept." LS, *ibid.* Also on June 9, Governor John A. Dix of N. Y. wrote to USG. "I have
read repeatedly your financial plan, and there is not a suggestion in it, in which I do not fully
concur. I am especially pleased that you recommend the withdrawal of all circulating notes
under ten dollars. That was the French limit, and it was by means of it that the German
indemnity was paid. There is not the slightest difficulty in getting as large a basis of specie
for our paper currency. If the country will have the wisdom to adopt your plan, I am satisfied that it will prove an effectual remedy for our financial embarrassments." ALS, *ibid.*

On June 10, Gamaliel Bradford, Boston, wrote to USG. "For some years I have maintained on every possible occasion that the only hope of escape from our financial difficulties
is to give to the Executive the direction as well as the execution of a financial policy   The
great attention which your 'Memorandum' has excited shows how eagerly the public mind
accepts this conclusion. It would be a great step in advance if your next message or report
to Congress would contain a recommendation that the Secretary of the Treasury be admitted to a share in public debate on the subject on the floor of the House   If in the mul-
titude of advice which is thrust upon you, you should care for a farther elaboration of this

point, I should be only too happy to submit the results of Long & thorough study upon it" ALS, *ibid.* On the same day, a *"Friend"* wrote to USG on U.S. Senate stationery. "I cannot leave Washington, without thanking you for your *financial Memorandum.* There are two things in that are very *impressive.* 1. *The return to Specie payments,* during your present term of office. 2. An *increase of revenue* to meet our need, and pointing to the renewal of duties on *Tea and Coffee.* It was *a great mistake* to take the duties from *Tea and coffee.* It should be put on as soon as next Congress meets. The present members will not wish to touch it till after the fall elections. I will not sign my name, as it may be supposed I am *interfering."* L, *ibid.*

On June 11, Daniel H. Chamberlain, Columbia, S. C., wrote to USG. "I am sure you need no endorsement to keep you true to the financial policy contained in your memorandum to Senator Jones: but it may not be unwelcome to you to receive an assurance that there are some *at the South* who believe with you that a return to specie payments is an instant duty, and the only way to avoid future financial disasters of the most wide-spread extent and character. I endorse with my whole heart and mind your memorandum and I firmly believe the whole American people will in six months be with you. At any rate, whoever is for you or against you, you *know* that you are in the path of honesty and good faith, and there can be no safety in any other path." ALS, *ibid.*

On June 15, Charles P. Culver, Washington, D. C., wrote to USG. "I have not only perused, but studied with deep interest, your views of the financial question that so deeply interests the people of this country at this time. They have the true ring of the old Jacksonian Democracy. I most heartily concur with you, that the only safe road out of our National embarrassments on this vexed question, is a speedy return to a specie basis for our circulating medium. As the speediest mode of reaching this condition, without materially disturbing values or embarrassing commerce, and at the same time aid you in carrying out your ideas of a specie basis, I would respectfully ask your consideration of, and attention to, the following plan or plans, and which require no legislation by Congress to carry into operation. The power is already vested in the Executive and his Secretary of the Treasury. . . ." ALS, *ibid.* An enclosed clipping suggested revised procedures for selling U.S. Treasury gold. Similar letters supporting USG's financial memorandum are *ibid.*

On June 7, 9, and 10, Fish had recorded in his diary. "I received a note from Speaker Blaine asking to see me: not being well I requested him to come to my house which he did. He speaks of the President's Memorandum on finance exhibiting considerable feeling; saying that if carried out it would be ruinous to the Republican party and the country; he said he should be inclined to adopt the words of Mr. Webster and say; 'that when his leader turned a sharp corner into a dark lane and changed the light which he had been accustomed to follow, that it could not be expected that they should keep company longer.' I told him that without adopting all the details of the President's plan, I believed the principles underlieing it were the only safeguards of the country. We then considered the bill he defending most of the provisions to which I took exception, admitting that personally he would not object to some of them. Our interview was interrupted by Mrs. Fish's illness, and I subsequently receive from him a copy of the bill and later in the evening he called again and I submitted to him certain proposed amendments all of which he thought were improvements to the bill and expressed the opinion that they might be assented to by the Committee, and he would endeavour to urge their acceptance." "In the afternoon Senators Jones and Stewart of Nevada called saying that the President had requested to have a bill drawn embodying the views of his Memorandum on the currency question to be introduced into the Senate. They asked my views as to the expediency of so doing. I deem it highly unadvisable, which, they tell me, is their opinion. They wish me to see the President to try and relieve him of the desire to have the bill introduced." "I speak with him on the subject mentioned yesterday by Jones and Stewart and endeavour to impress him with the impolicy of introducing any bill; in which view he finally concurs." DLC-Hamilton Fish. On June 20, USG signed an act to fix the amount of U.S. notes and redistribute national bank currency. See *U.S. Statutes at Large*, XVIII, part 3, pp. 123–25; *John Sherman's Recollections of Forty Years* . . . (Chicago, 1895), I, 508; Irwin Unger, *The Greenback Era: A Social and Political History of American Finance, 1865–1879* (Princeton, 1964), pp. 245–48; message to Senate, Jan. 14, 1875.

Speech

[*June 5, 1874*]

MR MINISTER: It gives me pleasure to know that the Republic of Nicaragua has been pleased to advance the rank of its worthy representative at Washington. The people of the United States are deeply interested in the prosperity of the American Republics, and will see with pleasure the completion of any work which may promote it. Especially will they regard with satisfaction the construction of ship canals between the Atlantic and Pacific Oceans whenever it may be found possible to construct them to advantage. The interest of this Government in such works has been frequently manifested. I appreciate the spirit in which you propose to devote yourself to cementing the good relations between Nicaragua and the United States, and shall be ready at all times to lend my aid to that end.

New York Times, June 6, 1874; Df, DNA, RG 59, Notes From Foreign Legations, Central America. USG responded to Emilio Benard, Nicaraguan minister. ". . . If, as is to be hoped, the Territory of Nicaragua shall be chosen for the union of the two great oceans, nothing, Mr. President, could be more gratifying to my country than the initiative taken by the Uni[t]ed States in this gigantic project. The energy of this great nation, its immense resources, its essentially enterprising character, and its ardent enthusiasm for all that is great, furnish a sure guarantee that the Inter-oceanic Canal, which has been regarded as a chimera by past generations, will become a brilliant reality whenever this nation shall lend it its powerful aid. . . ." *New York Times*, June 6, 1874. See *PUSG*, 23, 46–50, 221–23.

On Aug. 27, 1874, Secretary of State Hamilton Fish wrote in his diary. "Mr Benard (Nicaraguan Minr) having called yesterday, when I declined to receive him, calls again, to-day—Says he saw the President at Long Branch, the day that I left. Is anxious about the report of the Commission appointed to receive & consider the various reports as to the Routes of Interoceanic Communication across the Isthmus,—says Prof. Pierce is in Europe, expected to return in Nov October—had asked the Prsdt whether he could not be recalled or some else named in his place: that his own health will not allow him to remain here during the winter, their Congress will meet in Jany, wishes a Convention to be negotiated &

ratified this winter—& finally asked that our Minister to Nicaragua be instructed to converse with Members of the Nicaraguan Congress on the subject of the Canal, & assure them of the Presidents interest in the subject—Says Prsdt told him that Pierces expected return was so near at hand, & that it was not advisable to hasten it, or to make an appointment in his place—but that he thought Williamson might be instructed to confer with leading Members of their Congress. . . ." DLC-Hamilton Fish. On Sept. 14, Benard wrote to Fish announcing his return to Nicaragua. ". . . But not satisfied with all I have said in private conferences to his Excellency the President as well as to the honorable Secretary of State, I have the honor to reiterate to them now that, whenever it shall wish that the Isthmus of Nicaragua be designated as the preferable route, this Government ought to rely on it that mine will yield to the most liberal negotiations which the work demands and which may be in its power to concede. . . ." LS (in Spanish), DNA, RG 59, Notes from Foreign Legations, Central America; translation, *ibid.* Benard enclosed a pamphlet, "A Few Considerations Respecting the Nicaragua Ship Canal." *Ibid.* See Speeches, [*March 21, 1876*], [*Oct. 31, 1876*].

On [*Jan. 27*], USG had written. "The Sec. of the Navy may refer the Maps, surveys & reports of the different inter-ocean routes examined under his direction, with all information ~~in his~~ on the subject in his possession, to the Commissioners named to examine them." AN (undated), Wayde Chrismer, Bel Air, Md. See *PUSG*, 23, 49.

On Feb. 6, De Lancey H. Louderback, Chicago, wrote to USG. "I would like very much to join the new expedition to the Isthmus to select a route for the proposed 'Canal.' I have been in the telegraph business the last fourteen years and have a thorough knowledge of the business and can afford information needed in regard to a telegraph line over the same route if you propose to have one built. I would respectfully refer you to Hon. James. S. Negley James. B. Eads or J. E. Kingsley Continental Hotel Philada as regards my ability, and standing. Should you have nothing in this line will you please refer my letter to Capt. Selfridge as he may need a corresponding Secretary?" ALS, DNA, RG 45, Letters Received from the President. See *Chicago Tribune*, April 10, 1914.

To Elias W. Fox

———

Washington, D. C. June 5, 74

E. W—Fox Esq—

Dear Sir

Your letter of resignation of the office of the Surveyor of the Port of St Louis, Mo. is received. In accepting it it affords me great pleasure to say the office, since it has been entrusted to your charge, has been filled to the entire satisfaction of Govt officials over the revenue branch of the service, and to the best interest of the public service so far as can be observed here.

Your letter of resignation contains so much of information on the subject of the duties of the office that I shall forward a copy of it to your successor when appointed & confirmed.

Very truly

Your Obt Svt

U S GRANT

Copies (2), DLC-USG, II, 2. On May 30, 1874, Elias W. Fox, St. Louis, wrote to USG. "Respectfully referring to conversations held with you in the months of February and March last, I now tender you my resignation of the offices of Surveyor of Customs for the port of St. Louis, and Disbursing Agent for the Treasury Department, to take effect at the close of the present fiscal year, to wit: on the 30th June, 1874. In connection with the foregoing, I beg your indulgence to make a few brief statements concerning the character, importance, condition and efficiency of the office over which I have had the honor to preside. My chief duties have been those of a collector of the revenue from customs, and while every energy has been successfully bent to gathering every cent due to the government, a vast amount of labor outside the ordinary and routine duty of the office has been performed by myself and subordinates, in stimulating, encouraging and educating our merchants up to direct trade with foreign countries. During my term of office it has been demonstrated that merchants of the interior can compete in the importing business with those of the coast cities, and the efforts of our Representatives, kindly seconded by the officers of the government, have opened the doors of St. Louis to independent, economical and unrestricted trade with the nations of the wide world. . . . You are aware that we have a United States Marine Hospital at this port, and that in a large measure its management and care has devolved upon me. . . . It has been my pleasure to see (while Surveyor of the Port) the measures which will ere long provide a worthy edifice for the proper accommodation of the government business at this point. As one of the commissioners (by your appointment) to locate the building, I labored to secure the eligible spot where the work of erection has commenced, and as disbursing agent of the Treasury since the beginning of the enterprise, have done all in my power to further the interests of the government in that behalf. . . . I cannot close without offering a just tribute to the worth, fidelity, honesty and efficiency of the entire force of employees who have so successfully aided me in the conduct of the office. I think I can say I never saw a better organized or more smoothly working system than that which has obtained in my office. All the better the better things embraced in the Civil Service Reform Rules have been in practical possession or use here for a number of years—for great care has been taken to obtain men suitable for the work—to keep the force at the smallest possible number, and to perfect each one in his special line of duty. . . ." *St. Louis Globe*, June 11, 1874. On June 19, Levi P. Luckey wrote to John F. Long, St. Louis. ". . . As your confirmation as Mr. Fox's successor as Surveyor of the Port of St. Louis is received, I mail you the copy of Mr. Fox's letter of resignation as directed by the President and in accordance with his intention as expressed to Mr. Fox." Copy, DLC-USG, II, 2. See letter to John F. Long, Feb. 16, 1874; *HMD*, 44-1-186, 335–36, 342–43.

On Oct. 11, 1875, Fox, St. Louis, wrote to USG. "In a conversation held with you in Washington in the spring of '73 you gave me to understand that should a suitable opportunity occur, I would be remembered in your appointments. I beg to call your attention to the position of U. S. Marshal for the Eastern District of Mo. I believe that my appointment to that position would be favorably received by all your reliable friends in Mo. I have not asked for recommendations but have simply written the Atty Genl and Post Master Gen'l

Jewell giving references. If ever I needed a kindness in my life it is now." LS, DNA, RG 60, Records Relating to Appointments. No appointment followed.

On Jan. 11, 1876, USG wrote on Fox's card. "Consulate at Basle, Switzerland." AN, Columbia University, New York, N. Y. On Jan. 11 and 14, Secretary of State Hamilton Fish recorded in his diary. "The President directs that a letter be written to Mr Erni Consul at Basle asking his resignation with a view to the appt of Wm C. Fox of St Louis who is a personal friend." "I showed the President the papers of Mr Erni Consul at Basle with his own endorsement and ask him why he does not make a vacancy at La Rochelle now filled by a Democrat and recommended by Genl Mosby. He asks the salary—I tell him $1500   To this he answers that he doubts whether that will be sufficient but will let me know and that I need not take any action now." DLC-Hamilton Fish. On April 12, 1869, USG had nominated Henry Erni as consul, Basle; on Dec. 2, 1873, USG nominated Richard N. Brooke as consul, La Rochelle. On April 27, John S. Mosby had certified that he knew "Brooke for 8 years: that he is pecuniarily honest and trustworthy: that he is of good repute and steady habits: . . ." DS, DNA, RG 59, Letters of Application and Recommendation. On March 6, 1876, Fish recorded in his diary. "While sitting with the President Mr Fox of Mo sends in a request for the appointment of his son to some European Consulate. The President hands it to me remarking that this is the young man about whom he had spoken to me before & to whom he had promised the Consulate at Bale and requested me to find some place for him —I tell him there is no place where a change can be made but that on Saturday he had authorized me to appoint Mr. Farman recommended by Sen Conkling and Hoskins to Brunswick and he says he will appoint Fox in his stead." DLC-Hamilton Fish. Fox's card is in Columbia University, New York, N. Y. On the same day, USG nominated William C. Fox as consul, Brunswick, to replace John Greenwood, Jr., deceased. On Feb. 14, U.S. Representative George G. Hoskins of N. Y. had written to USG recommending Elbert E. Farman's appointment as consul in Germany, Italy, Switzerland, or France. ALS, DNA, RG 59, Letters of Application and Recommendation. Related papers are *ibid.* On March 27, USG nominated Farman as agent and consul gen., Cairo. See Endorsement, Dec. 3, 1875; Elbert E. Farman, *Along the Nile with General Grant* (New York, 1904).

On Nov. 10, 1872, Erni, Basle, had written to USG. "Permit me in my own behalf, and that of the inhabitants of Basle, who took a warm interest in the late political contest, to congratulate you to your re-election as President of the United States. It will give new impulse to the interests of this manufacturing community." ALS, USG 3.

To Nathaniel Carlin

Washington D. C. June 7th *1874.*

Dear Sir:

As I have not heard from you recently I write to make some enquiries and to make one or two conditional suggestions. First, I would like to know how you have the farm planted this season? the condition of crops, fruit &c. Next, I would ask the condition of the stock, how the mares have been bred, whether they are supposed to

be in foal &c. If you have any two-year-old fillies I think I would breed
them. If Jennie's three-year-old colt (filley) does not promise good
speed I would breed her to Peace Maker, (proper name Claymore.). If
she is likely to be fast I would prefere keeping her as an advertisement
for Hambletonian and for my own use when she is older. Hambleto-
nians sister has a filley colt by Messenger Duroc and will be stinted
to him again. I am anxious to get a horse colt from her to add to
the stock of the farm. She is large and the horse large and the sire of
some of the fastest trotting horses now living. Would it not be well
to put in this fall as much wheat and timothy as you can find ground
suitable to grow timothy upon? There is no use to attempt to raise
grass on poor soil. Has lime been tried on any of the fields? If so with
what success?

Yours Truly
U. S. Grant

N. Carlin, Esqr

ALS, CSmH.

To Domingo F. Sarmiento

Washington, D. C. June 12, 1874,

His Excellency D. F. Sarmiento
President of the Argentine Republic
Dear Sir:

I have the honor to acknowledge the receipt of your kind favor of
January 9th, received through Col. Davidson, and I shall take great
pleasure in complying with your request to communicate through
Mr. Garcia,[1] at Paris, my views upon the subject of the enquiry you
were kind enough to address to me.

I am very glad that you comtemplate employing our engineers upon the works of improvement in progress in your growing
Republic.

I have the honor to be
Your obt. svt.
U. S. Grant.

Copy, DLC-USG, II, 2. A notation dated June 12, 1874, indicates that this letter was "Sent to Col. Hunter Davidson Barnum's Hotel Balto, Md." Hunter Davidson graduated from the U.S. Naval Academy in 1847 and joined the C.S. Navy in 1861. His extensive Civil War service included command of submarine and torpedo operations on the approaches to Richmond. See Hunter Davidson, "Electrical Torpedoes as a System of Defence," *Southern Historical Society Papers*, II, 1 (July, 1876), 1–6; "Davis and Davidson," *ibid.*, XXIV (1896), 284–91; Dunbar Rowland, ed., *Jefferson Davis Constitutionalist: His Letters, Papers and Speeches* (Jackson, Miss., 1923), VII, 107–10, IX, 19–22.

1. Probably Manuel R. Garcia, Argentine minister.

To Senate

To THE SENATE OF THE UNITED STATES:

The Plenipotentiaries of Her Britannic Majesty at Washington have submitted to the Secretary of State for my consideration, a draft of a Treaty for the reciprocal regulation of the Commerce and Trade between the United States and Canada, with provisions for the enlargement of the Canadian Canals and for their use by United States vessels on terms of equality with British vessels. I transmit herewith a Report from the Secretary of State, with a copy of the draft thus proposed.

I am of the opinion that a proper Treaty for such purposes would result beneficially for the United States. It would not only open or enlarge markets for our productions, but it would increase the facilities of transportation from the grain growing States of the West to the seaboard.

The proposed draft has many features to commend it to our favorable consideration: but whether it makes all the concessions which could justly be required of Great Britain, or whether it calls for more consessions from the United States than we should yield, I am not prepared to say.

Among its provisions are articles proposing to dispense with the arbitration respecting the fisheries which was provided for by the Treaty of Washington in the event of the conclusion and ratification of a Treaty, and the passage of all the subsequent necessary legislation to enforce it.

These provisions as well as other considerations make it desirable that this subject should receive attention before the close of the present session. I therefore express an earnest wish that the Senate may be able to consider and determine before the adjournment of Congress, whether it will give its constitutional concurrence to the conclusion of a Treaty with Great Britain for the purposes already named, either in such a form as is proposed by the British Plenipotentiaries, or in such other more acceptable form as the Senate may prefer.

U. S. Grant

Washington, June 18. 1874.

Copies, DNA, RG 130, Messages to Congress; (printed) *ibid.*, RG 84, Netherlands, Correspondence. Another copy of this message, dated June 17, 1874, is *ibid.*, RG 59, Reports to the President and Congress. On June 17, Secretary of State Hamilton Fish wrote to USG transmitting a draft of this treaty. Copy, *ibid.* On June 17 and 18, Fish recorded in his diary exchanges with USG. "I explain to him the general provisions of the Reciprocity Treaty with Canada, as proposed: he requested me to prepare a message to the Senate expressive of general approval of the policy, and asking their advice whether he shall proceed to celebrate the Treaty. The Message to be sent in to-morrow" "I call on the President, & he signs a message (without recommendation) to the Senate transmitting the unsigned draft of the Reciprocity Treaty" DLC-Hamilton Fish. In May and June, Fish spoke frequently with Edward Thornton, British minister, and George Brown, Canadian emissary, concerning treaty details, and on May 29 and June 9, Fish recorded cabinet deliberations in his diary. *Ibid.* On June 18, the Senate referred the matter to the Committee on Foreign Relations and ordered USG's message and accompanying materials printed for confidential use. *Senate Executive Journal*, XIX, 356. On June 22, the Senate postponed consideration of the treaty until the next session of Congress and removed the injunction of secrecy. D, DNA, RG 59, Miscellaneous Letters. On Feb. 3, 1875, the Senate resolved that it was "not expedient to recommend the negotiation of the treaty for reciprocal trade." *Senate Executive Journal*, XIX, p. 502. On Jan. 28, Fish had recorded in his diary a discussion with Thornton predicting this end for the treaty. DLC-Hamilton Fish. The issue of a reciprocal trade treaty with Canada vexed foreign policy during USG's presidency. See *PUSG*, 19, 491–92; *ibid.*, 20, 32; *HRC*, 44-1-9, 44-1-389, part 2; Nevins, *Fish*, pp. 868–69, 919–20.

On May 28, 1874, Archibald Baxter and a secretary, New York City, "acting for the Committee appointed at a Meeting of the New York Produce Exchange, held 27th inst.," wrote to USG transmitting resolutions urging rapid consummation of a reciprocal trade treaty with Canada. LS, DNA, RG 59, Miscellaneous Letters. See *New York Times*, May 28, 1874. Probably in June, "Citizens of Detroit" petitioned USG and Fish on "the very great importance [o]f renewing reciprocal trade with the Dominion [o]f Canada." DS (filed June 9), DNA, RG 59, Miscellaneous Letters. On June 20, representatives of the Book Trade Association of Philadelphia wrote to USG denouncing the proposed reciprocity treaty as "inimical to the best interests of the productive industries of the United States, and to the revenues of the Government." DS, *ibid.* In Jan. [*1875*], Giles B. Stebbins, "of Detroit," Washington, D. C., wrote to USG. "Allow me,—not as an individual citizen, but as charged and authorized to represent 200,000 American workmen and $150,000,000 of capital in 'National Association of Lumbermen,' and also the large interests of the 'National Wool-Growers Association,'—to ask your attention to the sheet herewith enclosed. It is a condensation of fact and argument, not only against the proposed 'Reciprocity Treaty' with Canada, but against *any* such Treaty with *any people.* I would enter an *earnest protest* against any such Treaty—either with the *Sandwich Islands* in the distance, or Canada near at hand, deeming it a *bad and dangerous precedent*—for reasons you will find in the enclosed document." ALS (docketed Jan. 16, 1875), *ibid.* The enclosure, *Facts and Testimonies Against the So-called Reciprocity Treaty with Canada,* is *ibid.*

On Sept. 2, 1874, John C. Hamilton, New York City, wrote to USG, Long Branch. ". . . BLAINE is out warmly against the proposed treaty with Canada; and I learn that the statement is widely circulated that it opens our Atlantic and Pacific COASTING trade; and is not what I suppose it to be—a provision for mutuality as to the Lake navigation. A synopsis of the treaty gives the former view—Morton's you have seen. It would appear, that the administration cannot afford (after the grave mistakes as to indirect damages) to have this treaty rejected & yet it will be rejected.—nor yet I doubt whether it ought to be approved by the Senate. Might not action as to it be DEFERRED, while a confidential unofficial channel might be employed to impress upon the Dominion Gov't (previous to the meeting of Congress) a *conviction;* that, while the Imperial government of Great Britain lasts, *no* reciprocity treaty can be made; and that a severance of that tie, without proposing annexation, would probably ensure its success. It is an evidence of the intense desire for such a treaty, that when Galt came here—*money* was used to *purchase influence* in its favor. I happened to learn this *at the time.* I think it may be correctly remarked; that exceptional treaties are not desireable things.—An act of Congress imposing very light revenue duties on Canadian products might accomplish all that is desireable. True—such act act could be repealed, & this would not *satisfy* the Dominion. I do not wish it to be *satisfied.* I do not believe that it is wise to have the vast productions of the West liable to the incursions or interruptions of an adjacent foreign power—Northern america down to the gulf of Darien ought to be under the exclusive rule and policy of our Government. One of its founders was much of this opinion—A letter of my fathers signed by Washington (the draft in his hand being in the State Department) of Nov 14. '78,' is singularly interesting—and *suggestive* on this subject. Doubtless; CUT the tie with GBritain and Canada &c are ours. In a political history I am just completing of events since 1814 this matter is discussed; and I hope events will enable you, with due regard to *personal* & *national honor,* to be the great instrument of extending the bounds of our Republic. Such a policy well digested would be an assurance of uninterrupted peace to the American people, or of the United States—or of GBritain here, or of Mexico. One flag to wave over all this North America. It can be done, and who more able to do it than the person to whom I most respectfully address my best wishes. . . . P. S. Unless I pass there on my way to Mr Binney I will mail the pamphlet. The enclosed slip is evidently from the same pen in this days Herald—called Long Branch—Is there not a *spy* near Head Quarters?" ALS, USG 3. On Nov. 9 and 13, Hamilton wrote to USG. "Under the kind permission to address you again on the subject of the proposed treaty with Canada I merely write to say, that I am not aware of any new arguments in its favor, but am convinced you will think that it should be got rid of without any debate in either House of Congress. I beg leave to enclose to you a slip shewing the ground of Butlers opposition to it—2d: a copy of a resolution which I obtained from Philadelphia, passed by the Republican State Convention of Penns-a, and 3d: that of the Wool Manufactures Convention held in this City which, in the main, involves the interest of nearly all the Wool growers of the

U States. What truth there is in a statement that our Wool value is greater than that of the whole boasted cotton crop, I do not know; but the census shews these two important facts—*One*, that in the last two decades, while the production of cotton has only increased *one fifth*, that of Wool has *doubled*.—The *other*, that, while the production of cotton is confined essentially to only *nine* States, that of Wool is an important product of *all* the States, with only four or five exceptions. I find there is also dissatisfaction in Canada with this treaty. I beg leave to add, that, on the whole view of this subject, I suppose, whatever may be the merits or demerits of this treaty, these conclusions must be admitted—that a conflict with so many and such great home interests ought not to be risked; and more especially that a discussion of the questions raised in the Pennsylvania Convention, as well as by Speaker Blaine—as to the respective powers of the Senate and of the House with regard to it, *must not take place*, which can only be avoided by a prompt early withdrawal or a quiet rejection of it, of which you are the best judge. I propose in a few days to ask your indulgence, but *once more*, in reading some remarks upon another matter of vital importance, as to neither of which topics would any reply be needed. We expected Ulysses yesterday, and hope, when the season is a little more advanced to have him form some pleasant acquaintances in the circle of our near friends." "In a former note the mode of meeting the embarrassment as to the previous partial recommendation of the proposed treaty with Canada was adverted to. The more reflection which has been given to the subject the stronger is the conviction that the suggestion by the President in his Message as to the withdrawal of all foreign powers from territory contiguous to the United States is very desireable—*1*. on the grounds of a homogeneity of policy were these territories—a part of the United States. *2*—The prevention of territorial collisions almost unavoidable because of the long line of contiguity—and likely to be increased hereafter   *3*. the unreasonableness of the exercise of power by a nation or people of *one* continent over a nation or people of another Continent—*4*—the danger to the peace of the U S thereby being to any unavoidable degree more or less subject to be involved in the controversies which will arise from time to time, and perhaps are not now remote between European powers because of their differing Institutions, or because of their political or religious convictions or biasses, or of their real or supposed conflicting interests—dangers which our early history proves it required the most prudential wisdom to avoid. In the present state of affairs I know of nothing that would more probably extricate the Republican party, whose dominance, in reality involves the continued welfare of this country, than by bold broad views on the part of the President. What appear to be needed are two things—One, to present to the public mind some large object of expectation and of policy to be accomplished; and thus to raise it far above mere temporary or partial subjects of opinion or of feeling. This would be done by the suggestion of the establishment by an enlargement of the Union of one great American System—far above the control of any foreign influence and with power to assert its entire Independence of all other regions of the World. It was the cherished policy of the American Revolution and of the Founders of our National Government. If to this could be superadded a suggestion of such broader provisions of International law as would liberate the Ocean from all possible tyranny or violation of its freed Seas, then and thus, and only then and thus would the general welfare of this Great Republic, as respects other countries, be permanently established and secured. . . ." ALS, *ibid.*

To Mary E. P. Bouligny

———

WASHINGTON, D. C., June 19, 1874.

MRS. BOULIGNY:

To-morrow being so near the adjournment of Congress, and so many bills being presented to me for my action, which are passed during the last two or three days of a session, I find, greatly to my regret, that it will be impossible for me to accompany your excursion to Mount Vernon; and equally so for the members of the Cabinet, as I shall need their attendance to-morrow in the examination of bills.

I sincerely trust that the excursion will be an enjoyable one in every respect.

Very respectfully, yours, U. S. GRANT.

P. S.—When accepting the invitation to accompany the pilgrims to Mount Vernon the reasons for detaining me at home did not occur to my mind.

Washington Chronicle, June 21, 1874. Mary E. P. Bouligny was the widow of John E. Bouligny, U.S. Representative from La. (1859–61), who remained loyal to the Union until his death in 1864. She had organized an excursion to George Washington's grave to promote the Centennial celebration. See *HRC*, 46-3-37; [Mary E. P. Bouligny], *Bubbles and Ballast: Being a Description of Life in Paris during the Brilliant Days of Empire* . . . (Baltimore, 1871).

On June 18, 1874, Thursday, Levi P. Luckey wrote to Secretary of the Navy George M. Robeson. "The President directs me to say that the Marine Band may accompany the excursion to Mount Vernon on Saturday next, if it interferes with nothing more than the regular concert in the Ex. Mansion Grounds on that day." ALS, DNA, RG 45, Letters Received from the President.

To Congress

———

TO THE SENATE AND HOUSE OF REPRESENTATIVES OF THE UNITED STATES—:

I respectfully invite the attention of Congress to one feature of the bill entitled "An Act for the government of the District of Columbia and for other purposes." [1]

Provision is therein made for the payment of the debts of the District in bonds to be issued by the Sinking Fund Commissioners, running fifty years and bearing interest at the rate of 3.65 per cent per annum, with the payment of the principal and interest guaranteed by the United States. The government by which these debts were created is abolished and no other provision seems to be made for their payment. Judging from the transactions in other bonds, there are good grounds, in my opinion, for the apprehension that bonds bearing this rate of interest, when issued, will be worth much less than their equivalent in the current money of the United States. This appears to me to be unjust to those to whom these bonds are to be paid, and, to the extent of the difference between their face and real value, looks like repudiating the debts of the District. My opinion is that to require creditors of the District of Columbia to receive these bonds at par when it is apparent that to be converted into money they must be sold at a large discount, will not only prove greatly injurious to the credit of the District, but, will reflect unfavorably upon the credit and good faith of the United States.

I would recommend, therefore, that provision be made at the present session of Congress to increase the interest upon these bonds, so that when sold they will bring an equivalent in money, and that the Secretary of the Treasury be authorized to negotiate the sale of these bonds at not less than par, and pay the proceeds thereof to those who may be ascertained to have valid claims against the District of Columbia.

U. S. GRANT

Executive Mansion,
June 20, 1874.

Copy, DNA, RG 130, Messages to Congress. *HED*, 43-1-288. On June 20, 1874, U.S. Senator William B. Allison of Iowa, "Committee to Inquire into the Affairs of the District of Columbia," and seven others responded to USG's message. ". . . The idea that there is anything like repudiation in the bill is a mistake. The bill does not compel any holder of District securities to take bonds for them. It merely gives him the option to do so, or to retain them and receive payment thereof when the District may be able to pay. The changes made in regard to the District government do not discharge or impair its contracts or liabilities. The bill, therefore, is not repudiation, nor is it unjust to any holder of the District securities which may be funded under it. As to small creditors, such as laborers and so forth, the bill contemplates their payment in money. . . ." *SRC*, 43-1-473. Allison then spoke. "I will only add to the report that the committee have the best reasons for stating that the President, after being made familiar with all the facts and circumstances, is satisfied with the provision in the bill." *CR*, 43–1, 5273. Federal obligations for D. C. bonds remained a contested question for years. See Endorsement, Sept. 23, 1875; *HRC*, 43-1-627; Alan Lessoff, *The Nation and Its City: Politics, "Corruption," and Progress in Washington, D. C., 1861–1902* (Baltimore, 1994), pp. 107–13.

On July 22, H. M. Sweeny, president, and Moses Kelly, treasurer, Sinking Fund, Washington, D. C., wrote to USG. "The enclosed brief has been placed in our hands having reference to the character of the bonds to be issued under Act of Congress approved June 20. 1874, in payment of certain indebtedness created by the late authorities of the District of Columbia and, in view of the great importance of the questions presented, not only as affecting the interests of creditors but also the credit of the United States whose faith is pledged for the protection of these bonds, we take the liberty of submitting them for your consideration with the request, if it meet your approval, that the opinion of the proper law officer of the Government may be furnished us thereon." LS, DNA, RG 60, Letters from the President. The enclosure is *ibid.* On Aug. 11, Attorney Gen. George H. Williams wrote to USG. "I enclose my opinion upon the question submitted to you by the Sinking Fund Commissioners of this District. Since learning of the purport of the decision, the attorney representing those at whose instance the question was submitted to you, has desired me not to furnish to the Sinking Fund Commissioners a copy of my opinion, and he seems to think that a compliance with his request would be satisfactory to you. I shall feel bound by the directions endorsed by you upon the letter of the Sinking Fund Commissioners, to furnish them a copy of this opinion, unless otherwise instructed. Please advise me as to your wishes upon the subject." LS, *ibid.* On Aug. 12, Orville E. Babcock endorsed this letter. "Give copy to the Sinking fund Commers if copy has not been furnsh by Atty Gn" AES, *ibid.* On Aug. 11, Williams reported to USG that the Sinking Fund commissioners did not have the power or obligation to make bonds payable in coin: ". . . In my opinion their duty as to the preparation of the bonds will be discharged in entire conformity with the requirements of the law, by making them payable in *dollars* simply, without introducing any qualification therein respecting the *kind of money* in which they are to be paid. . . ." LS, *ibid. Official Opinions of the Attorneys-General*, XIV, 445–48. See *HED*, 43-2-1, part 6, pp. 118–23.

On March 29, 1875, Williams wrote to USG answering questions concerning the redemption and destruction of D. C. bonds. Copy, DNA, RG 60, Opinions. *Official Opinions of the Attorneys-General*, XIV, 554–57.

1. On June 20, 1874, USG signed this bill abolishing the D. C. territorial government, under attack for financial mismanagement, and establishing an appointed commission of three to govern on an interim basis. See *PUSG*, 21, 193–200; *U.S. Statutes at Large*, XVIII, part 3, 116–21; *SRC*, 43-1-453; *HRC*, 44-1-702; Lessoff, *Nation and Its City*, pp. 97–105.

On June 23, USG nominated Alexander R. Shepherd, William Dennison, and Henry T. Blow as D. C. commissioners. On the same day, the Senate rejected Shepherd, a controversial nomination, prompting USG to nominate Alexander G. Cattell; Cattell declined the nomination. On July 3, Babcock telegraphed to Secretary of the Interior Columbus Delano. "Will you please send Commission for John H ~~Ketcham~~ Ketcham as Commissioner for the Dist at once." ALS (telegram sent), DNA, RG 107, Telegrams Collected (Bound). On June 24, Dennison, Columbus, Ohio, had telegraphed to USG. "I accept district Commissionership with which you have honored me and will leave for Washington in a day or two," Telegram received, DLC-USG, IB. On June 26, Blow, St. Louis, telegraphed to USG. "Have just returned from the country and desire to accept the honor if my business engagement will permit, Cannot procure a copy of the act, how much of my time should be spent in Washington, in next six months in discharge of my duties of Commissioner, Please answer," Telegram received, *ibid.* In 1874, Blow wrote to USG resigning as commissioner. William Evarts Benjamin, Catalogue No. 27, Nov., 1889, p. 5. On Jan. 5, 1875, USG nominated S. Ledyard Phelps to replace Blow.

On June 10, 1874, J. Hazel Dean, Washington, D. C., had written to USG. "By the Bill, on District Affairs, presented to the Senate and House, I see three Commissioners are to be appointed by your Excellency. I am sure your excellency will select good men, but may I suggest that men above these local mongrel politics are what we want. We need such men as J. G. Berrett, formerly Mayor, here, who everybody believes would reflect credit on the Government and city. We don't want any dead men like Doctor Blake around either. Appoint live men. However, we all are satisfied your excellency will make the best selection to suit the largest portion of the people—" ALS, DNA, RG 48, Appointment Div., Letters Received. On June 23, U.S. Representative Richard C. Parsons of Ohio wrote to USG. "I leave the City tomorrow a. m. & Cannot do myself the honor of calling upon you. But in the interest of the Administration, & of the Country, I desire to make a suggestion— Should Gov *Dennison* decline the appt of *Commissioner*, I wish to advise you to appt Amasa Stone Jr Esq of Cleveland—. . ." ALS, *ibid.* On June 24, U.S. Representative John Coburn of Ind. wrote to USG. "I have the honor to recommend in case of a vacancy in the office of Commissioner of the District of Columbia the Hon Charles A Ray of this city late of the Supreme Court of Indiana for the place, . . ." ALS, *ibid.* On June 29, U.S. Representative Charles B. Farwell of Ill., Chicago, wrote to USG. "I see by the papers that the gentlemen whom you have named as commissioners to close up the affairs of the late District govern- ment do not accept, and I take the liberty of suggesting the name of Hon. A. H. Burley of this city as one who is eminently qualified for one of these places. He is the same gentleman whom Gen. Logan & myself recommended for Asst. Treasurer at this point about a year since   Should you appoint Dr Burley. I can assure you he will fill the position to your en- tire satisfaction" ALS, ICHi. On July 2, U.S. Representative Amos Clark, Jr., of N. J., Eliza- beth, telegraphed to USG. "If Commissioner for District of Columbia not appointed yet, I respectfully suggest name of Jno. H. L. Stratton, Ex member of Congress from Mount Holly, New Jersey, A man of irreproachable character, and sound judgment." Telegram re- ceived, DLC-USG, IB.

On July 3, Levi P. Luckey wrote to Elihu B. Washburne, Paris. ". . . The Commission for the District is completed this morning by the appointment of Gen. Ketchum, of N. Y., who, with Gov. Denison & Henry T. Blow, of Mo, will have Control of the District until Congress gives us some other form of Government. You would not know Washington now. It will soon be the Paris of America. The President & Mrs Grant are now alone, as the boys are all away. I think they feel very lonely. I was greatly disappointed that you did not come home & take the Treasury, though I do not doubt the decision being for the best. Yet, it would have been very nice to have you here for the next three years, and your counsels of great benefit. Mr Bristow is starting in on a good work in the department & will purify it. It certainly needed it badly. . . ." ALS, DLC-Elihu B. Washburne.

On July 11, John B. Motley, Washington, D. C., wrote to USG. "In the year 1871 I was commissioned by the late Governor, Henry D Cooke, a Notary Public for this District. The commission expires on the 18th inst, and as I am desirous of renewing it, I beg that you will request your Attorney General to state, whether or not in his opinion, the Commis- sioners of the District of Columbia have power to appoint Notaries Public in and for said District." ALS, DNA, RG 60, Letters from the President. On July 17, Samuel F. Phillips, solicitor gen. and act. attorney gen., wrote to USG. ". . . The conclusion is obvious, that the Commissioners of the District of Columbia have full power to appoint Notaries Public in and for said District." Copy, *ibid.*, Opinions.

To William W. Smith

Washington D. C. June 20th *1874.*

DEAR SMITH;

On the adjournm[e]nt of Congress—Tuesday or Wednesday next [1]—Mrs. Grant and I start on a little trip to the Kanahwa.[2] During our absence our household will be moved to Long Branch, so that we will be here only a day or two on our return. If you will drop a line to Babcock saying where you will have the Alderneys shipped to —Whether to Wheeling or Pittsburgh—I will direct that they shall be so shipped. They are thoroughbreds, and with one of them there is a heiffer calf about three weeks old.

Kindest regards to Emsy and the children. We have heard from Nellie several times since her arrival in England. She is very well and had a pleasant trip.[3]

Yours Truly

U. S. GRANT

ALS, Washington County Historical Society, Washington, Pa.

1. Congress adjourned on Tuesday, June 23, 1874. On this day, Levi P. Luckey telegraphed to cabinet officers, excepting Secretary of War William W. Belknap and Secretary of the Navy George M. Robeson. "The President will go to his room at the Senate at 12. Oclock today" Telegram sent, DNA, RG 107, Telegrams Collected (Bound).
2. See letter to William S. Hillyer, July 1, 1874.
3. See letter to Otis H. Tiffany, May 14, 1874.

To John A. J. Creswell

Washington, D, C, June 24, 1874,

MY DEAR SIR:

As I expressed to you verbally this morning, when you tendered your resignation of the office of Postmaster General, it is with the deepest regret to me that you should have felt such a course necessary.

You are the last of the original members of the Cabinet named by me as I was entering upon my present duties still in it, and it makes me feel as if old associations were being broken up that I had hoped might be continued through my official life.

In separating officially I have but two hopes to express: First, that I may get a successor who will be as faithful and efficient in the performance of the duties of the office you resign: Second: a personal friend that I can have the same attachment for.

Your record has been satisfactory to me, and I know it will so prove to the country at large.

Yours very truly
U. S. GRANT.

HON. J. A. J. CRESWELL P. M. GENL.

Copies, DLC-USG, II, 2; Dickinson College, Carlisle, Pa. On June 24, 1874, Postmaster Gen. John A. J. Creswell wrote to USG. "After more than five years of continuous service, I am constrained by a proper regard for my private interests to resign the office of Postmaster General, and to request that I may be relieved from duty as soon as it may be convenient for you to designate my successor. For the generous confidence and support, which you have uniformly extended to me in my efforts to discharge my duty, I shall not attempt to express the full measure of my gratitude. It is sufficient to say, that my relations, official and personal, with yourself, and with every one of my colleagues of the cabinet, have always been of the most agreeable and satisfactory character to me. Rest assured, that I shall continue to give to your administration my most cordial support, and that I shall ever deem it an honor to be permitted to subscribe myself . . ." ALS, USG 3.

On the same day, Secretary of State Hamilton Fish recorded in his diary. "The President states that he has called the meeting to lay before the Cabinet the resignation of Mr. Creswell; Post Master Genl. The President wishes to take a man from the South and thought of Settle. Phillips' (Solicitor General) name proposed; received with favour, but it was doubted whether he would accept the office. The President then said unless he could think of of any other man from the South he might be willing to go to New England. I suggested to the President the name of Eugene Hale, which he approved and proposed it to the Cabinet; each one of whom cordially endorsed it. Robeson offered to find him and ascertain if he would accept—found that he had left for Harrisburg an hour or two since. He telegraphed him at different points on the road. In the contingency that he should not accept the name of Lott Morrill was suggested and I suggested to the President, Schofield and McVeagh of Pennsylvania. He says he wishes to give Schofield a life appointment—but inclines to Mac Veagh." DLC-Hamilton Fish. On June 26, U.S. Representative Eugene Hale of Maine, Washington, D. C., telegraphed to USG. "I arrived late last night, regretted not seeing you this morning   I am hardly in condition to undertake the P O Dep't July first and have hoped that Mr Creswell would hold for a month or two if agreeable to you—Will telegraph decisively tomorrow" Telegram received, DLC-USG, IB. On June 27, Hale, Altoona, Pa., telegraphed to USG. "I accept the place of Post Master General and will be in Washington to qualify on the first day of July." Telegrams received (2—at 3:45 P.M.), ibid. On July 1, Fish recorded in his diary. "The President having returned from West Virginia calls a Cabinet meeting at 10½ o-clock . . . Hale decline the Post Master Generalship on the ground of ill health and necessity for relaxation. The question of a successor arising the President first spoke of Senator Morrill of Maine; then named Judge Settle and Mr. Blow; it being conceded that Morrill would not accept the Attorney Gen'l. named Solicitor General Phillips. I wrote the names of G. W. Schofield and John Scott on a card and handed them to the Secy. of the Treasury, who subsequently handed them to the President; each of the Cabinet present expressed approval of Schofield's name. President reserving final decision, says he thinks he will offer it to him during the day." DLC-Hamilton Fish. See Creswell to U.S. Senator Zachariah Chandler of Mich., July 2, 1874, ALS, DLC-Zachariah Chandler. On July 2, James F. Casey, collector of customs, New Orleans, and nine others telegraphed to USG. "The south needs a representation in your Cabinet   we recommend L. A. Sheldon for postmaster Genl" Telegram received (at 10:33 P.M.), DLC-USG, IB. See letter to Hamilton Fish, July 2, 1874; Proclamation, July 22, 1874; *New York Times*, June 26–27, July 2, 1874.

To *William S. Hillyer*

———

Washington D. C. July 1st *1874*

DEAR GEN.L;

Enclosed I send what you ask for in your note of this date. I deeply sympatize with you and Mrs. Hillyer in your great affliction. I just returned last evening from a little trip to the Kanawha Valley [1] and am therefore very busy. I will endeavor nevertheless to get down to see you before leaving the city.

Very Truly Yours

U. S. GRANT

GN. W. S. HILLYER

ALS, Hillyer Papers, ViU. William S. Hillyer, who had recently lost an infant daughter, died July 12, 1874, in Washington, D. C. See *Washington National Republican*, July 13, 14, 1874.

On May 17, 1873, Hillyer, New York City, had written to Gen. William T. Sherman. "Some weeks since Gen Grant wrote a letter to Mayor Havemeyer in which he was kind enough to suggest me as a proper person to fill one of the Commissionerships under the new charter. Upon presenting the letter the Mayor suggested a Commissionership of Police. A number of our leading citizens endorsed me—Such men as William Orton Wm A Darling & Lt Gov Robinson   Upon hearing of the Mayors suggestion Gen Grant wrote a second letter endorsing my fitness for that position having had the experience of the Provost Marshal General on his staff. . . ." ALS, DLC-William T. Sherman. On Oct. 31, U.S. Senator George E. Spencer of Ala. wrote to Hillyer. "I had a long talk with the President this morning   He spoke most affectionately & kindly about you,   I told him words would not not keep the 'wolf from your door'—Havemyer did write the most abusive letters about Bliss and the President thinks his course towards you was for the purpose of snubbing him, I have not seen Casey though he is here I called twice to see him. The President would I am satisfied appoint you today if there is a vacancy. If Dutcher is elected he will I think appoint you to the Darling's place. You had better come here & tell the President how bad you are off & how much in need of a place you are. I told him & I know it made an impression upon him. He had your letter before him while I was talking I have to leave Monday morning for Alabama. I have a mean fight on my hands & must be there or will suffer by it—Grant is your friend. If you will urge your own case you can do more than any one else. Keep a stiff upper lip and do not get discouraged" ALS, Hillyer Papers, ViU. On Feb. 13, 1874, USG nominated Hillyer as appraiser of merchandise, New York City; on March 9, USG withdrew the nomination.

On April 25, Orville E. Babcock wrote to Adam Badeau, consul gen., London. "... Hillyers name was withdrawn and will not go in again—You know just as well as I do why such things are done for him. He is known perfectly. I spoke to the President about the papers, he thinks Hillyer has none of any importance. I would not ask him for them for if he give he would expect too much in way of return. He is a poor drunken shyster—I think. . . ." ALS, MH.

1. On May 28, Levi P. Luckey wrote to Williams C. Wickham, vice president, Chesapeake and Ohio Railroad, Richmond. "The President directs me to acknowledge the receipt of your letter of the 21st inst., and convey to you his sincere thanks for the pass over your road which you were kind enough to enclose. He desires me to say that he hopes to avail himself of it as soon as Congress adjourns, as he and Mrs. Grant propose about the last week in June to visit the Springs, leaving here in the morning and remaining there over night; and if the hotels are open at that time, as I presume they will be, they will remain there two nights and a day. They will then go on to Charleston, returning home again over the same route." Copy, DLC-USG, II, 2. See *PUSG*, 16, 493.

On June 25, USG and Julia Dent Grant left Washington, D. C., for six days in West Va., beginning at White Sulphur Springs. On June 27, USG spoke to a crowd at Charleston. "It affords me pleasure to visit my friends at Charleston. About thirty years ago—but that makes me older than I thought—when I was a cadet at West Point, I promised my aunt, Mrs. Tompkins, and the other relatives referred to by Colonel Smith, residing in this valley, to visit them, and not until now have I been permitted to make good the promise. I am sorry that I cannot remain with you longer than two days." *Washington Evening Star*, June 29, 1874.

On July 2 and 3, Wickham telegraphed to USG. "Have forwarded your dispatch to H D Whitcomb he will answer. His address after today is Richmond" "I have heard from H. D. Whitcomb that he will accept the position you name" Telegrams received (the second at 11:35 A.M.), DLC-USG, IB. On July 2, USG appointed Henry D. Whitcomb to a board of engineers created to survey the mouth of the Mississippi River. See Proclamation, July 3, 1874; Angus James Johnston, II, *Virginia Railroads in the Civil War* (Chapel Hill, 1961), p. 18.

On Sept. 1, Wickham wrote to USG. "The government is I doubt not interested in having Gilbert C Walker defeated for Congress in this district—I think then it should exert some influence upon the selection of a candidate—Of the persons spoken of for nomination I am satisfied that only Mr John Ambler Smith can make a successful run The others if nominated can not avail themselves of the dissatisfaction in the Conservative ranks with Walker Under these circumstances it strikes me as proper that the Government should take steps to prevent any one holding office under it from going before the people in a manner which will lose us this district" ALS, NHi.

To Hamilton Fish

Washington D. C. July 2d *1874,*

DEAR GOVERNOR:

On thinking over the question of a successor to the Postmaster Gen.l. the name of Marshal Jewell occurs to me as about the most fitting, and if he would accept it, there would be no more pleasant associate to introduce into the Cabinet. Please telegraph him to know if he will accept the position, and if so to notify you by telegraph and start for Washington the earlyest day practicable. The office will be in charge of the First. Asst. P. M. Gn.[1] until he qualifies.

Very Truly Yours,

U. S. GRANT

HON. HAMILTON FISH, SEC. OF STATE.

ALS, DLC-Hamilton Fish. See letter to John A. J. Creswell, June 24, 1874. On July 2, 1874, Secretary of State Hamilton Fish twice wrote to USG. "I send herewith a package received to-day from Hamburg which I presume to be the one ~~one~~ spoken of ~~which~~ by Govr. Jewell ~~wrote some~~ f" Copy, DLC-Hamilton Fish. "I have sent the telegram to Gov. Jewell as requested." ALS, Babcock Papers, ICN. On July 3, Marshall Jewell, U.S. minister, St. Petersburg, wrote to USG. ". . . I am unable to express to you my thanks for this renewed manifestation of your confidence and accept with great pleasure, not because this position which I hold by your favor is not agreeable . . . but a position in your cabinet is preferable to any other . . ." William J. Novick, *Heirlooms of History*, III, no. 47. On July 29, Jewell, London, telegraphed to USG, Long Branch. "Shall postpone sailing till saturday eighth to Look into postal matters and call on your daughter unless you telegh haste" Telegram received, DLC-USG, IB. On Aug. 24, Fish wrote to USG. "In the absence of the usual request from the Post Office Department, I take the liberty to send herewith, for your signature, the Commission of Governor Jewell as Postmaster General, who it is understood will be here tomorrow. . . . P. S. The date of the Commission is left blank subject to your decision." Copy, DNA, RG 59, Reports to the President and Congress. On Dec. 7, USG nominated Jewell as postmaster gen., a position he had assumed on Sept. 1.

On Oct. 21, the Union League of America, William A. Newell, chairman, met at Baltimore and adopted a resolution praising USG for adding Jewell and Secretary of the Treasury Benjamin H. Bristow to the cabinet. DS, USG 3. Other resolutions praised Jewell and Bristow for "inaugurating a new and healthier order of things in their Departments and in their efforts to rid the Service of corrupt and inefficient Officers;" urged the administration "to weed out *all corrupt* and *inefficient* Officers wherever found, as the most important Step towards regaining the impaired confidence of the people;" and declared that "the Surest means of Strengthening the Republican Party and overcoming the influence of the White Leagues of the South is by reorganizing the Union Leagues in that locality, and that a proper recognition of our order at this time would be fraught with good results." *Ibid.*

1. On July 3, Orville E. Babcock had telegraphed to James W. Marshall, 1st asst. postmaster gen. "The President will be pleased to see you at the Executive Mansion this morn-

ing" ALS (telegram sent), DNA, RG 107, Telegrams Collected (Bound). On Aug. 20, Marshall wrote to USG. "I learn from the papers this morning that Mr Jewell has arrived in this country. Agreeably therefore to the understanding between us when you requested me to accept temporarily the position of Postmaster General, I hereby tender my resignation of that office to take effect whenever Mr. Jewell is ready to enter upon the discharge of the duties thereof. Permit me also in this connection to thank you most sincerely for the confidence reposed in me and for your uniform courtesy and kindness to me." ALS, Georgetown University, Washington, D. C.

On July 2, William R. Holloway, postmaster, Indianapolis, had telegraphed to Babcock recommending U.S. Representative James N. Tyner of Ind. as 1st asst. postmaster gen. Telegram received, DLC-USG, IB. On Feb. 26, 1875, USG nominated Tyner as 2nd asst. postmaster gen.

Proclamation

To all who shall see these Presents, Greeting:

Know Ye, That reposing special trust and confidence in the Integrity and Ability of Henry Mitchell, of the United States coast survey, I do appoint him to be a Member of the "Board of Engineers under the provisions of Section 3 of the Act approved June 23, 1874, for the purpose of making 'a survey of the mouth of the Mississippi River with a view to determine the best method of obtaining and maintaining a depth of water sufficient for the purposes of commerce, either by a canal from said river to the waters of the gulf, or by deepening one or more of the natural outlets of said river,'" and do authorize and empower him to execute and fulfil the duties of that office according to Law, and to have and to hold the said office, with all the powers, privileges and emoluments thereunto of right appertaining, unto him the said Henry Mitchell, subject to the conditions prescribed by law.

In Testimony whereof, I have caused these Letters to be made patent and the seal of the United States to be hereunto affixed.

Given under my hand, at the City of Washington, the Third day of July, in the year of our Lord, one thousand eight hundred and seventy-four, and of the Independence of the United States of America, the Ninety-eighth.

U. S. Grant.

Copy, DNA, RG 59, General Records. See *HED*, 43-2-114. Similar commissions were prepared for Theophilus E. Sickels, W. Milnor Roberts, and Henry D. Whitcomb (see letter to

William S. Hillyer, July 1, 1874). Born in 1830 in Nantucket, Mass., Henry Mitchell joined the U.S. Coast Survey in 1849, specializing in hydrography. On July 2, 1874, Secretary of the Treasury Benjamin H. Bristow wrote to USG recommending Mitchell. Copy, DNA, RG 56, Letters Sent.

On June 22, USG had signed legislation creating a board of commissioners to study levees and other means of flood prevention on the Mississippi River. See *HED*, 43-2-127; *PUSG*, 24, 227–29; telegram to William P. Kellogg, April 17, 1874. On June 24, Levi P. Luckey wrote to Secretary of War William W. Belknap. "The President directs me to say that he will be pleased to have you appoint Paul O. Hebért, of La., and Jackson E. Sickles, of Ark, as the two civilians on the Levee Commission" ALS, DNA, RG 94, Letters Received, 2661 1874. Probably on July 3, USG wrote. "Direct Sec. of War to send to the Sec. of State the names of Civil Commissioners appointed on Levees and opening the mouth of the Miss, together with their titles so that Commissions may be made out and signed before I leave the City." AN (undated), *ibid.*, RG 77, Letters Received.

On June 16, U.S. Senators Stephen W. Dorsey and Powell Clayton of Ark. had written to USG. "We beg to recommend to you Jackson E Sickels C. E. for appointment as one of the Citizen Engineers authorized to be appointed by you in conjunction with three officers of the Engineer Corps of the Army to enquire into and report upon some plan for Leveeing the Mississippi river. Mr Sickels is an Engineer of large experience and first class ability, and has had considerable practicable experience in leveeing the Mississippi which will be useful to the Board—." LS, *ibid.*

On June 17, James B. Eads, Washington, D. C., wrote to USG. "Mr. G. W. R. Bayley, civil engineer, of New Orleans, desires his name submitted for consideration in the selection of the Commission of Engineers to be appointed by Your Excellency, to investigate and report upon a permanent plan for the reclamation of the alluvial lands of the Mississippi. . . ." ALS, *ibid.* On June 18, U.S. Representative Stephen A. Hurlbut of Ill. wrote to USG. ". . . While in command of the Dept of the Gulf, Mr Bayley was Engineer in charge of Levèes &c under my orders. I know him well & certify him to be amply qualified, . . ." ALS, *ibid.* U.S. Representative Benjamin F. Butler of Mass. and fourteen others favorably endorsed this letter. AES, *ibid.*

On June 22, U.S. Senator James L. Alcorn of Miss. wrote to USG. "The organization of Commission of Engineers under the act of the present session of Congress, to examine and report on the subject of the Levees of the Mississippi is one of deep concern to the whole people of the delta; and I might say of the country—With every confidence in your good judgement I venture nevertheless to Suggest the name of a gentleman eminently qualified for the place. Minor Merriwether of Memphis Tennessee, is a gentleman of the most sterling integrity—the most unquestionable qualification—unmistakably incorruptible—with the largest measure of indefatigable industry—I was closely associated with Mr Merriwether for three years on the public levees of the Mississippi;   Our board paid him a salary of 5000$—regarded as extravagant at the time—but paid most cheerfully, his work having been approved by the country—I have known him as Chief Engineer on Several Rail Roads and everywhere he has been shown the man I describe. Modest and unpretending he has made no application for the appointment—I make it for him, and endorse him as equal to the task—he will reflect credit on the government and will win your confidence for capacity Skill and honesty should he be appointed—If need be I can procure any number of names in support of this recommendation—" ALS, PHi.

On June 23, Governor William P. Kellogg of La. and Stephen B. Packard, U.S. marshal, La., Washington, D. C., wrote to USG. "We respectfully recommend the appointment of Gen James Longstreet and Col David S. Walton as suitable and desirable persons to be appointed on the Commission to investigate the method of improving the mouth of the Mississippi River" LS, ICHi.

Also on June 23, T. Haskins Du Puy, New York City, wrote to USG. "I am a Civil Engineer of 31 years valuable experience in all the branches of my profession, and hereby make respectful application for appointment by you to some one of the several positions in your gift—The Mississippi River Examination, or a Commissionership of the D. C. would be specially acceptable—Refering you to A. J. Drexel Esq of Phila—G. W. Childs Esq of Phila—and John Hoey Esq of N. Y. who have all known me many years" ALS, DNA, RG 77, Letters Received.

On July 1, Henry W. De Puy, Washington, D. C., wrote to USG. "I have the honor to apply for appointment as one of the three engineers from civil life, to act in conjunction with three from the war department and one from the coast survey, to examine the mouth of the Mississippi and report upon a plan for rendering it navigable by ships of large tonnage. . . ." ALS, *ibid.*

On July 6, William B. Franklin, Hartford, wrote to USG. "A nephew of our Classmate W. F. Raynolds, who appears to be connected with the 'Daily Commercial' of Toledo has written me to asking you to have his Uncle put on the Board for examination of the Mississippi River with reference to the protection of the alluvial lands from overflow &c I hardly know whether Raynolds himself wants the position, but I think he would make a good member of such a Board. Anything that he will take hold of, and at which he would work hard, he is apt to do well. I think the Nephew has a notion that the place is a very soft one, and would therefore suit the declining years of his Uncle. I judge from the law that he is much mistaken in his surmise. With kind regards to Mrs Grant . . ." ALS, *ibid.*

On July 9, U.S. Representative Frank Morey of La., New Orleans, wrote to USG. "I have the honor to respectfully request the appointment of *Henry A. Peeler* a young Engineer of good reputation and ability (and who is a good Republican) as Secretary of the Engineer Commission to examine and report upon the Levees of the Miss. River—" ALS, *ibid.* On July 20, Belknap wrote to Maj. Gouverneur K. Warren, president, board of levee commissioners, Newport, R. I. "On the 2nd July, the President sent me the enclosed card, supposing he had the selection of Secretary for your Board. I have informed him that he was mistaken and also notified Mrs. Barnes, who was interested in the appointment of her brother. I deem it my duty to enclose this card to you, as it may give you an intimation of the Presidents suggestion in the matter. I do this however, without his knowledge, and with the statement that it is not to be considered as an order: it is simply a suggestion for the consideration of the Board." Copy, *ibid.*, RG 107, Letters Sent, Military Affairs. On July 30, Warren wrote to Brig. Gen. Andrew A. Humphreys, chief of engineers. ". . . After a great deal of consideration of numerous applications, the Comn on July 23d appointed Mr: Chas. B. Fauntelroy of La. to be Secretary . . ." LS, *ibid.*, RG 77, Letters Received.

On July 11, U.S. Representative J. Hale Sypher and four others, New Orleans, wrote to USG. "We learn that an application is being made by the New Orleans Chamber of Commerce, to your Excellency, to substitute the name of Prof C. G. Forshey for that of Mr J. E. Sickles, on the Board of Engineers ordered to report a 'plan and system for reclaimation of the Mississippi Delta', on the ground that Mr Sickles is also on the board for the survey of the mouth of the Mississippi River. . . ." LS, *ibid.*, RG 56, Asst. Treasurers and Mint Officials, Letters Received. On July 30, Henry T. Crosby, chief clerk, War Dept., wrote to Caleb G. Forshey, New Orleans, to explain that Jackson E. Sickles and Theophilus E. Sickels were not the same person. LS (press), *ibid.*, RG 77, Letters Received.

To Adolph E. Borie

———

Long Branch, N. J.
July 6th /74

MY DEAR MR. BORIE:

We are now established at Long Branch and would like to have a visit from you and Mrs. Borie for as long a time as you can stay with us. Next week Mrs. Grant & I go to Saratoga[1] to spend a few days, but this need not effect your coming at this time. The house and servants will all remain, and will be at your service 'till we get back if you will come now. The Childs'—next door—will keep you company.

I do hope you will come early for I believe the change will do you good. Mrs. Grant joins me in love to Mrs. Borie and yourself.

Yours Truly
U. S. GRANT

ALS, PHi. See letter to Adolph E. Borie, Aug. 2, 1874.

1. On June 22, 1874, Hathorn & Southgate, Washington, D. C., wrote to USG. "It would afford us much pleasure to have the honor of entertaining yourself and family at Congress Hall Saratoga Springs, at any time, or length of time, agreeable to your Exellency the present season, not forgetting the coming College Regatta July 17th Hoping should you honor us to make your visit agreeable . . ." L, USG 3. See *Washington Evening Star*, July 14, 15, 1874.

On July 11, Orville E. Babcock, Long Branch, wrote to George Crompton, Worcester, Mass. "I am in receipt of your letter of the 10th. I have submitted it to the President, who says he regrets to have to report his inability to be at Worcester on the 15th. He finds that he will not be able to leave New York before Tuesday morning (or perhaps Monday night), and that he does not see how he can be at Worcester and keep his engagements of long standing. . . ." *Dedication of the Soldiers' Monument at Worcester, Massachusetts, . . .* (Worcester, 1875), p. 86. Charles Devens also sent USG an invitation to this dedication. William Evarts Benjamin, Catalogue No. 42, March, 1892, p. 8.

To Hamilton Fish

———

Long Branch, N. J.
July 7th 1874

MY DEAR GOVERNOR:

I understand that Gen. M. C. Meigs, Qr. Mr. General, is a candidate for diplomatic honors now that he is elegibl for retirement. He is a highly educated man and I think would be well qualified for such service. You may therefore if you please tender him the mission to Russia. I know the Sec. of War is anxious that he should be relieved from his present duties for which his early education never fitted him. Graduating in the Engineer Corps he has never served with troops and knows therefore nothing of their wants.

On Monday next, Mrs. Grant and I start for Saratoga where we will spend the week. To-morrow we go to the city to allow her to do a little shopping before starting on the trip. Will probably remain in the city until Thursday afternoon.

Please present Mrs. Grants and my kindest regards to Mrs Fish and family.

Yours Truly

U. S. Grant

Hon. Hamilton Fish
Sec. of State

ALS, DLC-Hamilton Fish. On July 13, 1874, Secretary of State Hamilton Fish wrote to USG, Saratoga Springs. "I did not receive your letter in time to be sure that an answer could reach you at Long-Branch   If you have decided to offer the Russian Mission to Genl Meigs, I have nothing to say—but will, on my return to Washington, within the next three or four days, make the tender, as you desire. But, assuming from the tone of your letter that you have not definitively made up your mind, I trust that a frank & candid expression of opinion on my part will not be deemed obtrusive—I think there can be no question but that the acceptance of a diplomatic position, by an officer of the Army—whether on the Active or on the Retired list, risks a resignation   I enclose a copy of Sections 1222–1223 of the 'Revised Statutes'—the former applying only to Officers on the *Active* list—the latter to *all* Officers of the Army—To have the position declined would not be adviseable. With the highest estimate of Genl Meigs character, ability, and attainments, I think that if the special education he has received, and the experience of so many years in the Quarter Masters Department have not fitted him for the duties of his present office, it is not to be expected, at his time of life that he will be able to fit himself, for the very delicate and important duties of a diplomatic position near one of the first Powers of the World—duties, requiring great practical adaptability, as well as previous study, and experience in public law, & familiarity with international politics and policy—Mr D'Israeli has lately stated in Parliament that an International Crisis was nearer at hand than is generally supposed—Russia and the Eastern question will figure in such Crisis—Pardon me, my dear General, should I seem a little sensitive in respect to having one who is held to be unfit to discharge the duties of a Bureau in the War Department, as competent to the most important Diplomatic duties under the Department of State—This however is only, half serious—But there is an objection, to which I allude with some hesitancy, but under a firm impression of its real seriousness—The interests of the Country & the continued ascendancy of the Republican party, in my judgment, are identical—& we cannot shut our eyes to the fact that the hold of the latter upon public sentiment and sympathy is not as strong as it was—There is a deep and a growing restlessness and jealousy of Military influence, & ascendancy, and this jealousy is being fostered and worked upon by the Democratic press, and will be turned to the disadvantage of the Republican party in every possible way. Genl Meigs appointment to a Diplomatic Mission will not be recognized as a concession to any peculiar eminence, or to any prominence as a Statesman, a Politician, or a Diplomatist, in neither of which capacities is he known—it will be very far from satisfying the Politicians of the Republican party, and will be attributed, erroneously no doubt, but none the less certainly, to some other consideration. These objections are so strong to my mind that I feel it a duty to suggest them. If however, in view of what appear to me very strong reasons for not making the appointment, you still desire the tender of the position to be made, I will make it on my return to Washington whither I expect to go within a few days—so soon as I can arrange some matters of business here. Mrs Fish unites with me in kindest regards to Mrs Grant & yourself." ALS (press), *ibid.* On July 3, Fish had recorded in his diary. "Gen'l. Babcock is anxious to have General Meigs appointed to some diplomatic position in order to make a vacancy in the Quartermaster Generalship for Rufus Ingalls." *Ibid.*

On July 11, Orville E. Babcock, Long Branch, wrote to Fish, Garrison, N. Y. "The President directs me to send you the enclosed memorandum, relative to officer on the *Active list* holding civil appointments. Gen Meigs can retire at his own request, having served *thirty years.* The act I referred to when I spoke to you, is the one quoted in mine, and you will see that it was approved July 15th 1870. Badeau, left in 69, Sickles also (I think). All well at the Presidents. He goes to Saratoga Monday, by the night boat to Albany   Please remember Mrs Babcock and me to Mrs Fish, and other friends" ALS, *ibid.* On July 13, Fish wrote to Babcock, Saratoga Springs. "I have this morning your note of 11th with extract from Act July 1870. There is another section which I think is conclusive, as to retired Officers. I enclose a copy of both Sections 1222-& 1223 as embodied in the Revised Statutes— the limitations in the former Section (a re-enactment of the Act of 1870) to Officers on the Active list makes the latter section more significant—" ALS (press), *ibid.*

On July 18, Secretary of War William W. Belknap wrote to Babcock, Long Branch, concerning personnel changes in the q. m. dept. ". . . I have no feeling about it whatever, excepting a desire to carry out the Presidents wishes, at the same time feeling that as far as Genl Van Vliet is concerned he has been treated with every kindness and consideration. He speaks so strongly and positively about remaining at Leavenworth, that perhaps it would be as well to let him stay there. Please obtain the President's wishes upon the subject, reading this letter and these telegrams to him, when he has time to hear them, and return them to me. I expect to leave here on Friday evening." Copy, DNA, RG 107, Letters Sent, Military Affairs. On July 20, Monday, Belknap telegraphed to Babcock. "The following telegram just recd from General Van Vliet.   as it will now be disagreeable to meigs at Least for me to be in his office I repeat my earnest Request to have my orders repealed and I remain here   it will settle the matter at once and to the satisfaction of all. Wrote you on this subject on Saturday. I presume that under the circumstances the course suggested by Van Vliet is the best   please telegraph me presidents wishes in the matter" Telegram received, DLC-USG, IB.

On Aug. 21, Babcock wrote to Belknap. ". . . now let us pray that Meigs will accept. If he does not lets tell him that he owes it to the President to ask to be retired . . ." Carnegie Book Shop, Catalogue 335, no. 24.

On Sept. 6, Sunday, Brig. Gen. Montgomery C. Meigs, Washington, D. C., wrote to USG. "I have considered with the deliberation their importance deserves the subjects of our conversation of Wednesday last. I shall ever retain a lively sense of your kindness, and of the confidence you reposed in me, and were I so situated pecuniarily that I could in justice to those dependent upon me, give up my position in the army, my decision might be different. It would be a high honor to close my life in the public service, by a few years in the Russian Mission. But after careful consideration I am compelled to believe that to accept it, would end my connection with the military service. I long since put aside all projects for advancement out of the army & I have not been able to make a provision for my family, which would justify me in giving up what that now offers, or which would enable me to meet worthily the expenses of the Russian Mission, which are larger than its large salary. It would probably last half a dozen years & when it ended, I should have no means to support my family for the rest of my life should that be prolonged. I do not doubt that the laws were intended to prevent the acceptance by officers of such preferment, unless they were willing to retire entirely from the rolls of the Army, and if the words of the law now admit of any other construction I believe that they will be amended, when such construction, is known to have been put upon them. I am therefor unable to accept the honorable mission you have proposed to me, and I remain as heretofore your friend but doubly obliged for the very great honor done me and for the delicate and considerate kindness with which the offer was made" ALS, USG 3. See Nevins, *Fish*, pp. 726–28.

On May 19 and 22, 1875, Fish recorded in his diary. "Genl Meigs calls at the office and shows me a letter from the Secty of War purporting to be written by direction of the President detailing him to Europe to visit & collect information as to the Military affairs there . . ." "Bristow has heard of the order sending Meigs to Europe for 18 months and infers that the object is to bring Ingalls in his place; that a day or two since he says while in the Presidents room ~~and~~ Belknap came ~~coming~~ in; the President & Belknap had inquired of him whether he could not pay Meigs salary '*in Gold*' while in Europe through his fiscal agent there, that he replied that he had no such agent in Europe & was thankful that such was the case. He says that he learns that Mr Watson who was formerly assistant secretary of the Treasury last summer when the effort was making to send Meigs to Russia in order to put Ingalls in his place had stated that he had in his possession the history of a transaction which would expose Ingalls and must prevent his confirmation and must show him unworthy of trust   He understood that the papers had been withdrawn from file in the War Department but that he had secured copies which he would make public in case of Ingalls appointment" DLC-Hamilton Fish. See Belknap to Meigs, May 21, 1875, copy, DNA, RG 107, Letters Sent, Military Affairs; *HED*, 44-1-110, 2; Belknap to Fish, May 27, 1875, copy, DNA, RG 107, Letters Sent, Military Affairs. On May 28, Special Orders No. 104 detailed Col. Rufus Ingalls as act. q. m. gen. in Meigs's absence. Df, *ibid.*, RG 94, ACP, 2457 1875; printed, *ibid.*, RG 192, Orders Received.

On July 31, 1876, Robert F. Hunter, Washington, D. C., wrote to USG alleging collusion among Meigs, William Pettibone, and William Fitch in the prosecution of fraudulent claims. ALS, *ibid.*, RG 92, Consolidated Correspondence, Frauds. On the same day, USG endorsed this letter. "Refered to the Sec. of War for investigation." AES, *ibid.* On Aug. 14, Secretary of War James D. Cameron wrote to USG. "I had the honor on the 2nd of August to receive from you a communication from R. F. Hunter alleging certain charges against Quartermaster General Meigs, with directions to have them investigated. The papers were referred to General Meigs who has returned an answer, the substance of which is as follows: —Mr. Hunter was an Agent of the Quartermasters Department engaged in examining certain claims under the Act of July 4. 1864, and was discharged about June 1. 1876. He alleged that General Meigs was derelict in his duty—1st. in suppressing investigation into certain fraudulent acts of Messrs. Pettibone Fitch and others whom Hunter characterized as the 'Montgomery County Ring,' and—2nd. in discharging Hunter because of his Agency in developing the frauds of said Ring. In reply to these charges, General Meigs forwards copies of papers showing that on the 14th. of June he forwarded to this Department all the documents relating to Pettibone, Fitch and others, recommending 'that the

War Department and Treasury Department place them before the Department of Justice for investigation in order that if reason sufficient appear, all those implicated may be brought to Justice.' The papers were sent to the Department of Justice on June 22nd. This effectually disposes of the charge of suppressing investigation. In regard to the charge of discharging Hunter, General Meigs reports that when he returned from Europe on April 1. 187[6] he found the expenses of these agents were at the rate of $27.000, a year, and in view of the limited appropriation for incidental expenses of the Quartermasters Department, he directed that enough of these Agents be at once discharged to reduce the expenses one half. Eight Agents were discharged May 1st, two of whom were reinstated for given reasons, and Mr. Hunter was discharged simply to reduce expenses for which there was a very limited appropriation. There seems to me to be nothing in this matter that reflects in any way on General Meigs integrity or official action, and I recommend that no further action be taken." LS (press), *ibid.*

To William W. Smith

———

Long Branch, N. J.
July 7th. /74

DEAR SMITH:

I have your favor of the 2d inst. I can not give you the pedigree of the Alderneys I sent you. They were raised here, at Long Branch, by Mr. John Hoey from the best of imported stock. As he does not raise stock for sale however he has never registered it.

We got here on Saturday last[1] and found Jesse who says that he thinks beyond doubt he passed his examination for admittence into Cornell University.[2] Buck had been here but left again before we arrived and will not be back before the 20th   Soon after his return— he, Otis & Jesse expect to take their tramp out to your house, going by the cars to Huntington.[3]

Love from all to Emsy and the children.

Yours Truly
U. S. GRANT

ALS, Washington County Historical Society, Washington, Pa.

1. July 4, 1874.
2. See *PUSG*, 24, 260–61; Jesse R. Grant, *In the Days of My Father General Grant* (New York, 1925), pp. 176–78.

On Aug. 16, Julia Dent Grant, Long Branch, wrote to Olive Cole. "I learn this morning from Jesse, my dear Mrs Cole, that there is a probability of Willie's not coming to Cornell this autumn. I do hope he will come It will be a great disappointment to Jesse & I think to Willie also . . ." ALS (facsimile), Catherine Coffin Phillips, *Cornelius Cole: California Pioneer and United States Senator* (San Francisco, 1929), Plate II. For Willoughby Cole, see *PUSG*, 20, 325.

3. See letter to Adolph E. Borie, Aug. 2, 1874.

To Levi P. Luckey

[*Long Branch, N. J.*
July 11, 1874]

Enclosed find some receipts pertaining to the Rawlin's estate found here. Please place them with other accounts of the same sort.[1] I wish you would go through the drawers of the table in my office and put all the bank checks in "bands" for filing; and all the receipts for money paid in files for reference. There may also be letters that required action that have been neglected. If so forward such to me if you cannot act upon them. All others either destroy or file. I doubt now whether I shall return to Washington until we return for good in the fall . . .

Bruce Gimelson, Autograph Auction No. 9, March 1, 1973, no. 293.

1. See *PUSG*, 24, 144–48. On Nov. 10, 1874, Joseph M. Carey, associate justice, Wyoming Territory Supreme Court, Chicago, telegraphed to USG. "At Governor Campbells request I accompanied Mrs Rawlins remains here & placed same in hands of friends They will reach Danbury wednesday" Telegram received (at 6:48 P.M.), DLC-USG, IB. On April 30, 1875, Levi P. Luckey wrote to H. Horton Smith, New York City. "The President directs me to write you and ask what you think, now that bonds are so high, of selling enough to pay off the indebtedness on the Brooklyn House. He feels disposed to do it if you approve—Whenever the deeds are completed, from Mrs. Hurlbut send them down and the President will sell a bond and pay her the $1.000. . . . P. S. Write me the amount of claim against Brooklyn House and rate of interest it is drawing." Copy, *ibid.*, II, 2. In a deed dated Feb. 27, Orris T. and Mary W. Polley, Danbury, Conn., transferred to Sarah A. Hurlburt and the Rawlins children a Brooklyn property, accepting in payment $13,000, assumption of a $4,500 mortgage, and responsibility for "an assessment for the improvement of Prospect Park in said city of Brooklyn." DS, USG 3. On July 6, Luckey wrote to USG. "I recd. your letter this morning and have carried out your instructions. The interest due $867.00 I receipted for, and the enclosed draft for $650.25 represents ¾ which you desired sent to you. The remaining ¼, of $216.75, I deposited to your credit with Sherman & Grant after changing it into currency netting $252.51. I received 16½ per cent premium for the gold. If you turn over the draft to Mr. Smith will you please let me know that I may make the proper entry in your account, or inform me the rate should you exchange it for currency. I thought I would call your attention to the fact that Jimmy now, since Mrs. R's death

is entitled to ⅓ of the interest instead of ¼ as you have put to his credit. I did not know but that might have escaped your recollection when you wrote to me. It is exceedingly hot here." Copy, DLC-USG, II, 2. On April 13 and Oct. 30, 1877, James B. Rawlins, New York City, signed receipts. "Received on the 16th of Feb from Genl Grant three-hundred and fifty dollars ($350.00) for myself and two hundred dollars ($200.00) for my sisters making ($550) five hundred and fifty dollars in all." "Received from U. S. Grant Jr. $145 on the 13th of October and $100 on the 30th of October" DS, Mrs. Paul E. Ruestow, Jacksonville, Fla.

On Jan. 2, Luckey had written to Ulysses S. Grant, Jr. "I send you the Rawlins account book. I wanted to draw off a statement showing each year by itself, so you might file it with the other papers. Hereafter it might save the same work in case your father might wish to refer to it in that shape. I compared the payments to Smith with his account book, which he brought over with him, at my request, the last time he was over, and they agreed. He has since written to me concerning the first payment made to him, which had no date in his book & did not appear in the account book. It was made in July 1873 from July interest then collected, & in 1873 I had only the receipts from rents. So it is all correct in every partic- ular. You might show your father the statement, as it shows more plainly how the balances stood for each year. At the end of 1873 he had $533.01 left in his hands. At the end of 1874 the account was about even. During 1875 the rents were over $400. more than the general payments, and the interest over $600, more than paid to Smith, so that a balance of over $1000. was on hand at the beginning of 1876; and as you will see from the statement, over $600. accumulated during 1876, making the balance of $1712.69" ALS, USG 3.

To George H. Williams

———

Long Branch, N. J.
July 13th 1874.

Hon. Geo. H. Williams
Atty. Gen.
Dear Sir:

It seems from letters which have been shewn me that the Sec. of War has embodied in an order effecting the the W. U. Tel. Co. an opinion given by Hon. Reverdy Johnson as Asst. Atty. Genl.[1] Subse- quently to giving the opinion Mr. J. wrote a letter to the company that they owed the Govt. a large sum of money under his construc- tion of the law, say five or six millions of dollars, but that if they would acknowledge the binding effect of his construction there would be no prossecution for recovery of the money. I know nothing of the cir- cumstances that has led to all this, but it looks wrong to me—some- thing like "Black Mail" to say to a company that you owe so much but you will be let off if you will do certain things that I know you would not do if you could help yourself. If I knew all the facts possibly my views might be different; but as it is I think it important enough to call your attention to this matter, and to ask that you look into it as Atty. Gen.

The Sec. of War not being in Washington I have not written to him on the subject. When he does visit the Capital however I wish you would call his attention to this matter.

Yours Truly
U. S. Grant

ALS, DNA, RG 60, Letters from the President. On July 23, 1874, Attorney Gen. George H. Williams wrote to Reverdy Johnson, Baltimore. "I have received a letter from the President, and also one from Senator Conkling, in reference to some communication that you have made to the Western Union Telegraph Company, to the effect that suit for penalties will be commenced unless they adopt your construction of the acts of Congress, touching the duties and liabilities of telegraphic companies. Will you be kind enough to furnish me with a copy of that communication, if such a one exists, and also advise me as to what action you have taken, or propose to take in the matter? I suggest that you confer with me upon the subject, before you commence the suit for penalties against the Company." Copy, *ibid.*, Letters Sent. See Williams to U.S. Senator Roscoe Conkling of N. Y., July 22, 1874, *ibid.*, Letters Sent to Executive Officers; letter to George H. Williams, Aug. 2, 1874.

1. On Jan. 7, Williams had written to Johnson. "You are hereby retained as a Special Assistant to the Attorney General of the United States, in matters of controversy between the Government and various Telegraph Companies. . . ." Copy, DNA, RG 60, Letters Sent. Williams directed Johnson to report to Col. Albert J. Myer, chief signal officer.

To Alexander II

To His Imperial Majesty, Alexander II—
Emperor and Autocrat of all the Russias.
Great and Good Friend:

Mr. Marshall Jewell, who has for some time been accredited to your Imperial Majesty in the character of Envoy Extraordinary and Minister Plenipotentiary of the United States, having accepted the responsible duties of Postmaster General of the United States, has accordingly been directed to take leave of your Majesty. Mr. Jewell, whose standing instructions had been to cultivate with the Russian government relations of the closest friendship, has been directed, on leaving St. Petersburg, to convey to your Majesty the assurance of my sincere desire to strengthen and extend the friendly intercourse happily subsisting between the two nations. The zeal with which he has fulfilled his former instructions, leads me to hope that he will execute this last commission in a manner agreeable to your Majesty.

With the most sincere wishes for the happiness of your Majesty and for the prosperity of Russia, I am

> Your Majesty's Good Friend
> U. S. GRANT.

WASHINGTON, JULY 20, 1874.

Copy, DNA, RG 84, Russia, Despatches Received. See letters to Hamilton Fish, July 2, 7, 1874.

On July 5, 1874, John E. Bacon, Columbia, S. C., wrote to USG. "I have the honour to enclose a letter (copy) from Ex Gov' James L Orr & also endorsements from Gov F J Moses, & S J Lee, Speaker of the House of Representatives—also from the Senator & Members to the Legislature from Edgefield, my native County, recommending me for a Foreign appointment especially to St Petersburg, where I was Secretary of Legation under Mr Buchanan in 1858 & 9. Though I have the unqualified endorsement of Gov Moses & Speaker Lee, I do not desire to intimate that I am a radical. I never held any political office but was the nominee of the Reform Party for Congress against Hon R B Elliott. I am a conservative Republican & voted for Grant against Greeley.... As I desire to be fully understood, I will simply add, that I am a Son in law of the late Gov F W Pickens; having married his daughter while I was Secretary of Legation at St Petersburg. . . ." ALS, DNA, RG 59, Letters of Application and Recommendation. On July 24, U.S. Representative Robert B. Elliott of S. C., Columbia, wrote to USG recommending Bacon. LS, *ibid.* Related papers are *ibid.*

On July 30, William E. Stevenson, Parkersburg, West Va., telegraphed to USG, Long Branch. "I Concur with other west Virginians in recommending Col T B Swann for Minister to Russia" Telegram received, DLC-USG, IB. Also in 1874, U.S. Senator Arthur I. Boreman of West Va. wrote to USG recommending Thomas B. Swann as minister to Russia. William Evarts Benjamin, Catalogue No. 27, Nov., 1889, p. 5.

On Sept. 14 and 15 and Nov. 8, Secretary of State Hamilton Fish wrote in his diary. "President having visited Washington I call at the White House—He began by asking what I thought of transferring Jones from Belgium to Russia, & Read from Greece to Belgium   I reply that I do not think that Jones has done any thing to entitle him to such a prominent Mission as that of Russia—that he has been very amiable & attentive & hospitable to Americans in Brussells, & has made himself very Acceptable; all speak kindly of him—but that his official correspondence & record would not justify such advancement, that while Brussells is the most important point in Europe for gathering the political & diplomatic news & gossip, Jones has never sent us more than clippings of newspapers which we take at the office, & which of course is all public long before we get it—Moreover, that I do not think it wd be politic to give to Illinois, (which has had three Missions, ever since his Administration began,) two of the four first class missions Russia as well as France— He replies that Jones will come home, at any rate next Spring, & that then he will not give Illinois another Mission in his stead—. . . I told the President that I thought it would be adviseable, & wise, to appoint to Russia some person whose name would at once strike the

Country favourably—perhaps some literary man, & I name James Russell Lowell, that such a nomination would conciliate a large class who at present are not exactly hostile, but cold & indifferent toward the Administration—The President makes no response to this suggestion" "He refers to Russian Mission—thinks I had better inform the Russian Govt that the time of the convening of the Senate is so close that he will wait for their Confirmation —I ask what he thinks of the name I suggested yesterday (Lowell) he replies that he dont want to give favours there—I speak of the high character of the man, & the importance of a good appointment—He then speaks more warmly of Lowell, & thinks it would be popular—I state that people have written to me about Burnside—he unhesitatingly rejects the suggestion—says Burnside is a nice gentlemanly person, but has proved a failure everywhere—would rather appoint William B. Franklin but he is a Democrat—Wants a first rate man—such a man as Senator Edmunds—I remind him that Edmunds is not eligible until after 4th March, the compensation of the Minister having been raised, while Edmunds was in the Senate He suggests appointing Schuyler temporarily—I object to a temporary appointment, & think that Schuyler is too young for so prominent a Mission—Moreover Schuyler has a book on Russia, in the press in England, & wishes to leave St Petersburgh before its publication, to be relieved of official responsibilities" "Show to the President a letter from Judge Pierrepont, respecting a Foreign Mission, he requests me to write him that he wd be glad to offer him either of the four higher missions that might be vacant; that Russia alone is vacant, that he wd be delighted to offer him that if he would accept it—" DLC-Hamilton Fish.

On Nov. 21, Postmaster Gen. Marshall Jewell, Boston, telegraphed to USG. "The appointment spoken of here would I think be of the most satisfactory kind all our friends would be pleased with it and in my opinion none offened." Telegram received, DNA, RG 59, Letters of Application and Recommendation. A related telegram is *ibid.* Jewell likely referred to the rumored offer of the Russian mission to James Russell Lowell. On Nov. 28 and Dec. 3, Fish wrote in his diary. "Called upon the President, found Jewell with him— mention Russell Lowells declension of Russian Mission Jewell speaks of E. D. Morgan —President says that but for a possible wish to give something else to NY, he would not object to offering the Russian Mission to Morgan Says he is tall, large & of an imposing presence, won't say much, or do foolish things, & will give good dinners—after a little pause he request me to write & offer him the Mission" "I show to President Govr Morgan's letter of Dec 2, declining the tender of the Russian Mission & asked if he had any one in view for the appointment upon his answering in the negative, I inquired whether the name of Judge Swayne of the Supreme Court had occured to him, he thinks that Swayne has not yet reached the age for retirement & does not wish to precipitate his resignation, that the appointment of successor on Supreme Bench at this time might be embarassing, that Judge Cartter of District Court would be greatly disappointed if he should again be passed by & that while Cartter has the ability, learning fit for the place & is strong in his convictions upon essential points of differences, there are things in his conduct & manner, not wholly suited to the position—He would prefer therefor that Swayne should remain on the Bench, until towards the close of his own term, but will be most happy to give him some recognition of the kind proposed by me,—if the opportunity presented at time he may retire—On my saying that I had no person whom I was prepared to recommend for Russian Mission, he said that Mr Maney of Tennessee (of whom he has previously spoken to me in high terms) will be a very fitting person, that Secretary of Treasury knew him well Bristow hower on being appealed to replied very coldly 'Yes, I know him, he is a good fellow, I know Maney'—the subject thereupon dropped—" DLC-Hamilton Fish.

On Dec. 5, James H. Wilson, New York City, wrote to Adam Badeau, consul gen.,

London. ". . . Generals Bristow, Belknap, Porter and Babcock, and the President have commended me strongly to Mr. Fish for the Russian Mission, as a matter of course without my
solicitation, but somewhat to my personal gratification. Mr. Fish is however master of the
situation (as I will explain when we meet) and while he listens with attention to my friends,
gives no indication of what he will do. He had already offered it to Lowell, and has it is
thought, since tendered it to both Holmes and Whittier—how it will all turn out I have
no means of knowing, but in view of the fact that I am neither a poet nor 'inside politics,'
I have no great expectations. I have no desire to embarrass the President nor Mr. Fish, and
the only part I have taken in the matter has been to have them assured of that fact. . . ."
Typescript, DLC-James H. Wilson.

On Dec. 8 and subsequently, Fish recorded in his diary. "During the session of the
Cabinet, President writes on a card & hands to me a few lines inquiring whether I think
Williams wd like nomination to Russia adding that he had no person in view to fill his place
as Atty Genl   I reply that I have no knowledge on the subject but will endeavor to ascertain—" "December 9th . . . speak of Russian Mission & with President's allusion of yesterday with Attorney Genl's name in connection therewith   I tell I have not made any inquiry
to ascertain William's views   that I had no person in my own mind to suggest for the
place, but doubt whether nomination of Williams wd be well recd either by Senate or the
country—He speaks very kindly of Williams & thinks the Senate does not object to his
discharge of the duties of Atty Genl but that there is objection to his wife who he thinks
has been imprudent & that Williams has merely been guilty of not paying any attention to
what was done   I concur with him entirely in these views stating however that I think the
prejudice altho' unjust is very strong against both of them—He agrees in this view &
thinks it may be as well to say nothing about the nomination, adding at same time that he
had never thought of whom he sd nominate in his place as Atty Genl & had no one in view
therefore. I call his attention to the importance of filling Russian Mission, stating that I
thought it desirable that it sd be some person who had already filled some prominent position & wd be known to the country—He said that excepting for giving another mission to
Ohio, he wd have no objections to name Govr Dennison,   I suggested also the name of
Gov Hays of Ohio—they were both passed by   he proposed Henry T Blow of Mo & it relieved me from any necessity of objecting by saying 'he knew he cd not accept it' on acct of
his wife's health—I asked if he had thought of Gov Dix,   he said he had not, but doubted
whether it wd be acceptable to him to go to such a climate at his age & after having held
the Mission to France wh ranked above that at St Petersburg,   I then suggested the names
of Govs Claflin & Clifford of Massachusetts,   he said he wd not care to offer it to Claflin,
but that the suggestion of Clifford was first-rate & that I might offer it to him—" "Dec
29th . . . He directs that at the next meeting of the Senate Mr Bocker be nominated for Russia, and Mr Jones transferred from Belgium to Turkey—I call his attention to the fact that
Turkey is not a higher mission than Belgium, the grade, and the salery, of each being the
same. I inquire whether I shall telegraph to Bocker of the intent to make his transfer. He replies in the affirmative but presently said that he had received a letter from Jones requesting promotion but doubted whether he would care to be transferred to Turkey and desired
me not to telegraph today." "January 2d 1875 . . . Referring to his recent request, to suspend telegraphing to Mr Bocker about the mission to Russia he said he had done so, thinking of Williams   That he thought well of Williams and liked him thinking that he was very
harshly judged. I told him that there would be opposition in the Senate that some of the
Sentators had spoken to me lately in terms of severe censure of the Attorney General and
further stated that there were things connected with the administration of his office which
had not been exposed but created a very bad impression and that while I was personally

attached to Williams and thought well of his ability and character for integrity I was
satisfied that the nomination would be unpopular with the senate and people and would be
a challenge for criticism and censure which would be avoided by leaving him in his present
position   He assented to this view and authorized me if I thought proper to telegraph to
Bocker offering to him the mission to Russia although he expressed the opinion that it was
not worth while to consult him." DLC-Hamilton Fish.

On Jan. 8, 1875, Manning F. Force, Cincinnati, wrote to USG. "Mr. Lincoln when president, used to say he liked to talk with all sorts of people about public matters, and called
such a talk a—public opinion bath. May I write a letter by way of a sprinkle. As you are
looking for a person to fill suitably the Russian Mission, may I mention Bayard Taylor, as a
name worth considering. He has had some diplomatic experience; he was secretary of legation at St. Petersburg. He speaks Russian as well as French and German, the languages
used at the Russian court   He is, I understand, held in high esteem by both the Czar and
prince Gortschakoff. Though he has been a stockholder in the New York Tribune for many
years, he has not sympathized with its recent politics but continues a staunch republican.
At the same time his appointment would have a good influence on some who are ready to
regret that they dropped out of the republican ranks. I am not personally acquainted with
Mr. Taylor, and do not know that he is a suitable person, and I certainly do not offer to recommend him or any one for the office. I simply suggest that his name be put on the list
of persons to be inquired about, and from whom on inquiry, you make a selection." ALS,
DNA, RG 59, Letters of Application and Recommendation. On Jan. 5, Fish had recorded
in his diary a conversation with USG. "I show him a note from Sen Sherman receommend-
ing Bayard Taylor for the Russian mission   he says that he has also received a note making the same recommendation, that he would as soon think of appointing W. W. Phelps,
that each of them might be competent to fill the mission but neither would represent the
Government." DLC-Hamilton Fish.

On May 9, 1873, U.S. Representative Leonard Myers of Pa., Philadelphia, had written
to USG. "At the suggestion of several distinguished gentlemen of this City I respectfully
urge that you will appoint Hon. George H. Boker, to the Russian Mission—Pennsylvania
not only has no member of your Cabinet but no Mission of the First Class. . . ." ALS, DNA,
RG 59, Letters of Application and Recommendation. On Jan. 11, 1875, USG nominated
George H. Boker as minister to Russia. See *PUSG*, 22, 407; *ibid.*, 24, 108.

To John F. Long

————

Long Branch, N. J.
July 20th 1874

DEAR JUDGE,

Being reduced down to a pair of carriage horses and one saddle
horse I have made arrangements for the shipment of Butcher Boy if
he is still serviceable as a buggy horse, with good care. Will you do
me the favor to send this down to the farm, at my expense and tell
Carlin to deliver the horse to Adams Ex. Co for shipment without

delay unless the horse is becoming decrepid from old age. If I get him here I will keep him as long as he and I live.

Yours Truly

U. S. GRANT

ALS (written on an envelope), CSmH. On July 27, 1874, John F. Long, surveyor of customs, St. Louis, wrote to Nathaniel Carlin, Sappington, Mo. "If you have not yet responded to the requisition of the President, for the shipment of *Butcher Boy*, had you not better do so at once. From his peremtory note, to that effect, it would seem of the first importance, for you to either comply or give him satisfactory reasons, for non complyance,   May I ask your early attention to this matter, as the President, is doubtless looking for the arrival of his *pet horse.*" ALS, OClWHi. See Jesse R. Grant, *In the Days of My Father General Grant* (New York, 1925), p. 113.

On July 20, Long had written to USG. "Judge Krum has just returned your Letter (which for a better understanding of the matter I left with him to consider of.) and with it the enclosed penciled remarks upon the subject of *your note:*—Among the list of appointees for this office, was the name of Thos. S. Long—as an outside Inspector: which the *Acting* Secretary Conant *disapprovs*, on the 'presumption that he is a relative.' and he does not like to have more than one of the same family in the same office!—I would like to retain him —he is poor & my securities asks it." ALS, DNA, RG 56, Miscellaneous Letters Received. USG endorsed this letter. "Refered to the Sec. of the Treas. I have no objection to the appointment indicated." AES (undated), *ibid.*

On Aug. 10, John Kiernan, "Chief Farrier U. S. Army," St. Louis Barracks, wrote to USG. "I have the honor to respectfully call your attention to enclosed slip from 'St. Louis Democrat' of July 31st, and a correction which I made in the same paper of Aug. 4th. In stating to your Excellency that my visits to the farm are of so frequent occurrence—as to make it simply an impossibility for such a disease, or any other, to make its appearance and exist without my knowledge, I would also call your attention to the injuriousness of such reports. I consider them very ill-advised, and when without a shadow of foundation, much worse. The filly referred to was in reality suffering from the effects of a snake-bite, which resulted in the filly's death, as stated. Anxiety to disabuse your mind of a false impression as the state of the stock on the farm will, I trust, be my justification for trespassing on your Excellency's time.—The condition of the stock was never better than at the present time." LS, USG 3.

To Levi P. Luckey

———

DATED Long Branch July 21 *1874*
To L P Luckey ex Mansion W
Orders of Secy of War Seem to be sufficent for the present   ask him to exercise his Judgement should further despatches Come & Consult me by telegraph should he deem it necessary

U S GRANT

Telegram received (at 5:40 P.M.), DNA, RG 94, Letters Received, 1495 1874. On July 20, 1874, Lt. Governor Alexander K. Davis of Miss. twice wrote to USG. "Serious disturbances are anticipated in the City of Vicksburg, occasioned by ~~differences of opinion relative to~~ the approaching City Election which is to take place on the 4th of August, statements from prominent Citizens both verbal and in writing are constantly being received by me, to the effect that from the preparations that have been made should an outbreak occur the sacrafice of life and property would be immense, Armed bodies of men are parading the streets both night and day, the City Authorities are utterly unable to protect the lives and property of the Citizens—regretting the necessity—I am constrained to ask that Two (2) Companies of United States Troops be at once ordered to Vicksburg to ensure the Citizens against domestic violence which is imminent. Please to answer at once," "The Adjt Genl of the State reports Three (3) Companies of State Militia Two (2) White and One (1) Colored in open rebellion in the City of Vicksburg. An order was issued on the 9th of June by Gov Ames upon the Captains of said Companies to turn over to the Adjt Genl all Arms Ammunition &c in their possession property of the State.—The Adjt Genl. attempted to execute this order to day and was met by a ~~prompt~~ positive refusal to comply. He reports that these Arms are in the hands of men organized and unorganized who are setting at defiance the laws of both the City and State. I consider it absolutely necessary that Troops be at the earliest possible moment stationed in the City of Vicksburg to prevent impending riot and bloodshed—The unorganized condition of the State Militia render the Executive powerless to execute the laws and preserve the peace in the present emergency This appeal is made in conformity with Article 4 section 4 of the Constitution of the United States, Please answer at once," LS (press), Ames Letterbook, Miss. Dept. of History and Archives, Jackson, Miss.

On July 21, Peter Casey and Lazarus Lindsay, Vicksburg, telegraphed to USG. "We understand a petition has been made to you for troops at this place during the coming municipal election, The need of them is only in the imagination of violent politicians and we really believe everything will go off quietly, Presence of troops will do harm," Telegram received (on July 22), DNA, RG 94, Letters Received, 1495 1874. Also on July 21, Richard F. Beck, mayor, Vicksburg, telegraphed to USG. "I am advised that Leut Gov Davis acting Gov has demanded of you a federal Military force for this city for the astensible purpose of preserving peace now and during approaching Municipal election. I desire to advise you that this was done without consultation with me and that it is wholly unnecessary, the peace of the city is undisturbed I believe the Election will be a quiet one and the presence of troops will be Esteemed only as a menace to one class of our population in the interest of the political schemes of another. I am assured of the aid of all good citizens in preserving peace and am confident I can maintain without Military interference, I respectfully ask that no troops be allowed in the town nor at the day of Election, In making this request ~~In~~ I represent the Entire property holding Element of the city, Answer," Telegram received (on July 22), *ibid.* On July 22, Secretary of War William W. Belknap telegraphed to USG, Long Branch. "Peter Casey Postmaster, Lindsay U S Commissioner and R T Breck mayor have remonstrated against troops being sent to Vicksburgh. Lt Governor and Acting Governor Davis telegraphs that he has forwarded by mail communication giving full particulars Have Suspended orders for the movement of troops to Vicksburgh until the receipt of these particulars expected by mail after consultation with Attorney General concluded this was the best course" Telegram received, DLC-USG, IB; LS (telegram sent), DNA, RG 107, Telegrams Collected (Bound).

On July 23, Beck telegraphed to USG. "Lt Gov Davis makes allegation refusal of the military organization of this city to surrender the state arms, a pretext for requesting the presence of federal troops The arms were distributed here against the wishes of the whites but a portion of them are in their possession,   to a demand for their surrender they replied that they would comply if the demand should be enforced as to both blacks and whites,   no steps were taken to enforce it. Col French commanding military day telegraphed Gov Davis saying an order to disarm all the military in this city would be executed by him promptly & peacably   Davis refuses to send such order and indicates his purpose to procure federal troops to accomplish the purpose. There is no insurrection or unusual commotion here and troops are only desired in order that their presence may ensure the advantage of one class of the population and against the other   All that are under my control and are used in the interest of peace and order, only   the business men & property holders of the city with great unanimity unite with me in the request that no troops be sent" Telegram received, *ibid.*, RG 94, Letters Received, 1495 1874. On the same day, Davis telegraphed to Belknap renewing his request for troops. Telegram received (at 5:38 P.M.), *ibid.* Also on July 23, T. Warren Cowan and five others, Vicksburg, had telegraphed to USG. "The undersigned committee of the people's party of this city representing nine tenths of the tax paying portion of community, beg leave to protest against the granting of Lt Gov Davis' request for troops   on behalf [*of the*] principals We disavow any intention of resorting to violence or any other unfair means in the pending contest,   we desire only a fair and legal election and deprecate military interference as calculated to befall defeat this end and wholly unnecessary   The impending contest involves no political issues and there is greater excitement than is natural in a community struggling to free itself from debt, taxes and corruption   We appeal to you as chief magistrate of the nation not to strike us down in our efforts to accomplish this end" Telegram received, *ibid.* On July 24, Belknap twice telegraphed to USG, forwarding the telegrams from Davis and Cowan. Telegrams received, DLC-USG, IB; LS and ALS (telegrams sent), DNA, RG 107, Telegrams Collected (Bound).

On July 28, Maj. Thomas M. Vincent, asst. AG, telegraphed to Belknap, New London, Conn., conveying a telegram dated July 27 from Maj. Edward R. Platt, asst. AG, Vicksburg, to Col. William H. Emory, New Orleans, reporting that "those whose interests would suffer most in the event of a riot feel confident there will be none." Telegram received, *ibid.*, RG 94, Letters Received, 1495 1874. On the same day, Belknap endorsed this telegram. "Sent this to Prest at Long Branch July 28. 74 and said that in my judgment not advisable to send troops unless necessity more apparent.... Telegd Vincent same time that above had been sent to the President & troops would not be sent unless he so instructed" AES, *ibid.*

On July 29, Governor Adelbert Ames of Miss. telegraphed to USG. "Regret to inform you that I find upon returning here that a serious & alarming condition of affairs exists at Vicksburg. infantry and cavalry organizations exist & it is reported a number of pieces of artillery have been sent to the city & these bodies organized & armed without authority and in violation of law assume to be guardians of the peace,   this is a political controversy, one side the Democrats represented by the whites claim they fear frauds on the part of their opponents, the Republicans consisting mainly of blacks claim that they fear frauds and also violence on the part of the democrats. At one time a collission and bloodshed was feared by all.   now, by the republicans but by the democrats,   It is believed only because they have become masters of the Situation, it is they who oppose the presence of troops at this time,   Of the causes of this lamentable state of affairs it is now useless to speak. I only seek peace & protection for all,   Can there be any serious objections why troops should not be sent there,   no harm can result for troops are in many of our cities,   at this moment in two of the cities of this state, their presence may be great good, it may save many lives, even one would more than compensate for the harm which, if any I do not see to result from such presence,   Will it not be the best (least?) of evils to have troops there for any emergency" Telegram received, *ibid.* On July 30, Thursday, Belknap telegraphed to USG conveying the substance of this telegram. ". . . In my Judgement there is not good reason for sending the troops & I suggest that if you answer the governor. That you say that you do not deem it an emergency requiring the presence of troops. I expect to be at LongBranch on saturday morning" Telegram received, DLC-USG, IB. On [*July*] 31, Belknap telegraphed to Henry T. Crosby, chief clerk, War Dept. "Telegraph from Washington the following and show it to Genl Vincent, and Genl Sherman,   Hon A. Amos Jackson Miss,   Contents of your dispatch have been submitted to the President,   He declines to move the troops except under call made strictly in accordance with terms of the Constitution" Telegram received, DNA, RG 94, Letters Received, 1495 1874.

Also on July 31, Miss. Senator Charles E. Furlong and thirteen others, Vicksburg, telegraphed to USG. "We the citizens and property owners of this city desire to express to you our views of the situation here because we understand a call has again been made for U. S troops to preserve the peace of our city at the coming election   we having a full knowledge of all the facts consider the call unwarranted & believe that there does not exist a necessity for the aid or interference of the federal Govt in our local affairs & in support of which position we refer to Col Platt A A Genl and C & C   his excellency Governor ames has not been here & was only a few hours in the state when his call was made   our city has all to gain and nothing to lose by a fair honest & peaceable election   we believe that the presence of U. S. troops would cause an excitement which does not now exist   our wishes are for a quiet peaceable election which we are assured we will have without the aid of federal troops" Telegram received (at 8:30 P.M.), *ibid.*

On Aug. 2, Octavius L. Pruden, White House clerk, telegraphed to Orville E. Babcock, Long Branch, conveying a telegram dated Aug. 1 from Ames to USG. ". . . Lieut Gov and acting Gov Davis some days since made application for Troops to suppress Domestic violence at Vicksburg   he made his call at least designed it to be strictly in accordance with the terms of the Constitution   no reply to his communication has been received Imitating that they were defective in that particular   my Telegram was made with a knowledge of the existing correspondence. Domestic violence does exist and has existed for some time" Telegram received, *ibid.*

On Aug. 4, Furlong telegraphed to USG. "The election just closed was the most peaceable and orderly ever held here   a full vote no disturbance the peoples ticket elected" Telegram received (at 8:20 P.M.), *ibid.* See Proclamation, Dec. 21, 1874; William C. Harris, *The Day of the Carpetbagger: Republican Reconstruction in Mississippi* (Baton Rouge, 1979), pp. 634−36.

Speech

[*July 22, 1874*]

LADIES AND GENTLEMEN AND MEMBERS OF THE GRAND ARMY OF THE REPUBLIC: It has afforded me very great pleasure to have met the members of this organization to-day and to participate in your ceremonies. I never had the honor of meeting so many of the citizens of Paterson before, and my acquaintance with them has been limited except on occasions of travel. I am glad to have had the opportunity of visiting your city, but at this late hour you cannot expect a speech from me. I could not if I would, and I would not if I could.

New York Times, July 23, 1874. On May 29, 1874, Levi P. Luckey wrote to Charles Burrows, Paterson, N. J. "The President directs me to acknowledge the receipt of your cordial invitation—in behalf of the Grand Army of the Republic of New Jersey, and the citizens of Paterson—to attend the Re-union on the 22d of July next, and express his sincere thanks for the courteous attention. He desires me to say that if he is at Long Branch at the time so he can attend, it will afford him great pleasure to do so; but expects that according ~~according~~ to other arrangements which he has contemplated for July, he will not be able to visit Paterson on the 22d." Copy, DLC-USG, II, 2.

On July 22, Secretary of State Hamilton Fish telegraphed to USG, Paterson. "I have some papers requiring your Signature   will they reach you if Sent to Long Branch by to-morrows mail" Telegram received, *ibid.*, IB. On the same day, USG endorsed this telegram. "Will return to Long Branch to-morrow morning" AES, *ibid.*

On July 31, Henry W. Leonard, Jersey City, wrote to USG. "not having had an opportunity at our Reunion at Paterson N. J. on the 22.nd inst, allthought speaking to you about other matters . . . I would most respectfully call your attention to the efforts which were made last winter by my friends the Hon Marcus L Ward. I W Scudder and others at Washington, . . ." ALS, DNA, RG 94, Applications for Positions in War Dept. On Dec. 16, Leonard wrote to USG seeking a consulship. ALS, *ibid.*, RG 59, Letters of Application and Recommendation. Related papers are *ibid.* No appointment followed.

Proclamation

To ALL WHO SHALL SEE THESE PRESENTS, GREETING:

Know Ye; That reposing special trust and confidence in the Integrity and Ability of John A. J. Creswell, a Counsellor at Law, admitted to practice in the Supreme Court of the United States, in pursuance of the provisions of the Act of Congress approved June 23d 1874, creating a Court for the adjudication and disposition of moneys received by the United States under the award of the Geneva tribunal, I do hereby designate and appoint him to appear before said Court as Counsel on behalf of the United States and to represent the interest of the Government in said Court and in all claims filed for indemnity for losses under the provisions of the aforesaid Act, subject to the supervision and control of the Attorney General. And to have and to hold the said appointment with all the powers and privileges

thereunto of right appertaining, unto him the said John A. J. Creswell during the pleasure of the President of the United States for the
time being.

Given under my hand this 22d day of July, in the year of our Lord
one thousand eight hundred and seventy-four, and of the Independence of the United States the Ninety-ninth.

U. S. GRANT.

Copy, DNA, RG 59, General Records. On June 20 and July 1, 1874, Secretary of State
Hamilton Fish recorded in his diary. "I called upon the President and found the Secy. of the
Treasury, Attorney, General & Commr. of Internal Revenue. . . . I mention the possibility of a compromise in the Geneva Award bill; and that there may be a Commission, and
the following names were mentioned in this connection: Hezekiah G. Wells: Michigan.
Martin Ryerson. N. J. Kenneth Rayner. Mississippi. The President then said 'Stop I want
to put Cornelius Cole [ex Senator, California] on;' to which I remonstrated. President then
said, he might do for Counsel. The Attorney General thought he would not be fit for Counsel, and I begged the President to look in some other direction for a place for Cole." "The
designation of a Counsellor at Law to act before the Court of Commrs. of Alabama Claims
was brought up, and the name of F. A. Barlow was proposed; but the President objected
peremptorily; he subsequently wrote Creswell's name on a card & asked me to speak with
him on the subject; which I did, he declines on the ground that his motives for resignation might be misinterpreted, which I reported to the President, who will speak with him."
(brackets in original), DLC-Hamilton Fish. On July 6, Orville E. Babcock, Long Branch,
wrote to Adam Badeau, consul gen., London. ". . . How do you like the new P. M. G. Marshall Jewell. Creswell made up his mind some 8 months ago that he would go out, He will
remain in W. will be Counsel for the Geneva Award Commission, so he has lost nothing pecuniarily in the change—. . ." ALS, MH. On June 24, U.S. Representative Lyman Tremain
of N. Y., New York City, had written to USG. "Permit me to recommend Ex Attorney General Francis C Barlow for the position of Counsel for the Govt in the Geneva Award Commission. Energetic, able, thorough, incorruptible his appointment would be universally accepted as an eminently good one, You know him well, & I need add nothing by way of
commendation. Learning that he would be willing to accept the place, I take pleasure in
presenting his name to your Consideration" ALS, DNA, RG 59, Letters of Application and
Recommendation. Related papers are *ibid.* See *PUSG*, 19, 232–33; *ibid.*, 24, 400; letter to
John A. J. Creswell, June 24, 1874.

On June 21, Fish had written to USG. "In thinking of names of some Democrats from
New York & Pennsylvania these occur to me John V. L. Pruyn—New York Francis Ker-
nan—New York—Smith Ely Jun—New York Chas. R. Buckalew—Penna Geo. W. Woodward—Penna Edgar Cowan—Penna Saml J. Tilden—New York Some one of whom may
possibly meet your views." ALS (press, tabular material expanded), DLC-Hamilton Fish.
On June 23, USG nominated George W. Woodward as judge, Court of Commissioners of
Alabama Claims; on the same day, he withdrew this nomination.

To James W. Marshall

———

Long Branch, N. J.
July 24th /74

Hon J. W Marshall
Postmaster Genl
Dr. Sir

    I understand that two of the large iron steam ships built by the Pacific Mail Company, to carry the mails between San Francisco and China, under their contract heretofore made with your department, are about ready & that the company are anxious to dispatch them at once to the Pacific, and have, to that End, applied for their inspection and acceptance—This Service is so important to the Commercial and general interests of the country; and the Company have expended so much money in their endeavor to comply with their part of the contract, by building the largest and fastest steam ship ever produced in this country (wholly of American Material) that I think you had better at once Examine the subject and accept these ships, provided the law will permit you to ~~do so~~ continue the service, and they shall, on inspection, be found fit for it—This will be in accordance with the views Expressed by the late Postmaster General in his last report —with the recommendations of the Several Committees to whom Congress referred the subject at the last Session [& wi]th the often declared policy of the administration. As the Service is ~~already~~ now being performed by the company in their Ships already accepted for the mail service without extra charge, and as these ships after acceptance must be sent around Cape Horn, nothing further will be necessary till Congress again meets, when they can take all necessary action & make any further appropriation for the continuance of the service

Very Truly Yours
U. S. Grant

LS, Georgetown University, Washington, D. C. On Aug. 5, 1874, Postmaster Gen. James W. Marshall telegraphed to USG, Long Branch. "In conformity with the opinions of the solicitor General and attorney General Just rec'd By me I shall immediately request the

secretary of The Navy to have the new steamships inspected for the china mail service"
Telegram received, DLC-USG, IB. See *PUSG*, 21, 276–77; *ibid.*, 23, 298–99; *SMD*, 43-2-83, 2–3, 43-2-94; *HRC*, 43-1-598.

To Richard J. Oglesby

Long Branch, N. J.
July 31st 1874

DEAR GENERAL:

Your letter of the 24th inst. enclosing copy of resolutions of the National Lincoln Monument Association inviting me to be present, and to deliver the dedicatory address on the occasion of dedicating the National Lincoln Monument, at Springfield, Ill. was duly received.

I have kept the letter two days without answering to fully consider whether I can undertake a task so different from anything ever attempted by me before. My great admiration for Mr. Lincoln's character, talents and public services would tempt me if I felt able to do justice to the subject. But I do not, and therefore decline the honor—thanking the Association of which you are the President for confering it—and hope you will make a selection of some one who can and will do full justice to the memory and public services of our noble Martyred President.

I will endeavor to be in Springfield on the occasion of the National Lincoln Monument; but my official duties are of such a nature that I cannot always command my own time or see so far ahead as to enable me to engage positively to put in an appearance so far from the National Capitol on a specified day.

With great respect,
Your obt. svt.
U. S. GRANT

GENERAL R. J. OGLESBY,
PRES. NAT. LINCOLN MONUMENT ASSOCIATION.

ALS, IHi; ADf, USG 3. On July 24, 1874, U.S. Senator Richard J. Oglesby of Ill., Springfield, wrote to USG. "I have the honor to enclose herewith, a resolution of the National

Lincoln Monument Association, adopted in session to-day, respectfully inviting you to be present and deliver the dedicatory address, on the occasion of dedicating the National Lincoln Monument to the public, at Springfield, Illinois. In compliance with the spirit of the resolution, I venture to impress upon you the anxiety of the Association that you will find it consistent with your public duties, and your known and profound respect for the life and character of Abraham Lincoln, to accept this invitation. The day for the ceremonies has been definitely fixed for October 15, 1874, and we shall proceed with all necessary arrangements to have every thing in order by that time. We will communicate with you more fully upon the subject, should you desire any special information from the Association after you have signified your acceptance of the invitation, and will consult your convenience in all respects. I venture to suggest that it has occurred to the association that your acceptance of this honorable and imposing task is consistent with every consideration of propriety, and will in all respects be most felicitous. May I venture to hope that an early and favorable reply may be received, so that the Association may lay the arrangement before the public? If desirable, we will send a committee to call upon you with a view to any further arrangements, or to receive any suggestions from you as to other proceedings upon that day. . . . P. S. Will thank you to send your reply to Hon O M Hatch Sec. Springfield Ills. as I may at the time be away from both Springfield and Decatur" LS, USG 3; ADf, IHi. The resolution is enclosed in USG 3. See Speech, [*Oct. 15, 1874*].

To George H. Williams

Long Branch, N. J.
Aug. 2d /74

DEAR SIR:

Since my letter calling your attention to a letter which had been shown me from the Hon. Reverdy Johnson, asking the W. U. Telegraph Co. to recognize his construction of the law regulating services rendered by them for the Govt. I understand suit is about to be brought for the full amount of all forfeitures for which it is claimed that the company is liable under that construction. I hope you will not allow this until you have examined the subject yourself sufficiently to warrant you in recommendg that cours to be pursued. If the W. U. T. Co. was the property of a single individual, or wholly belonged to the officers of the Co. the course about to be pursued might be justified. But when it is ~~recollected~~ remembered that the stock is held by thousands of people, wholly irresponsible ~~o~~for the management of the company, many of them widows & orphans, and that such a suit is calculated to effect the stock disastrously, no matter how it may be decided in the end, it seems to me [that] a more equitable way might be devised to protect the Govt. If it is necessary to bring suit at all why not select such cases as will represent every ground under which it is claimed that the Co. is liable to forfeiture. Thus a test case would be presented to the courts which it seems to me would protect the Govt. in all the others, if the decission should be in favor of Mr Johnson's construction of the law, and would not effect injuriously —or not so injuriously—the value of the stock pending the trial. I hope at least you will let me know your own views on this subject before action is finally taken.

Very Truly Yours
U. S. GRANT

HON. GEO. [A] WILLIAMS ATTY. GN.

ADfS (bracketed material not in USG's hand), USG 3. On Aug. 3, 1874, USG signed a copy of this letter written in Orville E. Babcock's hand. LS, DNA, RG 60, Letters from the President. See letter to George H. Williams, July 13, 1874.

On Aug. 5, Attorney Gen. George H. Williams twice wrote to USG. "I have the honor to enclose herewith copies of certain correspondence showing what has been done by this Department, in reference to suits against the Western Union Telegraph Company, for alleged violations of the Act of Congress of July 24, 1866,   you will observe that Mr. Johnson states that he will not bring any such suits until after consultation with me in reference thereto." "Your letter of the 3d inst. is received. I am not aware of any intention to sue the Western Union Telegraph Company for the whole amount of their alleged forfeiture to the Government, for non-compliance with law; and, indeed, I doubt very much whether it would be legal to embrace all these claims for forfeiture, in one suit as there is a difference, of course, in the circumstances of each case. You have already been advised that Mr. Johnson will bring no suit without consulting me upon the subject, and I know of no reason why one or a few suits involving all the questions arising under the acts of Congress, might not be brought to test the correctness of Mr. Johnson's construction of that act. I suppose as a matter of course, should the court decide that Mr. Johnson's construction of the law is correct, the company would acquiesce in their decision, and would be ready to make some satisfactory arrangement in reference to the forfeitures already incurred, and hereafter conform to the requirements of the act of Congress as they were determined to be by judicial construction. I would not think it advisable to give the company to understand in any way that the Government, will not insist upon their compliance with the terms of the act, and that it will not if necessary, bring the necessary suits, to determine what the rights of the Government are in respect to the questions involved in the controversy." Copies, DNA, RG 60, Letters Sent to Executive Officers.

On Aug. 19, William Orton, president, Western Union Telegraph Co., New York City, wrote to USG. "I have the honor to enclose to you certain letters, constituting the material part of a correspondence recently concluded between Hon. Reverdy Johnson, as Assistant Attorney-General of the United States and the Western Union Telegraph Company. I respectfully request that you will refer it to the Attorney-General of the United States, for his judgment upon the principal question involved, to wit: Whether this company is liable to the United States for the whole or any part of the sum of $11.618.000 penalties asserted by Mr Johnson; and whether the name of the United States ought to appear as plaintiff in an action, the expressed and sole object of which is to coerce the company into acquiescence in legal principles which it believes erroneou[s] and oppressive. Although Mr Johnson, in making the claim contained in his letter, appears as an Assistant Attorney General of the United States, it has been evident that he is in fact acting only in the interest and under the direction of the chief of a bureau of a department. From this bureau, I wish to appeal to the United States. The subject seems appropriate for consideration by the head of the Department of Justice, but I am advised that applications by private persons for advice and opinions, are, by long established practice, disregarded by that department. Being thus unable to communicate directly with the Department of Justice, and being also desirous to bring this matter to your personal knowledge, I have taken the liberty to make this communication, and I now have the honor respectfully to request the submission of the whole case to the Attorney General, to whom the company will present their views of these questions if permitted. The Western Union Telegraph Company is a corporation whose stock is owned by a great number of persons throughout the country, including women, minors and others, who hold it for investment, who in no way participate in the management of its current affairs, and who certainly have had nothing to do with the technical breaches of law which, disputed as they are, constitute the sole basis for Mr Johnson's demand for so many millions of dollars. The institution of a suit in the name of the United States, upon a claim involving so large a possible liability, could not fail to exercise, temporarily, a depreciating effect upon the shares of the Company, which would benefit only the speculative dealers of Wall Street, and would seriously injure the body of stockholders who, though without fault, must thus bear all the loss. In the character of trustee for these stockholders, it is my duty to spare no proper effort to prevent the beginning of such a suit. I am advised, and am fully convinced, that the United States has no just, legal or other ground of complaint against this Company, and that the claims and the interpretation of statutes put forward by Mr Johnson are wholly and equally groundless. With the belief that a similar opinion in the mind of the learned Attorney-General will be the result of his examination, and that after such examination neither you nor he will permit the injustice and injury which would be the only result of such a suit, I confidently submit the whole case, and will hold myself ready, with the counsel of the company, to attend upon the Attorney-General at his convenience." LS, *ibid.*, Letters from the President. On Sept. 8, USG endorsed this letter. "Respectfully referred to the Atty General who will please give this matter a personal hearing and report his opinion to me on completion of the examination" ES, *ibid.* On Sept. 19, Williams wrote to Orton. ". . . I shall prepare an opinion as soon as I conveniently can, and if you desire to submit in support of your views anything more than what has been sent to me, it will be gladly received and promptly considered. . . ." Copy, *ibid.*, Letters Sent. On the same day, Williams sent a similar letter to Reverdy Johnson, Baltimore. Copy, *ibid.*

To Adolph E. Borie

Long Branch, N. J.
Aug. 2d /74

MY DEAR MR. BORIE:

Mrs. Grant and I will be glad to have a visit from you and Mrs. Borie now as soon as it may best suit your convenience. We are entirely alone now, the boys having left yesterday for a tramp through Western Pa[1] They will probably be gone about three weeks. Mrs. Sharpe will be here however room is abundant. Will you write me about the time you think you can come.

Mrs. Grant joins me in kindest remembrances to Mrs. Borie & yourself.

We have had three letters from Nellie in the last two weeks. She writes very cheerfully, and in her last letter speaking of her new Aunts that she has made the acquaintance of, that while she likes them all there is one she likes better than any of the others because she reminds her so much of Mrs. Borie.

Yours Truly
U. S. GRANT

HON. A. E. BORIE
EX. SEC. OF THE NAVY

ALS, The Filson Club, Louisville, Ky. See letter to Adolph E. Borie, Aug. 12, 1874.

1. See Jesse R. Grant, *In the Days of My Father General Grant* (New York, 1925), pp. 140–49.

To William W. Belknap

Long Branch, N. J.
Aug. 5th /74

DEAR SIR:

In designating applicants for appointment to the Army I do not recollect, the name of Kinzie, of Chicago, son of the late Paymaster of that name. I promised Gen. Hunter,[1] his Uncle, last fall that he should be appointed. You may therefore add his name now if it is not already on the list.

Very Truly
U. S. GRANT

GEN. W. W. BELKNAP
SEC. OF WAR

ALS, DNA, RG 94, ACP, 3702 1874. On Dec. 24, 1873, Frank X. Kinzie, Chicago, wrote to USG requesting an appointment to the U.S. Army. ALS, *ibid.* On Dec. 7, 1874, USG nominated Kinzie as 2nd lt., 20th Inf. Maj. Robert A. Kinzie had died on Dec. 13, 1873.

1. On Aug. 1, 1874, David Hunter, Washington, D. C., wrote to USG. "On behalf of my brother, Medical Director Lewis B. Hunter, of the United States Navy, now on the Retired List, I most earnestly beg the appointment of Cadet at the United States Military Academy, West Point, for his son Charles H. Hunter, to enter in the year 1876. when he will be in his eighteenth year, having been born in Philadelphia, on the 23d of December 1858. Med. Director Lewis B. Hunter has been all his life in the Navy, has served twenty one years at sea, his last sea service having been as Medical Director to Admiral Porter at the capture of Fort Fisher. Dr Hunter has a large young family, and is greatly in need of this kindness," ALS, *ibid.*, Correspondence, USMA. On Dec. 24, USG endorsed this letter. "Refered to the Sec. of War. Special attention directed to this application when appointments to the Military Academy are next made." AES, *ibid.* Charles H. Hunter graduated USMA in 1880.

To Julia C. Conkling

————

Long Branch, N. J.
August 5th 1874,

MY DEAR MRS. CONKLING;

Mrs. Grant & I will be pleased if we can have you & Miss Bessie spend next week with us at the Branch, where we will try to make your time pass pleasantly. Bring the Senator too, *just for company while traveling*, and to look after the baggage.

Very Truly Yours
U. S. GRANT

ALS, DLC-Roscoe Conkling.

To Hamilton Fish

————

Long Branch, N. J.
Aug. 6th /74

DEAR GOVR

Your letter announcing your departure from Washington, and the illness of Mrs. Fish, and one after your arrival home, were duly received. I hope by this time Mrs. Fish has entirely recovered.— When you return to Washington I wish you would pass this way and spend at least a day with me. Should you not contemplate an early return I would like to see you some day next week. I have no business that will not keep so I set no particular day but leave you to select such time as may be most convenient to you.

Very Truly Yours

U. S. GRANT

HON. HAMILTON FISH
SEC. OF STATE

ALS, DLC-Hamilton Fish. On Aug. 7, 1874, Friday, Secretary of State Hamilton Fish, Garrison, N. Y., twice wrote to USG. "I have a letter from Baron de Schwartz-Senborn, the new Austrian Minister, asking when he may have an opportunity to present his letter of Appointment—As a presentation for this purpose, is more formal, & should, as I think, be made at the seat of Government, I have replied that you were at present absent from Washington, & the presentation could take place on your return, & that I would enquire & inform him when you expect to be in Washington. The Doctor advises Mrs Fish to try the Sea air   I will, consequently, accompany her on Monday, (if she be well enough then to leave home) to the sea-shore, & will leave her there, & expect to be in Washington on Wednesday. If Genl. Babcock will have the goodness to let me know, (there) if any time is fixed for your being in Washington I will inform the Minister." "I am this Evenig in the receipt of yours of yesterday. I wrote you this morning announcing my expectation to accompany Mrs Fish to Long Island, on Monday. Should she be well enough to make the journey on that day, I will return to N. Y. on Tuesday, & if the connection of trains & Steamboats will allow, will take the Boat for Long Branch on Tuesday (otherwise on Wednesday) on my way to Washington—" ALS (press), *ibid.* See Fish diary, Aug. 12, 1874, *ibid.*

On Aug. 5, Wednesday, Fish had written to USG. "Baron Lederer, will, with your permission call upon you at Long Branch, on Saturday next at about noon, to present his letters of recall—He has submitted the remarks with which he proposes to accompany the presentation—of which I enclose a copy: also a reply by you for your approval—He may desire to have the copy of your reply—should you give it to him, there is a another copy for the files of the Department." ALS, ICarbS; press, DLC-Hamilton Fish. On July 31, Fish had written to USG on the same subject. ALS (press), *ibid.* See letter to Hamilton Fish, Sept. 2, 1874.

To John Hoey

———

Long Branch, N. J., 10 August 1874

I have some important business with him [*Governor Fish*] of a public nature such as filling the Russian mission . . . and then too there is a further embarrassment in the way. I had accepted an engagement with John Hill [1] . . . to visit the mining and manufacturing regions of Northern New Jersey . . . had to break the engagement after he had made all arrangements for the trip . . .

Brackets in original, Swann Galleries, Sale No. 1374, May 31, 1985, no. 110. The catalog described this letter as explaining USG's cancellation of a meeting with a "Mr. Dinsman," presumably William B. Dinsmore. See *PUSG*, 24, 10–12.

On Jan. 31, [*1874*], John Hoey, New York City, wrote to USG. "I dont often trouble my friends in Washington in reference to positions for any one. I am often asked, and all occasions decline. But the present case is one that I feel an interest in on a/c of the applicant being the Son of one of the founders of the American Express Co, Mr Fargo who writes me in his behalf is President of that Institution. Mr Livingston who makes the application wants to be made Paymaster in the Army. You will see from his letter to Mr Fargo that he pays me the Compliment of thinking I have some influence with you, and asks that I may call your attention to his Name as an applicant. I shall be pleased to know (if you can do so consistently) that his name will be considered when you send in your list of Candidates for the position he seeks. I trust you are quite well, and that Mrs Grant and Miss Nellie are enjoying good health. Mrs Hoey and Josie send their remembrances" ALS, DNA, RG 94, Applications for Positions in War Dept. The enclosures, Crawford Livingston, St. Paul, to William G. Fargo, Jan. 3, 187[4], and Fargo, Buffalo, to Hoey, Jan. 20, 1874, are *ibid.* No appointment followed.

1. Born in 1821 in N. Y., John Hill moved to N. J. in 1845 and served as U.S. Representative (1867–73).

To Benjamin H. Bristow

———

Long Branch, N. J.
Aug. 11th /74

Hon. B. H. Bristow,
Sec. of the Treas.[1]
Dear Sir:

If you have made no offer of Agency for the Govt. to transact the business of exchanging new bonds for old ones—in Europe—I would suggest the name of Hon. A. G. Cattell.[2] He was successful on the former occasion of exchange of bonds, and necessarily gained experience, and made acquaintances, which it will be well to avail ourselves of.

If you have offered the place to any one else, or if you think better of another choice, I do not ask that you should make this appointment without further consultation.

Very Truly Yours,
U. S. Grant

ALS, DLC-Benjamin H. Bristow. On Aug. 13, 1874, Secretary of the Treasury Benjamin H. Bristow wrote to USG. "I have your note of the 11th inst touching the appointment of

a general Agent of the Treasury Department in connection with the sale and delivery of
5% bonds abroad, and in reply have the honor to say that I had a note from Genl Babcock
last week expressing your desire to have Mr Cattell appointed such Agent to which I made
no reply for the reason that I hoped to see and confer with you in person on the subject before taking action. I have not tendered the Agency to any one; and I entertain serious doubt
whether under the contract made with the Bankers it is desirable or proper to appoint such
an Agent. However I desire to talk over this matter with you fully before taking action,
and if agreeable to you I will come over to Long Branch for that purpose next week." ALS
(press), *ibid.* On Aug. 14, Orville E. Babcock, Long Branch, wrote to Bristow. "The President directs me to acknowledge the receipt of your favor of the 13th, and to say that he will
see you on the matter you refer to: the appt of Mr Cattell, and to say that he will be pleased
to have you telegraph on receipt of this what day you will be here, that he may be at home
—I would add to his message that he has been intending to leave the middle or last of the
week for the Catskill Mts, yet he may not go. I mention this simply to post you. I enclose a
letter from Senator Sargent, recommending Mr Cattell. There are other recommendations
from prominent friends. Will you please return this letter to me. I send it simply to inform
you—" ALS, *ibid.* On Aug. 15 and 17, Bristow telegraphed to Babcock. "I can go over any
day after Monday that suits the presidents convenience.   please advise me" "Will the president be in New York any day this week   I cant leave here until to morrow & must return at
once   I want to see him few minutes only" Telegrams received (the first on Aug. 16),
DLC-USG, IB. See letter to Benjamin H. Bristow, Aug. 30, 1874.

On July 14, Babcock, Saratoga Springs, N. Y., had written to Bristow. "The President
directs me to drop you a note and say that if on the 22nd, when you have opened the pro-
posals for funding the national debt you wish to consult with him, on that or other matters he will be pleased if you will run down to the Branch, to see him, and stay at his cottage while there. You can leave W. on the 9. Pm train of the 22nd for N. Y—and arrive in
N. Y. in time to take the 7.30. boat for the Branch reaching the Branch at 9.30. Am of the
23rd. If you will telegraph to me on the 22nd that you will come I on any ~~special~~ particular train I will meet you at the depot and drive you to the Presidents, and if by chance he
has company, you will find plenty of room at my place. He expects to leave here so as to be
home Saturday—I hope Mrs Bristow is quite well, and if she has returned that bring her
with you to the Branch—We have room in abundance." ALS, DLC-Benjamin H. Bristow.

On July 27, Bristow telegraphed to USG, Long Branch. "Parties telegraph this morning acceptance of my modifications of their bid, and will be here to-morrow to close up the
matter. Meantime they ask that no announcement of the amount of their firm bid be made
until to-morrow." Telegram received, DLC-USG, IB. On July 29, Babcock, Long Branch,
wrote to Bristow. "On reaching home this morning I submitted the copy of the Syndicate
Contract to the President and explained the points you wished me to explain. He says he
is glad it has terminated so well, and that he not only believes the entire loan will be placed
but that it will make way, in his opinion, for the 4 per cent bonds and for specie payments.
He directs me to say that, in his opinion, Senator Cattell, from his thorough knowledge of
the matter, and his extensive acquaintance with the financial people of Europe, is perhaps,
the most suitable person to take charge of the matter in Europe, and that if you agree with
him he will be pleased to have you offer the position to him. The President and family quite
well &c." Copy, *ibid.*, II, 2. See Ross A. Webb, *Benjamin Helm Bristow: Border State Politician*
(Lexington, Ky., 1969), pp. 141–49.

1. On June 1, USG had nominated Bristow as secretary of the treasury in place of
William A. Richardson; on the same day, USG nominated Richardson as judge, U.S. Court
of Claims. On June 12, USG authorized John F. Hartley, asst. secretary of the treasury, to
serve as act. secretary in Bristow's absence. DS, Joseph W. P. Frost, Eliot, Maine. See Ham-

ilton Fish diary, June 1, 1874; Nevins, *Fish*, pp. 708–11, 714–16; Webb, *Benjamin Helm Bristow*, pp. 134–37.

On April 5, Vice President Henry Wilson, Philadelphia, had written to USG. "*Private.* . . . I venture to write you *in confidence* a few ~~lines~~ Suggestions. When you have read this I beg you to destroy it. I keep no copy. Never have I written you a word that I did not think would be for the good of the country, the Republican party and your own. I write so now. You will remember I spoke to you about Mr. Richardson's nomination. It is now said he is to go out of the Treasury. I never felt so anxious as I did about his going into that great position. I knew he must fail—that the country would be against him, as it is. His appointment injured your administration. This was so in Massachusetts. He has no support there or in Congress. Since I have been in Washington the past few days I have heard the strongest condemnation of his unfitness. I have nothing against him but he is not up to the needs of that position of great responsibility. Few are up to it. If he is to go out I beg you for the sake of the country, the party, and your own to get the ablest man you can. I hear a pressure is made for Delano—that Schenck is thought of. There are able men high in office that say that there are things in the Interior Department that are not right, and that they will yet come out. No risks should be taken now. There are difficulties enough. Discontent is everywhere. We are passing through a Storm of criticism and denunciation. You can carry us through the Wilderness as you once did. I think I know the people. We have a hard fight before us to carry the next house. I have pressed this upon our friends in Congress. You can do more to save the House than the Republican members can to Save themselves. If you could get one of such business men as Gov. Morgan, of N. Y., Wm Gray, of Mass., Mr. Drexel, or Joseph Patterson of this city at the head of the Treasury I am sure it would be a good thing. All would recognize their honesty and knowledge of Finance. If you cannot get a business man for that post and take a lawyer would not Mr. Hoar be a good man. You know him. He is able, honest—the nation knows it. He is a firm Republican and *your true friend ever.—I know it.* His appointment would give peace in Mass—would give you Strength. Men feel and say Gen. Butler has all influence and power. Men would then say 'the President favors no man or faction   He recognizes Butler & his friends, and he recognizes Mr. Hoar and other men that dont agree with Butler. The President is all right and means to be fair and just to all.' Hoar's appointment at this time would tend to peace, would strengthen the party and help you. I have no doubt of this. Gen. Butler and [o]ne or two others at first might not approve it, but that would do no harm. It is the growing idea that a few men have too much power that hurts the party & yourself. All shades of opinion & all sections of the Republican party would be recognized—no man & no section proscribed. I hope you will save the next House—rally the party—unite it—lead it to victory & close your Administration as you did the war in a blaze of glory. This is my hope, wish, and prayer." Copy, Michael Hutchison, Point Clear, Ala.

On April 15 and subsequently, Secretary of State Hamilton Fish recorded in his diary. "I call upon the President . . . The question of a possible change in the Cabinet arising, he says that Richardson is shortly to leave the Cabinet and would probably have presented his resignation before this time but for the pending investigation in Congress—that he had last evening with Messrs. Dawes & Boutwell, in which Dawes, (Chairman of the Committee of Way and Means prosecuting the Sanborn investigation) said that there was no evidence affecting the character of honesty or charging corruption upon the officers of the Treasury in connection with these Claims, although there had been much loseness and improvidence and that they had come to conclusion that Mr. Richardson had better withhold his resignation until close investigation. With respect to a successor he had thought to advance the Secretary of the Interior, Mr. Delano—At the close of the interview he decided that it would not be advisable to make such appointment. He was at loss whom to name;

would select no one from New England, the whole of which seemed covered with 'Butlerism' or Anti 'Butlerism', that New England with less population and less representation in the lower House of Congress than New York and but little if any more than Pennsylvania, but with twelve Senators to Pennsylvania's two, had for many years past had all the time one and much of the time two members of the Cabinet. He would like therefore if a proper man could be found, to make a selection from Pennsylvania—Suggested two names, asking me if I knew Joseph Patterson of Philadelphia of whom he spoke very highly; and he also spoke very highly of Don. Cameron's capacity and character but his relations to the Senator seemed to be an obstacle to his having the position." "24 April . . . After the adjournment of the Cabinet Mr. Robeson spoke to me about Washburne as Secretary of the Treasury having previously suggested the same name. I advised him to speak with the President. In the evening he calls at my house, has seen the President, who expressed himself pleased with the suggestion, but did not know whether the selection would be agreeable to the other members of the Cabinet. That Washburne might be inclined to interfere and meddle with other Departments than his own; he apprehended that I might not like the selection and had referred to Washburne's having endeavoured to make the principal appointments in the Department of State during his temporary occupancy. Robeson thinks the President would make the appointment if I express myself as having no objection." "Saturday, April 25th 1874. I call upon the President and refer to Mr Robeson's suggestion of Washburne's name for the position of Secretary of the Treasury, and express my own satisfaction with such a selection, should he think proper to make it. I mention my fear that Washburne might be a little indolent, with a heavy detail business and would therefore require a very efficient Assistant, . . ." "Friday, May 1, 1874. Mr. Delano (Secretary of the Interior) calls at my house in the morning before I start for the Department and says, that last year when Richardson was appointed Secretary of the Treasury, or about that time, Carpenter and other Senators had told him the President had said that Richardson was to remain until July only then he should appoint Delano—the same thing had since been repeatedly told him and it had also got into the newspapers; that now there seemed a doubt, and should any other appointment be made he should have to regard it as a want of confidence and an intimation on the part of the President that he wished him to resign his present position. He wished my advice as to whether he should go to the President and speak with him on the subject—I decline giving any advice, but inquire whether the President had himself ever given him any assurance or had authorized the indications made him. He answered no, whereupon I told him he had no right, in my judgment to regard the expressions made as the fixed opinion of the President. . . ." DLC-Hamilton Fish. See *ibid.,* April 10, 1874.

On May 4, William E. Chandler, Washington, D. C., wrote to Elihu B. Washburne, Paris. "*Personal* . . . In view of the fact previously known to but few, now rumoured publicly that the President wishes you to go into the Treasury Dept I think you ought to know my opinion of the political situation. Up to the time of the President's veto we were drifting helplessly on a lee shore; and were tolerably sure to lose the next House; & after that possibly, probably, the Presidential fight. Now the Presidents veto has changed all that. With a vigorous administration of the Treasury by a western hard money man we can save the House. Therefore much depends on the Treasury appointment *and I do not consider you at liberty to refuse it. . . .*" ALS, DLC-Elihu B. Washburne. On May 5, Fish recorded in his diary. "Before the meeting of the Cabinet, General Belknap and myself being present, the President said to me that he thought he could do no better than to name Washburne as Secretary of the Treasury; but he did not wish to positively offer it to him yet; and instructed me to telegraph to Washburne, and without either saying that I was or was not authorized so to do to ask him whether he would accept the position in case it were offered him. I subsequently drew a telegram . . . submitted it to the President who approved it and authorized me to send it." DLC-Hamilton Fish. The draft of the telegram is *ibid.* On May 7, Washburne wrote to USG. "I yesterday received telegraphic despatches from Gov. Fish and Mr. Robeson both to the effect that if the Secretaryship of the Treasury should be tendered to me it was important that I should accept it. I infer, therefore, that in case I would accept, it was your purpose to offer me the high and responsible position. For such a mark of your confidence and for that further proof of your personal consideration and kindness I wish to present to you my profound and grateful thanks. No man can administer the vast affairs of the Treasury Department who has not the most perfect health and the greatest powers of endurance. It is with infinite regret that I am obliged to say that I feel that my own health is not equal to the position. I cannot be where there is work to do without doing it with all my might. While in the lazy life I lead here my general health is very good, yet my old troubles give me constant admonitions. For the last three weeks I have been suffering a good deal from those same old ague pains which produced that terrible congestive chill I had at your house in July 1866 and the effect of which I have always felt and always shall feel to the last day of my life. Indeed I think I shall be obliged to go again this summer to seek the waters of Bohemia for my health. I am certain, therefore, that if I should go into the Treasury, I should break down before the end of the summer. It would, under such circumstances, be alike unjust to you and your administration to accept the appointment if tendered. I feel obliged, therefore, to telegraph Gov. Fish that considerations of health and family would compel me to decline if offered. Though it would have been a good deal of a sacrifice for my family to break up and leave here now while my children are all so well placed at school, still I should not have hesitated at it had I believed my health equal to the task. I know of nothing that I would not do were it in my power to gratify your wishes. It would have been a great pleasure to have shared with you the labors and responsibilities of your administration, particularly at this time when I am in such thorough sympathy and accord with your views on the great and paramount question of the currency. Renewing to you the expressions of my deep sense of obligation and the assurance of my sincere friendship, . . ." ALS, ICHi.

On June 2, William Dennison, Columbus, Ohio, wrote to USG. "Let me make to you my hearty congratulations on your appointment of Genl Bristow as Secretary of the Treasury, which, I cannot doubt, the country will warmly approve." ALS, USG 3. On June 3, Maj. James S. Brisbin, Omaha, wrote to USG. "I wish to thank you for appointing to office Col Bristow. While in command in Kentucky in 1864 65 66 & 67 and 8 I came to know Bristow very well & learned to regard him highly. I think he is one of the very best men in the Country honest capable & fearless. It gives your old friends great pleasure to see you call such men around you. I am confident Bristow will make an able Secretary of the Treasury and an agreeable member of the Cabinet. We were all much gratified with the veto of the finance bill & your action has saved us many wild cat speculations and put the Country on a better money basis than ever since the war   The correctness ease and facility with which you administer the Govermnt astonishes enemies as well as your friends. It is very gratifying to your old Army friends as they feel it evidences the fact that an Army officer (a soldier) may also be a good civil officer and fit for something else besides filling a station in a small Fort on the top of the Rocky Mountains   Your son Fred was here once to see us since he has been with Genl Sheridan. I was astonished to see how he had grown If they open the pay corps I wish to goodness you would make Fredrick a Paymaster. I will write him a strong letter any time he wants it. I was in Washington for a day or two last winter and saw Col Backcock but saw you were busy & so did not ask to see you   I know how busy you always are, but I feel you will be glad to hear from me for in this case the letter comes from not only a friend but who belongs to a class of men who never bother you for office & who prize you for yourself & not the official position you happen to hold In after years when no longer President it is in our famalies you will find rest & a welcome greater than if you were President. May God bless & prosper you alway General . . . P. S. Gen Ord sends regards" ALS, PHi.

2. On June 23, USG had nominated Alexander G. Cattell, former U.S. Senator from N. J., as D. C. commissioner; Cattell declined the position.

To Adolph E. Borie

Long Branch, N. J.
Aug. 12th /74

MY DEAR MR. BORIE:

Mrs. Grant and I are delighted to hear that Mrs. Borie is pleased with our proposed Western trip, and will accompany us. I am sure you will enjoy it and come back satisfied that the boasting of the Western people about their country is based on reality. Of course there will be plenty of room for Zella. We will have an entire car to ourselves and can stop, if any of the party should require it, any place on the road. I will arrange to go through Pittsburgh, Columbus, Cincinnati & Indianapolis on the way out; spending time enough in Cincinnati to take a birds-eye view of the place. Returning we will stop at Springfield and Chicago, and come by the Lake shore to Cleveland, thence to Pittsburgh and home.

You can visit us at Washington, and start from there, or meet us at Harrisburg, as you may prefer.

Mrs. Grant's and my love to all.

Yours Truly
U. S. GRANT

ALS, PHi. See letter to Adolph E. Borie, Sept. 22, 1874.

Endorsement

Respectfully refered to the Sec. of State.—Please ascertain from the Sec. of the Treas. or the Sec. of the Navy, wheth[er] it will be convenient to send a vessel this Summer—and to accommodate the three Icelanders with a passage up and back,—as they request in the accompanying petition.—It seems to me desirable to have Alasca settled, if it can be done, by an industrious hardy people, accustomed to a rigorous climate as the Icelanders are.

Please forward reply to the address of John Olafsson—the leading Icelander in this country—care of Marston Niles,[1] 16 Wall Street, New York City.

U. S. GRANT

AUG. 17TH /74

AES, DNA, RG 59, Miscellaneous Letters. Written on a petition of Fridjov Fridriksson *et al.*, Milwaukee, Aug. 2, 1874, "the day of the festival in remembrance of the settlement of Iceland one thousand years ago." "We the undersigned, born and brought up in Iceland, who have emigrated to the United States; beg leave to lay before your Excellency the subject of Icelandic emigration, and to present a plan by which, as we believe, the immigration of Icelanders to the United States can be made very extensive, and by which also an immense territory of the United States, which otherwise will probably for a long time remain uninhabited by any civilized race, can be settled. This territory is Alaska. By both Americans and the people of most European countries, it is considered too northerly-lying and too cold. The population of Iceland is about seventy thousand, and it is bent on emigrating. Since our forefathers landed there, one thousand years ago, the climate has gradually but greatly changed. Neither trees nor grain can now be made to grow there. By degrees it has become more and more barren; and many of the inhabitants would now starve, if it were not for the fish which abound on the coast, and for their herds of cattle, which enable them to purchase corn in foreign lands. It is little more than a year since emigration from Iceland began. There are now in the United States towards three hundred Icelanders, and in Canada towards two hundred; and those in the former country are mostly in Wisconsin and the neighboring states. This seems a small emigration; but it is in reality large, considering the suddenness of the movement, and the great difficulty of obtaining in Iceland a market for commodities sufficiently to raise money for the voyage; and considering above all the fact that the Icelanders are perhaps more than any other people, attached to their own countrymen, customs, laws and language, and that as yet no region has been found so far adapted in climate to receive a large Icelandic immigration, that the emigrating Icelander might be able to feel that either he was about to join his countrymen in a new and better land, or else that in a few years the bulk of his countrymen would follow him thither. Were the Icelanders to begin to establish themselves in such a region, the mass of the Icelandic population would leave their barren cliffs without a regret, because they would consider ~~that~~ the grand body of their country men, wherever they might dwell, to be their real country. . . . The region which we desire our men to look at is but a small portion of that vast territory, being only Kodiak Island, and the neighborhood of Cook's Inlet, and the long peninsula of Aliaska. We judge that two or three weeks upon the coast of the territory will be sufficient for our purposes, which are only to confirm the report of Dall in respect to these portions of the territory. We are most desirous to begin this summer, lest Canada (a country where our people might perhaps thrive for the present but which does not seem to us a desirable place of settlement for our race ~~but only for the present, thrive~~) should secure permanently the immigration of Icelanders which is just beginning. The Icelanders are poor, and the voyage from Iceland to Alaska (even by way of the Panama isthmus) is a long one; but we are sure that if a small Icelandic colony can only be established there, and if the settlers thrive, they will soon be able to bring over their relatives and friends, and that in the future the bulk of the population of Iceland will find their way thither. We have requested Mr Marston Niles, of 16 Wall Street, New York, to bear this memorial to your Excellency, together with an English translation of it, and otherwise to represent us with your Excellency. With deep esteem and great respect for the the President of the United States, . . ." DS (43 signatures; in Icelandic), *ibid.*; translation, *ibid.* See William H. Dall, *Alaska and Its Resources* (Boston, 1870). On Dec. 15, Jón Olafsson, New York City, wrote to USG concerning the expedition's findings. Copy, DNA, RG 59, Miscellaneous Letters. *Report of the Icelandic Committee from Wisconsin on the character and resources of Alaska* (Washington, 1875). On Dec. 19, U.S. Senator Frederick T. Frelinghuysen of N. J. wrote to USG. "Permit me to introduce to you my friend the Hon Nathaniel Niles—who is accompanied by Mr. Olefson, the Commissioner from the Icelanders to examine Alaska. These gentleman will occupy your time very briefly." Copy, DNA, RG 59, Miscellaneous Letters. A related letter of Dec. 5 from Frelinghuysen to USG is *ibid.*

On Aug. 22, Secretary of State Hamilton Fish had written to USG, Long Branch. "On the receipt of the Memorial of the Icelanders in Wisconsin I immediately sent a copy to the Treasury and one to the Navy Department, and am today in the receipt of an answer from the Navy, of which I enclose a copy for your information. It is physically impossible for the Committee to get to Alaska and return in time to send their report to Iceland by the first week in October when the last mail thither can be despatched. I enclose therefore a reply (under an open envelope) for your consideration, and if it meet your approval, to be mailed to the address named in the petition. In the reply I make no illusion to the enquiry of the Navy Department, as to the source whence the expenses of the Commission are to be defrayed. Should you desire a different reply to be made, I will make such as you shall direct. Some time in May last you directed the appointment of Dr. James Scoot of Ohio, as Consul at Honolulu in place of Mr. Mattoon, to whom you directed a letter to be sent requesting his resignation. The letter was sent on the 19th day of May; ample time has elapsed but Mr Mattoon has not forwarded the resignation. Little doubt can be entertained that he received the letter, as a letter was received from our Minister to that Country referring to Mr Mattoons contemplated withdrawal from the Consulate and Mr. Mattoon's friends in this Country seem to have been informed of it and are active in asking his retention. I enclose herewith an appointment of Dr. Scott and suspension of Mr. Mattoon, for your signature, in case you think best to make it at present. Possibly you may think proper to wait the expiration of four years from the date of Mr. Mattoon's appointment. A change seems necessary in the Consulate at Canton and I send also a Commission for Robt. M. Tindall, of Mississippi, who is the gentleman recommended by the entire Republican Delegation from that State, and who was agreed upon in case the change became necessary" Copy, *ibid.*, Reports to the President and Congress. On Aug. 20, Fish had written to Secretary of the Navy George M. Robeson, enclosing a copy of the petition. LS, *ibid.*, RG 45, Letters Received from the President.

On Jan. 27, Judge Robert A. Hill, U.S. District Court, Jackson, Miss., *et al.*, had written to USG recommending Robert M. Tindall for consul, Canton. LS (46 signatures), *ibid.*, RG 59, Letters of Application and Recommendation. On Feb. 3, Governor Adelbert Ames of Miss. endorsed this letter. "Respectfully referred to the President. It is the understanding of the Republican party that Dr Tindall shall have (of course by the consent of the President) the Consulate at Canton India now held by Dr Jewell of this State. The party is a unit in asking it—in which I join them." AES, *ibid.* On Dec. 8, USG nominated Tindall as consul, Canton.

On June 20, Thomas Spencer, consular agent, Hilo, had written to USG. "It is no Ordinary Occasion that Prompts me to adress You, and did I not Concider it Vital to the interests & honour of Our Beloved Country I should not have the Pleasure of adressing You at this time. By the last mail from the U States we learned that their was and effort being made in Washington to superseed C S. Mattoon Esq as U S Consell at Honolulu,   I speak for my self and every american Citisen resideing on these Islands that we here this news with the most prefound regretts and all as one join in the Prayer that he may be retained It is No Ordinary Man that Can fill this Office & be beloved by his Country men respected by all   I have been a resident of these Islands for the last 23 years   I have business connectios with his office largely during that time and I must bespeke for mr Mattoon that in him I find a Gentleman a patriotic noble man one we are all proud off . . ." ALS, *ibid.* On June 29, J. Bates Dickson, Honolulu, wrote to USG. "Rumors from Washington reach us that efforts are being made to supersede Mr. Mattoon, the present U. S. Consul at this port. During my residence here of seven years, I have at intervals been employed at both the Legation and Consulate—and am familiar with the history of both offices and I believe I but express the unanimous opinion of all true Americans here, when I say that at no time since the offices were established has either been as worthily filled as by the present incumbents. By his uniformly courteous conduct, strict attention to business, just and impartial descisions, Mr. Mattoon has greatly endeared himself to this Community. For the first time in the history of this Consulate its its affairs are *honestly* managed. I have made these Islands my home, but I am as much a citizen of the United States now as when I entered the Army from Galena in 1861 and what little influence I may have I wish to use to advance the interests of my country here or at home—Personally I am wholly disinterested in this matter of the Consulate, but beleiving it would be very detrimental to the interests of the U. S. Government and to those of American Citizens here to have Mr. Mattoon leave us at present, I earnestly request you to give to this letter from a former neighbor and companion in arms some weight in your decision should the question of superseding our present Consul come before you" ALS, *ibid.* See *PUSG,* 7, 495. On the same day, Calvin S. Mattoon, Honolulu, wrote to USG seeking retention as consul. ALS, DNA, RG 59, Letters of Application and Recommendation. Related papers are *ibid.*; *ibid.,* Consular Despatches, Honolulu. See *PUSG,* 20, 275–76. On Aug. 22, USG suspended Mattoon.

On April 3, 1869, USG had nominated James Scott as secretary, Washington Territory. On Dec. 6, 1872, U.S. Senator John Sherman of Ohio wrote to USG. "The name of Dr James Scott of Lebanon Ohio will be presented to you for Consul at Honolulu: Dr Scott —is a very prominent Citizen of Ohio—for many years a member of our Legislature— the Editor & proprietor of a leading Republican paper—at one time Secretary and Ex Officio Governor of Washington Ter'y, and has held other positions of trust & responsbility He possesses the qualities and experience that eminently befit him for the position as Consul at Honolulu and I most heartily join in the application for his appointment" ALS, DNA, RG 59, Letters of Application and Recommendation. On the same day, Benjamin F. Wade, Washington, D. C., wrote to USG recommending Scott. ALS, *ibid.* Related papers are *ibid.* On July 27, 1874, Sherman, Mansfield, Ohio, wrote to Fish that Scott "got the impression from the President that he would be appointed and made arrangements accordingly." ALS, *ibid.* On Dec. 8, USG nominated Scott as consul, Honolulu.

On Jan. 15, James J. Cooper, Philadelphia, had written to USG. "I would most respectfully ask for the appointment of Consul at Honolulu. I enlisted in the Penna Volunteers U. S. Service, as a Private in april 1861, and was honorably discharged as Captain, December 5th 1864. For further reference I would refer your Excellency to the accompanying recommendations. Hoping that they may receive your favorable consideration . . ." ALS, *ibid.* Related papers are *ibid.* On June 5, USG nominated Cooper as consul, Seville. On

Jan. 12, 1876, Robert Lynch, Seville, wrote to USG. "You will have the kindness [t]o excuse my writing to you on [a] painful subject for the Government, that you so well represent. The late consul that the Amn Government sent here, James J. Cooper, was a great swindler and he availed himself of being representing here his own country to cheat as many respectable people as he could. He got from me fifty dollars which he came to ask, not as J. J. Cooper but as the Amn Representative in this city, saying that he was expecting orders from the Secretary at Washington as to how he ought to draw for his wages, and that as soon as he got them 'he, the Amn Consul' should pay all and be thankful. He also asked my brother, to pay for him a bill for wine that he drank (—although he is a member of a Temperance Society—) amounting to thirty five dollars, and after a long time of cheating him he tried to prove, with false witness, at law that the wine was a present that he receive[d] from my brother, but the seller of it said that it was ordered to by him by J. J. Cooper. Althoug he was condemned they could not collect that money from him because they did not want to give an scandal. Different times he tried to get more money from me saying always that 'he was not satisfied with the V-Consul' and giving me to understand that if I came to terms he should appoint me V-Consul as he had power to do so with any person whom he had confidence in. But as I did not give him more money, as he required, he went to *sell out* the V-Consulate to some body else. Few days before he left, he signed me the enclosed note, which I beg from you to be so good as to send it back, if you consider that the Government ought not to pay, or can not discount it, from his salary as captn. in the army and in that case I will try to collect it through some friend. Hoping to get your pardon for addressing myself to you in this matter, . . ." ALS, *ibid.*, Miscellaneous Letters. The enclosure is a promissory note for fifty dollars from Cooper to Lynch, dated July 15, 1875. Copy, *ibid.*

On May 11, 1874, Mrs. Robbins, Washington, D. C., had written to USG. "I came to you a few days since with reference to a consulship for Capt F A. Hussey of Maine a relative of the Hon' Owen Lovejoy of Ill. There are few removals by death and seldom by resignations. Is it not the fact that in order to obtain a vacancy it must be made   If I mistake not it is being done every day. Capt Hussey has made application at the State Department for the Consulate at Honolulu now filled by Mr Mattoon of this City. We are aware of the fact that complaints have been made against said incumbent. I know Mr & Mrs Mattoon personally   they have no children.   they are independent outside of his salary.   he has valuable property in this City and was for a long time a salaried officer of the Gov't before receiving this appointment which he has held for several years. Capt Hussey has never rec'd anything from Gov't. notwithstanding he lost his vessel during the war, which was seized by the Confederate Gov't and sunk in the Savannah river.   he had returned from a foreign voyage, knew nothing of the existing troubles had no war risk and of course rec'd no insurance.   he is a gentleman of experience and conversant with Consula[r] business. well qualified to fill that office.   he has a wife and three children,   If you could in your wisdom see fit to make this appointment you could do no harm to the present incumbent and would do a great deal of good to this family recently embarassed pecuniarily." ALS, *ibid.*, Letters of Application and Recommendation. No appointment followed.

In an undated note, USG had written. "Senator Sherman suggests the apt. of Wm Penn Nixon, of Cincinnati O. as Consul to Honolulu in place of Mattoon, incumbent." AN, Columbia University, New York, N. Y. On Jan. 27, 1871, Sherman wrote to USG. "In pursuance of our conversation this morning I submit the name of Hon Wm Penn Nixon of Cincinnati as worthy to fill and entitled to receive an appointment as a Minister Resident or Commissioner or first Class Consulate—He is a lawyer by profession—has been a member of the Ohio Assembly, long connected with the Cin. Chronicle and is a gentleman of education character and abilities" ALS, DNA, RG 59, Letters of Application and Recommendation. No appointment followed. On Sept. 12, 1875, USG wrote to George W. Childs introducing William Penn Nixon. Samuel T. Freeman Catalogue, Dec. 10, 1928, no. 224.

1. Marston Niles resigned as lt. commander, U.S. Navy, as of Dec. 25, 1871, to practice law in New York City. See *New York Times*, May 29, 1916.

To Hamilton Fish

———

Long Branch, N. J.
August 17th /74

HON. HAMILTON FISH;
SEC. OF STATE:
DEAR SIR:

Mr. Steinberger expresses a willingness to return to the Samoan Islands, without pay unless provided hereafter by Congress. I wish you would commission him with such powers as may be consistent with law and the best interests of the country. Mr. Steinberger will leave here this evening for the purpose of consulting with you on this matter and I therefore give him this letter to carry and deliver to you in person.

Should Mr. Steinberger return to the Samoan islands I think it would be well to time his departure so that he might be sent on a vessel of War ~~that~~ which might ~~be sent~~ go ~~there~~ without detriment to the service, or extra cost to the Navy department.

Mr. Steinberger contemplates a short visit to Europe, the object of which he will explain, and I would suggest that he be given dispatches to carry if there are any at the present time worthy of being sent by special Messenger.

Very respectfully
your obt. svt.
U. S. GRANT

ALS, DNA, RG 59, Despatches from Special Agents. On April 10, 1874, Secretary of State Hamilton Fish recorded in his diary. "Mr Steinberger's letters of 14 March and 8 April respecting Samoan Islands were read. I mention the general very creditable character of Steinberger's report and the President directs that it be communicated to Congress, that while he does not favor annexation or a protectorate he would recommend the appointment of a Commissioner to the islands with a salary of from three to five thousand dollars—" DLC-Hamilton Fish. See *PUSG*, 24, 101–3.

On June 4, Albert B. Steinberger, Washington, D. C., wrote to USG. "I have the honor to make application for the position of Consul General for Melbourne, Australia—If the jurisdiction of the office embraces all of Polynesia Government action in Samoa would not be attended with extraordinary expenditure. May I hope that my efforts in the South Pacific will prove an endorsement for me" ALS, DNA, RG 59, Letters of Application and Recommendation. Related papers are *ibid.*, including a letter of March 29, [*1869*], from Col. Rufus Ingalls, New York City, to Secretary of War John A. Rawlins, recommending Steinberger as Mexican Claims commissioner. On July 3, 1874, Fish recorded in his diary a conversation with USG. "He wishes to send Steinberger to the Samoan Islands. I tell him we can appoint Steinberger Consul and give him specific diplomatic powers for some special object, but cannot give him a salary: the President requested me to allow his accounts." DLC-Hamilton Fish. See letter to Principal Chiefs of Samoa, Dec. 11, 1874.

Letter of Introduction

Long Branch, N. J.

August 18th /74

This will introduce Gen. H. G. Wright, U. S. Engineers, and the mixed board of Army & Civil Engineers of which he is president, to the representatives of the United States—Ministers & Consuls—in Europe. This board visits europe professionally, and will appreciate facilities extended to them in aid of the accomplishment of the object of their visit as a favor to their government as well as to themselves personally. I bespeak for them such kind offices as may be of service.

U. S. GRANT

ALS, DLC-Cyrus B. Comstock. Lt. Col. Horatio G. Wright headed a commission to survey the mouth of the Mississippi River. See Proclamation, July 3, 1874; *PUSG*, 10, 406.

On June 24, 1874, USG had written to ministers and consuls. "This will introduce to you Genl. Edwd F. Winslow who visits Europe for purposes of business & pleasure   Gen. Winslow served with distinction in the Union Army during the late rebellion, & is a worthy gentleman. I shall be pleased if you will extend to him such courtesies as you can during his stay in your vicinity" Copy, DLC-USG, II, 2.

On July 2, USG wrote to Elihu B. Washburne, Paris. "I take pleasure in introducing to you Dr. Geo. H. Mitchell, who formerly was a Surgeon in our army, and at one time served near me at Nashville, and is now a resident of New York." Copy, *ibid.*

On [*July*] 12, Sunday, USG, Long Branch, telegraphed to Secretary of State Hamilton Fish. "Cannot Passport be sent to A. T. Stewart who sails for Europe on wednesday Next" Telegram received (on July 13, at 10:00 A.M.), DLC-Hamilton Fish.

On July 24, U.S. Representative Charles B. Farwell of Ill., Chicago, wrote to USG. "My two young friends George & Charles Holt, sons of D. R. Holt Esq, a leading lumber merchant & citizen of my district, will start from here within ten days for an extended tour in Europe. These young men are intelligent and educated, and are fine specimens of american boys. They go abroad for pleasure and I ask a letter of introduction to our foreign representatives for them." ALS, DNA, RG 59, Miscellaneous Letters. On July 27, USG endorsed this letter to Fish. AES, *ibid.*

On Dec. 8, USG wrote to ministers and consuls. "I take pleasure in presenting to you Major Geo. A. Gordon, U. S. A. who proposes traveling in Europe for pleasure and for information. Maj. Gordon is commended to you as a gentleman worthy of such courtesies as you may be able to extend to him while he remains in your vicinity." Copy, DLC-USG, II, 2.

On Dec. 19, USG wrote to ministers and consuls. "This will present to you Mr. John S. Ricker of Milwaukee Wis., who proposes traveling in Europe with his family for pleasure. Mr. Ricker is commended to you as a gentleman worthy of such courtesies as you may be able to extend to him while he remains in your vicinity." LS, Milwaukee Public Library, Milwaukee, Wis.

Also in 1874, USG wrote similar letters of introduction for S. Warren Ingersoll, George Schneider, William A. Bartlett, Dr. W. H. Barrett, Samuel D. Hastings, R. S. Newbold, and Mrs. E. R. Stevans. Copies, DLC-USG, II, 2.

To Benjamin H. Bristow

Martha's Vineyard, Mass.
Aug. 30th /74

Hon. B. H. Bristow,
Sec. of the Treas.
Dear Sir:

Your letter of the 25th inst. was handed me just as I was going aboard of the City of Peking on Wednesday last.[1] Since that I have had no opportunity of answering it until now. In fact there has been no necessity for haste about it, nor for answering at all except that I wish to correct one or two impressions you have: first: in regard to increased deposites with Jay Cooke, McCullough &Co. by the Navy department. This is due to the Sec. of the Navy particularly. Some time after the failure of Jay Cooke &Co. in this country the Sec. of the Navy, in company with the Sec. of the Treas. called on me and stated substantially that if the Navy account was then withdrawn from the English house it would break it, and the Government would loose the amount then on deposite—a half million or thereabouts—beside something in the neighborhood of 200 thousand due from the First Nat. Bank of Washington. By increasing the deposite one Million security could be obtained for the entire sum due from both houses.

There were other considerations urged also for this course—if I remember them correctly—such such as saving other houses by buying from them exchange when there was no demand for it in this
country &c. The telling ground for increasing govt. deposite was
however that near seven hundred thousand dollars would be saved by
it. With some little reluctance I approved the course recommended
more by the Sec. of the Treas. than by the Sec. of the Navy. I doubt
now whether the course pursued was the wise one or not—think
rather it was not—but be that as it may it was pursued with my approval entirely in the interest of government. Since that time the Sec.
of the Navy has kept a Navy Paymaster in London, to whom all remit-
tances for the Navy are sent, and who has instructions not to keep
one farthing of it with McCullough. All London drafts by nNaval officers however are on Jay Cooke, McCullough &Co. and are accepted
by the latter but payied by the Paymaster. Apparently therefore as
sums are drawn for, and accepted by Mc the account goes down, and
up again when money is payied by the Paymaster insted of the house
accepting them. As the securities are disposed of, and the money realized government gets the money and the account is permanently
reduced that amount.—In my letter to you I may have been a little
ambiguous as to my authority for saying that I had formed the idea
that Cattell was to intimate with McCullough while in London, kept
his office in his bank &c. In fact do not remember what I said on this
subject as I kept no copy of my letter. But the opinions I formed on
this subject come more from what Gov.r Jewell told me. His information however probably came from rival banking houses that would
be glad to have the account themselves, and should be received with
a grain of allowance, and should be ingnored entirely when the word
of Mr. Cattell to exactly the contrary is had.—Now in regard to
Mr. Bigelow?[2] I have never heard a word against his integrity or his
capacity. I have however against his fitness for the head of such a position as he is being intrusted with. If I understand the matter the
agent in charge with of the exchange of bonds has large amounts of
them in his possession before the exchange is made. A man so entrusted should all the time have his wits about him. When the former
negociations were going on Mr. B. was on several occasions, while in

London, in such a condition as not to know where he was or what he was doing. This was carried to such an extent that Mr. Cattell had to remonstrate with him for it, in presence of his wife, and exact from him a written pledge not to take another drop of liquor while in London. This pledge I believe he kept. In regard to sending Mr. Cattell again of course I do not urge it. My interest in his behalf was first believing in his entire integrity and fitness,—he having been once tried —and my desire to accommodate the Sec. of the Navy.—I dislike McCullough more than any living American,[3] but I could not let any dislike for him cause loss to the government or thwart the success of an important governmental negociation; and I would not like it to stand in the way of the accomplishment of proper interests of friends who have always been ~~tried~~ true. The house of McCullough & Co. cannot be of use now however and unless I am incorrectly informed, are being got rid of as fast as possible. I understand that another house has been designated to disburse the Navy account—the house of Seligman &Co.[4]

It seems to me that prudence would dictate that some well known responsible person should be assigned to take principle charge of the negociations in London. Whether it be Mr. Cattell or another I leave entirely to your judgement, or whether another be appointed atall I leave until I can hear from you again. I will be at Long Branch on Tuesday next.[5]

Very Truly yours
U. S. GRANT

ALS, DLC-Benjamin H. Bristow. On Sept. 2, 1874, Secretary of the Treasury Benjamin H. Bristow wrote to USG. "General Babcock handed me on yesterday your letter of the 30th Ulto from Martha's Vineyard I hope it is not necessary to assure you of my entire freedom from all personal feeling in the matter to which your letter relates. What I have done has been prompted by a sense of duty only. I entertain a sincere conviction that the appointment of an Agent outside the regular officers, and Clerks of this Department would not only be unauthorized, because it is unneccessary, but might lead to mischievous consequences. The fullest consideration of the matter strengthens this conviction. If we have no officer in the Department fit to be trusted with this London business, surely it is time to make some changes. What do you say to sending Mr Taylor, the Comptroller? I sent Mr Bigelow because I found him at the head of the Loan Division, and was assured by persons in whom I had confidence that he was a suitable person. I made careful inquiry into his capacity, and his conduct when he was in London before. I heard of one irregularity on his part, indeed he frankly admitted it, but assured me it had occurred but once, & then under peculiar circumstances; and made the most solemn promises that it should not occur again I sent my private Secretary with Mr Bigelow with a private cipher, and instructions to cable me often, and to advise me of the slightest irregularity on the part of Mr Bigelow, or any other clerk. In selecting other clerks I have inquired closely into their capacity, integrity and habits, and feel confident that no mistake has been made in the selections. The locks of all safes are so arranged that it is impossible that loss should occur without the connivance of four persons. I am quite sure that the irregularities of Mr Bigelow have been greatly exaggerated; but in view of your suggestion I prefer to send some officer of the Deptmt to London to take charge of the business, and will send any one of them upon your suggestion. I am reluctant to annoy you with matters personal to myself, but since General Babcock informs me that the Honerable Secretary of the Navy has sent you a copy of his letter to me I have deemed it proper to send you by General B a copy of my reply. In this connection I take the liberty to suggest that any new Depository to be designated abroad should be required to give security just as National Banks, and other designated Depositories at home are required to do. The law has very carefully guarded such deposits at home, and I see no reason for discriminating in favor of foreign bankers." ALS (press), *ibid.*

On Aug. 25, Bristow had written to USG. "Your letter of the 23d inst was received this morning. In view of your statement that the Honble Secretary of the Navy would be here before your letter could reach me, and would confer with me about the matter to which your letter relates I have delayed my answer until late in the afternoon but regret to say that it has not been my good fortune to meet him. I am extremely reluctant to interpose any further opposition to your wishes in the matter of the proposed appointment of Mr Cattell as general financial agent of this Department & to superinten[d] the refunding operations now abou[t] to begin in London, and would certainly offer no further objection if I did not believe that your Excellency is misinformed as to certain facts that seem to me should be fully considered in determining the matter. In calling your attention to these facts as they appear to me I am sure you will believe me actuate[d] by no other motive than a sens[e] of official duty and personal regard for yourself. It would [be] much more agreeable to me personally to adopt at once the suggestion from you in favor of Mr Cattells appointment, and I am sure I might have saved myself from most persistent, not to say extraordinary pressure from the friends of Mr C. whom I should like to oblige if I could do so without doing violence to my own sense of duty. Upon receiving the expression of your desire for the appointment it seemed to me that I owed it to you, as well as myself to state frankly the reasons why I thought the appointment unnecessary, and when I found that my opinion in this regard was not accepted as a proper conclusion, I thought it due to perfect frankness to state to you certain information recently received by me, which seemed to me to make it highly improper that Mr Cattell should be sent to London as the Agent of the Treasury Department That information consisted partly of the state of the account of Jay Cooke McCullough &Co with the United States. Upon my statements to you on this subject you were pleased to direct that Mr Cattell be not appointed for the present. In your letter of the 23d inst you say you are assured that the recent deposits with Jay Cooke McCullough &Co are apparent, not real. Of course you will understand that it is not agreeable for me to feel bound to assure you that on this point ~~your opinions~~ the representations made to you are not supported by the monthly returns of J. C. McC &co on file in the Fourth Auditors office. On the contrary the records of this Department show conclusively that the house of Jay Cooke McCullough &Co has received large deposit in cash from time to time since the financial panic of last Autumn, down to a very recent date and that the balance due from them to the United States has actually been increased since the first day of June last. In support of this statement I beg to hand you herewith a statement made up from the returns of J. C. McC &c[o] showing their receipt, disbursement, and monthly balances from June 1871 to July 31st 1874 the date of the last return. In this connection I hand you also similar statement of the account of Baring Bros from July 1868 to July 1871. A comparison of these statements will serve to illustrate & confirm what I said to you in our interview at your house last week   It do not deem it necessary to repeat the statement made to you at our last interview connecting Mr Cattell in my mind with the account of Jay Cooke McCullough &Co. It may be proper however, in view of what you say of Mr Cattell's denial of intimacy, with Mr McCullough to say that my statement to you on that subject related more to his (Mr C's) intimacy with another member of the house than ~~to~~ with Mr McC. I have not failed to note what you say of Mr Bigelow. Before sending him abroad I made careful inquiries as to his capacity, habits and integrity and have received the most favorable opinions about him except from a few who have taken great interest in Mr Cattells appointment. He is certainly capable, and at the head of his division has shown himself faithful & diligent. I have sent with him the most competent and reliable clerks in the Department. However I have no other desire in the premises than to conduct the refunding in a business-like manner to a successful termination, and it will give me pleasure to substitute for Mr Bigelow any one you may suggest as better qualified for the work, and who enjoys your confidence more fully. Let me repeat to you, Mr President, that Cattells appointment would be a serious mistake. I sincerely hope you will concur with me in the conclusion that this business ought to be conducted by officials of this Department   I send this communication by special messenger because I deem the subject very important, and because I do not know where to reach you after tomorrow morning. . . . P. S. I have omitted to say that the work to be done by Mr Bigelow and his assistants in London is precisely what they would have to do if the exchange took place here instead of in London—nothing more nor less." ALS (press), *ibid.*

1. Aug. 26.
2. John P. Bigelow of Mass. served as chief, loan div., Treasury Dept.
3. See *PUSG*, 24, 490–91.
4. See *ibid.*, pp. 217–18. On May 2, 1876, Secretary of the Navy George M. Robeson wrote to USG. "I have the honor to submit herewith a withdrawal of the Nomination of Seligman Brothers made to the Senate on the 28th March last, and also an accompanying substitute, for Joseph Seligman, Isaac Seligman, and Leopold Seligman, trading under the name, style, and firm of Seligman Brothers, to be special Fiscal Agents of the Navy Department, at London England." Copy, DNA, RG 45, Letters Sent to the President. On May 26, the Senate confirmed Seligman Brothers as special fiscal agents, London.
5. Sept. 1, 1874.

Speech

[*Aug. 31, 1874*]

I am very much obliged to you, gentlemen, for the invitation which you extended to me, and the kindness which you have shown for me. I have enjoyed the trip with unusual interest, as much of the excursion has carried me over territory with which I was not before acquainted. My reception on this camp meeting ground, and my enjoyment of the exercises here have been very gratifying to me. I am sorry that so much trouble has been given in my reception, but that has been the fault of the committee, and no fault of mine, as all the entertainments have been thrust upon me, and I have been met at every turn in my visit with some kindness for which I am deeply grateful.

Boston Evening Transcript, Sept. 1, 1874. On Aug. 31, 1874, Micah J. Talbot, president, Camp Meeting Association, Martha's Vineyard, Mass., addressed USG before he departed for New Bedford, Mass. "We desire to express our gratification at your visit, Mr. President, and we hope you have enjoyed the hospitalities which the Vineyard has been able to offer to you. It is our prayer that the blessing of God may attend you and bring you safely to your home." *Ibid.* Later, USG spoke at New Bedford. "Allow me, Mr. Mayor, through you, to return to the citizens of New Bedford my sincere thanks for the cordial reception given me today. It is only a repetition of the enthusiasm which has met me in every place in Massachusetts. I am not unmindful of the history of your commerce and your patriotism. I wish you continued prosperity. Again I desire to return you my thanks." *Ibid.*

On Aug. 27, USG and Julia Dent Grant, along with Vice President Henry Wilson and others, had arrived at Martha's Vineyard for an annual Methodist gathering. USG's visit included trips to Cape Cod, Nantucket, and Naushon Island. See *ibid.*, Aug. 28, 29, 31, 1874; Arthur R. Railton, "When Grant Took the Island: President and Party Visit Martha's Vineyard in 1874," *Dukes County Intelligencer*, 29, 1 (1987), 3–25.

On Aug. 28, C. C. B. Waterman, Sandwich, Mass., wrote to USG. "As you have seen the location of Provincetown and the fitness of its Harbour for a great naval Depot you can appreciate the necesity for its ocupation for that purpose—particularly as forces are constantly at work looking in the future toward so far closing the Entrance of the Harbour of Boston against the ingress or egress of ships that are likely hereafter to constitute our naval power—. . ." ALS, DNA, RG 45, Letters Received from the President.

To William W. Belknap

LONG BRANCH, N. J., September 2, 1874.

General W. W. Belknap, Secretary of War:

The recent atrocities in the South, particularly in Louisiana,[1] Alabama[2] and South Carolina,[3] show a disregard for law, civil rights and personal protection that ought not to be tolerated in any civilized government. It looks as if, unless speedily checked, matters must become worse, and life and property there will receive no protection from the local authorities until such authority becomes powerless. Under such circumstances, it is the duty of the government to give all the aid for the protection of life and civil rights legally authorized. To this end I wish you would consult with the Attorney General, who is well informed as to the outrages already committed, and the localities where the greatest danger lies, and so order troops as to be available in cases of necessity.

All proceedings for the protection of the South will be under the Law Department of the government, and will be directed by the Attorney General, in accordance with the provisions of the Enforcement act. No instructions need, therefore, be given the troops ordered into the Southern states except as they may be transmitted from time to time on advice from the Attorney General, or as circumstances may determine hereafter. Yours truly,

U. S. GRANT.

Washington Evening Star, Sept. 4, 1874. On Sept. 3, 1874, Secretary of War William W. Belknap telegraphed to USG, Long Branch. "~~Have~~ Your letter to me on Southern outrages is admirable. I desire to publish it. May I do so?" ALS (telegram sent), DNA, RG 107, Telegrams Collected (Bound). Also on Sept. 3, Secretary of the Treasury Benjamin H. Bristow and Attorney Gen. George H. Williams telegraphed to USG. "We think it very important that your letter to the Secretary of War should be published. It is well considered, has the true ring and needs no revision." LS (telegram sent), *ibid.* On the same day, USG telegraphed to Belknap. "You are at liberty to do as you think proper with regard to giving to the public my letter of yesterday" Copy, *ibid.* Also on Sept. 3, Williams issued a circular to U.S. attorneys and marshals in Ala., S. C., Tenn., Ga., Miss., and La., embodying USG's policy. *New York Times,* Sept. 4, 1874. See *HED,* 43-2-262, 1218, 1225, 1247–48.

On Aug. 3, 1874, Paul Drane, "Colored," Mayfield, Ky., had telegraphed to USG. "In Election today We have not had justice   threatened to mob us because we tried to get to the polls," Telegram received (on Aug. 4), DNA, RG 60, Letters from the President.

On Aug. 6, Mortimer H. Goddin, Huntsville, Tex., wrote to USG. "Private & Confidential . . . This country is in a state of perfect anarchy! are you going to stand with folded arms and allow men because they are loyal to the Government of the United states hung by mob law, or shot at night in jail; while felons justly heretofore sentenced to the state Penitentiary for *Murder* in the first degree pardoned by the powers that be—in order to seek their fiendish vengence on some innocent witness against them? Such is the condition of Texas this day—While Grand juries unlawfully empaniled, are finding false indictments against every Republican officer—state or county—for the avowed and express purpose of dismissing them from office, and placing them in jail—because they cannot by conspiracy *pay* or *bail out,* there to be shot, or taken out and hung at midnight, and purjured witnesses to acquit the offenders" ALS, *ibid.* Goddin served as presiding justice, Walker County. See William L. Richter, *Overreached on All Sides: The Freedmen's Bureau Administrators in Texas, 1865–1868* (College Station, 1991), pp. 189–90.

On Sept. 1, Isaac Bourne, Silver Creek, Miss., wrote to USG. "I will Drope you a few lines to Let you know how ~~ye~~ We is in Pos up pun By the White Peapel in Laurence County and in linclon County Miss.   thae tak up the Corlded Peapel and Haung thim. By a subpecsin and mak thim tall antheng Whare it be so or not. We are Prass so We Cant Stand it.   if the law Woant Pertect ous We dont What to Do.   we ask you for insistans from you Els not let ous have the Chace to Do that" ALS, DNA, RG 60, Letters Received, Miss.

On Sept. 2, A. Freeny and seven others, La Grange, Ga., wrote to USG. "the republican party Troup County requested of me and the County Executive committee to write you in refference to our next election as we haṣve been so badly oppressed at the polls heretofore & was not allow a Citizen chance to vote.   we therefore thought it proper to ask you what steps would be best to pursue in the next campaign. We was oppressed at the last Governor & President's Election ~~that~~ so that there was not more than half of us could or did vote   They dealt with us in such a manner that one half of us ~~col~~ could not get to the polls until in the later part of the Evening.   when they saw that they had scatered the crowd, they allow the remainder to come up and vote. Is that right? They had a whole lot of names on a piece of paper of which they said had not ~~pay~~ paid their tax of which cause lots that had paid to not vote. What shall we do with such? Sir in every Condition we are oprassed. Where as our election ~~come~~ will come off next fall for Congressmen & Legislatur men, and we perceive that that their will be riots and bloodshed at the ~~pools~~ polls without some ~~protectection~~ protection from the higher authorites & whereas their has been already ~~300~~ Three hundred Guns laid up for shooting purposyus by the Dimocratic party.   these Guns they intended to use the Day of our nomination but as God was merciful to us, we escaped without any fiut at all   inshort they are allow to take out Grant's Military arms   we have non. They have a little County Court here of which is ruing the colored people henceforth and forever, it ough to be done away with   I Sir I am requested to ask you what must we do next fall? be shot down at the polls or be driven from the polls like Dogs? I am a Candidate for the next Legislatur, but Sir I am expecting nothing more nor less than a riot. Will you therefore send the Garrison down here for peiace & for nothing but peiace? I mean on the Day of our Election of which will come off next some time in next month. Dear Sir aint their no possible way, whereby that Taxs may be sot a side until after the Election   if theris any possible way please let us know immediately. The Election is drawing near and We want to get every thing in shape to meet it. Please let us have and answer from you soon as this reach you   I will close by asking you to Write soon . . . dont send any answer to the ordinary for he is a full Dimocrat and will not let us know what you said" L, *ibid.*, Letters Received, Ga. Enclosed is an undated anonymous letter to USG. "this Letter is Swore by 20 Black men of Tipton   we dont sign No Names to it because the White men Mighty Catch up with us   we hafter slip our Letters to you if We can So We says to you the White men is fixing for War evry day & the tells us to Lookout for ourselves for the Exspects to Kill us all out & We thought We mus fix for them & We went to town to buy amination & the wont sell it to us & that is the case in in evry Little town We send & therefore We Called Our Collar togather & Write to you to send us men to stand Untill we gets Redy thats all we ask them Let us get Reddy for war before the starts on us & if you pleas send us men to Stand untill We is Reddy for them & then you maie turn them aloose   there air 300 men in Covington Reddy for Drilling & We here with our hands Empty   Sen us Rainforcement if you pleas   We dont want them to fight   We Wants them to keep peace untill We Gets Reddy   We knows whats the matter with them this Civil right Bill is the cause of it & We demand it ~~past~~ passage" D, *ibid.* On Oct. 24, Freeny wrote to USG. "Since I have return from the Convention held at Chattanooga Tenn. and also from dodging Klu. kluks &c. I thought it best to give you the ~~return~~ condition of our Election and ask you whether such elections is fair & whether they must pass. If your honor let such as I will state to you pass I dont know know what side to appeal for justice   I am comepell to say that we will never have a fair Election while all rascals are appointed to at the ballot Box To tear up Tickets & deal wronfully. So far as learn thus has been the case time and again in Troup Co. Nevertheless our Election Taking place on the seventh of this month I. AFreeny several weeks before the Election, went seventy one miles to see the Governor and ask him to have two men of Each party to stand at the Ballot Box. Governor Smith told me it was not his place to appoint them, he said it was the Ordinary place to appoint them; therefore I return to the Ordinary & ask him kindly for satisfaction to Each party to appoint 2 managers of Colored & 2 White in other words two Dimocrats & Two

Radical   The Ordinary replyed to me that he had nothing at all to do with the Election & said that he did not want me to say any more to him about it   Therefore I could not find anyone in Town to appoint mangers   Nevertheless Voting Day come on. Early in the morning seven hundred Colored men & me in the midst of them assemble at the court house and ask for two republican men to be appointed as managers   no, no, cried the Dimocrats you can not get any appointed here   The crowd continue to gether. we declared that we would not vote unless some man was there that would see that we got a fair Election. ~~White~~ while we was at the Polls the Dimcrats to show that they was not going to give a fair Election put a large Goods box in the Court house door & nail a rope ~~out~~ on top it turn the hollow side in the Court house shut all the Doors of the court house but the one that the Box was in & put all Dimocratic managers in side & one on Top the Box to receive Tickets and hand them to the them that was in side   there fore we saw that they was going to ~~raS~~ rascal us out of the Election   we concluded not to cast a vote   to this end we all left the Polls and never voted at all   For we are convual convergence that we can beat them   we has about 12 or 13 hundred majority   further more there was several hundred persons tried to pay their Tax So as they could get a chance to vote but could not find the man to pay Tax to and when they did find him he refuse to own his names or take the money for I fail my self to pay ~~T~~my Tax at the proper time & was requeste[d] to pay Two Dollars, & never got chance to pay it until after I was nominated as Candidate for the Legislator, they refuse to take it. Numbers went to take up Execution that they had out against them and they would not let them. The devil ment that is carried on here I am unable to state   Shall such Election as this pass? I ask your honor is you going to suffer to see such pass as a fair Election? Is it not in your Power to issue fair Election when Governors & ordinaries wont do it?   if ~~so~~ not what shall we poor Freedman's do? Our Governor is a Dimocrat but I suppose you are aware of it. We therefore petition your honor for a ~~rel~~ reelection   over two thousand persons are infavor the reelection in this County. I will close by asking you to answer soon as this reach you   I am a colored man that writes to you . . . P. S. We are comepell to say that we are gaged down here, & subject to be Kill if we speak about our rights   People are crowding my house most every day asking me to get permission from you to imigrate. they say the way they are cheated out their crops & out of Election they dont feel dispose to stay here.   there is know place under the sun for them to go therefore I persuade them to remain   the Condition of Colored people is starvation   I ~~do~~ has done every thing that could for them in the way of speaking and hold them to gether" ALS, *ibid.*, Letters from the President. On Sept. 16, C. M. Leary, Jonesboro, Ga., had written to USG. "Give me & We as a Colored Race of People Heare in the South of Parte of the World A Cerfycation of our Sivelerite Heare in the Stat of Georgia   We as Publikine Heare in Clayton Conty is mad a Nomathion and is Nomathion a Colored Man for a Candidate Vitined   if we Gaine the Race for the purpuis of a Repzener of Clayton Conty as a Member in Legslatra Hall in Atlanta Ga and the Demicrate Says if we gaine the Electhione I wont Reach Atlanta alive and I Expecte they will Try and kill me Before then and So By this Mr Grante Send ous word Whort to Done Wether to Hold to Whort We got or Tun a Luse and So if you pleas Sir you as aprisdene Send ous word Whort to Done   if you Says Hold we will & Die and Whort Ever you Say Done We Will Done it for We as Black apublekine inten to have I Rigth in Law or the Las man Die atrying if you Says to for we are Not get our Regthe in Law Hear in Georgia   I Hav a Grete Aele to Write But will Clos off untill answ form you Give me answ By Saturday if you please" ALS, *ibid.*, Letters Received, Ga.

On Sept. 23, H. H. Montgomery, Sharon, Miss., wrote to USG "& his Cabinet." "That there is a desperate state of things in this country which is driving us to desperation cannot be denied. This state of things has been brought about by the Reconstruction Acts, and the consequences natural to them. 1 A large portion of our best citizens are disfranchised 2 A large population of ignorant brutal negroes were enfranchised 3 A vast number of the scum of the North & North west flooded this country in pursuit of offices & plunder after these acts were passed. These organized the negroes into Loyal Leagues, & made them believe that it would be death for one of them not to vote for the ticket these carpet baggers put out. They got some good negroes into those Leagues, who said: We would like to vote with you white people, but it would be at the peril of our lives to do so. Indeed one negro in Vicksburg voted the Democratic ticket there in 1868 and the whites had to protect him from the negro mob to save his life. Now these carpet baggers have the negroes organized into military clubs that meet & drill & beat drums a good part of the night 1 to 3 times a week. They are political clubs too. Some negroes in Madison county Miss, tried to get out a new county ticket that would not have all *imported* men on it. What did the carpet baggers do? They visited the meetings of the negroes and told them: 'If you do not vote for the ticket put out we will have you prosecuted for perjury and put you in the Penitentiary' That is bold is it not? Every county officer is an imported man. One is a scallawag—the most corrupt, perhaps, of all. The State officers are imported men—one a native, but imported here again recently. The man who is reputed to be Gov. of the State is there by blackmail. His nomination cost some body of the North a great deal of mony I have heard. What is he doing for the good of the State? Nothing. Taxes have run up to nearly $50-on the thousand dollars. In towns & Cities far beyond that. All just to fund & pamper a set of villians! The negroes now say, they will have their rights. That is the lands of the South. These carpet baggers have promised them over & again these lands, if you vote for us. They drill & say they expect to kill the whites from the cradle up—unless they see some white woman to whom they may take a fancy! Yet when La. wants to rid her self of such an incubus & stanch as W. P. Kellogg you order U. S. troops to La. to hold him there and wrench millions of money from that people and drive them (the whites) from the State. The devil must have instigated you to do that. For the taxes of that State amount to confiscation. Why dont you come down here under disguise, insted of feasting at Long Branch, and see what is being done by these monsters? Hate to the Southern whites has governed Congress since the war in all its acts—not love for the negro. Those spiteful, malicious men—That Stevens & Cha's Sumner—are gone and we are glad of it, and hope that Butler, Bingham and Grant & his Cabinet may soon go, if they do not change their course in running the Gov'mnt As it is run it is the most stupendous fraud, and oppressive grinding ever heard of—claiming to be Republican As you act as if Autocrat order all these Carpet baggers out of the South We would then have peace. The negro would be quiet in a little while and go to work. But kept up as he is 1 to 3 nights in the week, he is not fit to work. Hence short crops, debt and half starvation are natural. But if the blue bellid yankees were away there would be none to plan to keep the negroes excited. I send you a slip which I hope you will read—an editorial and something from Schurz whom you know. Before the war I was union and voted against sesession, and believed if the northern polititcians had had any comon sense all the questions could have been settled. When Lincoln, out side of the Constitution, called for troops to invade the South I did hope that every man who was fool enough to come to the South as an invader might be killed or die. I am yet sorry they did ever get away. All the love for them passed out of me. I loved the government & constitution as they were. But both are gone now. We have a Dictator who claims to be President under the constitution. The things will not gingle. I hope something will occur make you & Congress change your course toward the South." ALS, *ibid.,* Letters from the President. The enclosure is *ibid.*

On Oct. 1, Enoch D. Rushing, Pleasant Plains, Ark., wrote to USG. "I hope you will pardon me for writing to you but being an American citizen of 65 years I have presumed to do so. The war in this state was so coercive by the confederates that all men under 50 years were forced to go into the confederate Sirvice, or go North   the old men like myself, were forced to Shout for them or they had to leave their homes or be killid   in my immediate neighbord ther was murdured for their devotion to Union John Dicamp Farmer Shot Parson Stout campellite Hung John Pierce Farmer Hung John Laney Farmer Hung Parson John Murry Shot   in this county 54 were killed at home all old men   I could give all their names. I left home got to the federal Army and never returnd untill after the Surrender. when the Rebel Army returned home in this county & State they all had arms   when the reconstructions laws were in progress, They all opposed it and every man that was in favor was proscribed all over the land, Socially & otherwise   in 1868 The celebrated K Klux Klan become very conspicuous   They notified union both back and white to bi ware if they Voted the radical Ticket Hell was their portion   many cases of this kind which intimedated many rpublicans from the poles   your humble servant Recd two which I have yet.   since that time all over this state The Union Element to which was all the friends of the goverment ever had since the rebellion, have been abused by Schourging murdured and with unceasing, have continued ever Since, and Since the genrl goverment have enfranchised nearley all and State all of them, the friends of the Union are in a worse condition at this time then they were Since the Surrender.   through the Policey of the govorner of this State and a new constitution now pending giving, the power of the whole State goverment in their hands, with the execution of the Laws, all Sensible men knows that the Republicans of this State have no show for Justice whatever. therefore a dark gloom is hanging over us. I do not know how many friends of goverment have been murdured in the South Since the Surrender. The Natural enquiry arises in my mind if the genl goverment had power to put down an armed rebellion it seems to me it has power to Protect ~~its~~ its friends afterwards Say 3000 Union men have been murdured and Schourghed Since the Surrender, does a man owe Allegience to a goverment that cannot nor will not protect him in person and property. I will leave that to wiser men then me to answer.   now this day all their ancient hatred, are coming to light since their enfranchisement. as an evidence ~~is~~ this appears in many ways. One is they are setting forth all the old Seceders, for office as in this County, the grand cyclops at least admited to be Henry Niel, for county & Brobate Judge and for Representative a Senator of the confederacy, to wit Jackson S Trimble and for Smaller offices Such as clks Sheriffs &c Crepled Rebels, whom now urges their claims, upon the ground, they were wounded, in the glorious lost cause, as they claim. There is another enqurey arises in my mind where a goverment is able, and through kindness and Courtisy, to an enemy, and thereby Shed the Blood of its friends, whether or not it does not partake of crime of Shedding friendly blood, in other words the goverment Should through neglect for we know it has the power Suffer an enemy to do it,   it looks very unnatural to me to Shed a friends blood or Suffer it to be done I could help it. There is agloom over the loyal Element of the South.   in Ancient times light Sprang from the East.   we hope for light from the East. we hope that the Southern Convention of Republicans may offor or open up away for our rilief   if we do not get help from that Source or Some other available way, Unionism, in the South is a myth.   its friends will have to leave as I fully believe, or many of them will loose their lives." ALS, *ibid.*

On Nov. 9, Isaac Loveless, former sgt., Co. H., 46th U.S. Colored Inf., Somerville, Tenn., wrote to USG. "I take the opetunety of Writting you A few Lines to show you the condision that We collard People is in in tenn for votin the Republican ticket   We are With Bread or meet an With out help We Will Perish   We are all most Povity stricken to death Now an We ask you to Look at our condish an do some thing for us   We are dependin on you for help   We are here among demercrats an they say that they in tend to starve the dam negros out that vote the Radical ticket the ~~Reasn~~ Reason of that We say that We intend to Run you the third time for Presidency Now dear sir if you are the friend of the colard men Pleas help us for if there Ever Was a need time now is the time I Want you to Bring to your mine When I Was under your command at vicks Burg missip you know how Bad you hated to see your men Without somthing to eat it is ~~W~~ With us now Like it Was With us in time of the War an if We Evr needed help We need it now dear sir I never throught When I Was in the armey that I ever Would come to this now Sir you may think that We are Lazy But the Land holders say We shall not Work for them an you know that Put us in a Bad fix Look at this Letter inquier aBout it an see for your self Whether I tell the truth or not dear sir our chance is slender here an We ask you to Look for us a Little While for We need som one to Look for us now dear sir if you can do us no Good Give us ease By Writting to us I hope When you Get this that My name may sound in years as it did at the serender of vicks Burg Pleas Writ soon . . . if you think of us as you once did We know that you Will help us . . ." ALS, *ibid.*

On Dec. 4, Mary Sellers, Uniontown, Ky., wrote to USG. "It is with painful emotions I seat myself to inform you of the trouble caused by the hanging of 3 colored men in this county by a Mob who took them out of the Morganfield jail Tuesday 1st inst! The evidence was not sufficint to convict these men in court of Justice but these *demons* composing this mob took the law in their vile hands! George Moore the name of one of these unfortunate men was son in law of Mary Sellers husband to Milly Moore 'He left her with a child 3 years old & in a delicate situation' & no one to help her but sisters & a poor old Mother— The Mother is Mary Ewell who was a faithful servant in the family for many years: George Moore stated in court he knew nothing of the burning of the buildings of which he was accused 'farther then that Alex Ramsey' come to his house 'at 3 O clock A. M. & woke him up saying come & go with me to the 'Mill—after they got there Ramsey said to George Moore take a drink with me—Georg did drink with him Ramsey said stay here till I come back 'He went to a Coopers Shop & returned with an arm full of Shavings 'George Moore left there & went home' He saw no more of Ramsey: This is all the evidence against George Moore they could produce in court—Alex Ramsey has a brother George Ramsey who was one of the unfortunate men hung (only 18 years old) These brothers leaves a poor widowed Mother with four helpless children: Now my kind good friend I would like to know if SOMETHING cant be done with these outlaws: It is certanly known this Mob was composed of the Uniontown people 'For the commanded all the horses belonging to the Livery Stables—no strangers were in or around the town during the time' Will you be kind enough to proceed in this matter & have our wrongs righted' I would be greatly obliged if you will take some steps in this matter & have these terrible characters brought to justice' by so doing you will relieve the aching of many hearts who love & esteem you for your goodness & justice to our people" ALS, *ibid.*

On Dec. 27, James Moffat, Sr., and James S. Moffat, Weatherford, Tex., wrote to USG. "we have Setled on 160 Achres of state land in the railroad Belt 2½ miles west of weatherford we had it surveyed as a homestead by the county Surveyor 5 years ago now ~~now~~ J. P. Shirly has commenced a Suit against me to put me out of my house and take my Homestead this I know is contrary to Justice but there is no Justice. here in a Justice court for northren men or negroes these Southren Officers of the Rebel army have taken Several Homesteads from the freedmen—now they have commenced to put us northren men out of house and home as they did the Negroes these officers have sold our teem at Sherif Sale on acount of a Jugment given on a forged note against us after Selling our teem they are now going to have a lawsuit to get our homestead at Weatherford on the 4th of December I wrote Govr Coke before they sold my Catle but got no answer I also reported about the forged note to the Grand Jury the Democratic authoreties in Weatherford will give us no Justice   we are poor and have no money to pay lawyers   under these Circumstances President we hope you will do something for us to save our Homesteads from these land Sharks . . . we hope we will get an answer to this letter as soon as possable" LS, *ibid.*, Letters Received, Tex.

In Dec., Charles O. Fisher and many others, Savannah, petitioned USG. "The undersigned citizens of Georgia most respectfully take the privilege of appealing to your Excellency in regard to their condition, and in the name of a half million people of this State to invoke the power of the Government to interfere in their behalf in the following matter, Viz: Five colored men swore out a warrant before a U. S. Commissioner in Randolph County against one Kenny of Terrell county, Georgia for interfering with their free exercise of the right to vote at the election for State officers in October last. Kenny was arrested under the warrant and brought to Savannah for trial 'where the case broke down.' The grand jury of Randolph county then found a true bill against the colored men for perjury and three of them were arrested by the sheriff of Terrell county under a bench warrant issued by the Judge of the Superior Court for that circuit. One of the men escaped and the other two were tried found guilty and in all probability will be sent to the penitentiary for at least five years. Now here are citizens seeking in the U. S. Courts justice which is denied them in State courts; and this very effort of theirs to obtain justice is charged against them in the State courts as a crime and punishment inflicted by the State authority in contempt for the authority of the U. S. Courts. If these men committed perjury it seems to us the offense is punishable only in the court in which the offense was committed. Our general condition in this respect is briefly as follows: The free exercise by our people of their rights as citizens is constantly interfered with by parties hounded on by the Democratic press and politicians. When the matter is brought before the U. S. Court, notwithstanding there is a plain violation of law, from some cause or other the violators of law are not punished. In the State courts where we are admonished to bring our grievances no colored men or republicans are ever put on the juries, nor is it possible to convict a democrat for any violation of the rights of a colored citizen. If a colored man is murdered in Georgia by a democrat it is only sufficient for the juries and officers of the law to know that it was politics or 'insolence' on the part of the murdered man and investigation ceases. If a citizen is to be arrested by a State court, for seeking to enforce the laws of the United States, go through the mockery of a trial and sent to the penitentiary by that court—liberty is but a name and half of the people in this State will be effectually deprived of their human rights guaranteed by the constitution of our country. We send you herewith Mr. President a copy of the proceedings of the trial of the colored men above mentioned and an editorial in regard to the matter taken from the Telegraph & Messenger a newspaper published at Macon in this State recognized as an able and influential journal—the letter and editorial both having been written by the Editor H. H. Jones by which it will bee seen that the trial was a mere farce—the lawyer who defended the prisoners conceding that they pwere guilty of the crime charged. We implore your Excellency to check these outrages by having the proper officer of the law for this State to have the colored men whose rights were so grossly interfered with and whose liberty has been so foully abridged, brought before the proper tribunal on writ of *habeas corpus* and a careful and impartial legal investigation be had of the case in question or by such other means as may seem best to your Excellency. We believe that if the State has the right to refuse us justice in its own courts and punish us for seeking it in the United States Courts that the days of civil liberty are at an end in Georgia, for colored citizens and all who dare be their friends. We most respectfully and earnestly ask your Excellency's attention to our prayer." DS (docketed Dec. 29), *ibid.*, Letters from the President. The enclosures are *ibid.*

1. See Proclamation, Sept. 15, 1874.

2. On Aug. 24, U.S. Senator Daniel D. Pratt of Ind., Logansport, wrote to USG. "I send you inclosed the letter of Mrs Wayne, an accomplished Southern lady, but educated at the North. While Engaged in investigating Ku-Klux outrages I stopped for a week at Livingston and took much testimony. It was & had been one of the hardest places in Alabama in respect to outrages upon the blacks & whites of Republican faith. The work of expulsion of loyal White men is nearly completed. The father of this lady was among the tried & faithful during the war. He then held the office of Judge of Probate, but when I saw him felt in daily peril. He is an excellent gentleman & was very kind to the committee & furnished them valuable information. This letter has been slow reaching me. I hope you will cause a detachment of troops to be sent to that locality & thus stop these murders & [ho]use bur[ni]ng[s]." ALS, DNA, RG 60, Letters from the President. *HRC*, 43-2-262, 1223. On [*Aug.*] 2, S. A. Wayne, Livingston, Ala., had written to Pratt. ". . . Mr W P Billings a Northern gentleman was murdered last night between the hours of 7½ or 8 o clock, by a band of assassins, within half a mile of his plantation—His body was found next morning by some of the negroes on his place & taken to his house—He had attended a meeting of Republicans about six miles from this place & was returning peacefully to his home unarmed & unsuspicious of danger when waylaid by a band of men & murdered—. . ." ALS (misdated July 2), DNA, RG 60, Letters from the President. *HRC*, 43-2-262, 1223. On Sept. 18, Wayne wrote to USG. "I feel more like addressing you as my dear Father & Friend for such you have proven to me & mine—but—Oh, my God! you have no conception of the trouble we are in—War is declared in our midst and though the U. S. troops are here the Ku Klux are worse than before they came—And who are they fighting? The poor defenseless negroes —Why? for voting or rather expressing their determination to vote the Republican ticket —This evening the lives of my husband—father & brother were threatened—with the intention of making them renounce their principles—God only knows what the end will be—I have seen the Capt & Lt stationed at this place—& they say the only hope is Martial law—& that is the only remedy—Since I last wrote you some four or five negroes have been killed in this County—& the Ku Klux are now at Belmont 16 miles from this place in force & will probably murder as many more—They are exasperated against the three white Republicans in this place because they refused to go with them on one of their raids last weeks—hence the threats against their lives—My Father left this evening & I pray God he may not return until Martial law is declared—Oh my dear Sir *you can save* the country—oh protect the Union loving men against those who despise it & are doing all to overthrow it—I write you this not thinking my enlisting in the cause will help it, but because I feel it my duty to let you know how great our trouble is—No excuse can be given by these murderers—for since the assassination of Mr Billings not one single Republican meeting has been held in this county—And this is what the Democrats are fighting for— Unless Martial law is declared hundreds of the poor negroes will be killed—even now they do not sleep in their houses & are hunted down like wild beasts by the Democracy because they will not vote their ticket—Oh! My dear Sir act & be our friends   God knows the innocent only suffer—& the blush of shame mantles my cheek when I read the pitiable excuses in the Democratic papers—apologizing for their cowardly deeds—No brave man is afraid of a few of them in open daylight but a hundred or two banded together; making night hideous with their demoniac yells is enough to make the stoutest heart quail—I have written you hurriedly—There is no security in the mails & I send this by a U. S. Paymaster who arrived here this afternoon & leaves to night—Again I beg you to help us in this dreadful emergency—No U S Marshall has been here & if they were to come they could not punish these murderers immediately—& they ought to be dealt with severely & imme-

diately—This is private & I write as to my own dear Father & confide to you our troubles —We have lived in the midst of it since the war & it is more terrible now than ever—Every Union man will be killed if active steps are not taken by the Goverment to stop it—I am ever your true & loving Union woman" ALS, DNA, RG 60, Letters from the President. On the same day, Capt. William Mills endorsed this letter. ". . . in my opinion nothing but the strong arm of the U. S. Governmt aided by martial law will protect all citizens irrespective of color—" AES, *ibid.* On Sept. 19, Pratt endorsed to USG a letter from Wayne. AES, *ibid.* HED, 43-2-262, 1226. On Nov. 12, 1875, Pratt, commissioner of Internal Revenue, wrote to USG. "I am urged by Mrs. Wayne, of Livingston, Alabama, to see you in person in reference to the disturbed condition of that part of the State, and the danger to human life of Union people who reside there. Her father, Judge James A. Abrahams, whom you personally know, was recently attacked by three ruffians in the night-time on his way home from a session of the Board of Commissioners. He was shot, but not fatally. The particulars are given in a letter from his daughter to Mrs. Wayne, now before me. I enclose an article on the subject cut from the Alabama State Journal of November 9. Mrs. Wayne has explained the condition of affairs there to the Attorney General, to whom I refer you for further particulars. What she ardently desires is that you will order United States troops to Livingston to extend protection to Union people who are compelled to remain at home and look after their property,—as is the case with her father. I wish to add that when taking testimony in that part of the country in the fall of 1871, as one of the Committee appointed by Congress, I became acquainted with Judge Abrahams and family, and much interested in their welfare. I have no doubt he needs the protection his daughter seeks for him." LS, DNA, RG 94, Letters Received, 5768 1875. A clipping is *ibid.* On Nov. 13, AG Edward D. Townsend telegraphed to Maj. Gen. Irvin McDowell, Louisville. "The President directs you to station a company of troops at Livingston, Ala. immediately to be governed by instructions under which the troops are now serving in your Department, in regard to lawful aid to the civil authorities in case of emergency, and protection to life. Acknowledge receipt." ADfS, *ibid.* Related papers are *ibid.*

On Sept. 20, 1874, Theodore Nunn, Autaugaville, Ala., had written to USG. "from 1850 to 1861 I was a Secessionist Because I thought I had cause and a Right to be and During the Confederate Struggle I did every thing in my Brain mussles and Breeches to sustain the cause   after subjugation I very Reluctantley taken the oath to be a faithful citizen of the united States and went and asked President Johnson to Pardon me   he did and Since I have tried to be as good and faithful a citizen to the united States as I could be and to be as faithful and as honest to it as any one who acted or bore Arms in its Defence and I hope to continune to do so as long as I live   But Sir allow me to say to you that you know the Southern People Although Subjugated are as Brave and can do as good fighting as any People on the face of gods Earth and let me say to you that the action of the Radical Party in my opinion to wards them is such, that in my opinion will arouse all good men of Every Section and Climate in there Sympathey Except a fiew North Eastern States   I want Peace and I want no Rupture in this goverment and I intend to do all I can to have Peace But allow me to say that I fear the actions of the Administration the 14 & 15 amendments and worse than all the Civil Rights Bill together with the great actions of the Powers that be will to centralize and Declare a Dictator over this goverment which in my opinion will never be until after some of the worst Tragadees that has ever bien Performed will be and let me Beg of you as our Ruler to Stop and reflect before it is too late   I am over 50 years of age   I never held office nor wanted office nor never Expect to and as I want Peace and to see no other Rebellion Let me beg you to act with more reflection more Caution and more Prudence for the sake of the Countrey for the sake of all good People and for god sake let us have Peace" ALS, DNA, RG 60, Letters from the President.

On Sept. 21, William M. Brooks, Selma, Ala., wrote to USG. "I endorse on the envelope which encloses this letter the words 'Private and Confidential,' hopeing by that means to secure with more certainty the attention of your Excellency to the within printed Address. This Address is signed by hundreds of our best and most substantial Citizens of all classes professions and occupations; and on their behalf I respectfully invite its careful perusal and consideration. Regarding you as the President of the whole people and as under the highest obligations to give them an impartial hearing without distinction of party or race we earnestly invite speedy investigation of the truth of the various charges preferred by Congressmen White, Hays and others against the White people of this state. Let the investigation be conducted by officers of the Federal Army or such other honest capable and impartial men as your excellency may appoint   Being a stranger to you it is proper perhaps that I should say enough of myself to give you an opportunity of learning who and what I am. I am a Lawyer by profession and before the war was one of the Judges of the Circuit Court of this state. I was President of the Alabama state Secession Convention and am a life long Democrat. In common with my fellow citizens I have long since 'accepted the situation in good faith and conducted myself accordingly. I beg leave to assure you that no factious opposition to your administration will be made by the White People of this state, but that on the contrary we are ready to sanction with pleasure such of its acts as our judgement approves. On On behalf of the White people of the state I earnestly invoke a fair and speedy hearing and even handed justice" ALS, *ibid.* Brooks enclosed a Sept. 15 petition to USG by "Citizens of Selma," refuting charges of racial oppression. Clipping, *ibid.*

On Oct. 3, "REPUBLICAN CITIZEN," Greene County, Ala., wrote to USG. "We, the people of the State of Alabama, colored population assembled this day in the beat of Falkland, in the name of the Almighty God, do petition with all of our hearts, asking thee to make a dividing line between the republican party and the democratic party. We cannot live together. They are killing and Ku-Kluxing us both day and night; killing harmless women; running our wives and children through the woods; run your school-teacher off, and whipping some to death. We have for the last nine years been cheated out of everything that we have made. President Grant, who stands at the head of the republican party, look on our struggling condition, living here with outraged Ku-Klux. But if God be our helper, we intend to carry this coming November election. For heaven's sake do something for us, for we have to have better living than we are living." *HRC*, 43-2-262, 1236.

On Oct. 30, Alpheus Baker, Eufaula, Ala., telegraphed to USG. "Hon Alex. White and Republicans just arrived here are telegraphing attorney General Williams for authority to dispose the troops here over the country so as to carry the election in their favor   will you permit our troops to be so employed" Telegram received, DLC-USG, IB.

On Nov. 17, Elias M. Keils, Eufaula, wrote to USG. "I regret to say we have reign of terror in this (Barbour) County. The County officers elected on the Republican ticket on 3rd inst, are threatened by the 'White League' with murder if they undertake to hold their offices—This League openly declare their intentions, that no Republican shall hold office in this County—The League means what they say, as we (I) have the most abundant proof in the foul murder of my only son, and the premeditated attempt to murder me on the 3rd of Nov. inst, simply because I was U. S. Supervisor at the Spring Hill Precinct, acting and Commissioned as the Republican Supervisor—Can we have protection? The U. S. Marshal says he is powerless. Pardon me—If we had a rigid earnest Judge of our District Court, in place of Judge Busteed, resigned, it would do a great deel to give us peace and law in Alabama—" ALS, DNA, RG 60, Letters from the President. On Dec. 24, Keils, Washington, D. C., testified before the Select Committee on Affairs in Ala. *HRC*, 43-2-262, 1–9. On April 24, 1875, Keils, Washington, D. C., twice wrote to USG. "I have endeavored to see you very often during the last *four months*, but have failed—My wife has made every effort in her power to see you on numerous occasions, and all without success—The object of my Wife was to see if you would caus[e] me to be employed by the Government to ferit out and to prossicute the murderers of our child, and the destroyers of the ballot box at Spring Hill, Barbour County Ala, on the day of the last November election—I enclose you a paper with a brief account of the outrage—Two State Courts have been held in that County since this outrage, and no indictment found against any of the mob—The evidence was overwhelming, but ther[e] is no redress in the State Courts there,—and will not be—There has been indictments found in the U. S. Court at Montgomery against *a few* of the Mob—The others have not been indicted, some of them not identified—The U. S. Dist. Attorney (McAfee) will do his duty as far as he can, as will Ex. Gov. Parsons who is retained to assist him—But they have not the time to hunt out all or near all of this Mob—. . ." "I wrote you to day, and do not wish to make myself troublesom—But to show you more fully the magnitude of the outrages in Barbour County Ala. it may not be out of place to say, I had been Judge in Alabama for nearly five years, and was elected by majority vote of more than two thirds in said County—. . ." ALS, DNA, RG 60, Letters from the President. The enclosure is *ibid.* On May 17, Keils again wrote to USG requesting "the appointment of Judge in Dakota Territory, or an Auditorship in some of the Departments here—Or I would like to be employed to assist the U. S. Dist. Attorney in the prossecuting of those guilty of outrages in the South—This latter I would really prefer, because I think I can do much good. . . ." ALS, *ibid.*, Records Relating to Appointments. On Jan. 1, 1876, Keils wrote to USG concerning appointment as territorial judge. ALS, *ibid.* No appointment followed. See Sarah Woolfolk Wiggins, *The Scalawag in Alabama Politics, 1865–1881* (University, Ala., 1977), pp. 95–98.

On Dec. 14, 1874, the House of Representatives passed a resolution requesting Belknap to describe troop deployment in Ala. at the time of the Nov. 3 election, and to state "whether said troops acted independently or as a *posse* of the United States marshal." *HED*, 43-2-110. AG Edward D. Townsend wrote an undated memorandum. "The President in giving orders relating to ~~suppression~~ prevention of violence, riot, or bloodshed, couches them in general terms—'Keep the peace'—'Prevent bloodshed'—leaving it to the officers concerned to exercise sound discretion as to how to accomplish the purpose. . . ." ADf (docketed Dec. 18), DNA, RG 94, Letters Received, 3579 1874.

On Dec. 22, USG wrote to Speaker of the House James G. Blaine. "I have the honor to transmit herewith for the information of Congress, a Memorial forwarded to me by a Convention of Colored Citizens assembled in the City of Montgomery, Alabama, on the second of this month." Copy, DLC-USG, II, 2. *HED*, 43-2-46; *HRC*, 43-2-262, 1074. On Dec. 2, Philip Joseph, Montgomery, had written to USG and Congress. ". . . For three or four months past especially, our lives, and the lives of nearly all republicans in this State, have had no protection except the fear of the authority and laws of the United States. But for the presence of United States troops, and civil officers of the United States, hundreds of the active and earnest republicans of this State would have been assassinated. But even with the protection of these agencies, many of our race were shot down and killed at the polls on the 3d day of November last only because they chose to exercise their right to vote, as in the cases of Mobile and Barbour Counties, where Norman Freeman, Bill Jackson, and William Kinney, (in Mobile,) and Alfred Butler, George Walker, and W. C. Keils, white, and others (in Barbour) whose names are at present unknown, were killed, and a large number wounded. Many of the victims of the White League in Barbour County were found dead in the woods and partially eaten by vultures; and these crimes will go utterly unnoticed or unpunished by the State courts. The obvious reason is, that the grand and petit juries, the judges, and the civil officers as a mass, and the sentiment of the people justify, approve, excuse, or connive at these atrocious crimes. . . . Our race have now met in convention to consider solemnly the question of their future destiny in this State and in this country. We have no reason to expect from our political opponents, now dominant in this State, the exercise of justice, mercy, or wise policy. Not recognizing the value of our labor, their leaders declare our presence as a curse to the State, and profess to look with pleasure upon our *exodus* from the State. The solemn question with us is, Shall we be compelled to repeat the history of the Israelites and go into exile from the land of our nativity and our homes, to seek new homes and fields of enterprise, beyond the reign and rule of Pharaoh? The question presses upon us for an early solution. We linger yet a while to learn what will be done to avert these evils by the power that made us free men and citizens, and whose honor and good faith stand pledged to make that emancipation and citizenship something more than a delusion and a mockery. We present these facts for the consideration of the Government of the United States, and ask its immediate interference in the terrible situation that it has left us after solemnly promising to guard us in the enjoyment of the privileges that it has given to us—namely, all the rights of citizenship." *HED*, 43-2-46, 6, 9–10; *HRC*, 43-2-262, 1078, 1080. See also *SMD*, 43-2-107.

In [*Jan., 1875*], Blaine wrote to USG. "In accordance with Mr. Albright's request I enclose his letter—which gives a shocking picture of affairs in Alabama" ALS, USG 3. On Jan. 3, U.S. Representative Charles Albright of Pa., Mobile, had written to Blaine. "Thinking that you might perhaps desire to have some idea of the situation here I drop you this note. *First.* A Republican government does not exist in Ala, there may be the form of it but so far as the protection of life and property of Union men white or black is concerned, it is a mockery a sham and a delusion. *Second.* The spirit of intolerance, proscription and intimidation is worse than it was at any time since the war and I doubt whether it was worse in 1861. *Third.* That the hatred is confined to office holders is a mistake. To be a Republican whether an office holder or not is to be put under the ban—and the feeling is even stronger against the Southern Union men than those from the North. Unless some relief comes the White Union men will feel compelled to leave or surrender their manhood and give up their political convictions *Fourth.* The poor blacks are at the mercy of the land owners and their old masters they do the work and get nothing for it. Their faith in God and confidence in the Republican party are evidences of moral heroism grandly sublime The wonder is not that some under the great pressure that exists have gone over to the Democrats but that as a race they have been as true and loyal to the Republican party. *Fifth.* The situation is truly alarming and nothing but decided bold and aggressive legislation will save (I will not say the Republican Party) but) the constitutional rights of the true men of the South—To commit the colored ~~men~~ people to the care of the men who tried to destroy the government and who are assuming their old arrogance and race superiority is to turn the index finger on the dial plate of Christian civilization backwards—and to allow to be perpetrated a crime and stupendous infamy that will darken and pale the fading ~~the~~ years of the 19th Century and that will almost make the celebration of our centennial, a day of lamentation and sorrow. My dear sir, I use strong words—but I remember that the evil is great and the remedy to overcome it must be proportionately strong. I believe therefore in stretching the Constitution to the utmost limit to bring relief to the Southern states in protecting the rights of all—*It is moral degradation to be a Union man and a Republican here* I will be glad if you will let the President see this letter. We remain here to morrow and then go to Eufaula—Livingston &c . . . P. S. The testimony will present a chapter of barbarism that will shock the world." ALS, *ibid.* See *HRC*, 43-2-262.

3. On Aug. 26, L. Cass Carpenter, editor, *Daily Union*, Columbia, S. C., had written to USG. "The telegraphic accounts of the recent trouble at a place called Ridge Springs in

this state were most grossly exagerated. There was no threatened uprising of the negros nor was there the least ground for anticipating such a thing. The whole thing was put up by the democratic whites for the purpose of intimidating the negroes from voting. It arose in this way. A colored militia company was quietly drilling in the town not interfering with any one nor desiring to do so. The white democrats determined to put a stop to the drill and ordered the company off but it very properly refused to go. It was a company of the national guard of the state and has as much right to drill as a white company had. When refusal was given word was sent to Augusta Georgia distant but a few miles when three or four hundred men armed and equipped immediately started for the place carrying terror wherever they went. They stopped and searched railway trains insulted and frightened passengers delayed the US mails all on the pretext of searching for seditious persons. This was kept up for four days. The Judge of the circuit Hon R. B. Carpanter went to the scene of trouble but could do but little. The rioters even dragged a man from the cars by his side because they feigned to suspect him of being one of the leading 'niggers' as they call them. The Sheriff of the county dares not go home for fear of his life and is now in this city. He is a white man and a native of the state. Open threats have been made by these Georgians that they will tend to the counties along the border of that state when the day of election comes. I have been in ten counties in the state within the past two weeks and find the negros quietly and peacably at work in the fields and workshops. They are no more disposed to oppress or abuse the whites than they were ten years ago or five years ago. They desire to live in peace and quiet, and are striving to do so. These cries of 'negro insurrections' are only the basest pretexts for deeds of blood committed upon these poor defenseless people. I am among them every day and know something of the feelings that exist. I write this that your Excellency may be apprised of the actual facts and not prejudiced by the partisan reports of the democratic associated Press." ALS, DNA, RG 60, Letters Received, S. C.

On Sept. 25, Governor Franklin J. Moses, Jr., of S. C., telegraphed to USG. "The state of affairs in Edgefield County in this state has been for the last ten days of such a character as to threaten the lives & the destruction of the property of law abiding & peaceful Citizens   I have Exhausted my Efforts with the peaceful & legal means at my Command to restore the usual situation   armed bands are assembled at various points in the County and have demanded the surrender to them of the state arms in the hands of the regularly organized militia of the state   from this action a reign of terror Exists   I issued my proclamation on the twenty second inst Commanding these armed bands to disperse & retire to their homes within three days and hereafter to refrain from a repetition of such actions they are still under arms   I am powerless to Enforce my orders Except by the use of the inexperienced state Militia the employment of which I fear would hasten a Conflict which I desire to avoid   having Exhausted all means at my Command I Call upon you under the Constitution of the United states for such assistance as will Enable me to restore the peace & quiet of the County and to this end I ask that you will send immediate orders to Colonel H M Black Commanding United states forces here to report to me with such of his Command as it may be found necessary to employ   please answer as speedily as possible" Telegram received (at 8:00 P.M.), *ibid.*, Letters from the President. On Sept. 26, Williams telegraphed to Moses. "I have to say, by direction of the President, in answer to your telegram of yesterday to him, asking for troops to aid in suppressing disorders at Edgefield, that a company of U. S. troops is now stationed there, and it is expected and believed that it will afford adequate protection to the lives and property of citizens." *Washington Evening Star,* Sept. 26, 1874.

On Oct. 9, Joseph E. Glover, Jr., U.S. commissioner, Walterboro, S. C., wrote to USG. "We expect to have Trouble with the Blacks of our State if They do not Elect Their men to Office, next month,   Some of loose tongue do not hesitate to say They expect there will be a War of Races Soon, and when it comes The will whipe out the White Man,   from what I can learn, I believe Life & Property to be in danger, especially along the Southern Countys of our State, therefore I respectfully request that One Company of U. S. Troops be Located at or near Walterboro, a few days before the Ellection to remain untill all Excitement has passed away,   Their Presence alone will have a good affect, and if an outbreak occurs They will be on the Spot to assist the Civil Officers in keeping the peace. Hopeing you will do what in Your Judgement You consider best for us in these trying times. . . ." ALS, DNA, RG 60, Letters from the President. See Richard Zuczek, *State of Rebellion: Reconstruction in South Carolina* (Columbia, 1996), pp. 140–47.

To Hamilton Fish

Long Branch, N. J.
Sept. 2d /74

HON. HAMILTON FISH,
SEC. OF STATE,
DEAR SIR:

Your letter of yesterday enquiring when I will be in Washington and can receive the Austrian and Spanish Ministers is received. I shall be there all day on the 14th & until one o'clock p. m. on the 15th if not until the departure of the night train. It will be entirely convenient therefore to receive the two Ministers separately on the two days, each at twelve o'clock M, or at any hour that may [be more convenient

Very Respectfully
your obt svt.
U. S GRANT.]

AL (signature clipped; bracketed material not in USG's hand), DLC-Hamilton Fish. On Sept. 1, 1874, Secretary of State Hamilton Fish wrote to USG. "The new Austrian, & also the new Spanish Minister, are ready to be presented, when you shall return—Neither is at this moment in Washington, but will come on, on being advised of the time of your readiness to receive them—Should you intend to pass two or three days here, it might be desirable to present them on different days, to avoid the conflict of rank between them, the Austrian having arrived some weeks before the Spaniard—As it may be necessary to summon them from Newyork, I would like to know in advance at what date you will be here, & whether you will receive them on separate days, or would prefer to have both presented on the same day—Will you have the kindness to let me be informed on both points, at as early a moment as your Convenience will permit." ALS (press), *ibid.*

On Sept. 14, USG greeted Baron William von Schwarz-Senborn, who had presented his credentials as minister from Austria-Hungary. ". . . One so favorably known at home with whom my own countrymen there, as well as citizens or subjects of most other States on the globe, have recently, on a memorable occasion had satisfactory intercourse, cannot be otherwise than cordially welcomed by the United States. . . ." *New York Times*, Sept. 15, 1874. Schwarz-Senborn had served as general manager of the 1873 Vienna Exhibition. For the presentation of the Spanish minister, see Speech, [*Sept. 15, 1874*].

To Henry T. Crosby

DATED Long Branch n J 9/2 *1874*
To H. T. CROSBY CHF CLERK WAR DEPT W D C
Send Dent Sharp[1] now with Gen Babcock in Washn to fill vacancy at Military academy

U. S. GRANT

Telegram received (at 6:40 P.M.), DNA, RG 94, Correspondence, USMA. On Sept. 2, 1874, USG, Long Branch, telegraphed to Orville E. Babcock. "Failures at West point leaves a vacancy among appointments at large   send Dent Sharp up to try his chances   I have telegraphed chief clerk War Dep't" Telegram received (at 6:40 P.M.), *ibid.* Earlier on Sept. 2, Henry T. Crosby, chief clerk, War Dept., had telegraphed to USG. "The Secretary is absent and cannot be reached by telegraph. The Superintendent of Military Academy reports the failure of new Cadets at large Hearn, and Ray. He also telegraphs that an alternate might be sent, but would have to make up lost time, as the class started on first September   Geo. W. Goode of St. Louis, is the only remaining Alternate you have specially designated. Shall await your orders as to the persons to be appointed, if any are." LS (telegram sent), *ibid.*, RG 107, Telegrams Collected (Bound). On Sept. 3, Secretary of War William W. Belknap telegraphed to USG. "Your instructions about Dent Sharp received and carried out." Copies, *ibid.*; *ibid.*, RG 94, Letters Sent, USMA. On the same day, USG telegraphed to Col. Thomas H. Ruger, superintendent, USMA. "Please inform me as early as possible the result of young Sharps examination for admission to the Academy   He will arrive there probably today" Telegram received, USMA.

On Sept. 4, USG telegraphed to Ruger. "If there is still a vacancy at large at West Point Please give young Hoyt Grandson of Genl Scott first chance & Berard second. Notify them & after examination notify War Department so that appointment can be furnished   These come after Dent Sharp who should have reported yesterday of course" Telegram received, *ibid.* On Sept. 10, Belknap telegraphed to USG. "Gen'l. Ruger informs me that Messrs Hoyt and Sharp failed to pass and that Berard passed—" ALS (telegram sent), DNA, RG 107, Telegrams Collected (Bound). For Winfield S. Hoyt, see *PUSG*, 24, 441–42. John H. Berard did not graduate.

On [*Sept.*] 23, Belknap telegraphed to Ruger. "The President has appointed Douglass Howard of Galena Illinois a cadet to enter the present fourth class and has telegraphed him to go to West Point at once to be examined   If he presents himself have him examined and let the Physical examination be made by the Surgeon and assistant surgeon at West Point and if another surgeon is required one will be ordered from New York upon intimation to that effect   The President has the impression that although he starts nearly a month be-

hind his class he will do well as he is a very bright young man   notify me of result of examination by telegraph" Telegram received (stamped Sept. 24), USMA. On Sept. 26, Lucius S. Felt, Galena, telegraphed to USG. "Second despatch received. I telegraphed yesterday Howard's acceptance, wrote you," Telegram received, DLC-USG, IB. On the same day,
USG endorsed this telegram. "The boy must hurry as he is now a month behind." E (initialed, in Babcock's hand), *ibid.* On Oct. 3, Belknap telegraphed to USG. "~~Young~~ Young
Howard passed both Medical and Academic examinations" ALS (telegram sent), DNA,
RG 107, Telegrams Collected (Bound). Douglas A. Howard graduated USMA in 1878.

On Jan. 31, Fanny Wash Goode, "Near St. Louis," had written to Julia Dent Grant.
"Let me hope that it may not be unpleasant thus to renew acquaintance with one whom
you knew when we were both young. A bright & happy youth it was, for both. But with
my youth, has gone all the brightness from my life, & Time's wave which has carried you
on its topmost crest to Fortune, has stranded me, with hopes all wrecked   My friend Gen.
Harney has kindly promised to give you this, & to second my petition in behalf of my Son
George W Goode, for whom I wish to obtain a position at West Point. I have no claim to
favour Save that he comes of honest law abiding Tax paying Stock, & has himself a more
than ordinary share of brains & muscle. He is Eighteen years old   I think he has good
principles & he has all the education, I could afford him. If you can without personal inconvenience or Sacrifice of principle assist him, you will do a great kindness, to us both . . ."
ALS, *ibid.*, RG 94, Correspondence, USMA. On June 19, USG endorsed this letter. "Refered to the Sec. of War. This name may be placed on the list of substitutes, next below
those already named for next year. Should there be a vacancy this year, in Sept. after appointing all the subs. named he may then be aptd." AES, *ibid.* George W. Goode graduated
USMA in 1880. See *Julia Grant*, p. 47.

On July 23, Belknap telegraphed to Babcock, Long Branch. "Letter received. ~~Will~~
Go to NewLondon tomorrow evening. Will run over to Long Branch on Thursday or Fri-
day next week. Assignment of Cadets was made yesterday but order will ~~be~~ not be pub-
lished until I see the President. Will bring all papers with me. Weather delightful here—"
ALS (telegram sent), DNA, RG 107, Telegrams Collected (Bound); telegram received,
DLC-USG, IB.

1. Born in 1857 in Auburn, Mo., Frederick Dent Sharp was the second son of Alexander Sharp and Ellen (Nellie) Wrenshall Dent, sister of Julia Dent Grant. On Dec. 6,
1876, USG nominated Sharp as 2nd lt., 20th Inf.

To Benjamin H. Bristow

Long Branch, N. J.
Sept. 5th /74

GEN. B. H. BRISTOW,
SEC. OF THE TREAS.
DEAR SIR:

Some week before my late visit east Dr. Tiffany, of the Metropolitan M. E. Church, called on me in the interest of Dr. Sam.l C.
Blake as surgeon to the Marin[e] Hospital, Chicago, Ill.   I took

down in pencil at the time memoranda which I made at the time, and which I intended to read to you when you come up, but forgot.

"Dr. Tiffany asks for the Apt. of Dr. Sam.l T. Blake as surgeon of the Chicago Marine Hospital—present appointee was a compromise man—Dr. Blake will give satisfaction to most of the people— is worthy and well qualified, and is one of the sufferers of the Chicago fire—in his business-practice—particularly. The north side has not been built up like the balance of the city; and people w[h]o lived there for[mer]ly h[ave] scattered."

The appointment is entirely u[nder y]our controll and I know nothing about the present incumbent except what I here tell you, and nothing about Dr. Blake. Dr. Tiffany is well acquainted in Chicago and rendered important service by speaking daily early in the war in encouragement of enlistments while filling his pulpit regularly.

Very Truly Yours
U. S. GRANT

ALS (damaged), Boston Athenaeum, Boston, Mass. No appointment followed for Samuel C. Blake, formerly surgeon, 39th Ill. Ralph N. Isham continued as surgeon, Marine Hospital, Chicago.

To Benjamin H. Bristow

———

Long Branch, N. J.
Sept. 5th /74

DEAR SIR:

An application for the abolition of one office and the creation of another under the Appraiser of the Port of New York will be forwarded to you. From the statement made to me by the Collector & Surveyor of the port the change will be a benefit to the service. My particular interest in the matter however arises from the fact that I am desirous of getting a situation for Willie Hillyer, a most excellent young man of about twenty-one years, who I have known from his infancy, and who is left now with a widowed mother and four younger children than himself dependent upon him. I spoke to the Collector and Surveyor in his behalf and the accompanying recommendation is the result. I wish you would look into the matter and if you agree in the propriety of the change that you will authorize it.

In the matter of London Agent for the exchange of bonds[1] I leave it entirely to your judgement who, from the Treas to select. I have full faith in the integrity and ability of Mr. Bigelow, but stated to you what I had heard as to his unfitness in other respects.

Very Truly
Your obt. svt,
U. S. Grant

Hon. B. H. Bristow
Sec. of the Treas.

ALS, DLC-Benjamin H. Bristow. On Sept. 8, 1874, Secretary of the Treasury Benjamin H. Bristow wrote to USG. "I have your favor of the 5th inst relative to the appointment of Willie Hillyer to a position in the N. Y. Custom House. I have received no communication from the Collector or Surveyor on the subject, and the 'accompanying recommendation' mentioned in your letter was not received, having been inadvertently omitted, as I suppose. I have written Genl Arthur on the subject, and will be pleased to comply with your request as soon as I can get the information necessary to enable me to do so. I have asked Genl Hillhouse to go to London in charge of the refunding, and he is quite strongly inclined to accept unless his bondsmen shall interpose objection. He asked time to consult them. I think he is the very best man in this Department for the place, and he has an assistant who is well qualified to fill his place during his absence. I hope this will meet your approval. The Surgeon in Charge of the Marine Hospital at Chicago is, or has been strongly backed by Mr Farwell, and I have deemed it advisable to write him that I desired to make a change for the reason that the present incumbent gives very little attention to the Hospital. Referring again to the proposed removal of Mr Low, Supervising Steamboat Inspector I am inclined to think it would be well to give him an opportunity to meet the grave charges against him, and will adopt that course unless you shall see proper to direct otherwise." ALS (press), *ibid.* William S. Hillyer, Jr., served as clerk to the gen. appraiser, New York City. See letter to William S. Hillyer, July 1, 1874.

On Sept. 9, USG, Long Branch, telegraphed to Bristow. "WITHHOLD NOMINATION TO SUCCESSOR TO LOW AS INSPECTOR OF STEAMBOATS UNTIL MY ARRIVAL IN WASHINGTON." Telegram received (at 6:40 P.M.), DLC-USG, IB. On Sept. 4, Bristow had written to USG. "Referring to the order for the suspension of Mr Addison Low, Supervising Inspector of Steamboats for the second district, and the designation of Mr E. Platt Stratton as his successor, forwarded for your signature on the 25th ultimo. I have the honor to state a thorough examination of the affairs of the second Steamboat Inspection district by a competant Special Agent of the Department, has disclosed the fact that Mr Low has been faithless in the execution of the Steamboat law, that he has granted and permitted his subordinates to grant illegal indulgences to steamers and officers of steamers; that he has frequently over ruled decissions of the local inspectors, and that he has directed or influenced local inspectors to act, officially, contrary to their own judgment of right. The above on the representation made to the Dept. upon which its action in recommending the successor of Mr Low, was based. The facts are, however, submitted that your Excellency may direct what further course shall be taken. The commissions of Mr Stratton and the order suspending Mr Low are returned you that you may sign them or direct their cancellation as may seem best to you, after a consideration of this statement. Mr E. Platt Stratton, designated as Mr Low's successors, is hereby recommended Hon Henry J. Scudder as a suitable person, in every respect for the position." Copy, DNA, RG 56, Letters Sent. On Sept. 7, Bradley S. Osbon, secretary, National Board of Steam Navigation, New York City, wrote to USG. "I am directed by a resolution of this Board to foward the enclosed resolution which was passed at its third annual meetng held at Buffalo N. Y on the 2d and 3d insts." ALS, *ibid.*, Letters Received from the President. The Sept. 3 resolution urged USG and Bristow to name as head of steamboat inspections "a gentleman of integrity and of learning . . . whose judgment and rulings cannot be improperly warped or effected by any interested party, whether he be steamboat owner, officer, patentee or politician." Copy, *ibid.* On Sept. 12, Saturday, Addison Low, Albany, N. Y., telegraphed to Orville E. Babcock. "I shall be in Washington Monday morning" Telegram received, DLC-USG, IB. Low continued as supervising inspector of steamboats, 2nd District. See *New York Times*, Oct. 25, Nov. 15, 1875.

1. See letter to Benjamin H. Bristow, Aug. 30, 1874. On Sept. 15, Babcock wrote to Bristow. "The President directs me to say that Mr. F. Widdows, Clerk in 6th Auditor's Office is desirous of being detailed as one of the clerks to go abroad with bonds. He is recommended by the Met. M. E. Church, as a special favor to them." Copy, DLC-USG, II, 2.

Endorsement

Respectfully refered to the Sec. of State. If there is any thing that can be done for Wayne I should like to do it. If the Sec. will bear this in mind when I visit Washington—and will call attention to it when we meet with such members of the Cabinet as may be there at the time—we will see if it is practicable.

U. S. GRANT

SEPT. 5TH /74

AES, DNA, RG 59, Letters of Application and Recommendation. Written on a letter of Aug. 28 from Henry C. Wayne, USMA 1838, Savannah, to USG. "(Private) . . . The treachery of my former partner has ruined me nearly, and what little I may be fortunate in recovering is locked up in Arbitration, and for some time to come. The universal stagnation in business has so far rendered unsuccessful my search for Employment, and I am for the present without income. The state of Georgia being under Democratic Control, there is no opening for me politically in my own state, and therefore I am compelled, reluctantly, to ask if you can give me something to do, at least until I can get on my legs again." ALS, *ibid.* See Hamilton Fish diary, Sept. 14, 1874, DLC-Hamilton Fish. No appointment followed. On Dec. 2, 1873, USG had nominated Wayne as consul, Kanagawa; on Jan. 19, 1874, USG withdrew the nomination. See Nevins, *Fish*, pp. 742–43; Alexander A. Lawrence, ed., "Some Letters from Henry C. Wayne to Hamilton Fish," *Georgia Historical Quarterly*, 43, 4 (1959), 391–409.

To John M. Ogden, Walter Allison, and Richard K. Betts

LONG BRANCH, N. J., Sept. 5, 1874.

JOHN M. OGDEN, WALTER ALLISON, and RICHARD K. BETTS, *Committee of the Carpenters' Hall Company.*

Your invitation to me to attend the hundredth anniversary meeting of the Continental Congress in their hall on this day has, from accumulation of papers and letters during my recent visit East, escaped my attention until this moment.

Please excuse apparent neglect. It would have afforded me pleasure to attend your exercises on an occasion of so much interest. I hope they will be attended with all the interest such an occasion should naturally inspire.

U. S. GRANT.

New York Tribune, Sept. 7, 1874.

To John F. Long

Long Branch, N. J.
Sept. 7th /74

DEAR JUDGE;

Your several letters have been duly received and read, but as they did not need special answers, and as I get so many that do, I have not answered before. I have received the Fair tickets you were kind enough to send. We will be in St. Louis about the second day of the Fair—Tuesday. As we wish to run about, visit the farm &c. Mrs. Grant thinks we had better not go to a private house. The party will consist of Mr. & Mrs. Borie & maid, Mrs. Sharp Genl Babcock ~~my~~Mrs Grant & myself. Mrs. Sharp will stay with her brother but the balance of us would like rooms at the new hotel if it is opened,[1] if not then at the Planter's House—It was in accordance with my instructions to Carlin to sell off all the cattle. I hope he will manage the farm so as to make it self supporting.—You are right in leasing the Carondelet property when ever occasion presents itself. I shall be compelled to pursue the same course with White Haven if it continues expensive.

My kindest regards to you and your family.

U. S. GRANT

JUDGE JOHN F. LONG.

ALS, CSmH. On Oct. 5, 1874, Monday, at 9:00 P.M., USG and party arrived in St. Louis on a special train. On Oct. 10, USG and party left St. Louis. See *St. Louis Globe*, Oct. 5–6, 8, 10, 1874; Speech, Oct. 11, 1874.

1. The Southern Hotel reopened after renovation and refurbishing on Oct. 3. See *St. Louis Globe*, Oct. 4, 1874. USG and party stayed at the Lindell Hotel.

To Russell Sage

———

Washington, D. C. Sept. 7th 1874.

HON. RUSSELL SAGE
PRESDT. P. M. S. S. Co.
61 WALL ST. NEW YORK
MY DEAR SIR:

I avail myself of the first leisure since my return from my visit to Marthas Vineyard and vicinity to thank you for the delicate attention extended to my family on board your beautiful Iron Steamship "City of Peking." I congratulate you and through you your company —on the completion of two such magnificent iron Ships—entirely the production of American labor.

I trust the successful building of these iron ships will stimulate American Ship building, and thus greatly aid in regaining our lost Commerce, and building up a powerful carrying trade in American built ships.

Wishing your Company success in maintaining their great Steamship line.

I am, Yours truly

U. S. GRANT

Copy, DLC-USG, II, 2. Born in 1816, Russell Sage became a successful merchant in Troy, N. Y., served two terms in Congress as a Whig (1853–57), and later moved to New York

City, where he amassed a large fortune speculating in railroad and other stocks. For the Pacific Mail Steamship Co., see letter to James W. Marshall, July 24, 1874; Paul Sarnoff, *Russell Sage: The Money King* (New York, 1965), pp. 157–60, 193–98.

On Aug. 26, 1874, USG, Julia Dent Grant, Sage, and others boarded the recently completed *City of Peking* at New York City for an overnight trip to Newport, R. I., en route to Martha's Vineyard. See *Boston Evening Transcript*, Aug. 26, 1874; Speech, Aug. 31, 1874.

On June 18, 1876, Margaret Olivia Sage, New York City, wrote to USG. "My husband 'the Admiral' is too diffident to write to you, & so I will attempt to plead my own cause. Two of the last graduating class at West Point were found deficient, & failed to receive their Diplomas. One of these young men (Herbert J. Slocum of Cincinnati) is my nephew, & the other is Mr Guilfoyle, who was appointed by yourself, from the Soldiers Home in Baltimore. They, no doubt ought to be punished, but cannot their punishment be tempered with mercy? Cannot these young men be 'turned back,' & regain by studious habits, & exemplary atten- to duty, the respect of themselves as well as the approval of their fellow men?—My nephew I know would greatly prefer to do this, & Gen Sherman told me while on his recent visit to West Point, that it was all wrong for any one to *ask*, or to have a commission *given* to a young man under such circumstances.—I understand that there is an under current of feeling toward yourself, at the Point, growing out of your independant action in reference to *this* graduating class, & that these young men have been treated thus, to make issue with you. . . ." ALS, DNA, RG 94, Correspondence, USMA. On June 22, USG nominated Herbert J. Slocum as 2nd lt. See *PUSG*, 21, 497–98.

Endorsement

Sept. 14th 74

Referred to the Secretary of War: If the change can be legally made, or if the Government can legally receive back the arms previously issued to citizens of Kansas, I think it but fair to give them approved arms in place of those they now have.

U. S. GRANT

ES, DNA, RG 156, Letters Received. Written on a letter of Sept. 5, 1874, from Governor Thomas A. Osborn of Kan. to USG. "To enable me to protect the frontier settlements of this state Contiguous to the Indian Territory from Indian depredations, I made application to the General Government, through you for arms and ammunition under the Act of April 23rd 1808, providing for arming and equipping the Militia. The Secretary of war, to whom the application was referred, refused to issue the arms; assigning as a reason that the state was already indebted to the General Government for arms heretofore issued. . . . The frequent incursions, into the state, of hostile bands of Indians who murder and plunder our Citizens, notwithstanding the earnest and energetic efforts of Maj General Pope, Commanding this Department, to afford all possible protection, demonstrates the inability of the Government, with the present depleted condition of the army, to afford protection to our Citizens living near the line of the Indian Territory. These frequent outrages are de-

populating the Country Contiguous to the Indian Territory, and I have deemed it necessary to call into the service a few companies of the state militia for service in that locality.
The five hundred carbines furnished the state, by the Government in June last, are the only
arms we now have fit to be used in an encounter with the hostile Indians. By some means
they have been amply provided with the best guns manufactured in the United States, and
it would be worse than cruel to send into the field, to meet such an enemy, a body of troops,
armed with the old muskets, with which the state stands charged on the books of the War
Department. You will readily see that 500 guns is but a meagre number with which to protect our extended frontier. Sixteen citizens of Kansas are known to have been murdered by
Indians within the state since the 16th of June last and not one of the murderers has been
punished or even arrested by the Government, whose wards they are. But a few days since,
and even since the receipt of your letter, assuring me that the U. S. Army would protect our
state from invasion, six Citizens of Lawrence, engaged in surveying the public lands in
Kansas, under a contract with the Interior Department of the General Government were
brutally murdered by Indians. While the United States Government may be unable to
afford to the Citizen that full measure of protection which is so essential to his personal
safety, can she, in honor, do less than afford him the means of protecting himself? This
State has already expended, since her admission into the Union, more than $350.000 in de-
fending her citizens against hostile Indians whose good conduct was guaranteed by the
Government, and whatever may be the decision on this application for arms, we will endeavor to protect the lives and property of our Citizens at whatever Cost." LS, *ibid.* On
Sept. 18, the Kan. legislature passed a resolution asking USG to grant Osborn's request.
Copy, *ibid.* On Sept. 21, Secretary of War William W. Belknap wrote to Osborn authorizing additional weapons. LS (press), *ibid.*

On Aug. 21, Osborn had telegraphed to USG. "I have information through Indian agt
Stubbs and other sources that the Osage tribe of Indians have at a general council declared
war against this state. Depredations have already been committed by them on our Southern border. The state has but few arms & the United States troops heretofore guarding the
line being now in the Indian Territory at a great distance from the Osage reservation ex-
poses the frontier settlements of this state to great danger. With arms we can defend our
borders. Can you furnish me two thousand carbines and accoutrements and one hundred
thousand cartridges on account of the state of Kansas" Telegram received (at 10:27 P.M.),
ibid. On Aug. 25, Enoch Hoag, superintendent, Indian Affairs, Central Superintendency,
Lawrence, Kan., telegraphed to Edward P. Smith, commissioner of Indian Affairs. "Agent
Stubbs is now here and denies having made to any person the statement contained in the
dispatch of Gov. Osborne that the Osage Council had declared war against the State of
Kansas. Agent Gibson reports to day that the Osages are all quiet and on their reservation. Official proceedings of the said Council forwarded." Copy, *ibid.* On the same day, Isaac
T. Gibson, agent, Neosho Agency, Coffeyville, Kan., telegraphed to Belknap. "I have just
read Governor Osborn's telegram. He is misinformed. The Osages have not declared war
against the people of Kansas nor any body, nor have the tribe threatened to do so, nor have
they committed any depredation, whatever, on the contrary the Grand Summer Campaigne
of Plains Indians was broken by the determined loyalty of the Osages to the government,
~~They~~ Yet they feel grieved that the so called militia of Kansas treacherously and wantonly
murdered four unarmed Osages recently and stole at the same time over fifty head of po-
nies but they rely on the government to obtain for them just redress   All of them are on
their reservation and the head men are councilling in the interests of peace and civilization   Peace cannot be promoted by arming border men," Telegram received, *ibid.* Also on

Aug. 25, Belknap wrote to Osborn. "... on the 25th of June last an issue of arms and ammunition was made to the State, amounting in value to $10.260, and as the value of the
stores now asked for will be about $40,000, I am compelled to decline your request as I
doubt my authority to authorize the issue under the circumstances, the debt of the State
being already so large." LS (press), *ibid.* On Aug. 27, Levi P. Luckey telegraphed to Osborn. "The President directs me to acknowledge the receipt of your telegram of the 21st,
which was referred to both the War and Interior Departments, and say that it is the duty
of the General Government to protect the State of Kansas from invasion by Indians, and
that should there be a necessity for so doing the Secretary of War will send troops to Kansas for that purpose." Copy, DLC-USG, II, 2. See *HED*, 43-2-1, part 5, I, 534–35, 541–42.

On July 7, H. G. Kelley, El Paso, Kan., wrote to USG. "We Respectfully request the
aid of the Govermen for protection against the Savages who are on the war path and killing and scalping the citizens of the frontier of Kansas Without the least interruption   the
citizens are unarmed and unprotected   they are Said to be five tribes banded together
numbering about 3,000 woyers   to day they killed 4 men and left them lying in the road
scalped and mutilated and are stopping the Mails, and the familie are leaving the Country
as fast as possible and as we have all that we have in the world here it would be almost suicide to leave it and we humbly request the aid of the of the government   if you cant send
us Troops send us guns and amunition and we will protect our selvs as well as Possible
this morning the stage came back and said that they was stopped on the Ft Sill rout   as
I am writing there has been 4 wagons come from Colwell and say they are Meditating an
atact this eve   there has been several Companies organized but they have now arms but
Pistole and of a very poor sort   they would be but a little show against the Henry rifle
which the Indians are in possion of   if you or the Governmen armes the indians you had
ought to arme or protest the frontier and its citizens" ALS, DNA, RG 75, Letters Received,
Central Superintendency.

On Aug. 28, 1875, Celia C. Short, Lawrence, wrote to USG. "One year ago, Hon.
C. W. Babcock, Sur. Gen., informed you of the Cheyenne massacre of the Six Surveyors in
the South-Western part of this State. The deputy of that party, O. F. Short, was my husband and the flag-man, my son. In my desolation, I presume to solicit the attention of our
Honorable President, to the two (2) enclosed *printed* letters, believing them expressive of
'the people,' where-ever the 'facts' are known. Woman's power may be in her helplessness;
yet I am thankful Sir; that Republican *principles* was a part of my education and religion,
as taught in my girlhood years in the 'Banner State' of Illinois. In 1840—though scarcely
four years of age, I shed my first tears of bitterness, at the death of the lamented, Harri-
son. But the memories and scenes of the past eighteen years, has made *this State*, my home
forever; although not a relative within its boundaries. For months my pony has traverst the
'plains,' midst the narrow, fresh-beaten trail of Savage tribes, and where storm and night
over-took me, I threw my saddle upon the ground for a pillow and slept away from camp,
unarmed, for *I thought* the red-man my friend. But their treachery—has robbed me of a
loving husband, and a darling Son, fourteen years of age. With their life-blood, is this soil
made sacred to me. *Here* with a mothers pride, I have seen my little boys 'go with Papa to
vote for General Grant,' and four years later, heard their merry shouts,—'We will vote for
President Grant, Hurah!' Even in this day of mid-night; I pray to live, that by the guidance
of God; I may see my three remaining sons, with their little sister, grow up for usefulness
here, and happiness in the here-after: and to this end it is my chief desire, to have *means*
to *educate*; for 'It is not all of life, to *live.*' I shall this winter most respectfully—petition
Congress for an appropriation of ten-thousand ($10,000) believing I shall be sustained in

the same by our worthy President of the U. S. My papers are nearly in shape. The letter addressed to 'two houses' from the Superintendent of Ind. Affirs E. Hoag, strongly recommends my 'bill', and the one to him; by the Cheyenne agent, J. D. Miles, is full and handsomly written. Maj. Gen. Pope will use his influence in my behalf; also Gov. Osborn. Fearing I have intrude by this lengthy article, upon your patience and time, I would humbly beg your lenity." ALS, *ibid.*, Cheyenne and Arapahoe Agency. The enclosures are *ibid.* See *HRC*, 45-2-404.

On Dec. 24, 1874, Osborn had telegraphed to USG. "I am informed by Agent Gibson that parties of Osages have left their reservation, ostensibly to hunt. I fear a collision between them and the settlers in the southwestern part of this State, if they are not returned to their reservation." *Report of the Adjutant General to the Governor, 1875* (Topeka, 1876), p. 25. On Jan. 5, 1875, Smith wrote to Secretary of the Interior Columbus Delano. ". . . Respecting the cause of alarm in the apprehension of Gov. Osborn, I have to state that these Osages are the people, a band of whom were murderously attacked by a party of men—afterwards enrolled by Governor Osborn as Kansas militia—and four of their number brutally killed, and the band plundered of the property they had along with them. The Osages have repeatedly asked of the Government, and of Governor Osborn, that steps be taken to punish these murderers and return the property. As to the most prompt and efficient method of preventing the Osages from attempting retaliation for the murder of their brethren, I beg to venture the suggestion that it will be found in the putting forth of vigorous efforts on the part of the authorities of Kansas to comply with the manifest requirements simply of justice and humanity. . . ." *Ibid.*, p. 26.

Speech

———

[*Sept. 15, 1874*]

Mr. Mantilla: I am happy to receive you in the character which your credentials describe. The assurances which you offer on behalf of your Government of its disposition to strengthen the friendly relations between the United States and Spain are heartily reciprocated by me. The embarrassments to which you allude, which the Government of your country has for some time past experienced, both at home and elsewhere, deserve the sympathy of all wellwishers of Spain. I share the hope expressed by you that the day is not distant when, under the shelter of restored peace, Spain will be able to extend to all over whom she may claim jurisdiction the privileges of liberty, civilization, and social order. You set forth with correctness the motives to harmony and intimacy between our respective countries. It is hoped that both will be unremitting in their endeavors toward tightening the bonds between them. I have confidence in your professions of good will to that end, and you will find no cause to call in question a similar feeling on my part.

New York Times, Sept. 16, 1874. USG spoke after Antonio Mantilla presented his credentials as minister from Spain. ". . . Abandoned in the midst of her political and social reconstruction by the Chief Magistrate, whom she had elected to rule and govern her with the character of perpetuity rooted in her glorious traditions and in her secular habits, exposed to be a prey to turbulent factions, as she was to be a victim of unstable Governments, forced to sustain a triple contest with separatistic demagogy and decrepit absolutism, Spain, by the powerful exertions of her worthy sons and the visible protection of heaven, has succeeded in maintaining her integrity and in re-establishing order in the greater part of her vast territory against so many enemies conspiring for her ruin, and the day is not far distant when, under the shelter of peace, her present Government will be able whenever it wishes to extend to those who know how to appreciate them, all the benefits of liberty and civilization . . ." *Ibid.* Spain's first republic, declared in Feb., 1873, fell to monarchists in Dec., 1874. On March 16, 1875, Mantilla visited the White House and presented a letter, dated Jan. 16, from King Alfonso XII to USG. "The Spanish Monarchy having been re-established by the acclamation and assent of the people, and We having been called to govern it by reason of our legitimate heirship and the abdication of our well beloved mother, Queen Isabel the Second, We hasten to inform you of our accession to the throne. . . ." LS (in Spanish), DNA, RG 59, Notes from Foreign Legations, Spain; translation, *ibid.* See *Washington Evening Star*, March 16, 1875. On May 1, Secretary of State Hamilton Fish wrote to USG conveying Mantilla's request to present new credentials to reflect the change in government. LS, Babcock Papers, ICN.

Proclamation

―――――

Whereas, It has been satisfactorily represented to me that turbulent and disorderly persons have combined together with force and arms to overthrow the State government of Louisiana, and to resist the laws and constituted authorities of said State; and

Whereas, It is provided in the Constitution of the United States that the United States shall protect every State in this Union on application of the legislature, or of the executive, when the legislature cannot be convened, against domestic violence; and

Whereas, It is provided in the laws of the United States that, in all cases of insurrection in any State or of obstruction to the laws thereof, it shall be lawful for the President of the United States, on application of the legislature of such State, or of the executive when the legislature cannot be convened, to call forth the militia of any other State or States, or to employ such part of the land and naval forces, as shall be judged necessary for the purpose of suppressing such insurrection or causing the laws to be duly executed; and

Whereas the Legislature of said State is not now in session and cannot be convened in time to meet the present emergency, and the executive of said State, under Section 4 of Article IV of the Constitution of the United States and the laws passed in pursuance thereof, has therefore made application to me for such part of the military force of the United States as may be necessary and adequate to protect said State and the citizens thereof against domestic violence, and to enforce the due execution of the laws; and

Whereas, It is required that, whenever it may be necessary, in the judgment of the President, to use the military force for the purpose aforesaid, he shall forthwith by proclamation command such insurgents to disperse and retire peaceably to their respective homes within a limited time:

Now, therefore, I, Ulysses S. Grant, President of the United States, do hereby make proclamation, and command said turbulent and disorderly persons to disperse and retire peaceably to their respective abodes within five days from this date, and hereafter to submit themselves to the laws and constituted authorities of said State; and I invoke the aid and co-operation of all good citizens thereof to uphold law and preserve the public peace.

In Witness Whereof, I have hereunto set my hand and caused the seal of the United States to be affixed.

Done at the City of Washington this fifteenth day of September in the year of our Lord eighteen hundred and seventy four, and of the Independence of the United States the ninety-ninth.

U. S. GRANT

DS, DNA, RG 130, Presidential Proclamations; copy, *ibid.* *SD*, 57-2-209, 155–56. On Sept. 15, 1874, Secretary of State Hamilton Fish wrote in his diary. "Ascending the Stairs at the Prsdt, whither I had gone to present the new Spanish Minr, was met by the Presidents ~~Message~~ Assist. Priv. Sect (Sniffen) with a large Envelope, which he said contained a 'Proclamation' relating to Louisiana, signed by the President to which my signature & the Seal were desired. ~~the President~~ The document was without heading—dated the 98th instead of 99th year of Independence. I met Atty Genl who was anxious at once to give it to the Press—I promised to telegraph him, as soon as I returned to the office—& had the seal affixed, which was done about half past 12 oclk—It appears in the Evening papers —garbled—an erroneous copy having been given out at the Attorney Genls office, as he admits—No member of the Cabinet has been consulted as to the propriety of issuing ~~the~~

a Proclamation—In the Evening Bristow & Jewell call at my house, as I was ~~fully~~ prepared to leave for NY—they enquire if I had been consulted as to the Proclamation—~~I reply~~ Answering in the negative, I tell them what is above stated, as to its coming into my possession &c—they express surprise that a document of such importance and significance should be put forth without more of deliberation, & without consultation with the Cabinet—(They are new members—otherwise they wd not be surprised)   They suggest that the Prsdt who had intended going to Long Branch—should not quit Washn at this time— Concurring in this view, & ~~in company with~~ Bristow & Jewell & ~~I go~~ to Dr Sharps where the President is staying, & suggest to him whether it be adviseable that he leave the seat of Govt at this moment—His luggage was already on a Cart at the door—He immediately, on the first suggestion of ~~the~~ the question of propriety of leaving, decided that he should remain, & his trunks were brought into the House—A telegram was recd by him while we were there, ~~for~~ signed by a large number of names, Presidents of Banks Insurance Cos & prominent persons, many of whom were recognized by Bristow & Jewell, representing the restoration of entire order, in New Orleans—The President requests us to meet in Cabinet tomorrow morning at 9½—I subsequently went to Gov Jewells rooms, where he read me a telegram, from the Supt of the Postal service, who he says is a very trustworthy person, also representing the prevalence of peace & order—Bristow came in, & some discussion ensued as to the proper course to be pursued—~~the~~ a great difficulty seems to be presented, in the committal by the Prsdt in his Proclamation (that of ~~of~~ this day) to a recognition of the Kellog Govt   The new Govt (Penn's) comes into power, by a revolutionary movement, & by force of arms—It appears to me that it cannot be recognized, irrespective of the past committal in favor of the Kellogg Govt" DLC-Hamilton Fish.

On Aug. 19, Governor William P. Kellogg of La. had written to USG, Long Branch. "I regret to have to trouble you again about our affairs but the exceptional circumstances surrounding us, and the importance of the issues involved, render it necessary that I should make a brief statement of the situation. Louisiana is now the last state in the South-West except Mississippi, that remains true to the Republican party. We have a large majority of the legal voters of the State. Even our opponents now admit it and refuting their own often repeated assertions of last year, that a heavy colored vote was polled for the fusion candidates, assert in their published call, that all efforts to persuade the colored element to unite with them have failed, and consequently that other means must be resorted to. Accordingly they have abandoned the policy of fraud upon which they relied in 1872, and have returned to the policy of murder, violence and intimidation which they pursued in 1868 to such purpose, that out of nearly eighty thousand republican votes in the State barely six thousand votes were cast for yourself and the national republican ticket. The great majority of the republican voters of this state are colored, though we are daily receiving large accessions of white voters especially in the City of New Orleans where we shall probably poll from four to five thousand more white votes than at the last election. In the river parishes which are easily accessible, and where our numerical superiority is very great, we shall probably be able to preserve peace and bring out our full vote in the coming election without much trouble; but in the more distant parishes of the State, lying on the borders of Arkansas and Texas, where turbulence and lawlessness are chronic, much violence already prevails, and much more is anticipated before election. The State is doing, and will do all it can to suppress these internal disorders but there are influences of a very powerful kind which are being used against us. The eminently just and proper action of the National Administration in the affairs of Arkansas and Texas is represented as indicating a settled purpose on the part of yourself to 'let the South alone' and not to extend to any republican government in the Southern States the protection of the General Government, no matter what domestic violence may be set afoot. This impression has been industriously circulated in the parishes lying near the Arkansas and Texas line, and taken in connection with the decision of Judge Bradley releasing the Grant parish murderers, has had a very bad effect. At the same time while this impression is being circulated with regard to the attitude of the President, the pronounced hostility of these men to the National government remains as bitter as ever. By the redistribution of districts, this State is entitled to representation by six congressmen in the next congress. In five at least out of the six districts we have an undoubted republican majority and we can elect our candidates if we can have a fair election uncontrolled by violence. I have felt it due alike to the National Administration, and to the State Government that the coming election should be held clear of all suspicions of fraud such as have tainted previous elections in Louisiana. Accordingly I have approved and promulgated an act passed by the last legislature providing for an entirely new registration throughout the State. I have voluntarily pledged myself to give the opposition a clerk in every registration office in the State, and our new law gives them a commissioner at every poll. So far as the State Administration is concerned the next election will be one of the fairest ever held in Louisiana. But it is necessary that every republican voter should know that he will be protected if violently interfered with in the exercise of the rights conferred upon him by Congress and the Constitution, and should feel that he is not beyond the reach of the national arm. Except a handful of men at Colfax, we have no U. S. troops in the State, and have had none since the 19th Infantry were removed, which is now several months since. There are troops now stationed at Holly Springs Miss:, who I believe are designed for service in this state. If they were promptly assigned to the respective stations heretofore occupied by the 19th Infantry whom they have been sent to relieve, one great incentive to the outrages and violence now prevailing would be at once removed   The heated term here has apparently passed and the State is healthier than it has been for many years. Not a single case of Yellow fever has anywhere manifested itself, nor is there any epidemic disease prevailing. I respectfully and earnestly suggest that if the U. S. troops were returned to their posts in this State, such a course would have a most salutory effect and would prevent much bloodshed, and probably a formal call upon the President and a renewed agitation of the Louisiana question which otherwise a quiet fair election next November would for ever set at rest and fully vindicate your just policy towards us." LS, DNA, RG 60, Letters Received, La. *SED*, 43-2-13, 9–10.

On Aug. 25, Secretary of War William W. Belknap telegraphed to USG. "Lt. Otis leave extended to October Twentieth (20th). Prompt steps will be taken in connection with Louisiana matter referred to in your letter of August Twenty third—(23d)" ALS (telegram sent), DNA, RG 107, Telegrams Collected (Bound).

On Sept. 4, S. J. Ward, president, board of trade, *et al.*, Shreveport, telegraphed to USG. "The delaration of your excellency that the recent atrocities in the south particularly in Louisanna Alabama & South Carolina show a disregard for Law Civil rights & protection of property that ought not to be tolerated in any civilized government—accompanied by directions for troops to be sent to the three states mentioned. following closely upon the proclamation of Gov Kellogg offering a large reward for the parties implicated in the killing of six white men parish officals captured by the white people in a riot near the town of Coushatta in Red River parish and intimation that the killing was done by citizens of Caddo leads us to think that the origin & character of the Coushatta affair & other civil commotions which have occured in Louisanna has been misrepresented to your excellency or that your judgement of them has been colored by the grossly false reports of a partizan press & of parties who conceive that it is fair political strategy to misrepresent their political opponents   we assure your excellency most positively that Gov Kellogg is in Error in relation to the participation of the citizens of Caddo parish in what is known as the Coushatta affair   the disturbance terminated on the twenty eight of august   its intelligence of it reached Caddo on the morning of the twenty ninth of Aug in letters dated twenty seventh Aug stating that Eight hundred negroes were in arms threatening with extermination two hundred whites who had gathered to protect their homes & families and calling for help a body of mounted men embracing merchants & professional men & property holders left Shreveport at three oclock AM the twenty ninth of Aug   this force divided in two squads when twelve miles from Shreveport a the route Cushatta was met by a courier & turned back with the information that the trouble had been settled by the capture of six white & six negroes instigators & Leaders of the riot. Every man in the party returned to the city before ten oclock that night   the killing of the six white men occurred the following day sunday & the intelligence of it reached shreveport monday afternoon.   this simple state-ment offe acts susceptible of proof by hundreds of witnesses shows that gov Kellogg has been mislead   we are as Ignorant as yourself of the parties who killed the men but we do know that they were not from this parish   the statement is made in the executive depart-ment in new orleans that the troubles originate in the assemblage of a posse of whites & negroes by the sheriff of Red River, parish to than a movement on the part of the whits to force the republican officials to resigne   on the contrary we have the testimony of men of unquestionable veracity present before during and after the trouble that no such purpose was entertained that the action of the negroes was prompted by their white Leaders with a view of bringing about such a condition of affairs as would induce your excellency to send troops to the state which troops it was hoped and believed by the willey instigators of the trouble would overawe and intimadate the white people and prevent them from prosecut-ing the present political contest against the radical party   we shall not attempt to justify to your excellency the killing of the six white men but knowing as we do the deep and bit-ter wrongs our people have endured at the hands of the Class to which these men belong & knowing that our own Homes & families have been impoverished by the mischievous teachings and schemes of their kind that through their incompetency and dishonesty as of-ficals we and our fellow citizens have been well nigh reduced to beggary & our state to ruin we cannot participate in what of indignation their violent death may have stirred within your heart & the hearts of others who know not the fraction of our sufferings & grievances the white people of Louisanna are an Enlightened and christian people with large prop-erty and commercial interest at stake   their human feelings lead them to prefer peace & the supremacy of Law to riot & civil strife and it must be Evident to the mind of your ex-cellency that they would not imperil their property and other private interest & risk the lives and chastity of their families in a fierce warfare inspired by pure & simple brutality & hate against a race of people whom they know to be the only class of laborers upon whom they can rely for the tillage of their fields   we assure your excellency that their is no war of races in Louisianna further than that the ignorant and credulous negroes have been in several L[oca]lities of the state incited to violence against the whites by a pernicious class of Demagogues for the purpose of making political capital with the country out of the blood that might be shed   in the resolutions of our people and in the attempts of their press all the rights secured to the Negroes by the Constitutional Amenments have been endorsed whenever the whites have killed negroes the negroes have been the aggressors and have Either murdered whitemen or ravashd white woman   we are firmly convinced that the disturbances which have occurred in Louisianna were instigated by our political opponents and our share in them systematically misrepresented for the purpose of inducing your ex-cellency to send troops among us and direct the signed application of the enforcement acts in our state & we have no doubt it is designed so soon as your recent orders and instruc-tions are carried out that affidavits will be made by negroes and supple politica[l] hench-men against our most prominent and influential citizens and that they will all be arrested by U S. marshall or his deputies under the protection of your troops taken from their homes to go through the mockery of a trial while our people are left without leaders to organize and conduct the present campaign   before your excellency permits the arrests of our citizens to be made by federal officials on the affidavits of our political antgonists we earnestly entreat you to appoint a commission of fair mind[ed] men to visit this state & investigate the full truth and Enquire if there is any lawlessness a vigorous state goverment in the hands of competent & honest officals in whom the people have confidence cannot deal with to investigate the facts in relation to the disturbances that have transpired in various localities of the state & judge from the evidence of the partizans of the present state government—& the negroes are not the instigators   should your excellency deem that we are Entitled to this consideration we gurantee that full & amply testimony can be had & that the white people of the state or Least of this portion of it will give such a commission all the assistance in their power and acquiesce to its authority   we assure your excellency that the white people of Louisiana owning upwards of three hundred & fifty millions of property and largely interested in commerce and agricultural desire only to Elect and Establish a government of competent & honest officials under which all legitimate interests of all persons Irrespective of race color or previous condition of servitude will be protected we claim only a fair registration a fair Election and the fruits of this victory if we win it" Telegram received (on Sept. 5), *ibid.*, RG 60, Letters from the President. See letter to William W. Belknap, Sept. 2, 1874; Ted Tunnell, *Crucible of Reconstruction: War, Radicalism and Race in Louisiana 1862–1877* (Baton Rouge, 1984), pp. 173–204.

On Sept. 5, Rev. John Boyd and many others, "Committee of 1000 men," Caddo Parish, petitioned USG. "Please to mit us to call your attention to the Uncivilization, of the colored race and of the whole Southern States of the United States of America. We have nine years experienced: We have seen what the Struggle has been between the Two races and we fear much, We fear much, that if this question still rage as it have been these two races never can a gree in one Union to-gether, for now the white people of this state, have drawn off from us into white Legues, and has dis-franchised Us of all our rights of Citizenship, that the law have ever given us and we do ask of you Mr President, as the President of the United States, in the name of the almighty God what shall we do.   as we a race of people who stands on the Globe, Freedom we do wish to enjoy and to Enjoy all the rights of any other race of citizens in the United States, but Mr President these white people & of these ~~United States~~ Southern States, once who has held us Slaves, Do not, nor will not, let us enjoy The rights of a Citizenship and they Says in this State that none shall hold an Office but an honest white Man and Mr President? We do wish to ask you in the name of our God to please to make some other arrangements for us.   put us in a state to our selves or send us to our country, to Affrica where the white race say we belong to   Mr President. We had as Soon to be Sunk in the Bottom of the red Sea and to live here in the Southern States in the condition that we have been in for the last past 9 years. and we protend to be free, and Mr President it seems to Us, that it gets worst, and worst, and furthermore We will estate as they have told Us, That we should live off of our Radicalism, and civil-rights not With Standing, that we Disbelieve if we were in a Teritory to our selves But what we could do So, now. Mr President, We ask you and congress of the United States to investigate this matter, look at it ~~ju~~ that just as it is one ~~night~~ ningths of our both Men Women & Children are standing in Starvation, and poverty. Mr President. We Resolve that there is over 3000 names of Colored men is here present purposes this. and we will Send you list of some of the names of the people. Mr President. We now sign our reason for purposing this and it is this, in the first place. We work for half we make, and when it is aded up we dont get one fourth we make, in the Southern States. Mr President, how in the name of God! can a man and Family live at that. and if we go to law for our rights we are either shot or hung or runned off of the place, or out of the Parish or county. We have seen the Suffrage of our poor wives & children, and our mothers and sisters, going strolling about from place to place and homeless on accout of their Husband being kille[d] and runned off from their rights   Now Mr President! when ever there is a colored man holds a conversation with a white lady, or laughs when she is talking to him and is seen by a white man, of the Southern States he is either shot hung or runned out of the country. & it is said that he is trying or did Ravish her! Now. Mr President! look at the conditions of the United States in that respect, Mr. President! there is 1000 or more half white children born by colored women where we find more than fifty born by white women and now Mr. President there is one hundred colored men sleighing about white women where there is not five white men slain about colored women   the white men does as they please about colored women and the colored men are afraid to cheap. Mr. President what on earth do we want to stay in a country with such a race of people. Now, Mr. President, don't the constitutions of the United States call every man a citizen? We are not considered as citizens in the Southern States,   if a Republican form of government is that in which all the men have a share in, the public power we ask for ours. Give us peace or give a Territory to ourselves Mr. President. . . . Here is our prayer. We hope to D Be Delivered from among thes white people of the Southern States. Mr President any place that you destignate for our Locality We are willing to except of it. also we are willing to pay the United States Government, for our Locality or if the United States constitutions, or congress of the United States Sends us to Afric we are willing to go. Now Mr President. You are the first President. that ever was elected by these great nation of people and you all ways Says in you proclamation to let us have peace. Mr President We believe, that you will j̶ do justice by all; the people of the United States before God and man.   now Mr Presiden[t] we ask you to look at us as t̶h̶e̶ Moses did the children d̶i̶d̶ of Isreal as Abraham Lincoln was called a President that looked at all men as the Same. and Mr Lincoln is dead and you have taken his place. as Joshua did Moses in the days of old. Mr. President Grant there is a few us has Served unto you as Soldiers in the United States Government as, the children d̶i̶d̶ of Isreal did unto Joshua in the days of old   now General look at us, as Joshua did the children of Isreal when they was under bondage.   you help to release us from the jaws of Slavery and you had the largest part on your Shoulders, but General We ask you in great faith and Honor for we believe that the lord thy God is with you.   look with a Sympatizing eye. Now. General Grant. we believe that you are as faithful to us as you was to us when y̶ we stood in front of Richmond Virginia with you Seven days and night.   and now. We ask of you and congress. of the U̶n̶i̶o̶n̶ United States to please prepar a T̶ Territory for the colored race. of the Southern States   We hope Mr President. that you will work for us as you did for us. from 1861 up to 1865. We are told of the Danger of War   we are ready to acknowledge its hazard, and Misfortunce but we have a extraordinary Danger to apprehend at least, and mind constitute a majority of men. Virtue is true nobility, the Tide of improvement is necessary   Sir, Mr President you know we are True men and we are law abiding men. Mr President you have experienced that your-self   our hearts have ached long enough all over the entire Southern States   all of this has Sprung from the white Legues. You have led us, and we are willing to be led by you, as long as you do as you have done by us.   it is high time Mr President that we Should ocupey some Citizenship in the Southern States, for we realy do believe that Gable will soon blow the Trumpet. and yet! we are will nor b̶y̶e̶ ocupying citizenship w̶h̶i̶c̶h̶ that is all we want, and for God Sake. Mr President, give us our citizenship. in t̶h̶e̶ of the Mighty God look upon this. as the Almighty God did upon the children of Isreal. when they was under Bondage   Now Mr President we have had Committee of about 500. of our race going through the Southern States from one end to the other, holding corresponency with our people. of the Colored race and seen the Condition that they now Stand in and they have been traveling for the last past, four years & 8 months now the committee Majority have met and assembled to gether in the Parish of Caddo State of Louisiana and they Brought Lists from all points   the Committee will send in one state at the time   Mr President we dont want any Black Legues at all   all we want in the world is our equal rights and Citizenship   we have come perfectly Satisfied as to know, unless an alteration there is no peace for us.   our Female Sexes and our children and ~~our our~~ men part of them cant hide their nakedness, becaus the are cheated out of ~~th~~ what they make.   you will find a list of the Names in your other letter. We send our names in the Same." D, DNA, RG 60, Letters from the President; copy, *ibid.*

On Sept. 9, Robert H. Marr, New Orleans, telegraphed to USG. "by direction of the Committee of seventy of which I am chairman I submit the accompanying resolution & appeal to you adopted at a meeting last evening. . . . Resolved That this Committee on the part of the conservative people of Louisiana make the following appeal to the President of the U. States   To His excellency U. S Grant Prest of The United States of america. The Committee of Seventy a body which fully represents the Conservative people of Louisiana referring to Your recent order Placing a Portion of the armies of the US under the direction of the department of Justice for use in this & other Southern states would respectfully remind you that the People of this state whom we have the honor to represent have after two years of struggle against the Power of what they Consider an odious usurpation been remitted by your action & by the non action of Congress to the ballot as the only means of relief from their difficulties   The approaching election has therefore more than ordinary significance   the chances are against the Conservative Masses although they have an unquestionable majority since the machinery of Election is in the hands of the acting Govr a machinery carefully arranged by himself & his C[o]adjutors for the express purpose of defeating the popular will. The Conservative People however believe that they would be able to overcome even these advantages by a thorough organization & the greatest vigilance You Can imagine then with what surprise this Community received the intelligence Troops to be sent among us at the disposal of the atty Genl of the United States for the purpose of assisting the marshal of this district S. B Packard in carrying on prosecutions against our People   without intending the slightest disrespect & impelled by a sense of public duty we would remind you that in the opinion of the people of this State & w[e] believe of the country at large whether that opinion be well or ill founded the Present Government of Louisiana owes its blighting existence in a large measure to the Countenance & active support of the atty Genl himself & that this marshal to whose control the troops are really to be remitted was one of the most active participants in the Judicial & Political manoeuvres by which the usurpation was Called into existence that he has been ever since the friend & supporter of the acting Govr That he was the president of the last republican Convention in this State, whose nominees for Congress & other important positions are now before the people that he is at this time as he has been for many years the President of the state Central Committee of the republican Party of Louisiana and is therefore pledged as a bitter Partizan against the rights of the Conservative People.   with the federal troops under the orders of the President of The state Central Committee of the republican party it is manifest that a fair election is improbable   We may thus be foiled again in our efforts for relief. If we understand the sentiments of our people Correctly they have no objection to your sending troops to louisiana provided they Come to Secure Good order & a fair exercise of the franchise by both white & black especially as the present state Govt not having been chosen by the people & being Therefore without their affection or Confidence has shown itself utterly unable to administer the affairs of the state and preserve order   but we earnestly protest against your placing troops in Louisiana upon the eve of such an election as is now approaching under the control of civil officers both of whom are Thoroughly identified with the usurpation and one of whom is actually the President of the state Central Committee of the political party sustaining the usurpation—To Your Candor we appeal & ask whether this is just. If you will remove the present marshall of this district & appoint some one not identified with either party but enjoying the Confidence of both & such men may easily be found we will not object to the Coming of troops to Louisiana for the purpose of maintaining the peace & securing a fair election   The class of people whom we represent have nothing to gain by disorders but everything to lose. If you consider it your duty under the laws to employ troops here it seems to us that Justice would require that they should not be placed in any way directly or indirectly under the Control of a partizan Marshall who is an active supporter of the usurpation and the acknowledged leader of one of the parties to this Contest." Telegram received, *ibid.*

On Sept. 14, Kellogg telegraphed to USG. "under article four section four of the constitution of the U. S I have the honor to inform you that this state is now subject to domestic violence of a character that the state forces under existing circumstances are unable suppress and the legislature not being in session and not being able to be convened within the requisite time to take action in this matter I respectfully make requesition upon you to take measures to put down the domestic violence & insurrection now prevailing" Telegram received (at 7:10 P.M.), *ibid. SED,* 43-2-13, 13; *SD,* 57-2-209, 155. Also on Sept. 14, Kellogg sent a similar telegram to USG "Via Long Branch." ". . . I send this second despatch fearing the first has been intercepted." Telegram received, DNA, RG 60, Letters from the President; telegram received (at 11:40 P.M.), DLC-USG, IB. On the same day, Kellogg telegraphed to Attorney Gen. George H. Williams. "After a lengthy preamble D B Penn issues the following   'Constrained from a Sense of duty as the legally elected Lt Govr of the state (acting (Govr In the absence of Gov McEnery) I do Hereby issue this my proclamation Calling upon the militia of the State embracing all persons between the ages of Eighteen & forty five Years, without regard to Color or previous condition.' To arm & assemble under their respective officers for the purpose of driving the usurpers from Power —. . . D. B. PENN Lt. Gov. & actg Gov. & Commder in Cheif of Louisiana state militia. The situation at present is Critical   the white legue & large numbers have had a fight with the Metropolitan police in the vicinity of the U. S CustomHouse—quite a number have been killed & wounded on both sides   the militia and police are in possession of the state House at present but a very small force of the US troops have arrived here   the league are determined on over throwing the state Govt   troops should be ordered here from Alabama & the Nearest stations at the earliest possible moment" Telegram received (at 9:30 P.M.), DNA, RG 60, Letters from the President. Related telegrams are *ibid.*

Also on Sept. 14, David B. Penn, New Orleans, telegraphed to USG. "Hopeless of all other relief, the people of this State have taken up arms to maintain the legal authority of the persons elected by them to the government of the State against the usurpers, who have heaped upon them innumerable insults, burdens, and wrong. In so doing they are supported by the great body of the intelligent and honest people of the State. They declare their unswerving loyalty and respect for the United States Government and its officers. They war only against the usurpers, plunderers, and enemies of the people. They affirm their entire ability to maintain peace and protect the life, liberty, and equal rights of all classes of citizens. The property and officials of the United States it shall be our special aim to defend against all assaults and to treat with the profoundest respect and loyalty. We only ask of you to withhold any aid or protection from our enemies and the enemies of Republican rights, and of the peace and liberties of the people." *SD,* 57-2-209, 154.

On Sept. 15, Maj. Gen. Irvin McDowell, Louisville, telegraphed to Gen. William T. Sherman. "The following telegram just received. The following has just been received from Lieut Col. Brooke third Infantry Comdg troops New Orleans   Gov Kellogg informs me that he has made requisition on the President for troops under the Constitution. He fears

it has been intercepted and desires genl Emory to so inform the President   W. H. EMORY
The Louisville morning papers state that governor Kellogg is in the Custom House" Telegram received, DNA, RG 108, Letters Received, 1524 1874. Also on Sept. 15, AG Edward
D. Townsend telegraphed to Lt. Col. John R. Brooke, New Orleans. "The President directs
me to say previous orders are not to be observed. You will preserve peace and order to the
best of your ability. Orders that you may give for that purpose you may use your own judgment about publishing, but in all cases of special orders for the suppression of violence
submit them to the Secretary of War, for approval. . . ." ADfS, *ibid.*, RG 94, Letters Received, 3579 1874. On the same day, Townsend telegraphed to Col. William H. Emory,
Holly Springs, Miss. "Since despatch of this morning the President directs me to say to
you, If possible preserve peace. Proclamation has just been issued in accordance with Constitution and laws. If there is any unsafety to person use all the means at your command
to give protection until you receive final instructions—" ADfS, *ibid.*

Also on Sept. 15, Albert H. Leonard *et al.*, Shreveport, telegraphed to USG. "we respectfully beg leave to represent to your Excellency that the Kellogg government as such
has ceased to exist, in North Louisiana,   in every parish the fusion officers will quietly
take possession to day   every thing has been done peacibley & without bloodshed   the
colored people seem to participate in the enthusiasm of the whites   we pledge to your excellency the ready obedience of the past to your government & ample protection to all citizens black & white in every right and privilege" Telegram received, *ibid.*, RG 60, Letters
from the President. On the same day, Samuel H. Kennedy *et al.*, New Orleans, telegraphed
to USG. "Kellogg Government completely deposed   perfect confidence restored,   we feel
that we are free once more and thank God for the calmness & courage of our citizens   not
a single case of lawlessness   the colored population & all other citizens perfectly secure in
their lives and property   a load of degradation and oppression lifted from our people and
we are now hopeful and encouraged for the future   Business men greatly encouraged   as
loyal citizens of the United States we confidently rely upon you for the recognition &
guarantee of the Govt of the state under McEnery and Penn who have the confidence of
the good & true men of Louisiana" Telegram received (at 5:25 P.M.), *ibid.* Also on Sept. 15,
William G. Brown, superintendent of public instruction, and Charles Clinton, auditor, New
Orleans, telegraphed to USG. "Armed mobs reported all over city   leaguers much more
formidable than supposed appear to be coming in from abroad   five days delay will we fear
cost hundreds of lives   prompt action is necessary" Telegram received (at 8:15 P.M.), *ibid.*

On Sept. 16, Fish wrote in his diary. "At half past 9, Secr of State, Secr of Treas,
P. M. G. & Atty Genl met the President in Cabinet—Atty Genl has a telegram from Marshal Packard, not differing much from other accounts as to the general order prevailing,
though evidently with a feeling in favor of the deposed party—The Adjutant Genl was sent
for, & brings a telegram from Genl Emory—The U. S. forces in N. O. are less than 300,
including some on their way thither—Emory says his forces will be insufficient in case a
conflict occurs with the ~~State~~ 'Citizens' party—as it is called—President asks if it be expedient to Convene Congress—I do not think it adviseable at present to decide so to do—
the regular Session is only about 80 days distant—the fall Elections are soon to take place.
Congressmen will not be pleased to be absent from their Districts, pending the election
& as very many of them are Candidates for re election, it would jeopard the Republican Ascendancy in the next Congress—The suggestion of an Extra Session met no affirmative
response—Kelloggs weakness & imbecillity were denounced by the Prsdt & others—Williams urges that there is an undoubted majority of 20.000 of Republicans in the State—
The ~~rest~~ others present, (including the Prsdt) refer to the fact that there has been no official counting of votes, & that although Kellogg may have recd more votes than McEnery
there were great frauds on both sides, & no legal return of votes honestly given—Jewell

remarks on the Controlling influence of New Orleans, as really representing the State—refers to the telegram from his Superintendent, & that order being established, it ~~being~~ is evident that a majority of the wealth, intelligence & business interest of the place, acquiesce, & approve of the new Govt   I express the opinion, that events manifestly indicate that what has occured, is the result of a well matured & carefully organized scheme, extending certainly through the State of Louisiana & probably acting in Concert with organizations elsewhere—That to recognize the new Govt wd be encouragement to lawlessness & usurpation, & to attempts at the violent overthrow of existing Governments—Williams says, in support of the idea, that the movement was premeditated, & one of concert, that large quantities of arms, & military equipments have been taken into La & other Southern States—that 'White leagues' & 'Rifle Companies' have been organized throughout the South, & are regularly drilled, meeting at night, & going through various Military evolutions, such as pitched fights, bayonet exercises &c—Bristow says that Genl Emory told him that there is a strong sympathy among the regular troops in La with the 'Citizens' party, & against the Kellogg party—& in Confirmation of this a telegram appears this morning in the public prints, that the U. S. troops cheered the forces of the usurping or Revolutionary party—Townsend is asked how many troops can be concentrated in N. O—he replies about 1,000 within 15 to 20 days—I enquire whether there be not some naval vessels at Key West or elsewhere, which might be sent there in case of need—President wrote a card (which subsequently he destroyed) ordering Adm Reynolds (Acting Secr of Navy) to order to N. O all the vessels, which can conveniently be sent there—In answer to an enquiry of mine, as to the Condition of the Forts on the Mississippi, below N. O. the Prsdt says they are in a very dilapidated Condition—he is not sure whether any force is there, or any Armaments—Bristow asks if I make the enquiry in Connection with the passage of Naval Vessels up the River—I answer no—not at all—but that if there be any extended Conspiracy, involving other States, and even in respect to La alone, it is important not to allow a show of the seizure, or occupation—of the forts—that while they could not interfere with Naval vessels, they might interfere with Commerce, & the moral effect of their occupation wd give the appearance of the inauguration of Civil war—Bristow threw out, (apparently tentatively) the idea of a revocation of the Proclamation of yesterday—but I cannot remember that it excited any Comment—It was suggested but without any particular notice that unless some new emergency arose, the Prsdt should wait the expiration of the five days named in his proclamation—I remark that if there be a possibility of conference a Compromise might be effected, whereby both claimants are to withdraw, & an election be held, either under the Control of Federal Authorities, or ~~by~~ the joint control of the two contending parties—The Prsdt at one time spoke of Sending Genl Sheridan down—at another time, of ordering McDowell, (within whose Division La is)—Bristow suggested Genl Terry which met with general approval—& the idea then came of a Proclamation of Martial law, & making Terry Governor—A further meeting of the Cabinet is to be held at three o'clk this afternoon   At three oclk Bristow, Jewell, Williams & I met at the White House—President was absent, detained until near four—He read a paper on the Condition of Affairs in Louisa Concluding with a declaration that he would not Convene Congress—on a suggestion by me that it might not be expedient, to make a declaration at this time, on that point he said that the paper which he read was not for publication—He declared very emphatically against a proclamation of Martial Law—saying (with a logic which I did not comprehend, & on which Jewell & I each expressed dissent) that he would much more willingly declare Martial Law, if there had not been, & were not doubts of the legality of Kellogg's claims to the Governorship—It was suggested that some discreet person representing the Govt ~~might be~~ might be influencial in bringing about an understanding between the contending factions, & prevent further violence—Bristow, half jokingly, proposed that I go—he afterward told me that he was more in earnest than in jest—I objected to going—saying that no member of the Cabinet could go many miles in the direction of N. O. without its being telegraphed all over the Country, & his influence thus destroyed, but suggested some discreet man, naming Admiral Rodgers, whose movements would not necessarily excite suspicion as connected with this Affair—Genl Cowan (of the Interior) was named by some one else—Various propositions were made, but without definite result—All were agreed that the Revolutionary Government could not under any Circumstances be recognized—the President then drafted a notice which he suggested might be given to the Associated Press, to that effect, & intimating Military orders at the expiration of the five days indicated in the Proclamation—This was subsequently changed into the form of an order through the War Department to the Military Commander in Louisa, that under no circumstances could the Insurgent Govt be recognized, & that further orders were reserved until the expiration of the five days named in the Proclamation—The President thinks there is no reason for my remaining longer at present in Washington—I prepare therefore to go to NY this Evening—After the first Cabinet meeting this morning Judge Lyons of Va (who, it seems, is a Brother-in-Law of Penn the ~~Acting~~ Lieut. Govr of Louisa on the McEnery ticket) called, to say the the the entire white population of the South, would consider any force, to re-instate the Kellogg Govt as an act of War, which would be resisted, & urged that the Penn Govt be recognized. I told him that was impossible—the most of concession that the Insurgents could expect, was a military Government—he thought that would be better than the restoration of Kellogg" DLC-Hamilton Fish.

Also on Sept. 16, Townsend telegraphed to Emory, New Orleans. "The President directs that you prevent the taking of money from the Treasury of Louisiana until further orders are received—" ADfS, DNA, RG 94, Letters Received, 3579 1874. On the same day, James F. Casey, collector of customs, New Orleans, telegraphed to USG conveying a message from business leaders. ". . . I have been ~~requested~~ asked to sign the above, The Statement that the City is perfectly quiet, is true, and business is proceeding as usual, property and persons are safe from insult or injury from the Citizens, unless from some rowdies or drunken men." Telegram received, *ibid.*, RG 60, Letters from the President.

On Sept. 17, 10:30 A.M., USG wrote. "The Sec of the Navy will order the Colorado the Worcester and the Dictator to New Orleans without delay" AN, Wayde Chrismer, Bel Air, Md. On the same day, Emory wrote to USG. "As a friend of your administration generally but more particularly of that part of it which embraces this unfortunate and disturbed portion of the country, I beg I may be pardoned the liberty of suggesting to you, as a measure which will be followed I am sure with the best results, that the persons engaged in the insurrection against the State authorities of Louisiana, in the present month of September, may be pardoned and exempted from prosecution by the Civil authorities. The outburst embraced nearly every white man in the community; but the promptness with which they yielded to the mandates of your proclamation when they were made to know that it applied to them, even when laboring under the most maddening impulses prompts me to make this request. I believe that Governor Kellogg, if he was permitted to express his wish by the excited people around him, would join me in this request." Copy, DNA, RG 393, Dept. of the Gulf, Letters Sent. Also on Sept. 17, Thursday, Belknap, Columbus, Ohio, telegraphed to Townsend. "Say to President that there is universal expression of opinion among men of all parties sustaining him in firm stand he has taken in Louisiana matters, if not there, telegraph this to him, Will be in washington saturday morning" Telegram received, *ibid.*, RG 94, Letters Received, 3579 1874. On the same day, Orville E. Babcock wrote to the act. secretary of war. "The President directs me to say that you will please order eight (8) companies of the 22d US Infantry under command of the Colonel to New Orleans without delay." LS, *ibid.* Belknap again telegraphed to Townsend. "Telegram recd.   as the insurgents have disbanded & surrendered consult President as to revocation of order moving twenty second Infant   I think that order might now be revoked   consult him before action. I will be home saturday morning" Telegram received (at 10:03 P.M.), *ibid.* Townsend endorsed this telegram. "The President saw this and declined to change order except as to the Colonel & the company at Fort Brady." AE (initialed, undated), *ibid.*

Also on Sept. 17, Moses Greenwood and William M. Burwell, New Orleans, telegraphed to USG. "Whereas various reports have gone abroad representing this city as being in a disturbed & riotous Condition & deeming it our duty to Correct this erroneous impression, be it resolved that this Chamber of Commerce of Neworleans hereby testifies to the peaceful & satisfactory Condition of this city & the remarkable cheerfulness & Energy which now appears to be infused into the business & financial circles   resolved that all the information in possession of this Chamber shows that in the Country parishes of the state a peaceful acquiescence in the late change of Governors & officers of the state has taken place   Resolved that the members of this Chamber feel perfectly assured that the present state Govmt. will fully accord to the Colored people of this state all the rights & privileges of citizens & would deeply deplore any act of the General Govt of the United states whereby the popular will should be set aside   Resolved that the foregoing resolutions be transmitted to the leading Chambers of Commerce of the Country with a request that they give us their Cooperation & sympathy in carrying out our views as Expressed above. Resolved that the officers of the Chamber are instructed to dispatch by telegraph Certified Copies of the foregoing resolutions to the Prest of the US. Extract from Minutes" Telegram received (at 1:35 P.M.), *ibid.*, RG 60, Letters from the President. On the same day, Mayor Harvey D. Colvin of Chicago and nineteen others telegraphed to USG. "We are confident the People of the Northwest will sustain you in your prompt & decisive action to put down insurrection in whatever quarter" Telegram received (at 2:35 P.M.), *ibid.* U.S. Senator John A. Logan of Ill., Cairo, also telegraphed to USG. "The Situation in Louisiana is such that in my Judgment there can be but one course pursued that is to promptly reinstate the deposed *Gov* if the whole army & Navy be required to do it" Telegram received (at 4:45 P.M.), DLC-USG, IB. Also on Sept. 17, John R. Lionberger, president, Third National Bank, St. Louis, *et al.*, telegraphed to USG. "As merchants bankers & Business men loyal to the Government of the U S we beg your attention   Since the panic of last Sept & the floods of June our people at the cry of help have given their fortunes to those of the South   the cotton Season is here & with a war the crops would be ruined & devastation would stalk through the land   a greater monetary convulsion would come upon the west than ever before.   we beg that conciliatory measures may be adopted by the Government or at least that more time be given in order that a peaceful Solution of the difficulty may be reached" Telegram received (at 11:40 P.M.), DNA, RG 60, Letters from the President.

On Sept. 18, Townsend telegraphed to Emory. "I am directed by the President to say that your acts to this date so far as they have been reported and received here officially, are approved, except so far as they name Colonel Brooke to command the City of New Orleans. It would have been better to have named him as commander of the United States forces now in that City. ~~Without reference to irregularities, claimed by the opposition to the Kellogg Government in the election of 1872 in the State of Louisiana, t~~The Kellogg [~~organization of State~~ State] Government ~~has been recognized in all the forms necessary to make that the de facto~~ [existing at the time of the bgining of the present insurrectionary movement must be recognized as the lawful] state Government, until some other Government can be legally supplied. Upon the surrender of the insurgents, you will inform Governor Kellogg of the fact, and give him the necessary support to reestablish the authority of the State Government. If at the end of five days given in the Proclamation of the 15th instant, there still exists armed resistance to the authority of the State, you will summon a surrender of the insurgents, ~~a surrender of their arms and persons, either to be paroled or imprisoned, as may be advisable at the time~~. If ~~these terms are~~ [the demand is] not quietly submitted to, ~~they~~ [it] must be enforced at all hazards. This being an insurrection against the State Government of Louisiana to aid in suppression of which the U. S. Government has bee[n] called upon, in the forms required by the Constitution and Laws of Congress thereunder, it is not the province of the U. S. Authorities to make terms with parties engaged in such insurrection." ADf (initialed by USG; bracketed words in USG's hand), *ibid.*, RG 94, Letters Received, 3579 1874. *SD*, 57-2-209, 156–57.

Also on Sept. 18, Stephen B. Packard, U.S. marshal, New Orleans, telegraphed to USG. "Associated Press dispatches state Louisiana Republicans in Washington are dissatisfied with General Emory's course yesterday in retaining the McEnery police on duty and not disarming the whole league,   Genl. Emory's course was prudent and proper,   there was pressing necessity for a police force to be on duty last night & the Metropolitan police organization could not be put on duty,   the prompt energetic movement of Genl Emory yesterday saved our city a conflict & bloodshed & meets the approval of Republicans here" Telegram received, DNA, RG 60, Letters from the President. On the same day, Edward C. Billings, Northampton, Mass., telegraphed to USG. "I suggest that Louisiana will not be protected from domestic violence unless illegal police is displaced and legal police restored and that the dispersion should not be treated as a surrender but as the disbanding of an insurgent body without terms except such as re-instated law creates" Telegram received, DLC-USG, IB. Also on Sept. 18, M. Hutchins, Maysville, Ky., telegraphed to USG. "You have pinned the Country's enemies by moving immediately upon their works,   A grateful people is the result" Telegram received, *ibid.* On the same day, William H. Smith, act. secretary of the interior, telegraphed to Babcock. "I have just recd the following telegram Mt Vernon Ohio Oct. 18th   On my way to Washington   Every body sends thanks & congratulations to the President—will reach Washington tomorrow   C DELANO" Telegram received, DNA, RG 107, Telegrams Collected (Bound).

On Sept. 19, Postmaster Gen. Marshall Jewell wrote to Elihu B. Washburne, Paris, about La. affairs. ". . . Grant means business in this thing. He is not mad about it, nor does he use any hard language, and he does'nt smoke or say much, but his eyes are *sot in his head*, and he will never make it up as long as theres an insurgent pretender in the chair, and does not hesitate to call out all the force in the United States. He is cool and collected, and thoroughly determined, and grows a little black in the face when talking about it, but that's all." ALS, DLC-Elihu B. Washburne.

On Sept. 20, Thomas Cottman, Waukesha, Wis., wrote to USG. "Knowing the people of Louisiana as I do, it can scarcely be considered presumptive in me to express to you an opinion on the unprecedented condition of the State of Louisiana. I had an opportunity of testing the sentiments of the people during my visit in June last & conferred freely with Kellogg on the subject & with the leaders of the present difficulty whose names do not appear in public requesting each party to be circumspect in expression as what was said by one would be made common to both. At that time Kellogg had an opportunity of quieting turbulence. He did not embrace it & now the sword of Damocles is impending over him ready to drop at any moment. My relations with Kellogg have been of the most amicable character   When he was appointed Collector of Customs he was commended to me by Govr Dick Yates & the Secretary of the Treasury—In the election between Kellogg & McEnery I gave the preference to McEnery & being in Louisiana immediately preceding the election visited my old stomping ground, the Parish of Aescension & though a very small parish it gave Kellogg 1700 majority, which was not disputed by either Returning Board. But since that time there has been a revolution in popular sentiment. I will name to you some of the original Republicans, who still adhere to the party but are opponents of Kellogg—. . . From information that I consider reliable the State is likely to be disgraced by the assasination of both Kellogg & Packard—Sicilians & Spaniards from the Mediterranean Coast are to be found in Barretarria who would make away with them for fifty dollars a piece which in my opinion is bound to occur through some source. They say Attorney General Williams order to U. S Marshals makes Satraperies of all the Southern States as effectually as any Eastern Potentate ever conferred upon his distant dependencies—I have no idea that a fair election could be held under Kelloggs registration & will not be by either side unless presided over by Military *authority*—Whilst I was in New Orleans every spoke favorably of Col Jas Casey except in connection with his deputy Herwig who they execrated   I am perfectly aware of the difficulties which beset you in this emergency & the necessity for prompt action, but there lurks danger of ulterior consequences, which might be avoided by the experience of such old statesmen as Govr John A Dix & Thurlow Weed of NewYork—It is impossible to adapt abstract principles with the rules square to human actions. Experience the result of practical experiment, with the knowledge thus acquired is more available than any ratiocination upon Theory—I hope you will not take this amiss as I can only plead for it good intentions—" ALS, *ibid.*, RG 60, Letters from the President. See Joseph G. Dawson III, *Army Generals and Reconstruction: Louisiana, 1862–1877* (Baton Rouge, 1982), pp. 165–80; Endorsement, Sept. 23, 1874.

On Jan. 13, L. J. Higby, New Orleans, had telegraphed to USG. "new election will ruin Louisiana   all is well with Kelloggs financial policy   refer to Senator Howe" Telegram received (at 7:43 P.M.), DLC-USG, IB. On Jan. 22, William E. Chandler, Washington, D. C., wrote to USG. "Personal . . . I most respectfully but earnestly urge that the administration ~~mak~~ make no change of attitude with reference to Louisiana   A new election ~~as~~ now, as proposed would be absolutely and certainly fatal to the loyal men of the state. Beyond all doubt or peradventure it would result in a rebel-democratic victory; and the complete and entire overthrow of Governor Kellogg and his adherents; not because they ~~are~~ have not a majority of the voters, but because it will be impossible under any proposed auspices to get the full Republican vote to the polls and to prevent illegal democratic votes. Rather than desert ~~the~~ Governor Kellogg now it would have been better to have abandoned him a year and half ago, before the ~~contest and~~ long and arduous conflict which is about resulting in complete victory only delayed by the fatal suggestions of a new election. Will not the President adhere to his well considered and triumphant policy—which has given a state ~~triumph~~ victory to the Republicans of Louisiana who ~~labored to secure a presidential victory~~ entered the fight in 1872 mainly to secure success in the Presidential contest; and who are now entitled ~~to participate~~ to the same consideration and fairness ~~to~~ to which they would ~~have~~ be entitled if the Presidential election depended ~~on them~~ upon sustaining them." ADf, DLC-William E. Chandler. On the same day, J. H. Oglesby, New Orleans, telegraphed to U.S. Representative Lionel A. Sheldon of La. "Funding bill passed Endorsed by our very best people   none of us here desire a new Election   please show this to president Grant" Telegram received (at 5:40 P.M.), DLC-USG, IB. Also on Jan. 23, Packard, New Orleans, telegraphed to USG. "Republican state Central Committee met this Evening   full attendance from all parts of state   adopted resolutions thanking you for your efforts in sustaining legally elected state Government respectfully protesting against any congressional action in favor of a new election in this state & instructing me as chairman to telegraph you the fact and to forward a copy of the resolutions to our delegation in congress" Telegram received (on Jan. 24, at 12:40 A.M.), *ibid.* On Jan. 24, Lt. Governor Caesar C. Antoine of La., New Orleans, telegraphed to USG. "Dispatches from members of Louisiana delegation inform me that you signify your opposition to congressional interference with our government   permit me in behalf of the colored population of this state to thank you for this

renewed evidence of friendship for and care of my race   this is added to our many obligations to you & your administration" Telegram received (at 10:50 P.M.), *ibid.*

On Jan. 27, Fish recorded in his diary. "The President reads a draft of the proposed
Message to Congress on Louisiana which had been prepared by the Attorney General at
the request of the President. With the exception of Mr. Richardson, who finally concurred,
every member present advised strongly against any message being sent; the President
adopted the advice of his Cabinet." DLC-Hamilton Fish.

On Jan. 19, Jules Lanabère *et al.*, New Orleans, had written to USG. "Being informed
a Successor to Col. Casey, present Collector of N. O. is soon to be appointed; we earnestly
recommend the appointment of W. R. Crane Esq. a true and tried Republican, the choice of
our people to secure the reform, unity and success of the Republican Party in this State—"
LS (5 signatures), DNA, RG 56, Collector of Customs Applications. A related petition of
Jan. 27 is *ibid.* Casey continued in office. See *PUSG*, 19, 449–50; *ibid.*, 22, 337–40.

To John C. Brown

———

EXECUTIVE MANSION, Sept. 19, 1874.

Hon. John C. Brown, Governor, Nashville, Tenn.:

SIR: Your dispatch of yesterday has been received and referred to
the United States District Attorney for the Western District of Tennessee for a report, as there is now no official information of his proceedings here. When his report is received I will give you a more
definite answer, or have the Attorney General do so. I will state, however, that it is very gratifying to know that the State authorities of
Tennessee are disposed to suppress and punish a class of lawless acts
so dangerous to life, and so opposed to every political, financial, and
moral interest of the State. But the Constitution makes it my duty to
enforce the acts of Congress, and Congress has passed laws giving
the United States jurisdiction in such cases as are referred to in your
dispatch. No special order has been given to the Federal officials in
Tennessee, further than the circular of Sept. 3, of the Attorney General, which is general in its nature, and constitutes instructions to
all Marshals and District Attorneys whenever violations of said acts
may occur. I will add that the State and General Governments, as you
are well aware, may have concurrent jurisdiction over the same offense, as, for example, in cases of counterfeiting, and the action of the

State authorities in such cases does not prevent the General Government from proceeding against the offenders.

U. S. GRANT.

New York Times, Sept. 20, 1874. On Sept. 18, 1874, Governor John C. Brown of Tenn. telegraphed to USG. "There were sixteen negroes Committed to the Jail of Gibson Co in this State charged with a conspiracy to take the lives of the white Citizens of the neighborhood on the night of the twenty fifth of Aug eighteen Seventy four (1874)   a party of disguised men violated the Jail & took these prisoners forcibly from the Jailor & killed four & wounded two the remainder escaping & now being at large.   the next day I offered a reward of five hundred dollars each for these unknown offenders   the State Court being then in Session took immediate Cognizance of the outrage & the labors of the regular & special term have resulted in the detection & indictment of forty one of the guility parties the majority of whom have been arrested & ~~will~~ the remainder will be if they have not fled the Country they are indicted under the Second & third Sections of the act of the General assembly of Tenn of eighteen Sixty nine (1869) & Seventy (70) passed the thirtieth (30) of January eighteen Seventy (1870) entitled an act to preserve the public peace & which is in full force the Sections are as follows: Sect two (2) Be it further enacted that if any person or persons disguised or in mask by day or by night shall enter upon the premises of another or Shall demand entrance or admission of the house or enclosure of any citizen of this State it Shall be considered prima facie that his or their intention is to commit a felony & such demand shall be deemed an assault with an intent to commit a felony & the person or persons so offending shall upon conviction ~~Shall~~ be punished by imprisonment in the Penitentiary not less than ten years nor more than twenty years—Sect three—Be it further enacted if any person or person so prowling travelling riding or walking through the towns or country of this State masked or in disguise shall or may assault another with a deadly weapon he or they Shall be deemed guilty of an assault with an intent to commit murder in the first degree & on conviction thereof Shall Suffer death by hanging provided the Jury trying the cause may Substitute imprisonment in the Penitentiary for a period of not less ten years nor more than twenty one years'   The State authorities have manifested the most earnest desire to enforce them against the guilty parties & have demonstrated by these indictments & arrests not only their disposition but ability to enforce the law & protect all citizens without regard to race color or previous condition of Servitude   these efforts I can assure You will no sense be relaxed until the majesty of the law is fully vindicated   notwithstanding with these efforts with the results Stated the united States marshall & Commissioner for the western Division of Tenn with the aid of detachment from the Government garrison at Humboldt have arrested & are continuing to arrest citizens & conveying them under guard to Memphis nearly one hundred miles distant to answer for Same offence charge against by the State Courts   as Governor of Tenn I do most respectfully but earnestly protest against this exercise of Jurisdiction by the U-S Commissioner & marshall without reference to the question whether the offences are proper Subjects of proper cognizance by the united States Courts but alone upon the ground that the peace of society will be more certainly preserved & the rights of Citizens as well protected by conceding Jurisdiction to the State Courts & &   I therefore respectfully ask Your Excellency order that no further arrests be made by the marshall & that the parties already in his custody be turned over to the proper local tribunals for trial & punishment—I undertake to assure your Excellency that no effort will be Spared to enforce the laws & protect the citizens by the officers of the State Govt throughout the borders of this State & believe the local authority is ample to protect people of every race & condition in life   an early reply is respectfully Solicited" Telegram received (at 4:50 P.M.), DNA, RG 60, Letters from the President. On May 3, 1875, Governor James D. Porter of Tenn. telegraphed to USG. "The Gibson County Klu Klux Cases are set for trial in the State Court today, the witnesses are held in custody by United States authorities at Memphis as witnesses in Causes pending there,   I respectfully ask that they be delivered to the state authorities there," Telegram received, *ibid.*, Letters Received, Tenn.

On Aug. 23, 1874, M. C. Manson and four others, Lebanon, Tenn., had written to USG. "After my address to you I hasten to inform you of the sad Event which taken place at Hartsville in Trousdel Cty Tenn on 21th of Aug 1874.   the afair is a great one too and that is this, one of our School Teachers was killed which you know is very cruel and the White people Says they cant do any thing to prevent it or ~~prote~~ protect us   the Col people of the adjoining county are coming in to our ~~Twn~~ Town for they cant ~~com~~ ~~Say~~ Stay there for the night Riders are troublling them too great to Stay there at their homes.   the person that was killed was a Leady   we want to know What to do   tell us what to do.   we want to get your advise   please tell us What to do   we want aid and if you can help us we Shal be glad that you would let us know whether you can ~~can~~help us or n[ot] and if you can please let us hear What you can do for us   we have no ~~per~~ protecting power here and we want you to say What you can do for us   if you will ~~pe~~ back us we will protect our ~~self~~ selves.   we trust that we are not flattered by Writting those lines.   we hope that the answer be agreeable   we want the promise of the U. S ~~protecting~~ protection   Mr Pres.t not only the promise but we want the aid Truly and if you will not help us send us the arms and Say that you will help us   be as good as your word and we will Stand for our Selves untill we die.   please Send us word Whether you will help us or not   please Answer this letter right a way" LS, *ibid.*

On Sept. 25, Reverend H. W. Harris, Grand Junction, Tenn., wrote to USG. "we the Colored citizens of Grand Junction Tennessee and vicinity of Said town & State met on the 24th of sept 1874 to look after the entres of the colored race, and the Great Cause that called our attention to this object were because there have been So much murdering of our race duering the month of August 1874 in Some parts of our state. and as it has gone So far, and we ar not able to help our Selves, we have Considered it best for our race to be Colonize into Some territory to them Selves.   we think it will be best for us.   we think it Will berry a great Eald of animosity.   we think it will Save many ~~lif~~ lives.   we think it Will killed the Ku Klux and all these Night Riders that comes to our houses at ~~on~~ Night When we are Sleep and murder us in cold blood: we think if we were Colonize it would be better for them and us too, because they would not have to ride at night when they ought to be in bed at home taking ~~of~~ care of their families. now I have Said a nough on the Subject that you might understand what we Want. So now mr president we Want you and Congress of the United states to do all you can for us. And *mr* President I want you to instruct me on this great Subject all you can. Sir please give me all the light on the Subject you possible can that I might be able teach my race here. Mr president if there is not Some steps of this kind taken for us we never can become intelligent peopel in World. Now Mr grant Sir we colared ~~pelpel~~ peopel have Stood up for you Every Sence we have knowen you.   we Casted our Votes for you twice   we stood to you in the War and I beleave this our Colared race will Stand to you untill your eyes are chilled with death. these Colored peopel will all die for you to day. they have a great love for you. So we want you to do all Can for us. I will now state the spirit of the race in tennessee and mississippi   they all wish to be Colonize in a territory or state to them Selves, and they also Wish to be Colonize ~~un~~ under the lows of the united states, and to live under that ~~law.~~ low. Notice to the president and Congress if you Will designate Some Sutable States or territory for the race, and move us there by the Exspencis of the United states and provied provission for us one year we ar willing to pay for the land What Ever Congress. Charges we ar willing to pay all of the Exspencis back to united states agan   we are Truly willing to make all Exspencis good if the Congress of the united states request it of us.—Mr President we have many Reasons that ar Compelling us to do this and we all think they ar good Reasons   the white race have murder larg Nombers of the Colored Sence the war and ar yet at it to day, and we think they will be at it as long as we ar a mong them. and we can help our Selves. there fore we think it best for us to be to our selves. if we try to bye their land they they it put to us at $20 & $30 & $40 & $50 an ~~acers~~ acre   I Could Say great Eald mar but have not time. Please let me here from you as soon as this comes to hand   give me all the news. All of us Send our love to you" L, *ibid.*, Letters from the President.

On Jan. 29, 1875, William E. T. Atkins, Paris, Tenn., wrote to USG. "Pleas excuse me for writing to you   I would not have don so but my life is in Danger & it is no use in appealing to the civil courts here for they are all friends of the partys   A few days before the election A possel of fellows about ten in number; Went to Colored mans to whip him becaus he was going to vote for Coln Maynard   the negro resisted and shot some of them with bird shot   they run and left their horses   next day they went back & got their horse   he knew their horsees: I am a U. S. D. I found out their names. Now they threatten my life   they say they will waylay me & shoot me like a dog   I tell you a man can shoot a negrro or a man that voted for Horace Maynard without any danger. If you pleas send your troops down here & reorganise and apoint a militarry govenor   I am & old Rebel soldier   Nothing more at presnt" ALS, *ibid.*, Letters Received, Tenn. In 1874, U.S. Representative Horace Maynard of Tenn. had written to USG concerning Tenn. politics. William Evarts Benjamin, Catalogue No. 42, March, 1892, p. 15. Maynard ran unsuccessfully for governor in Nov.

On March 8, 1875, USG nominated Maynard as minister to Turkey. On March 6, 1869, Thomas H. Pearne, editor, *Knoxville Whig, et al.*, Washington, D. C., had petitioned USG. "The undersigned respectfully, recommend the appointment of Hon. Horace Maynard, of Tennessee, as minister to some one of the European courts. For this appointment, as it seems to us, there are adequate *personal* reasons, arising from Mr. Maynard's long, able and distinguished services in the cause of his country; his extensive and varied acquirements, political, literary and judicial; his ripe scholarship; his thoroughly tested fidelity to the great principles of justice and liberty, underlying our entire system of Government; his natural endowments and his unswerving constancy to the national cause. There are, also, general and political considerations deserving of notice. The principal offices of the Government, including the judiciary and the foreign appointments are filled from other sections of the Union than the South. We do not mention this to complain; yet the fact is undeniable and it affords a strong argument in favor of the request we prefer: i. e. provided persons can be found in the South qualified for the position sought. Of all we know in that section, none surpass—very few equal—Mr. Maynard, in eminent qualifications for the office desired. We therefore, respectfully, but earnestly, call your atention to our wishes herein and to the reasons upon which they are based." DS (24 signatures), DNA, RG 59, Letters of Application and Recommendation. On Jan. 2, 1875, Secretary of State Hamilton Fish recorded in his diary a conversation with USG. "I asked him if he had any one in mind for Turkey—He had not but enumerating the positions held by the southern states asked if I could think of any one from either of them. I suggested the name of Gov Aiken, he objected saying he would appoint no one who was keeping a list of his former slaves with their estimated valuation, with the declared intention of being at some future time indemnified by the United States. I ask him if such were the fact with respect to Aiken; he says that Gov Morton was his authority who had many times told him that Aiken had had told

him—I expressed doubt as to the accuracy of this, that knowing Aiken intimately and having often talked with him on the present condition of the south and of his own affairs he
having expressed himself quite satisfied with the result of the War and had more than once
and the last time in October last told me that he would not if could have slavery back. The
President then said he would rather appoint McGrath and authorized me to write to him"
DLC-Hamilton Fish. On Jan. 4, Monday, Levi P. Luckey wrote to Fish. "The President directs me to say that if you have not offered the Turkish Mission, as suggested last Saturday,
please not to do so." Copy, DLC-USG, II, 2. On Jan. 4, and subsequently, Fish recorded
in his diary. "Received a note from the President through his Secretary countermanding
the request made to me Saturday that I should offer the mission to Turkey to Judge Mc-
Grath; it seems some Iowa men have been speaking to him of Governor Kirkwood and he
now inclines to offer him the place as I learn from Allison and Wilson of Iowa who called
to see me during the afternoon" "January 5th . . . While in Cabinet I receive a note from
Sen Allison enclosing a telegram from Governor Kirkwood with regard to the Turkish
mission and requesting delay; the President requests me to reply that he will hold it over
until Monday next—" "January 26th . . . I recommend the appointment of Eugene Schuyler as minister to Turkey and Horace Maynard to Belgium   The President is willing to
appoint Maynard to Turkey or Belgium but wishes to give one of the places to some Iowa
man." "February 2d . . . Sen Wright and Mr Donnan of Iowa call and state that the President had, some time since, offered to the Iowa Delegation the appointment of some person
for Turkey, Ecuador, or Peru: and that they had had a meeting and agreed upon Mr W. G.
Donnan, a member of the House for the present year. That Donnan had not much Diplomatic experience (which was quite apparent) but that they valued his good sense and felt
sure that he would make a competent Minister   Mr Donnan stated that he would be glad
to go to Turkey; and that Sen Wright had seen the President who had no objections if the
appointment were agreeable to Mr Fish   He suggested that the pay of Peru was better
than Turkey, but that he was afraid of the climate as he was desirous of taking his wife. Mr
Cadwalader told him that the climate was better in some of the South American States
than it was in Turkey; but he replied that he thought that it was earthquakey and his wife
would not like it   Mr Wright spoke of Mr Donnan as a lawyer of promise, and that he
would be agreeable to the Republicans of Iowa   Mr Cadwalader said that he would mention what had been said to the Secretary of State" DLC-Hamilton Fish. U.S. Representative William G. Donnan of Iowa returned home after his term ended on March 3.

To Charles Bockman

———

[*Washington, D. C., Sept. 20, 1874*]
. . . thank you for your kindness in keeping my mare Becky so
long. . . . during the Summer it was my intention to visit you and
make the arrangements then. But I was kept so running about that I
did not find the time to go before the 14th of this month when I was
oblig'd to be in Washington to entertain an old club—of which I was
an original member—formed in the City of Mexico in 1848 during

the occupancy of that City by the U. S. Army.[1] We dine together annually—the surviving members of us—so far as we can get together
on the 14th of Sept., the anniversary of our entrance into the City.
I expected to return immediately to the Branch. . . . and then to pay
you a visit or to send a groom to bring Becky away. But the La.
troubles breaking out has kept me here. . . . Will you please inform
me who there is in the neighborhood who keeps horses to whom
I can send the mare and colt? I would rather keep them in Orange
County now for the Winter than to send them to my farm in Mo. and
will avail myself thereby of breeding again to one of the fine horses
in that County. . . .

Typescript (ellipses in original), Philip Fitzhugh Stryker, Washington, D. C. See *PUSG*,
24, 165–66; letter to Charles Bockman, Oct. 26, 1874.

1. See *PUSG*, 24, 211; Richard Hoag Breithaupt, Jr., *Aztec Club of 1847: Military Society of the Mexican War, Sesquicentennial History 1847–1997* (Los Angeles, 1998), pp. 39–43.
   On Sept. 14, 1874, Ambrose E. Burnside, Providence, R. I., telegraphed to USG.
"Sever illness of my wife's mother deprives me the pleasure of being with you to day" Telegram received, DLC-USG, IB.

To Adolph E. Borie

Washington D. C. Sept. 22d *1874*

MY DEAR MR. BORIE:

The La. war apparently having blown over I think there is but
little doubt but I shall be able to get away to make our expected trip.
Mrs. Grant & I confidently expect you & Mrs. Borie to accompany
us. I believe the trip will be beneficial to you and very pleasant. As
stated before we will have an officer's car to ourselves and can stop
at any time. We will probably start on the fourth instead of the second, of October as I befor stated. ~~to you before~~. But I will inform you
in time of the exact date and hour.

Mrs. Grant's and my kindest regards to Mrs. Borie and yourself,

Yours Truly

U. S. GRANT

ALS, PHi. See letter to Adolph E. Borie, Sept. 25, 1874.

Endorsement

———

Refered to the Sec. of War. I think McDowell had better be advised
not to remove troops from New Orleans for the present

U. S. GRANT

SEPT. 23D /74

AES, DNA, RG 94, Letters Received, 3579 1874. Written on a deciphered telegram of
Sept. 22, 1874, from Admiral Christopher R. P. Rodgers and Benjamin R. Cowen, asst. secretary of the interior, New Orleans, to Orville E. Babcock. "Situation unsteady and liable
to sudden change but not threatening at present. Kellogg proposes to seize arms soon and
trouble may result. His government can only stand at present by support of U. S. troops.
There are about one thousand troops in the city. The time of many of them expires in November. Two companies of these leave town by order of McDowell to Alabama, and one by
change of station within the Department. No vessel of War has arrived. We advise strongly
against the removal of any of the force at present here." Copy, *ibid.* Rodgers and Cowen had
been sent to report on the political situation in La. See Proclamation, Sept. 15, 1874.

On Sept. 21, Rodgers and Cowen had telegraphed to AG Edward D. Townsend. "If
Government at Washington does not desire its Civil officer here to treat with officer on the
so called Penn Government as such, relative to further political action, it should be so intimated immediately." Copy (deciphered), DNA, RG 94, Letters Received, 3579 1874. USG
endorsed this telegram. "The Marshal & Dist Atty. of La. should be instructed that if any
negociations are being conducted between Govr Kellogg, or any other State Authorities,
and the predended state authorities they must not take part in such negociations. The
Govt. must not be committed directly or indirectly by state Civil or Military officers in any
recogniti[on] of any of the parties to the late insurrection as having claim to official position, in" AE (undated), *ibid.*

On Sept. 23, "a Lover of Justice," New Orleans, wrote to Julia Dent Grant. "Take
warning you husbands life is in danger   he will be assassinated if he dont MAKE Kellogg
resign and allow the People of Louisiana a true and honorable election. Men are now on
their way to Washington to FULLY EXECUTE the DESIGN of putting U. S. Grant out of
the way. And are Sworn to do So. Warn him Warn him before it is to late   Let us be free
and WE WILL OBEY THE LAWS of the State of Louisiana. This is ALL True . . . Profit by
this." L, Babock Papers, ICN. On Sept. 17, "A Northerner," Cincinnati, had written to [Ju-
lia Grant]. "If Grant *reinstates* Kellogg—he will suffer. Southerns, do not want to have Kellogg & niggars over them. Casey, is very unpopular   Grant, may follow Kellog—if he
does, he will be Shot at" L, *ibid.*

In [*Sept.*], William Alexander, president, "N. O. Colored Club," wrote to USG. "Your
Excellency will find herein enclosed a list of names of the colored citizens of New Orleans,
belonging to a colored organization, and who are sincerely desirous of sustaining the Mc-
Enery & Penn Government. There are thousands of others who think as we do, but owing
to the very short delay since the government has changed we were not able to obtain their
names. We have great confidence in your Excellency, & trust that you will not ignore the
sentiments of the good colored citizens of the state of Louisiana." ALS (docketed Sept. 24),
DNA, RG 60, Letters from the President. An undated petition to USG in support of La.
gubernatorial contender John McEnery, signed by Alexander and ninety-six others (most

by mark) is *ibid.* Printed copies of a similar petition to USG are signed by "merchants, representing the commercial interests of New Orleans." DS (docketed Sept. 24), *ibid.*

On Sept. 25, "We the Colored people of New Orleans" petitioned USG "to in formed you of the present Condition of our Setuation as it exist in these times amonge the White leaguers democratic party, the peoples party the Conservative Party and the reformers party and all others partys that is now Combine together in arms, against the White republicans: and all So the negros as they Calls us) you Can rest asure of Whate we tell you of those White leaguers they have got not less then 30.000. to 25.000. Guns mixt up With fix ammunation and they have Swarn to Take there revange but What they ll have the State under democratic Cantroll if they must kill every negro that is in the State they declares that Just as Soon you Shall With drew the Troops from Louisanana there Will not be One republican to be found in the State We Whould not Tresspass upon you in Weary your paitian to our long letter but there is one thing that Louisiana needs now and for 20. years to Comme is martial Law, because Whiles these rebles Will Continue With there Schemme to over throw the Government and murdar republican and put up the flage of Jeff davis and the blue ribon of Penn & Mcenery they Can not be Conqured unless you Whould Send us General Benjamin, F. Butler here for only Six months and if he dont Cure them of there deseased We be Willing to be reinstated as, We, were before butler Came to town We Call your attention again in reguards of the White leaguers you may depend on What We have all ready Said, that the White leaguers have got guns enought to masecre every man that do not Want to be a White leaguers democrate, the White leaguers Wants the Troop a way from the City but We do not Want there are hundreds of our Colored peoples Who Whould get regersted but they are realy afried to at tempt it if you Will demend the guns from them and give us a fare Chance at the ballot box We Can Shoot, 3. to there one and have enought to Spare them to helpt them on the Way We bege leife to be excuse for our bad gremmer. We Omite our names at present on account of our W.: L.: friends you may Publish if you See Cause, So that our masters may See the Writing of there old Slaves on connait l'ami au besoin" D, *ibid.*

On Sept. 27, Secretary of War William W. Belknap, New York City, telegraphed to Townsend. "In my judgement the six Companies of seventh cavalry should be ordered to Louisiana and sheridan telegraphed also to send some cavalry from Texas If he can spare them see the President & if he concurs issue above orders telegraph me the result, the regiment of Infantry from Platte may be held in readiness to go if necessary" Telegram received (at 9:57 A.M.), *ibid.*, RG 94, Letters Received, 3579 1874. On the same day, Townsend telegraphed to Belknap. "The President has directed that ~~six~~ the cos. of Cavy and also the Infy regt—be sent at once. Sheridan is desired to communicate with Emory as to point to which they will be sent and to furnish the squadron from Texas if it can be spared." ADfS, *ibid.* On Sept. 28, Belknap telegraphed to Townsend. "I HAVE BY PRESIDENTS DIRECTION TELEGRAPHED TO GENL. SHERIDAN THAT THE REGIMENT OF INFANTRY BE NOT MOVED TO LOUISIANA UNTIL FURTHER ORDERS. HE WILL ACKNOWLEDGE THE RECEIPT OF THE TELEGRAMT TO YOU" Telegram received, *ibid.* Related telegrams are *ibid.*

Also on Sept. 28, Cowen, Washington, D. C., wrote to USG. "I have the honor to report that in compliance with your verbal directions I left here on Thursday, 17th inst, for New Orleans. At the time of leaving here no information had been received from that city as to the effect of your proclamation of the 17th inst., and it was not known what measures the insurgent government of Mr. Penn would take in regard to the demand made for its surrender. The five days within which you had demanded the surrender of the Penn government would expire on the 21st instant, and it was your desire that I should reach New

Orleans on the previous day in order to be present at the expiration of the time above referred to, to observe the course of events, and report my views of the situation gleaned
from consultation with leading men of both parties. I reached New Orleans on Sunday,
20th instant, at midnight. The situation had in the meantime so far changed, as will be remembered, as that the so-called Penn government had surrendered possession of the State
offices to General Emory, commanding the Department, and Governor Kellogg had resumed his official functions. Immediately on my arrival I called upon U. S. Marshal Packard at his office in the Custom House, and from him obtained a statement of the circumstances which had followed the receipt of your proclamation;—the surrender of the Penn
government; the restoration of Governor Kellogg,—and the existing condition of things
in the city. For several days previous to my arrival in New Orleans, and subsequent to the
surrender, several of the leaders of the Penn party, including McEnery and Penn, had been
in conference with a like number of the Republican leaders of the State with a view to the
adoption of some terms of settlement of the unhappy condition of affairs, and to agree upon
some basis of future political action in the State on the part of Governor Kellogg, particularly in regard to regulations for registration, preparatory to the November election. Those
negotiations were terminated on Monday, 21st, by the withdrawal of the Penn representatives, which withdrawal was occassioned, ostensibly, by the refusal of the friends of Governor Kellogg to accede to the demand for a reorganization of the State Returning Board.
The demand was that Governor Kellogg should secure the resignation of three members
of the Board—allowing two members to remain—and that two of the three vacancies thus
created should be filled by the appointment of two men named by the opposition, and that
the four members should themselves select the fifth, who might be a Republican, but must
be acceptable to the opposition. A similar arrangement had been made in regard to the Advisory Board, and acceded to. The termination of the negotiations created considerable excitement throughout the city, and the responsibility for the refusal of Governor Kellogg's
friends to accede to the demand of the opposition in regard to the State Returning Board
was placed upon me by some, at least, of the leaders of the opposition. Such charge was entirely unfounded. Although I was informed of the details of the negotiation during its progress by the friends of Govr Kellogg, which information was afterwards confirmed by the
statement of the spokesman of the opposition in the conference committee, my advice
was not asked nor given in regard to the subject matter of difference. The only opinion I
expressed in regard to the conference while it was in progress was relative to the terms of
the preamble to the articles of agreement, which purported to be with certain gentlemen
'representing the government of Governor Penn,' thus to some extent recognizing the legality of Penn's usurpation. My disapproval of the proceeding, if the expression of a mere
doubt of its propriety in the above respect could be called disapproval, was on account of
the fact that some of the representatives of Govr Kellogg in the conference were State and
U. S. civil officers whose *quasi* recognition of the leaders and representatives of an insurrectionary movement, styling itself a regular and legal government, might prove a serious
embarassment in the event of any subsequent legal proceedings against the actors in said
insurrection. In expressing the doubt referred to, however, it was done with the assurance
that it was merely my own opinion, for which neither the President nor any one else could
be held in the remotest degree responsible: that not knowing of the pendency of the negotiations until my arrival in the city, I was without instructions concerning it, and could
not, therefore, by any possibility, express the views of any one but myself. I was exceedingly reluctant to express any opinion in relation to the conference, or in regard to any
other question of State policy, lest any such expressions might be misconstrued into a desire on your part to interfere in the details of State policy, or party management, which I
very well knew you were especially anxious to avoid. A few moments after the close of the

conference I was in the presence of Governor Kellogg, who asked my advice as to what course he should pursue. I told him, unhesitatingly, that I would at once issue a proclamation proffering the opposition the representation that had been agreed upon in the Advisory Board, and two members whom the opposition might name upon the State Returning Board, with such other details as might be considered necessary to convince the opposition that it was his desire and intention to have an honest registration and a fair election. I thought that such a course would be a gracious act on the part of the fully reestablished Governor, which could not fail to exert a harmonizing influence, and that it would be the more beneficial because of its voluntary character, and because it could not be said to have been wrested from him by compulsion. I felt sure that Governor Kellogg would issue such a proclamation in time for publication in the evening papers of the 21st, or at farthest in the morning papers of the 22d. I had the assurance from prominent citizens who were in entire sympathy with the Penn movement that such a course would be accepted as an evidence of good faith on the part of Govr Kellogg, and that all their influence should be exerted to induce his opponents to quietly submit to his rule, at least until the next session of Congress. But no such proclamation was issued. The argument urged by the opposition for the reorganization of the State Returning Board, was that there were no members of the Board who belonged to the opposition party. After most careful enquiry, I had reason to believe that this was an error. There were upon it at that time State Senator Anderson, President *pro tem* of the Senate who was elected in 1872 as an anti-Republican, and ex-Governor J. Madison Wells, a member of the conservative party. On the 23d, I had quite a lengthy interview with a number of prominent gentlemen of the city who were in entire accord with the insurgent movement, and who professed the ability to express the views of a majority of the opposition to Governor Kellogg in the city and State. After they had fully set forth their reasons for the apprehension that it was the determination of Govr Kellogg to maintain his control over the State Returning Board at all hazards, and thus prevent a fair election, I asked whether, in the event of Governor Kellogg's appointing two members of that Board that the Penn party should name, they would quietly submit to his authority, and exert their influence in good faith to allay the excitement and the hostility to Governor Kellogg throughout the city and State. After considerable hesitation and consideration the reply was in the affirmative. This conversation I reported at once to two of the republican members of the conference committee, and advised them to recommend Governor Kellogg to act accordingly. Immediately thereafter I left New Orleans for this city. On my arrival here I found the following telegram awaiting me: 'New Orleans, Sept. 26th 1874. Hon B. R. Cowen Asst. Secy. Interior. Washington. D. C. Our proposition likely to be accepted. It is satisfactory. Inform me early. I refer to our conversation in St Charles Hotel. S. B. Packard. U. S. Marshal.' This telegram referred to the suggestion above cited, just before I left New Orleans, and I replied that I thought it would be acceptable, but preferred that it should be the voluntary act of the Governor. The many prominent citizens of New Orleans whom I met talked with the utmost freedom of the recent troubles, and the causes which produced them. They had much to say of the unhappy condition of the commercial and industrial interests of the city and state,—were very bitter in their denunciations of Governor Kellogg, and seemed to consider him as the author of all their troubles. Without exception they expressed themselves as unwilling to live under his administration, and preferred a military government. They were avowedly skeptical as to his desire for a fair registration and election, and expressed the belief that he was plotting to secure a republican victory at the November election by unfair means. They drew a sad picture of the effects of the laws in force in regard to taxation, which were burdening them beyond endurance, and destroying the business of the city. While there is no doubt but that the character of the existing financial legislation of the State is such as to justify the most unmeasured censure, almost all the more objectionable features of it, as I have reason to believe, were enacted before Governor Kellogg's official term began, and he has been unable to change the system which he found in force at the time of his inauguration. If good men of all parties had rallied to his support at the outset and exerted all their influence in behalf of reform, instead of seeking to embarass and destroy him, he might have been able in some measure to ameliorate their condition. But with a large majority of the capital, the intelligence and the business experience of the city so bitterly arrayed against him, his efforts towards reform were necessarily futile. Instead of endeavoring to placate this hostility, the social and political leaders of the city seem to have increased it by their sympathy and active coöperation until it culminated in the lamentable events of the 14th. . . ." LS, *ibid.*, RG 59, Miscellaneous Letters.

On Oct. 7, Belknap telegraphed to USG, St. Louis. "So many appeals have come for troops that I have called on Sheridan for a Regiment. He will send the thirteenth (13) Infantry Col. Morrow. Six Companies will go at once and the others as soon as practicable" ALS (telegram sent), *ibid.*, RG 107, Telegrams Collected (Bound).

On Oct. 10, La. Senator William Harper, Caddo Parish, wrote to USG. "We the Under signed Colored citizens of the parish of Caddo & the State of Louisiana. We called a mass meeting in the city of Shreveport, and adoped the following resolutions, and also ratify them.   all the people of this parish and the Surrounding parishes, Endorses the petition of that thousand & thirty eight men Sent to you from this parish dated the 5th day of September A. D. 1874. and reaching you on the 18th day of Sept. So stated in New. York. herald, of the 19th inst.—Now. Mr President We resolve that We are poor laboring class of people and we are with-out money, for what little we did have, our Freedmans-Bank closed on us, and we are now with-out homes and not many white Friends for the white League made most all of them turn their backs on Us—and mr President we know no other but replying to you and Congress to give us a Territory to our-selves.   now Mr President Great God of Isreal, we have tried these white people and we wants to live with these people in peace, but mr. President it is impossibly for us to live with these white people in peace, and hold up our hands for an Office. there is not but one way to live here among these white people here in the Southern States in peace, and that is for every colored man to hold up his hand & declare that he will never hold an other Office in the Southern States, and Mr Prsd't if the colored men in the Southern States, Still hold up their hand for ane Office, for God almighty's Sake take the colored people and the white people apart from one another or put the colored people in a State to them-selves, or send them across the red Sea, to Africa. for A part of us ins not got as much assurance as a dog, for we may go, to law about any case what ever it may be, for if a white man shoots one of us five times and we shoot him one time, we have to go to State prison, or parish or County prison and leave him out side with the game.   and Mr President the white men of these Southern States will not let the colored people have what they make, because the colored people do not enjoy one Seventh of their labor.   as far as letting them enjoy the rights of citizen of United States, that question is dead   mr President we are not the Office holder and we are not the Office Seekers, but we are the ones that makes the cotton & the corn and Splits rails and cuts the wood and clears the land and we are the people that is Suffering, for Some of our people will freeze to death this winter, for the want of clothing   that is the report that our committee brings in to us and we are compelled to believe it, on acout of what we see in this State where we are living   mr President you have done us a great favor by sending the United States Troops here to stop this murdering that have been going on, for these last six or seven months. We give you great thanks for what you have done. We also pledge our Selves to the Truth and nothing but the truth So help us God. we know no other chance to live with these white people in the God's world but to leave them or keep the whole entire Southern States Stockated with ~~Sou~~ Soldiers, because here what prooves it You remember mr President once when these Southern white people attempted to draw the whole entire Southern States from the northern States & Stockated with Slaves. that prooves thy correcily. what they will do now Mr President let us confer your mind to the facks that Occured in our midst, & they have already disfranchised us. of our Registration a great many of us, and you may be Sure that they will disfranchise us at the ballot box. at the day of the election for the majority of the Supervisor is Democrats, and larg majority too." ALS, *ibid.*, RG 60, Letters from the President.

On Oct. 11, Théodore Daussaint, New Orleans, wrote to USG charging that Democrats had illegally naturalized foreigners to boost voter rolls. ALS (in French), *ibid.*

On Oct. 14, U.S. Senator J. Rodman West of La., Chattanooga, telegraphed to USG. "Convention passed unanimously Judge Shoemakers resolution sustaining your La. actions" Telegram received, DLC-USG, IB. Southern Republicans met in Chattanooga to discuss recent violence and upcoming elections. See *New York Tribune*, Oct. 13–15, 1874.

On Oct. 27, Townsend telegraphed to Col. William H. Emory, New Orleans. "The President would like to know your views as to stationing troops in New Orleans on day of election. The object being to confirm every individual in his legal right to vote, cannot points be selected near polls where attempts to overawe voters, likely to result in riots, may be made, and troops stationed there a day or too beforehand? It would not be desirable to have soldiers at or too near the polls, as all appearance of military interference except to secure voters their right to vote, should be avoided—Reply to me—copy by mail" Copy, DNA, RG 94, Letters Sent. *SED*, 43-2-17, 62. On Oct. 28, Emory telegraphed to Townsend. ". . . The whole city and riverfront completely commanded. The troops in taking exercise move about the city daily. The City occupies narrow strip extending ten miles along river, is divided into fifteen wards, and usually has polls opened at more than one hundred places. The frauds charged, if true, are already consumated in the registration, and every man having certificate of registration is entitled to vote. To change position of the troops now and place them near the polls would be inconvenient owning to the number of polls, if not impracticable . . ." Copy, DNA, RG 94, Letters Received, 3579 1874. *SED*, 43-2-17, 62.

On Nov. 4, Philip Clayton, consul, Callao, wrote to USG. "The President, I trust will excuse the liberty I have taken in presenting my views upon his act in recognizing Kellogg as Governor of Louisiana—It seems that the opposition can find no other ground of attack to his, thus far, successful administration of the Government & they are prostituting the learning of those who have obtained the highest legal reputation to that object— The regulations & the law prevent the publication of my views on political questions, & even if they did not I have not the vanity to suppose there effect would be felt—It is however a gratification to offer the humble tribute to one who I conceive has come up to the full measure of his duty & shown an unwavering fidelity to the trust imposed & the confidence bestowed—" ALS, USG 3. The enclosed memorandum is *ibid.*

On Nov. 7, J. D. Bruns and four others, New Orleans, telegraphed to USG. "The committee of seventy have the honor to inform your excellency that on the second day of this month at a General election holden in this state under the auspices of the acting Governor Wm P Kellogg the conservative party was entirely successful and will have in the next legislature a clear majority upon a joint ballot It is a well ascertained fact that thousands of our colored fellow citizens voted the conservative ticket—We address you now to make a solemn but respectful protest against the further occupation of the state by military forces & to request their withdrawal with the return of our people to power we can assure you that the civil law will become supreme that its sacred obligations will be recognised both by the ruler & the ruled and that there will be ample protection guaranteed to life & liberty within our borders   at present and for some weeks past the state house has been garrisoned by united states soldiers and our city has presented more the appearance of a military post than of a great commercial metropolis while the agricultural interests of the state have been greatly hindered by the operations of a part of the army in the country parishes —The returning board is to meet on the 11th of this month for the purpose of canvassing and compiling the election returns and will be assembled in the state house   We cannot but consider it extremely improper that the important civil work with which that board is charged should be executed in the midst of the bayonets of the federal government inter arma silent leges   at the commencement of the new era which seems dawning upon our people, we wish to assure you and the People of the united states of our devotion to the principles of the constitution and of our stead fast purpose to uphold the cause of public liberty and good government." Telegram received (at 5:55 P.M.), DNA, RG 60, Letters from the President. On [*Nov. 16*], USG wrote. "If troops in New Orleans still occupy the State House have them removed to their barracks or to where they are to be quartered for the winter." AN, *ibid.,* RG 94, Letters Received, 3579 1874. On Nov. 17, Emory telegraphed to Townsend. "The troops moved as directed. It will slightly increase estimated expense for Quarters. While in State House strict orders were observed not to interfere with free ingress or egress of citizens or with state affairs." Copy (telegram received on Nov. 18), *ibid.*

On Nov. 9, E. Allen and eighty-five others "who voted the Democrats Ticket," Caddo Parish, had written to USG. "We wish to ask your permittion of sending you a pettition and elso estate to you the reason why we did not or could not vote as we wished to here in this parish and also estate to you the reason why we colored people voted the White Peoples's Ticket,   We was threatined by our employers, that we should leave our crops, and our wives and our children, and Mr President We have laid in the woods long-enough on the account of Voting, and we know that we would have to be killed or run of from our wives and children and crops, if we had had not voted the People's, Ticket and loose very thing that we have got in the world.   they swore by the God who made them that they would not give no one any ~~one~~ work, who voted the Republican Ticket, and they have turned off a Great many who voted the Republican Ticket, and we who voted the Democrat Ticket, is still working   Now Mr President please look at this,   we have done saw the action of the United States moove   how on Earth can we call our-selve Free People? when we was driven to the Polls, and made vote the white man's Ticket, like hogs & dogs, and like beef cattle, with revolvers, and made vote the white man's Ticket,   the majority of colored people who voted the Republican in this parish, their lives aint worth $10,   they are threatined by the Democrat party   Mr President We are not in favor of Troubling you so much, but we see there is no other chance in the world for us to live, but for us to go to you, as the children did Moses, in the days of old   Now Mr President, We look at you and send our prayers to you as the the christian people do to god Almighty to give us aid. Mr President as We have asked you part of us, to give us a Territory to our selves or send us to Africa, for the Mount of Money that we have been cheated out of for the last past 9 years will pay for any Territory that you will mind designate for us. Mr President we see that we can not live here and enjoy our citizen-ship and if we continues here among these white People who held us slaves once We will have to live in War, ~~and~~ or just give up and be slaves at once and now Mr President We dont want no War here among us, and if stay here, and things working on like they are we will be scouting like Indians is, for here is many of our race, has to ~~be~~ lye in the Woods every night, to keep from being killed   Mr President We hope that when this reaches you that you will Say, the work shall be done.   if there is any way to give us an Understanding We greatly and hope, and Trust in the almighty God, that you will give us, an answer. Whether you think that there is any possible chance of giving us a Territory to our selves or not, for we is not Free, here, and we can not have no free privolege. Mr. President, look back in, 1868, right here in caddo Parish and in Bossier, our race was slaughtered as same as hogs on the account of an Election. that is been the very same way here in 1874. Mr President what kind of a country do you Call that. a man can not vote to Suit himself, be caus in 1868, they claim the Election then, as they do now, and they aint ʂ no more Titled to it know than they was then. now Mr President let us call your attention to another Fact. these White men says here boldly and Public, that they can take guns and revolvers, and kill as many black men as they want to, and the law will protect them in it, and we believe it, too, and the reason of it because every white man that killed a blac man is walking about, big and nothing is done to him, for we know 15 or 20 ʷ that killed black men and are walking bout here safer than we ᵃʳᵉ we are, and theɏre is not any law in this parish for a colored man and any way the white people say do it is done wright or wrong. Great God Mr President give us permission to ask congress to give us a Territory to our selves. Or send us to Africa. the Majority of the colored people all over the southern states is in favor of this but as most of them are afraid to sign their names afraid these white people in the southern states will kill them and in the next column you will find a few of our names who voted the Democratic Ticket and we are as true republican's as ever was   Mr. President Ecuse us if you please: for talking so much to you at one time, but it is so seldom that We ever get chance to talk to you that We can not help our selves. but as fore said to you about us voting the White Peoples Ticket We knew that we was ruining our selves in Government affairs, but We thought that our lives and our wives and our children's ̶l̶i̶v̶e̶s̶ and our childrens Lives, was much better to us at the present Time and voting a Republican Ticket, and looseing all or one of them at one time, for Mr President if we look, at a white man's and Grunt too loud, We are prisoned in angry, and then there is no law for us. none of us is not going to get none of our crops hardly this year, for the White people has said so. We believe they mean it, and We will ask you again & again to give ̶u̶s̶ us a Territory to our selves. O! merciful God Mr President, look at us and help us, as Joshua did the children ̶d̶i̶d̶ of Isreal in the days of old. Democrats! may have all the Elections in the world but just give us a Territory to our selves." L, *ibid.*, RG 60, Letters from the President.

On Nov. 10, U.S. Representative Frank Morey of La., Monroe, telegraphed to USG or Attorney Gen. George H. Williams. "Strong feeling against execution of writs for offences against enforcement act, caused by arbitrary and illegal action of State District Judge —Election has injured us—My election assured,   No political complication involved— Friends of Administration all agree that vigorous execution of law now our political salvation. Law can now be enforced without danger. Chief Justice, and General Morrow now here—All wish to know Administration policy in this matter before moving further" Telegram received (in cipher, at 1:12 P.M.), *ibid.*, Letters Received, La.; copy, *ibid.* Morey served until June 8, 1876, when his election was successfully contested.

On Nov. 28, 1874, M. Arthur *et al.*, "Committee of 80. men) colored Republicans," Caddo Parish, wrote to USG. "We wish to ask your permission to inform you, of the condition that We now stand in, as we are colored men, and so called legal voters, of this State, and of the United States. We take the Honor to Say to you and congress of the United States that We are some of the men who voted the Republican Ticket in this parish & State and we have assembled to gethir today, to inform you and Congress that the White people of this Parish have threatened to murder us, and also discharged us from our Labor, and have runned a part of us from our crops and have took all we made, and have killed some of our Kin, and have threatened not to Employ none of us another year, unless We agree to be a Democrat, and vote the Democratic Ticket, at every Election, but Mr. President We have not never voted the Democrat Ticket, and never will but we expect, for it to create War here but We can not help it for the way these White people here in These Southern States, is Going on with us if we stay here among them, War will Be gin. We as colered men Belonging To the Republican party and True Republican and We disire to live in peace, and Harmony and to Enjoy all the rights of a citizen ship. but under the Law the Demo-crats have Got on us, and trying force, on us, it is impossible ~~unless they put us back like they did~~ for us to live under the law that the Democrats have got on us and trying to get on us unless they put us back where they had us in 1854 & 1855 and so on. Now Mr Presi-dent We are not in favor of troubleing the President so much but we are bound to tell you that here is Several of us who have to lay in the Woods from our families on account of Voting the Republican ticket and here is white men hundred of them Geting resolutions after Resolutions to crush the rights of a colored man, on account of ~~his~~ our political rights. Great God mr President how can we stand that and labor and keep the country up too, for we are the only race that keeps the country up and we are the ones that have to take the punishment for Every race on this Earth has more privolege than we colored men here in these Southern States   Even to the Beast, and the Varmant in the woods has more privolege with their kind than we do with our Nation. now Mr President, We have before asked you and asked ~~congr~~ your concent, to ask congress of the United States, to Give us a Territory to our selves or send us to Africa. Whil'st all other nation of people is colonized in the World, for God all mighty's sake mr President, turn your Eyes toward us, and help us to be colonized too   We is not alone in this State for the State of Texas and Arkansas is working for the same thing that is of our race. Mr President as we are now shaded under a Republican Government that we can not live in peace, what will we do when the Demo-cratic party become Victorious all over the United States. We Resolve to ask the Executive Department which we has supported in the pass, and in the name of God and the almighty God that there will be something another done for our peace. We think that it is high time that our people should be protected in this civilization. We have a lawful right to ask for that Aid. Expressive, first, We are men of a Nation. We are men of feelings   We are men born of a Woman   We are men of flesh and blood, and of feeling   We are entitled to the life and rights of Liberty and the persuit of Happiness   We do not Desire the power of all of the Government, but we want what the Law and constitution Garantee us. We want it with out Waring for it   We had that to do once under power of the White Northern abolishing Party, and we did it well, Equal with any other men, and if necessary we will do it again we are been stricken down in our manhood long enough. as we hope to Save the Union we have a right to Enjoy it. our political rights which have have been Guaruntee'd to us, by the constitution of the United States, and We are being Disfranchised of them every day.   as we now stand it is a matter of impossibility for us to support our selves as a people should Do. When the Northern abolishing party Emancipated us, they Guaranteed a portion cit-izen rights and We also look for it now. We do not desire no War What ever, but it seems as we will have to ~~st~~ do some thing another. Mr President, apart of our race in this part of the country is nearly naked becaus they have been Swindled so much out of their rights. you will find a list of our names in the next Sheet. Mr President We hope you will Excuse us for Troubleing you so much preferance of our Governor of the State   the reason why we do this we knew that you has thousand times as much power as he has, and ~~all~~ also the Democrats in this State got their Blood Hounds, blood thirsty and they over thrown the State Government in three days, and our Governor Kellogg was afraid to poke his head out and you know it is ten times worster with we poor men. Now Mr President it looks possibly that We might get a Territory to our selves, for all the merchants and the farmers have swore by the God who made them that they will not rent us nor sell us, nor let us, have any thing to Eat nor to drink nor to wear. Nor no land to work, unless we pay the cash money for it. Mr President You know that wont do, for we is not Got the cash. for what little cash we colored people had the Freedman's Bank had it and ~~they~~ it closed upon us and now it looks like the whole world is closed upon us, for our race is is Dying up all over the Southern states with the Neumonia on account of not having clothes, and they are Suffering. under them circumstances We are bound to perish, and be clothless it is our special duty to mention these things we have to handled and be with Every day. We know no body else to ask but you. General Grant if you were to come down in the Southern states and take a visit of our Situation which We have so long-endured you would think it and know it impossible for us to stand it. in the General observation of our people We should be colonized or something should be done for our people, be cause We are a lost people for when we go to law here ~~again~~ for our rights we would make better speed by being in the Woods praying to a tree, for dependence and ever lasting life, and when we dispute a Democrat's words, to Jail we will Go, and there we will stay, until the Democrats Gets ready to turn us out, and he wont turn us out until we say we will work for them. all of our crops is gone now. They have got it Mr President you must Excuse us, but we are telling you the Truth and nothing but the truth so help us God. the united State Troops is here all among us but the the Democrats killed four colored men in 25 miles of this place this week. and they are still a killing they tell us they aint killed none, but what they will kill after the first day of January, and they say if they dont kill us then they will sleigh us like hogs when the soldiers leave here. We pray God you may look at this and use your best judement in the name of the almighty God. . . . please turn us an Answer by some meins." L, *ibid.*, Letters from the President. See Joseph G. Dawson III, *Army Generals and Reconstruction: Louisiana, 1862–1877* (Baton Rouge, 1982), pp. 183–97; Joe Gray Taylor, *Louisiana Reconstructed: 1863–1877* (Baton Rouge, 1974), pp. 297–304; telegram to William P. Kellogg, Dec. 9, 1874.

To Thomas W. Cook

[*Sept. 23, 1874*]

MY DEAR SIR,

Your favor of the 6th inst. not giving the name of your son, my reply to his request for an autograph letter must be through the father. I have no doubt however but he is a good, dutiful boy, and has all the promise now that one of his age could have; otherwise he would not solicit a father's attention with so much certainty of having it complied with. I advise him that he always keep on such terms with his parents that he can, at all times tell them "the truth, the whole truth, and nothing but the truth," and his future will be at least happy and honorable. Add too that my late visit along the eastern shore of Massachusetts was a most pleasurable one to me and one I hope to enjoy again more leisurely made.

Very Truly, your obt. Sevt.
U. S. GRANT

Profiles in History, Catalog 28. On Feb. 26, 1877, Culver C. Sniffen wrote to Thomas W. Cook, New Bedford, Mass. "The President directs me to forward the enclosed autograph letter to you; he supposed he had mailed it to you long ago." *Ibid.*

To Adolph E. Borie

————

Washington D. C. Sept. 25th 1874,

MY DEAR MR. BORIE:

When I stated that we would leave here on the 4th of October it was with the impression that that would be Saturday. We will leave on Saturday the third, but at what hour of the day I cannot tell until I hear from Col. Thom Scott who kindly offered to furnish us a car for the trip. As soon as I learn the hour of the day at which we will leave I will either telegraph or write to you.

I have had numerous invitations for our entire party at private houses during our visit, but have declined them and have secured rooms for us at the new Lindell Hotel, just completed. The St. Louis Fairs call together the largest crouds of any such associations in the United States. In the first place they are open to the entire country, and the premiums are the largest. Stock raisers, Machinists & Manufacturers assemble there both to advertise & find a market for their wares, and to find where and what to purchase. Seventy-five thousand people is not an unusual number to be found on the grounds at one time, and I believe about that number can be seated to witness exihibitions of stock. We will visit the Fair grounds at least on the day my horses are to trot.[1] The white faced colt you have probably seen in the grounds in front of the White House when you were sec. of the Navy is one of them, and a colt of his another.

Yours Truly
U. S. GRANT

ALS, PHi. On Sept. 25, 1874, Orville E. Babcock wrote to Thomas A. Scott, president, Pennsylvania Railroad, Philadelphia. "The President's arrangements are now such that he proposes to leave Washington on Saturday the 3d at such hour as will best suit the Rail Road. He wishes me to inform you and ask you to inform him what hour will probably be best to leave here." Copy, DLC-USG, II, 2. See letter to John F. Long, Sept. 7, 1874.

1. For a list of USG's horses at the St. Louis fair, see *St. Louis Globe*, Oct. 4, 5, 1874. Cash prizes were awarded for horses in different categories, including $150 for "Roadsters (in harness) stallions, 5 years and over." ". . . After considerable delay, the judges tied the blue ribbon upon the head of President Grant's Claymore, by Peacemaker. It is seldom that we take exceptions to the action of committees, but in this instance we feel compelled to dissent. In our opinion, as well as in the opinion of nearly every judge of this noble animal upon the ground yesterday, this award was regarded with amazement and astonishment, in such a collection, comprising, as it did, the very best horses in the country. In all due deference, it seemed to us that the ribbon was given as a compliment to the President and not to the animal. Parties who came here hundreds of miles to compete for these premiums, complain, and as we think with good reason, that an injustice had been done them. The committee making the award was composed of the following well-known gentlemen: General John McDonald, Archie Taylor, Captain Bartle, Colonel Buckmaster, Colonel Conner and H. Page. Two of the above committee disclaim having any agency in the award." *Ibid.*, Oct. 7, 1874.

While in St. Louis, USG drove a buggy and team belonging to John McDonald, supervisor of Internal Revenue. On Dec. 1, McDonald signed a receipt for $1758.50 from USG for two horses, a buggy, and associated items. DS, USG 3. Related receipts are *ibid.* McDonald alleged that this transaction was faked to hide the fact that he had given the team to USG. McDonald also claimed that he paid USG's hotel bill and manipulated the prize committee. See his *Secrets of the Great Whiskey Ring* (Chicago, 1880), pp. 95–109.

To Julia Dent Grant

[*New York City, Sept. 28, 1874*]

DEAR JULIA;

I find that it has been arranged to have the Lord Mayor of Dublin, with the company which accompanied him to this country meet me for a short time at the Army & Navy Club rooms this evening. This will probably detain me until about 12. If Buck has returned ask him to come with the bearer of this.—To avoid the croud the party with me come out the side door and Gen. Hawley, who looked for Buck to bring him with us, could not find him.

ULYS.

ANS (on "Army & Navy Club" stationery), Ulysses Grant Dietz, Maplewood, N. J. On the evening of Sept. 28, 1874, USG, Ulysses S. Grant, Jr., U.S. Representative Joseph R. Hawley of Conn., Col. Rufus Ingalls, and Lt. Col. James B. Fry attended the Park Theatre, where they saw Mark Twain's *The Gilded Age.* See *New York Times,* Sept. 25, 29, 1874; George C. D. Odell, *Annals of the New York Stage* (New York, 1927–49), IX, 556–57.

To Hamilton Fish

Washington D. C. Oct. 2d *1874*

MY DEAR GOVERNOR:

Your personal letter of the 22d of Sept. was duly received, and duly answered: but I did not Mail it. Kowing your indisposition to accept the place of Sec. of State in the first ~~place~~ instance, and your frequently expressed desire since to again enjoy the privileges of private life, and that you yielded your own desires only at my earnest solicitation, and that of your associates in the Cabinet I do not see how I can again ask you to change your determination as much as I regret your having taken it. I do not agree with you however in the statement that "it will be no difficult task to select a sucessor who will fill the place with more ability." I think the public will agree with me in the statement that more ability, efficiency and honest effort has not been in the place of Sec. of State for many Administrations back.

As New York will hold an election early in November, and change now might have some effect upon the result,[1] I ask that all consideration of the question of your resignation may be defered until that time.

I leave here to-morrow for St. Louis where I will remain until the 14th. After that I will be in Chicago until the 20th. Letters addressed accordingly will be duly received

With great respect
your obt. svt.
U. S. GRANT

HON. HAMILTON FISH
SEC. OF STATE.

ALS, DLC-Hamilton Fish. On Sept. 22, 1874, Secretary of State Hamilton Fish, Garrison, N. Y., twice wrote to USG. *"Personal . . .* You are aware that for a long time, it has been my desire to retire from Official life—Nothing has retained me in the position which unsolicited and unexpected you urged upon me,—which I accepted with diffidence and hesitancy, & have continued to hold at no small sacrifice, but my attachment to yourself and

the assurances often received from you, of your desire that I remain. The State Department, above all others cannot be administered except with the most unreserved confidence given to its Head by the Executive—When that confidence is shaken, or when the influence of the Head of the Department in the Administration of its Affairs, or the formation of its policy, is overshadowed by others, a sensible, or a sensitive man will appreciate that the time for his retirement has arrived. A series of recent events leads me to the belief that my continuance in office is no longer useful, and to the apprehension that I have not the control, or the influence in matters relating to my own Department, which are necessary, not only to a confident, and satisfactory discharge of the delicate and Complicated duties of the office, but also to the independence of feeling, without which the high position which I have held in your Administration cannot be worthily occupied. If I am not mistaken in this impression, my resignation and retirement to private life, will bring me a relief which I have long desired. The only regret which will attend them, will be the less frequent opportunity of personal association and intercourse with yourself; & with the friends with whom I have been closely associated in connection with my official position during the past five and a half years. I therefore enclose herewith my resignation of the Office of Secretary of State of the United States. To find a successor more competent than I have been, will be no difficult task—you will however find none who will bring more of disinterested & loyal effort, to promote the honour, dignity, and welfare of the Nation, & of your Administration, or who will prove more anxious for your own personal & official welfare and success than . . ."
"As you are aware, it has long been my desire to be relieved of the duties of official life. Believing that my retirement may now take effect without inconvenience to any public interests, I feel authorised to consult my own wish for the quiet of private life, and therefore respectfully tender my resignation of the Office of Secretary of State of the United States, to take effect as soon as my successor shall have qualified and shall enter upon the duties of the Office. Appreciating the honour you did me, by the unsought, & unexpected appointment to a position under your Administration, & with the best wishes that its future, as its past may tend to the honour, & to the best interests of the Nation, & with the most sincere regard for yourself . . ." ALS (press), *ibid.* Fish's drafts of these letters are *ibid.* On Oct. 1, USG telegraphed to Fish, New York City. "Can you not come to Washn tonight & attend cabinet meeting tomorrow" Telegram received, *ibid.* On the same day, Fish, New York City, telegraphed to USG. "Regret that it is impossible for me to go to Washington tonight—I am obliged to go immediately to Garrison" Telegram received, DLC-USG, IB; ALS (press, telegram sent), DLC-Hamilton Fish. On Oct. 2, Fish, Garrison, wrote to USG. "Your telegram met me yesterday afternoon on my way to the Station for this place—half way up. I had an important appointment here for to day, and had no change of clothes in Newyork, and my keys &c wherewith to obtain clothing or any thing else, in Washington, were all here—I was therefore forced to proceed, & to express my regret at not being able to Comply with your request to return to Washington last night—which I would certainly have done had it been practicable. I wish very much my dear General, an opportunity to Converse with you, frankly & fully, on the subject of a letter which I addressed to you on 22d of last Month, of the reception of which, however, I have no acknowledgment. Had I known of your being in Newyork, I should not have failed to go there, and regret exceedingly that I had not learnt of your being there, until after you left, as also, the impossibility of going last Evenig to Washington. If you are to remain there for a few days, I will go on, or if you pass through Newyork on your way West, or stop in Philadelphia, I will, if agreeable to you, meet you, on being advised of the possibility of doing so—" ALS (press) and ADf (initialed), *ibid.*

Intrigues by Orville E. Babcock and Secretary of War William W. Belknap prompted Fish to tender his resignation. On Oct. 24, Fish wrote in his diary after discussing his concerns with USG. "... He very warmly & earnestly said, that so far from having lost his Confidence I now had it more fully & implicitly, and that no one had, or Could have his confidence more fully than I have. That while he saw that things had occurred, which should not have been allowed, they had in every instance been the results entirely of thoughtlessness, & without the slightest idea of interfering with the appropriate duties of my Department, & more especially without any want of respect for me. I thanked him for the assurance of his continued confidence & friendship—& while I accepted his assurance that the acts &c complained of had been inadvertent & thoughtless, they had become so frequent & constant, as to indicate a habit to which I could no longer accommodate myself, and that I could not remain except with an understanding that in the future there should be more of reserve, & of care, & that the interference of the part ~~by~~ of (or by others through) Babcock, or from other quarters, or from the other Departments, unless regularly presented in Cabinet discussion, whether such interference be directed to the policy, or the disposal of the Offices under the State Department, should cease—He thought that I might rely upon it that, attention having been directed to the matter, there would be no recurrence of any cause of complaint—& reiterated the expression of wish that I should continue in office— I replied that relying upon the assurance he gave that I might not apprehend any further cause of complaint I would reconsider & withdraw my resignation—. . ." *Ibid.* See Fish diary, Sept. 21–22, Oct. 3, 1874, *ibid.;* Nevins, *Fish,* pp. 734–39.

On June 22, Belknap had written to Maj. William Myers and Capt. Stephen C. Lyford. "You are selected by the President of the United States to take charge of the arms and other military stores, which have been prepared by this Department for presentation to His Highness the Mikado and other high officials of the Japanese Empire, and to accompany them to the seat of government of that nation. After you have executed this commission, you will visit and examine the military organizations and works of the Empire to as full an extent as may be permitted by the authorities, and upon completion thereof you will return to the United States. . . ." Copy, DNA, RG 107, Letters Sent, Military Affairs. On July 1, Belknap wrote to Col. Alexander E. Shiras. "It is the President's desire that Major Bell of the Commissary Dep't. perform, during Gen'l. Myer's (Q. M. D.) absence, the duties now in Gen'l. M's charge—. . . I have so informed Gen'l. Meigs—" ALS, *ibid.,* RG 192, Orders Received. On Sept. 14, Fish wrote in his diary about a conversation with USG. "I ask him if he had signed or authorised any Commissions to Gnl Meyer & Col Lyford through the War Dept to the Emperor of Japan. (in this Connection see Binghams No 110) He says he believes that he authorised the presentation of some Arms or Military equipments, to the Emperor—that Genl Meyer wanted to visit Japan, & he authorised his going—I mention the purport of Bingham's despatch, that these Officers were 'Commissioned by the President through the War Department'—that this is I believe the first time that any Dept other than the State Dept. has given Commissions to a foreign Government—that once before the War Dept had undertaken to Commission an Officer (Gen Meyer of the Signal Service) to a Scientific congress In other cases even to such Congresses or Conferences they had been Commissioned by the State Dept—That the making of presents to foreign Sovereigns, of Arms &c had frequently taken place—but always through the Department entrusted by law with the Correspondence with Foreign Governments. That it was not only a breach of Comity & of courtesy & of the respect of one Department toward another, but of Law for the War Dept. to undertake to issue Commissions to Foreign States, or to hold Correspondence, or to make presents except through the proper Department—That I could not allow this to pass without remonstrance but did not wish to cause any rupture, or hard feeling, but I could not allow it to pass unnoticed lest it fall into a precedent—He said he was sure that no disrespect, or want of official Courtesy to me or the Department had been intended—that it had been from thoughtlessness

—To which I replied that it was strange that the War Department, & Army men who are very tenacious of Etiquette, & of what is due to themselves, should be so very thoughtless of what is due to others—That I believed I understood the influence through which this had been brought about—(alluding to Genl Babcock) & was tired of its interference with my Department. In the Course of the Conversation I referred to the misunderstanding between China & Japan, & to the jealousy of the former—that the presentation of Arms by the U. S. to Japan, however insignificant the amount or quantity, would be greatly magnified, & at this time was injudicious—had I been consulted I would have advised against it at present—" DLC-Hamilton Fish. See also letter to Hamilton Fish, July 7, 1874.

On Sept. 19, Culver C. Sniffen wrote to Fish. "The President directs me to say that he will be pleased to have a Commission prepared for John B. Bowman of Kentucky to be Minister Resident to Ecuador in place of E. Rumsey Wing to be recalled." Copies, DLC-Hamilton Fish; DLC-USG, II, 2. Fish opposed this appointment. John B. Bowman, related to Belknap by marriage, declined the position. E. Rumsey Wing had died on June 11. On Jan. 12, 1875, Levi P. Luckey wrote to Samuel M. Wing, Louisville. "Your letter of Nov. 20th was duly received by the President, and its answer has been delayed through various causes. The picture alluded to did not arrive and the reply was delayed awaiting its receipt and then your letter was mislaid and but just found. The picture has never been received. The Secretary of State promised to ascertain fully the regulations in force in Ecuador in regard to the removal of bodies from that country. He expressed much regret that the remains of your son were not at once placed upon a Steamer and sent home." Copy, *ibid.* On July 18, 1876, USG signed a bill appropriating $1,000 to remove Wing's remains from Ecuador to Ky. See Fish diary, Sept. 14, 1874, DLC-Hamilton Fish; Nevins, *Fish,* pp. 731–32, 734; *PUSG,* 24, 322–24; *CR,* 44–1, 1353–54, 1400; *U.S. Statutes at Large (Private Laws),* XIX, 34.

1. At the election on Nov. 3, 1874, N. Y. Republicans suffered a serious setback, as did Republicans elsewhere.

On Nov. 3, Charles H. T. Collis, Philadelphia, telegraphed to USG. "Philada retains her position with eleven thousand majority" Telegram received (at 7:25 P.M.), DLC-USG, IB. On the same day, Henry H. Bingham, Philadelphia, telegraphed to USG. "We Carry the Entire State ticket & the legislature   Robbins democrat elected in the Myers Harmer district   Negley Republican defeated   we think that we gain a Congressman in Schuylkill District   Freeman Oneil & Kelly elected" Telegram received (on Nov. 4, at 1:40 A.M.), *ibid.*

Also on Nov. 3, U.S. Representative James B. Sener of Va., Fredericksburg, telegraphed to USG. "Douglas Majority in My Native place twenty six   a gain for me of one hundred & sixty three with postmaster griffith voting open ballot against me" Telegram received, *ibid.* Sener lost his reelection bid.

On Nov. 4, U.S. Senator Matthew H. Carpenter of Wis., Milwaukee, telegraphed to USG. "Wisconsin has breasted the wave   we hold our representation in Congress and have regained our legislature" Telegram received (at 4:09 P.M.), *ibid.*

On Nov. 6, Gen. William T. Sherman, New York City, wrote to his aide Col. Joseph C. Audenried. ". . . The results of the elections has completedly stupefied the Republicans, and if the Democrats only act with moderation and prudence—no great harm will result. Genl Grant and his immediate surroundings have been selfish and mean, and have alienated the Country and many of his Old Friends are not only alienated but deeply angry. When Johnson and his Cabinet were scheming to damage Grant, as you know I substituted myself—and went to Mexico, and afterwards many times I stood between him and conflict with the Cabinet. You have seen how he has returned it. I am not sorry that he has caught the inevitable consequence, but I shall not quarrel with him or anybody. . . ." RWA Inc.

Auction Catalog No. 39, June 1, 1996, no. 95. On the same day, John Bigelow, Highland Falls, N. Y., wrote to William M. Huntington, *New York Tribune* reporter, Paris. ". . . The horse jockies about the White house made Grant believe that the people wanted him for a third term and no one could make him 'let go.' The only way to get rid of him was to sink ~~the~~ his boat. ~~which floated him~~. . . . The change of 100,000 votes in this State in two years shows that Grants power like Tweeds & Louis Napoleons was all imaginary. . . . John Sherman (the Senator from Ohio) says Grants regards this Election as the defeat of the Repub. party but not of him. It will require so much of the Strength of the Republican party to keep Grant down with all the patronage for two years under his control that they will have none to Spare for rallying again to resist the Democrats. Nor do I think the result to be regretted. . . ." ALS, American Philosophical Society Library, Philadelphia, Pa.

On Nov. 19, John Tyler, Jr., Tallahassee, wrote to USG. "It is with no pleasure that I impart to you, through the Floridian of the 17th Instant, the loss of the State of Florida to the Republican Party. The Majority against it in the Legislature is increased to five on joint ballot by the election of Dr Hicks of the Methodist Church from Dade County; and this majority will doubtless be confirmed & strengthened through the prestige of the general Democratic triumph, at least in effective action. It is, moreover, the year for the reapportionment of the state. Further than this, the Conover & Dyke balance of power ticket in Leon County for the Legislature, for which the Democratic vote was thrown under resolution of the Democratic State Executive Committee, in despite of the Mandamus issued at their joint instance by the Democratic Judge White, has been thrown out by the Board of Canvassers, so that now Senator Conover is as dead politically in the State as if he were shot, for he stands no where with the Republican Party, and if he seeks a lodgement with the Democracy they have, of course, their own special men to prefer over him. He may possibly somewhat recover himself by a continued affiliation as a subordinate Democratic tool with Dyke and the Floridian, and by further inducing you, in your Federal appointments here, to ignore Southern Republicans and advance to official position Southern Democrats in their place. Again, by the throwing out of the Dyke and Conover ticket for this County the majority for Purman is reduced to about 150, and although he goes to the House of Representatives on this meagre majority, as a member of the 44th Congress, he will sit there almost alone from the Southern states, and with Republicans in 'Minimis,' almost as a solitary '*Carpetbagger*,' scorned under the force of the general political change by his Northern Republican associates, and utterly contemned by the Southern Representatives. His '*Honor*' will thus attach to him simply as the shirt of Nessus, unless he has the obtusity of the hide of a Rhinoceros. The '*Practicality*' that has been quietly, and in its own peculiar way, at work in all this business, may still be questioned, but the '*efficiency*' of the work will scarcely be doubted. I am, Mr President, so far as I am permitted to be, your friend &c" ALS, Tyler Papers, College of William and Mary, Williamsburg, Va. On Sept. 21, Tyler had written to USG. "At length, Govr Steirns on the one side, and Senator Conover on the other side, have done the first sensible thing since the accession of the first to the Gubernatorial chair, and of the last to the Senate, *but this only through the absolute force of Circumstances, & not through either a disposition to do right, or their prescient political sagacity.* After having between them brought about the inevitable destruction of the Republican Party in the State, and seeing before them plainly their own individual destruction, through their miserable games with the Democracy, on the right & on the left, the first playing his cards with Judge Westcott, a very small man in every sense, and the latter with Dyke and Bloxham, two utterly rotten political dishclouts, and the first, if not the last, rotten in more senses than one, both sides opening the back door of the Republican House to the Democrats OFFICIALLY until these had gotten possession of the Republican Citadel,—now, at last, they have made a virtue of necessity, and to save themselves rather than the Party, have coalesced their factions and thus again the Party & Legislature may be considered secure in the State. Suffer me to add the wish that you will not turn from a third term. The condition of the Country demands your Continuation in the Executive Chair. Leave it, and we shall soon again have Civil Commotions, in the North as well as the South. The necessity of Caesarism is becoming more & more apparent every day. To my own mind it has been plain ever since the close of the War, and all that the New York Herald has said upon the subject is but a rehash of my own Articles & Essays on the Subject, as Walton of the Sentinel says he told in New York last year when the Herald first opened on the subject, he being then in that City. I am satisfied—have long been satisfied—that all the Chief Military men of the Country, North & South, as well as all the chief Capitalists of the Country would sustain the movement. *Grasp the situation & take a third term.*" ALS, *ibid.* See Jerrell H. Shofner, *Nor Is It Over Yet: Florida in the Era of Reconstruction 1863–1877* (Gainesville, 1974), pp. 293–95, 301.

On Nov. 30, "a meeting of the Convention of the Republicans of the City of Baltimore" adopted a "Preamble and resolutions" for presentation to USG, Secretary of the Treasury Benjamin H. Bristow, and Postmaster Gen. Marshall Jewell. "Whereas, It has been conclusively proven by the results of the late elections and other transpiring events, that the mass of the Republican voters of our state have no longer any confidence in the ability of the Federal Officers in this City to manage party affairs, . . . we urgently request the National Administration to relieve us of the onerous burden inflicted upon us by the aforesaid unworthy officials, and do earnestly urge their removal and the appointment of prominent Republicans in their places, as the surest means of regaining lost confidence. . . ." DS (2), DNA, RG 56, Letters Received from the President.

To Hamilton Fish

Washington D. C. Oct. 2d *1874.*

Dear Governor;

This will introduce W. C. Depauw,[1] Esqr, Pres. of Star Glass Co, New Albany, Ind. This company, Mr. Mullett[2] informs me, manufactures a good plate glass, practically equal to the imported Article. Mr. Mullett is anxious to procure it for the New State Department, and my own sympathies are decidedly in favor of using home productions in all governmt works, where atall practicable to do so. This matter will be placed more fully before you by Mr. Mullett probably, and also by the Sec. of the Treas.

Yours Very Truly
U. S. Grant

Hon. Hamilton Fish,
Sec. of State,

ALS, DNA, RG 59, Miscellaneous Letters.

1. Known for investing skillfully and supporting Methodist charities, Washington C. DePauw included plate glass works among his many enterprises. See Lawrence M. Lipin, *Producers, Proletarians, and Politicians: Workers and Party Politics in Evansville and New Albany, Indiana, 1850–87* (Urbana, 1994), pp. 181–97.

2. Alfred B. Mullett moved as a child from England to Ohio, studied architecture and engineering, and practiced in Cincinnati. Becoming act. asst. supervising architect of the Treasury Dept. during the Civil War, he rose to supervising architect and designed notable buildings for the federal government in several cities. See letter to Ministers and Consuls, May 22, 1875.

Speech

[*Oct. 11, 1874*]

It affords me great pleasure to visit your beautiful country, a country which I have never seen before, though I have been far on all sides of it.

It is rich in soil, and of surpassing beauty. Without saying anything at this time about the policy which I think should be adopted with regard to this Territory, I will say that I am pleased with such evidences of advancement among you, and hope you will be encouraged in cultivating the soil of so rich and magnificent a country.

St. Louis Globe, Oct. 12, 1874. On Oct. 11, 1874, 3:45 P.M., USG arrived by train with Adolph E. Borie, William S. Harney, and others at Vinita, Indian Territory. Elias C. Boudinot spoke. "It is with great pleasure that, in behalf of the people of this place, I welcome you and your distinguished companions to the Indian Territory. Never before has our Territory been honored by a visit from the President of the United States. In Indian parlance you are called the Great Father, but we of the Cherokee Nation, who have for more than a generation abandoned the manners and customs of savage life, and adopted in their stead the principles of your civilization, delight to address you by that title, so simple, yet so grand, by which you are known and honored throughout the civilized world. Mr. President, you have crossed the threshhold of the Indian territory to a country larger in area than the six New England States, and unsurpassed in natural wealth by any section of country of equal extent. In your journey to-day you will pass for two hundred and forty miles through portions of the four principal civilized Indian nations, the Cherokee, Creek, Choctaw and Chickasaw, numbering in the aggregate some 50,000 souls, of whom about 20,000 are negroes and whites. Whatever differences of opinion there may be among the Indians of this Territory respecting questions of public policy concerning them, I am sure all unite in the conviction that you, Mr. President, are the true and steadfast friend of the Indians and will exercise your great influence on all suitable occasions to protect our interests and encourage and sustain us in our efforts to secure all the rights and privileges to which our advanced civilization entitle us. The recommendations you have made to Congress in your annual messages with regard to this Territory, I believe are cordially indorsed by a large proportion of the intelligent part of our people. Wishing you a safe and pleasant journey, and trusting you will see evidences of that high degree of enlightenment the Indians of these nations claim to possess, I again bid you welcome." *Ibid.* See letter to Robert S. Stevens, Oct. 26, 1874; Thomas Burnell Colbert, "Visionary or Rogue?: The Life & Legacy of Elias Cornelius Boudinot," *Chronicles of Oklahoma,* LXV, 3 (Fall, 1987), 268–81.

On July 2, Alfred M. Wilson *et al.,* Fayetteville, Ark., had written to USG. "The undersigned members of the bar of Fayetteville Arkansas, state that we are personally well acquainted with Majr E. C Boudinot, formerly of this City, and take great pleasure in saying that he is a gentleman of a high order of legal ability, and in our judgment is eminently suitable for for the position of Dist Atty. of the U. S. for the West. Dist of Arkansas   We therefore most respectfully request that such appointment be conferred upon him   May of us have often met him in legal contests at this bar and elsewhere in bye-gone days and *know whereof we speak*" LS (11 signatures), Duke University, Durham, N. C. On July 17, Newton J. Temple, Fort Smith, Ark., wrote to USG resigning as U.S. attorney, Western District, Ark. ALS, DNA, RG 60, Letters Received, Ark. A related letter is *ibid.* On Dec. 14, USG nominated William H. H. Clayton to replace Temple.

On Aug. 7, Attorney Gen. George H. Williams wrote to USG. "You will receive two blank commissions by to-nights mail—one for N. S. McAlfee, as U. S. Attorney for the Northern District of Alabama, in place of John A. Minnis, resigned. He is recommended by Mr. Minnis and Senator Spencer, and I have heard no objection to his appointment; and the other for W. H. H. Clayton as U. S. Attorney for the Western District of Arkansas, in place of N. J. Temple, resigned. He is the brother of Senator Clayton, and is recommended by both the Senators and others from Arkansas. All that I have heard upon the subject, is favorable to him." Copy, *ibid.,* Letters Sent to Executive Officers. On [*July*] 31, John A. Minnis, Montgomery, Ala., wrote to USG. "Having recieved and accepted the nomination of the Republican party of Montgomery County; the Candidacy for Judge of the City Court of Montgomery—I hereby tender to you my resignation . . ." ALS (misdated), *ibid.,* Letters from the President. A letter from Minnis to Williams recommending Nicholas S. McAfee as his replacement is *ibid.* On Dec. 11, USG nominated McAfee as U.S. attorney, Northern District, Ala.

Speech

[*Oct. 12, 1874*]

I have been very much gratified, in passing through your country, to note so many evidences of progress among your people. I am glad to see you engaged in the raising of stock, and I think, in a country so well adapted as this to that branch of industry, you cannot fail to become wealthy and prosperous. I have always endeavored to protect the Indian from wrong and injustice and to give them every civil right. In future years, should I again have the pleasure of passing through your country, I hope to see great fields of cot[t]on and other products that your soil and climate is well adapted to produce.

I have no doubt but that, in time, you will become among the most wealthy citizens of the United States. You have a soil and climate that justifies me in saying this to you. I am much pleased to meet so many citizens of the Choctaw Nation.

St. Louis Globe, Oct. 13, 1874. On Oct. 12, 1874, USG spoke at Caddo, Indian Territory, in response to a welcoming address interpreted by Peter P. Pitchlynn. *Ibid.*

On Aug. 13, John H. B. Latrobe, Newport, R. I., had written to USG. "When I had the pleasure of seeing you at Long Branch I left with you an address to the Choctaws & Chickasaws, which you were kind enough to say you would read. You there must have seen the great wrong that had been done to me by Mr Shanks, availing himself, most unjustifiably of his late position as ch'n: of the Committee on Indians, to put upon record a most unwarranted attack against me and others, which *he alone of the committee ever saw*. In my address, I refer to his conduct while in the Indian Nation as a subcommittee to circulate statements about me as cruel as they were unfounded; and advices from there satisfied me that, instead of acting as a judge he was pursuing me and others as a detective, refusing to hear testimony but on one side—after Mr Shanks re-election to Congress, he has followed the same course of hostility with a vindictiveness I am, even now, unable to account, for except on the supposition that he has ulterior-personal motives, looking to his own interests or the interests of his friends—all this I refer to now, because my attention has been called to the fact that you have the appointment of a commissioner to proceed to the Indian territory, and report upon the condition of things there. If this resolution was passed at the suggestion Mr Shanks, I have no doubt that he desires the appointment of one who will corroborate his violence and aid his views—and with no other object than to prevent injustice and obviate evil purposes, I write to ask, that in making the appointment you will as far as practicable select a commissioner, who, without prejudice and above influences, will hear both sides, if there *are* two sides and report the truth. After half a century as a lawyer, and having won, at all events, a good name among those who know me best, it is not only mortifying but painful in the extreme, to have to meet the malignant violence with which I have been pursued, directly and indirectly, by the person referred to, and in writing to you, as I do, I feel that I am appealing to one who desires to do justice and to prevent wrong—" ALS, DNA, RG 75, Letters Received, Choctaw Agency. During a congressional investigation, Latrobe had been accused of fraud while representing the Choctaws and Chickasaws in 1866 treaty negotiations. See *HRC*, 42-3-98; W. David Baird, *Peter Pitchlynn: Chief of the Choctaws* (Norman, 1972), pp. 191–93.

On April 6, 1875, Lemon Butler and Matt Perkins, Caddo, telegraphed to USG. "We have employed no one to attend to our business of any color   if any one interefering with it, it is not legal   we Aimed to meet Congress but money was scarce" Telegram received, DNA, RG 75, Letters Received, Miscellaneous.

On April 14, Coleman Cole wrote to USG. "I Coleman Cole Principal Chief of the Choctaw Nation, Do beg and request unto you, that you will cause a true copies for the use of the authorities of this Nation, all the names of the Individual Claimants, with the accompanying Evidences, and to what amount shall be allowed to these Individual Claimants, to be found in the Treasury Department or, any of the Department   Whereas by the treaty of 22nd June, 1855, Choctaws assuming to pay the Individual claims under the 12th article of the said Treaty by accepting the net proceed of the sale of the Land in the State of Mississippi. And now therefore, I have the hounour, under the act approved Oct. 21st A. D. 1859, Establishing the Court Claims in the Choctaw Nation to as certain and determaine Every Claims separately and to adjudicate them, call on your honor, to forward those copies as soon as practicable, in order to Enable the proper authorities of this Nation carry out more fully and justly according to the 12th article of the Treaty of 1855, as contemplated." ALS, *ibid.*, Letters Received, Choctaw Agency.

On June 26, Cole wrote to USG and Secretary of the Interior Columbus Delano. "I herewith Respectfully inform you the affairs of my people; and in Enclosed papermark A. you will find the statement of Green Thompson, County Judge, Blue County as to Mr Morris bad conduct; another paper market B. you will find that G. W. Ingalls U. S. Indian Agent has granted a License to Maxwell and Morris to trade with the Choctaw Indians: another paper market C, you will find what the Sherriff of Blue County said about the License of Maxwell &. Morris: another paper market D. you will find the Choctaw Commissioner said about Maxwell &. Morris doing business without complying with our Local laws. And another paper market E you will find a bound given by Maxwell &. Morris, with John A. Filch, and John Dorchester as securities of five thousand dollars, filed with him. And this is not all. G. W. Ingall U. S. Indian Agent has granted License to whiteman Sweet, which from the best information that I have in my office shows that he has been in company with Choctaw rogue who is charged with stealing hogs. When the petetion got up to go before U. S. Agent Ingalls, my understanding is two of them went and signed the petetion, and U. S. Agent G. W. Ingalls has granted him the License, without my consent, after promising me that he will not take notice to any such petetion he told me that he had issued order for Mr Sweet to be removed out of the Nation, and said he will not with drawed his order   And Now, he has revoke his order, and acted contrary to what he said to me. Now for my humble judgment if this is the way he goes, and not stoped by the head Department, No peace for the future, and the life ~~and the life~~ is not safe. . . . I am of the opinion that the subject of Trade rests primarily fall within the authorities of the Choctaw Nation, and not the white authorities or white introders to go to U. S. Agent to get a permit from him and step into Choctaw country without the consent of the proprietor outragous and hurt full. This is taking our Country without right. When I ask of him to take away his white introders from my Country, that we may see more peace, and live in peace, And he answers me, that he is going to do it, And then to act contrary to what he said to me, as stated above is very ungentlemen with me, may be because I am an Indian. . . . it is no use to hate the Indians becaus they have large County. But white men Coming in the Indian Territory Cursing and vilafying the Indian the life is in danger. G. W. Ingalls has been here long Enough to have all the introders out of the Nation but he has not the first one out. We the Choctaws like to have Every white introders out of the Indian Territory. I like to here from you very soon, if it to be done by military force let it be done, to which It seems to me that I have no way making him do that. I am confidently hope you can do it or, make him do it. If it is to done by Marshal let it done, but he says he is going to do it, and never done it. I am just ready to say to him this is man I want him to go out, and if possible I like to here from you very soon. You may be pleased to give any aid, you may be good to Extend. Will be gratefully Appreciated." ALS, *ibid.* The enclosures are *ibid.*

On Nov. 1, Cole wrote to USG. "You will please find a certified Copy of A, Resolution expressive of the approval of the General Council of the General Council of the Choctaw Nation of the able report of the House Committee on Indian affairs during last session of Congress &c   will you be pleased to answer me on receipt of the same" LS, *ibid.* The Oct. 29 resolution supported *HRC*, 43-2-151, which opposed establishing a territorial gov-

ernment for Indian Territory. ". . . the Choctaw Nation in Council assembled express the
hope that the great Government of the United States will make said report of said committee the base of its intercourse and dealing with the Choctaw people for all time to come . . ."
Copy, DNA, RG 75, Letters Received, Choctaw Agency. Another resolution, dated Oct. 27,
requested Cole to resubmit copies of previous memorials to USG. Copy, *ibid.*, Letters
Received, Central Superintendency. See *PUSG*, 24, 485–86. On May 10, 1876, Cole again
wrote to USG. "Respectfully memorialize unto your Honor, That I have heard so much con-
fution about Territoriatizing the Indian Territory which we occupy, without our consent,
which they cannot do it without violating all the Treaties, which we have our country in
fee simple titles to our land, and the appurtenances, and so is decided by the United States
Suprime Court, and Committee of 43rd Congress second session. The reversion of the lands
of our nations, Provided for in the acts of 1830, and the Patent granted to the Indians, is
but a declaration of the doctrine of Escheat that attaches to all fee simple titles to land, because the land will not die when one man dieth. These views will be sustained in our faver
by reference to all the Treaties. It is very true that we hold our real Estate in common. The
title is only vested in Choctaw Nation, and nothing more then five men owning one solid
section in your State. On the face of our Patent (we got from the United States) Epluribus
Unum, to live on it. Our land described. Which contain a condition, that shall revert to the
United States, if the tribes become Extinct. We have unrestricted right of Self Government
by Treaty Stipulations. So we have organized free Government for our own Safety and
for the race of man. It does not justify on the part of the Christian Government attempt to
forcible Extermination of the Indians or their Expulsion from their lands as conditions of
forfeiture which is detrimental to the well fair and happiness, to both." ALS, DNA, RG 75,
Letters Received, Choctaw Agency. On May 31, USG signed an order establishing rules
for the "presentation and determination of all claims for damage to or destruction of property arising" from railroad construction through Choctaw and Chickasaw lands, as stipulated by 1855 and 1866 treaties. DS, *ibid.* On Dec. 19, Attorney Gen. Alphonso Taft wrote
to USG. "I have the honor to return herewith the communication of Coleman Cole Principal Chief of the Choctaw Nation which you were pleased to refer to me on the 18th ult, in
regard to the 'net proceeds claims' of the Choctaw Indians. . . . I regret that I feel compelled
to decline undertaking to comply with his request for an exposition of the treaties to which
he refers. While I should with pleasure answer any question of law which he might see
proper to propound in connection with those treaties, to attempt an interpretation *at large*
of their various provisions would be departing from the long established practice of this
Department." Copy, *ibid.*, RG 60, Letters Sent to Executive Officers.

On Jan. 8, Pitchlynn, Washington, D. C., had written to USG. "I have been informed
by letters from home that the Principal Chief of the Choctaws, Coleman Cole, has written
to you in regard to my business relations with the United States as Choctaw delegate
Mr Cole has made repeated efforts to induce the General Council to withdraw the authority conferred upon me more than twenty years ago, and since repeatedly reaffirmed, to represent the Nation as its delegate, which the Council has invariably refused to do. The character of his efforts may be inferred from his statement repeatedly made, that if the Council
would pay his expenses he would come here and get without difficulty within a month,
upon his own unaided application, the amount of the claim I have so long been trying to
recover. The object of this letter is simply to ask as a matter of justice that you will furnish
me a copy of any written communication the chief may have made to you in regard to myself or my business as delegate, and that if you should conclude to act upon his representations, you will allow me to be heard before you make your decision" LS, *ibid.*, RG 75, Letters Received, Choctaw Agency. See Baird, *Peter Pitchlynn*, pp. 200–202; Angie Debo, *The*

Rise and Fall of the Choctaw Republic (1934; reprinted, Norman, 1961), pp. 165–66, 206–7; *HMD*, 44-1-40.

Speech

———

[*Oct. 12, 1874*]

I shall remember with pleasure my visit to the Indian Territory. I see on every side evidence of prosperity. In this latitude you must possess a climate well adopted to the growth of cotton and other profitable crops. I have always tried to see you protected in every right guaranteed in your treaties, and while I hold my present position I shall endeavor to see that you are protected in the enjoyment of your personal and civil rights. With industry and a proper observance of the laws of the country and the rights of others, you cannot fail to become prosperous and useful citizens.

St. Louis Globe, Oct. 13, 1874. On Oct. 12, 1874, Pleasant Porter, Muskogee, Indian Territory, welcomed USG. "The Creek Council, now in session, instru[c]t me to express to you their appreciation of the great honor you have conferred upon them in visiting the Indian Territory. The Indian race look upon you as the friend of their people; they feel confident you, while occupying the elevated station you now fill with so much honor to the whole country, will guard sacredly the rights of all, however weak and defenseless they may be. In behalf of all the people, and with sentiments of high regard for you personally, we bid you welcome to our country." *Ibid.* See John Bartlett Meserve, "Chief Pleasant Porter," *Chronicles of Oklahoma*, IX, 3 (Sept., 1934), 318–34.

On Nov. 4, Samuel Checote, principal chief, Creek Nation, authorized twenty dollars for a "special appropriation for Beaded Pouch Presented to U S Grant—" D, Oklahoma Historical Society, Oklahoma City, Okla.

Speech

———

[*Oct. 14, 1874*]

GENTLEMEN OF THE ARMY OF THE TENNESSEE:—It always affords me very great pleasure to meet with those with whom I have had the honor of serving during the conflict through which the nation has passed in recent years, and especially to meet with the Army of the Tennessee.

I have had the honor of rendering the first service that I did in the field during the war with the nucleus of this army. It fell to my good fortune to be the commander of what composed the main body of men constituting the Army of the Tennessee. The same good fortune permits me to renew the association to-night.

I hope the meeting you are now having will be a pleasant and profitable one to you all, and that you may live, all of you, to meet for many years again in these annual reunions.

Report of the Proceedings of the Society of the Army of the Tennessee, at the Eighth Annual Meeting, . . . (Cincinnati, 1877), pp. 249–50. On Oct. 14 and 15, 1874, the Society of the Army of the Tennessee met at Springfield, Ill., in conjunction with the dedication of the Lincoln Monument. Gen. William T. Sherman presided as president of the society.

On May 11, Secretary of War William W. Belknap had written to Sherman. "I have the honor to acknowledge the receipt of your communication of the 8th instant, asking permission to remove your Headquarters to St. Louis, Missouri, in the month of October next, and to inform you that it has been submitted to the President of the United States. With the assent of the President consent is given to your moving your Headquarters to St Louis, as you desire. . . ." Copies, DNA, RG 107, Letters Sent, Military Affairs; DLC-William T. Sherman. On Oct. 24, Sherman, St. Louis, wrote to Belknap reporting his removal from Washington, D. C., on Oct. 15 and his readiness "to execute any duties that may be devolved on me by proper authority." *HED*, 43-2-1, part 2, I, 5. On Nov. 17, Sherman, Washington, D. C., wrote to Ellen E. Sherman. ". . . I called on the Secretary of War in his office, and on the President who was more than usual cordial, pressed me to stay to Lunch, which I did with Mrs Grant, Fred & his wife—They all enquired particularly after you all, and when I assured Mrs Grant that we were firmly established in St Louis, from which we would never again budge, she insisted that we would soon tire and come back here—But I was equally Emphatic to the contrary—They have a party there tonight for Fred's wife, to which of course I will go, and both the General & Mrs Grant urged me to drop in on them to dinner at 6. PM—any day—. . ." ALS, InNd. See *Memoirs of Gen. W. T. Sherman* (4th ed., New York, 1891), II, 453–54.

Speech

——————

[*Oct. 15, 1874*]

Mʀ Cʜᴀɪʀᴍᴀɴ Lᴀᴅɪᴇꜱ & Gᴇɴᴛʟᴇᴍᴇɴ:

On an occasion like the present I feel it a duty on my part to bear testimony to the great and good qualities of the patriotic man whos earthly remains ~~lay buryed beneath~~ rest ~~in~~ beneath the Monument ~~unveiled~~ now here dedicated. It was not my fortune to make the personal acquaintance of Mr. Lincoln until the begining of the last year of the great struggle for National existence.

During those years of doubting and dispondency among the many patriotic men of the country Abraham Lincoln never for a moment doubted but that the final result would be in favor of peace, union and freedom to every race in this broad land. His faith in an All Wise Providence directing our arms to this final result was the faith of the christian that his Redeemer liveth. Amidst obloquy, personal abuse and hate undisguised, and which was given vent to without restraint ~~from~~ through the press, upon the stump and in private circles he remained the same staunch unyealding servant of the people, never exhibiting a revengeful feeling towards his traducers: but he rather pitied them, and hoped for their own sake, and the good name of their posterity that they might desist. For a single moment it did not occur to him that the man Lincoln was being assailed, but that a treasonable spirit, one willing to destroy the existence of the freest government the sun ever shined upon, was giving vent to itself upon him as the Chief Executive of the Nation only because he was such executive. As a lawyer in your midst he would have avoided all this slander—for his life was a pure and simple one—and no doubt would have been a much happyer man: but who can tell what might have been the fate of the Nation but for the pure, unselfish and wise Administration of a Lincoln?

From March 1864 to the day when the hand of an Assassin opened a grave for Mr. Lincoln, then President of the United States, my personal relations with him were as close and intimate as the nature of our respective duties would permit. To know him personally was to love and respect him for his great qualities of heart and head, and for his patience and patriotism. With all his disappointments from failures on the part of those to whom he had entrusted command, and treachery on the part of those who had gained his confidence but to betray it, I never heard him utter a complaint nor cast a sensure for bad conduct or bad faith. It was his nature to find excuses for his adversaries. In his death the Nation lost its greatest hero. In his death the South lost its most just frient.

ADf (undated), William H. Scheide, Princeton, N. J. This draft is written on five leaves of "State of Illinois Executive Department" letterhead. Another undated but probably earlier draft in USG's handwriting is in InFtwL. USG's speech contributed to elaborate festivities surrounding the dedication of the Lincoln Monument, Oak Ridge Cemetery, Springfield, Ill. See *Illinois State Journal,* Oct. 12–16, 1874; *Oak Ridge Cemetery: Its History and Improvements, . . .* (Springfield, Ill., 1879).

Addressee Unknown

STATE OF ILLINOIS, EXECUTIVE DEPARTMENT.
SPRINGFIELD. Oct. 15, 1874.

MY DEAR MR. ——: The great American traveler, Mr. Borie, and I are this far on our return from "swinging round the circle." We have been in Texas, through the entire width of the Indian Territory and Kansas, across the Missouri at two points, then the same with the intervening States from Pennsylvania to the Mississippi River. At least it will be so when we get back. After the unveiling of the Lincoln statue we go to Chicago by the roundabout way of Wisconsin. Mr. Borie has seemed to enjoy his trip very much. His health has apparently been better than at any time since I first knew him. He has indulged in coffee and other articles of diet of which he is very fond, but dare not take ordinarily with impunity. If he holds out, upon his return I have no doubt that he will become an explorer of the fleet. . . .

Very sincerely yours,
U. S. GRANT.

New York Times (ellipsis in original), Dec. 5, 1880. This letter was likely addressed to either George W. Childs or Anthony J. Drexel.

To Adam Badeau

Washington D. C. Oct. 25th *1874.*

MY DEAR GENERAL:

Your letter stating that Mr. Sartoris & Nellie had been at your house in London was received while Mrs. Grant & I were in Chicago attending the wedding of Fred. to Miss. Honoré.[1] Fred's wife is beautiful and is spoken of by all her acquaintances, male & female, young & old, as being quite as charming for her manners, amiability, good sense & education as she is for her beauty. Mrs. Grant and I were charmed with the young lady and her family,—father & Mother, sister & four brothers. We expect them to spend the winter with us, [and] as Mr. Sartoris & Nellie will be here in January we will have I hope quite a gay household. Buck is in a law office in New York City and is a student at the same time in Columbia Law school.[2] Jesse entered Cornell University, without a condition, although he has never attended school but three years, then in an infant class. My boys are all growing up. Fred. with no surplus flesh, weighs 193 lbs. and Buck, who is a spare looking young man, weighs 160 lbs. twenty pounds more than I weighed at forty years of age. As my children are all leaving me it is gratifying to know that, so far, they give good promise. They are all of good habits and are very popular with their acquaintances and associates. We have had—Mrs. Grant has—a letter from Nellie this morning. But as I was busy I have neither read it nor heard its contentnts; therefore do not know whether it was written before or after her visit to London.

Although remiss in writing I am always glad to hear from and take as warm an interest in your wellfare as though I wrote frequently.

Yours Truly
U. S. GRANT

GEN.L A. BADEAU
CONSUL GEN.L ENG.

ALS (facsimiles), DLC-USG, IC; Munson-Williams-Proctor Institute, Utica, N. Y. See Badeau, pp. 474–75.

1. On Oct. 20, 1874, Frederick Dent Grant had married Ida M. Honoré, daughter of Henry H. and Eliza Honoré. See *Chicago Tribune*, Oct. 21, 1874; *Washington Post*, Sept. 6, 1930. On Oct. 19, USG "accompanied by Gen. McArthur, ex-Secretary of the Navy Borie, United States Commissioner Philip Hoyne, and one or two other gentlemen, visited the present Post-Office and the new Government building in course of erection. With both places the President expressed himself much pleased. At about noon a large number of the leading gentlemen of the city assembled at the Palmer House, on the invitation of the proprietor, to take lunch with the President. Previous to sitting down to lunch, the President gave a short reception, during which almost all the gentlemen guests were presented to him by Gen. Webster and Phil Hoyne. At lunch the President sat on the right of Mr. Palmer, who had on his left Gen. Webster, ex-Secretary Borie occupying the seat at the right of the President. There were about 150 guests present, . . . The lunch was a very pleasant affair, no speeches being indulged in, and at its close the President, together with Gen. Webster and one or two friends, went out for a quiet drive round the city. In the evening the President and family dined at the res[i]dence of H. O. Stone, Esq." *Chicago Tribune*, Oct. 20, 1874. See also *ibid.*, Oct. 18, 1874; letter to J. Russell Jones, Nov. 1, 1874.

2. Ulysses S. Grant, Jr., who had graduated from Harvard on June 24, was associated with Alexander & Green. See letter to J. C. Bancroft Davis, Sept. 5, 1875.

To Charles Bockman

———

Washington D. C. Oct. 26th 1874

MY DEAR MR. BACKMAN.

Your kind letter was received just as I was about starting for the West on my recent trip, hence the delay in answering. I want to avail myself of your offer of a colt from Messenger Duroc, and hope to get a horse colt to keep as a stallion. I have on my place a number of thorough bred mares from any one of which I would be willing to breed. But all of them are in foal now and I would not like to send them on so long a trip. I will however try to purchase one here in the east between this and spring, and if I succeed in getting one to suit will send her on about May.—If you will be kind enough to have one of your boys put Beckey on the cars directed to the care of Adam's Ex. Co. Jersey City, I will have her brought home and sent to my farm in Mo. I send a letter with the same Mail as this to Mr. Hoey asking him to ship the mare from Jersey City. A man from my farm will be here in a few days with a pair that I am having brought for my own driving, and I will send Beckey, with two of my wornout carriage horses, back by him. Those I am having brought I drove during my stay in St. Louis and found them pleasant and fast. They are said to have gone in 2 41½ to-gether, and the slowest one in 2 37 single in a trial trip or heat.

I shall take the earlyest opportunity I can to pay you a visit on your farm, and to go without so much company as attended me on the last occasion. In the mean time I shall hope to meet you here or elsewhere.

Very Truly Yours
U. S. GRANT

ALS, Munson-Williams-Proctor Institute, Utica, N. Y.

To Thomas A. Scott

———

Washington, D. C. Oct. 26, 74

DEAR COL.

We returned on Saturday from a most delightful trip. We went as far South as Dennison, Texas, and as far North as St. Joseph, Mo. At all points we received the kindest attention from the Rail-road people.

We found the car in most excellent order and thoroughly cared for by the Porter. I am much indebted to you for the use of the car, and for the assistance your letter gave us.

Please accept many thanks, not only from me but from all the party.

Very truly yours
U. S. GRANT

HON. THOS A. SCOTT
PRESDT PA. R. R. CO PHILA, PA.

Copy, DLC-USG, II, 2. See following letter; letter to Adolph E. Borie, Sept. 25, 1874.

To Robert S. Stevens

———

Washington, D. C. Oct. 26, 74

DEAR SIR:

At my first leisure I send you a line to thank you for the many courtesies extended to me and my party in the long trip from St. Louis to Springfield—all portions of which were interesting and beautiful—especially the ride through that truly beautiful garden—the Indian Territory.

I hope my predictions, viz, that the development of that country within the next few years will necessitate a double track on your line of Railroad to do the business, will be realized.

Our entire party enjoyed the trip and often referred to it and to your polite attentions.

Very truly yours

U. S. GRANT

COL. R. S. STEVENS

GEN. MANAGER OF THE MO. KAS. & TEX. R. R.

SEDALIA, MO.

Copy, DLC-USG, II, 2. Robert S. Stevens was an outspoken N. Y. Democrat before moving to Kansas Territory in 1857 to practice law and to advocate free-state principles. Active in the relocation of tribes to Indian Territory, Kan. politics, and railroad construction, he became gen. manager of the Missouri, Kansas & Texas Railway in Sept., 1869. See V. V. Masterson, *The Katy Railroad and the Last Frontier* (Norman, 1952).

On May 10, 1872, Levi Parsons, president, Missouri, Kansas & Texas Railway, New York City, had written to Orville E. Babcock. "You will see from the enclosed extract from a letter received from Major O. B. Gunn, our Chief Engineer, from the Indian Territory, that there is a very bad state of affairs existing there—I do not know what we are to do—It seems almost impossible for us to get our men to remain there—Our station agents are threatened with death constantly—One day recently, two Indians came to one of our stations each with two revolvers and drew them upon the agent and threatened to kill him, he being without arms to defend himself—I do assure you, it is not pleasant for an ordinary Railway employé to be situated where he is liable to be assassinated at any moment just for the amusement of the thing—The Government has sent down a few infantry troops but they do not help matters any—They drive the bad characters and desperadoes away from the terminal points and simply scatter them down the line; which does more harm than good—I have written the Dept of the Interior and also Genl Sheridan requesting a Company of cavalry to do patrol duty from the end of our track through to Texas, a distance of less than 100 miles—We are shortening this distance very rapidly every day, and if the Government could give us one Company of Cavalry to do patrol duty, they would be able to keep order and give us the needed protection—I think if any Company has ever been entitled to the protection of the Government in its work, it is ours—We have not asked them for anything, but have pushed the work through the Territory without any aid whatever—If the Government cannot spare a Company of regular Cavalry, can you not get us a Company of volunteers—Unless something is done we shall be obliged to stop our work—Many of our men refuse to remain in such a desperate country without any protection whatever—Murders on the line of our road average from one to two a day—Please my dear General give this matter your earnest attention for I feel sure you can get the Department to do something for us—" LS, DNA, RG 94, Letters Received, 1485 1872. The enclosure is *ibid.* On May 29, Secretary of War William W. Belknap wrote to Parsons. "I have received, by reference from the President, your communication of the 10th instant, enclosing extracts of a letter from the Chief Engineer of your Road setting forth the condition of affairs on its line, and your request for military protection of your employes in the Indian Territory. General Sheridan, who was advised of your application, has just informed me that the conditions of affairs in the Indian Territory is not such as is represented in the report of Mr Gunn, . . . and thinks that your Company would not ask for any additional force if correctly advised of the condition of affairs in that section of the country." LS (press), *ibid.* See *PUSG*, 20, 202–8; *HED*, 42-3-1, part 5, I, 464–65, 481, 622.

To J. Russell Jones

Washington D. C. Nov. 1st *1874.*

DEAR JONES:

While in Chicago attending Fred's wedding I received a letter from you enclosing a plat of Sec. 15 as it is proposed to be laid out, and copies of Overton's[1] letter to you and your reply. I have not lost your letter I do'nt think but have mislaid it so that I can not now lay my hands on it. I remember the substance however.—I visited our land in company with gentlemen who have property in the same neighborhood. They tell me the property is worth now about $500 00 pr. lot, which is I suppose about $4000 $\frac{00}{100}$ pr. acre after taking out streets & allies. The city is building up very fast to the city limit West, and immediately North of us workshops and residences, with one very fine public school building, have gone up since my last visit. My judgement is that all the owners of land in our section should agree to a subdivision of it so as to give those owners who wish the opportunity to sell their land to the best advantage. Every lot improved on the tract enhances the value of the balance. After such a subdivision you, Smith and I might divide our lots equitably so that sales can be made by either party at their option. I have got to sell mine right along from the 4th of March /77 to get something to live upon. That land and my farm are the bulk of my estate and must be put in a condition to produce something when my salary seases.

I met Ben.[2] in Chicago and sent by him some messages to you. No doubt he delivered them.—Mrs. Grant's and my kindest regards to Mrs. Jones & family.

Yours Truly
U. S. GRANT

ALS, IHi. See *PUSG*, 23, 242–45.

On April 2, 1874, Levi P. Luckey had written to W. N. Belt, St. Louis. "The President is in receipt of your letter of the 30th ult. He would be glad to have you give him your judgment of the value of the land in Jefferson County." Copy, DLC-USG, II, 2. See *PUSG*, 15, 372–73; *ibid.*, 18, 32.

1. William H. Ovington was a business associate of J. Russell Jones.
2. Possibly Jones's son, Benjamin C.

To John F. Long

Washington, D. C.,
November 9, 1874

DEAR JUDGE: I have yours in relation to the payment of interest on the Jane Orr tract. Please pay off the loan with any money you may have on hand of mine. This calls to mind a circumstance in connection with Elrod's (the overseer's) accounts. He wrote me that Mr. Orr wished to sell for $2000. I sent him the full amount, but he afterward informed me that he had purchased for $1900. If there is a chance to see, I would like to know if I am credited with the other $100.

Carlin just left here last evening. He showed me four bills which he owed, amounting in the aggregate to $600, which I think are all right and should be paid. Please pay them or let Carlin have the money to do so. I will send you another check in a few days, so that you may have money of mine on hand at all times to meet any proper engagements I may have.

I have now about twenty-two brood mares. I want to increase the number to thirty between this and spring. I told Carlin that when he found a mare that suited in pedigree and price he might purchase but before doing so to consult with you; that if purchase could be made he would find the money to do so with you.

I have partially engaged a young Pennsylvania farmer to take charge of my farm.[1] He is honest, practical and industrious, I know. Yours truly,

U. S. GRANT.

Clipping, Grant Family Scrapbook, USGA. On Oct. 26 and Nov. 2, 1874, Levi P. Luckey wrote to John F. Long, St. Louis. "The President directs me to send the enclosed notice of protest to you, and his check for $765.00. He wishes you would pay the note and collect the money of Mr Hatch, and give him credit on his account with you." "The President directs me to acknowledge the receipt of your letter of the 30th ult. He is glad that part of the Hatch & Phare note is taken up, of course, and approves of the balance being paid by you if not taken up by Hatch at maturity of the extension. As to the three hundred dollars of Mrs. Orr's, the President says that when he bought the land he paid cash for it, and did not suppose there was anything of the kind against it. Mrs. Orr is the one to pay it, but he does not suppose she is able or ever will be perhaps, and you may pay the interest only, if you think best, or pay principal and interest both. Use your own judgment in the matter." Copies, DLC-USG, II, 2. See *PUSG*, 20, 127–28.

On Oct. 30, George H. B. White, asst. cashier, National Metropolitan Bank, Washington, D. C., had written to USG. "I have sold $2.000. of the $5.000 Reg. Consols 1867 and your account has credit by proceeds $2.340. The three certificates for $1.000. Registered in your name as trustee are enclosed herein" ALS, USG 3.

1. See letters to John F. Long, Nov. 29, 1874, July 13, 1875; letter to Nathaniel Carlin, Aug. 24, 1875.

To Benjamin H. Bristow

———

Washington D. C. Nov. 14th 1874.

Hon. B. H. Bristow;
Sec. of the Treas,
Dear Sir;

This will be presented by Maj. W. Fearin, of New Orleans, a lawyer of that city and a gentleman who I take pleasure in introducing. The Major has professional business with the department which he will state, and will ask nothing I am shure that he does not think right.

Respectfully &c
U. S. Grant

ALS, DLC-USG. Born in 1832 at Huntsville, Ala., John Walker Fearn graduated from Yale in 1851 and worked as a lawyer and diplomatic secretary. During the Civil War, he served on the staffs of C.S. Army officers Joseph E. Johnston and William Preston between overseas missions. See *New York Times*, April 9, 1899.

On March 7, 1875, Edward M. Hudson, New Orleans, telegraphed to USG. "In behalf of those recommending Walker Fearn for Judge I respectfully request his nomination," Telegram received, DLC-USG, IB. No appointment followed.

Endorsement

———

Respectfully refered to the Sec. of State. The writer of this is an old army surgeon and an acquaintance of mine of many years standing.

His son, of whom the letter speaks, I have known almost from his infancy, always favorably.

U. S. GRANT

Nov. 18TH /74

AES, DNA, RG 59, Letters of Application and Recommendation. Written on a letter of
Nov. 10, 1874, from Joseph H. Bailey, Kent Cliffs, N. Y., to "My Dear Friend," presumably
USG. "I am slowly recovering after a fearfull accident some 6 or 7 weeks since & barely
able to write a little for the first   I request you will ask Mr. Fish to give a position in his
Department to my son Dr. T. H. Bailey, he is every way reliable & you may recommend
him—without hesitation,   by complyin you will place me under renewed obligations"
ALS, *ibid.* A related letter is *ibid.* See *New York Times,* April 3, 1883.

To John F. Long

————

Washington, D. C. Novr. 29th 1874.

DEAR JUDGE.

I hasten to return your letter of the 27th to Carlin just received
and read by me. I am too busy—having but just commenced my
Message to Congress to write at length, but wish to say that the
business directions to Carlin I approve of. But there is an impression
you have—and which you necessarily took from one of My letters,
—which does Carlin injustice and which I will correct. Carlin did
not say that six hundred dollars would pay his present debts nor did
he specify any amount. He said to me that there were four bills which
ought to be paid at once, and proceeded to give the amounts of each
and to whom due, the figuring I did in my head from memory when
I came to write. I cannot say even that he left me under the impression that there were no more bills. The fact is he had turned over
to him the farm and stock with nothing to sell but the cattle and a
few pigs, and not enough to feed the balance untill a new crop could
be raised; with correction your instructions are timely and good.—
In the course of a few days I will send you a check for $1000.$\frac{00}{100}$.
Should more be necessary to pay up my taxes and indebtedness elsewhere I will send it. I want Carlin also to pick up during the winter
four or five more brood mares when he can do so on favorable terms.
I will forward you means from time to time, to meet his bills. Ford

made the contract with Carlin. The amount agreed upon ~~was~~ as I understood it, $800.00 per anum. He finding everything himself except he has the house to live in and necessarily gets his fuel from the farm. The man who goes in the spring gets $600%⁄₁₀₀ with fuel. In addition I allow him a liberal garden plot with team and time to do the plowing. The balance of the work is done out of his own time. . . .

yours Truly,
U. S. GRANT.

Copies, CSmH; OClWHi. On Nov. 28, 1874, Levi P. Luckey wrote to John F. Long, St. Louis. "The President directs me to enclose you his check on the Citizens National Bank of this City for $367.50 and say that he will, within a few days, send you enough more to make up the amounts you will have to pay out for him. He would write you himself this morning, but he is just commencing the preparation of his Annual Message and has not the time. He says to say to you to pay Carlins bills which you think are all right, and renew your caution to him about making expenditures." Copy, DLC-USG, II, 2. See letter to John F. Long, Nov. 9, 1874.

Draft Annual Message Fragment

[Dec. 1, 1874]

into the past, in respect to Executive controll in Southern States, into the necessity for exercising the authority that was exercised, and, if possible, to provide by legislation, as near as can be, how and when, and to what extent, Executive authority should be exercised over a state, or in the regulation of the affairs of an individual state. I am not unmindful of the fact that the Country has gone through four years of a fearful struggle for existence; I was reminded of that fact monthly and sometimes daily, for the whole period of that four years by leaden & iron messengers that there was a tremendous combination to break up this union: I have ~~been~~ not been permitted to forget the fact from the ~~more incessant~~ paper bullets which have been incessant ever since that interference then was not only condemned, but that those who interfered are under the constant scrutiny—not fair scrutiny ready to justify and uphold where right, and to point out wrong where committed—of critics who assume to direct affairs without responsibility, and, I am sorry to say, in many instances without consience. In the South this class was termed, during the great conflict "Bomb Proofs." In the North they were termed "Home Guards." They paraded, drilled, danced and drank *Lager,* and entered the service on condition that they should not be required to leave their homes except in case they were invaded. But for these two classes I verily believe we should have the most perfect quiet to-day. I speak of this with feeling, but without being able to point out the correction. It cannot be corrected by legislation. Public opinion will have more to do with the settlement of all questions of feeling that unsettle us sectionally. Let the North see the good and not always the bad in southern state affairs; and let the better class of society South condemn, and aid in bring to justice, the violaters of the law, good order & good morals, and of the public peace, and there will be but a short duration of existing trouble.

ADf, ICarbS. A note at the start of this draft states "Expurgated from 6th Annual Message Dec. 7—74." N, *ibid.* On Dec. 1, 1874, Secretary of State Hamilton Fish recorded in his diary USG's remarks in cabinet on his proposed annual message. "He reads, apparently more in jest than in earnest some sheets which he says he thinks of bringing in, after what he may have to say on the condition of the Southern States & the question of reconstruction—They might be well for a heated Congressional debate or a rough newspaper article, very strong & very just, but wholly beneath the dignity of his official position or of an official document. After reading them, he remarks this is just what I want to say, but don't think I can—" DLC-Hamilton Fish. See Draft Annual Message, [*Dec. 7, 1874*], note 4.

To John F. Long

———

Washington D. C. Dec. 1st *1874.*

DEAR JUDGE;

Knowing that it will be the 4th of Dec. before you can get a check back to Washington for collection, sent today, I enclose you one for $1000%⁄₁₀₀ with which to pay my taxes in Mo. I will send more soon, and by the 3d of Feb.y. will have in your hands enough to pay the last installment on my Carondelet property.

Yours Truly

U. S. GRANT

ALS, MoSHi. See letter to John F. Long, Jan. 29, 1875.

Draft Annual Message

[*Dec. 7, 1874*]

Since the convening of Congress one year ago the Nation has undergone a prostration in business and industries such as has not been witnessed, ~~in this country~~ with us, for many years. Speculation as to the causes for this prostration might be indulged in without ~~profit~~ profit, because as many theories would be advanced as there would be independent writers—those who expressed their own views without borrowing—upon the subject. Without indulging in theories as to the cause of this prostration therefore I will call your attention only to the fact, and to some plain questions as to which it would seem there should be no disagreement.

During this ~~suspension of business and industries~~ prostration two essential ~~comodities~~ elements of prosperity have been most abundant; labor & Capital. Both have been largely unemployed. Where security has been undoubted Capital has been attainable at very moderate rates. Where labor has been wanted it has been found in abundance, at cheap rates compared with what,—of necessaries & comforts of life—could be ~~procured~~ purchased with the wages demanded. Two great elements of prosperity therefore have not been denied us. A third might be added; Our soil and climate is unequaled, —within the limits of any contiguous territory ~~for the~~ under one Nationality—for its variety of products to feed and cloth a people, and in the amount of surplus to spare to feed less favored peoples. Therefore, with these facts in view, it seems to me that wise statesmanship, at this session of Congress, would dictate ~~a policy~~ legislation ignoring the past,—~~except so far~~ but ~~to~~ to directing in proper channels these great elements of prosperity to any people. Debt; debt abroad, is the only element that can,—with always a sound currency —enter into our affairs to cause any continued depression in the industries and prosperity of our people. A great ~~exigency~~ conflict for National existence made necessary, for temporary purposes, the raising of large sums of money from whatever source ~~it could be attained~~. obtainable. It made necessary—in the wisdom of Congress:—and I do not doubt their wisdom in the premises, regarding the necessity of the times—to devise a ~~National~~ system of National currency, which ~~it~~ proved im~~possible to keep~~ to be of a quality to keep on a par with the recognized currency of the civilized world. ~~The latter~~ This begat a spirit of ~~of~~ speculation—(the currency being of fluctuating value, and therefore unsafe to hold for legitimate transactions, ~~requiring money~~, [naturally became a subject of speculation in itself] to present themselves)—involving an extravigance & luxury not required for the happiness or prosperity of a people, and involving, both directly & indirectly, foreign indebtedness. ~~This debts how~~ These two causes however have involved us in a foreign indebtedness, contracted in good faith by borrower & lender, and should be paid—~~I trust all of them will be, and do not doubt for a moment the full payment of that contracted by the Nation~~—in the coin, and according to the bond, agreed upon when the debt was contracted, gold, or its equivolent. The good faith of govt, and, ~~American U~~ corporations cannot be violated towards foreign creditors without National disgrace. But our commerce should be encouraged; American ship building and carrying capacity increased; forign markets sought, for products of the soil and manufacturer's, to the end that we may be able to pay these debts. Where a new market can be created for the sale of ~~one of~~ our products, either of the soil, the mine, or the manufactury, a new means is discovered of utilizing our idle capital & labor ~~for~~ to the advantage of the whole people. But in my judgement the first step towards accomplishing this object is to secure a currency of fixed stable value; a currency good where ever civilization reigns; one which, if it becomes superabundant with our people will find a market with some other; a currency which has as its basis ~~in~~ the *labor* necessary to produce it, which will give to it its value. Gold & Silver are now the recognized mediums of exchange the civilized world over; and to this we should return with the least practicable delay. In view of the pledges of the American Congress when our present Legal Tender system was adopted and debt contracted there should be no delay—certainly no unnecessary delays—in fixing, by legislation, a method by which we will return to a specie. ~~basis as rapidly as possible.~~—To the accomplishment of this end I direct your special attention. ~~Such promi-~~

nence do I wish to give this subject in your minds that I depart from
the usual method of reporting to Congress the opperations of the
government for the year, in the order of conventional rank of departments, leaving special recommendations for the last, and put this
first.

I firmly believe firmly that there can be no prosperous and permanent revival of business and industries until a policy is adopted—
with legislation to carry it out—looking to a return to a specie basis.
at an early day. It is easy to conceive that the debtor and speculative
classes may think it of value to them to make so called money abundant until they can throw a portion of their burdens upon others. But
even these, I believe, would be disappointed in the result if a course is
should be pursued which will keep in doubt the value of the *legal tender* medium of exchange   A revival of productive industry is needed
by all classes. By none more so than the holders of property, of whatever sort, with debts to liquidate from realization upon its sale. But
admitting that these two classes of citizens are to be benefited by expansion, would it be honest to give it? would not the general loss be
too great to justify such relief? would it not be just as honest and
prudent to authorize each debtor to issue his own *legal tenders* to the
extent of his liabilities? than to do this would it not be safer—for
fear of over issues by unscrupulous creditors—to say that all debt obligations are obliterated in the United States, and now we commence
a new, each with whatever possessing all he has in possessions? at
the time? These propositions are too absurd to be entertained for a
moment by the thinking andor the honest people. Yet every delay in
preparation for final resumption partakes of this dishonesty and is
only less in degree as the hope is held out that a *convenient season* will
at last arrive when the good work of redeeming our pledges has at
last arrived. It will never come, in my opinion, except by positive action by Congress, or by National disasters which will destroy,—for a
time at least,—the credit of the individual and the state at large.

A sound currency might be reached by total bankruptcy and discredit of the integrity of both nNation and of individuals.

I believe it is in the power of Congress, at this session, as to devise such legislation as will reneiw confidence, revive all the indus-

tries, start us on a career of prosperity to last for many years, and to save the credit of the Nation and of the people. Steps towards the return to a specie basis is the great requisite towards this devoutly to be sought for end. There are others upon which I may touch upon hereafter.

A ~~National~~ Nation dealing in a currency below that of specie, in value, labors under two great disadvantage: Firs, having no use for the worlds acknowledged medium of exchange, Gold & Silver, ~~it the latter~~ these ~~is~~are driven out of the country because there is no demand for them; Second; the medium of exchange, in use, being of fluctuating value—for after all it is only worth just what it will purchase of gold & silver; metals having an intrinsic value just in proportion to the honest labor it takes to produce them—a larger margin must be allowed for profit by the manufacturer and producer. It is months from the date of production to the date of realization. Interest upon Capital must be charged, and risk of fluctuation in the value of that which is to be received in payment added. Hence high prices, acting as a protection to the foreign producer who receives nothing in exchange ~~except what is known to be of unvarying value.~~ for the products of his skill & labor a currency good, at a stable value, the world over. It seems to me that nothing is clearer than that the greater part of the burden of existing prostration—for the want of a sound financial system—falls upon the working ~~man and salaried men~~ man, who must, after all, produce the wealth, and the salaried man who superintends ~~the conducting of all~~ and conducts business. The burden fall upon them in two ways; by the deprivation of business, and by the decreased purchasing power of their receipts.

It is the duty of Congress to devise the method of correcting the evils which are acknowledged to exist, and not mine. But I will venture to suggest two or three requisites which seem to me as absolutely necessary to a return to specie payments, the first great requisite. The legal tender clause to the law authorizing the issue of currency by the National Govt. should be repealed, to take effect as to all contracts entered into after a day fixed in the repealing act. Provision should be made by which the Sec. of the Treas. can purchase gold as it may become necessary from, time to time from the

date when specie redemption commences as full security against re-
laps[e.]   To this might, and should be, added a revenue sufficently
greater than current expenses to insure an accumulation of gold to
sustain the redemption. I commend this subject to your careful consideration, believing that a favorable solution is attainable, and that
if reached by this Congress that, the present and future generations
will ~~hold in high esteem the Congress that come to their timely relief. will~~ ever greatfully remember it as their deliverer from a thral-
dom of evil and disgrace.

Mem

With resumption free banking may be authorized with security, giving ~~the same~~ equal protection to bill holders as is ~~now~~ given by present laws. Indeed I would regard *free banking* as essential. It would
give ~~the much required~~ proper elasticity to money. As more money
~~is~~ should be required new banks would be started, and in turn ~~they
would~~ banks wind up their business when it was found that there
was ~~to much~~ a superabundance of money. Capital is the safest judge
to decide just how much currency is required for the transaction
of the business of the Country. It is unsafe to leave the settlement of
this question to Congress, the Sec. of the Treas. or the Executive.
Congress should make the regulation under which banks may exist
but should not make banking a monopoly by limiting the amount
that ~~shall exist~~ of redeemable paper currency that shall that shall be
authorized [1]

Mem.   ~~Revenues should exceed expenditures to enable secure
the accumulation of gold~~.

~~Int. improvements~~.

Such importance do I attach to this subject, and so earnestly do I
commend it to your attention that I give it prominence by introducing it at the begining of this message.

State

In connection with this subject I call the attention of Congress to
a generally conceeded fact that the great proportion of the Chinese
immigrants who come to our shores do not come voluntarily, to make
their homes with us, and their labor productive of general prosperity,
but ~~by~~ come under contracts with head men who own them almost

absolutely. ~~in a state of bondage.~~[2] In a worse form does this apply to Chinese women. Hardly a perceptable percentage ~~visits~~ of them perform any honorable labor, but they are brought as prostitutis, to the disgrace of the communities where settled, and to the great demoralization of the youth of those localities. If this evil practice can be legislated against it will be my pleasure as well as duty to enforce any regulation to secure so desirable an end.

Treas.

The report of the Sec. of the Treas. which, by law, is made directly to Congress and forms no part of this message, will shew the receipts and expenditures of the govt. for the last fiscal year; the amount received from each source of revenue, and the amount paid out for each of the departments of govt. It will be observed from this report that that the amount of receipts over expenditures—in other words the reduction of the National debt—has been but $2.344.882.30. for the fiscal year ending June 30th 1874, and that for the current fiscal year the estimated reduction will, ~~in the absence of legislation to increase revenue or diminish expenditures~~, not much exceed Nine Millions of dollars. In view of the large National debt existing, and the obligation to add one pr. cent per Annum to the sinking fund—a sum amounting now to over $34,000,000.00 per annum I submit whether revenues should not be increased or expenditures diminished to reach this amount of surplus. Not to provide for the sinking fund is a partial failure to comply with the contracts and obligations of the Govt. At the last session of Congress a very considerable reduction was made in rates of taxation, and in the number of articles submitted to taxation. ~~and~~ tThe question may well be asked whether not, in some instances, unwisely. In connection with this subject too I venture the opinion that the means of collecting the revenue, especially from imports, ha~~s~~ve been so embarrassed by legislation so as to make it questionable whether or not large amounts are not lost by failure to collect, to the direct loss of the treasury, and to the prejudice ~~of the~~ interest honest importers?

The Sec. of the Treas. in his report, favors legislation looking to an early return to specie payments, thus supporting views previously expressed ~~by me~~ in this message. He also recommends economy in

appropriations; ~~especially for public buildings~~; calls attention to ~~a~~the
loss of revenue from repealing the tax on tea & coffee, without benefit to the Consumer; Recommends an increase of 10 cents a gallon on
whiskey and ~~recommends~~ further that no modification be made in the
banking and currency bill passed at the last session of Congress unless modification should become necessary ~~in~~ by reason of the adopt-
~~ing~~on of measures for returning to specie payments. To ~~those his~~
these recommendations, ~~so far as here innumerated~~, I cordially ~~agree~~
join my recommendation.

(Here to add suggestions on the tariff)

Tarriff

~~This is a subject which has never been considered, it seems to me in
entirely its true light~~. I would suggest to Congress the propriety of
readjusting the tarriff so as to increase the revenue and at the same
time decrease the number of articles upon which duties are levied
Those articles which enter into our manufactures, and are not produced at home, it seems to me should be entered free. Those articles
which we produce ~~some of~~ a constituent part of, but do not produce
~~any one necessary constituent~~ the whole, that which we do not produce should enter free also.

~~That which we must import should be free. part of the constituent part of should enter free~~. I will instance fine wool, dyes, &c, ~~du-
ties upon which go directly to the cost of manufacturing woolen
cloths and injure the market for that which is produced at home
by diminishing the demand for it. I will mention the highest class
of wools as the principle among many. It~~ These articles must be
imported to form a part of the Manufactury of the highr grades of
woolen goods. Chemicals used as dyes, in medecines compounded, in
manufactures, in various ways come under this class. The introduc-
tion~~s~~ of such wools as we do not produce, free of duty would stimulate the manufactury of goods requiring the use of those we do produce. ~~as an admixture~~, and therefore would be a benefit to home
production. There are many articles entering into "home manufacturies, which we do not produce ourselves, the tariff upon which increases the cost of production. All corrections in this regard are in the
direction of ~~drawing~~ bringing labor and capital in harmony with each

other, and of supplying one of the elements of prosperity so much
needed.

~~War~~ Army

The report of the Sec. of War, herewith attached, and forming a part
of this message, gives ~~a~~ his all the information ~~necessary~~ concerning
~~thise~~ ~~branch of the public service~~ opperations wants & necessites of
the Army ~~for the past year~~, and contains many suggestions and recommendations which I commend to your special attention. There
is no class of government employees harder worked than is the
Army,—officers & Men,—none who perform their task more cheerfully and efficiently, and under circumstances of greater privations
& hardships. Legislation is desirable to render more efficient this
branch of the public service. All the recommendations of the Sec. of
War I regard as judicious, and I especially commend to your attention the ~~propriety~~ of following: the consolidati~~ng~~on ~~the~~ of Govt. Ar-
senals; ~~to~~ the restoration of mileage to officers traveling under orders:
the exemption of money received from the sale of subsistence stores
from being covered into the Treasury; the use of appropriations for
the purchase of subsistence stores without waiting for the begining
of the fiscal year for which the appropriation is made; for additional
appropriations for the collection of torpedo material; for increased
appropriation for the Manufactury of arms: for relieving the various
states from indebtedness for arms charged to them during the rebellion; for droping officers from the rolls of the Army, without trial, for
the offence of drawing pay more than once for the same period: for
the discouragement of the plan to pay soldiers by checks; and for the
establishment of a professorship of Rhetoric and English literature
at West point. The reasons for these recommendations are obvious
and are set forth sufficiently in the reports attached. I also recommend that the status of the Staff Corps of the Army be fixed—where
this has not already been done—so that promotions may be made,
and vacancies filled as they occur when as ~~each as~~ each grade is reduced below the number that may be fixed by law. The necessity
for such legislation is specially felt now in the Pay Department. The
number of officers in that department is below the number adequate
to the performance of the duties required of them by law.

Navy

The use of the Navy, in time of peace, might be further utilized by a direct authorization of the employment of Naval vessels in explorations and surveys of the supposed navigable waters of other ~~n~~Nationalities on this continent; specially the tributaries of the tributaries of the two great rivers of South America; the Oronoco and the Amazon. Nothing prevents under existing laws, such exploration except that expenditures must be made in such expeditions beyond those usually provided for in in appropriations. The field designated is unquestionably one of interest and one capable of large developement of commercial interests, advantageous to the peoples reached, and to those who may establish relations with them.

P. O. Dept.

Education of the people entitled to exercise the right of franchise I regard essential to general prosperity everywhere, and as ~~essentially~~ specially so ~~with~~ in Repuplics where birth, education, or previous condition does not enter into account ~~with the value of the ballot cast~~. in giving suffrage. Next to the public school ~~do I think the free inter-communication of communication~~ through the mails ~~comes~~ the post office is the great educator of   Our vast territory; the rapidity ity with which new ~~places~~ sections are being settled, ~~up~~, thus increasing the carrying of mails in a more rapid ration than the increase of receips is not so alarming; ~~but deserves fostering~~. The report of the Postmaster General, herewith attahed, shews that there was an increase of revenue in his department in 1873 over the previous year of $1,674,411. dollars, ~~but that the deficiency to be supplied from from the general treasury had been increased. was $3,041,441,468.91~~ and in increase of cost of carrying the Mails of $3,041.468.91. ~~The amount drawn from the general treasury was $5,259,933.55~~   The report of the Postmaster General gives interesting statistics of his department, ~~all going to show such as the number of post offices, miles of rail way, mail carriage numbers of letters carried, weight of mails transported, number of letters exchanged with forign nations, &c~~. and ~~all compared~~ compares them with the same statistics of a year a ago; showing a grouth in every branch of the department,   A postal convention has been concluded with New South Wales, an exchange of postal cards established with Switzerland, and the negotiations pending for several years past with France which have terminated in a convention with that country which went into effect last August.

An international postal Congress was convened in Berne, Switzerland, in Sept. last at which the United States was represented ~~by~~ in the person of Mr. Blackfan,[3] an officer of the postoffice department of much experience and of great qualification for his position   A convention for the establishment of an international postal union was agreed upon and signed by the delegates of the ~~Convention~~ Countries represented, subject to the approval of the proper authorities of the countries represented.

I respectfully direct your attention to the report of the Postmaster General and to his suggestions in regard to an equitable adjustment of the question of compensation to rail-roads for carrying the mails.

Law

The whole subject of Executive interference with the affairs of a state is repugnant to ~~the~~ public opinion, to the feeling of those who, from their official capacity, must be used in such ~~interference~~ interposition and to him, or those, who must direct. ~~such interference~~. Unless most clearly on the side of law such interference becomes a crime: with the law to support it ~~ist~~ is condemned without a hearing. I ~~would~~ desire therefor ~~the most rigid investigations~~[4] that all necessity for Executive ~~med~~ direction in local affairs may become unnecessary and obsolete. I invite the attention, not of Congress but of the people of the United States to the causes and effects of these unhappy questions. Is there not a disposition on one side to magnify wrongs and outrages? on the other side to belittle them or justify them? If public opinion could be directed to a correct survey of what is, and rebuking wrong, and in aiding the proper authorites in punishing it, a better state of feeling would be inculcated, and the sooner we would have that peace which would leave the states free indeed to regulate their own domestic affairs. I believe on the part of our citizens of the southern states—the better part of them—there is a disposition to be law

abiding citizens: and to do no violence either to indiviual rights, or
to the ~~rights~~ laws ~~over them~~ existing. But do they do right in ignoring the existence of violence ~~of~~ and blood-shed in resistance to constituted authority? I sympathize with their prostrate condition, and
would do all in my power to relieve them:—acknowledging that in
some instances they have had most trying governments to live under,
and oppression in the way of taxation for nominal improvements ~~but
without giving~~ not ~~given~~ giving benefits equal to taxation—but can
they proclaim themselves entirely irresponsible for the condition?
They cannot. Violence has been rampant in some localities and has
either been justified or denied by those who could have prevented.
The theory is even raised that there is to be no further interference on
the part of the general government to protect citizens within a state
where the state authorities fail to give protection. This is a great mistake. While I ~~execute~~ remain Executive all the laws of Congress, and
the provisions of the Constitution, including the recent amendments
added thereto,—will be enforced with rigor but with regret that they
should have added one jot or tittle to Executive duties. Let there
be fairness in the discussion of Southern questions, the advocates of
both, or all, political parties giving honest, truthful, reports of occur-
rences, condemning the wrong and upholding the ~~wrong~~ right, and
soon all will be well. Under existing conditions the Negro votes the
republican ticket because he knows his friends are of that party. Many
a good citizen votes the opposite not because agrees with the great
principles of state which separate party, but because, generally, he is
opposed to Negro rule. This is a most delusive cry. Treat the Negro
as a citizen and a voter—as he is, and must remain—and soon parties will be divided, *not on the color line*, but on principle. Then we will
have a Union not calling for interference in one section that would
not be exercised under like circumstances in any other.

    I respectfully suggest to Congress the propriety of increasing
the number of Judicial Districts in the United states to eleven, ~~in-
stead of nine as at present~~ [the present number being nine], and the
creation of two additional Judgeships. The territory to be traversed
by the Circuit Judges is so great, and the business of the courts so

~~constantly~~ [steadily] increasing, that it is growing more and more impossible for them to keep up with the business requiring their attention. Whether this would involve the necessity of adding two more Justices of the Supreme Court[5] to the present number I submit to the judgement of Congress.

Int.

The attention of Congress is invited to the report of the Sec. of the Int. and to the legislation asked ~~asked~~ for by him. The domestic interests of the people are more intimately connected with this department than with either of the other departments of govt. Its duties have been added to from time to time until they have become so onerous that without the most perfect system and order ~~ist~~ will be impossible for any ~~one man~~ Sec. of the Int. to keep trace of all ~~the~~ official transactions by his authority, and in his name, and for which he is held personally responsible.

The policy adopted for management of Indian Affairs, know as the peace policy, has been adhered to with most beneficial results. It is confidently hoped that a few years more will relieve our frontiers from danger of indian depredations. I commend the recommendation of the Secretary for the extension of the Homestead laws to the Indians; and for some sort of territorial government for the Indian Territory. A great majority of the indians occupying this territory are believed yet to be incapable of maintaing their rights agains the more civilized and enlightened white man. Any territorial form of Govt given them therefore should protect them in their homes and property for a period of at least twenty years, and before its final adoption should be ratified by a majority of those effected.

The report of the Sec. of the Int. herewith attached, gives much interesting statistical information which I abstain from giving an abstract of but refer you to the report itself   The Act of Congress of 1862 prosciling the oath which pensioners must subscribe to before drawing their pensions cut off from this bounty a few ~~persons~~ survivors of the War of 1812 then residing in the Southern states. ~~They have not yet been restored~~ I recommend the restoration of this bounty to all such. The number of persons whos names would thus be restored to the list of pensioners is not large; they are all old men who could have taken no part in the rebellion, and the services for which they were awarded pensions was in defence of the whole country,

Agriculture

The report of the Commissioner of Agriculture, herewith accompanying, contains suggestions of much interest to the general public, and referrs to the approaching Centennial and the part ~~the Govt. may~~ his department is ready to take in it.

I feel that the Nation at large is interested in having this exposition a success and commend to Congress such action as will secure a greater general interest in it. Already many forign nations have signified their intention to be represented at it, and it may be expected that every civilized nation will be.

Civil Service

The rules adopted to improve the civil service of the government have been adhered to as closely as has been practicable with the opposition with which it meets. The effect I believe has been beneficial on the whole and has tended to the elevation of the service. But it is impracticable to maintain this without direct and positive support of Congress. Generally the support which it nominally receives is from those who give it their support only to find fault when the rules are apparently departed from. Removals from office, without prefering charges agains parties removed are frequently sited as a departure from the rules adopted for Civil Service reform, and the retention of those against whom charges are made by irresponsible persons, and without good grounds for their charges, ~~ais~~ is also condemned. Under these circumstances therefore I announce that if Congress adjours without positive legislation on the subject of "Civil Service Reform" I will regard such action as a disapproval of the system, and will abandon it except so far as to require examinations for all appointees to determine their fitness. Competitive examinations will be abandoned.

The gentlemen who have given their services, without compensation, as members of the Board to devise rules and regulations for the government of the Civil Service of the country have shown much zeal ~~in~~ and earnestness in their work,[6] and to them as well as to myself it will be a source of mortification if it is trown away. But I repeat again that ist is impossible to carry this system to a successful issue without general approval and assistance, and positive law to support it.

I have heretofore pointed out stated that three great elements of prosperity to any people which we yet still has: the nation: Capital, unemployed labor, skilled & unskilled, and products of the soil [still remain with us.] To direct the employments of these is a problem deserving the most serious attention of Congress. If employment can be given to all the labor offering itself prosperity necessarily follows. I have expressed the opinion, and repeat it again, that the first requisite to the accomplishment of this end is the substitution of a sound currency in place of one of a fluctuating values. This secured there are many interests that might be fostered to the great profit of both labor and Capital. How to induce Capital to employ labor is the question. The subject of Cheap transportation is one which has occupied the attention of Congress, and at the last session a Committee was appointed to look into this matter, and to report at this session.[7] It is to be hoped that this Committee will be able to throughw much light on the subject and also be able to suggest a practicable solution of it. It is important, ofand of general interest to all sections alike, and may well be regarded as a work for the Nation at large and not one to be left to individual enterprise. Should such work be undertaken it will serve directly to givinge employment to many thousands of hands, and indirectly to the employments of other tens of thousand. Next in importance to this is a revival of ship building, and particularly of iron Steam ship building. The United States is now paying over $100,000,000 00 per annum for freights and passage to foreign ships —to be carried abroad and expended in the employment and support of other peoples—beyond a fair percentage of what should go to forign vessels, estimating on the tonage and travel of the each respectively. Nations. It is to be regreted that this disparity in the carrying trade exists, and to correct it I would be willing to see a great departure from the usual course of government in supporting what might usually be termed private enterprises. I would not suggest as a remedy direct subsidy to American steam ship lines; but I would suggest the direct offer of ample compensation for carrying the mails between Atlantic Seaboard ~~Citizens~~ Cities and the Continent, on American owned and American built Steamers, and would extend this liberality to vessels carrying the mails to south American states, and to Central America & Mexico; and would pursue the same policy from our Pacific seaports to foreign seaports on the Pacific. It might be demanded that vessels built for this service should come up to a standard fixed by legislation, in tonnage, speed and all other qualities, looking to the possibility of government requiring them at some time for war purposes. The right also of taking possession of them in such emergency should be guarded. I offer these suggestions believing them worthy of consideration in all seriousness, effecting all sections and all interests alike. If anything better can be done to direct the country into a course of general prosperity no one will be more ready than me [I] to second the plan.

City Govt.

Forwarded herewith will be found the report of the Commissioners, appointed under an Act of ~~this~~ Congress, ~~at its first session~~ [approved June 20th 1874], to wind up the affairs of the District ~~of Columbia~~ Government; ~~and of also the report of the Board of Health~~. It will be seen from the former report that the [net] debt of, the District of Columbia ~~is as follows~~:

~~The net debt of the District~~, less securities on hand & available;[8] ~~as follow~~ [is] Bonded debt issued prior to July 1st /74 $8.883.940.43. Three sixty-five (3.65) bonds, Act of Congress June 20th 1874 $2.088.~~943.43~~ 168.73 Certificates of the Board of Audit $4.770.558.45, (making in all $15.742.667.61. less) special improvement assessments chargeable to private property, in excess of any demand against such assessments, $1.614.054.37. Less Chesapeake & Ohio Canal Bonds (above par in value) $75.000.00. Less Washington & & Alexandria R. R. Bonds $59,000.00. ~~In~~ [in] the hands of the Commissioner of the Sinking Fund. $1,748.054.37. leaving actual debt, less said assets, $13.994,613.24. In addition to this there are claims prefered against the Government of the District amounting in the [Estimated] aggregate—~~estimated~~—of [to] $3.147.787.48, ~~but~~ of which the greater part ~~must~~ [will probably] be rejected,—~~and cannot enter into~~ [This sum can, with no more pro-

priety be included in] the debt account of the District government
~~any more~~ than can the thousands of claims against the general government ~~can~~ be ~~estimated~~ [included] as a ~~part~~ [portion] of ~~its in-
debtedness~~ [the National debt]. ~~Here I will venture the one remark
that I have The District of Columbia should be regarded the as National Capital grounds; is an object of so much interest to the whole
people;—the whole District being sort of National public grounds,
claimable by every free and independent citizen as in part theirs,—a
Territory of which all citizens, naturalized~~

[In my opinion the Dist of Columbia should be regarded as
the grounds of the National Capital in which the entire people are
interested

I do not allude to this to urge generous appropriations to the
Dist but to draw ~~its attention~~ the attention of Congres[s] in framing
a law for the government of the ~~City~~ Dist. to the ~~manne~~ magnificent
scale ~~in~~ on which ~~it~~ the City was ~~laid out~~ planned by the founders
of the government the manner in which for ornamental purposes the
Streets reservations ~~avenues~~ and avenues ~~are~~ were laid out—and the
proportion of the ~~actual~~ property actually possessed by the Genl go
—I think the proportion of the expenses of the government and improvement to be borne by the general government—the City and
Dist should be ~~fully~~ carefully and equitably defined—]

I feel much indebted to the gentlemen who concented to leave
their private affairs, ~~to~~ [and] come from a distance to attend to the
business of this District;[9] and for the able and satisfactory manner in
which it has been conducted. I am sure their services will be equally
appreciated by the entire country.—

[I especially invite your attention to the recommendations of the
~~Funding Commission of the Dist—as relating~~ Commissioners of the
Sinking fund relative to the ambiguity of the act of June 20th 74—
the interest on the Dist bonds—and the consolidati~~ng~~on of the indebtedness of the Dist.

It will be seen from the accompanying full report of the Board of
Health ~~accompanying~~ that the sanitary condition of the Dist is very
satisfactory—

In accordance with Sectio 3 act apprvd June 23d 1874 I ap-

pointed a board ~~of Engineers~~ to make a survey of the Mouth of the
Missippi river with a view to ~~obtaining~~ determine the best method
of obtaining and maintaining a depth of water sufficient for the purposes of commerce &c. ~~The e board has not yet submitted its completed its report—work. As the report is received it will be submitted to Congress, and~~ in accordance with an act entitled "an act to
provide for the appointment of a commission of Engineers to investigate and report a permanent plan for the reclamation of the alluvial basin of the Missippi River subject to inundation." I appointed a
commission of Engrs—neither board ~~have~~ has yet completed ~~ther~~
its labors—when their reports are received they will ~~f~~ be forwarded
to Congress without delay.] [10]

ADf (bracketed material not in USG's hand), ICarbS. The full message includes synopses
of foreign relations, especially involving Japan, Great Britain, Spain, and Mexico; unsatisfactory expatriation and citizenship laws; new ships constructed for the U.S. Navy; and political unrest in La., Ark., and other Southern states. Copy (printed), DNA, RG 130, Messages to Congress. *Foreign Relations, 1874,* pp. iii–xxii. On Oct. 27, 1874, and subsequently,
Secretary of State Hamilton Fish recorded in his diary. "President mentions that he wishes
two subjects considered in connection with his Annual Message to Congress. First. With
reference to proposed Reciprosity Treaty, with Canada; and suggests that it should be recommended to reject the treaty, as inexpedient, while this country is suffering under an irredeemable currency. I remind him that the treaty had been submitted only to Senate, and
without any recommendations but simply as a proposal of Congress; and that every indication pointed to the failure of its adoption, and that an executive recommendation proposing its rejection would be inconsistant with its submission to the Senate, and might be regarded as an act ~~toof~~ discourtesy towards Great Britain and Canada. And that the annual
message being addressed to both Houses there would be an inconsistency in referring
therein to a treaty which was pending before the Senate alone, in executive session. Second subject—The want of equivalent advantages in the navigation regulations and trade
between the United States and Cuba   He thinking it may be expedient to adopt some retaliatory legislation. He wishes it noted as a subject of consideration." "November 17th . . .
President recurs to the discriminating tariff of Spain agt our ports in Island of Cuba, working very disadvantageously to the United States, notwithstanding that the same tariff applies to imports from all other countries, but in consequence of our proximity & greater
trade, working more disastrously against the United States—To the inquiry, whether he
will recommend any retaliatory legislation, he thinks it will be sufficient to state the facts
& leave Congress to act—I remind him that the facts have already been communicated to
Congress and that without specific recommendations, it is not probable that Congress will
take action—Without definitely deciding on this point he expresses the opinion that Congress should do so, . . . In Cabinet, while speaking of subjects for the Message the President requested me to recommend to Congress an appropriation for the payment to San
Domingo of the second year's rent of the Samana Bay. I advise agt any allusion to the Subject in the Message, arguing that the subject had better originate in Congress under a resolution calling for information whether any amount was due—President assents not to in-

troduce Subject in his Annual message, reserving possibility of submitting it in a special message—" "November 24—. . . Various questions in connection with the Message, resumption of specie payment, tariff, and internal taxation are discussed, also question of government of Alaska" "Tuesday—December 1 . . . Message discussed—President reads a rough draft of what he proposes to say with reference to currency & resumption of specie payments   Very decided in its tendency & positiveness—Rather roughly & carelessly written—Some criticisms were made, & alterations of style & of thought were suggested, & adopted by him. . . ." "Decr 3rd . . . President read draft of his message, excepting that part relating to currency & finance which he had read on Tuesday—in the main a very good document, better written than some former ones, subjected to more criticism in a friendly spirit & more discussion than on any previous occasion—The part relating to reorganization of Southern States especially Arkansas was modified after considerable discussion—Bristow, Jewell & myself urging modifications, Delano, Williams & Robeson atty opposing them—Assertions of questionable powers on the part of the Executive & the expression conceding certain powers to Congress were those objected to on constitutional principles . . ." DLC-Hamilton Fish.

On Nov. 29 and Dec. 6, correspondents reported from Washington, D. C. "The President has written a portion of his message, and will devote several hours each day to labor upon it till it is completed. The message this year is awaited with unusual interest, in the expectation that it may have an important influence upon the political situation. The President's views upon most of the important topics which he will discuss in his message are, however, already well known through his official statements or acts. . . ." "The President's Message is not yet quite complete, owing to a delay in receiving the report of the District of Columbia Commissioners, a reference to which will be added to the Message to-morrow morning. Copies of the Message are being made to-day for Congress and the representatives of the press associations. . . . The President says that although he did not commence the preparation of his Message until a week ago yesterday, some of the newspapers previously prognosticated its contents, although he had consulted nobody as to what it should contain. . . ." *New York Times*, Nov. 30, Dec. 7, 1874.

On Dec. 7, U.S. Representative James A. Garfield of Ohio wrote in his diary. "Happily the President was induced to keep out of his message his scheme for employing the laborers of the country by large appropriations. I rejoice that he holds firmly in favor of specie payments." Harry James Brown and Frederick D. Williams, eds., *The Diary of James A. Garfield* (East Lansing, Mich., 1967–81), II, 400. On Dec. 3, a correspondent had reported from Washington, D. C. "It is no secret that several prominent members of the Republican Party have endeavored to persuade the President and Secretary of the Treasury to make no recommendation for a speedy return to specie payments. Their arguments are directed wholly to the effect upon the Republican organization, and they fear that the taking of a positive and radical position with respect to specie payments will result in hopeless division of the party." *New York Times*, Dec. 4, 1874.

On Dec. 11, Gerrit Smith, Peterboro, N. Y., wrote to USG. "I must not bore you with my frequent writings—But occasionally I write something, which, I think, you will read approvingly. The accompanying Circular closes with an extract from your recent Message, which I am happy to say is a highly satisfactory Message. I hope you are blest with good health." ALS, Gilder Lehrman Collection, NNP. See Smith's broadside dated Peterboro, Dec. 12, "Will the American People never cease to oppress and torture the helpless poor?," an appeal for "the pending Civil Rights Bill." Smith died on Dec. 28.

On Dec. 24, Elihu B. Washburne, Paris, wrote to Fish. ". . . As the true text of the Message is read, the portion of it in regard to Cuba, is highly commended as statesman-like, moderate and just. You will have heard before receiving this of the scandalous misrepresentation of this part of the Message which was telegraphed to Europe by Reuter's Telegram Company. That false version of the Message created a bad impression here and was a means of very materially depressing the Bourse. It was not until the full text of the Message was received here that the fraud was discovered.... As this despatch in some measure concerns the President, I would feel particularly obliged to you if you would call his attention to it." LS (press), DLC-Elihu B. Washburne. *Foreign Relations, 1875,* I, 452–53. On Jan. 11, 1875, Fish showed Washburne's dispatch to USG. Hamilton Fish diary, DLC-Hamilton Fish. On Nov. 30, 1874, a Reuter-Havas agent, New York City, had written to Orville E. Babcock. "Once more I dare to intrude upon your valuable time. The important moment is approaching when I am called upon to secure the most rapid transmission of the Annual Message. Although I am still under the full impression of the decided answer which you gave me last year, I venture to remind you of the great difficulties which I had to overcome and which rendered the Presidential Message, as telegraphed to London, almost valueless in consequence of the confounding of the Treasury Report with the Message by the misreading of one cipherword. I will not undertake to impress you again, esteemed General, with the necessity of the most rapid cable transmission of a document, the value of which can not be rated highly enough, but I dare to ask you if you would condescend and allow me to prepare a telegraphic summary which I would entrust with you until the message has been handed over to the Representatives of the Nation. The benefit of such a concession on your part to the Representative of two Companies, embracing Europe Asia and South America, is immeasurable in so far as misstatements or misinterpretations can be prevented. Another reason why I should not be placed on equal footing with the Representatives of the American Press is the difference in time between America and Europe.— From the steps of the Capitol President Grant's words without exception are handed over to the American Press and sent off by a flash over the telegraphic wires, but I have scrupulously to select every word of importance, carefully preventing any possible mistake. If it is in your power, esteemed General, to grant such a concession please inform me by telegraph, and I shall, at the proper time, pay my respects to you at Washington." ALS, ICN. On Dec. 3, Babcock drafted a reply. "... I have again to repeat my inability to comply with your request and hope that you will consider the declension in no way personal to yourself." ADf (initialed), *ibid.* On Dec. 22, *The Times* (London) editorialized: "... We have now the unpleasant duty of informing our readers that we and they have been deceived.... we reproduced what purported to be an exact extract, given between inverted commas, from General GRANT's Message respecting the state of affairs in Cuba. The full text of the Message has now reached us, and we find that no such language had been used by the PRESIDENT. The agent of Baron REUTER at New York has evidently deceived him, and has been the means of deceiving the whole of Europe. Instead of the bellicose language attributed to the PRESIDENT, the words actually used were so colourless and pacific that no Foreign Secretary of England, overweighted with the responsibility of his position, could be more discreet than General GRANT was. The paragraphs which we trustfully reproduced were, in fact, nothing more than the unauthorized anticipations at New York of what might have been spoken.... Many on this side of the Atlantic were induced to believe that the PRESIDENT had made a desperate attempt to revive a decaying reputation by the suggestion of foreign war, when, in truth, he had spoken with a degree of moderation and self-restraint which could not have been surpassed by the responsible Minister of any European country...." See also *The Times* (London), Dec. 8, 23, 1874. On Jan. 26, 1875, Egbert T. Smith, Brook Haven, N. Y., wrote to USG. "Having been introduced to you at the time of your second Inaugeration and having not long since returned from Louisiana I take the liberty to write you in relation to Louisiana affairs   From the outset I have approved your course as the old Spirit of the Rebellion is there almost as strong as during the war . . . I will also state that I heartily concur with you in relation to Cuba (so does nearly every body) as lain down in your Message to Congress   I stopped in Havana upon my return from New Orleans and there is no doubt but the Rebellion has gained ground and that Spain is not as near crushing it as at the close of the third year of the war. She never can do it and as President Tyler said to Congress after the Texas insurrection had lasted five years 'It is time high time this war had ceased.' If I may be allowed to express a wish I would say I hope after this Louisiana Rebellion is done Congress will recognize her Independence. It would make Cuba Free. There would be no war with Spain but other nations would follow our example as in the case of the South American States and the Republican Party would be stronger than ever. With my best wishes for your Personal and Political welfare . . ." ALS, USG 3.

On Jan. 19, John A. Bingham, U.S. minister, Tokyo, wrote to USG. "I have read with great satisfaction your last annual message. Your recommendation that the interest accrued & to accrue on the Simonoseki indemnity hitherto paid by Japan to the United States be appropriated to the Education in Japan of American and Japanese youths is honorable alike to you & to our Country. The proposition is so politic & wise and will do so much, if adopted and carried out in good faith, to advance American influence and American interests in Japan that an English paper published in Yokohama has already been swift to denounce it and to utter such words concerning it as the writer doubtless thinks will prejudice the Japanese not only against the measure but against our Government & Country. That the Japanese are pleased with your message I have every reason to believe. This assault having been made upon your recommendation I took occasion to call the attention of the Foreign Minister of Japan to your Message with which he seemed to be much pleased: and without making any reference to the article or the conversation it is very significant that he has since sent me a dispatch dated yesterday saying that his government has authorized Mr. Yoshida the Japanese Minister at Washington to represent Japan at the Centennial & that a commission will also soon be appointed to attend the exhibition & exhibit Japanese productions &c. Of all this I have acquainted Mr Fish in two dispatches by this mail, in one of which I enclose the article by the English press referred to. When I declined to press the payment of the Indemnity in the absence of instructions last year the English Press made my conduct the subject of comment & my government the subject of abuse, as they did also when I received the unpaid balance of the indemnity in pursuance of my instructions. There is an exceeding jealousy of America among Europeans here which I have no doubt was the cause of the complaints made against me concerning which I wrote Mr Fish in my despatch No 131 last year & called your attention thereto in former letters. I deeply regret the result of the October & November Elections, but I do not attribute that result to any dissatisfaction with you or with your Administration but to the unhappy divisions among our friends in Congress & out of Congress on questions of vital importance to the country which divisions ought to have been & could have been healed. After the solemn pledge of the Republicans in the Acts of 1862 & 1869 to redeem in coin the legal tender notes & the Bonds of the United States there should have been no intimation in Congress or out of it among Republicans of a purpose to repudiate the plighted faith of the party & of the nation. As I understand it, there were such intimations so understood by the people and hence in the Elections they repudiated repudiation and the very appearance of repudiation. All that has been lost can be recovered, by wise & just action before the final vote of 1876. In my opinion the party cannot hold its own with the people by continuing as it has for the past two years to assail its own men & measures without any good cause or even colorable excuse. It seems to me that some of the men so clamorous against the party & its most active members manifestly to make room for their own advancement have been taught a lesson by which if they are wise they will profit. It is not good at this age of the world to play the role of the over-righteous who Eighteen centuries ago in the public streets & upon all occasions proclaimed that they were *not like other men.* Our party I hope will stand by all that is good that has been tried & proved & accepted by the people in its past record—and will claim in the future as in the past to follow its own judgement upon all questions Subject only to the requirements of the Constitution & the laws & not the judgement of the Enemies of the party & of the Country. Be pleased to accept for yourself & Mrs Grant the assurance of my hearty wishes that the New Year may be to both of you a year of happiness and prosperity." ALS, *ibid.* See *Foreign Relations, 1875,* II, 783. On Dec. 16, 1874, J. A. McKnight, Lawrence, Kan., had written to USG. "Having been a boy yourself, and having started at the foot of the 'Ladder of Fame,' and now safely landed at the topmost round, you will understand and consider the feeling which prompts me to the act of addressing you. Sir, I have read your last annual Message, and my admiration of the sound judgement therein displayed, is unbounded. But there was one passage, in which you refer to allowing a certain number of young men to learn the Japanese language, to aid in the more satisfactory mode of a National intercourse with that Realm, and that is the passage of which I presume to speak, and enquire. It is obvious that Congress will [a]ct and [ac]cept that suggestion, and a number of *favored* young men, will receive those appointments. I am now 19 years old, and have fought the battle of Life for myself, for about 7 years. Have traveled some little in the western part of the United States,—In Nevada, Idaho, Utah, Montana, Wyoming, and Colorado; have gained some knowledge of the world and humanity, and am now struggling for an education, attending, at present, the Kansas State university. My means are limited. I have a great desire to do something for my Country, and to succeed in life myself. . . ." ALS, DNA, RG 59, Miscellaneous Letters. On Dec. 21, J. R. Branson, Franklin College, New Athens, Ohio, wrote to USG. "Having seen in your late message your submission to Congress of the propriety of devoting a portion of the Simonsky Indemnity fund if not the whole of the income from it, to the Education of a number of young men in the Japanese language, to be under obligations to serve the Government a specified time as Interpreters at the legation and the consulates in Japan and being desirous of going to that Country and study that language, I have come to the conclusion to give to you my offer to be one of those young men, . . ." ALS, *ibid.,* Letters of Application and Recommendation. No appointments followed.

1. See next text for remarks on this subject not incorporated into the annual message.
2. In an undated letter, George M. Rodgers, Chicago, wrote to USG. "I respectfully submit the enclosed prints, requesting that advise be furnished me in regard to marked portion of same, Viz: Can I either for myself or for a (Southern planter Co) go to China and contract with Chinese labor, to come with *me,* and work on *my* plantation, for three or five years" ALS (docketed Jan. 11, 1875), *ibid.,* Miscellaneous Letters. The enclosed clippings are *ibid.*
3. Joseph H. Blackfan graduated from Princeton in 1844 and entered the post office dept. as a clerk in 1853. On Nov. 29, 1874, a correspondent reported from Washington, D. C. "Mr. Blackfan, Superintendent of the Foreign Mail Bureau of the Post Office Department, who has just returned from Switzerland, speaks in enthusiastic terms of the success of his mission to the Postal Congress. . . ." *New York Times,* Nov. 30, 1874. See *Washington Post,* Nov. 25, 1883.
4. The remainder of this paragraph supplanted the Draft Annual Message Fragment, [*Dec. 1, 1874*].
5. On Dec. 5, T. Follett Ware, New York City, wrote to USG. "We have rumours here

that there will be a vacancy on the Supreme bench in which case may I as one of your firm supporters call to your attention the name of the Hon. Francis L. Smith of Alexandria Va —he is one of the leading lawyers of the country & would be an ornament to the highest court & whose appointment would give eminent satisfaction to the entire country. An old line whig in politics, a friend of Mr Clay, & always admired for his conservative views. May I beg your kind consideration of my letter in case a vacancy does occur . . . ps Mr Smith is a most intimate personal friend of Mr Saml Shoemaker of Baltimore Md." ALS, DNA, RG 60, Applications and Recommendations. Congress did not enlarge the Supreme Court; no appointment followed.

    6. See *PUSG*, 22, 297–300.

    7. See *HRC*, 44-1-360. No bill passed. Congress had received several communications concerning cheap transportation. See, for example, *HMD*, 43-1-147 and *SMD*, 43-1-104.

    8. On Dec. 5, Babcock wrote to D. C. commissioners. "The President will be pleased if you will send him the following information—as early to-day as convenient. Net debt of the Dist. of Col. less securities on hand and available. Amount of certificates issued by Board of Audit to date. Amount needed to complete outstanding contracts for improvements." Copy, DLC-USG, II, 2. On the same day, William Dennison, Henry T. Blow, and John H. Ketcham, D. C. commissioners, wrote to USG supplying the requested financial information. LS, USG 3.

    On Dec. 19, Levi P. Luckey wrote to Secretary of the Treasury Benjamin H. Bristow. "The President directs me to request you to be good enough to have H. Res. 119 just referred to you, extending the Board of Audit for the District, examined & reported upon as soon as possible, as there are many poor workmen in the City whose payment, he understands, awaits his approval of the Resolution." ALS, DNA, RG 56, Letters Received from the President. On the same day, Bristow wrote to USG. "I have the honor to return herewith House Resolution No. 119 'to continue the Board of Audit to examine and audit the funded and floating debt of the District of Columbia;' and to state that no reasons are known to this Department why the same should not become a law." Copy, *ibid.*, Letters Sent to the President. See *CR*, 43–2, 13–14, 33–35.

    9. See message to Congress, June 20, 1874, note 1.

    10. See Proclamation, July 3, 1874.

Draft Annual Message Fragment

[*Dec. 7, 1874*]

So much for what I believe a solemn pledge by the Goverment; Now there remains a duty no less solemn, to the Citizen who pays the taxes that support and save the credit of the Nation—

At the present time there is a large surplus of Capital in the principle centers of trade awaiting employment. This would, to the casual observer, indicate that more paper money exists than is necessary for the transaction of the business of the Country. The truth is however,—from my reading [of] the signs of the times—that since the financial panic of last Summer, holders of "ready money" have become exceedingly timid believing that legislation would necessarily result on the subject of finance by this Congress. Inability to see what this legislation ~~was to might~~ may be:—whether contractive or expansive—whether prices were to be increased or lessened—whether the possible legislation might not produce another panic which would give undue value to ready capital either to lend at usurious rates, or for the purchase of bonds, stocks or real estate, far below its value— has led to ~~hoarding~~ rejecting ~~to~~ loan unless an amount of security is given ~~that~~ which will secure a return at the shortest possible notice.

There is another fact which seems plain to me. The Eastern & Middle states, from their wealth, density of population being largely a Manufacturing, ~~people~~ Mercantile and Commercial people, requiring at all times ready capital at hand, have accumulated the money of the country to them, to ~~their~~ the detriment of the balance of the country and of themselves. ~~too.~~ To a great extent the consumption of the articles produced, or traded in, has been stopped by the lack of means—cash—to be obtained where abundance of property is owned to give security if the money was to be obtained on that security.

To you belongs the task of passing such a financial bill as will relieve and set free the industries of the Country—that will be in harmony with the repeated pledges of Congress, and of the republican party platforms: that will be equitable to all sections of the Country.

My own views are,—after as careful a study of the subject as I have been able to give it—the remidy is in free banking, with restrictions that look to specie resumption at as early a day as [is] practicable. Resumption cannot commence until there is specie in the country to redeem with. While the precious metals are not used as currency they become simply articles of commerce. All suplus will go to the best market, regardless of the condition of trade between us and foreign nations. With the balance largely in our favor the surplus, would go just as freely as if the balance was the other way.

Thus it looks plain to me that something should be done to keep these metals at home until there is [a] sufficient quanty of it to redeem in specie. After that the subject will take care of itself. I would repeat therefore the suggestion that the revenue of the country be so increased that the goverment may increase its coin reserve, and that the banks be required to hold, as a part of their reserve, either all or a fixed part of the coin interest which they receive upon the bonds held as security for their circulation.

With this, *free banking*, I think, would be entirely safe and would not only not prove an expansion—in the end—but a contraction. As now situated the mass of prosperous farmers and planters of the Country are so located that they cannot use ~~the~~ banks for deposite. In the fall or early winter the proceeds of their years labor come in, —requiring at that season of the year a very large amount of ready Capital to transact the business of the Country—and is ~~thus~~ taken home and locked up only going out in ~~driblets~~ [small sums] as purchases have to be made or wages paid, ~~thus~~ through the year. In this way [except once or twice a year] a large proportion of the Capital of the Country is prevented from performing its function of keeping alive industry & enterprize ~~more than once or twice a year~~. With banks convenient this money would be deposited and used over and over. Manufacturies would spring up where they do not exist now because unencumbered real estate would command the means for their establishment.

I submit these views for your consideration, hoping that something better may be adopted, but earnestly urging that speedy action may be had on the subject of *Banking* & *Finance*, or that the declaration be made that no action ~~shall~~ will be taken. The business interests of the Country demand that the action of Congress on this subject should be known at an early day.

ADf (facsimile, bracketed material not in USG's hand), USGA. This text was omitted from the final version of the annual message.

To William P. Kellogg

Washington D. C.
Dec. 9th 1874.

To Govr W. P. KELLOGG.
NEW ORLEANS. LA.

Your dispatch of this date just received. It is exceedingly unpalatable to use troops in anticipation of danger. Let the State authorities be right and then proceed with their duties, without apprehension of danger, and if they are then molested the question will be determined whether the United States is able to maintain law and order within its limits or not.

U. S. GRANT.

Copies, USG 3; DNA, RG 60, Letters from the President. *SD*, 57-2-209, 158. On Dec. 9, 1874, Governor William P. Kellogg of La. telegraphed to USG. "Information reaches me that the White League purpose making an attack upon the state House Especially that portion occupied by the Treasurer of the state   the organization is very numerous and well armed and the state forces now available are not sufficient to resist successfully any movement they make   with a view of preventing such an attempt and the bloodshed which would be likely to result should an insurgent body again take possession of the State House and in dispersing them, I respectfully request that a detachment of U. S. troops be stationed in that portion of the st Louis hotel which is not used for any of the state officers where they will be readily available to prevent any such insurrectionary movement as that Contemplated" Telegram received (at 3:00 P.M.), Belknap Papers, NjP. *SED*, 43-2-13, 16; *SD*, 57-2-209, 158.

On Dec. 10, Kellogg telegraphed to USG. "I transmit the following dispatch by request Ex Gov Wells President of the returning Board . . . New Orleans, Dec 10th 1874 To PRESIDENT GRANT, Authentic information in possession of the returning Board justifies them in believing that an attack is intended upon the st Louis Hotel now occupied as a state House wherein the returning Board holds its sessions and where the returns of the late Election are deposited   the board has nearly completed a careful and impartial canvass of the returns in compliance with law and Expect to make promulgation therefrom as soon as the same can be properly compiled   the members of the Board are being publicly and privately threatened with violence and an attack upon the state House which is likely to result in bloodshed is also theatened,   by request of the Board I respectfully ask that a detachment of troops be stationed in the state House so that the deliberations and final action of the Board may be free from intimidation and violence,   J. MADISON WELLS, Prest of state Returning Board" Telegram received, DNA, RG 60, Letters from the President. *SED*, 43-2-13, 16.

On Dec. 16, Secretary of War William W. Belknap wrote to AG Edward D. Townsend. "The President directs that Gen'l. Emory be instructed to make arrangements to be in readiness to suppress violence ~~to suppress violence~~, and to have it ~~so~~ understood, that he will do it—" ALS, DNA, RG 94, Letters Received, 3579 1874. See Endorsement, Sept. 23, 1874; message to Senate, Jan. 13, 1875.

To Hamilton Fish

Washington D. C. Dec. 11th *1874*

DEAR GOVERNOR:

Suppose on the arrival of King Kalekaua to-morrow you with the party that accompanies him come directly to the White House. I will be here to meet you.

I think Monday will be the evening for the reception, and Wednesday for the dinner. If you will give the official notification for the reception—in the order we spoke of—I will be much obliged.

Very Truly Yours

U. S. GRANT

HON. HAMILTON FISH
SEC. OF STATE

ALS, DLC-Hamilton Fish. On Dec. 11, 1874, Friday, Secretary of State Hamilton Fish wrote to USG. "I have just now learnt that King Kalakaua will reach Washington tomorrow at half past Eleven—If you have no objections, I will endeavor to arrange the first visit for tomorrow afternoon at about three or four o clk, as may be agreeable, mutually, to you, & to him   In Company with the Secretaries of War & Navy, I go at half past ten to meet him at a Station a short distance from the City—Shall any thing be said about a reception on Monday Evenig, or a dinner at any subsequent date   I will call in the morning, before going to meet the King, to receive any instructions you may have to give" ALS (press), *ibid.* Illness prevented King Kalakaua from meeting USG the next day. See Hamilton Fish diary, Dec. 12–13, 1874, *ibid.*

On Dec. 4, King Kalakaua, San Francisco, had telegraphed to USG. "Kalakaua, King of the Hawaiian Islands, sends greetings to his great and good friend the President of the United States of America. He acknowledges a generous reception, characteristic of a warm-hearted people, and will hasten to express in person those sentiments of sincere respect and lasting friendship entertained toward the President of the great nation he so worthily represents." *New York Tribune,* Dec. 5, 1874. On the same day, a reply was telegraphed from Washington, D. C. "The President of the United States extends the cordial welcome of the nation to his great and good friend, His Royal Highness Kalakaua, on his arrival in the United States, and tenders his personal congratulations on the safety of his voyage. The President anticipates with great pleasure the opportunity of a personal greeting, and assures His Highness of the sincere friendship which in common with the people of the United States he entertains for His Royal Highness, and hopes that his journey across the continent may be guarded by a kind Providence." *Ibid.* On Dec. 5, Fish recorded in his diary. "Allen & Carter (Hawaii) think the King will probably leave San Francisco to-day, but have no positive information on that point, nor whether he will come through without stopping nor the number of persons in his suite. I desire them to obtain information on those points & to let me know—. . . They then converse on proposed Reciprocity Treaty, & I indicate to them the difficultyies which I anticipate, not only on general objections to any Reciprocity Treaty, but also as arising from the pendency of a Reciprocity Treaty with Canada which will be opposed on other grounds than those which would apply only to a Treaty with Hawaii—. . ." DLC-Hamilton Fish.

On Dec. 8, Levi P. Luckey wrote to Gen. William T. Sherman, St. Louis. "The President wishes me to write you and say that on the arrival of the King of the Sandwich Islands he will have to entertain him by giving a reception at which all departments of the government, civil and military, will be invited to be present. Also a dinner at which he wants the Cabinet, the Chief Justice & others & the heads of the Army & Navy to be present. If you can come on the President says that we will telegraph you the time &c. Awaiting your reply, . . ." ALS, DLC-William T. Sherman.

On Dec. 14, Fish wrote to USG. "A note from Mr Allen informs me that the King is still quite indisposed, & unable as yet to make any appointment—he hopes to be able to do so tomorrow" AL (initialed, press), DLC-Hamilton Fish. On Dec. 19, Fish recorded in his diary. "The President last night had a Reception for the King at which were present the members of the Cabinet; Senators, Members of the House the Diplomatic Corps, The Supreme and District Courts and officers of the Army and Navy on duty here. On the arrival of the King the President met him in the vestibule and escorted him into the 'Blue Room' where Mrs Grant and the ladies of the Cabinet and part of the company were already assembled. . . . When Mrs Williams entered she was received in a cold and distant manner by Mrs Grant and subquently complained of it and enquired of Genl. Babcock and others what was the cause." *Ibid.* On Dec. 22, USG hosted a dinner for King Kalakaua. Hamilton Fish diary, Dec. 22, 1874, *ibid.* See *PUSG*, 24, 70–73; Proclamation, Jan. 22, 1875; *Foreign Relations, 1875*, I, 669–79; Gavan Daws, *Shoal of Time: A History of the Hawaiian Islands* (New York, 1968), pp. 201–3.

To Principal Chiefs of Samoa

To their Highnesses
The Taimua and Pule or Principal Chiefs of Samoa
Great and Good Friends

I have received through Col. A. B. Steinberger whom I sent to your Islands as a special agent of the United States the interesting letter of the 3d of October 1873 which you were pleased to address to me,[1]   I am gratified to learn from that communication that peace prevails in your country

This is among the greatest blessings vouchsafed to nations and I hope that your enjoyment of it may be without interruption—You also inform me that the Samoan government had adopted a flag—

This is an interesting event in your history. My prayer is that as it is an emblem of your unity and independence these may ever remain inviolable except by the general consent of your people—

Your course generally as reported to me by Col Steinberger deserves my cordial approval and encouragement which I offer you,   I trust that you will persevere in well doing   although the chief city of the United States whence I am writing to you, is far away from your Islands being near the coast of the Atlantic ocean, our Territory extends to the shores of the other ocean in which your Islands lie at a not much greater distance from San Francisco than is the City of Washington which is our Capital—Being then much nearer to us than to any European nation, on this account alone, it would be natural were there no other reasons that we should take a lively interest in your welfare, and in all that concerns you—

The Staff, the Fly Flap, and the "Sacred Mat" which you intrusted to Col Steinberger, were safely delivered by him and were received by me in the spirit with which they were offered—You may be assured that, I am duly sensible of the significance of these gifts—

Colonel Steinbergers course during his first mission has so far met my approval and he seems to have made himself so acceptable to you, that I have authorized him again to visit you for the purpose of informing me of the progress of your affairs since he left you—I pray you therefore to receive him kindly and to continue to him the good will which you showed on the former occasion

I pray God to have you in his safe and holy keeping—
Written at Washington, this 11th day of December 1874

U. S. GRANT

Copy, DNA, RG 59, Despatches from Special Agents. *HED*, 44-1-161, 77, 44-2-44, 66, 104. See letter to Hamilton Fish, Aug. 17, 1874. On Dec. 11, 1874, Secretary of State Hamilton Fish wrote to Albert B. Steinberger, Washington, D. C. "The President having determined to authorize you again to proceed to the Samoan group in the character of a Special Agent of the United States, you will embark for those Islands at San Francisco in a man of war on board of which the Secretary of the Navy has been requested to direct you to be provided with a passage. The expense attending this and of your mission generally must be borne by yourself, and will in no event be recognized as a proper charge against the government. Pursuant to the suggestion contained in your letter from Baltimore of the 19th of November last, the President has addressed the accompanying sealed communication to the Timua or Pule of Samoa; a copy of which is also furnished for your information. You will make proper arrangements for presenting the original. The special Passport with which you are also herewith provided, describes your official character. I annex hereto a list of articles which have been furnished by several of the Departments, which will be entrusted to you as presents as suggested by you. There is no doubt from your report and from information received from other sources, that the Samoan group is naturally fertile and has many resources. Its position, too, in the Pacific is commanding and particularly important to us. It is more than doubtful, however, whether these considerations would be sufficient to satisfy our people that the annexation of those Islands to the United States is essential to our safety and prosperity. In any event, supposing that the general sentiment should be favorable to such a measure, I am not aware that it has received such an expression as would require an acknowledgment by the government and warrant measures on our part accordingly. It is deemed inexpedient without such a call from the public to originate a measure adverse to the usual traditions of the government and which, therefore, probably would not receive such a sanction as would be likely to secure its success. Under these circumstances, your functions will be limited to observing and reporting upon Samoan affairs and to impressing those in authority there with the lively interest which we take in their happiness and welfare." Copy, DNA, RG 59, Diplomatic Instructions, Special Missions. *HED*, 44-1-161, 76, 44-2-44, 102–3.

On May 12, 1875, Tagaloa and thirteen others, "Taimua of Samoa," Mulinu'u, wrote to USG. "We have received, from Colonel A. B. Steinberger, your very excellent letter, which was written on the 11th December, 1874. Our joy is very great, and our thankfulness to your Excellency, in that you have been pleased to regard us, and accept our letter and our petition which were sent to you. That was indeed a red letter day for us, and all the people of Samoa, on which Colonel Steinberger first gave us your letter, and we perused it, and we also again looked upon the person of Colonel Steinberger who had returned to Samoa. Then, thus was our thanksgiving, 'the will of God is good,'—it is He who has enabled you to regard us, and to appoint him to Samoa to become a source of light in all matters which will give right and solidity to our Government and the Laws which have been set up in Samoa. You are aware, our weakness and ignorance is very great, our land has not been accustomed to these affairs;—it is, as it were, a new thing to us. Our anxiety was very great, during the time that we had not received an answer, whether you would accept our wish or not, as also from false stories of vagrants in Samoa. But now their stories are things of the past, we have no longer any doubts, our thoughts are only those of thanks and rejoicing because of your letter, and Colonel Steinberger who is the full pledge of your kindness towards us. On account of this we are now of good courage and have confidence, and also great strength. All the encouraging words in your letter are very good to our thinking, we will heed them. We are very grateful indeed for the present from your Excellency, and your Government,—the weapons which were brought by Colonel Steinberger to us, to strengthen our Government, because since he reached us and gave us these weapons, our Government has not been hampered in any way, no one has attempted to originate quarrels as was our foolish custom in days gone by. Although we are well aware that we can be of no use to you and your Government, it is right for you thus to show friendship to us, but it is on account of your free-will to us and our land that you have given us these handsome presents. We have received from Colonel Steinberger the new flag, which was made for our Government, we deliberated whether we would receive it. We have resolved to accept it gratefully, because it is a very beautiful flag, and we have now adopted it as the sign that our country is one, and desirous of establishing a new Government. We are also very desirous of keeping stedfast our present prosperity, and that by God's will, it may not again be interrupted. We are about to commence this year fresh plans which we hope will give unity to our Government, we are now in fact beginning this with Colonel Steinberger. His zeal is very great in helping us and showing us things that are right and useful. We still esteem this gentleman very highly on account of his love and humility and great forbearance, inasmuch as great is our inexperience and slowness of comprehension at present. But he is not disheartened on that account, on the contrary, it is as though our darkness and slowness are the cause of his being more zealous and energetic by night and by day to make things plain to us, just as is the true love of a father to his children. Our pleasure in Colonel Steinberger is still very great, and our prayer to God is that he may be pleased that nothing in his providence may happen to cause his speedy removal from amongst us, but that he may remain with us in Samoa till his death. Our reason for this is that we are well aware that this gentleman is very useful indeed to our land, through him our Government is for the first time strong, and able, as it were, to stand and walk about, so also with all arrangements regarding our Laws. Captain Erben, the Commander of the war-ship 'Tuscarora' has also been with us for some time; the zeal of that gentleman in encouraging us was indeed great, the behaviour also of the officers and all his crew was excellent before us and all the Samoan people,—all that they did in Samoa was very good indeed. The words which we have written in this letter are not many lest you should get weary in reading it, but your letter we shall preserve that future generations of Samoans may peruse it. We send our best respects to your Excellency. May the ever-living God be pleased to preserve your Government for ever." D (in Samoan), DNA, RG 59, Miscellaneous Letters; translation, *ibid.*

On Oct. 19, Malietoa I, Mulinu'u, wrote to USG. "I now write to your Excellency so as to give you some ideas of our Government in Samoa. Mulinu'u is the capital of Samoa, the Laws of our Government are established there. We have formed two Houses, the House of Lords (Taimua), and the House of Commons (Faipule); these two houses make all the Laws for Samoa. We have appointed for our various Districts Governors, Judges, Magistrates and other Officers. I, & all the Chiefs, and people are very pleased with the Laws because by the Laws we know what is bad, it is not good if people are let have their own way in badness. We are very thankful that Colonel Steinberger the Premier has arrived here it is like the love of God to our country   our wish is still to have this Gentleman with us because these people are so obstinate,   now, the darkness is passing the sun is rising and the people are getting clearly to understand Laws. We are very pleased with this wise and kind hearted Gentleman,   the Samoans sympathize with him on account of his very hard work,   he has no rest from teaching us all things so that we might all become wise. There is another thing I want to mention to your Highness. There are a number of White men from different Countries who have lived in Samoa for many years who are spreading bad reports against the Samoan Government, and the Premier. Some White men are angry because the Premier has not given them any Offices; notwithstanding their hinderance, slander, and spreading reports against this Gentleman, we pay no heed or attention to them. This is my desire that I will communicate to you the President of the United States, and Congress, that Colonel Steinberger the Premier remain in our country until his death, and that you will respect his work of love to the Samoan Government, and that this country

may still prosper, and that all the Great Nations may protect it. This is all my letter to your
Excellency the Highest Chief   May God Almighty make you prosper" DS (in Samoan),
ibid., Despatches from Special Agents; translation, *ibid. HED*, 44-1-161, 96.

On Oct. 30, Le Mana and fifteen others, "Taimua of Samoa," wrote to USG. "This is
our letter to your Excellency to give you some information respecting our Government
now a days. We are very pleased because we have got a Government, we thank God for his
great goodness in permitting us to have this quietness, and also that our country is happy,
it was not so in years gone bye. We are also thankful for his goodness in that you sent us
the Gentleman Colonel A B Steinberger, he is a light to our path all the time. We are still
very pleased with Col A B Steinberger and we wish to help him because he does every thing
justly and he is so indefatigable, and he is also always so very careful in every thing regarding this our Government, and he is so lenient with us and makes such allowances for
our stupidity and darkness   That is why we so much wish that it would please God Almighty that we still remain as one with this Gentleman in Samoa   We think now that
soon the darkness will leave Samoa and that light will come so that we might rejoice in it,
also all the comming races of Samoa. There is something else we want to explain to your
Excellency. 'There is a great deal of our land that was sold anyhow during our wartime to
different people of various nations now residing in Samoa; now all this land is to be sold
at Public Auction on the 17th day of January of the comming year by order of S S Foster
Consul of the United States of America   The reason why we mention this is that you
might see how it is, and give us your decision regarding it because it is all dark to us.' We
have not had an investigation into land titles because of the great press of work that the
Premier Col A B Steinberger and we have to do. These are just a few remarks that you
might see how things are. We send our greatest love to your Excellency. May it please God
that your Nation may prosper for ever." D (in Samoan), DNA, RG 59, Despatches from
Special Agents; translation, *ibid. HED*, 44-2-44, 5–6.

On Oct. 29, Steinberger, Mulinu'u, had written to Fish resigning as U.S. agent. LS,
DNA, RG 59, Despatches from Special Agents. *HED*, 44-1-161, 124. On Dec. 14, Fish recorded in his diary a conversation with USG. "I read to him Steinbergers resignation of his
claimed position as Agent of this Government and mention to him that Steinberger calls
himself premier of the King of Samoa and that he had sent a large bundle of papers among
them a proposed treaty between the United States and the King of Samoa   I ask him if he
wishes the letter replied to. He says no take no notice of it." DLC-Hamilton Fish.

On Jan. 20, 1876, Malietoa wrote to USG. "We have this day appointed Frank Platt a
special Commissioner to the government of the United States—to present the present
state of affairs in our Kingdom, and The said Frank Platt is granted diplomatic powers, as
well as being bearer of despatches—to beg from Your Excellency Peace, Amity, Friendship
and the protection of your moral support as a great nation" LS, DNA, RG 59, Despatches
from Special Agents. *HED*, 44-2-44, 70. On Sept. 7, 1875, Tuesday, Frank Platt, New York
City, had written to USG. "After the interview with you last Thursday I addressed Mr Fish
asking whether he had any despatches for the Samoan Islands, but up to this time have
[heard nothing] from him—I leave to night for SanFrancisco & will depart from there—
on the 13th inst   I should be most happy to serve you in any way—if it is possible for me
to do so address Grand Hotel San Francisco—With kind wishes for for the health and
prosperity of your Excellency, . . ." ALS, DNA, RG 59, Miscellaneous Letters. Probably on
Sept. 9, USG endorsed the docket. "If we should have any thing, it may go to the care of
this writer" AE, *ibid.* On Jan. 23, 1876, Steinberger wrote to USG. "May I beg that your
Excellency will [se]e all of my despatches & have them [pr]inted. I wish to assure Your

[Ex]cellency that all attempts from [the] US Consul & the English Officers [to] reach your kindly letters to [m]yself have *failed.* I mention [th]is because I wish ever to preserve [in]violate your confidence in [my]self. A weak nation—but it [is] as one man; prays for your [re]cognition—this will protect them [ag]ainst 200 German & English [tra]ders who have ruled them thro' [the] dread of a 'man of war'—The action of the 'Tuscarora' [& Ca]pt Erben will live forever in [the] grateful remembrance of these [pe]ople." ALS, *ibid.,* Despatches from Special Agents. *HED,* 44-2-44, 68.

On Feb. 24, "the Taimua and Faipule" (upper and lower houses) "of the Government of Samoa" wrote to USG. "This is our letter to inform you of great troubles which have come on us since the departure of Mr Platt bearer of dispatches from our Government to the United States Government. These troubles which have come on our government and disturbing the peace of such is all caused by S. S. Foster—U. S. Consul and the English Ship of war the Barracouta and the foremost among them is the English Missionaries. They have now arrested Col. A. B. Steinberger our Premier by order of Malietoa who was our King, and he is now a prisoner also, on board of the English Ship Barracouta. This scheme was concocted we find by Mr Turner the Missionary and Captain Stevens of the British ship of war the Barracouta,   between those two, they have led Malietoa astray, . . . On the 15th day of Feby. the Ship of war with the English Missionary Mr Turner, went to that Island and returned again with Malietoa to reïnstate him in his office. Ever since we are persecuted by the Captain, the two Consuls and the Missionaries to receive Malietoa again and place him in the position he formerly held, but we are decided and united not to have him again as our king, and still another thing they are persecuting us about is to give ourselves under the British protection and to throw up our desire to be protected by the United States of America. This is the reason we will await patiently for a United States Ship of war to assist us to investigate the meaning and cause of this persecution they are bringing on us. We all send your Excellency our love." D (in Samoan), DNA, RG 59, Despatches from Special Agents; translation, *ibid. HED,* 44-2-44, 70–71. See message to House of Representatives, May 1, 1876; R. P. Gilson, *Samoa 1830 to 1900: The Politics of a Multi-Cultural Community* (Melbourne, 1970), pp. 293–321; George Herbert Ryden, *The Foreign Policy of the United States in Relation to Samoa* (New Haven, 1933), pp. 112–42.

1. See *PUSG,* 24, 102–3.

To Anthony J. Drexel

Washington D. C. Dec. 15 *1874*

MY DEAR MR. DREXEL:

Mrs. Grant and I will be pleased if we can have the company of Mrs. Drexel, Miss Fannie & yourself for a week, commencing next Monday week. Our next State dinner is on Tuesday week, to the Supreme Court, and we would like to have you here for that. I invite Mr & Mrs. Childs for the same time.

Mrs. Grant and Nellie join me in kind regards to Mrs. Drexel, yourself and all the other members of your family.

Yours Truly

U. S. GRANT

ALS, Gallery of History, Las Vegas, Nev. For the state dinner, see *Washington Evening Star*, Jan. 6, 1875.

To Louis I

To HIS MAJESTY. LOUIS I.
KING OF PORTUGAL.
GREAT AND GOOD FRIEND:

Mr. Charles H. Lewis, who has for some time resided near the Government of Your Majesty in the character of Minister Resident of the United States, being about to return to his country, I have directed him to take leave of Your Majesty. Mr. Lewis, whose standing instructions had been to cultivate with your Government relations of the closest friendship, has been directed on leaving Lisbon, to convey to Your Majesty the assurance of our sincere desire to strengthen and extend the friendly intercourse now happily subsisting between the two Governments, and to secure to the people of both nations a continuance of the benefits resulting from that intercourse. The zeal with which he has fulfilled his former instructions leads me to hope that he will execute his last commission in a manner agreeable to Your Majesty.

Your Good Friend,

U. S. GRANT.

WASHINGTON, 18TH DECEMBER, 1874.

Copy, DNA, RG 84, Portugal, Despatches. Born in 1816 at Lewiston, Va., and trained as a lawyer, Charles H. Lewis served as secretary in the Reconstruction government of Governor Francis H. Pierpoint. On March 1, 1870, USG nominated Lewis as minister to Portugal. On Dec. 18, 1874, Fish wrote to Lewis, Lisbon. "Mr. Benjamin Moran, having been appointed to succeed you in the mission to Lisbon, I have now to acquaint you with the fact, and to enclose, herewith, a letter addressed by the President to His Majesty the King of Portugal, announcing your recall. . . ." Copy, DNA, RG 59, Diplomatic Instructions,

Portugal. See Fish to Lewis, Sept. 14, Oct. 27 (2), Nov. 13, and Dec. 10, copies, *ibid.*; Hamilton Fish diary, Dec. 9, 1874, DLC-Hamilton Fish; *PUSG*, 21, 463–64.

On Nov. 27, Fish had written to Robert C. Schenck, U.S. minister, London. "*Private* ... The President desires to mark his appreciation of Mr Moran's long & valuable services, & at the same to respond to the expressions of almost Every American who has been in London, during Mr Moran's long association with the Legation there, by advancing him, & as he expects that within a very short time a vacancy will exist in the Mission to Lisbon, he contemplates naming him thereto—He has decided to transfer to Lon[don], as Secretary of Legation, Mr H[of]fman, now occupying the Secretaryship in ~~London~~ Paris, & who, intimated his desire to be thus 'promoted,' at the time when it was supposed Mr Moran might have come into one of the places in this Department—Precisely how soon the vacancy may arise in Lisbon, is not at present known—While I desire that you be informed of the probable change, it is requested that for the present no publicity be allowed to the contemplated changes—All very busy getting ready for Congress—" ALS, OFH. See *PUSG*, 24, 337; *The Times* (London), Dec. 22, 1874.

On March 26, 1869, Wickham Hoffman, Paris, had written to Adam Badeau, Washington, D. C. "I wish you would hand this letter to Genl Grant, and say a word in its support. Washburne is kind enough to send me word that he wants me to stay here, and I shall be glad to stay till he is posted in the routine business of the legation. This would probably be for the interest of the service. But when he is so posted, if the Gen. could conveniently give me promotion, I should like it." ALS, DNA, RG 59, Letters of Application and Recommendation. On April 7, Badeau wrote to Fish concerning Hoffman. ALS, *ibid.* A related paper is *ibid.* On June 22, 1874, U.S. Senator Oliver P. Morton of Ind. wrote to USG. "R. R. Hitt, Esq., of Ogle County, Illinois, has been with me as Secretary for the last three years. He is a gentleman of the highest character, a ripe scholar and linguist, a man of rare intelligence and reading. He wishes to go abroad to spend two or three years, and would be glad to have a position as consul, preferring a post in Germany or Italy. He has mentioned Berlin, Dresden, and Naples as places at one of which he wished to live. I am very anxious personally to have Mr Hitt's wishes gratified. . . ." LS, *ibid.* Related papers, including letters from U.S. Senators Richard J. Oglesby and John A. Logan of Ill., and Daniel D. Pratt of Ind., are *ibid.* On Dec. 9, USG nominated Hoffman as secretary of legation, London, and Hitt as secretary of legation, Paris.

Proclamation

Whereas it is provided in the Constitution of the United States that the United States shall protect every State in the Union, on application of the legislature, or of the executive (when the legislature cannot be convened), against domestic violence; and

Whereas it is provided by the laws of the United States that, in all cases of insurrection in any State, or of obstruction to the laws thereof, it shall be lawful for the President of the United States, on application of the legislature of such State, or of the executive (when the legislature cannot be convened), to call forth the militia of any other State or States, or to employ such part of the land and naval force as shall be judged necessary for the purpose of suppressing such insurrection, or of causing the laws to be duly executed; and

Whereas the legislature of the State of Mississippi, now in session, have represented to me, in a concurrent resolution of that body, that several of the legally elected officers of Warren County in said State are prevented from executing the duties of their respective offices by force and violence—that the public buildings and records of said county have been taken into the possession of, and are now held by, lawless and unauthorized persons—that many peaceable citizens of said county have been killed, and others have been compelled to abandon, and remain away from, their homes and families —that illegal and riotous seizures and imprisonments have been made by such lawless persons—and, further, that a large number of armed men from adjacent States have invaded Mississippi to aid such lawless persons, and are still ready to give them such aid; and

Whereas, it is further represented, as aforesaid, by said legislature, that the courts of said county cannot be held, and that the Governor of said State has no sufficient force at his command to execute the laws [t]hereof in said county and sup[p]ress said violence, without [c]ausing a conflict of races and [e]ndangering life and property to an alarming extent; and

Whereas the said legislature, as aforesaid, have made application to me for such part of the military force of the United States as may be necessary and adequate to protect said State and the citizens thereof against the domestic violence hereinbefore mentioned, and to enforce the due execution of the laws; and

Whereas the laws of the United States require that, whenever it may be necessary, in the judgment of the President, to use the military force for the purposes aforesaid, he shall forthwith, by proclamation, command such insurgents to disperse and retire peaceably to their respective abodes within a limited time:

Now, therefore, I, Ulysses S. Grant, President of the United States, do hereby command said disorderly and turbulent persons to disperse and retire peaceably to their respective abodes within five days from the date hereof, and that they refrain from forcible resistance to the laws, and submit themselves peaceably to the lawful authorities of said county and State.

In Witness whereof, I have hereunto set my hand and caused the seal of the United States to be affixed.

Done at the City of Washington, this twenty-first day of December, in the year of our Lord eighteen hundred and seventy-four, and of the Inde[p]endence of the United [Sta]tes the ninety-ninth.

U. S. GRANT

DS, DNA, RG 130, Presidential Proclamations. On Dec. 19, 1874, Governor Adelbert Ames of Miss. telegraphed and wrote to USG. "Whereas it is provided in the Constitution of the united states article four section four that the united states shall guarantee to every State in the union protection to each state against domestic violence on application of the legislature of such state & whereas in the county of warren in the state of mississippi several of the legally elected & acting officers of said county including the sheriff thereof by force & violence on the part of lawless persons have been compelled & have been prevented from executing the duties of their respective officers & the public property including the Court house the jail together with the prisoners lawfully confined therein & the p̶ records of said County have been taken possession of by like force & violence & are still held by such lawless & unauthorized persons contrary to & in defiance of the laws of said state & whereas in consequence of such illegal acts as aforesaid many of the peaceable citizens of said county have been Killed & a large number through fear of violence have been compelled to abandon their homes and families and forced to seek protection by flight & concealment are still unable peaceably return to and occupy their respective abodes and whereas certain lawless armed & riotous persons in flagrant violence of the constitution & laws of the united states of the state of mississippi have made illegal searches of the private houses and persons of citizens of said County of warren and such lawless armed and riotous persons have also Imprisoned and held for a number of days many of the Citizens of said County including public officers without any legal authority or process of law whatever and whereas a large number of armed men from adjacent states have invaded the state of Mississippi in aid of such lawless and riotous persons and acts therein and others have signified their willingness to assist such lawless and riotous persons whenever Called upon & whereas the courts of the County have been paralized to such Extent that they cannot be held & thus rendered incapable to suppress such violence and to enforce the laws & whereas the Executive of the state has no sufficient force at his command by calling out the militia for other adequate power to suppress such domestic violence to Execute the laws & to guarantee full protection to all citizens irrespective of race Color or condition without causing a conflict of races & there by endangering life and property to an alarming extent   therefore resolved by the senate of the state of mississippi the house of representatives concurring that the president of the united states *be, is* hereby Called upon and urgently requested by use of the military power at his command to suppress such domestic violence to restore peace and order in this state & to guarantee to all citizens the Equal Impartial Enjoyment of their Constitutional & legal rights   Be it further resolved that his Excellency the Governor of this state be & is hereby authorized and requested to transmit forthwith the foregoing resolutions properly attested to his Excellency the president of the united states" "I transmit the accompanying concurrent resolution of the Senate and

House of Representatives of the State of Mississippi as requested therein." Telegram received and LS, *ibid.*, RG 60, Letters from the President. The enclosed resolution, dated Dec. 18, is *ibid.* On Dec. 19, USG telegraphed to Ames. "Your dispatch of this date is received, and the proclamation called for by the law in such cases, will be forthwith promulgated." Blanche Butler Ames, comp., *Chronicles From the Nineteenth Century: Family Letters of Blanche Butler and Adelbert Ames . . .* (1957), II, 77. Political and racial tensions had provoked violence in Vicksburg on Dec. 7. See *ibid.*, pp. 68–81, 96–97; telegram to Levi P. Luckey, July 21, 1874; *HRC*, 43-2-265; William C. Harris, *The Day of the Carpetbagger: Republican Reconstruction in Mississippi* (Baton Rouge, 1979), pp. 645–49.

On Dec. 5, Capt. Arthur W. Allyn, 16th Inf., Jackson, Miss., had written to Maj. Edward R. Platt, asst. AG. "I have the honor to report for the information of the General Commanding, certain matters which have come to my knowledge: and which I deem it desirable that he should know. An armed organization, called 'the Tax Payers League' has taken possession and holds the County Court House, of Warren Co. Miss at Vicksburg. The sheriff of the County has been forced to resign, and an appointee of the League is holding his place—The board of Supervisors have scattered and disappeared, to avoid being compelled to accept the forced resignation of the Sheriff—No disorder, or disturbances have as yet taken place—though it is reported that a large number of men are in arms, to support the movement and resist the militia if called out to reinstate the officials—The Governor will use what means, he has at his disposal, and they are limited, to replace the officers—Not more than two hundred men can be armed, as the supply of arms will only equip this number, and there being no funds in the State Treasury for this purpose, the militia, if organized, will have to be organized near the seat of the trouble at Vicksburg. It is rumored that resistance will be made and if it is, the State Government will appeal to the President for aid, . . ." ALS, DNA, RG 94, Letters Received, 3579 1874. Presumably on Dec. 19, USG wrote a note. "The Sec. of War may telegraph the Commanding officer of troops stationed in Jackson Miss. that if the legislature ~~are~~ is threatened with violence from unauthorized persons they must be protected in the proper discharge of their duties." AN (undated), *ibid.* On Dec. 19, Orville E. Babcock endorsed this note to [Secretary of War William W. Belknap]. "The President directs the above." AES, *ibid.* On Dec. 19, 2:30 P.M., Belknap wrote a note. "The Adjutant General will give the necessary instructions, by telegraph, without delay—" ANS, *ibid.*

On Jan. 4, 1875, Ames telegraphed to USG. "The majority of the legislative Committee sent to investigate affairs at Vicksburg report to me a great feeling of insecurity prevails there and that Certain officials Cannot safely discharge their duties the sheriff of the Co reports to me that armed defiance of all law and lawful authority hold full sway at the Court House Consequently I am compelled to ask you to send troops there to uphold and protect the lawful authorities—" Telegram received, *ibid.* On the same day, AG Edward D. Townsend telegraphed in cipher to Lt. Gen. Philip H. Sheridan, New Orleans. "The President has sent the following despatch to the Secretary of war with directions to comply with the request of Govr Ames as far as practicable—. . . The Secretary of War authorizes you to send troops from New Orleans, ~~of~~ or other point in the Divisions of the South ~~of~~ or of the Missouri, as you deem best—acknowledge receipt." ADf (initialed, telegram sent), *ibid.*; copy, DLC-Philip H. Sheridan. On Jan. 14, Ames testified before a congressional committee investigating unrest in Vicksburg. *HRC*, 43-2-265, 536–51.

On Dec. 20, 1874, Jo. Miller, Okolona, Miss., had written to U.S. Representative Alexander H. Stephens of Ga., addressing the letter initially to USG. "Will you permit me most respectfully to address you in a petionary way in reference to the darkie down South. I am a short sighted being & no politician, I did think howere that when he was made free that the abolitionists would be satisfied when this *'national disgrace was taken away'* but I was mistaken and am still mistaken. How the problem of is his freedom would be solved I could not see in reference to his relation with the white man But I think I do see how things are now & how they will be under the enforcement act & civil rights bill. In all societies sociality goes off in to clans   In England there are 3 or 4 classes that never go to the same school though they are all white. This society does in & of its self & will always do ʻaAs birds of a feather will flock together'. Excuse me I dont propose to argue the question, for you know all about it. It is no less clear that the 2 races never will, never can legislate together, conjointly, in peace. You yourself sd 'Let us have peace.' Mr President I thank you for that word. If the above proposition be true how is the latter to be secured. I can concieve of but 3 ways   1 is by the bayonet which is contrary to the genius of this government another is to seperate the races by congeress, concentrating the negro in a given space, a territory, a country of his own, in which he could in all things enact, act, and do as to him might seem good just and right; unmolested by the white man & protected by the general goverment in all his rights as a citizen   the ⅓ & last to let the white man make the laws alone; I would respectfully suggest that congress be so advised to do. Mr Alexander Stephens I penciled the above thoughts designed for the President direct but upon 2nd consideration I conclude to submit them to you as I had to Lamar & Beck. It is true that in our region we are getting along fairly with the darkie though he is morose, sour, & sullen dissatisfied & murmuring, works but poorly wishes to live on credit with the merchant, improvedent & wasteful, but you know him   For any uprising on his part our old confeds say the are ready for him   Crops are very short, how he is to live I see not. He will concentrate himself but I fear it will be only after much suffering & blood-shed   I therefore submit this thing to you to ponder over   Can nothing be done to save the Country, the negro, the white man" ALS, DLC-Alexander H. Stephens.

On Dec. 28, A. M. Dowling, Macon, Miss., wrote to USG. "the writer of this note is an old Man; was a Democrat up to 1851.—Was opposed to Secession, was a union Man during the war; threatened with arrest, together with others, but as we always had been and were then obedient & Submissive to the powers that were, better Council prevailed: Have never joined any Loyal Leage, or any white mans party; am looked upon with distrust by both Colours; Have only attended one potical Meeting Since the Surrender, and that for only a Short time, which was a republican, & only for a Short time: Have voted for both parties, Have always desired to vote for & Sustain the powers that be, but from present indication, it looks to me that the white people are being driven to the wall: The only intimidation for more than two years in east Mississippi So far as I know, has been by the negroes, and a man near my own age informed me this morning, and he is entirely trust worthy, that Several negroes told him during the 'Biggy Vally Riot' that they were Strong enough and that if the whites drew a drop of the negro blood, they would clean them out, would not leave man, woman or child in the South of the Southern whites, and that *all the yankees would help them.* The negroes do all the Marching & drumbeating drilling and *efforts at intimidation* & *Overawing,* that is done in this portion of the State: They had even went So far before this Biggy Vally Riot, as to notify Some Men who had been guarding their premises of nights, that they had to abandon the practice; this was done by a crowd of armed negroes at night, the negroes were unknown to the man, who is a reliable man. Now permit me to express my honest opinion, that if you Could place yourself among them roughly clothed in a blue Soldiers Coat and inter mix among them for a few weeks, or Months at Most, even without encouraging them more than Say you are a yankee and were a friend to the negroes—you would learn that all the trouble is attributable to the So Called Carpet baggers, aided by a few designing Southern men who are destitute of principle, and Seeking office for the purpose of Stealing, if not to Steal directly, certainly indirectly in every conceivable manner, So as to enrich themselves and impoverish the Country. The most Succissful mode is by the Lobbying System in the Legislature and the passage of laws that they may desire, by which means the Ring Consiting of all Colours, get the offices, the whites of course all that is worth having, and then by a united effort & action, they Controle officers & Jurors So as to hold the Ring harmless, while the rank and file of the negroes are left to Suffer: The Masses of the whites are as kind, indulgent & make even More than fair Setlement with their labourers, while most of the Little plantation and cross road Stores, encourage them to Steal & Sell to the Stores—these Stores generally plant from 10 to 40 aces in Corn & Cotton & probly mak 5 to 10 bales Cotton & from 100 to 300 Bushels corn & before the crops are all geatherd will have 1000 to 1500 Bu Corn & Send to market 50 to 100 Bales Cotton, paid for with whiskey & tobacco, and under the laws & Manipulations of Officers in Selections of and Controle of Jurs, you Cant reach them.   yet the negro, if let alone, are a quet inoffensive people.   yet let a Squad of Soldiers be Stationed near them, or even pass through the Country, under the Controle of Certain leads in every district, white or black, they become restless & turbulent and alsorts of intimations & rumors are Set afloat. To be used abused and legislated for by non tax payer who have no interest in common with the Masses, ought not be forced upon any people who are as much disposed to be good citizens as the Southern whites are. Multiplied thousands of Southern who have been & been trying to vote Republican ticket, will unite with the opposition if they are not respected by the powers be, or if their rights are not respected, for 9 or 10 years is long enough to learn that they are disposed to be good Citizens, but really it Seems that the more quit and unobtrusive a man is judging from the testimony of the Chief Justice of Ala in the Case of one of the Livingston prisonr, the More Certain of persecution. But I had no idea of Saying any thing except on Mississippi affairs—I have not been liable to Military duties for 20 years & of Course was not in the Rebellion and only remark that I have but a Short time longer to live and desire that all Should be peace & prosperity . . . The within account of the Bigby Valley Riot, is thought to truthfully written, and certainly not higly coloured." ALS, DNA, RG 60, Letters from the President. The enclosure is *ibid.*

On Jan. 13, 1875, Miss. Senator Finis H. Little wrote to USG. "I have the honor to enclose herewith a copy of resolution adopted by the Joint Republican Caucus of the Legislature of Mississippi which I am directed to transmit to you." LS, *ibid.* The enclosure stemmed from a caucus on Jan. 12: "Whereas, The peace of the State of Mississippi is now in a condition of such imminent peril as to demand imperatively the services of a United States Marshal, in the Southern district thereof, who will perform the duties of his office in an honest, impartial, and fearless manner; and Whereas, We recall with pride and gratitude the untiring, unremitting, fearless and successful services, of the Honorable Michael Shaughnessy, late United States Marshal of said distirct, in searching out, day and night, in time past, the 'Ku Klux' and 'Crusader's' secret military organizations, who were engaged in murdering, and outraging, and in hounding from burning and desolated homes, the peaceable and inoffensive colored people of the State, until the said Secret organizations were utterly broken up, and the leaders thereof arrested and brought before the bar of justice by the said M Shaughnessy, as United States Marshal: Therefore, Be it resolved: That, our Senators and Representatives in Congress be requested and instructed to take such steps as will cause a removal from the Office of United States Marshal for the Southern District of Mississippi, of the present incompetent incumbent thereof, and to urge for appointment to said office, the Honorable Michael Shaughnesssy, . . ." Copy, *ibid.* On June 23, 1874, USG had nominated John L. Lake, Jr., as marshal, Southern District, Miss.; he remained in office. See *PUSG*, 21, 390; *ibid.*, 24, 435–36.

On Jan. 30 and Feb. 16, 1875, Ames wrote and telegraphed to USG. "I take pleasure in recommending Genl. W. W. Dedrick of this state for an appointment at your hands. He is an Ex Union officer who has been located in the south since the war—he has labored zealously in the cause of human freedom which is the real issue here—he has been maligned because of such efforts as have all of us—he is an educated, capable gentleman and will reflect credit upon the government. I would earnestly recommend his appointment." ALS, DNA, RG 60, Records Relating to Appointments. "The republican party by a caucus the legislature being here at the Capitol unanimously endorsed Mr Brannigan as District Atty I speak the wish of our party when I ask his retention   I would ask that you carefully examine an official report made to the secretary of Treasury bearing upon the character of James McKee" Telegram received (at 11:41 P.M.), *ibid.* On Jan. 13, Little had written to USG. "I am directed by the Republican Caucus of Members of the Legislature of Mississippi to forward the inclosed resolution to you" ALS, *ibid.*, Letters from the President. The enclosure supporting Felix Brannigan's retention as U.S. attorney, Southern District, Miss., is *ibid.* On March 9, USG nominated William W. Dedrick to replace Brannigan. On June 13, 1873, Andrew D. White, Ithaca, N. Y., had written to USG. "Understanding that the name of Mr Wm Wirt Dedrick has been mentioned in connection with the Dist. Attorneyship for the Southern District of Mississippi—it gives me pleasure to state that my acquaintance with Mr Dedrick began during his course as a Student at the State University of Michigan when he distinguished himself as a Scholar, writer & speaker—and that everything that has come to me since, regarding him leads me to believe that his appointment would be useful to the public service & creditable to the administration" ALS, *ibid.* On Sept. 22, 1874, Dedrick, Vicksburg, wrote to USG. "I venture to thank you for your late action in regard to 'Ku Klux' atrocities in the South; and also your action with reference to the Louisiana insurrection. They demonstrate to the people only *more conclusively* your unerring Judgment and absolute reliability in the right. The utterances of democratic leaders had of late beyond doubt excited some distrust in the minds of Southern republicans, but their entire confidence in you is now fully restored & stronger than ever. If Congress passes a civil rights bill which you shall sign it will be very dificult to hold back the body of the republican party in the Southern states from forcing a third term upon you *nolens volens.* It is certain that every delegation to the national convention will be instructed for you, whatever the party in other sections may think or do about it. Your late action has reminded me of a remark made in my presence by General Rawlins when Secretary of War which is almost too good to be forgotten. Judge Dent was about being brought forward as the Conservative Candidate for Governor of Mississippi and in Company with him I visited Secretary R. on some private business in which he was my attorney. After transacting the business which was very brief Judge D. broached the matter of his prospective candidacy. Gen Rawlins listened a few moments when turning to Dent he said earnestly, 'Judge you may be a republican, and this may be a republican movement, but I shall advise Grant to use *his own army* to reconstruct Mississippi. He didnt call upon You Sir to help him capture Vicksburg and he dont need rebel forces now to help him reconstruct the state'. It is becoming pretty evident that if *Grant sets out to Capture a third term He will 'use his own army'* *to do it with.* To any fair minded person however, it is clear that your official action has ever been guided by the dictates of patriotism, reason and common sense. Justum et tenacem propositi virum   Pardon this letter which I have not the slightest idea you will ever read It is not written however in a spirit of officiousness & hence I trust will not give offense—" ALS, USG 3. See *PUSG*, 23, 391–92; Harris, *Day of the Carpetbagger*, pp. 462, 664.

On Feb. 4, 1876, U.S. Senator James L. Alcorn of Miss. wrote to USG. "*Personal . . .* I have the honr to enclose the application made by myself & Senator Bruce for the removal of Dist Atty Dedrick and the appointment of Mr H. R. Ware to the office of U. S. District

Attorney for the Southern district of Miss. My acquaintance with Mr Ware is Slight, the information which I have, and I have taken care to be correctly informed, is altogether favorable to the appointment,   mr Ware is a gentleman of education, having been I am told, a class mate of Secty Bristow, is a good lawyer, a man of courage, and of unquestioned integrity,   He was a Confederate Soldier & lost a leg in that Service, is a republican of strong conviction," ALS, DNA, RG 60, Records Relating to Appointments. The enclosure is *ibid.* On Feb. 5, Ames telegraphed to USG. "District Attorney Dedrick requests me to telegraph you and ask that you give him a hearing before removal. He says his Court, now in session, will continue about a week longer when he will hold himself ready to meet all charges. This he asks in the name of justice and for the preservation of his good name." Press copy, Ames Letterbook, Miss. Dept. of Archives and History, Jackson, Miss.; telegram received, DNA, RG 60, Records Relating to Appointments. On Feb. 6, Dedrick, Jackson, telegraphed to USG. "My abrupt removal unexplained would cause me irrietrievable injury   have had no intimation of any thing save personal warfare   could you not suspend action & give opportunity to vindicate myself   no wrong or neglect of duty can be Substantiated   Court in session investigation election outrages   will report first train after adjournment   your slightest wish for resignation willould be respected after vindication" Telegram received (at 11:00 P.M.), *ibid.* On Feb. 16, Attorney Gen. Edwards Pierrepont wrote to Alcorn. "I saw the President this morning; and he has not changed his mind about the district Attorney. . . ." Copy, *ibid.*, Letters Sent to Executive Officers. On Feb. 28, William H. Harney *et al.*, Jackson, petitioned USG to retain Dedrick. ". . . We regard him as one of the very best republicans in this State, standing squarely up to every issue and giving no uncertain sound for the right,   He enjoys in an eminent degree the confidence of the entire Colored people. Whatever *may* have been true as to his inexperience when he first went into the office cannot now be urged against him, as he has discharged the duties of his position twice in the Federal Courts held in his District and is thus more familiar and better acquainted with the duties incumbent upon him, than any other man who would be likely to get the appointment. We but speak the sentiment of our people, when we say that his retention in his present position will give universal satisfaction. Believing that you are always willing and ready to accede to the reasonable wishes of your friends: . . ." DS (14 signatures), *ibid.*, Records Relating to Appointments. On July 8, USG nominated Luke Lea to replace Dedrick. For Lea, see *HRC*, 43-2-265, 301–11.

To George H. Sharpe

Washington, D. C. Dec. 22d 1874

DEAR GENERAL:

Your letter of the 28th of Nov. in relation to the continuance of the Society Meetings of the Army of the Potomac was duly received, but I really forgot to answer it until my attention was called to it a day or two ago by General Babcock.—I am not prepared to give much advice on the subject, but it strikes me as desirable to keep up these meetings at least until the centennial. After that it might become a question whether it would not be well to consolidate all the Army Societies into a single society with a name denoting "Union."

> Very respectfully
> your obt. svt.
> U. S. GRANT

GEN. GEO. H. SHARPE.

ALS, PHi.

To Nathaniel Carlin

———

Washington D. C. Dec. 26th *1874*

DEAR SIR:

Enclosed I send you a letter from Mr. Akers, of Lawrence, Kansas. I have written to Mr. A. saying that I would enclose his letter to you and authorize you to select from among the stallions that he wishes to dispose of one to keep on my place the next season. I will make the terms with Mr. Akers. You might select about eight mares to breed to his horse and continue the rest with our own. If you have an opportunity to sell Hambletonian in the spring you might sell him, or dispose of him something on the terms I will take a horse from Mr. A. I am glad to hear that the horses and colts are doing so well. I repeat, if the mares you are driving are likely to make a good team I would continue driving them. If they are not likely to fulfill your expectations then breed them.

I really am not able to send you the Articles you ask for. I have already paid out this year some $12.000%⁄₁₀₀ on the farm and have not got the means to go further. When I go out in the Spring I may make arrangements to put the place on a good footing.

> Yours Truly
> U. S. GRANT

N. CARLIN, ESQ.

P. S. Write to Mr. Akers on receipt of this.

ALS, CSmH. On Feb. 6 and 12, 1875, B. F. Akers, "Kansas Stud Farm," Lawrence, wrote to Nathaniel Carlin, Kirkwood, Mo. "I enclose you a list of my Stallions, that I propose to let make season away from home—and are not contracted for—'Erie—' 'Bullock' 'Rhode Island' 'Comus' 'Bay Star' & 'St. Nicholas'   all except 'Bay star' are on the catalogue   he is by 'Daniel Lambert' a son of Ethan Allen and out of a Throughbred imported mare—can trot in about 2.35 7 years old. Rhode Island was the horse I thought had better come there as a great many around st. Louis want to see if they cannot get another Gov. Sprague—" "Yours recd—Rhode Island is in Providence   am going after him in a few days—& will leave him at st. Louis on my return—I have some very fine & fast colts by him in Providence both Stallions & mares   I shipped them there last fall, and concluded not to sell them, after shipping them for that purpose—do not know of a team such as you want. Will fix up an article on R. I. & his colts for you soon." ALS, OClWHi. See letter to Nathaniel Carlin, April 24, 1875.

On Sept. 21, 1874, Culver C. Sniffen had written to Carlin. "The President directs me to return the accompanying bill of Fidel Ganahl and the sight draft to the order of Geo. W. Griffen, on himself for $24.93/100. in payment of the same. The Draft was paid on the 19th instant. He requests me to say that he paid a bill a little while ago of about the same amount for wagon repairs to a man by the name of White. The President would like to have you forward accounts regularly, as agreed, that he may keep out of debt." ALS, OClWHi. On Sept. 25, Levi P. Luckey wrote to Carlin. "The President wishes me to call your attention to the fact that you have forwarded no account since last May. He is desirous that you send your statement to date, including all amounts received and paid out by you to date & also any sums which may be owing for purchases you have made and not yet paid for." Copy, DLC-USG, II, 2.

On Dec. 4, Orville E. Babcock wrote to Christopher C. Andrews, U.S. minister, Stockholm. "The President desires me to acknowledge the receipt of your letter of the 3d of Oct, and of the acorns, which you were kind enough to gather and send to him. He wishes me to convey you his sincere thanks. He has had them sent to his farm near St. Louis, with instructions to plant them as you direct in your letter." LS, Andrews Papers, Minnesota Historical Society, St. Paul, Minn.

To Adolph E. Borie

———

Washington.
Dec. 27th 1874

MY DEAR MR. BORIE:

Mrs. Grant and I will be glad to have the company of you, Mrs. Borie and your two nieces—the Yankee and the Britisher—for the week commencing Jan.y Fourth. Our state dinner to the Supreme Court will be on Tuesday the 5th at which I want you all present. Jesse will be here and possibly Buckey to escort the young ladies.

The harmony among the republican Senators in the passage of the Finance Bill I think argues well for the country and the party. The same harmony was exhibited in the House, and if they come back feeling as they did when they went away, and will pass the bill [1] without delay, I think the republican party will grow stronger as the days lengthen and the nights shorten. I feel very confident for the future of our country and party.[2]

My love,—and Mrs Grants—to you all.

Yours Truly

U. S. GRANT

ALS, PHi. "Mr. and Mrs. Borie, Miss Borie and Miss Leach" attended the state dinner held on Jan. 5, 1875. *Washington Evening Star*, Jan. 6, 1875. See also *ibid.*, Jan. 11, 1875; Hamilton Fish diary, Jan. 5, 1875, DLC-Hamilton Fish.

1. On Dec. 22, 1874, the Senate debated and passed a bill providing for resumption of specie payments; on Dec. 23, Congress recessed until Jan. 5, 1875. See message to Senate, [*Jan. 14, 1875*].
2. On Dec. 22, 1874, Secretary of State Hamilton Fish had recorded in his diary. "The President called attention to the Government advertising being given to papers which were personally abusive of either the whole or a part of the administration   that while he had no objection to criticism on any of the measures or policy of the administration, he thought it proper to withold the patronage of the Government from papers which personally attacked any member of the Government and requested each member of the Cabinet in their selection of papers for advertising to withold them from any paper which heretofore had, or which shall hereafter personally, assault any member of the administration." DLC-Hamilton Fish. On Dec. 24, Orville E. Babcock wrote to Secretary of the Treasury Benjamin H. Bristow. "The President wishes me to say that he does not wish to exclude th[e] *N. Y. Graphic* in request about advertisements, but wishes to include it among those to whom advertisements are to be given." ALS, DLC-Benjamin H. Bristow.

To Onslow Stearns

———

Washington.
Dec. 27th /74

DEAR GOVERNOR:

Mrs. Grant and I will be pleased to have the company of you, Mrs. Stearns, and the two young ladies for a week, commencing Monday, Jan.y 11th. During that week—~~Tuesday~~ Saturday— Mrs. Grant will have her reception which will give the ladies an opportunity of seeing many of the ladies in Washington society, and on Tuesday evening ~~evening~~, preceding, there will be a public reception. I hope you will all be able to come but if not come as many as can.

Please present my kindest regards to Mrs. Stearns and daughters, in which request Mrs. Grant joins ~~you~~ me.

Yours Truly

U. S. GRANT

GOV.R O. STEARNES

ALS, New Hampshire Historical Society, Concord, N. H. USG wrote on the envelope:
"Postmaster please forward if not in Concord." AN (undated), *ibid.* Born in 1810 at Bil-
lerica, Mass., Onslow Stearns worked as a railroad manager, was elected Republican
N. H. senator (1862), and served as governor of N. H. (1869–71). See *Washington Evening
Star*, Jan. 18, 1875.

Calendar

1874, JAN. 2.   USG order amending "the Tariff of Fees . . . so that hereafter a single fee of twenty five cents shall be charged for the services required in sealing cars coming from countries adjacent to the United States, . . ."—Copy, DNA, RG 130, Orders and Proclamations.

1874, JAN. 3.   Anthony Comstock, Brooklyn, to USG. "I have the honor to address you this letter, in the interests of morality and common humanity; and on behalf of the youth of America. I beg in the first place, with the greatest respect for yourself, and the most profound reveraence for your High office, to call you attention to an interview you did me the great honor to grant me, a little less than one year ago. If you remember Sir: his honor, Ex-Governor Cooke introduced me, and I gave you a brief detail of the manner of conducting, and the character, of the business of Obscene Literature. At the close of that short interview, you said to me, in the presence of Gov. Cooke and others, 'that so long as you were in the Presidents Chair, no pardon should be ever granted to any man who was convicted for the offense of sending the same through the Mail.' There was at that time two or more applications for pardons before you, which were denied. I presume Sir: you have forgotton this, and in the midst of the great and mighty duties and cares of your high Office, when some Senator or Representative has presented a petition signed by respectable men from their locality, that you have been led to grant their request. This is as I look upon the Pardon by your Honor, of the following named persons, Seth H. Hunsdon, James Patterson, John R Thomas, all of Albany. The petition to the two first I know contained very many respectable and influential names: but Sir I have felt and now feel that you were imposed upon, and did that, that had all of facts been laid before you you would never have granted. The Secrecy of the Mails affords great advantages. The two first carried on the business of sending out *Obscene books*, and articles for the *prevention of Conception and procuring of Abortion*, for seven years, without even their wives and families knowing it. When they were arrested 84,000 Circulars and 10,000 books, and articles for indecent and immoral use was found in their possession. It is not strange then that the petitioners to your honor for the pardon of these men should be deceived if their own wives knew it not. The entire business almost, was done under some four or five fictitious names or Aliases, so that it was not possible for the men to know of the business of these men. Again, *there were several distinct and seperate charges that were not tried.* They sent their Obscene books and articles to boys and girls, to married and unmarried alike, thus inciting the young to crime. John R. Thomas, is a poor, low, ignorant man a Sail-maker by trade, but advertised, and doing business through the mails, as *Dr J.* R. Thomas. He was an *Abortionist*; and was convicted for violating the Mail in this respect. He set him self up as a celebrated physician while he was nothing but a low ignorant Scoundrel. I beg to submit, that, the business of Obscene literature, does not consist in, obscene books alone, but while the books excite the passions, the dealers in them, provide means for gratifying the Same. Nearly every Circular of Obscene books, sent out for circulation among the youth of our land, *and very largely in our Schools and Seminaries*, are classified as follows, first the Obscene books, which excite the passions, then the Female or Male organ, made of Rubber, to be used for Self-Abuse, then articles for the prevention of Conception, articles for aiding seduction and then comes the *abortionists*, with their instruments and medicenes. All the above is part and parcel of Obscene Literature. That you may judge of the extent of this terrible evil, I beg your indulgence, while I present to you what has been unearthed and destroyed, in a little more than one year. I have seized about (15) fifteen tons of Obscene Matter, including, medicenes &c for *Abortion.* I have found this vile matter in some of our best schools, Colleges, & Seminaries, in the hands of the sons and daughters of our best families. I find by inquiry of the heads of Insane Assylums, that nearly one half of all the inmates of their Assylums are there from Self-Abuse, induced in many instances by Obscene books or pictures. From letters seized in the hands of the persons I have arrested I find, information that convinces me that hundreds and thousands of young women, and married women die every year, *killed by the nostrums sent out through the U. S. Mail* by the wretches, who advertise themselves as *doctors*, and engage in this business. Thousands and tens-of-thousands of the youth of our land fall every year into disgrace, shame, and untimely graves, through the Curse of Obscene Literature. The Action of the Courts, thus far, has been very benefitial and timely, in their dealings with these men. I have arrested over 100 in little more than one year. Nearly half have been convicted, and the balance await trial. There are hundreds to be arrested. The pardons thus far granted has given these men new hope. The business is lucrative and they can afford risks. I now, beg most respectfully, to ask, that in the future, an opportunity may be granted me to present all the facts, before *any* of the 40 or more men that I have caused to be convicted shall be pardoned. O Sir, I appeal to you, not for mercy to the family of one man, who is, or has been convicted, but rather for mercy to the young who are being corrupted, and demoralized by this monstrous and nefarious business. I appeal to you in the name of every young man, and young woman in our Schools, Colleges, or Seminaries, not to pardon more of these men. Have mercy upon the innocent, and those that are led astray, upon the weak ones; but O Sir, I pray you in the name of all that is *pure*, and *good*, in our homes, and through out our land, spare the young, from the nefarious business in which these men engage. Let them not, exult and say, 'The President, is opposed to the work in which you are engaged. I know you are not but they say so."— ALS, DNA, RG 60, Letters from the President. On Nov. 24 and Dec. 16, 1873, USG had pardoned the three men condemned by Comstock.—Copies, *ibid.*, RG 59, General Records. On March 3, USG had signed a bill promoted by Comstock concerning obscene literature and its circulation through the mails. See *CG*, 42–3, Appendix, 168–69; *U.S. Statutes at Large,* XVII, 598–600; Heywood Broun and Margaret Leech, *Anthony Comstock: Roundsman of the Lord* (New York, 1927), pp. 128–44, 166–68.

1874, JAN. 3. George W. Fishback, *St. Louis Democrat,* to USG. "I take great pleasure in recommending to your favorable consideration my friend & associate Mr Newton Crane who desires to obtain a diplomatic or consular appointment. . . ."—ALS, DNA, RG 59, Letters of Application and Recommendation. In the same month, John F. Long, St. Louis, wrote to USG recommending Newton Crane, "whose failing health" required an overseas appointment.—ALS, *ibid.*

Related papers are *ibid.* On Jan. 19, Orville E. Babcock wrote to Secretary of State Hamilton Fish. "The President directs me to say that he has no objection to the appointment of Mr. Crane of St. Louis as Consul to Manchester, and would be pleased to have you bring the papers in the case when you come to the Cabinet meeting to-morrow."—Copy, DLC-USG, II, 2. On Feb. 6, USG nominated Crane as consul, Manchester, replacing Charles H. Branscomb.

On Jan. 17, Levi P. Luckey wrote to Branscomb, Manchester. "The President directs me to acknowledge the receipt of your letter of Dec. 18th and assure you of his sincere thanks for your thoughtful kindness in sending him the handsome rug, and convey to you his regards."—Copy, *ibid.*

1874, JAN. 5.　To Senate transmitting commercial and extradition treaties with Salvador.—Copies, DNA, RG 59, Reports to the President and Congress; *ibid.,* RG 130, Messages to Congress. On Feb. 28, USG authorized Secretary of State Hamilton Fish to exchange ratifications of the extradition treaty.—DS, DLC-Hamilton Fish. On March 4 and 13, USG proclaimed the ratifications of the extradition treaty and the commercial treaty, respectively.—Printed in DNA, RG 56, Letters Received from the President.

Also on Jan. 5, USG had transmitted to the Senate an extradition treaty with Honduras.—Copy, *ibid.,* RG 59, Reports to the President and Congress.

1874, JAN. 5.　To Rear Admiral John L. Worden, superintendent, U.S. Naval Academy. "This will introduce a St. Louis friend of mine, Judge Treat, who visits the Academy to see a Nephew who is now a cadet. The Judge will appreciate the attentions he may receive as I will also."—ALS, MoSHi.

1874, JAN. 5.　Levi P. Luckey to cabinet officers. "I am directed by the President to say that he will be pleased to have permission given to such clerks as may desire, to attend the noon day prayer meetings in Lincoln Hall during the present week, between twelve and one o'clock."—Copy, DLC-USG, II, 2. On the same day, Luckey wrote to individual cabinet officers.—LS, DNA, RG 45, Letters Received from the President; *ibid.,* RG 56, Letters Received; *ibid.,* RG 59, Miscellaneous Letters; *ibid.,* RG 60, Letters from the President.

1874, JAN. 6.　To Senate transmitting an agreement to extend the time for ratifying two treaties with Peru.—Copies, DNA, RG 59, Reports to the President and Congress; *ibid.,* RG 130, Messages to Congress. A copy of the agreement is *ibid.,* RG 59, Reports to the President and Congress. On Dec. 6, 1870, USG had twice written to the Senate transmitting commercial and extradition treaties with Peru for ratification.—DS, *ibid.,* RG 46, Presidential Messages, Foreign Affairs, Peru.

Also on Dec. 6, USG had transmitted to the Senate extradition treaties with Guatemala and Nicaragua.—DS, *ibid.,* Guatemala; *ibid.,* Nicaragua. The Nicaraguan treaty is *ibid.,* RG 84, Spain, Commercial Treaties, Conferences, and Conventions. On March 31, 1871, the Senate approved the treaty with Guatemala, which failed to ratify the treaty; the issue remained unresolved until 1903. See *List of Treaties Submitted to the Senate, 1789–1934* (Washington, 1935), 75–

76; Christian L. Wiktor, ed., *Unperfected Treaties of the United States of America, 1776–1976* (Dobbs Ferry, N. Y., 1976), II, 385.

1874, JAN. 6.   William H. Winder, Kalamazoo, Mich., to USG. "I am desirious of obtaining an appoint as a Cadet at West Point   But as I am a colored boy and have no Parents or influential friends to assist me in procuring an appointment or even a trial I take this method of addressing you asking you to point out the proper source to which I should apply to accomplish my object. I am seventeen years old, and have been to school five years   I think I posess the necessary qualifications ~~to admit~~ mentally and physically to admit me to the institution if I had a proper trial"—ALS, DNA, RG 94, Unsuccessful Cadet Applications.

1874, JAN. 7.   USG endorsement. "Refered to the Sec. of the Treas. This is a copy of a letter the original of which has been mislaid."—AES, DNA, RG 56, Applications. Written on a letter of July 21, 1873, from John A. Bingham, minister to Japan, Cadiz, Ohio, to USG. "William G. Finney formerly a citizen of Ohio & for many years a clerk in the Treasury Department desires to be re-appointed in that Department. I have no doubt he was one of the most efficient of the clerks of his grade in the Department. If in your judgment the civil service will not suffer, by suspending the rule in Mr Finney's case for a competitive examination I pray you to do so, as I have no doubt he will if restored to the service discharge his duties most acceptably."—ALS, *ibid.*; copies (2), *ibid.* William G. Finney had resigned upon what proved to be false charges. See Francis Miller to George S. Boutwell, June 7, 1871; John S. Crocker to William A. Richardson, Dec. 15, 1873, *ibid.* As of Oct. 21, 1875, Finney worked in the money order div., 6th Auditor's office.—ADS, *ibid.*

1874, JAN. 7.   USG endorsement. "Refered to the Sec. of the Int."—AES, DNA, RG 48, Appointment Div., Letters Received. Written on a letter of Jan. 6 from U.S. Senators Powell Clayton and Stephen W. Dorsey of Ark. to USG. "We respectfully recommend the appointment of Mr. D. B. Sickels of New York City, to the position of Government Director of the Union Pacific Railroad, in place of Mr. David S. Ruddock, of New London, Connecticut, reported to us as an inmate of an Insane Asylum at this time. Mr. Sickels is an accomplished engineer, is familiar with Railway business, and is in every way fully competent to make an efficient Director of the RailRoad."—LS, *ibid.* On June 7, 1876, David B. Sickels, Washington, D. C., wrote to USG. "I have the honor to enclose herewith a petition signed by several of the leading merchants and bankers of the City of New York requesting my appointment as one of the Commissioners of Public Schools in the event of the reorganization of the Board. I beg leave to ask that it may be filed with my other letters endorsing my application for the office of Consul at Bangkok, Siam, which application, I am informed has been referred to the Honorable Secretary of State."—ALS, *ibid.*, RG 59, Letters of Application and Recommendation. The enclosed petition and related papers are *ibid.* On Aug. 2, USG nominated Sickels as consul, Bangkok.

On Jan. 11, 1871, U.S. Senator Orris S. Ferry of Conn. had written to USG. "I take pleasure in recommending D. S. Ruddock Esq, of New London, Conn.

for appointment as Govt Director of the Pacific R. R. Co. Mr Ruddock has been an untiring and self-sacrificing laborer in the Republican party from its origin and as the principal Editor of a Daily Newspaper in New London has rendered efficient service. He is an upright and reliable gentleman and his appointment would gratify a large circle of friends and be of material benefit politically in our State"—ALS, *ibid.*, RG 48, Appointment Div., Letters Received. Related papers are *ibid.*

On Feb. 16, 1875, U.S. Senator Frederick T. Frelinghuysen of N. J. wrote to USG. "My brother in law Mr. J. N. A: Griswold of New-Port. R. I wishes the appointment of Government Director of the Union Pacific R. R Co—He is a gentleman of integrity—of extensive business information—well informed in R. Road matters—and has a marked capacity for understanding extensive & complicated business transactions—I dislike to recommend a relative for position, & would not, do so did I not know that he possessed the characteristics I have stated—I dont know or think that it is any objection to his appointment but it is proper that I should inform you that Mr Griswold is interested & an active director in the Chicago Burlington & Quincy R. R Co—I do not know that there will be any vacancy or change in the direction of the Union Pacific R. R. Co—but if there is I am satisfied Mr. G. would well & faithfully discharge the trust, and would be much gratified by the appointment—"—ALS, DNA, RG 48, Appointment Div., Letters Received.

On Feb. 17, 1874, James W. Husted, speaker, N. Y. assembly, and three others wrote to USG. "Hon. F. B. Brewer Member of Assembly for the second term from Chatauqua County is visiting Washington in relation to a matter which he will present to your Excellency. . . ."—LS, *ibid.* On Feb. 24, 1875, U.S. Senator Roscoe Conkling of N. Y. wrote to USG. "I have the honor to state that Mr. F. B. Brewer, now a Government Director of the Pacific Railroad, appointed last year, wishes to retain his place, if it be agreeable to you. He is a man of excellent character, who was highly commended, and I think deserves the commendation he received."—LS, *ibid.*

On Jan. 15, 1876, U.S. Representative Clinton D. MacDougall of N. Y. *et al.* petitioned USG. "We the Undersigned Representatives in Congress from the State of New York, Most respectfully ask you to appoint the Hon. W. J. Heacock, of Gloversville, Fulton County, New York, to fill the next vacancy which may occur in the 'Board of Directors of the Union Pacific Railroad. Mr. Heacock is one of the leading Republicans of New York, in which state he has filled with honor many important places of Public trust. We heartily recommend him for the office desired, and endorse him as a man of ability and strictest integrity—"— DS (14 signatures), *ibid.* On Feb. 9, Conkling favorably endorsed this petition.— AES, *ibid.* Conkling also endorsed a letter of Feb. 1 from N. Y. Senator Webster Wagner. "Respectfully submitted to His Excellency The President, with the remark that Mr Heacock is a fitting valuable man for the trust suggest. I have already verbally presented the case to the President."—AES (undated), *ibid.*

On Jan. 24, U.S. Representative John H. Baker of Ind. had written to USG. "We beg leave respectfully to ask you to appoint Col. Alba M. Tucker as one of the Government directors of the Union Pacific Railroad. Col. Tucker has had nearly twenty years experience as a railroad man. . . ."—ALS, *ibid.*

On Feb. 25, U.S. Representative James A. Garfield of Ohio wrote to USG. "I respectfully recommend the appointment of the Hon. George W. Steele of Ohio, as one of the Directors of the Union Pacific Rail Road on the part of the United States—Mr Steele is a prominent, and most worthy citizen of Ohio, ~~and~~ has been a prominent member of the Ohio Legislature, and enjoys the confidence of the people of the state—His residence is Painesville, Lake Co Ohio—"—ALS, *ibid.*

1874, JAN. 7. To House of Representatives. "In reply to the resolution of the House of Representatives of the 15th of last December, requesting a revision of the estimates for the expenses of the Government for the fiscal year ending June 30th 1875, I have the honor to transmit herewith amended estimates and replies from the several departments."—Copy, DNA, RG 130, Messages to Congress. *HED*, 43-1-36. Replies from cabinet officers are *ibid.*

1874, JAN. 7. Levi P. Luckey to A. T. Stewart & Co., New York City. "The President directs me to enclose his check for $344 00 the amount of your bill, which please be kind enough to receipt and return to me."—Copy, DLC-USG, II, 2. Letters from USG's secretaries to Stewart concerning bills are *ibid.*, II, 1, 2. USG's secretaries also wrote letters concerning payments to Brooks Brothers, New York City; Arnold, Constable & Co., New York City; and J. & J. Darlington, Ivy Mills, Pa.—Copies, *ibid.*, II, 2, 3.

1874, JAN. 8. To Congress. "In compliance with the Act of Congress approved March 3, 1873, entitled 'An Act to authorize inquiries into the causes of steamboiler explosions,' I directed the Secretaries of the Treasury and Navy Departments to create a commission to conduct the experiments and collect the information contemplated by the act. Such a commission was created and I have the honor to submit ~~a~~ herewith a report of ~~their~~ the results of their labors to the present time."—Copies (2), DNA, RG 130, Messages to Congress. *HED*, 43-1-46.

On July 30, Secretary of the Treasury Benjamin H. Bristow wrote to USG. "You will perhaps remember that in June 1873, Messrs. Copeland, Crawford, Holmes, and Robinson received from the Secretaries of the Treasury and Navy jointly, by authority from you, an appointment authorizing them to inquire into the causes of steam boiler explosions, etc., under the direction of D. D. Smith Esq, Supervising Inspector General of Steam Vessels. I have to-day received a communication signed by Messrs. Robinson, Copeland, Crawford and Holmes, setting forth the action of the Commission and making grave charges against Mr. Smith, involving both his efficiency as Chairman of the Commission and his integrity in the expenditure of the appropriation made by Congress. . . ."—Copy, DNA, RG 56, Letters Sent. On Dec. 7, USG nominated William Burnett as supervising inspector gen. of steamboats, to replace David D. Smith.

1874, JAN. 9. USG note. "Retire Gen. Cullum"—AN, DNA, RG 94, ACP, 692 1873. Col. and Bvt. Maj. Gen. George W. Cullum retired as of Jan. 13.

1874, JAN. 10.   Isaac F. Quinby, U.S. marshal, Rochester, N. Y., to USG recommending the reappointment of Timothy E. Ellsworth as collector, Niagara District.—ALS, DNA, RG 56, Collector of Customs Applications. On March 5, 1869, Governor Lucius Fairchild of Wis. had written to USG supporting Ellsworth.—ALS, *ibid.* Related papers are *ibid.* On Feb. 19, 1874, USG renominated Ellsworth.

1874, JAN. 10.   U.S. Representative John P. C. Shanks of Ind. to USG. "I most cheerfully call the favorable attenion of the President to the case of E. J Curtis present Secretary of the Territory of Idaho, and recommend his reappointment. Having spent some months in Idaho during the past Summer, and having traveled over the Territory much during that time, I state that the people are satisfied with the official conduct of Mr Curtis. If the accounts of Secretary curtis are correct, I ask that he be reappointed"—ALS, DNA, RG 48, Appointment Papers, Idaho Territory. On Jan. 30, USG nominated Edward J. Curtis to continue as secretary, Idaho Territory.

On Aug. 18, 1876, U.S. Senator William B. Allison of Iowa, New York City, wrote to USG. "I. earnestly recommend to you E. M. Stedman for appt to the position of Secretary of the Territory of Idaho. When a vacancy occurs or is made, Mr S. is very competent to fill the position. in every respect Having been twice a member of our legislature & being a business man of knowledge & experience. I hope you will appoint him. He is the person I mentioned to you in our last intervew"—ALS, *ibid.* On Aug. 20, USG endorsed this letter. "Referred to the Sec. of the Int. If a change of sec. in Idaho is to take place—and I understand there is—I approve this recommendation."—AES, *ibid.* No appointment followed.

On [*Dec.*] 8, U.S. Delegate Stephen S. Fenn of Idaho Territory wrote at length to USG. "I call your attention to the Official action of Edward L Curtis, who has held the Office of Secretary of Idaho Territory since some time in the year 1869, and desire that after consideration you take such steps in the matter as you may think its importance demands. I charge that said Curtis, Secretary of Idaho as aforesaid, has during his whole term of office or nearly so been unfaithful to his Trust, and has certified yearly to the correctness of vouchers for disbursements, made by him in that capacity, that have been overcharged and in many cases fraudulent if not wholly fictitious. . . ."—ALS, *ibid.* On Jan. 11, 1877, 1st Comptroller Robert W. Tayler wrote to Secretary of the Interior Zachariah Chandler. ". . . The accounts of Mr Curtis do not show anything apparently wrong, and have been allowed; If wrong has been done by him in the expenditure of public moneys advanced to him, it does not appear from anything in the knowledge of this Office, . . ."—LS, *ibid.*

1874, JAN. 10.   Ellen E. Sherman, Washington, D. C., to USG. "Doctor *C. C. Cox,* is no doubt well known to you, as he is to me, as the Lieut. Gov. of Maryland during the War, afterwards Commr. of Pensions, and always a staunch Republican, & a very polished, cultivated scientific man. His health is almost too delicate for the exposure which the practice of his profession involves, and I beg to add mine, to the many other petitions that he receive the place which Commissioner

Baker may soon leave. . . . Dr. Cox is as warm a friend to you as you have in the country."—ALS, DNA, RG 48, Appointment Div., Letters Received. James H. Baker continued as commissioner of pensions. For Cox, see *PUSG*, 21, 197–98.

1874, JAN. 11.   Silas N. Palmer, probate judge, and many others, Vermillion, Dakota Territory, to USG. "We the undersigned Citizens of Clay County Dakota Territory, formerly Subjects of Christian (VIIII) ninth King of Denmark, Would respectfully represent that owing to the remoteness of Consul and Vice Consuls (for our native Country) from this Territory (there being none in said Territory) and the great inconvenience we are necessarilly put to under these circumstances to do business with our native Country We would ask and earnestly pray that our worthy Citizen and fellow countryman Rasmus. M. Rasmussen be appointed Vice Consul for this Dakota Territory . . ."—DS, DNA, RG 59, Letters of Application and Recommendation. Related papers are *ibid.*, none written with any awareness that USG could not appoint a Danish consul.

1874, JAN. 12.   John G. Thompson, Houston, to USG. "Hon Webb Flanagan Son of Hon J. W. Flanagan U S. S. arrived in Houston the tenth and left the 11th inst   during his stay here; he entered into a special agreement with Judge M N Brewster of this place to the effect that he through his father Hon J. W. Flanagan would secure the Office of Collector of Customs of the Port of Galveston for Judge Brewster—Judge Brewster agreeing to pay the Hon Webb Flanagan One thousand dollars for his and his fathers services in that behalf, in fact advancing half the said fee—whereupon Dispatches were sent to the Hon Flanagan Sr engaging his services &c &c. While I have nothing to say about the present Collector pro or con—I and others who are aware of this agreement as above suggested only wait with some interest to see the result of this matter being somewhat anxious to know if such influences are to control the Federal Patronage of Texas, as there is a slight suspicion here that father and Son understand each other in a business way. The enquiry suggests itself quite forcibly is a man who seeks by such appliances and influence to secure an important Federal Office likely to be the most suitable man for the position he thus seeks, and is he likely to take proper care of the public interests, should he succeed as above.—These and similar enquiries are quite practical"—LS, DNA, RG 56, Collector of Customs Applications. On Dec. 7, USG nominated Benjamin G. Shields as collector of customs, Galveston.

On April 4 and 19, 1875, Charles Matthews, "Special Texas Correspondent Chicago Inter Ocean," Galveston, wrote to USG. ". . . What I wish particularly to call your attention to is the case of B. G. Shields, Collector of this Port. He has succeeded in palming himself off as a Republican although his actions since his confirmation show clearly that he is at heart a Democrat. The majority of his appointees are of the worst class of Democrats and it is a most notorious fact that several of them openly stated 'that they would not accept' unless the 'nigger' clerks and Inspectors were removed. Some of the most noted ex-confederates and Democrats, who talk as though the war was still going on and who made themselves very conspicuous by their open abuse of Republicans and Republican Institutions, have been appointed to positions and sent to distant points in the District where they can give vent to their feelings without endangering their chief. My idea in writing to you is party to show the true character of Shields but principally to explain the effect such an appointment will have on our Party. The leading local Republicans, who control conventions &c, are greatly dissatisfied and as the day is not far distant when we will be called upon to elect Delegates to the Presidential Convention I think that the interests of the Party demands that our Federal Officers should not be obnoxious to the masses of the Republican Party. Shields has without cause removed all the Ex-Union Soldiers who were employed in the Office when he took possession: He has since employed two others but it was at the instance of District Judge Morrill and others whom he dare not refuse. . . ." "Enclosed you will find a brief article which I 'clipped' from a late issue of the Galveston Mercury: It will satisfy you of the truth of the charges made by me against Shields in a former communication. The Mercury was formerly an Independent Journal but is now Democratic. It is the Official Organ of the U. S. It seems to me that the Federal Officers here ought to start a good Daily Paper and run it in the interests of Republican Party; By requiring Government employes to contribute to the support of a Republican Paper we could very soon weed out Shield's Democratic friends."—ALS, *ibid.*, Letters Received from the President.

On Aug. 15, 1876, U.S. Senator Oliver P. Morton of Ind. wrote to USG. "Adolph Zadek, of Texas, would accept the position of Collector of the Port of Galveston. Mr. Zadek is a leading German Republican, a gentleman of prominence and influence in Texas, and in every way qualified to perform with credit the duties of that office. I am assured that his appointment would meet with the hearty approval of Texas Republicans, and it would be much appreciated by . . ." —LS, *ibid.*, Collector of Customs Applications. On Aug. 18, USG endorsed this letter. "Refered to the Sec. of the Treas. I am inclined to believe that this change should be made."—AES, *ibid.* Related papers are *ibid.* Shields continued as collector; Adolph Zadek served as U.S. commissioner, Western District, Tex., as of Sept. 30, 1877.

1874, JAN. 12.   John B. Van Petten, Sedalia, Mo., to USG. "I beg leave to solicit your clemency for an esteemed neighbor Dr. W. F. Boyer. In common with the people of our City generally I hereby affirm that he is considered one of our best and most useful citizens. Our whole Community was shocked to hear of his trouble on account of one Jackson Bolend and soon quite generally regarded him the victim of unfortunate circumstances. He seems to have taken a mortgage or trust deed on property of this Bolend to secure a debt which property was already mortgaged. When Bolend afterward was put into bankruptcy in view of costs and trouble Dr Boyer gave for little or no consideration a quit claim deed of said property to Bolend's Assignee. So he virtually relinquished his debt as he could not expect much but trouble and expense from the bankrupt court as most any of us would have done. It appears this Bolend to save a homestead or to gratify malice has since denied Dr Boyer's debt though he has admited it in the presence of some of our best men. Dr Boyer has been regarded by this Community quite unanimously ~~regarded~~ as an honorable man. He is a good Physcian and is most respectably connected. Your clemency in his behalf will be a favor to our City and especially to a most estimable citizen his Father Mr. Henry Boyer. In view of all the circumstances his case appeals strongly for your favorable consideration."—ALS, NjP. On Nov. 4, USG pardoned convicted perjurer William F. Boyer.—Copy, DNA, RG 59, General Records.

1874, JAN. 13.   Matthew R. Barr, Republican committee chairman, Erie, Pa., to USG. "The Daily dispatch has very little political influence or standing"—Telegram received (at 4:25 P.M.), DNA, RG 56, Letters Received from the President. On the same day, Thomas M. Walker, Erie, telegraphed to USG. "The Erie daily dispatch has no political Standing or influence of any consequence"—Telegram received (at 4:26 P.M.), *ibid.* On Jan. 10, Orville E. Babcock had written to Secretary of the Treasury William A. Richardson. "The President directs me to let the nomination of James R. Willard to be Collector of Customs Dist. of Erie, Pa. go to the Senate on Monday next. You will remember that you had the nomination over here on the 5th inst. & carried it back with you. Will you please have it sent over or another one prepared to go to the Senate on Monday."—Copy, DLC-USG, II, 2. On Jan. 12, USG nominated James R. Willard, owner of the *Erie Daily Dispatch*, as collector of customs, Erie.

1874, JAN. 13.   Emily L. Pitcher, Detroit, to USG. "Knowing the old friendship which existed through many years between yourself and my late husband, Dr. Zina Pitcher, I feel that I may, as his wife, be allowed to address you about a matter in which I am greatly interested myself, and in which my dear husband would have been equally so, were he living. You doubtless can recall to mind Dr. Pitcher's long & arduous service in the old United States' Army   He entered in the year 1822 and was stationed at the extreme frontier Posts, at that time almost inaccessible. He ever held you in great esteem and only a few weeks before his death he spoke of you as an old and tried friend. May I, dear Mr President, in the name of my beloved husband beg you to act in behalf of my son in law, Silas B. Coleman who desires the appointment of Pay Master in the Army. Dr Pitcher had great respect and affection for Mr Coleman, being a young man so free from vices and of so honorable a nature   His letters of recommendation you will receive   If possible, do what you can for him, for the sake of my dear and honored husband"—ALS, DNA, RG 94, Applications for Positions in War Dept. Related papers are *ibid.* No appointment followed.

1874, JAN. 14.   USG pardon for convicted embezzler Horatio Jenkins, Jr.—DS, DNA, RG 59, General Records. On April 3, 1869, USG had nominated Jenkins as collector of Internal Revenue, Fla.; on Dec. 1, 1873, USG nominated Alva A. Knight to replace Jenkins. See *SRC*, 44-1-309.

1874, JAN. 14.   William S. Clapp, Carmel, N. Y., to [USG]. "I am the Son-in-law of Daniel Drew of NewYork—having married his only daughter. I expect to spend some time in Europe for the education of my youngest son, leaving in the Spring or sooner—and should like very much to represent my Government there in a *Consulate* either in France, Italy, Germany or Austria. I am in my 52nd year, of unquestioned health and habits, classically educated, by profession a

Baptist clergyman, have spent some fifteen months in Europe in 1864 & 5, am familiar with the French & Italian Languages—always a Republican—represented my district in the New York Legislature last winter, and could have been returned for this Session but I gave way in favor of Hon Hamilton Fish Jr—Is there the least chance for me to obtain a Consulate? It is my first application for a political favor, and doubtless there are thousands ahead of me for the same position. Mr Fish informs me that he believes the Slate is *full.* If there is a chance for me between this and the 1st of May next I will come on to Washington at your call, and bring ample recommendations if they are required. Collector Arthur —of New York is a friend of mine from boyhood"—ALS, DNA, RG 59, Letters of Application and Recommendation. No appointment followed. See Clifford Browder, *The Money Game in Old New York: Daniel Drew and His Times* (Lexington, Ky., 1986), p. 79.

1874, JAN. 15, Thursday.   William A. Purrington to USG. "I called on you last Thursday to state certain facts in connection with my appointment, but not seeing you I was unable to do so. The facts are these. When you were good enough to offer me an appointment, I had no suggestion to make as to where it should be, knowing that you would do what was best; and your selection of a position fully bore me out in that belief. Yet I cannot but feel that it would be a poor return for your kindness to allow any considerations of self interst to blind me to the fact that I may greatly inconvenience others in my present position. . . ."— ALS, DNA, RG 60, Letters from the President. USG wrote an undated endorsement that is filed with a note of July 3 from Secretary of State Hamilton Fish concerning Purrington. "Refered to the Sec. of State. If there is a vacancy to the Italian legation cannot Mr. Wm Purrington be appointed to it?"—AES, *ibid.*, RG 59, Letters of Application and Recommendation. On March 2, 1875, Fish recorded in his diary a conversation with USG. "He had spoken to me last evening, suggesting the nomination of Wm A. Purrington, now consular clerk at Rome, for Marshal of Consular Court in Japan   He says his son Ulysses is very anxious for his transfer from Rome where he says the climate is injuring him—I tell him that the Marshal is required to give a bond of $10.000 and suggest that the Secretaryship in Brazil is vacant and probably may suit him better; he assents and requests me to make out his nomination tomorrow or Friday"— DLC-Hamilton Fish. On March 8, USG nominated Purrington as secretary of legation, Brazil. See *New York Times,* Oct. 27, 1926.

1874, JAN. [*16*].   Bishop Matthew Simpson, New Orleans, to USG. "Detained for passports   spanish consul here will issue for self & company if spanish minister will telegraph him so   please authorize him   ship sails tomorrow night or next morning"—Telegram received (on Jan. 17, at 12:22 A.M.), DNA, RG 59, Miscellaneous Letters. Simpson was en route to Mexico via Havana to inspect Methodist Episcopal missions.

1874, JAN. 17.   Levi P. Luckey to E. D. Atchison, Memphis. "The President directs me to acknowledge the receipt of your letter of the 9th inst. and tell you of his regret that the letter you speak of having written several months ago, did not reach him. He learns with sorrow of the death of Col. Leatherman, who during his last hours remembered him and desired to leave him a token of his remembrance and friendship. He wishes me to tender you many thanks for your kindness in the matter and care of the colt, which he says you may ship at your convenience to N. Carlin (for U. S. Grant) care of the United States Express Co. St. Louis, Mo. when it will be placed on his farm"—Copy, DLC-USG, II, 2. For Davidson M. Leatherman, see Lincoln, *Works*, VI, 179, 324, 431; Johnson, *Papers*, 9, 47–48.

1874, JAN. 17. U.S. Senator Aaron H. Cragin of N. H. to USG. "I wish you would delay action in the matter of the pension agency at Portsmouth N. H. till I can see you tomorrow morning."—Telegram received, DNA, RG 107, Telegrams Collected (Bound). On Dec. 6, 1869, USG had nominated Daniel J. Vaughn as pension agent, Portsmouth, N. H.; on March 19, 1874, USG renominated Vaughn.

1874, JAN. 17. Charles Parker, Houston, to USG. "I have the honor to make application herewith for an appointment in the Pay Department of the U. S. Army in case additional Paymasters are made: If additions are made to the Ordnance Corps *only*, I would be pleased to accept an appointment in that branch of the service. My reasons for making this application may be found in the accompanying letter from the Governor of the State of Illinois endorsed by Senators Logan and Oglesby and General R. S. MacKenzie as well as other papers now on file at the War Department."—ALS, DNA, RG 94, Applications for Positions in War Dept. On March 1, 1873, Governor John L. Beveridge of Ill. had written to USG. "I write you in the interest of Charles Parker Esq. late Capt in 9th U. S. Cav. who was discharged under G. O No 1. 1871. The captain is under the impression that his discharge was a mistake,—however he casts no blame upon any office of the Government. His desire is to be restored to the same rank in either branch of the service. Capt Parker served in my Regmt, the 17th Ill. Cav. and I always found him a faithful and efficient officer, and his habits of life in my opinion are good. Since he left the army he has resided in Texas, and for the last two years has been Supervisor of Education in that State. I humbly pray that he may be restored to his former standing in the army."—ALS, *ibid.*, ACP, 1590 1871. Related papers are *ibid.* See Parker to USG, March 7, 1871, copy, DLC-Lyman Trumbull. On April 18, 1874, Secretary of War William W. Belknap wrote to AG Edward D. Townsend. "The President has returned to me the enclosed nominations & directs that Capt. Charles Parker be (mustered out by Act order No. 1—1871—) be re-appointed Captain in 9th Cavalry vice Humfreville—"— AN (initialed), DNA, RG 94, ACP, 1590 1871. See *Calendar*, April 30, 1874.

1874, JAN. 21. USG endorsement. "Refered to the Sec. of War. Please call special attention."—AES, DNA, RG 94, USMA, Board of Visitors. Written on a letter of the same day from U.S. Senator William G. Brownlow of Tenn. to USG. "It would be personally very gratifying to me if you would appoint Hon. Oliver P. Temple of Knoxville Tennessee as a visitor to West Point. Mr. Temple is now and has long been a Judge of the Chancery Court. He is a man of scholarly at-

tainments and undoubted loyalty and his appointment would be acceptable to
the friends of the Administration throughout the state"—ALS, *ibid.* On Dec. 26,
1873, Charles H. Fowler, president, Northwestern University, had written to
USG. "I wish to bring to your attention, and commend to your favorable consideration the name of Prof. Julius T Kellogg Prof. of Mathematics in the
Northwestern University, as a suitable person to ~~be app~~ serve on the Examining Com. of the Military Academy at West Point, and respectfully ask for his
appointment."—ALS, *ibid.* On Jan. 8, 1874, U.S. Senators William B. Allison
and George G. Wright of Iowa wrote to USG. "We respectfully recommend the
appointment of Rev. A. B. Kendig of Cedar Falls Iowa as visitor from the State
of Iowa to the West Point Military Academy for the year 1874—"—LS, *ibid.* On
Jan. 15, Nathan S. Davis, Chicago Medical College, wrote to USG. "I take pleasure in stating that I have been personally acquainted with F. K. Bailey M.d. of
Knoxville, Tennessee for many years. He is a man of the highest integrity; a physician of large experience and high professional attainments; he served faithfully as Surgeon with the Army in subduing the Rebellion, and would do credit
to the State of Tennessee as a representative in the *Board* of *Visitors* to the Military School at West Point."—ALS, *ibid.* On Jan. 29, U.S. Representative God-
love S. Orth of Ind. wrote to USG. "I respectfully recommend Captn William A.
Brown of GreenCastle Indiana, as a suitable person to recieve the appointment
of Visitor to the Military Academy at West Point, and have reason to believe
that his appointment would be acceptable to our Delegation in Congress, and
also to our people—"—ALS, *ibid.* On Feb. 3, U.S. Representative Frank Here-
ford of West Va. wrote to USG. "I have recd a letter from Genl Alfred Beckley
one of my constituents living at Raleigh C. H Raleigh Co W. Va requesting that
he be appointed one of the Visitors to West Point   Genl Beckley is a graduate
of West Point, but resigned many years ago because he had a growing family
and his pay in the army would not support him—He is anxious to visit the scene
of his earlier days—..."—ALS, *ibid.*, Correspondence, USMA. On Feb. 6, Marshall Jewell, U.S. minister, St. Petersburg, had written to USG. "You will perhaps
reccolect my speaking to you last spring in regard to appointing Prof. Francis
Wayland of New Haven one of the Board of examination at West Point this year
& you suggested that I should remind you of it about the first of March. I think
you will find him every way qualified and I hope he may obtain the appointment"
—ALS, *ibid.*, USMA, Board of Visitors. On June 23, 1873, Jewell, Hartford, had
written to USG on the same subject.—ALS, *ibid.* USG appointed Oliver P.
Temple, Amos B. Kendig, Francis Wayland, Charles S. Hamilton, Commodore
Christopher R. P. Rodgers, Thomas P. Morgan, and James D. Cameron to the
board of visitors, USMA, for June, 1874. See *New York Times,* May 30, June 3–5,
Dec. 3, 1874.

1874, JAN. 21.   Anonymous, New York City, to USG. "If you do not wish your
party and your *good name* entirely used up, you will not allow your officers here
and at Washington—having charge of the fraudulent transaction cases, softly
termed '*Irregularities,*' bought off, which is now being done. The great case of
Woodruff & Robinson, of this city, which your detective, Jane, said was the worse
that ever came under his observation—where the irregularities amounted to

over $2,000.000.00—is now quite out of sight. Every paper in New York, even the 'Times,' has been '*fixed*,' and nothing more is said about it. A poor man is broken down at once, with the slightest cause—but these Million-airs, rob and cheat the Government, and it is 'all right' with them. Read this truth from an *old merchant* & One of Your *Staunch friends*."—L, DNA, RG 56, Letters Received from the President. Customs fraud cases in New York City provoked controversy over the investigative methods of Benaiah G. Jayne, special agent, Treasury Dept. See *HMD*, 43-1-264, 173–75, 180–81, 219, 231; *New York Times*, Dec. 24, 1873, Aug. 22, 1874.

1874, JAN. 23.   USG speech. "*Gentleman:* I am very happy to see you in the capacity in which you present yourselves—in your relations as an association of health boards. Your objects are highly commendable and entitled to great consideration by all classes. It is not my province now to say more than to express my wish that your objects may be successful. Again I thank you for your attendance."—*Washington Evening Star*, Jan. 23, 1874. USG spoke in response to A. W. Boardman, president, National Health Council. "*Mr. President:*—We have come as a delegation of the municipal boards of health from some of the principal cities of the Union, to whom has been committed the all-important trust of the health of the people, the preservation of which constitutes a state. Our province is rather deeds than words; and so we merely desire to thank you heartily for your invitation to visit the head of the nation, and cordially to wish for you that best blessing of heaven—good health."—*Ibid.* See also *Chicago Tribune*, Jan. 24, 1874.

1874, JAN. 23.   USG order promulgated by Secretary of State Hamilton Fish directing executive depts. to organize displays for the Centennial exhibition and creating a board to coordinate these activities.—DS, DLC-Hamilton Fish; DNA, RG 45, Letters Received from the President; *ibid.*, RG 56, Records Relating to Government Participation in Expositions; (2) *ibid.*, RG 59, Miscellaneous Letters; *ibid.*, RG 60, Letters from the President; *ibid.*, RG 94, Letters Received, 1326 1874.

1874, JAN. 23.   Benjamin Thomas, Weatherford, Tex., to USG. "I wish to state that I am a Couloured man and have been robed and Badly treated by those who have been in rebelion against the united States   I and my family have been turned out of doors out of my own house and farm   this has taken from me 1000 dollars worth of labour   I have aplied to the authorities and went myslf to Governor Davis but nothing has been done for me   we Couloured people can get no land here to setle on as there is such a strong prejudice against us   we wish to know if the President or the Government at Washington can do any thing for 2 familys are turned out and they are making Efforts to turn more of us out of our Houses and farms after setling on State land acording to the Homestead law and paying all expenses   Several murders have been commited here but nothing done to Arrest the murderers   they are still here at large   I live 3 miles West of Weatherford and Hope to get an answer to this . . . I hope the

President will Investigate this affair for we are all Suffering and our children not Educated and they want to have us poor and to Slave for them as we did Before   the rebels Here all the Setlers lands   they Claim and turn them out of doors *both Black and Whites*"—ALS, DNA, RG 60, Letters from the President. On Nov. 8, Thomas again wrote to USG. "I am a couloured man and live 3 miles West of Weatherford Parker Co Texas   I wish to Say as I Stated Before that the couloured people are Suffering here and cannot get their rights among the democrats   we are alowed no Showing here in law   they Steal murder and turn poor people out of their Houses by false pretences forged deeds and old confederate Claims   we are Here Overrun by peace Breakers and disturbers threatening Couloured and poor white Setlers from the north with death and to be put out their of their Claims Because they are not Democrats   here the coulered people are brught to great Suffering here and all over Texas though the rebel papers lie and say that the couloured people are treated right all over Texas which is a false hood   Both Couloured and White people do not know when they will be murdered for Speaking the truth   these people have taken my homstead from me my plantation Houses and will do the Same with other Black and White Setlers if something is not done for us Imediately ion old Confederate Certeficate Claims   they give no quarter or Showing to an actual Setlers Claim here in Parker, C   the Grand Jury would not hear me in Weatherford when I looked for Justice   for Gods Sake President do something for me. . . . Part of my homestead is on Rail R land   these people have no deed or title to it   they are now about to remove the fences around my plantation   I hope the president will Send an Officer to put this man out of my Homestead under the U. S law"—ALS, *ibid.*

1874, JAN. 24.   USG endorsement. "Refered to the Sec. of War. Let this application appear for the class of /76, with spl. attention called."—AES, DNA, RG 94, Correspondence, USMA. Written on a letter of Jan. 22 from John S. Mosby, Warrenton, Va., to USG. "The bearer—Major Scott—who is one of your earliest & warmest friends in Va—has a son, a youth of great promise, who desires to get the an appointment as cadet at West Point. You could not confer a favor on one more deserving or who will do more honor to you & the country. He is a member of one of the most distinguished & influential families in this State many of whom are your supporter."—ALS, *ibid.* On the same day, James C. Scott, Warrenton, wrote to USG requesting appointment to USMA.—ALS, *ibid.* On Feb. 27, John Scott, Warrenton, wrote to USG acknowledging the endorsement. ". . . Let me express to you Mr President my unfeigned thanks for this mark of favour shown to my son & the great honour done my family. We the 'Grant Conservatives' of this District, mean by a large majority, to elect your *tried* adherent Col. *Mosby* to Congress next fall and I have enclosed herewith a published article from my pen, as the Key note of the campaign."—ALS, *ibid.* Scott did not attend USMA. See John Scott, *Partisan Life with Col. John S. Mosby* (New York, 1867).

1874, JAN. 24.   John McDonald, supervisor of Internal Revenue, St. Louis, to Orville E. Babcock. "The weather being favorable for shipment, I send you by

Express to day a box of Game, some young Bear Meat, two saddles of Antelope, two dozen Grouse, two Quail, and two pair Pheasants; which you will please share with President Grant with my compliments. . . ."—AL (torn), Babcock Papers, ICN. On Jan. 30, Babcock drafted a reply to McDonald acknowledging receipt of the game. ". . . The President and Secty of War send many thanks— . . ."—ADf (initialed), *ibid.*

1874, JAN. 25.   Vincent A. Witcher, Washington, D. C., to USG. "I have several times called to see you not to ask for an office but to shake your hand and say to you that whilst Predjudice & pashion is runing Mountain High & great injustice I believe has been done you the time will come when your Administration will be aptly compaired with those of Madison & Monroe & lastly but not leastly to say, I hoped to have the pleasure of stumping the Kanawha District for you in 76   I canvassed it last fall for Mr Hall but would rather canvass it for you than any man living simply because I think you have been fearless and concientious   I shall return to our state on the 30 and consequently shall not see you   I have nothing to ask and only write this in obedience to the dictates of a Rebell Soldier's judgement who tries to rise a bove section & predjudice . . . P S I Allso wished to say if an occasion should Demand it I would be found on the side of the government as I was in the Army of the Confedracy"—ALS, USG 3.

1874, JAN. 26.   Julian Allen, New York City, to USG. "It is almost criminal to discharge so many from the Brooklyn Navy Yard now. It adds to the general distress."—Telegram received (at 10:00 A.M.), DLC-USG, IB.

1874, JAN. 26.   Mrs. Jasper A. Maltby, Chicago, to USG. "I hear the Office of Inspectress of Customs, at the Port of Brownsville Texas is to be vacant very soon. I should like the appointment very much indeed. I have a Brother living there with whom I should make my home. I am so very unfortunate as to be obliged to earn my own living. Knowing of your many deeds of kindness to others, I have taken the liberty of asking this favor. I have many friends both here and elsewhere who will give all the recomendations you may require. And I hope I am not entirely forgotten by yourself and family,"—ALS, DNA, RG 56, Letters Received from the President. On March 5, Levi P. Luckey wrote to U.S. Representative Benjamin F. Butler of Mass. "The President directs me to refer the enclosed letter to you, with the view of getting the place of Matron in the Wisconsin Orphans Home for Mrs. Maltby. She is the widow of rather a leading democratic politician before the War, who, however, took his stand for the Union the moment secession commenced; volunteered early; came out a General, and died soon after the War, leaving his family poor."—ALS, DLC-Benjamin F. Butler. No appointment followed. Melvina A. Maltby received a pension in 1878. See *SRC*, 45-2-83.

1874, JAN. 27.   To Senate. "I transmit for the consideration of the Senate, with a view to its ratification, a Protocol relative to a claim on the government of Chile, in the case of the ship 'Good Return.'"—Copy, DNA, RG 59, Reports to the President and Congress. On March 2, the Senate ratified this protocol.

1874, JAN. 27.   Gardner Rand, Troy, N. Y., to USG. "I last week received to add to my collection of autographs, a letter written by President Lincoln to yourself when Lieut General.   my object in writing is to find out if possible, if it is an original which it has every appearance of.   and unles[s] you have the original I think that this is it. Below is a copy of it. 'Executive Mansion Washington April 14th 1865   LIEUT GENL GRANT Please call at 11. AM to-day instead of 9. as agreed last evening. Yours truly (signed) ALINCOLN.' If you will be so kind as to favor me with an answer if but a line. I should be greatly obliged"—ALS, IHi. On Feb. 5, Culver C. Sniffen wrote on this letter. "If you will send the original I will soon decide for you. Mr Lincoln was assassinated on the night of the 14th April 1865, you will remember. Send it to me & I will ask the President."—ANS, *ibid.* See *PUSG,* 14, 484.

1874, JAN. 29, Thursday.   To Edwards Pierrepont. "Yesterday I had invitations sent to you and Mrs. Pierrepont to our next State dinner and intended them to be accompanied by an invitation to you to come on Monday next and spend a week as our guests. Both Mrs. Grant and myself will be pleased if you can come, and will endeavor to make the time pass pleasantly to both you and Mrs. Pierrepont."—Diana J. Rendell, Inc., List 32 [Oct., 1991], no. 53.

1874, JAN. 30.   Arthur C. Ducat, Chicago, to USG. "An application to you for the appointment of my Son Arthur C Ducat Jr to a Cadetship at large in the Military Academy at West Point was forwarded to you through Lt Genl P H Sheridan. I learn from my friend Hon J A Garfield that the application from its date did or will reach you until after your appointments are made. This is to request that should any of your appointments not accept, or should there be from any other cause a vacancy that you appoint my son. . . ."—ALS, DNA, RG 94, Correspondence, USMA. On Feb. 2, Brig. Gen. Montgomery C. Meigs, Washington, D. C., wrote to USG. "I enclose a note from Colonel Ducat, whom I knew after the battle of Chickamauga, on the staff of General Rosencranz at Chattanooga. He then seemed to me to be a zealous soldierly officer, useful and intelligent. If you can appoint the youth, I should expect good service from the son of such a man as Colonel Ducat appeared to me to be."—LS, *ibid.* Arthur C. Ducat, Jr., graduated USMA in 1879. See Lt. Gen. Philip H. Sheridan to Orville E. Babcock, June 9, 1874, copy, DLC-Philip H. Sheridan.

1874, JAN. 31.   USG endorsement. "Refered to the Sec. of State. Please answer Senator Boreman whether an apt. can be given."—AES, DNA, RG 59, Letters of Application and Recommendation. Written on a letter of Jan. 29 from U.S. Senator Arthur I. Boreman of West Va. to USG. "Allow me to bring to your notice Mr: Robert W. Simmons, of Parkersburg, West Virginia, for appointment to a consulship or some other foreign position. Mr: Simmons is a coloured man of a bright mind naturally & of very fair acquirements, and is also a very sprighly and ctive business man, and, I feel assured, would perform the duties of such post with credit to himself and to the satisfaction of the administration. I assure you I should be more than gratified if you could favor him with an appointment."—ALS, *ibid.* On Feb. 1, 1873, Boreman had written to USG recommending Robert W. Simmons for appointment to Liberia or Haiti.—ALS, *ibid.* No appointment followed.

1874, Jan. 31.   Maj. Stephen V. Benét, Washington, D. C., to Orville E. Babcock. "I have received the Official appointment of my Son, for West Point—When opportunity offers, will you do me the favor to thank the President in the heartiest manner for his kindness. I would gladly do so in person, but am well aware he is overrun with visitors, & my going would be an additional bore to him. With many thanks for your interest in the matter, . . ."—ALS, USG 3. James W. Benét graduated USMA in 1880.

1874, Jan. 31.   Ludwig August Frankl, Vienna, to USG. "Deign to permit the undersigned, as President of the first European Congress of directors and heads of institutions for the blind, which met at Vienna, during the holding of the World's Fair, under the auspices of the Imperial and Royal Ministry of Religion and Public Instruction, to submit to Your Excellency the report of the proceedings of said Congress, together with an account of the foundation of the new educational institution which he had the honor to establish himself in 1872 at the Hohe Warte, near Vienna, for the benefit of fifty blind children. The touching interest taken by Your Excellency in every humanitarian work leads the undersigned to hope that you will favorably receive these publications, which embrace both the scientific and the social view of the question. The object is to shed light into the souls of unfortunate human beings—who, according to statistics, number more than a million—whose eyes are closed to the light of day, and whose minds, imploring our assistance, aspire to a deliverance which can only be given by instruction and by a moral and religious education."—LS (in French), DNA, RG 59, Miscellaneous Letters; translation, *ibid.* Frankl was a poet and educational reformer.

[*1874, Jan.*].   Mary Anna Longstreth to USG. "A letter, received a few weeks ago from our friend Jonathan Richards, was so cheering that I thought it would interest our highly esteemed President, and encourage him in his benevolent plans for the Indians. We sympathize with him cordially in the trials and persecution he is sometimes called to endure for righteousness' sake. May he abundantly receive the blessing promised to those who suffer in the cause of truth, justice, and mercy,—the reward of peace in this life, and an unfading crown of glory in the world to come! Believing he will be interested, also, in the account of the reception of the Indians at our meetinghouse, I enclose that with a copy of the letter from Jonathan Richards to my Sister, who is actively engaged in working for the Indian Schools under the care of our Society."—ALS (docketed Jan. 19, 1874), DNA, RG 75, Letters Received, Wichita Agency. The enclosures are *ibid.* See *HED*, 43-1-1, part 5, I, 591–93; [Margaret Newlin], *Memoir of Mary Anna Longstreth* (Philadelphia, 1886).

[*1874, Jan.*].   Ellen L. O'Dowd, sister of "the late Brigadier General James L Kiernan," Brooklyn, to USG seeking an appointment for her husband "Charles O'Dowd to any position where he could earn a comfortable livelihood for us."—

ALS (docketed Jan. 14, 1874), DNA, RG 107, Appointment Papers. No appointment followed.

On March 13, 1869, James L. Kiernan, Washington, D. C., had written to USG. "I held high positions in New York before the war. I gave them up to enter the army; I served in the army faithfully and was repeatedly wounded; I also served in civil life, canvassing in many States for the Union cause from 1864 to 1869. I have impoverished myself in my fight, military and civil, for the Union. I ask the position of U. S. minister to *Portugal* or *Turkey* which I consider I deserve by my merits in the Union cause and which I am adapted for by education and experience as U. S Consul"—ALS, *ibid.*, RG 59, Letters of Application and Recommendation. On April 17, Kiernan wrote to Secretary of State Hamilton Fish. "Senator Wilson informs me that some party impressed you with the idea that I 'drank'; I pronounce this statement made to you by 'some party,' either ignorantly or maliciously, *utterly false* and I must state that my whole life disproves it. . . ."—ALS, *ibid.* Related papers are *ibid.* See *PUSG*, 10, 512.

[*1874, Jan.*]. "Your memorialists, of the Third Legislative Assembly of the Territory of Wyoming," to USG claiming "the Chief Justice of this Territory Jos W Fisher to be incompetent for so highly responsible a trust as that which he now holds. . . ."—D (docketed Jan. 12, 1874), DNA, RG 60, Letters Received, Wyoming. On Dec. 17, 1875, USG renominated Joseph W. Fisher as chief justice, Wyoming Territory. See *PUSG*, 19, 399–400.

1874, FEB. 1. J. W. Dougherty, San Francisco, to USG. "I am intending to take the precaution to mark this letter private, that if possible it may reach your own eye, as it concerns a matter of vital importance to me. My husband is owner in one of the Alabama claims, and our circumstances are such that we are in urgent need of the money. For several years we have looked forward to their settlement as a relief from poverty—for my husband is an invalid, and for a long time has not been able to attend to any business—but it has always been the 'hope deferred that maketh the heart sick.' We have tried to sell the claim, or get an advance on it, but since the French claims delays, no confidence is felt in government claims, and our efforts have failed. Since the assembling of Congress daily we have watched the papers hoping against hope for favorable news, but, so far, without success. Lately we have heard, indirectly, that the Committee on Claims had decided to recommend an immediate settlement, paying directly to the owners—but, that the President had opposed it, advising the appointment of a number of commissioners to decide who it was to go to. This, if true, we fear may make a long delay; and as each name is mentioned in the arbitration made at Geneva I thought perhaps if you knew how exceedingly in need we are, you could be induced to let it be paid right away. We are reduced to that point that we only have the *dreadful* alternative of dependence on unwilling relatives. You have been so generous and humane in your Indian policy that I cannot but cherish a hope that you will give heed to other tales of distress. And I have studied your face and actions badly if I am mistaken in the belief that if you once will to have a matter accomplished that you do not succeed. Pardon me for intruding my private affairs upon your attention, but believe that stern necessity only led me to the step. Can you give this matter your consideration? And would it be possible for you to spare a clerk for a few minutes to let me know if I can have any hope?"—ALS, DNA, RG 59, Miscellaneous Letters.

1874, FEB. 2.   Mary J. Barnett, Walnut Grove, Ky., to USG indicating financial distress and requesting leave for her son 2nd Lt. Charles R. Barnett, USMA 1868, to visit her ailing daughter. ". . . She is the same little girl that wrote to you a year ago for your Photograph and you sent it to her. She got crippled, in a play at School nearly a year ago and has been confined to bed ever since with a low nervous fever. And ever Since the 6th of last April has been dieing by inches. . . ."—ALS, DNA, RG 94, ACP, 5014 1872.

1874, FEB. 2.   William Weir, Fort Winnebago, Portage, Wis., to USG. "Today I have mailed to you, a copy of The Wisconsin State Register a Republican news paper published in Portage by Messers Brannan & Turner—At Vicksburg I gave you a copy of said paper in it you read a part of my military History   Before I served under you when you were Asst Q. m. at Detroit—I had served under Generals. MaComb, Scott, Gains, Taylor, Worth, & our most distingushed Generals since the days of Gen Scott—. . . I am still doing duty under Orders that I received from Gen Thos S. Jesup. In charge of what there is left of the old military Reservation at this Post—When Col Abercrombie he was Capt of Co K when I joined 1st U. S. Infy saw me here at the commencment of the last war he asked me what I was doing   I told him I was left here guarding Indians   The Col. said that was what he had been doing until he received orders to take all soldiers under his command & go into Virginia & fight Rebels & that as I was an old U. S. Regular Soldier that I should go. I obeyed the Cols Orders   You know all about what the Indians did while we were fighting the Rebs & what trouble we have had since the close ~~of close~~ of the war. &c. The white men here that have the most to say about Indians are not Soldiers. They never carried the knapsack & musket   It was Lieut Staffard & twenty soldiers that captured Big Hawk & his band   Peace Commissionrs could not remove Big Hawk from Wisconsin Yellow Thunder & a small band of Winnebagoes are still around the Old Fort— I was one of the U. S. Soldiers that took *yellow* Thunder & his band prisoners thirty years ago. . . . The Indians stands in fear of soldiers. I found that out when the Army left this Post. I was left in charge. When the Indians did destry public property I put one in black hole.   hundreds came into the Fort & demanded that I should release the prisoner   After all the Big Chiefs talked, I said that if the Indians did not behave that I would send for the soldiers & remove every Indian that there was then around the Fort   That the Indians feared & promised to be good & pay all damages &c   I then released the prisoner & had no more trouble in making Indians obey orders &c. Soldiers are the best friends The Indians have got. Indian Agents make all the money they can from poor Lo Indians. The Freed mans Bureau has been broken up. & If Goverment wants to save millions of Dollars they will give Army Officers full control of Indian Affairs. Dear General—We are cursed in Wisconsin with ~~with~~ a so called *Reform Party* headed by Wm R. Taylor whose Chief leaders are men, having brought with them from the German States loose ideas in regard to temperance Religion

& good morals; . . . You will observe that the so called reformers in Wisconsin have made political captial by lecturing & writing on the Indian Question. It is time that the scattred tribe of Winnebagoes should be all settled on their rese- vatn before another cold winter setts in"—ALS, DNA, RG 75, Letters Received, Miscellaneous. Related clippings are *ibid.*

On Jan. 17, 1876, Weir wrote to USG praising Wis. Senator Henry D. Bar- ron. ". . . He is preparing a speech on the subject of the third term, in which he will take high ground that there is no 'unwriten law' of the republic against it, . . . Gen. Stewart, Van Vliet, Asst Qr Mr General, U. S. Army, [h]as informed me that my claim for services as Agent in charge of Fort Winnebago Wis. 'has been refered to the Third Auditor of the Treasury recommending settlement from April 1st 1855, to Dec 31st 1855—9 months at the rate of $20 per month, $180 00' Pleas see that I am paid. All Quartermasters which I first served un- der are dead but yourself, and I respectffully ask to remain in charge of the Post while I live."—ALS, USG 3. On April 12, Weir wrote to USG charging Jeffer- son Davis with malfeasance in an 1853 land sale while serving as secretary of war.—ALS, DNA, RG 206, Miscellaneous Letters Received. On Nov. 10, Weir wrote to USG concerning the presidential election in Wis. and his position at Fort Winnebago.—ALS, *ibid.,* RG 92, Consolidated Correspondence, Fort Winnebago.

1874, FEB. 4. John C. Winsmith (or Winnsmith), Spartanburg, S. C., to USG. "Desiring an appointment from your Excellency, and not having the time, at present, to make a personal application at Washington, I submit a written state- ment in reference to myself, which I trust may receive your favorable consider- ation. Though I was an officer in the Confederate army, I joined the Republi- can Party when the war ended, and have zealously advocated its principles since then, even during the reign of terror which existed in this section of the coun- try. I thought it proper at that time to communicate to your Excellency the extent of the Ku Klux organization, which information you referred to Senator Scott, Chairman of the Committee on Southern Outrages. . . ."—ALS, DNA, RG 59, Letters of Application and Recommendation. Winsmith enclosed editorials he had written while editor of the *Columbia New Era.*—*Ibid.* Related papers are *ibid.* On Jan. 28, 1875, Winsmith again wrote to USG. "I observe a Bill is before Congress to establish the Western District of S. C. I desire to be appointed U. S. Judge for that District, and hope your Excellency may give me the appoint- ment. I have been practising as an Attorney for 16 years. Senator Robertson, Hon. A. S. Wallace and all the members of Congress from S. C. will inform you of my qualifications and fitness for the office."—ALS, *ibid.,* RG 60, Records Re- lating to Appointments. No appointment followed.

On Oct. 5, 1874, Winsmith had written to USG. "Confidential . . . When I addressed you on the 4th of February last, I desired that you would give me an appointment to office. I do not now desire any civil appointment from the Gen- eral Government. The State of South Carolina is now passing through a bloody ordeal, and as a citizen and as a Republican, I cannot think of absenting my- self from my post of duty. During the reign of terror here under Ku Klux rule, I thought proper to communicate to your Excellency the extent and power of

that infamous organization; and I even went so far as to respectfully suggest
to you the propriety of sending General Sheridan to South Carolina to crush the
hideous monster—Ku Kluxism. You, however, did not think proper to send him.
The result has been: a committee from Congress on Southern outrages at an
enormous cost to the Federal Government; a Marshall for S. C, Johnson, who
was notoriously guilty of receiving blackmail from the Ku Klux; Deputy Mar-
shalls and U. S. Commissioners who did likewise; a few trials and convictions
in the U. S. Courts; and then the pardoning of the criminals. I believed then, as
I believe now, that if you had sent Genl. Sheridan here, under your proclamation of martial law, and directed him to try the Chiefs of the Ku Klux Klans by
military commission, and if found guilty, to fortwith execute them, the world
would not have heard of a third rebellion in in La. and S. C. It was necessary not
only to cut off, but to sear, the hydra heads of Secession, Rebellion and Murder.
You will recollect what Genl. Jackson said in 1832, 'If there is Nullification, I will
hang Calhoun.' A third rebellion now raises its hideous front before us in the
upper and eastern counties of S. C. The pardoned Ku Klux, and the murderers,
who for a while fled the State, have returned. Now it is a 'war of races' they are
inaugurating. There is a Shotwell, associate of D. H. Hill, as Editor of the Charlotte, N. C, 'Southern Home,' a pardoned Ku Klux, who sends broadcast over
this section the seeds of rebellion, sedition and murder. There are many others
whose names I might mention. Suffice it to say there are men in all the Counties above referred to who are engaged solely in preparing for another butch-
ery of the white and colored Republicans: They have organized white leagues,
rifle clubs, and a secret police, not only in the towns but, also in country places.
There is a fixed determination, on the part of these bad men, never to acknowledge the results of the war. You are aware, Mr. President, that the negroes were
held in the Southern States, by a tenure of force, and that it required force to
make them free. I will here add: it will yet require *force* to secure their rights to
them. What I am now going to state will explain the conduct of those infamous
men to whom I have just referred: On the 8th inst, in Columbia, the Ku Klux
Klan in S. C. will nominate for Congress from the 4th Dist, Gen. J. B. Kershaw,
Grand Cyclops of the Ku Klux Klan in S. C—a man of smooth exterior, but a
viper at heart—an oily tongued hypocrite and a perjured villian—He accepted
his parol and took the oath of allegiance to the U. S. Govt; The evidence can
be produced to convict him not only of being the Grand Cyclops of the Ku Klux
Klan, but of actually initiating into the Klan at Camden S. C. a treacherous
and cowardly Judge—W. M. Thomas—who was elected as a Republican by the
S. C. Legislature. In the 8 Counties composing the 4th Dist—viz: Greenville,
Spartanburg, Union, York, Chester, Lancaster, Fairfield and Kershaw, there is a
clear Republican majority of 2,500 voters. This majority will be easily overcome,
unless some proper precaution is adopted, as the Ku Klux are organized to murder, & the Republicans are not. It is true there are detachments of U. S. Troops
in several of the towns; but there is no regular communication between them;
and there is no officer in chief command, who can at a glance comprehend the
danger threatened. There is no doubt but on the 3d day of Novr—Election day
—Georgians and North Carolinians, will be passed over the Air Line R. R, and

together with the rifle clubs and white leagues, take possession of the polling places. As during the reign of terror by the Ku Klux Klan, I took the liberty of suggesting to your Excellency what I conceived to be the remedy, I will now again, when I see the portentous threatenings of the coming storm of violence and murder, suggest to you the propriety of ordering Genl. Sheridan on a tour of observation through N. C., S. C., and Ga, to stop at Charlotte, Spartanburg, Union, Columbia and Atlanta. His presence here—the power of his great name and of his military renown—will cause the traitors to tremble, and to pause in the preparations for their bloody work. The force which Kershaw and his adherents can probably raise will be about 3 thousand men. I believe if General Sheridan comes soon the bloody plans of the Traitors and murderers will be thwarted. If he does not come, I verily believe we will have a re-enactment of the bloody scenes of 1870–1871. Mr. President; What I have written proceeds from what I conceive to be a sense of duty to my country. I am so situated that I know whereof I write. I was the Brig. Genl. appointed by Gov. Orr to command in this part of the State; and I held the same position under Gov Scott. I have watched these people for 28 years, and I know what they are doing now. I can scarcely be considered an alarmist, as I have been in more than 30 battles and engagements, and have been repeatedly wounded. Mr. Chamberlain will be elected Governor by 20 or 30 thousand majority; but the great fight will be in the 4th Dist for Congress. If Kershaw is allowed to carry out his wicked designs, he will always be a thorn in the side of our Governor & will presume to dictate to him. If Kershaw is thwarted, and we can have the troops to remain here for 6 months after the election, we will have every thing then so settled, that we can protect all our citizens in their rights under the Laws. I would add, in conclusion, that I believe there are 3 Generals in S. C. who do not belong to the Ku Klux Klan, and who do not entertain the designs of Kershaw, Hampton, Chesnutt, Gary & others, to overthrow the State Govt—and they are: Genl. James Connor, of Charleston, Genl. John Bratton of Winnsboro, and Genl Johnson Hagood of Barnwell."—ALS, *ibid.*, Letters Received, S. C. In [*Nov.-Dec.?*], Daniel H. Chamberlain wrote to USG concerning his inaugural address as governor of S. C., delivered on Dec. 1, 1874.—William Evarts Benjamin, Catalogue No. 42, March, 1892, p. 6. On Aug. 9, 1873, USG had pardoned Randolph A. Shotwell, convicted on Sept. 22, 1871, of conspiracy in N. C., sentenced to six years in prison, and fined $5,000.—Copy, DNA, RG 59, General Records. See Gordon McKinney, ed., "The Klan in the Southern Mountains: The Lusk-Shotwell Controversy," *Appalachian Journal*, 8, 2 (Winter, 1981), 89–104.

1874, FEB. 6.   To Congress. "I transmit herewith a copy of a communication dated the 22d ultimo received from the Governor of the State of New York, in which it is announced that in accordance with the invitation of Congress as expressed in the act approved July 2d 1864, that state now presents for acceptance a bronze statue of George Clinton, deceased, one of its distinguished citizens." —Copy, DNA, RG 59, Reports to the President and Congress. *HED*, 43-1-115. The Jan. 22 letter of Governor John A. Dix of N. Y. to USG is *ibid.*; LS, DNA, RG 59, Miscellaneous Letters.

1874, FEB. 6.   To House of Representatives. "I transmit to the House of Representatives, in answer to their Resolution of the 16th ultimo, a report from the Secretary of State, with accompanying papers."—Copy, DNA, RG 59, Reports to the President and Congress. *HED*, 43-1-114. On Jan. 16, the House of Representatives had passed a resolution requesting papers concerning Roderick F. Farrell, U.S. consul, Cadiz (1866–69), "who was instrumental in exposing the frauds on the revenue by certain Spanish Wine Merchants, and their agents."— D, DNA, RG 59, Miscellaneous Letters.

1874, FEB. 8.   James H. Slack, Standing Rock, Dakota Territory, to USG. "it is through the request of the Citizens of this Vicinity, that I write to You giving a discription of the condition of the Standing Rock agency the way the Indians are Scattered around   there are about Eighty miles of Country on the opposite of this river where the Indians have no right to, part of, Sioux Indians that belong to the agency, camp on this Side of the River and proul this County. So a white man cant live in this County with Safity.   there are a greate many men here now that wishes to Settle on the land, here which would be of benefit to the country also to the N. P. Rail Road, that runs through the upper end of this Scope of country.   we wish to know how it is that those Indians cant be taken accross the river where they belong. So it will the whites a chance to take farms and Settle this part of the Territory.   the Goverment Clothes and feeds the Indians why cant the be kept on their Resevation as well as to be Roveing the country as they do   if those Indians ever put away from this Side of the river this Spring there would be over fifty Settler take claims along this River that dare not do it the way it is now   the agent here has the power to take those Indians on their agency if he See propper but it appears as they do as please with him   we trust our President will Show us a favor and have those Indians taken to their agency, So that this Section of Country Can be Settled by parties that wish to take Claims a go to farming   it will of great benefit to the public in general."—ALS, DNA, RG 75, Letters Received, Grand River Agency. See *HED*, 43-1-1, part 5, I, 598–99, 43-2-1, part 5, I, 554–56.

1874, FEB. 9.   USG endorsement directing Secretary of the Treasury William A. Richardson to authorize a three-month extension of leave for Capt. George R. Slicer, revenue marine service.—Cohasco, Catalogue No. 30, Oct. 26, 1989, no. 116. On the same day, Orville E. Babcock wrote to Richardson on this subject. ". . . He is the only remaining child of old Mr. Slicer, for fifty years a Methodist preacher and his presence is necessary with his father during his remaining days—which cannot extend beyond the time asked."—Copy, DLC-USG, II, 2. On Feb. 11, Richardson wrote to USG reporting extension of Slicer's leave.—Copy, DNA, RG 56, Letters Sent to the President. Henry Slicer died on April 23.

1874, FEB. 9.   To House of Representatives. "I have the honor to transmit herewith the report of the Secretary of the Department of the Interior, to whom was referred the resolution of the House of Representatives of January 7, requesting 'a statement of the extent and nature of the contracts, purchases, and expenditures for the Indian service made since July 1, 1873, setting forth which, if any, of them were made or entered into without conference with the board of Indian commissioners appointed by the President, and the extent and description of contracts and vouchers objected to by said board, stating to what extent payments have been made thereon against their remonstrance.'"—*HED*, 43-1-123. On Feb. 5, Secretary of the Interior Columbus Delano had transmitted to USG the requested information and explained the cumbersome procedures for examining Indian accounts. ". . . The responsibility of finally acting upon these accounts being placed upon me by law, cannot be transferred or avoided. I shall, therefore, continue in the future as in the past, to exercise the most rigid scrutiny into their character, and shall act in accordance with my judgment and sense of duty in all cases, until Congress sees fit to provide some other method for their adjudication. . . ."—*Ibid.*

On Jan. 8, William Welsh, Philadelphia, had written to USG. ". . . Before I refer to the present lamentable condition of the Indian Office, allow me to thank you with all sincerity for your invariable kindness to me during the five years in which I have, at much cost of time and money, co-operated with you in your noble effort to save the remnant of our American Indians, and thereby to remove a fearful stigma from the nation. We all owe you a debt of gratitude for taking Indian Agencies from those who ordinarily were using them as party spoils, and for transferring them to the care of religious bodies, who expend hundreds of thousands of dollars annually in successful efforts to civilize and Christianize Indians. . . . At our recent appointed interview, I felt constrained to inform you that since the last letting of contracts for supplies, a powerful Indian Ring, comprising men whom I named to you, had been formed, and that in some unaccountable way it had acquired such an influence in the Interior Department that, if unchecked, it would undermine your merciful policy by destroying the confidence of Congress, and thus hindering the appropriations necessary to promote Indian civilization. As you will remember, I further said that my belief in the integrity of the Secretary of the Interior had not been impaired, and that having thoroughly cordial relations with him, I desired to exert every persuasive influence before invoking your aid. As these efforts have failed to procure the reforms in the Indian Office necessary to protect the Indian and the Government, I now present the case to you in an open letter, as I do not feel free to confer with you privately about the duties of a Cabinet officer . . . If the whole Indian service could be placed under the entire control of the Society of Friends, the many forms of demoralization, now so baleful in their influence, could be checked, Indian civilization promoted, and I do believe a million of dollars a-year saved by the Government. There is a devotion to this cause in the Society of Friends that I do not find as marked in any other religious body, and this, with their large experience, gives them peculiar facilities in procuring and supervising conscientious agents. . . ."—William Welsh, *Indian Office: Wrongs Doing and Reforms Needed* (Philadelphia, 1874).

1874, FEB. 10. USG order to credit Edward Haywood, State Dept. clerk, for disbursing "five hundred dollars, during the month of February 1874, from the fund for the expenses under the Neutrality Act, the object of which it is deemed inexpedient now to be made known."—Copy, Hamilton Fish diary, DLC-Hamilton Fish. On the same day, Secretary of State Hamilton Fish recorded in his diary. "The President signed the approval of the payment of $500.00/100 out of the Neutrality Appropriation in order to pay Mr-Cadwallader."—*Ibid.*

1874, FEB. 10. U.S. Senator Aaron A. Sargent of Calif. to USG. "The signers of the accompanying paper proposed to call upon you in behalf of the matter named in it; but I suggested that it was probably unnecessary, & a mere letter showing their interest in the subject might be placed on file. They assented to that view, & I beg leave to submit such letter. . . . The signers are all of the Pacific Coast Rep. delegation except Mr. Tremaine who is a personal friend of Simpson."—ALS, DNA, RG 94, ACP, S128 CB 1863. The enclosure is a petition of Feb. 9 from U.S. Senator William M. Stewart of Nev. and seven others to USG. "The undersigned respectfully represent that they have a high regard for Gen. M. D. Simpson of the Commissary Corps, and due appreciation for his excellence as an officer. They beg leave, in view of his qualifications, his services and character, to protest earnestly against his being passed over ~~officer~~ by the promotion of any junior officer of the Corps over his head to the position of Commissary General. They confidently rely on your sense of justice in this matter, & suggest, beyond personal considerations, that the deprivation of an officer, properly fitted for advancement, of the promotion earned by meritorious services, would be an injury to the public service, which they strongly deprecate."—DS, *ibid.* On Feb. 15, Secretary of War William W. Belknap wrote to AG Edward D. Townsend. "*Confidential* . . . The President directs that Gen'l. Eaton Com'y. Gen'l. be retired from active service. . . ."—AL (initialed), *ibid.*, 5178 1874. Related papers are *ibid.* On June 17, Maj. Gen. John M. Schofield, San Francisco, wrote to USG. "Understanding that it may soon be necessary to select an officer to fill the vacant position of Commissary General, and without wishing to say anything to prejudice the claims of any officer of superior rank, I deem it my duty to submit my opinion of the claims and qualifications for that office, of Lieutenant Colonel Simpson, who for several years, has served upon my staff as Chief Commissary of the Military Division of the Pacific. . . ."—ALS, *ibid.*, S128 CB 1863. On Feb. 5, 1875, Leland Stanford, San Francisco, telegraphed to USG. "General Simpson is highly esteemed here for personal worth and faithful service his many friends will be much gratified should he be appointed Commissary General to me it would be a personal favor of the strongest kind,"—Telegram received (on Feb. 6), *ibid.* On Dec. 7, 1874, USG had nominated Lt. Col. Marcus D. L. Simpson, USMA 1846 and asst. commissary-gen., as col.; on Dec. 22, the Senate reconsidered and rejected this nomination. On Jan. 9, 1875, USG renominated Simpson; on Feb. 3, the Senate confirmed Simpson's promotion. On Jan. 9, USG also had nominated Col. Alexander E. Shiras, USMA 1833, for promotion to commissary-gen. with rank of brig. gen. See *PUSG,* 17, 113–14.

1874, FEB. 14. Felix R. Brunot, chairman, Board of Indian Commissioners, Pittsburgh, to USG. "My very great anxiety in regard to the condition of Indian affairs in Wyoming Ter. I hope will excuse me for addressing a letter to you directly on the subject. To send troops to the Red Cloud and Whetstone Agencies, as is proposed by General Sheridan and approved by the Interior Department as I learn from this mornings telegram in the newspapers, will give the Sioux just cause for making War; and the moment the troops march across the North Platte, the lives of the whites at the Agencies and of the settlers all along the border will be in imminent peril. The end will probably be, that after a vast expenditure of life and treasure, it will be again found in the summing up that the Government will have been in the wrong. The act of sending the troops would be an infraction of the solemn pledge of the Government made through the original Board of Army Peace Commissioners, ratified by the Senate. The killing of Appleton in a quarrel with an Indian—and the murder of the two officers in another quarter by individual murderers certainly does not justify such an infraction on our part; or the attack upon a whole tribe, the bulk of them anxious to be at peace, and guilty of no wrong. If—as there is good reason to believe—the conduct of the Agents and their confederates at these Agencies has been such as greatly to embitter a portion of the Indians against the whites, and there is danger to themselves and the Agency employees in consequence—the Agencies should at once be withdrawn, and troops so disposed as to give protection to the settlements along the Border until a better understanding shall be reached. Permit me to say that I fully appreciate the difficulties of the position, and know the strong influence both in the West and elsewhere that is bent upon having an Indian War if possible, right or wrong—But your prudent and just control has defeated all such influences for nearly five years, and I do not despair of its success now. Of course if the *War* does come, it will be charged upon the *Peace* policy. The industrious manipulation of the Telegraph, the bloody incidents of an Indian War, and the sensational reports of newspaper warriors, will for a little deceive, as to its origin—but the truth will be developed in due time, and the righteous indignation of the people be visited upon those who shall be found to be responsible."—Copy, DNA, RG 94, Letters Received, 563 1874. See Secretary of War William W. Belknap to Secretary of the Interior Columbus Delano, Feb. 21, Df (undated), *ibid.*; copy, *ibid.*, RG 107, Letters Sent, Military Affairs. On Feb. 26, Delano wrote to Belknap a letter that USG approved. ". . . The sole purpose of the Interior Department in asking for troops at Red Cloud's and Spotted Tail's Agencies, was to prevent, and not to cause, hostilities. It was supposed that these troops would be used as a protecting, and not as an aggressive, force. The information received by this Department from the two Agents of the Agencies alluded to, seems to justify reasonable apprehensions that the Minneconjous, Sans Arcs and Unkapapas, who have never attached themselves to either of these Agencies, and who were known to be in the neighborhood, were likely by their influence to produce disturbances and to endanger peace. It was believed by the Agents, and others in that vicinity who advised with the Department, that a military force nearer these Agencies than any at that time existing, would serve to prevent the depredations of the hostile Sioux, who had not joined the Agencies, and thereby probably dissipate the danger of a war with any of the Sioux tribes. . . ."—LS, *ibid.*, RG 94, Letters Received, 563 1874. On March 18, Bishop William H. Hare, Red Cloud Agency, Wyoming Territory (via Fort Laramie, March 19), telegraphed to Delano. "We consider it essential that the Department shall decide whether authority of Agent or Commanding Military Officer is superior on this reservation. We think the situation does not demand that he be authorized to act independently of the Agent or contrary to his advice. Messenger will wait at Fort Laramie for response."—Copies, *ibid.*; *ibid.*, Letters Sent. On March 20, Delano telegraphed to Hare. "I am directed by the President to say that the duties of the Military Authorities and of the Indian Agents are distinct and independent, and that neither is subordinate to the other in exercising their several legitimate powers. Should a difference arise in regard to any definite questions report it for settlement by the President."—Copies, *ibid.*; *ibid.*, Letters Received, 563 1874. On the same day, Lt. Gen. Philip H. Sheridan, Chicago, telegraphed to AG Edward D. Townsend. "Your telegram of this date transmitting telegram of W. S. Hare Chairman of Commission &c at Red Cloud agency & reply of the President thereto has been rec'd   My views on the subject are the same as those of the President & for that reason in my letter of Instructions to Gen'l J C Smith I forbid the holding of any Councils with any Indians or Indian Chiefs   see copy sent to Washington through regular Channels to which no objections has been made   it is to be hoped that Goodhearted but Inexperienced men may not disturb the peaceable solution of the trouble at the red Cloud and Spotted Tail agencies which bid so fair of settlement   before their arrival I went so far in order to avoid any Mistakes of Subordinate Commanders as to direct that they should hold no Communication either by telegraph or mail with the Indian bureau except through Superior headquarters"—Telegram received (at 11:30 P.M.), *ibid.* Related papers are *ibid.* See also *PUSG*, 24, 112–14; *New York Times*, Feb. 14, April 18, 19, May 9, 1874; *HED*, 43-2-1, part 5, I, 397–407, 559–62.

On Feb. 20, a correspondent reported from Washington, D. C. "The President yesterday, . . . referred, in the first instance, to the apparent effort again renewed to misrepresent and pervert the results and effect of the Indian policy thus far enforced by the Administration. That policy, he said, had been so far successful in settling Indians upon reservations, and in inducing several prominent savage tribes to abandon their roving and pillaging habits, as to warrant him in adhering to it, and he should continue to do so. The opposition, he remaked, was incited by the residents on the frontier, traders, and others, who saw their chances of making money reduced by the efforts of the Government to deal honestly with the Indians. Political management had also much to do with it, and out of Indian outbreaks political, as well as pecuniary, fortunes are sought to be made. In regard to the integrity of the service at present, the President remarked that the haphazard statement that the service was more corrupt now than ever before was proven false by the record, which showed that there was scarcely as much corruption now in a whole year as in a week in former days. . . . 'With all our efforts,' said the President, 'some men have succeeded in circumventing and cheating us, but as fast as discovered they have been broken up and cast out.' He expressed himself very positively against any control of Indian affairs by the army, except the punishment of refractory tribes who refuse to accept the Government's proffer of kind treatment for good behavior. . . . The President expressed the utmost confidence with the policy of treating the Indians in good faith, and as a result of such treatment he pointed to the fact that, notwithstanding probable outrages of swindling flour contractors, which he regarded as the cause of the disturbance among the Sioux, yet several of the leading tribes, notably the Ogallallas and the Brules, now stood firm for peace, whereas, heretofore, the firing of the first gun had always cemented the Sioux nation for war. In his last message to Congress the President said he had cordially approved the recommendation of the Secretary of the Interior to abolish the payment of annuities in money. The Indian had no use for money, and it was simply a source of corruption and demoralization to him. The same amounts should go to him in clothing, stock, and implements for tilling the soil. . . . The President then referred, with considerable severity of expression, to what he termed 'the dishonest course of a portion of the public press in its treatment of the Indian and kindred questions.'. . . He cited, as an illustration of this systematic purpose of misrepresentation, the case of Indian Commissioner Smith. This officer, he said, had for months rested under a load of vindictive charges, never uttering a word of complaint, but inviting the most searching investigation, and giving his accusers a free field. Many of the newspapers had assailed him most virulently before trial, and now that he was not only exonerated but the integrity of his action completely vindicated these same papers were absolutely silent, ignoring the facts, while the Commissioner himself could contemplate the result with only such gratification as could be given by the personal misfortune of a wife driven to an insane asylum by the assaults of personal and political enemies upon the good name and fame of her husband. In truth, the President remarked, there should be a new statute for the punishment of lying. In conclusion, he said the country, when correctly informed, would clearly see the benefits of the policy of keeping faith with the Indian thus far pursued, and he was so confident of its correctness and of its ultimate complete success that he should resolutely adhere to it."—*New York Times,* Feb. 21, 1874.

In a letter docketed May 2, Alfred E. Cole, Mount Vernon, Ind., wrote to USG concerning Indian policy. ". . . My plan is this—To induce all the tribes to concentrate and settle in a Territory selected for that purpose and to educate and teach them to cultivate the soil. All this could be done with far less expense to the government, than to pursue the present policy. Some may think that it will be impossible to accomplish this; but my idea is that it *can* be accomplished. I would be willing to undertake this grand enterprise. I would need very little help. I am no office seeker, but am prompted by a sense of duty, and out of sympathy for the Indian. Neither do I want a large compensation. I merely want enough to live on. I have served 3 yrs in the Second Minnesota Cavalry during the rebellion. . . ."—ALS (undated), DNA, RG 75, Letters Received, Miscellaneous.

1874, FEB. 14. Judge Connally F. Trigg, U.S. District Court, Knoxville, to USG. "The bearer of this note is the wife of Thomas G. Boyd who is now confined in the penitentiary of the State of Tennessee for a offence against the U. S—Mrs Boyd is a lady of merit and is anxious to obtain a pardon for her husband who has been confined for 12 months. I appreciate her anxiety and on her account I cheerfully unite with many other gentlemen of position in the State, who I learn have joined in applying for a pardon, in asking that your Excellency

may extend the clemency she asks if it can be done consistently with your duty.
I forbear any expression of opinion on the merits of the case as I did not try it
—"—ALS, OFH. Thomas G. Boyd had committed pension fraud. No pardon
followed. See *New York Times,* Jan. 8, 1882.

1874, FEB. 15.   Little Berry Camp, Nueces, Tex., to USG seeking office as a Republican. "... through a long life, one half of which time has been spent in Texas,
I have had the confidence of my countrymen so as to get any position that I
was capible of filling,   I have served in eight Legislative Assemblies.   resigned
my seat rather then take the oathe to the Confederacy in 1860,   I was one of
22 Loyal men of the Convention of 1866 who protested against the Constitution framed by that body. but now (from my political antecedents alone) I could
not be elected to the humblest office in the gift of the people ..."—ALS, DNA,
RG 56, Applications. A related letter is *ibid.* No appointment followed.

1874, FEB. 16.   USG endorsement. "Refered to the Sec. of the Interior."—AES,
DNA, RG 48, Miscellaneous Div., Letters Received. Written on a letter of the
same day from Abby Dustan, Washington, D. C., to USG concerning a pension
for Abigail Hall.—ALS, *ibid.* On June 11, Hall, Hampstead, N. H., wrote to USG.
"I have rote to them about my Pension and I cannot get any answer from them.
the last papers ware Sent out there more then Six months ago, and I have not
hurd any thing from them Since. My Son Jacob B Hall was killed July 18 1863
at Fort Wagner and I have ben trying to get my pension ever Since and have not
got it yet. I should like to know the reson why I can not get it. I am most 73 years
old and I need my pension now if ever. I am anxious to hear from it and hope I
Shall Soon."—ALS, *ibid.* Hall was granted a pension as of April 21, 1875.

1874, FEB. 16.   2nd Lt. J. Estcourt Sawyer, Plattsburg, N. Y., to USG. "I have
the honor to apply for one of the vacancies in the Pay Department of the Army,
basing my claim for the appointment solely upon my Fathers long, and faithful services of 47 years in the Navy, and with whom you were personally acquainted, while he commanded the Naval Station at Sacketts Harbor N. Y.   I
have served in the Volunteer Navy during the late Rebellion and since 1867 as
a 2d Lieutenant of Artillery in the Army. This appointment which I solicit would
enable me to give a home to my Mother during her life time. I inclose a letter
from Mr Agustus Ford of N. Y City, a mutual friend, who has known me since
childhood, and as my Father was known to you in the years gone by, a brother
officer. I ask that if possible you will appoint me to one of the vacancies in the
Pay Dept"—ALS, DNA, RG 94, Applications for Positions in War Dept. On
Feb. 20, Augustus Ford, New York City, wrote to USG recommending Sawyer.
—ALS, *ibid.* On Dec. 7, USG nominated Sawyer as 1st lt.

1874, FEB. 17.   To Congress. "I transmit herewith a communication from the
Secretary of State and accompanying papers."—Copy, DNA, RG 59, Reports to
the President and Congress. *SED,* 43-1-27. A report on the 1873 Vienna International Congress on patents is *ibid.*

1874, FEB. 17. Levi P. Luckey to U. S. Senator Zachariah Chandler of Mich. "The President tells me to write an invitation to you and Mr Brush for tomorrow evening at half past seven o'clock, to spend the evening socially; with a game of whist &c. As it is an awkard sort of invitation to write & have you fully understand, I send it as a personal note."—ALS, DLC-Zachariah Chandler. On April 23, Edmund A. Brush, Detroit, wrote to USG praising his veto of the currency bill.—ALS, USG 3.

On Sept. 19, Culver C. Sniffen wrote to Brush. "The President directs me to acknowledge the receipt of your favor of the 16th instant and in explanation of the failure of an early acknowledgment of your very kind invitation, to say, that in laying it aside for the purpose of answering it personally, it unfortunately got overlooked, and of this he was reminded only, by the receipt of your second letter. He very much regrets the oversight and hopes you will be kind enough to accept the explanation. The President begs you will be kind enough to present his compliments and sincere thanks to the Governor General and say that he could not have accepted his courteous invitation, because it is not permitted the President to leave the United States during his term of Office. He could, however, have accepted an invitation to sail in your Yacht, earlier in the season."— Copy, DLC-USG, II, 2.

On Jan. 1 and Dec. 9, 1876, Brush wrote to USG. "It needs not I should say, that I wish you a Happy New, Year in which are included all of yours, especially Mrs Grant, & very many recurrents.—I have a want.—You have heard & hear, the expression of this sentiment more times than you had men in the Army with which you saved the Republic, but my want is not in that category. I don't want a Foreign Mission—nor a Domestic Mission—nor a Mission to the Heathen— nor to be an Attaché to any body—nor a place in the Customs—or the Post office—or the Revenue—nor a commission in the Army—nor a Navy Yard—nor any appointment in any special or general Service—nor any office whatever it be except the office of a good friend, never uncertain.—The Gov. Genl of Canada has sent me a particularly good photograph of himself, with his autographic signature at the bottom.—His Countess has done the same.—These likenesses are framed & hang in the parlor of my home—I think by this time, a General who has had a million of men under his command, can't fail to know what my want is.—Unless I get the photographs, I shall explain more fully.—" "I have sent to Mrs Grant a Memorial.—In this brief renewal of an intercourse, the memory of which has been filled with the pleasantest recollections, I am unwilling to let the occasion pass, without recurring to what I have heretofore said about the ingratitude of Republics, & the characteristic forgetfulness of this Republic—Caesar was no more potent at Rome nor had more caps thrown up in his honor, than you, among this people, when you refused Lee's sword.—The ingrained selfishness of what are falsely called politics, the true sense of which is an honorable & elevating pursuit, but which here, means only the struggle for power & what comes of it, forced you unwillingly into a position, distasteful, irksome & at war with your inclinations & the training of your life,—And for this concession, greater & harder to you, than the hardships, anxieties & perils of the war, for whose victorious end they were your debtors, you have received the compensations steadily accorded to every of your predecessors, from Washington, Jefferson, Adams, Jackson down, & from which nothing saved Lincoln but the horror of his assassination.—History, not remote, will do you justice, because she cannot help it—The dispassionate & fair minded do it now—When the froth subsides the water will come clear—It will then be seen, that as long as party strife of Ins & Outs exists, to which the elements of envy, selfseeking, untruth & malignity are never wanting, no combination of honor & conscience will ever serve to avert the shafts of detraction, harmless though they fall, short of their mark.—My affilations are not with the party you represent, but so neither are they apart from a moral sense, a common sense, & a well earned countrymans grateful sense, of what you have done.—"—ALS, USG 3. See "Representative Men of Michigan: First Congressional District," *American Biographical History of Eminent and Self-Made Men, . . . Michigan Volume* (Cincinnati, 1878), pp. 25–26.

1874, FEB. 17.   James Rollings, Lovelady, Tex., to USG. "I am a colored man & Black Smith, have been running a shop at Lovelady a little more than a year. I am a Poor man dependent on my labor for a living. In the fall of 1872 I was arrested by Parties claiming to be U. S. authorities on the charge of manufacturing Tobacco and Iron. I was carried to austin & gave bond for my appearance at Court . . . They did not sustain the charges & I was acquitted. I Proved clearly that so far from manufacturing either of the articles named, I knew nothing about it & could not have done so had I desired it. When I was acquitted I was told to go home, & also that I was clear of it. I was not told nor had I the slightest idea there was any charge of cost or any other chargees to be presented against me until day-before yesterday the U. S. Dpty Marshall came here & locked up my shop on the plea of $30.00 Thirty dollars cost against me   Now to sum the matter up. I was totally inno of the charge which I proved clearly & to the satisfaction of all. It has cost me between Two hundred & seventy five & three Hundred dollars. Such treatment is not justice or equity nor do I think the U. S. intends treating her subjects in that manner . . ."—ALS, DNA, RG 60, Letters from the President.

1874, FEB. 18.   Secretary of War William W. Belknap to USG. "I have the honor to return Senate Bill No 367, authorizing the Secretary of War to deliver to the State Authorities of Rhode Island a certain gun, with remark that no objection to its approval is known to exist. Senate Bill 29 to authorize the Secretary of War to ascertain amount of expenses incurred by Territorial Authorities of Dakota for arms, &c., in 1862—received with the enclosed bill—will be returned as soon as report is received from the Adjutant General."—LS, Duke University, Durham, N. C. On Feb. 19, Belknap wrote to USG reporting no objection to Senate Bill 29.—Copy, DNA, RG 107, Letters Sent, Military Affairs.

1874, FEB. 19.   USG pardon for Merritt S. Leggett, convicted of embezzlement on June 19, 1873, sentenced to one year in prison and fined $1,550.—Copy, DNA, RG 59, General Records. On March 1, 1873, E. Harvey, Louisville, had written to USG concerning Leggett, ". . . called *now* the defaulting clerk—of Col H. B. Reese, Paymaster U. S. A. He with a friend or rather an acquaintance, became very much intoxicated, an *unusual* thing for him, and they became impressed with the desire for 'play'. Accordingly they entered such a place and he lost all the funds with him. By that time he was crazed litteraly by the Liquor he was still plied with there—The 'tempter' of course was at work. In his *own* safe at the Office was the amount of $3000: 300 with which he was in the morrow to pay off troops at Lebanon. The idea then presented itself of regaining what he had lost by using a part of that; possessed himself of a part—played and lost it—*so* with the remainder—. . . they have incarcerated him, and perhaps will send him to the Penetentiary. It will surely be his death, for he is a man of good principles, generous and noble, holding for years a high position among the order of 'Masons,' with a wife and two children denpendent upon him, one a poor helpless little cripple—. . ."—ALS, *ibid.*, RG 153, 278½ BMJ 1873.

1874, FEB. 19. To Congress. "I have the honor to transmit herewith a memorial upon the cultivation of timber and the preservation of forests, and a draught of a joint resolution prepared by the American Association for the Advancement of Science, together with a communication from the Commissoner of the General Land-Office upon the same subject."—*SED*, 43-1-28; *HRC*, 43-1-259, 3.

1874, FEB. 20. To Benjamin Murphy authorizing the extradition of Alexander D. Hamilton, "charged with the crime of embezzlement of Public Moneys," from Mexico to N. J.—Copy, DNA, RG 59, General Records. On Feb. 16, William A. Lewis, corporation counsel, Jersey City, had telegraphed to USG requesting the authorization.—Telegram received, *ibid.*, Miscellaneous Letters.

[*1874, Feb. 22*]. To Willie U. S. Grant Levison, Sacramento. "I am only just this morning—the anniversary of the birth of Washington, in receipt of your letter of the 1st of January, inclosing your photograph and copy of a letter from your father to me on the occasion of your birth. I am very glad to receive both your letter and the photograph, and to know that I have so promising a little namesake away off on the Pacific coast. Inclosed I send you in return my photograph—a very poor one, I am sorry to say, but the best I have."—*New York Times*, March 21, 1874.

[*1874*], FEB. 23. Secretary of State Hamilton Fish to USG. "Unless I shall learn from you that it will be inconvenient for you to receive them, I propose, tomorrow, at twelve o'clock, to introduce to you Messrs Chin Lan Pin and Huber, Commissioners on the part of the Chinese government to inquire into the condition of Coolies in Cuba. They will be accompanied by Mr Chin Ling as Interpreter."—LS (misdated 1873), Babcock Papers, ICN. On Feb. 24, Commodore Daniel Ammen, Washington, D. C., wrote to USG. "My old friend Judge Huntington is the neighbor of the Chinese Commissioner, who usually lives at Hartford Conn. He hopes that the State Department will be able to forward the Commissioner's wishes as to the coolies on the island of Cuba, where he will go for the purpose of inquiring into and mitigating the wrongs that are supposed to be perpetrated on the coolies. It seems to me if you could have any thing done to forward the objects of the Commissioners visit it would be greatly in the in-

terest of humanity & would be appreciated by the Chinese Government. Judge
Huntington although a life long Democrat was at the last Presidential election
your active supporter and friend and is a gentleman who has the affection of all
who know him."—ALS, DNA, RG 59, Miscellaneous Letters. See *Report of the
Commission Sent by China to Ascertain the Condition of Chinese Coolies in Cuba* (1876;
reprinted, Taipei, 1970).

1874, FEB. 23.   Mary G. Webster, Huntington, Conn., to USG. "I am a little
girl 15 years of age and so of course not through going to school   I have never
writen any letters to an honorable man like yourself and don't know much about
writing to our great and good President but I shall try and not make any mistakes especially in spelling for my Mother had rather see anything than a poor
speller. My Grandpa Gilbert was a soldier in the war of 1812 served his time
out and was honorably discharged,   he died 14 years ago leaving my Grandma
a widow with five children and a property prized at $1100.   three of her chil-
dren have died since then, the other two are daughters in moderate circumstances. As Grandpa was not married until after peace was declared Grandma
was not entitled to a pension under the act. I don't know what I want, but she
is old and feeble now, and I want some way contrived so that she shall have a
pension. I write without her knowledge"—ALS, DNA, RG 48, Miscellaneous
Div., Letters Received.

1874, FEB. 24.   U.S. Representative Isaac W. Scudder of N. J. to USG. "Mr
George C. Thomas formerly a Jersey man and late of the United States Army
desires to be appointed paymaster in the Army, should a bill now pending in
Congress be passed, which will give the President that power. . . ."—ALS, DNA,
RG 94, Applications for Positions in War Dept. George C. Thomas, USMA
1836, continued as q. m. clerk. See *PUSG*, 17, 542–43; *ibid.*, 18, 23–25.
     On Sept. 2, 1876, Thomas wrote to Gen. William T. Sherman concerning an
effort to gain appointment as postmaster, Washington, D. C., in 1869. ". . . Accordingly I called at the White House the next morning, fell into the line of
those who were approaching the President, & when within five feet of him the
door opened from Genl Babcocks room & in marched Senator Zach Chandler &
seated himself by Genl Grant, &, then & there pursuaded him to appoint Judge
Edmonds, of Michigan, to the very office promised me the day before & which
office he still holds. As Chandler retired I approached the President, made
my bow to him & left the room, & there that matter ended. . . ."—ALS, DLC-
William T. Sherman. See *PUSG*, 20, 276–77.

1874, FEB. 25.   USG endorsement. "Accept to take effect Apl. 1st 1874."—AES,
DNA, RG 60, Letters from the President. Written on a letter dated Feb. 26 from
David B. Parker, Washington, D. C., to USG, resigning as marshal, Eastern Dis-
trict, Va. On March 3, USG nominated Charles P. Ramsdell to replace Parker.
     On March 12, 1869, Mayor Sayles J. Bowen of Washington, D. C., had writ-
ten to USG in Parker's behalf.—ALS, *ibid.*, Records Relating to Appointments.
On March 31, USG nominated Parker as marshal, Va. Upon the creation of two
judicial districts in Va. (1871), Parker became marshal, Eastern District. See
PUSG, 16, 486.

1874, FEB. 25.   USG order setting aside land for the S'Klallam Indians on the Skokomish River in Washington Territory.—DS, DNA, RG 75, Orders. *HED,* 45-3-1, part 5, I, 774, 47-2-1, part 5, II, 358, 49-2-1, part 5, I, 594; *SED,* 48-2-95, 641; *SD,* 57-1-452, 924. Subsequent orders were printed in the documents listed above except as noted. On April 9, USG ordered land set aside for the Muckleshoot Indians, also in Washington Territory.

On Feb. 14, USG ordered land within the Little Traverse Reservation, Mich., restored to the public domain.—DS, DNA, RG 75, Orders. Printed (dated Feb. 4) in the last three documents listed above.

On March 23, USG ordered the Pyramid Lake Reservation set aside for the Piutes in Nev.—DS, DNA, RG 75, Orders. On March 19, USG had ordered land reserved on the Walker River in Nev., also for the Piutes.

On April 9, USG ordered the Hot Springs Reservation set aside in New Mexico Territory for the Chiricahua Apaches.—DS, *ibid.*; facsimile, Jane F. Smith and Robert M. Kvasnicka, *Indian-White Relations: A Persistent Paradox* (Washington, 1976), p. 201. On Dec. 21, 1875, USG ordered part of the land restored to the public domain.—DS, DNA, RG 75, Orders. On Nov. 24, 1874, USG had ordered the Tularosa Valley Reservation in New Mexico Territory restored to the public domain.—DS, *ibid.*

On July 1, USG ordered land set aside in Arizona Territory for the Papago "and such other Indians as it may be desirable to place thereon."—DS, *ibid.* On Nov. 16, USG ordered land added to a reservation on the Colorado River in Arizona Territory and Calif.

1874, FEB. 26.   USG endorsement. "Refered to the Sec. of the Navy for his recommendation."—AES, DNA, RG 45, Miscellaneous Letters Received. Written on a letter from Charlotte A. von Cort to USG. "Your Petitioner Charlotte Avon Cort, would respectfully represent that she is the widow and sole Executrix of C. J. von Cort M. D. & Com. Surgeon, of Morrisiana N. Y, who invented sometime in the year 1861 a submarine explosive shell with its appliances and adaptations for sea coast and harbor defences; which invention was patented by the Patent Office at Washington in 1862. . . ."—DS, *ibid.* Von Cort, represented by Belva A. Lockwood, sought compensation for the subsequent use of her husband's invention. See *HRC,* 44-2-215.

1874, FEB. 26.   To Frederick A. Sawyer, asst. secretary of the treasury. "Permit me to return you my sincere thanks for the beautiful cane you were so kind as to send me, and also as well, for the compliment you pay me in choosing me to be its recipient. The artist has been very successful in symbolizing the issue of the rebellion, and I am proud to possess so fine a piece of work, and to possess it through your kindness."—Copy, DLC-USG, II, 2. On Feb. 9, Sawyer had written to USG. "When, a few years since, Rebellion raised it head in the land, one of its favorite emblems was a Palmetto tree around which a Rattlesnake coiled his slimy folds, with the legend *'Nemo me impune lacessit.'* The flags of Secession and Rebellion went down before the justice and power symbolized by the National Standard. In the cane I have the honor to send, the artist has represented this victory. The Eagle, the Symbolic bird of our country, holding in his beak the national colors, and guarding the interests of the Republic as he would those of his own offspring, has throttled the Serpent and disproved the proud boast of the legend. To no one could this emblem of the national triumph be more appropriately offered than to him who led our armies to final victory in the field, and under whose civil administration so much has been done to secure and consolidate the fruits of that victory. I therefore ask permission to offer it to you as a Small token of the high esteem and earnest friendship of . . ."—ALS, IHi. USG endorsed this letter. "Acknowledge receipt."—AES (initialed, undated), *ibid.*

Probably in Feb. or March, 1873, James L. Orr, minister to Russia, had written to USG recommending an appointment for Sawyer, former U.S. Senator from S. C.—William Evarts Benjamin, Catalogue No. 34, Jan., 1891, p. 23. On March 18, USG nominated Sawyer as asst. secretary of the treasury. On June 11, 1874, Levi P. Luckey wrote to Sawyer. "The President directs me to acknowledge the receipt of your letter of June 6th, tendering your resignation as Assistant Secretary of the Treasury and to say that the same is accepted to take effect on the receipt of this letter."—Copy, DLC-USG, II, 2. On June 22, USG nominated U.S. Representative Lyman K. Bass of N. Y. as Sawyer's replacement; Bass declined the nomination. On Dec. 7, USG nominated Charles F. Conant. See *New York Times*, June 23, July 2, 1874.

1874, FEB. 26.   U.S. Representative James A. Garfield of Ohio to USG presenting Daniel R. Tilden of Cleveland.—Parke-Bernet Galleries, April 27, 1954, 260.

1874, FEB. 27.   Walt Whitman, Camden, N. J., to USG. "Hoping, (should time & inclination favor,) to give you a moment's diversion from the weight of office & political cares—& thinking, of all men, you can return to those scenes, in the vein I have written about them—I take the liberty of sending, (same mail with this) some reminiscences I have printed about the war in nos of the N. Y. *Weekly Graphic.* I am not sure you will remember me, or my occasional salute to you in Washington. I am laid up here with tedious paralysis, but think I shall get well & return to Washington."—William White, "Whitman to U. S. Grant: An Addendum," *Walt Whitman Review*, XIII, 2 (June, 1967), 60–61. See Edwin Haviland Miller, ed., *Walt Whitman: The Correspondence* (New York, 1961–77), II, 280–81, V, 297–98.

On June 22, Whitman wrote to USG. "Would it be convenient to the President to personally request of the Attorney General that in any changes in the Solicitor Treasury's office, I be not disturbed in my position as clerk in that office—all my duties to the government being & having been thoroughly & regularly performed there, by a substitute, during my illness. I shall probably get well before long."—ALS, DNA, RG 60, Letters from the President. See Miller, II, 306–7.

1874, MARCH 3.   D. A. Robinson, Elizabeth, N. J., to USG. "The decease of Hon N. K. Hall of Buffalo Dist Judge for the Northern Dist of N. Y. leaves a vacancy on the Bench to be filled by your appointment. Of course the usual machinery will be put in motion and the claims of a score or more of gentlemen will be vigorously pressed and the selection finally made may or may not be the best. I was for many years a resident of Western N. Y., a lawyer by profession, and well acquainted with all of the prominent members of the Bench and Bar from Albany to Buffalo. Having usually acted and voted with the Democracy I am able to form unbiased and unprejudiced opinions of the prominent members of the opposite party with whom I am brought into personal contact   I take the liberty of suggesting the names of three gentlemen either of whom would make a most worthy successor to the eminent judge just deceased. 1st Hon Chas J. Folger of Geneva—late Asst Treasr of the U. S. at New York and now one of the Judges of the Court of Appeals   2nd Hon Chas C. Dwight of Auburn Justice of the Supreme Court. 3rd Hon James C. Smith of Canandaigua, Justice of the Supreme Court. . . ."—ALS, DNA, RG 60, Records Relating to Appointments. Letters recommending George Wolford, R. Holland Duell, Charles O. Tappan, James Forsyth, John C. Churchill, William Marvin, Norton A. Halbert, William A. Sackett, Edward Wade, and D. F. Gott, to replace Nathan K. Hall, are *ibid.* On April 2, USG nominated William J. Wallace, mayor of Syracuse, to replace Hall.

1874, MARCH 4.   USG endorsement. "Refered to the Sec. of the Int."—AES, DNA, RG 75, Letters Received, Miscellaneous. Written on a letter of March 3 from Alfred Morton, Richmond, to USG. "This will be handed you by *Thomas Cook, Chief* of the *Powhatan Tribe* of *Indians,* and *Thomas W. Langston* of the same tribe, who compose a committee representing the remnant of Indians now in Virginia—They desire to state to your Excellency the condition of their Tribe, which is now located on a reservation on the Pamunkey River, and they are known as the 'Pamunkey Indians' with whose history I am satisfied you are familiar—The reservation upon which these Indians are located, was made in colonial times, and afterwards regulated by state legislation all of which is matter of history. They are now informed by some person representing himself to be one *Charles Keokuk,* and an *agent* that it is the desire of the Government that the Tribe represented by Cook & Langston should sell out their reservation and consent to be removed to the West. These Indians do not wish to be disturbed and do not want to 'go west'—I do not know any thing about Mr. Keokuk, nor do I know what cause this tribe has for alarm and I trust the fears of their leading men are groundless—In the interest of humanity however, I give them this letter, assuring them that your Excellency will see that justice is done them, &c—"—LS, *ibid.*

1874, MARCH 4.   USG note. "Will the Com. of Int. Rev. please see *W. H. Cardwell,* and if temporary employment can be given him, say for one month, give it to him."—ANS, DNA, RG 56, Applications. Wyatt H. Cardwell, former sgt., C.S. Army, received a one month appointment as watchman on March 10.—*Ibid.*

1874, MARCH 4.   To House of Representatives. "I have the honor to transmit herewith replies from the several Departments in answer to the resolution of the House of Representatives of the 16th of January last, requesting 'a list of all expenses incurred by the various Departments for transportation of any matter which, before the abolition of the franking privilege, was carried in the mails.'"

—*HED*, 43-1-173. On Feb. 4, USG had written on the same subject. "I transmit to the House of Representatives, in answer to their Resolution of the 16th ultimo, the accompanying report from the Secretary of State."—Copy, DNA, RG 59, Reports to the President and Congress. This message was apparently not sent.

1874, MARCH 6. USG commutation of death sentence for John Broderick, convicted of murder in Ark., to five years in prison, citing "circumstantial evidence, and doubts . . . as to his guilt."—Copy, DNA, RG 59, General Records.

1874, MARCH 9. USG proclamation announcing the death of Millard Fillmore. —DS, DLC-Executive Orders.

1874, MARCH 9. Mary K. Colburn and Mary A. Burnett, Round Valley, Calif., to USG. "Possibly, you may recall a visit, some four years since, of two ladies, introduced by J. C. Clift M. C. from Georgia. We were then, on our return from South Western Georgia, bearing messages from the Freedmen of that Section. It was the termination of six years instruction in the South. On a previous occasion, we had the pleasure of meeting you at Savannah. We are now laboring among the Indians of California. From experience acquired at Tule River & Round Valley Reservations, we are convinced that the present Christian Policy is the Best, and that it will prove successful, wherever it is fairly tested. We do now most respectfully urge its continuance, notwithstanding the tide of opposition arrayed against it. The Fruit of Christian Effort is appearing in this Valley. Within the last month, Seven Hundred Children of the Forest have accepted Christianity & united with the Church, including the Chiefs and all the prominent leaders of the various Tribes. Class Leaders have been appointed from among their People, who with characteristic boldness, are now fighting the Battles of the Lord   Old & young are pressing into the Kingdom. About forty youths, in our Schools are reading with avidity the Word of Life; and hundreds are emerging from darkness, into the glorious light & liberty of the Gospel. A marvelous change has come over these Red Children, wrought by the Spirit of God, proving that Christian kindness can reach and soften, the wildest Savage. These Christian Indians, are praying for their Great Captain at Washington, well knowing the Author of the System which is so rapidly improving their condition. Their prayers also ascend daily, for their Agent, their Teachers, and all true friends, and even for their enemies. That the 'Father of All' may inspire with wisdom the hearts of those to whom are committed the destinies of this People, and that the humane Peace Policy, may be perpetuated, until the Indians shall rank as Citizens of our great Republic, and every Tribe, enlist under the Banner of the Captain of our Salvation, is the Hope & Expectation of yours, for God & Humanity"—LS, DNA, RG 75, Letters Received, Miscellaneous. On Aug. 30, 1875, E. B. Bateman and eight others, Round Valley, wrote to Edward P. Smith, commissioner of Indian Affairs. "We, the undersigned, employes on the Round Valley U. S. Indian Reservation, respectfully represent, that during the time of our employment on this reservation, we have, as we think, not only faithfully discharged the several duties assigned us, but have in addition thereto, performed that which the Church should have done, but failed to do, viz: The religious, or missionary work among the Indians. Under, and by the blessing of God, to whom be all praise, we have, we believe, been the means in connection with, and under the supervision of Agent Burchard, of effecting a social, intellectual and moral reform, unprecedented and unparalled in the United States. In the short space of less than two years, nine hundred and eighty-five Indians have embraced Christianity, and with rare exceptions are running well, comprising the entire resident population except a few little children, and as those scattered outside the reservation come in, they continue to swell our ranks. . . . The salaries contracted for on our coming here, and which were as small as honest, capable men could afford to work for, have in some cases, for the last several quarters been partly withheld, by the Government not supplying the Agent with the necessary means. . . . At the proposed consideration we predict a class of employes who will not only cheat the Indians and defraud the Government, but who will also debauch and demoralize the Indians, and speedily destroy the good which has been accomplished, . . ."—Copy, *ibid.*, Letters Received, California Superintendency. See Robert H. Keller, Jr., *American Protestantism and United States Indian Policy, 1869–82* (Lincoln, Neb., 1983), p. 163.

On May 18, 1875, USG signed an order establishing the northern boundary of the Round Valley reservation.—*HED*, 45-2-1, part 5, I, 635, 45-3-1, part 5, I, 738, 47-2-1, part 5, II, 317–18, 49-2-1, part 5, I, 529–30; *SED*, 48-2-95, 236; *SRC*, 48-2-1522, 113. On July 26, 1876, USG ordered land and buildings formerly occupied by Camp Wright added to the Round Valley reservation.—Copies, DNA, RG 153, Military Reservation Files, Calif. Printed in the sources listed above. See *PUSG*, 19, 446.

On March 9, 1874, John Beeson had addressed a Washington, D. C., meeting "in relation to the condition and needs of the Indians," and was appointed to present a memorial to USG. "Your memorialists respectfully represent that the testimony of distinguished military officers, such as the late General John E. Wool and General Harney, shows that all the difficulties with the Indians arise from the lawless conduct of white men. Therefore your memorialists respectfully ask that you, as the commander-in-chief, order an immediate cessation of war, and instead thereof authorize the president (Alfred Love) of the Peace Association in Philadelphia to send a delegation among the Indians, and investigate the cause of the difficulties; and in the meantime let the saying of the great Teacher be strictly observed, 'If thy enemy hunger feed him.'"—*Washington Chronicle*, March 10, 1874.

On March 15, Maj. Joseph G. Tilford, 7th Cav., Fort Rice, Dakota Territory, wrote to USG. "I see there has been a bill introduced in congress, to authorize you to appoint ten officers of the Army as a Board of Peace Commissioners for the Indians. In the event of the bill becoming a law may I ask that I be detailed as one of the officers constituting the Board?. . ."—ALS, DNA, RG 94, Letters Received, 1323 1874. Congress did not pass this legislation.

On April 27, Rev. Alfred N. Gilbert *et al.*, "citizens of Baltimore in Mass Meeting assembled," petitioned USG. "Your memoralists respectfully represent that, notwithstanding the combinend efforts of the Government and the churches during the past five years to secure peace and protection to the Indians, there has been constant war, and a succession of frauds and Massacres, which for atrocity and magnitude are equal to, if not greater than those of any former period. And your memoralists would further represent that it is not alone by the wickedness and whiskey of the lawless men, who infest the borders of every Indian tribe, that this war fraud and massacre are caused; but that official authorities inform us of the shameful fact 'That of all the appropriations made by Congress to pay the lawful debdts of the nation to the Indian tribes but a small part ever reaches them,' and that the failure of the Government to fullfil its treaty engagements with the Sioux in 1861 and with the Modocs in 1873 cost the nation more than a thousand lives and of several million of dollars   Therefore—Your memorialists would earnestly pray that before any new measures are pressed on any Indian tribes, Delegates, both men and women, nominated by 'The National Society for the promotion of Universal Peace,' and approved by the President of the United States, be appointed to visit the Indian tribes, not to dictate to, but to cousel with them as to terms of agreement and the best modes for the restoration and preservation of good will between the races"—D, *ibid.*, RG 75, Letters Received, Miscellaneous.

1874, MARCH 9.   Henri Stewart, Oswego, Kan., to USG. "Having implicit confidence in your willingness in answering *short* questions, I dare take this liberty, through utter ignorance of better authority in my case. I was born in the Indian Territory (Ft Towson) with an *american* for a father and a *half Choctaw* for a mother,—both died and were burried there. My only only question is; is there any inheritage, 'head right' or any *particular benefit,* to be derived by one of that class? Without burdening you with the trouble of giving the above facts extra attention it would be an inestimable favor if you could place me at the propper starting point. Our family was intimately connected with Geo. B. McClellan, while he was in command of Ft. Towson, and he could verify the above statement."—ALS, DNA, RG 75, Letters Received, Choctaw Agency.

1874, MARCH 12.   Margaret Bailey, Cincinnati, to USG. "I have taken the liberty of addressing you in the hope that you will aid me in a matter of great importance to me. Having made application for Increase Pension under Act of March 3rd 1873, for my children, my claim was *rejected.* because I was allowed a pension under Special Act of Congress. My husband was an old school mate of yours & was also at West Point. His name Dr George Bartlett Bailey Jr. son of Dr George B Bailey of Georgetown Ohio. He was killed at Guyandotte Va in 1861 while acting as Lieut: Col. of the 9th Regt West Va Vols., leaving me with very little means and five children. Hon Chilton White and others succeeded in getting me a pension. The Act of March 1873 gives $2 00 per month to each child under sixteen years from July 25 1866, and, as I draw only the same as widows of the same rank, I think I ought to receive the benefits of this just the same as other widows do who were not on the Pension Rolls by Special Act. I am now almost helpless with Paralysis and find it very hard to get along and this increase would be a great help. . . ."—ALS, DNA, RG 48, Miscellaneous Div., Letters Received. See *HRC,* 37-2-130.

1874, MARCH 12.   S. L. Deutsch, New York City, to USG. "I take the liberty to address you, in the name of Humanity to grant me a favor. A youth eighteen years old the son of a widow, but not her suport, I am very anxious to enter the Politechnic at West Point!—I would go to College in this City yet Mother is not able to aid me;   Mechanic or Merchant, I can and will not be!!!   Depending, Hoping & Expecting . . ."—ALS, DNA, RG 94, Unsuccessful Cadet Applications.

1874, March 14.   I. D. Cheauteaut, "U. S. chieef Marchall," Osage Agency, Indian Territory, to USG.   "your honor and magestey will please to Notice and See and cause this matter to be settle Beetune the osages and ther traders for god and ther Sake for I am an Eey wittness of Seeing Hiatt in co. and Dunnlap in co for this last three yeares sweendle the poor osges Bay the hool Sale bay Saling to them coffie at one Dollar Par Paund and Every thinng als accordinglley   your honnor will see that it is my Dautey to Notifide your honor of this the truth so help me god   sir you will Derict me of what to Dou &c &c"—ALS, DNA, RG 75, Letters Received, Neosho Agency. A copy is *ibid.* On March 27, Secretary of the interior Columbus Delano telegraphed from the White House to Benjamin R. Cowen, asst. secretary of the interior. "The President will receive Comr & Osage Indians at half past one to-day."—Telegram sent, *ibid.*, RG 107, Telegrams Collected (Bound). See *New York Times,* March 28, 1874; *HED,* 43-2-1, part 5, I, *533;* Peter J. Rahill, *The Catholic Indian Missions and Grant's Peace Policy: 1870–1884* (Washington, 1953), pp. 132–35.

On Dec. 14, Augustus Captin *et al.,* Osage Nation, Indian Territory, petitioned USG. "As your helpless Children we desire to call your attention to a matter of great interest to ourselves and families—We are half-breed Osages, being mixed with white blood: and many of us are educated having been educated: by the Roman Catholic Missionaries—. We live in the Osage Nation, Indian Territory as cittizens thereof: and under our Treaties with your Government, we have all the rights, privileges and benefits, that full blooded Osages have, in our Nation, and to all of our funds, and the public benefits—We have annuity funds paid to us *per capita,* the Same as the fullblooded Osages have; but we do not draw equally with the full blooded Osages, in our rations and provisions, issued to our Tribe by our Agent I. T. Gibso[n] and which has been purchaced by our Money. As our interests in our funds, are the Same, as those of our full booded cittizens, and as our provisions are purchaced with our own funds, we think we should have ~~our~~ an equal distribution with the full blooded Osages, in the rations and provisions, as well as Clothing bought with our Common funds. Besides this we feel that we should have the same assistance in our efforts, at farming and stock raising that the full blooded Osages get from our Agent.—we are very pour— we have been left in a destitute condition by the late war of the Rebllion, and by our bad and inhuman treatment in Kansas by the whites, and we need all the help we can get. The great majority of us are not able to help ourselves, we have but few work animals, and very few farming utensels and we are not able to buy any, and our Agent (Gibson) does not furnish us as he does the full blooded Osages,—we have abandoned the chace, and we are living a civilized life and are trying with all of our might and means to imitate civilized people. Our Treaties, and your laws under which our money is due our Tribe do not make any distinction among our people in our money matters, and we do not think our agent should make any distinction, when the laws and Treaties make non   We all have equal rights, and we petition you, our Great, Father to take steps ~~steps~~ as soon as possible to have us treated in all respects, like the full blooded Osages, as regards our funds, provissions clothing, live stock farming untensels, &c and as our efforts are in the right deretion, we hope that you, as our protector will encourage us, and that you will cause your agent, to inform us, at least twice a year what he does with our funds—. Now your Humble Petitioners will ever pray—as in duty bound as your Children—."—DS (42 signatures, 6 by mark), Marquette University, Milwaukee, Wis. See *HED*, 43-2-1, part 5, I, 530–31, 44-1-1, part 5, I, 778, 781.

1874, MARCH 16. Eliza Jane Taylor, St. Paris, Ohio, to USG. "i seat my self to rite you a few lins that i wanted to now weather i cold draw eny thing from the ware or pention ornot   tell me if can   i hase got a boy but we never was maried the man went to the wore   he promis to mary   iwanted weather i cold draw penion for him   some told me i cold and iwanted to no   i am very pore and ithout if cold it wold help me very mutch   i can proove that he promest to mary mee and dient and went to the ware   his name is Joseph D C Croco   he went in the second virgina rgiment . . ."—AL, DNA, RG 48, Miscellaneous Div., Letters Received.

[*1874, March 18*]. To [*Culver C. Sniffen*]. "Refer to Sec. of the Int. for his opinion as to the course that should be pursued in this case."—AN, Wayde Chrismer, Bel Air, Md. Sniffen endorsed this note. "(Judd, Reg. L. O. Springfield Dak. Mch. 18. Int."—AE, *ibid.* On June 9 and Dec. 9, USG nominated Luman N. Judd to continue as land office register, Springfield, Dakota Territory; the Senate rejected the first and confirmed the second nomination.

1874, MARCH 18. Frank Swain *et al.*, Warrington, Fla., to USG recommending changes among officials at the Pensacola Navy Yard. ". . . In closing: this Committee would Call to your attention the employement, of a great many boys among whom there cannot be found one collord of whom, there are sveral fully as competant, and it is strongly recomended that said patronage be equally distributed also   with thi[s] our humble pitition we Respectful[ly] a wait your early decision."—DS (14 signatures), DNA, RG 45, Letters Received from the President.

1874, MARCH 20. USG order. "The Consulate General of the United States in Italy having been transferred from Florence to Rome, and the Consulate General at Beirut in Syria having been discontinued, the Secretary of State, pursuant to authority invested in me by law, is directed to instruct the Consuls in Italy to regard themselves as subordinate to the Consul General at Rome . . . and the Consuls in Turkey to regard themselves as subordinate to the Consul General at Constantinople, . . ."—DS, DLC-Executive Orders. The order also amended consular regulations.

1874, MARCH 20. To Senate. "I transmit, herewith, for the consideration of the Senate, and with a view to its ratification a Convention concluded between the United States and Belgium on the 19th of March 1874, concerning Extradition." —Copy, DNA, RG 59, Reports to the President and Congress. On Feb. 6, USG had authorized Secretary of State Hamilton Fish to negotiate this convention. —DS, DLC-Hamilton Fish.

On March 9, 1875, USG wrote to the Senate transmitting a commercial treaty with Belgium.—Copies, DNA, RG 59, Reports to the President and Congress; *ibid.*, RG 130, Messages to Congress. On March 8, USG had authorized Fish to negotiate this treaty.—DS, DLC-Hamilton Fish.

1874, MARCH 20.   Nathaniel Wright, Cincinnati, to USG. *"Private. . . .* Probably I shall need to introduce myself to you, tho' you may remember me in connection with your visit to our City some years since; or in connection with a public demonstration here in support of your administration. My age has occasionally given me some prominence in such matters, being a month or two older than our Federal Constitution. One object of my letter is to protect a son from unjust charges & unfriendly influences. That son, Nathaniel Wright Jr. is at the head of the Registering department in the post office here. He is perfect master of the duties, faithful & diligent, often employed a large part of the night to keep every thing square. It is said that Thomas H. Foulds, former Post Master here, is manoeuvring to get that place for a relative of his   It is due to justice & the public weal that the department should know that Mr. Foulds is not a reliable man. I have for a long time been acquainted with him. He had for several years been a partner in business with my son, & for a long time we had entire confidence in his integrity, & had no suspicions to the contrary, till it was too late to avoid the consequences. . . ."—ALS (press), DLC-Nathaniel Wright.

On Jan. 6, USG had nominated Gustav R. Wahle as postmaster, Cincinnati, to replace Thomas H. Foulds. U.S. Senator John Sherman of Ohio had written to USG. "Please hold nomination of Post Master at Cincinnati until I can show you some telegrams"—ALS (undated), DLC-USG, IB.

1874, MARCH 21.   Col. Rufus Ingalls, New York City, to USG. "The bearer of this is Mr. Charles E. Moore, late of the Army—He graduated at West Point in the class of 1865—He desires to reënter the Military service—He has been in my office the past year and half—I believe him to be an accomplished gentleman, of good standing and habits—His Father is quite old, and has been long in service—If the young man can be restored, he will make a gallant officer—"— ALS, DNA, RG 94, ACP, 1631 1872. On April 11, Charles E. Moore, New York City, wrote to USG. ". . . I would respectfully ask the attention of the President, to the accompanying letters, and pledge myself, in the event of a favorable consideration of this application, to abstain from the use of intoxicating liquors during the term of my military service"—ALS, *ibid.* No appointment followed. A former 1st lt., Moore was cashiered on March 18, 1872. See *PUSG,* 19, 333–34.

1874, MARCH 23.   To Congress. "I have the honor to transmit herewith the report of the Board of Commissioners on the Irrigation of the San Joaquin, Tulare, and Sacramento Valleys of the State of California, and also the original maps accompanying said report."—*HED,* 43-1-290. See Donald J. Pisani, *To Reclaim a Divided West: Water, Law, and Public Policy, 1848–1902* (Albuquerque, 1992), pp. 128–32.

1874, MARCH 23.   Levi P. Luckey to Chester A. Arthur, collector of customs, New York City. "The President directs me to write you and suggest the propriety of transferring Mr. Houghton, a soldier with only one leg, from the Naval Office to one of the other departments of the Custom House."—Copy, DLC-USG, II, 2. On May 16, Orville E. Babcock wrote to Arthur on the same subject. ". . . The President will be pleased to know whether anything has been done in the case."—Copy, *ibid.* On March 16, 1875, USG nominated Charles H. Houghton as collector of customs, Perth Amboy, N. J. See *New York Times,* May 25, 1882.

1874, MARCH 25.   USG order establishing a reservation for the Jicarilla Apaches in New Mexico Territory.—DS, DNA, RG 75, Letters Received, New Mexico Superintendency. *HED,* 45-3-1, part 5, I, 760; 49-2-1, part 5, I, 567–68; *SED,* 48-2-95, 507; *SD,* 57-1-452, 874.

In [*March, 1876*], Governor Samuel B. Axtell of New Mexico Territory and other territorial officials petitioned USG, Secretary of the Interior Zachariah Chandler, and John Q. Smith, commissioner of Indian Affairs. "Your memorialists, citizens of the Territory of New Mexico, respectfully represent: *First:* That in the year 1873 a treaty was made with the Jicarilla Apache Indians by one Thos A. Dolan, and that soon thereafter an Executive order was issued, in conformity with the terms of said treaty, whereby a certain portion of country, lying in the North West part of the Territory of New Mexico, was set apart as the 'Jicarilla Apache Reservation': That a bill was introduced into the Congress of the United States to carry out and confirm the provisions of said treaty and was passed in the House of Representatives but not in the Senate, and that said treaty has therefore never been ratified or confirmed. *Second:* That the Jicarilla Apache Indians show no desire to locate on said reservation, but on the contrary are opposed to so doing and will never of their own free will consent to locate thereon. That there was no provision made in the aforesaid treaty for the appointment of an agent, nor any appropriation for the pay of an agent, or to defray the expense of erecting agency buildings &c, and that only the sum of $10.000. per annum was designated for the entire expense and subsistence of said Indians, which said sum would be utterly insufficient and inadequate to supply the actual wants of said Indians. That, by the provisions of said treaty, the said Indians are to receive their supplies from the Southern Ute Agency, situated in Southern Colorado, but even should the Jicarilla Apaches be forced or by any means induced to settle on said reservation, they would almost certainly be unable to draw their supplies from said agency as there could hardly fail to be a constant warfare and conflict between the two tribes. *Third:* That there is at the present time a reservation in the Southern portion of New Mexico, near Fort Stanton, known as the 'Mescalero Apache Reservation', at which said reservation there is an agent at present located, and that there are ample agency and other necessary buildings already erected thereon; that said reservation is well stocked with game, and in every way a suitable and proper section of country for the Indians; That the Jicarilla Apaches could be moved at a very small expense on to said reservation, and when once there could be maintained and fed with much less expense than at any other point, and thus save many thousands of dollars to the Government: *Fourth:* That the country now set apart as the Jicarilla Apache Reservation, is, for the most part, destitute of game, and in no wise the kind of country liked by, or suitable for, the Indians: *Fifth:* That the San Juan mines in South Western Colorado are among the largest and most promising mining Districts in the whole west and that they are approachable during the winter season through this reservation only, and further that during all seasons the supplies for the mines are at present required to be brought from a great distance and over almost impassable roads at much trouble and expense; and further, that the country immediately South of the Colorado line, embracing said reservation, has the finest natural advantages for a farming, agricultural and grazing Country, and that there are numbers of the citizens of the Territory desirous of locating farms and ranches thereon and of settling upon the same and building up and improving that portion of the public domain, thereby providing the necessary means of sustenance for the San Juan miners, together with easy access and egress, and also greatly benefitting this Territory by bringing under cultivation one of its richest agricultural districts. We therefore most earnestly recommend and request, in consideration of these facts, that the said treaty (it never having been confirmed according to law) be set aside and annulled, and that said Jicarilla Apache Indians be removed to the 'Mescalero Apache Reservation' and placed under the charge of the agent at that place, and that the lands now embraced within the limits of the Jicarilla Apache Reservation be duly declared to be open to settlement, as other public lands of the United States."—DS (28 signatures), DNA, RG 75, New Mexico Superintendency. On July 18, USG ordered the reservation returned to the public domain.—DS, *ibid.*, Orders. *HED*, 45-2-1, part 5, I, 638; 45-3-1, part 5, I, 761; 49-2-1, part 5, I, 568; *SED*, 48-2-95, 507; *SD*, 57-1-452, 874–75. See Veronica E. Velarde Tiller, *The Jicarilla Apache Tribe: A History, 1846–1970* (Lincoln, Neb., 1983), pp. 77–81.

1874, MARCH 25.   J. A. Barnes, Baton Rouge, to USG seeking appointment to USMA. ". . . I am a boy of 17 yrs white southern and *free born*   my Father was a Captain in the southern army and fought through the whole war, before which he was a slave holder,   I would disdain to hide the real truth from you so will add that he is now a warm democrat . . ."—ALS, DNA, RG 94, Unsuccessful Cadet Applications.

1874, MARCH 27.   U.S. Representative Austin F. Pike of N. H. to USG opposing the renomination of Henry P. Rolfe as U.S. attorney, N. H.—ALS, DNA, RG 60, Letters from the President. On Dec. 1, 1873, Joab N. Patterson, U.S. marshal, Concord, N. H., had written to USG recommending Rolfe's reappointment.— ALS, *ibid.*, Records Relating to Appointments. Related papers are *ibid.* Petitions to USG dated Nov. 25 recommending Charles P. Sanborn are *ibid.* On March 31, U.S. Senator Bainbridge Wadleigh of N. H. and two others wrote to USG recommending Joshua G. Hall.—LS, *ibid.* On the same day, Orville E. Babcock wrote to Attorney Gen. George H. Williams. "The President directs me to request that you will have prepared and sent to him the withdrawal of the name of Henry P. Rolfe to be U. S. Attorney for the District of New Hampshire & the nomination to that office of Joshua G. Hall of Dover New Hampshire."—LS, *ibid.*, Letters from the President.

1874, MARCH 28. Secretary of State Hamilton Fish to USG. "Mrs. Lieber sends me the enclosed letter, sealed, and requests me to forward it to you, which I take pleasure in doing, but have no knowledge of its contents—"—Copy, DLC-Hamilton Fish.

1874, MARCH 28. Moritz Ellinger, editor, *Jewish Times,* New York City, to USG. "If I am presumptous enough to address you, I must plead the encouragement given me by your Brother Orville Grant Esqr, who has been kind enough to take charge of these lines and present them to you. I am aware that you are partial to brevity and I shall therefore endeavor to be brief. My name is perhaps not altogether unknown to you, as I have had the honor to represent the German Republicans of this city and in that capacity had your ear several times. I have kept retired of late, but, intensely Republican as my sentiments are, I am sorry to see the mistakes which in my opinion are repeatedly made in neglecting to cultivate the German element and instead of attracting, alienating them from the Republican ranks. This has produced an apathy against the Republican party amongst the Germans, so that the German Central Committee was forced to accept a man as chairman of the Executive Committee, who if anything will repell the better element amongst the Germans. A reorganization is imperatively demanded and if not accomplished will lead to similiar results, as witnessed in the last elections. This reorganization can be only effected with the help, encouragement and assistance of the Administration and their representatives here. An attempt, I hear, is being made toof inducing you to replace the present efficient collector of Internal Revenue Mr M Friedsam. He is probably the best working Republican amongst the Germans, as he is equally efficient as officer; which is best attested by a reference to his official record. I hope and trust that you will receive my frank statement, as coming from one, who believes to serve you by laying these matters before you. Mr. Friedsam is perhaps the only man who has any considerable strength amongst the Germans and who has ever been ready to disregard personal interests when those of the Republican party had to be advanced. I must plead again the encouragement of your Bro, if I close by asking a favor, which, however, would prove of service to the party. I ask if that is possible, the appointment as Consul to one of the French ports of a man, who is equally proficient in the English, as he is in French and German languages, who is a man of great business capacities and almost pedantic punctuality, Mr Louis C Koppel. Of course I would ask this, if it can be done, without too great inconvenance. If the President should desire it, I would come to Washington, and in a personal interview discuss the reorganization of the German Republicans, and lay the matter before your Excellency more explicitly, than it is possible in such a brief note; I hope that you will pardon this liberty and permit me to assure you of my highest regard—"—ALS, DNA, RG 59, Letters of Application and Recommendation. No appointment followed for Louis C. Koppel, *Jewish Times* publisher. As of Sept. 30, 1875, Morris Friedsam no longer served as collector. See *New York Times,* Oct. 30, 1875, July 29, 1878, Oct. 23, 1879.

1874, MARCH 30.   James H. Wilson, New York City, to USG. *"Personal. . . .* I hand you herewith copies of correspondence which will explain itself. My brother sent it to me for my personal information; I send it to you for a similar reason, but as you will observe without his knowledge or consent. I may add in conclusion however that as he owes the office to you and you alone I am sure that his resignation is ready whenever you may choose to call for it though he is not at all likely to give it at the call of any body else. Knowing that he has not only been a faithful officer as well as a devoted friend to you, I do not suppose for one moment that you want his resignation at all, but should you think best to ask it, I trust you will in no case ask for it, till after the next term of his courts. Please drop him or me a line indicating your wishes, . . ."—ALS (press), DLC-James H. Wilson. On June 1, Orville E. Babcock wrote to Everett C. Banfield. "The President directs me to acknowledge the receipt of your letter of the 29th ultimo, tendering your resignation of the office of Solicitor of the Treasury, and to say that the same is accepted to take effect to-day."—Copy, DLC-USG, II, 2. On June 10, Charles B. Lawrence, Chicago, wrote to USG. "I take the liberty of uniting with other recommendations that will be sent to you, in favor of the appointment of Gen. Bluford Wilson, the present District Attorney in the Southern District of Illinois, to the position of Solicitor of the Treasury. . . ."—ALS, DNA, RG 56, Appointment Div., Treasury Offices, Letters Received. On June 17, Governor John L. Beveridge of Ill. and four others telegraphed to USG on the same subject.—Telegram received, *ibid.* On March 8, 1873, USG had renominated Bluford Wilson as U.S. attorney, Southern District, Ill.; on June 19, 1874, USG nominated Wilson as solicitor of the treasury.

1874, MARCH 31.   Levi P. Luckey to Alfred N. Duffié, consul, Cadiz. "The President directs me to acknowledge the receipt of the case of Sherry you were kind enough to send him and convey to you many thanks for your remembrance. The case for Genl. Dent I had sent to him at Fort Trumbull, New London, Conn. where he is now stationed. The President wishes me to ask you if you will be good enough to call on some Wine Merchant in whom you have confidence and get him four (4) quarter casks of best Sherry and have them shipped to him, directing in care of the Collector of Customs at New York. On Shipping the Sherry draw on the President for the cost, through any banker that suits the merchant, at sight."—Copy, DLC-USG, II, 2. On May 26, Luckey wrote to Chester A. Arthur, collector of customs, New York City. "I enclose you a letter received by the President from Messrs Galwey & Casado, of New York, relative to the shipment of some Sherry from Cadiz to you for the President. I enclose also the invoice, bill &c. The President wishes me to ask you to be kind enough to attend to the matter for him, and when the wine arrives to send him a bill of the expenses duties &c. that he may remit to you."—Copy, *ibid.* See *PUSG,* 20, 370.

[*1874, March*].   A. Alpeora Bradley and William L. Coakley to USG "and his Cabinet." "Your humble petitioner, A Alpeora Bradley, pray that you may be pleased to appoint him, *assistance* U S District Attorney, for the Southern district of Georgia: that the *colored* Republican voters of the State, may be represented in that department of justice. He was claimed as a Slave by ExGov Frank Pickings of Edgefiend S C, until the 13th amendment. Admitted to the *bar* of the Supreme ꓶ Court of Maine, Oct 4th 1866, and the same certified to by C W Walton, one of the Justiceses of the Supreme Judicial Court Sep—1869:—And to the circuit Court of South Carolina Feb 1870:—And was elected to the Georgia Senate in 1868 by a colored Republican vote of 4151, and did vote for President Grant, and the strate Republican ticket since its first inception. With these few statements of facts, we pray, that you will be please, to put the Petitioner in this *place*; that he may *prosecute* and defend his own race, from the multipled outrages, that has been, and are now being perpetrated in the State of Georgia."— DS (docketed March 28, 1874), DNA, RG 60, Letters from the President. No appointment followed. See *PUSG*, 19, 410–11; *ibid.*, 23, 30.

[*1874, March*].   John Gotshall to USG appealing his 1873 dismissal from the army on charges of drunkenness. ". . . The injustice of holding an officer criminally, and ruinously to himself, responsible for intoxication that has to be tested by an examination of his pulse, which may be influenced in its beats by a hundred causes apart from drink, is too plain to need comment. . . ."—LS (docketed March 16, 1874), DNA, RG 94, ACP, G120 CB 1867. See *SRC*, 46-2-525.

1874, APRIL 1.   U.S. Representative Lyman Tremain of N. Y. to USG. "I recommend the enclosed application of Mr M. H. Read for the Pardon of his son to your favorable consideration. Being again confined to my room I take the liberty of sending the fathers letter to me as my statement of the case to your Excellency. Mr Reed is Prest of the first National Bank & one of our most estimable citizens. I send also the Report of the trial. It presents a case of accidental unintentional killing of a man by an officer who was incensed by his stupidity   The blows by the hand & the bare foot could not have caused death except by the merest accident,   The character of the accused appears to have been that of a mild gentlemanly man. & I respectfully submit that the one years Imprisonment he must suffer (if pardoned) is sufficient to meet the claims of justice. Hoping that the answer to this application may be returned as soon as may be to me . . ."—ALS, DNA, RG 59, Miscellaneous Letters. On March 31, Matthew H. Read, Sr., Albany, N. Y., had petitioned USG for the pardon of Matthew H. Read, Jr., convicted of manslaughter and sentenced to three years in prison by a U.S. consular court at Shanghai.—LS, *ibid.* Related papers are *ibid.* On April 17, Secretary of State Hamilton Fish recorded in his diary that he had advised against pardon in this case and that USG concurred.—DLC-Hamilton Fish.

1874, APRIL 6.   Attorney Gen. George H. Williams to USG. "I have the honor to return herewith H. R. 1762, and to inform you that, in my opinion, there is no objection to its receiving your approval."—LS, OFH. See *U.S. Statutes at Large*, XVIII, part 3, pp. 27–28.

1874, APRIL 7.   USG speech upon receiving the credentials of A. Bartholdi, French minister.—*New York Herald*, April 8, 1874.

1874, APRIL 8.   Blanche K. Bruce, Floreyville, Miss., to USG. "I would respectfully recommend the reappointment of Capt. J. H. Pierce to the office of United States Marshal for the Northern Dist of Mississippi. Capt. Pierce has during his present term been a competent and vigilant officer and his reappointment will give general satisfaction to the citizens of the district."—ALS, Swarthmore College, Swarthmore, Pa. On May 29, USG renominated James H. Pierce.

1874, APRIL 9.   Secretary of War William W. Belknap to U.S. Representative George C. McKee of Miss. "Your letter of the 6th instant, inclosing papers relative to the rent and purchase of the land upon which the 'Grant Pemberton Monument' stands, has been received and duly considered. In reply I will state, that some time since authority was given to make some repairs upon this Monument, shortly after this, a letter from Dr. Booth to the President asking for compensation for the use of his land &c., was referred to me, and it was decided to take no action upon it. Should, however, it now be deemed best to purchase this land, and should you introduce a bill for this purpose, it seems to me that the sum named by you $1.000 00 should be in full payment of all claims for rent as well as for the land itself."—Copy, DNA, RG 107, Letters Sent, Military Affairs. On Aug. 19, Lt. Col. William M. Dunn, asst. judge advocate gen., wrote to David W. Booth, Vicksburg, on the same subject.—Copy, *ibid.* No action followed. See *HRC,* 44-1-558, 45-2-288.

1874, APRIL 9.   Sylvanus Cadwallader, Madison, Wis., to USG. "I write to inquire if you have yet appointed a Surveyor General for Arizona; and if not, whether you could consistently name me for the place. My journalistic experience in Wisconsin has never been satisfactory, and is less so now than at any time since the war. I think of emigrating to Arizona, and if made its Surveyor General, would purchase, if possible, the Tucson *Sentinel,* now owned by Mr. Wasson, late Surveyor General. Of my personal attachment you need no proof. Of my political, you should not long doubt were I in Arizona. With the old-time sentiment of esteem and affection, . . ."—ALS, DNA, RG 48, Appointment Papers, Arizona Territory. On June 1, USG nominated John Wasson to continue as surveyor gen., Arizona Territory.
    On Feb. 16, 1885, Frederick Dent Grant, New York City, wrote to Cadwallader. "General Grant directs me to answer your letter of the 11th inst and say 'that the incoming administration is democratic, and therefore, he could ask nothing of them.'"—ALS, DLC-Sylvanus Cadwallader.

1874, APRIL 9.   "Martha Washington," Va., to USG. "You are respectfully invited to be present at a tea-party to be given by myself at Masonic Temple, on the 15th instant, and to be continued on the 16th instant, in order to accommodate the many friends that I think would be pleased to see me, and renew old times and acquaintances. This party is given in celebration of my hundredth birthday, and if entirely convenient, please come dressed in the garb of ye olden times. . . ."—*Washington Chronicle,* April 15, 1874. Martha Washington impersonators conducted charitable events in several cities.

1874, APRIL 10.   USG veto of a relief bill for William H. Denniston.—Copy, DNA, RG 130, Messages to Congress. *HED,* 43-1-210; *SMD,* 49-2-53, 385–86. On April 8, Secretary of War William W. Belknap had written to USG that records did not support Denniston's claim that he served as 2nd lt., 70th N. Y.— Copy, DNA, RG 107, Letters Sent, Military Affairs. See *HRC,* 43-1-21; *SRC,* 43-1-102.

1874, APRIL 11.   U.S. Senator Abijah Gilbert of Fla., Jacksonville, to USG. "A dispatch has been received here that F. A. Dockray has been arrested by the Cuban authorities at Puerto Principe, ~~will~~ do everything you can to save his life"—Telegram received (at 9:25 A.M.), DNA, RG 59, Miscellaneous Letters. On the same day, Governor Marcellus L. Stearns of Fla. telegraphed to USG. "Frederick. A. Dockray a citizen of Florida is captured by the cubans at Puerto Principe & is in danger of Execution   will you Interpose to Save him"—Telegram received (at 8:46 P.M.), *ibid.* On April 14, Secretary of State Hamilton Fish recorded in his diary a conversation with USG. ". . . he said that Dockray was not entitled to any sympathy or commiseration from this Government being an absconding defaulter who had gone to Cuba to no good purpose but was in a bad way inasmuch as he did not dare return to the United States; that those people who, down in the insurrectionary lines and were caught by the Spaniards had no right to appeal to this Government for protection."—DLC-Hamilton Fish.

On April 17, U.S. Senator Simon B. Conover of Fla. wrote to USG. "In an interview which you accorded me to-day I brought to your notice the case of F. A. Dockray, a citizen of Florida, of whom telegraphic accounts sent from Havana report that he is under sentence of death pronounced by a military tribunal in Cuba. The offence for which he was so condemned, is said to be 'communication with the insurgents.' You informed me that the Government was apprised of the report alluded to, and that the Secretary of State had made communication on the subject to the authorities in Cuba, and that all proper efforts would be made to secure to Mr Dockray a fair and impartial trial and such protection as an American citizen had a right to expect at the hands of his Government. I felt it however to be my duty to give the subject more especial attention and solicitude, and hence I deem it due to myself, in this more formal manner, to renew what I endeavored to present to you this morning. . . ."—LS, DNA, RG 59, Miscellaneous Letters. Spanish authorities eventually commuted Frederick A. Dockray's sentence to imprisonment. On April 3, 1869, USG had nominated Dockray as collector of customs, St. Johns; on Dec. 21, 1870, USG nominated John S. Adams to replace Dockray. See *New York Times,* March 22, 1876; Jerrell H. Shofner, *Nor Is It Over Yet: Florida in the Era of Reconstruction 1863–1877* (Gainesville, 1974), pp. 237–38.

1874, APRIL 12.   Elizabeth Griffith, Goshen, Ohio, to USG seeking aid in securing a pension. ". . . my husband served three years in the army and got an onerable discharge & and was sent home sick and was sick with the chronick direa untill his death . . . I was left with a little babe five weeks old   I am the mother of eight living children   my age is forty one   I have worked so harde since my husband died that I am not able to support my little children any longer . . ."— ALS, DNA, RG 48, Miscellaneous Div., Letters Received. On May 18, Griffith wrote to USG on the same subject.—ALS, *ibid.* Griffith received twelve dollars monthly beginning in May.

1874, APRIL 13.   Secretary of War William W. Belknap to USG. "I have the honor to return Senate Bill 366, 'for the relief of Oliver Powers' late Private Company "K", 10th Tennessee Cavalry, with remark that this man is reported as having deserted at Athens, Ala. January 5. 1865. and at Gravely Springs, Ala. February 5, 1865. In 1868 application was made to the Adjutant General's office, in this case for a discharge, it being claimed that the soldier was captured when reported a deserter, . . ."—Copy, DNA, RG 107, Letters Sent, Military Affairs. The bill became law without USG's signature. See *SRC*, 43-1-47.

1874, APRIL 15.   J. William Gunesch, Vienna, to USG. "In my capacity as advocate in Vienna I beg to claim the aid and assistance of the Government of North-America and her august Chief against a flagrant violation of rights by which two highly respectable ladies, Austrian citizens are menaced by the Plenipotentiary at the Austrian Court Mr. John Jay. . . ."—LS, DNA, RG 59, Miscellaneous Letters. Gunesch charged that John Jay, minister to Austria, had broken the lease on two houses in Vienna rented for embassy use. See *New York Times*, Oct. 6, 25, 1874.

1874, APRIL 15.   Mrs. F. P. Willing, Crystal Springs, Miss., to USG. "In view of the fact that an application will be presented to you for consideration, in behalf of my husband, W. J. Willing Esq, for appointment as Dist. Atty. for the Southern Dist. of our State, I am prompted by a recollection of the many acts of kindness, you were pleased to extend to my Mother, while you were commanding the Federal Forces at Vicksburg, to address you this communication. You may have forgotten many of the circumstances, but my Mother, Mrs. R. F. Pettit, and, myself, then but a mere girl, were frequently at Head Quaters; and for the acts of kindness shown to ~~ourselves~~ us, by yourself, and, Gen. Rawlings, we shall ever entertain the best rememberances, coupled with gratitude for all you did for us. Mr. Willing is fully identified with the Republican Party of our State, and, has ever been a political friend and admirer, as well as, supporter of yours. He was a member of the Miss. Legislature for two terms, and, as a friend of our present Govenor, Genl Ames, did much to assist in securing his nomination and election, first as U. S. Senator, and afterwards of Govenor. During the years 1870 & 71. Mr. Willing was an active member of the Judiciary Committee of the H. R. and in 1872 was appointed by our present Congressman, Hon. J. R. Lynch, then Speaker of the H. R. as chairman of that committee. In addition to the evidences of his qualifications, as a Lawyer, for the position he seeks, allow me to refer you also, in reference thereto, and to his standing as to a Rebublican to, Hons J. R. Lynch, Jason Niles, Geo. C. McKee H. W. Barry, and A. R. Howe, our Representative in the present Congress, also, to Genl Alcorn and Maj. Pease

the present Senators from this State."—ALS, DNA, RG 60, Records Relating
to Appointments. On June 5, Secretary of War William W. Belknap, West Point,
telegraphed to Orville E. Babcock. "A movement is on foot to have O, C, French
a defaulter in Freedman's Bureau, appointed District Attorney in Mississippi, Please inform President, Your letter received, Thanks,"—Telegram
received, DLC-USG, IB. On June 8, William H. Gibbs, Miss. auditor, wrote to
USG recommending James M. McKee as U.S. attorney, Southern District, Miss.
—LS, DNA, RG 60, Records Relating to Appointments. McKee later served as
asst. U.S. attorney. See *PUSG*, 21, 331–32; Proclamation, Dec. 21, 1874.

1874, APRIL 15.   William H. Wisener, Sr., Shelbyville, Tenn., to USG. "My information is that a Young Artist living in this place, by the name of G. W. Jones
is an applicant to accompany, the Expedition to the South Seas, to witness the
transit of venus, in the capacity of Assistant Photographer. . . ."—ALS, DNA,
RG 45, Letters Received from the President. See *SED*, 46-1-31.

1874, APRIL 16.   USG endorsement. "Refered to the Sec. of War. Let special
attention be called to this application when apts. come to be made for the class
of /76"—AES, DNA, RG 94, Correspondence, USMA. Written on a letter of
April 15 from Judge Walter Q. Gresham, District of Ind., Washington, D. C., to
USG. "I respectfully request that my son, Otto Gresham, of New-Albany, Indiana, born on   day of February, 1858, be appointed a Cadet in the Military Academy, at West Point, for the Country at large—"—ALS, *ibid.* On May 2, 1876,
Gen. William T. Sherman telegraphed to Gresham, Indianapolis. "Just seen the
President. Impossible to make any promises, as the alternates will doubtless fill
immediately every vacancy made by failure from any cause   President thinks
the law requires the Academic Board to consent in all cases of failure—"—
Copy, *ibid.*, RG 108, Letters Sent. On May 3, Gresham telegraphed to USG.
"My Son Well up in mathematics failed in Grammar only   Will have him prepared   cant you give him another chance?   not able to Educate him Elsewhere
unless I resign—"—Telegram received, *ibid.*, RG 94, Correspondence, USMA.
On May 4, Ulysses S. Grant, Jr., wrote to Secretary of War Alphonso Taft. "By
direction of the President I enclose a telegram from Genl Gresham   The President says, that a vacancy may be retained for young Gresham in September, and
please notify Genl Gresham and the Academic Board."—ALS, *ibid.* Otto Gresham did not attend USMA.

1874, APRIL 16.   Orville E. Babcock to David Davis, U.S. Supreme Court. "The
President requests me to say that when he accepted the invitation to dine with
you on the 18th inst. he was under an impression that it was a different day of
the week. He had invited some friends to dine with him on Saturday, and he is
therefore reluctantly compelled to withdraw his acceptance, and hopes you will
excuse his oversight."—LS, David Davis Papers, IHi.

1874, APRIL 17.   Willis Drummond to USG resigning as commissioner, General Land Office, effective June 1.—LS, DNA, RG 48, Appointment Div., Letters
Received. On April 24, Sempronius H. Boyd, Springfield, Mo., wrote to USG. "I

herewith respectfully present myself to your favourable consideration as an Applicant for 'Commissioner of the General Land Office' soon to be vacated by the Honorable Willis Drummond. Mr President—I am about financially flattened, in consequence of defalcating Federal Officers and mail contractors to whom I lent my name as bondsman—. . ."—ALS, *ibid.* Also on April 24, U.S. Representative John W. Hazelton of N. J., *et al.,* wrote to USG recommending Maurice M. Kaighn to replace Drummond.—DS (23 signatures), *ibid.* Secretary of the Navy George M. Robeson favorably endorsed this petition.—AES (undated), *ibid.* On April 27, 28, and 29, USG received telegrams from William H. Benton, John F. Long, and others in St. Louis, urging Thomas C. Fletcher for the position.— Telegrams received, *ibid.*; DLC-USG, IB. On April 28, USG nominated Samuel S. Burdett to replace Drummond.

1874, APRIL 17.   Mrs. Edmunds B. Holloway, Independence, Mo., to USG seeking a cadetship for her son. ". . . *Thomas Thornton Holloway* is the youngest son of Edmunds B. Holloway, formerly Capt. of H. Company, 8th Regiment of Infantry, Reg. U. S. Army. and grandson of *Genl. William F. Thornton,* late of Shelbyville, Illinois. His Father fell in the very beginning of our Civil war; while in command of Missouri State Guards. Capt. Holloway's record in the Army is without blemish. Graduating from West Point at 21 years of age, he spent almost the whole of his life in active service. Was dangerously wounded in the Mexican war, & again in 1849, received injuries from which he never wholly recovered— This did not prevent him engaging in battle with the Indians of New Mexico— with success—in the fall of 1860. Influenced by the same motives which caused Gen. Lee, Johnson, Jackson, McIntosh, & others, to make the sacrifice—Capt. Holloway resigned his Commission and took up arms with the Southern people. These details are not very politic, perhaps, General Grant; yet in this, I atleast, pay your Excellency the compliment of shewing that this appointment is *not* asked as a *personal favor* to an old class-mate, and Comrade in arms; but because my son has shewn himself possessed of the qualities most requisite to form a good Soldier. . . ."—ALS, DNA, RG 94, Correspondence, USMA. Thomas T. Holloway did not attend USMA.

1874, APRIL 20.   Mortimer M. Benton, Covington, Ky., to USG. "Capt. J. M. Blackburn, the bearer, is the son of Dr. Blackburn, md, late of this city, and of a most respectable family—He was Clerk of the U S. Court in this City, having been a most consistent and active Union man in all the struggles of the Country against the late Rebellion—He is generous & confiding, and while acting as Clerk, he received considerable sums of money, that were paid into court, as the Register of the Court—and had indulged friends in the use of sums, who failed to respond, hence on his settlement, he fell in arrears, for which he was indicted in the District Court, ~~and~~ but getting time to make up his accounts for fees & with the assistance of friends he has paid off the claim in full—My own opinion is that Capt. Blackburn never purposed a wrong—but confiding too much in others was deceivd and furnished money when he should not, but no doubt that he always considered that he could & would make good when required—I cannot believe that he designed to defraud the Government or any person. He has

been subjected to much trouble & great mortification which has been severe
punishment for any delinquency, and he now hopes Your Excellency will grant
him pardon & cause the prosecution to be dismissed—I do hope that he may
find favor with the Executive and be fully discharged from further prosecution
for the case aforesaid."—ALS, DNA, RG 60, Letters Received, Ky. Related papers are *ibid.* No action followed.

1874, APRIL 21.   U.S. Representative Henry L. Dawes of Mass. *et al.* to USG.
"Believing that it is fit and proper to have one of the Judges of the Court of claims
appointed from the Southern States as much of the business of that court comes
from that section of the country—And as the recent death of Judge Milligan has
rendered vacant the only place filled from States lately in rebellion. We recommend the Hon Horace Maynard, as a man peculiarly fit to receive an appointment to fill this vacancy and give satisfaction to the country"—DS (93 signatures), DNA, RG 60, Applications and Recommendations. U.S. Representative
Roderick R. Butler of Tenn. and twelve others also petitioned USG on behalf of
U.S. Representative Horace Maynard of Tenn.—DS (undated), *ibid.* On April 22,
U.S. Representative Philetus Sawyer of Wis. *et al.* petitioned USG recommending Halbert E. Paine as judge, Court of Claims.—DS (7 signatures), *ibid.* Papers
recommending Paine for a similar vacancy in 1870 are *ibid.* On April 27, 1874,
Judge John Erskine, District of Ga., Savannah, wrote to USG. "The death of
Judge Milligan having created a vacancy in the Court of Claims, I beg, with respect & deference, to commend the name of the Honble A. T. Akerman to your
attention, as a man in every way qualified to fill the office of a judge, & peculiarly
fitted, in my humble judgement, for a position on the Bench of the Court of
Claims. As Mr Akerman is so thoroughly known to you, I will add nothing
more."—ALS, *ibid.* On June 1, USG nominated William A. Richardson, former
secretary of the treasury, as judge, Court of Claims, to succeed Samuel Milligan.

1874, APRIL 24.   USG endorsement. "Refered to the Atty. Gen. There is no
better or truer man than the writer of this letter. I have known him for more
than thirty years. His services in the late war however were in the rebel army."
—AES, DNA, RG 60, Records Relating to Appointments. Written on a letter
of March 31 from William M. Gardner, USMA 1846, Rome, Ga., to USG. "Having been associates, comrades and may I add friends in the past? I approach you
directly & frankly and perhaps informally—I desire to be appointed U. S. Marshall for the District of Georgia, or to some other Federal Office in that State
the duties of which I may be judged capable of discharging and the emoluments
of which may enable me to support a large & helpless family—You are the best
judge, if you recollect me at all, whether I am a fit man for appointment—I have
no political antecedents, belong to no political party and therefore have no political friends—I am what I have ever been a plain soldier, now a very necessi-
tous one—If appointed to office I shall execute the laws—& have had no part
in making them—I have asked for no endorsements—My old associates know
what sort of man I am—I think my appointment would be agreeable to many
Georgians—If the Government wants a faithful and zealous officer I think one
can be had in me—My politics are perhaps unusual—I stand to my friends

and trust they may stand to me as faithfully—"—ALS, *ibid.* No appointment followed.

1874, April 27.   USG endorsement. "Refered to the Sec. of War. Let attention be called to this application when apt. are made for the class of /76."—AES, DNA, RG 94, Correspondence, USMA. Written on a letter of April 20 from Amanda M. Mervine, Canandaigua, N. Y., to USG. "As the Widow of Rear Admiral Mervine who for the period of over half a century served his country with fidelity and zeal and as the mother of three sons who enlisted early in the war of the Rebelion and served until death in one instance, and wounds in another took them from the field of action, I come to you with a petition for which I crave your kindly concideration. I have a grand son, Edward Mervine Sturges, 17 years of age, who desires to enter West Point Academy. He is the son of a beloved daughter, long since deceased. Should you Mr President have the kindness to give him the appointment, I think I can promise that he will endevour to prove himself wothy of it. And for myself, my prayers and blessings shall always follow you, as they have done, ever since you were raised up for the salvation of your Country in her hour of peril."—ALS, *ibid.* Related papers are *ibid.* Admitted to USMA in 1875, Edward M. Sturges did not graduate.

1874, April 27.   Rear Admiral Henry Walke, Brooklyn, to USG. "I have the honor most respectfully, to address your Excellency as a friend, a companion in arms, and by your special kindness now a R. Admiral in the United States Navy, for which I shall ever be most grateful. I am apprehensive however that the permanence of my position on the retired list of the Navy may, at any time, be in jeopardy, by a gradual reduction of the Navy retired list. . . ."—LS, DNA, RG 45, ZB File. Walke remained on the retired list.

1874, April 28.   Felix R. Brunot, Pittsburgh, to USG. "The enclosed note is from Bishop Morris of the Episcopal Ch. in Oregon. I may add that I have some acquaintance with Judge Deady, and do not know of a Territorial judge of whose legal ability and moral qualifications I think so highly. I understood some months ago that efforts were to be made for the removal of Govr Potts of Montana. Having had some acquaintance with Gov Potts also, and opportunities to observe his administration, I venture also to express the opinion that he is man of ability and integrity in who whose removal the public interests would not be beneficially served, however much it may benefit that of individuals."—ALS, DNA, RG 60, Records Relating to Appointments. On April 8, Bishop Benjamin W. Morris, Portland, Ore., had written to Brunot concerning political attacks against Judge Matthew P. Deady, District of Ore.—ALS, *ibid.* Deady retained his position. On June 19, USG renominated Benjamin F. Potts as governor, Montana Territory.

1874, April 29.   Joseph D. Webster, asst. treasurer, Chicago, to USG. "Having been requested to do what I can to procure for Charles Mills an appointment to the Military Academy, I herewith submit a letter from his mother, and one from the Superintendent of the Relief Society under whom he has been employed for some time. I beg to commend Mrs. Mills' letter to your careful attention. I have made *careful inquiry* and can find no reason to doubt the statements therein contained. The death of her husband in Libby prison constitutes a good 'claim' in behalf of her son. . . ."—ALS, DNA, RG 94, Correspondence, USMA. Charles Mills did not attend USMA.

1874, APRIL 29. Orville E. Babcock to William E. Chandler. "Thanks for the letter for Col Whitley. The President told me this morning that he should not remove Young and has told Small so. Of course you will not use my name in this"—ALS, New Hampshire Historical Society, Concord, N. H. On April 28, Babcock had written to Chandler seeking a letter of introduction to Governor Ezekiel A. Straw of N. H. for Hiram C. Whiteley, investigating counterfeiters for the Treasury Dept.—LS, *ibid.*

1874, APRIL 30. Col. Edward Hatch, Fort Brown, Tex., to USG. "I have the honor to request that you will nominate and appoint J. Lee Humfreville late Captain 9th U. S. Cavaly to his old position in my Regiment, with former rank, . . . I beleive that the punishment inflicted on the men of his Co while absent's guarding the Rail Road surveying party—was the result of a zealous desire to preserve correct decipline ~~with~~ in his company under the most discouraging circumstances, and if a wrong has been committed by Capt Humfreville I beleive it was not from a desire to do so, but from an error of judgement, . . ."—Copy, DNA, RG 233, 43A-D1. Related papers are *ibid.* J. Lee Humfreville had been court-martialed on charges including drunkenness and illegally punishing his men. On June 22, Secretary of War William W. Belknap wrote to USG that he had found "no sufficient cause" to recommend reinstating Humfreville. "This is the case of which I spoke to you personally the other day."—Copy, *ibid.*, RG 107, Letters Sent, Military Affairs. On Feb. 19, 1875, Belknap wrote to Humfreville that USG had declined to reinstate him.—Copy, *ibid.*

1874, [*April-May*?]. Robert L. Stuart *et al.*, New York City, to USG inviting him to the cornerstone laying for the American Museum of Natural History.— William Evarts Benjamin, Catalogue No. 27, Nov., 1889, p. 10. USG laid this cornerstone on June 2. See *New York Times*, May 30, June 3, 1874.

1874, MAY 1. Levi P. Luckey to Flodoardo Howard, Washington, D. C. "Personal. . . . The President directs me to write you and say that since seeing you this morning he has examined into the matter of the physician here, and finds that it was established by Mr. Johnson and is not necessary any longer. As it comes out of the appropriation of the Surgeon General's office and is not authorized by law specially, he has concluded not to appoint a successor to Dr. Holston."—Copy, DLC-USG, II, 2. John G. F. Holston, White House physician, died the same day. See *PUSG*, 19, 416; William B. Atkinson, ed., *A Biographical Dictionary of Contemporary American Physicians and Surgeons*, 2nd ed. (Philadelphia, 1880).

1874, MAY 4. USG endorsement. "Refered to the Sec. of War to report whether ~~late~~ Lt. Campion, late of the U. S. Army may not be permitted to resign to take effect the date of his dismissal from the Army"—AES, DNA, RG 94, ACP, C1365 CB 1864. Written on a letter of April 4 from Richard Campion, Philadelphia, to U.S. Representative John W. Hazelton of N. J., on behalf of his brother William H. Campion, court-martialed in 1872 for misuse of funds. ". . . I am convinced that if Sec'y Robeson & yourself will make a personal appeal to the President he will grant your request   Sec'y Robeson told me in the presence of Mr Dobbins that (after our interview with the President) 'now it is my case and I will see that it ends all right,'   the plan I suggest will make it 'end all right.'   I trust Sec'y Robeson will make that effort, for when the President has the details of the case explained to him—his military experience will show him at once, that the case is one of only technical offences—to you sir I am unable properly to express my sentiments, my gratitude shall ever be yours—Please advise me of your views upon receipt of this"—ALS, *ibid.* On May 7, Belknap wrote to USG that Campion could not legally resign.—LS (press), *ibid.* On Feb. 24, Belknap had written to Secretary of the Navy George M. Robeson declining to reinstate Campion.—Copy, *ibid.*, RG 107, Letters Sent, Military Affairs.

On March 10 and 23, Maria Campion, Camden, N. J., had written to USG. "I address thee with a heart full of sorrow and grief on account of my Dear Son Wm H. Campion . . . Ever since he received his sentence he has bin a man of sorrow   he has bin in no business   said he could not ask for a situation any whare as he stood accused before the world of being a thief therefore he could not ask any one to give him situation in their business   It has made him almost a child as to sheading tears and his words is if the Goverment will give me back my *honor* and *good name* I can then look up as a man . . ." "I once more adress thee on behalf of my dear broken hearted Son . . . of his case I have reason to believe thee is well acquainted, . . ."—ALS, *ibid.*, RG 94, ACP, C1365 CB 1864. On Feb. 27, 1877, Maria Campion wrote to USG on the same subject.—ALS, *ibid.*

1874, MAY 5.   Silas Savage, Hartford, to USG concerning "French Spoliation Claims."—ALS, DNA, RG 59, Miscellaneous Letters. On Sept. 13 and Dec. 20, 1875, Savage wrote to USG on the same subject.—ALS, *ibid.* See *New York Times,* Dec. 12, 1884.

1874, MAY 6.   Christian S. Eyster and ten others, Denver, to USG. "The undersigned return thanks for nomination of Hon D. A. Cheever, as P. M. of Denver."—Telegram received, DLC-USG, IB. On May 5, USG had nominated David A. Chever as postmaster, Denver.

On Jan. 19, 1876, Alexander C. Hunt, Denver, telegraphed to USG. "No appointment ever made by you in this city ever gave so general satisfaction as Sumner"—Telegram received (at 7:10 P.M.), *ibid.* On Jan. 13, USG had nominated Edward C. Sumner as postmaster, replacing Chever.

1874, MAY 8.   Felix R. Brunot to USG. "I venture to remind you of our conversation on the 16th of March, in which, for myself and other members of the Board of Indian Commissioners, I suggested the desirability of placing the control of Indian affairs in a department, or independent office, whose head should receive a salary commensurate with the ability required and the importance of his position, and whose term of office should continue during the term of at least two or more administrations, subject only to removal for cause. . . . You expressed approval of the plan, and among other things said it would continue the present policy, and take the Indian service out of politics, but that you did not think Congress would adopt it, that you would consult some of the leading members on the subject and would inform me of your conclusions. I greatly desire to know your decision in regard to the proposed measure; the more so, because we are convinced that it will be impossible for the present relations between the Board of Indian Commissioners and the Interior Department and the Indian Office—so far at least as the original members are concerned—much longer to continue. Should Congress continue the Board with the duty of supervising all accounts and contracts of the Indian Office, and make its decisions final, the engagements of the members of the Board would hardly permit them to accept the duty. On the other hand, should the duty be imposed with no more power added than exists under the present law, they will hardly consent to continue a service which seems to them as vexatious and arduous as it is ineffective in the correction of abuses."—(ellipsis in source) Charles Lewis Slattery, *Felix Reville Brunot 1820–1898* (New York, 1901), pp. 222–23. On May 18, Levi P. Luckey wrote to Brunot, Pittsburgh. "The President directs me to say that your favor of the 8th inst. has just been brought to his attention though it was received at the office several days since. After your interview he did consult with the Secretary of the Interior on the subject of it, and found he not only approved but was anxious to have the Indian Bureau independent of the department. There were such questions before Congress, however, at the time that he felt that it would be idle to expect legislation on the subject until these questions were out of the way, particularly the financial question. Until this is settled he would consider it very unfortunate to have the subject of legislation on the Indian question brought up at this session. The reasons why are obvious. The President is, however, in favor of a separation of the Indian Bureau from all departments, with a view of making the policy adopted more effective. But the tenure of the office of the Commissioner, as suggested by you cannot be reached by any legislative action. An official appointed by the President, by and with the advice and consent of the Senate, and subject to removal under any circumstances, is subject to removal for any cause the appointing power may deem suficient. Nothing but a Constitutional provision can change this."—Copy, DLC-USG, II, 2.

On May 27, Brunot, Robert Campbell, Nathan Bishop, William E. Dodge, John V. Farwell, and George H. Stuart wrote to USG. "The undersigned, the remaining members of the Board of Indian commissioners originally appointed by you under the Act of Congress approved April 10th 1869, respectfully resign the office we have held under that appointment. We cannot take this step without expressing our warm appreciation of the high motives which have actuated you in the line of policy for the treatment of the Indian tribes announced in your inaugural message, and of your faithful and persistent adherence to that policy through much opposition and in despite of many obstacles, and at the same time thanking you for your ready and cordial sympathy with the efforts of the Board to promote that policy, and the kindly personal consideration which has always marked your your intercourse with its members. Your policy has attained by its success and the manifest righteousness of its foundation principles, a position in the judgement of the right minded people of the country which it is hoped cannot fail to render it permanent, nor can the evil deeds of individuals or small parties of savages, or the necessity which may arise to punish them, condemn the humane and just treatment of the Indians generally, save in the minds of those who on account of hatred or greed, denounce whatever seems to interfere with their schemes. It is not claimed that honesty and right dealing have been secured throughout all the ramifications of the Indian service, but many corrupt practices have been corrected, and enough has been accomplished to demonstrate that with proper organization it is possible to secure at least as great a degree of honesty in Indian affairs, as in any other department of the government. Some of the points where reformation is still needed were indicated in the last annual Report of the Board. We regret that it is not deemed expedient by the Hon. Secretary of the Interior to urge upon the present Session of Congress the legislation we recommend which would make the Indian Bureau independant of the Interior Department, with an officer of high ability at its head. The measure we consider of great importance for the perfection, as well as the perpetuation of the Peace policy, and its economic reforms, and we are glad to know that it meets your approval. Whilst we do not deem it necessary to present all the reasons which have decided us to resign, we may state, that should Congress as indicated in the Indian appropriation Bill which has already passed the House of Representatives—continue the Board of Indian Commissioners with all the 'duties imposed by existing laws, and requiring in regard to the examination of the accounts, contracts, and vouchers, that 'all such examinations and duties shall hereafter be performed in the city of Washington' we could not accept the duty—First, because under the existing laws the overruling of the decisions of the Board by the Interior Department would frequently render the labor of examining and deciding upon the accounts and vouchers as useless, as it is arduous and vexatious, and Second, because none of us can remove to Washington City to perform the duty. Experience has shown that a Board of Indian Commissioners clothed with proper authority, and acting in co-operation with the Department of the Interior but not under its direction or control, can hardly preserve harmonious relations with that Department; On the other hand, a Board not so constituted and under the influence or control of the Interior or Indian Department, would be a comparatively useless appendage to the service. Reiterating our entire confidence in the wisdom and justice of the Peace Policy, our conviction of the capacity of the Indians to receive all the civilization necessary for their welfare and the safety of the frontier settlements, and all the christianization needful to their salvation; we desire to express our satisfaction with the progress which so many of them have already made in this direction, and our regrets for the necessity which terminates our official connection with the service."—LS, DNA, RG 48, Appointment Div., Letters Received. On May 28, Thomas C. Jones, Delaware, Ohio, wrote to USG. "By the construction put upon the Statutes defining the duties of the Board of Indian Commissioners, it is assumed that they are required to supervise the action of the Commissioner of Indian Affairs and the Secretary of the Interior, in all matters relating to the allowance of accounts, the purchase of goods, and the general management of the Indian Bureau, as well as the conduct of all its subordinate officers. Finding that I cannot afford to devote the time required for the proper discharge of duties so responsible and important, I most respectfully that the President will be pleased to accept my resignation"—ALS, *ibid.* See *PUSG*, 19, 191–97; *New York Times*, Feb. 21, June 8, 1874.

On June 8, Thornton P. Pendleton, Oakland, [Md.], wrote to USG. "I see in this Morning Baltimore Sun that all of the Indian Commissioners Messrs Felix R Brunot and others have tendered their resination Having Applied, to be appointed one of them when the Board was created, and was assured, by my Friend Col, J, S, Mosby—that it was at one time determined to appoint me: yet for some cause, I did not get the appointment. I again solicit, that you will appoint me, to fill the place of one of those resigned. I take great interest, in the wellfare of the Indians: I have now a daughter, as an Episcopal missionary; under Bishop Hare, of the Diocesan of Niobrara; Near Yankton Station: I refer you to my Friends Honorable Simon Cameron, Honorable Senator Lewis, of Virginia, Judge Robert W Huges, & Col J S Mosby, and will furnish, the entire endorsement of all your Prominent Friends, in Virginia if need be. Please let me hear from you & direct answer to Berryville Clarke County Virginia."—ALS, DNA, RG 48, Appointment Div., Letters Received. On June 9, Robert L. Dashiell and Thomas M. Eddy, New York City, wrote to USG. "The corresponding Secretaries of the Missionary Society of the Methodist Episcopal church have the honor to present the name of Genl. Clinton B. Fisk of St Louis for appointment as one of the Indian Commissioners. He is a gentlemen of high character and eminent ability, and we assure you that his appointment would most acceptable to the Christian Public and especially to our own church, which has no representation either among the Commissioners or Inspectors. . . ."—LS, *ibid.* On July 3, USG appointed Clinton B. Fisk, Henry H. Sibley, and Theron R. Butler to the Board of Indian Commissioners. See *New York Times*, July 4, 18, 21, 1874.

1874, MAY 8. Henry N. Gassaway, Washington, D. C., to USG. "I have the honor to make application to you, for a commission as paymaster in the U. S. Army. I beg to inform you, in support of my application, that I have been in the volunteer service of the U. S. as a private (Co. F. 114th Pa. Vols.) and at the battle of Gettysburgh, lost the use of my right hand, by a gun shot wound through the wrist joint. When fit for duty again, August 26, 1864, I received commission as Second Lieut: Veteran Reserve Corps, and was assigned to duty with "K" Co., 21 V. R. C., which commission I resigned in March 1865. Failing in the effort to again resume the duties I laid down to enter the army, I sought in 1868 and obtained a position as clerk in the civil service, which I have retained in various capacities since. In consideration of the fact, that my wound incapacitates me from my former line of life, I make this application and beg to submit the accompanying endorsements as commendations thereto."—ALS, DNA, RG 94, Applications for Positions in War Dept. Among the enclosures is a letter of May 9 from Maj. Gen. Irvin McDowell, Washington, D. C., to USG. "Mrs. Chapman Coleman tells me her son in law Mr. H. N. Gassaway is to apply to be appointed Paymaster in the Army in the event of the passage of a bill making additions to the Pay-Department. She further informs me her son-in-law served and was wounded in the War as an officer of Volunteers! I take pleasure in asking your favorable consideration of his application and do so the more readily as I know you will be glad to do whatever is in your power for the family of one who has so many claims on his country men, as that eminently distinguished patriot J. J. Crittenden of Ky.!"—ALS, *ibid.* On Oct. 31, S. Lee Gassaway wrote to USG. "Fearing I might not have the courage to speak to you of my hopes and fears, I have concluded to write you a few lines on the subject. If when you are kind enough to receive me my heart should fail, I will hand you this. Accompanied by my Mother, I saw you several times last winter, when the Paymasters bill was pending, and expressed my earnest desire that my husband Henry N. Gassaway, should be made Paymaster. You always received & listened to me kindly. The bill I was watching so anxiously did not pass, but, do not The 'Revised Statutes' Adopted by vote of both of the houses June 22nd 1874, take precedence of all legislation prior to December 31st 1873. Sec. 1182 *fixes* the number of Paymasters at sixty, and I think there are not more than 44 at present. If this is so can you not under this law appoint Paymasters now, and if so, will you not appoint my husband?. . ."—ALS, *ibid.* On Jan. 18 and March 10, 1875, Mrs. Gassaway wrote to USG. "I have come again to trouble you about 'my Paymasters Bill.'. . ." "Mr Stephens called to see you the day before his departure, to ask you to give my husband one of the Paymaster Appointments you told him the list was closed, and he said nothing further! He gave me this letter, and told me that when the Appointments had been sent to the Senate to take it to you myself. He said he feared he had no influence—I have heard Mr Stephens speak of you many times General Grant in terms of the highest admiration, and I can but think that there must be a reciprocity of feeling between two such men, and that you, would be pleased to gratify a wish of his. . . . Through all my disappointment and it has been great, I have remembered your former kindness!"—ALS, *ibid.* On March 6, U.S. Representative Alexander H. Stephens of Ga. wrote to USG recommending Gassaway and praising John J. Crittenden as "one of the noblest men I ever knew."—Julia Sweet Newman, Catalogue No. 200, 1965, no. 146. No appointment followed; Gassaway worked as a Treasury Dept. clerk in 1877.

1874, MAY 11. Elihu B. Washburne to Orville E. Babcock. "The term of office of an old friend, Mr. Wann Surveyor of the port of Galena, will expire in July and a re-appointment will be necessary. All that will be required to have Mr. W. re-appointed will be to call the President's attention to the matter, at the time. I presume no one will contest the re-appointment of Mr. Wann."—ALS (press), DLC-Elihu B. Washburne. On June 3, Babcock wrote to Washburne. "I received your letter in good time. I spoke to the President about the renomination of Mr W, he said there was none. So I asked the Secty of the Treasury to send it over.   he did so. I took it to the senate and it was confirmed yesterday. . . ."— ALS, *ibid.* For Daniel Wann, surveyor of customs, Galena, see *The Biographical Encyclopædia of Illinois in the Nineteenth Century* (Philadelphia, 1875), pp. 54–55.

1874, MAY 12.   USG veto. "I return herewith without my signature a bill, H. R. No 1331, entitled 'An Act for the relief of Joab Spencer and James R. Mead, for supplies furnished the Kansas tribe of Indians.' I withhold my approval of said bill for reasons which satisfy me that the claim should not be allowed for the entire amount stated in the bill and which are set forth in the letter of the Acting Secretary of the Interior, dated the 7th instant, a copy of which, with its accompanying papers is herewith transmitted."—Copy, DNA, RG 130, Messages to Congress. *HED,* 43-1-249; *HRC,* 44-1-741, 45-2-376, 46-3-72, 47-1-309; *SRC,* 47-1-58; *SMD,* 49-2-53, 389. On May 7, Benjamin R. Cowen, act. secretary of the interior, had written to USG recommending further investigation of the claim of Joab Spencer and James R. Mead, former Indian traders.—*HED,* 43-1-249. Repeated efforts to pass legislation to pay Spencer and Mead finally succeeded in 1882.—*U.S. Statutes at Large,* XXII, 728–29.

1874, MAY 13.   Samuel P. Holt, Lynchburg, Va., to USG. "PERSONAL, . . . I herewith enclose certain papers, which I respectfully ask your Excellency to examine,   The accounts are *just*; I have rendered the services; the Government has had the benefit of my extra labor, and I am slow to believe that a great government, like the one over which you preside, will withhold the scanty earnings of an humble, and faithful, employee. The amount claimed by myself, is but a small item to the Government, while to me, it is of vital importance,   In, justice to myself, I would say, that I am a Republican, and as such have been a firm supporter of your administration,   I am one of the many friends you have in *this* section of Va who will urge your nomination for a third term, . . ."—ALS, DNA, RG 56, Letters Received from the President. Enclosures detailing Holt's claim for compensation for additional services rendered while asst. assessor of Internal Revenue, 5th District, Va., are *ibid.* On May 25 and June 8, Holt again wrote to USG. ". . . It is very true, that the amount which I am claiming is *small* and if my necessities did not call for every cent which I have earned, I would not trouble you with such insignificant matters,   In order to support myself and family, I was compelled to make some debts, while I was at work for the government, and now those debts are pressing me, and if I cant realize the amout *justly due me,* my property will be sold at a sacrifise, . . ." ". . . The debts contracted by myself, and which I expected to pay out of the money realized for my services, are now distressing me,   My last Bed is now in the hands of my *Land Lord,* and he is kindly waiting for a fiew days to see whither my accounts will be allowed and paid, . . . What is the pitiful sum of $1365.06 to the U. S. and yet to me, it is of *vital importance,* for with it, I can pay my honest debts and thereby save my Beds for my children,   I am not beggin, I am only asking to be paid for my labor, . . ."—ALS, *ibid.* See *SRC,* 44-2-569.

On Feb. 25, 1875, Robert W. Hughes, Norfolk, wrote to USG. "I take pleasure in bearing testimony to the personal character and fidelity and efficiency as a Republican of Saml. P. Holt esq. of Lynchburg. He has received the highest possible endorsement from the Republicans of Lynchburg and Campbell Co. where he lives, and deserves the confidence of the administration."—ALS, USG 3. On March 16 and 24, Holt wrote to USG. ". . . The great question now to be settled, is, can we successfully meet and overcome the recent success of the old secession party?. . . I know there are politicians in the Republican party, who are looking to the Presidential chair, such men will doubtless oppose a third term, but all such must stand a side for the present, If we expect, or even hope to succeed in electing a Republican President in 1876, we must go to work at once, and organize the party so as to secure your nomination. This can be done; the people are mightier than the politicians, . . . unfortunately for us as a party, there are too many Federal office holders, who are not in sympathy with the Administration, they hold their office for the pay, Such men add no strength to the party, but rather weaken it, Ex Rebel office holders wont do to trust in a close hand to hand fight, and the sooner they are disposed of, the better it will be for the party in the next Presidential Contest, . . . P. S. As I am not personally acquainted with you Excellency, I enclose a letter from Judge R. W. Hughes, to you, and I would add, that it would afford me much pleasure to canvas for your nomination and election as our next President," ". . . Unfortunately for us as a party there has been too many exrebels appointed to federal positions, . . . They are not capable of leading any party, and our recent defeats, is owing in part to the inefficiency of such men, they hang as dead weights on the party, they use their offices entirely for their own benefit, and not for the cause of Republicanism; We hear such men Complaining of northern men holding office, as if the lowest Carpetbagger in the South is not entitled to more respect than a perjered *ExRebel*, I am a native Virginian an old union man, and I thruthfully say that it would be fare better for our party, if we had more Carpetbagers, and fiewer ExRebels in Federal positions, This cry against Carpetbagers comes, not from the old Republicans, but from these elventh hour converts, they come for office, and not for any love they entertain for the administration, and the sooner they are rooted out the better for the party, With a sincere desire on my part to know that you will consent to serve the third term. . . ."—ALS, *ibid.* On Nov. 27, 1876, Holt again wrote to USG. "PERSONAL. . . . You will doubtless reckollect, that during the last Summer, I addressed you several letters, in which, I urged the propriety, (if not the actual necessity) of your being elicted President for the third term, I believed at that time, that the unsettled condition of the country, growing out of the deeprooted hostility of the Democratic Party to the Republicans, required the reelection of yourself, The condition of things at this time, satisfies not only myself, but many wiser heads, that the party has ered in not electing you for the third term; If Hayes, should be returnd as the President elect, it will be by counting Louisana, South Carolina, and Floriad, if that is done, I feele assured that there will be trouble, and that of a serious character; . . . I believe it would be advisable to increase the Secret Service, in all the Democratic States that your Excellency may be kept advised of every movvement made by the leaders of the Tilden or Democratic party, . . . Virginia has gone Democratic, by an over whelming vote, and if called on to support the Northern Democricy, would be a formidable foe to be within gunshot of the Federal Capital; . . ."—ALS, DNA, RG 60, Letters from the President.

1874, MAY 14. William McDanield, "Late a priveat Co H. 23th Regt O. V. V. I," Mount Vernon, Ohio, to USG. "thrugh the merceys of the Almighty god i am able to chat to you thrugh the Medium of the pen, two unfold to you the meny

obligation the people of the United States owes to me,   in July 24th 1864 at the
battle neigher Winchester Va. in Genl Hunters command i was taken prisoner
of war and taken two Danville Va. and hild their till Some time in october, 1864
i was paroled at aikens landing   before i left the prison i had formed acqua-
tence, with Some Union men of Danville who had a dispach, or the rebels plans,
and forci that held Richmond and Peatersburgh Va   they waunted to get it two
Secretary Stanton   this i dun Suckcessfull with great pearl of my life.   i reporte
to Secreatary, Stanton   he and Abraham Lincoln held a council over the disspaches   i then lay at Hicks Hospittal Marland   when i first notified Secreatary
Stanton of Smuglin the disspaches thrugh. he Scent a message to me. also. a pass
two report to Washington.   for all this President Lincoln and Secreatary Stanton gave me great prais and Said that i Should bee well reccompenced for it and
Should Abraham Lincoln lived and and Seccretary Stanton, i have no dopt, but
they would of dun Something nice for me.   for (this reason) they have my name
company and Regiment on (reccord) and the whole transaction.   they allso had
my name reccorded in the post.office department under postmaster Dennison a
bout July 1864 for Rought agent on the Sandusky Mansfield and Newark Rail
Road   this was dun by their askin, but never got no help from the United States
Goverment. President Grant i refur the Matter before you as a gentleman and
Soldier. . . ."—ALS, DNA, RG 48, Miscellaneous Div., Letters Received. In a
letter to President Andrew Johnson, March 10, 1868, McDanield mentioned
nothing about any pledge of assistance.—ALS, DLC-Andrew Johnson.

1874, MAY 15.   USG note. "Will the Sec. of the Treas. please see Miss Mattie
Hill, of Iowa, who lost a father & brother in the war, and has a mother and several younger brothers & sisters to support."—ANS, DNA, RG 59, Letters of
Application and Recommendation. Among related papers is an undated letter
from Martha A. Hill to the secretary of the interior. "I would respectfully ask
to be appointed to such a position in your Department as is usually occupied
by women. I am the daughter of a soldier. My father, Col. S. G. Hill, was killed
at Nashville, Tenn. Dec. 15th 1864. My Post Office address is Muscatine, Muscatine Co. Iowa. I would respectfully refer you to the accompanying letter."—
ALS, *ibid.*

1874, MAY 16.   Orville E. Babcock to Isaac F. Shepard, appraiser, St. Louis.
"The President directs me to acknowledge the receipt of your confidential letter of the 5th inst., and to say in reply that he does not endorse the appointment of Gen. McNeil. He would approve the appointment of Henry C. Wright
to this place."—Copy, DLC-USG, II, 2. Henry C. Wright replaced Shepard as
appraiser. See *PUSG*, 24, 117–18.

    On Dec. 1, 1876, John McNeil, St. Louis, wrote to USG. "The undersigned
your petitioner would respectfully represent that at the May term of the United
States district Court for the Eastern district of Missouri there was rendered
against him and his co-security Julius Hanike in the case of the United States
Versus William C. Jouette et al a judgement as suritities on a Bond of said Jouette
as distiller for the penal sum of *twenty seven thousand Dollars* ($27,000). That said
sum is largely in excess of all your petitioner is now worth and that his entire

property the savings of forty years of residence in St Louis—incumbered as it now is in consequence of loss of credit by this process—and the general depressed state of property at this time—would hardly bring the Government the costs in this suit. The petitioner when he consented to be security on this bond could not even dream that the principle a young man in the best position in society—enjoying the best of characters—and being the son of an old officer of the Army whose name while he lived was the synonim of honor—could by any chance engage in frauds on the Revenue or ever under any circumstances do that that would imperil his liberty and ruin his character. Nor did he for a moment suspect that he was to be under the influence of a set of officials who made honesty in this vocation ruin. But when these things were charged he withdrew from the Bond. He has never had one cents worth of interest in the manufacture or sale of liquor, and was merely on this Bond as a neighborly accomodation for a young friend. This suit and the necesary sacrifices in order to protect endorsers and cover all honerary and honest obligations has nearly ruined your petitioner and threatens his family with loss of house and home. He therefore Respectfully refering to his age and the fact that he has at all times loyally supported his Government to the extent of his abilities—would ask if it is either good pollicy or sound justice for that Government to ruin him—Justice has been vindicated. The Guilty have been punished—and frauds on the Revenue have been let us hope made too dangerous for repitition—should not mercy be extended to inocent sufferers? He therefore asks that the Attorney General shall be instructed to enter up satisfaction of the judgement in this case with all costs and that your petitioner be allowed to depart free of all incumbrance."—ALS, DNA, RG 60, Letters from the President. For McNeil, see *New York Times*, June 9, 1891.

1874, MAY 16, 2:00 P.M.   Abram J. Dittenhoefer, "Chairman of the German Executive Republican Co," Washington, D. C., to Secretary of State Hamilton Fish. "In the matter of Mr Andreas Willmann, of whom I spoke to you this morning in Connection with a Consulate, I have the honor to state that I have seen The President and gave him the names of St-Galen and Olten Switzerland, and Schiedam, Holland, either of which places, being Created Consulates without salary, Mr Willmann would accept, we have agents there now, The President made a memoranda thereof for the purpose of speaking to you. . . ."—L (probably in Simon Wolf's handwriting), DNA, RG 59, Letters of Application and Recommendation. Related papers are *ibid.* No appointment followed. See *New York Times*, March 5, 1878.

1874, MAY 18.   Secretary of War William W. Belknap to USG. "I have the honor to return House Bill 1776 'for the relief of George Yount' The records of the Third Missouri Volunteers show, that prior to the receipt of his commission as 2nd Lieutenant, Yount, while serving as an enlisted man, was wounded in action on May 22d 1863, left the regiment and did not return to, and enter upon duty under said commission, until March 7th 1864. This information was furnished the Military Committee, House of Representatives by the Secretary of War, February 21st 1873. There is no evidence of any service whatever, rendered by Yount, as an officer, prior to March 7th 1864, date of his return to his regiment, and muster in as 2nd Lieutenant, nor could he have rendered any as such, being absent from his command, disqualified by reason of wounds received while an enlisted man, (May 22d 1863) over three months previous to the date (September 1, 1863,) from which payment is allowed him in the accompanying bill. . . . *It is believed that the foregoing embraces objections to the approval of the Bill.*"—Copy, DNA, RG 107, Letters Sent, Military Affairs. This bill became law without USG's signature. See *SRC*, 43-1-200; *U.S. Statutes at Large*, XVIII, part 3, p. 552.

1874, MAY 19. To House of Representatives. "I transmit herewith in answer to the Resolution of the House of Representatives, of the 9th instant, a Report from the Secretary of State, with accompanying papers."—Copies, DNA, RG 59, Reports to the President and Congress; *ibid.*, RG 130, Messages to Congress. *HED*, 43-1-253. On the same day, Secretary of State Hamilton Fish had written to USG. "The Secretary of State to whom was referred the Resolution of the House of Representatives of the 9th instant, requesting the President to communicate to the House 'any correspondence between the State Department and other Governments as to the landing of Foreign convicts on our shores; and what legislation, if any, in his judgment is necessary to prevent such outrages,' has the honor to submit the following report to the President. The involuntary deportations to the United States by foreign officials of foreign convicts and of foreign paupers, idiots, insane persons, and others incapable of supporting themselves, has been frequently made the subject of official correspondence. Although the resolution of the House refers in terms only to the deportation of convicts, it is supposed that it will not be thought improper, in answering it, to transmit also correspondence relating to the other classes of involuntary emigrants. This objectionable practice has been the subject of official correspondence in previous administrations as well as during the present administration but inasmuch as it was necessary to terminate the researches at some point, it seemed that the spirit of the resolution would be answered by transmitting to the House copies of all the official diplomatic correspondence which has taken place since the 4th of March, 1869. . . . Respecting the inquiry 'what legislation if any is necessary to prevent such outrages' the Secretary of State is of the opinion that the Executive should be empowered summarily to prevent the landing of persons whom he may have reason to believe to have been convicts, or confirmed vagabonds, or persons permanently incapacitated from earning their own support and who may have been sent from their own country in whole or in part at the public expense, or at the expense of any public or professedly charitable institution or association, and to compel the vessels bringing them hither, to convey them away, . . ."—Copy, DNA, RG 59, Reports to the President and Congress. *HED*, 43-1-253.

1874, MAY 19. Secretary of War William W. Belknap to USG. "I have the honor to return House Bill No. 345, 'to relieve certain persons therein named, late members of Company "K," 58th regiment Illinois Volunteer Infantry, from the charge of mutiny,' and for the reasons stated in the enclosed report of the Judge Advocate General, I am of opinion that this bill should not receive the Approval of the President."—Copy, DNA, RG 107, Letters Sent, Military Affairs.

On Feb. 6, U.S. Representative John B. Hawley of Ill. had spoken in favor of this bill to revoke mutiny convictions against men who refused to obey orders after the apparent expiration of their service, explaining "that these men having all suffered imprisonment of several months, have suffered punishment enough for so slight an offense as simply refusing upon one occasion to go upon duty, and that not in the presence of the enemy or when they were required to fight. . . ."— *CR*, 43–1, 1273. This bill became law without USG's signature. See *U.S. Statutes at Large*, XVIII, part 3, p. 552.

1874, MAY 19.   Governor Adelbert Ames of Miss. to USG. "This letter with enclosure will be presented to you by Mrs Booth of Canton Missi who visits Washington to secure compensation for injury done her property during the War. Personally I know nothing of the facts, but I put unlimited faith in the statements of the writer of the enclosed letter, Mr T. B. Pratt the Dist Atty of that Circuit. Mr P. was a Union Soldier and would be slow in writing such a letter were he not convinced of the correctness of his position. I shall be glad to know that Mrs Booth receives full justice."—LS (press), Miss. Dept. of Archives and History, Jackson, Miss. On Jan. 13, 1875, the Senate Committee on Claims reported adversely on Martha A. Booth's claim for $11,500.—*SRC*, 43-2-518.

1874, MAY 20.   Attorney Gen. George H. Williams to USG. "I have the honor to return herewith the Act H. R. No. 2846, and to inform you that, in my, opinion, there is no objection to its receiving your approval."—LS, OFH. This bill repealed an act establishing a date to elect U.S. Representatives from Calif. See *CR*, 43–1, 3779; *HMD*, 43-1-184.

1874, MAY 20.   Lt. Governor Caesar C. Antoine of La. *et al.* to USG. "The Republicans here are very anxious that B. F Joubert should be nominated Collector of Internal Revenue for this District to Succeed Col Stockdale   his high character and sterling integrity especially Commend him for the position."— Telegram received (at 4:15 P.M.), DLC-USG, IB. On May 18, USG had nominated John Cockrem as collector of Internal Revenue, 1st District, La., in place of Sidney A. Stockdale.

1874, MAY 20.   U.S. Representative George F. Hoar of Mass. to USG. "Mrs B. W. Perkins is commended by many highly respected citizens of Worcester as a person whose claim against Russia is entitled to the consideration of our government, and to its aid in bringing it to the notice of his Majesty the Emperor of Russia."—ALS, DNA, RG 59, Miscellaneous Letters. See *Petition of Anna B. Perkins, of Worcester, Mass., Administratrix of the late B. W. Perkins, . . .* (Washington, 1867); Nevins, *Fish*, pp. 503–9.

1874, MAY 20.   Andrew Rothwell and William Stickney, Washington, D. C., to USG. "A General Convention of Ministers and Delegates of the Baptist denomination will be held in this city from the 22d to the 26th inst. On behalf of the Committee of Arrangements, the undersigned call to tender their respects to the President, and to ask of him the favor to make such order as will permit persons in the public employ, who may so desire, to attend the sessions of the

Convention.—No such general Baptist Convention has been held in this city, and no similar one will meet here for many years to come. We invite the President to honor the Convention with a visit, at Calvary Church corner of H and 8th streets."—LS, DNA, RG 59, Miscellaneous Letters. On May 25, USG received a large delegation from this convention at the White House.—*Washington National Republican,* May 26, 1874.

On April 22, Stickney had written to USG. "Accept my sincere congratulations for the veto message this day transmitted to Congress. I confess it was the first time I feared you might not be equal to the emergency—Thank God, you were, and our Country is saved from disgrace—"—ALS, USG 3.

1874, MAY 21.   USG pardon for F. E. G. Lindsey, imprisoned mail robber, recommended by persons "entertaining doubts as to his sanity at the time of the commission of the offence."—Copy, DNA, RG 59, General Records.

1874, MAY 21.   E. S. Frazer, St. Louis, to USG. "Though not personally acquainted with you, though a fellow townsman for more than twenty years. You will perhaps remember me as having attended your Son professionally, during a protracted and dangerous illness at the house of Mr Boggs, in this city during the war. I therefore beg you will allow me the liberty to Solicit your attention & interest in the case of my young friend Judson S. Post, (The bearer), I have read the official record and finding of the Naval Court Martial & finding in his case, by which he was dismissed the Service as Paymaster . . ."—ALS, DNA, RG 45, Subject File, Div. NI. No reinstatement followed. In 1868, Judson S. Post had been dismissed for drunkenness.—*SRC,* 46-3-843. See also *CR,* 44-1, 3478; *U.S. Statutes at Large (Private Laws),* XIX, 30–31.

1874, MAY 25.   Robert M. Kelly, Louisville, to USG. "Mr. Eli M. Kennedy of Bourbon County desires to be appointed to the mission to Bolivia, made vacant by the death of that gallant & noble gentleman John T. Croxton. Mr. Kennedy is a native of Bourbon County and has lived there always. He is a farmer of means and belongs to a family highly respected, and what is rare among men of his class in that county has been at all times a staunch union man and unwavering Republican. Hardly General Croxton, himself, was more noted in that community as a friend and upholder of the rights of the colored people. Like all of his views Mr. Kennedy has had to endure loss and obloquy from maintaining them. . . ."—ALS, DNA, RG 59, Letters of Application and Recommendation. Related papers are *ibid.* Papers recommending James Thomas, Wesley Ogden, and Moritz A. Jacobi for minister to Bolivia are *ibid.* On June 10, USG and Secretary of State Hamilton Fish reviewed "the list of applicants for Bolivia," expressed dissatisfaction, and postponed action.—Hamilton Fish diary, DLC-Hamilton Fish. For the nomination of Robert M. Reynolds, see *PUSG,* 24, 43–45.

On May 25, 1874, William H. Morgan, Annapolis, wrote to USG requesting appointment as minister to Bolivia.—ALS, DNA, RG 59, Letters of Application and Recommendation. On Feb. 12, Orville E. Babcock had written to Secretary of the Navy George M. Robeson. "The President requests me to say that he will be pleased to have you appoint Genl. W. H. Morgan of Kansas City, Mo. one of the Board of Visitors to the Naval Academy for this year; and to have the appointment prepared and sent to Genl. Morgan at Willard's Hotel as soon as practicable"—LS, *ibid.*, RG 45, Letters Received from the President. On March 2, 1875, U.S. Representative Stephen A. Hurlbut of Ill. wrote to USG. "Col. Wm H. Morgan formerly of the 25th Indiana Vols—requests to be considered as an applicant for Pay Master. You know him, his service, & his capacity and I simply give my old & valued comrade the advantage of being brought to the attention of the President"—ALS, *ibid.*, RG 94, Applications for Positions in War Dept. No appointment followed.

On May 26, 1874, P. Burgess Hunt, Lexington, Ky., telegraphed to Babcock. "Cant you get the President appoint me successor to the late Genl Croxton at Bolivia   I can furnish any papers he may require as to my fitness for the place. Genl Croxton & I were warm personal friends and had he named a successor I flatter myself he would have named me. I have never received an appointment from the President & I will feel very grateful to you if you will bring this matter before him"—Telegram received, *ibid.*, RG 59, Letters of Application and Recommendation. On Aug. 29, Herman W. Hasslock, postmaster, Nashville, telegraphed to USG. "It certainly will be for the best interests of the Party down here to keep supervisor K R Cobb in office."—Telegram received, DLC-USG, IB. Also on Aug. 29, Mayor Thomas A. Kercheval of Nashville telegraphed to USG on the same subject.—Telegram received, *ibid.* On Sept. 3, Secretary of the Treasury Benjamin H. Bristow telegraphed to USG, Long Branch. "Your message received,   No steps will be taken towards the removal of Supervisor Cobb until further orders from you."—Copy, DNA, RG 56, Letters Sent. On Dec. 10, USG nominated Hunt to replace Kenneth R. Cobb as supervisor of Internal Revenue for Tenn., Ky., Ala., Miss., and La. On Dec. 31, John M. Harlan and four others, Louisville, telegraphed to USG. "we earnestly hope that you will not withdraw the nomination of col Hunt from the senate   he is an honest true man who will fill the office with credit"—Telegram received, DLC-USG, IB. See *PUSG*, 19, 435.

1874, MAY 26.   To Senate. "I herewith transmit a report from the Secretary of State and accompanying it, copies of all the papers on file or on record in the Department of State, respecting the claim on Brazil concerning the 'Caroline.'" —Copy, DNA, RG 59, Reports to the President and Congress; *ibid.*, RG 130, Messages to Congress. *SED*, 43-1-52. On the same day, Secretary of State Hamilton Fish wrote to USG transmitting papers and suggesting "their transmission to the Senate, where a bill is now pending making an appropriation to enable the repayment in full of the sum paid by Brazil upon that claim."—Copy, DNA, RG 59, Reports to the President and Congress. *SED*, 43-1-52.

1874, MAY 26.   Orville E. Babcock to Secretary of State Hamilton Fish. "The President directs me to say that the several departments of the Government will be closed on the 30th inst., in order to enable the employés to participate in the decoration of the graves of the soldiers who fell during the rebellion."—LS, DNA, RG 59, Miscellaneous Letters. Babcock sent similar letters to all cabinet officers.

1874, MAY 27.   USG endorsement. "Refered to the sec. of the Int.   I approve the appointment of Gen. Smith."—AES, DNA, RG 48, Appointment Papers, New Mexico Territory. Written on a letter of the same day from U.S. Representative Horatio C. Burchard of Ill. to USG. "I respectfully recommend the appointment of Gen John C. Smith of Illinois as Receiver of the Land Office at Santa Fé New Mexico to succeed Eldredge N. Little resigned   Gen Smith is a competent man for the position a wounded and partially disabled soldier of the late war"—ALS, *ibid.* On March 17, USG had nominated John C. Smith as land office register, La Mesilla, New Mexico Territory; Smith declined this nomination. See *Chicago Tribune,* Jan. 1, 1911.

On April 22, U.S. Delegate Stephen B. Elkins of New Mexico Territory had written to USG. "Having been informed that the present Depositary & Receiver of public moneys at Santa Fé New Mexico will soon resign his position, I respectfully request, in case he does, the appointment of Abram G. Hoyt to fill the vacancy. Mr Hoyt is and has been for about three years a resident of New Mexico, is a graduate of Princeton College and formerly a resident of Wilkesbarre Pa. If appointed Mr Hoyt will make a good & faithful officer, he is a worthy young man a zealous republican & an earnest supporter of the present admintration"— ALS, DNA, RG 48, Appointment Papers, New Mexico Territory. Related papers are *ibid.* On May 26, USG nominated Abram G. Hoyt as land office receiver, Santa Fé.

1874, MAY 28.   Lt. Gen. Philip H. Sheridan, Chicago, to USG. "The bearer of this note is Mrs. Captain Arthur, widow of an officer of the 4th Infy. and sister of Col Thomson Morris, formerly colonel of same regiment. Her pension has been reduced for some reason, and in her distress she appeals to old friends to help her get it back. She thinks if she could only see you, that your influence would be paramount and I have taken the liberty to give her this note."—Copy, DLC-Philip H. Sheridan. Capt. Benjamin H. Arthur, 1st Inf., died in 1856; in 1875, Cornelia M. Arthur received an increased pension. See *HRC,* 43-1-717; *U.S. Statutes at Large,* XVIII, part 3, p. 668.

1874, MAY 29.   USG endorsement. "The recommendation of the Secretary of the Interior for the establishment of a Pension Agency at Portland Oregon is hereby approved."—ES, DNA, RG 48, Appointment Papers, Ore. Written on a letter of the same day from Secretary of the Interior Columbus Delano to USG. —LS, *ibid.* Also on May 29, USG nominated Stephen J. McCormick as pension agent, Portland.

1874, MAY 29.   USG proclamation extending Treaty of Washington articles related to fisheries and duties to Newfoundland.—DS, DNA, RG 130, Presidential Proclamations. *Foreign Relations, 1874,* pp. 1–3.

1874, MAY 30.   William McKee *et al.*, St. Louis, to USG. "We the undersigned Citizens of SaintLouis would most respectfully Solicit the appointment of Genl Eugene A. Carr Lt Col 5th U. S. Cavalry, to the Superintendency of the recruiting Service in this City *When* the next appointment Shall be made in December 1874. . . ."—DS (13 signatures), DNA, RG 94, Letters Received, 1670 1874. Carr, USMA 1850, wrote about an interview with USG at Long Branch on Aug. 14 concerning this position.—AD (undated), PCarlA. No appointment followed.

On June 5, 1875, Carr, Galesburg, Ill., wrote to USG recommending his nephew Eugene M. Carr for an appointment to USMA.—ALS, DNA, RG 94, Correspondence, USMA. Carr did not attend USMA.

1874, MAY 30.   J. T. Scott, New Orleans, to USG. "Mr. R. H. Burton son in law of Dr. Lindsay deceased (and at time of his death Collector of the Port of Shiedsboro Mississippi) now Seeks at your hands the Collectorship of Said Port. Mr. Burton is well known and well connected, and is intelligent and fully capable to attend to the duties of Said Office. Dr. Lindsay's family is in straitened circumstances and are in the main dependent upon Mr. Burton for Support. . . ." —ALS, DNA, RG 56, Collector of Customs Applications. On June 3, B. F. Lindsey, Shieldsborough, Miss., wrote to USG requesting the appointment to replace his deceased father, Caleb, as collector of customs, Pearl River, Miss. ". . . I have been his Special Deputy ever since you appointed him which is a little more than one year ago, and have endeavored to discharge the duties of the office to my own credit and to the benefit of the Government. I am a republican in principle—and the first vote I ever cast was during your second Presidential Campaign. My father was a Southern raised man, but a bold & avowed union man all through the war and therefore suffered from persecution, proscription and loss of all he had in the way of property. . . . This is a poor and desolate country in the way of making a living. My dear mother and sisters now live on a little piney woods farm about fifteen miles from this place the only legacy left by my father and although I am a 'farmers lad' yet the ground is too poor to make a living . . ."—ALS, *ibid.* On June 15, USG nominated Frank Heiderhoff as collector of customs, Pearl River.

On Dec. 16, Heiderhoff, Washington, D. C., wrote to USG. "Having been already kindly introduced to your Excellency by a member of the Mississippi Delegation, and not wishing to intrude again upon your time, I beg leave to inclose herewith a letter of introduction from Gov. Adalbert Ames, of Mississippi, a political and personal friend of mine; and to add that I desire your Excellency's kind consideration, when a successor to the late *Minister* to *Ecuador* is to be nominated. The Delegation of Mississippi in Congress tell me that they do not think that their State has the proportion of Federal patronage she is entitled to, and are desirous of pressing my appointment to the above or a similar position, as they know my fitness as well as my devotion to your Excellency's interests. Permit me, therefore, to hope for a favorable consideration of this application." —ALS, *ibid.*, RG 59, Letters of Application and Recommendation. The enclosure and related papers are *ibid.* On Jan. 15, 1875, Heiderhoff, Shieldsborough, wrote to USG. "I desire to say to you that the good men of the Southern States applaud the stand you have taken in defense of law and order, and that even many prominent men who have publicly put themselves on record on the side of an-archy, have done so through constructive compulsion, and the fear of social ostracism. A perfect system of moral, if not physical terrorism exists in Louisiana, Arkansas and Mississippi, from which the law-abiding can only be protected by the strong arm of the General Government."—ALS, USG 3.

On Aug. 28, 1876, Richard B. Avery, Bay St. Louis, Miss., wrote to USG. "I am an applicant for the position of Collector of Customs for this, the District of Shieldsborough, Miss. There is now no vacancy, but there should be, as the office is now held by one F. Heiderhoff, who is unfit morally and politically to hold office under a Republican President. At this time he is editing a Democratic paper—the Bay St Louis Herald—and particularly abusive of ex-Federal soldiers and Republicans. I have been publishing a Republican paper—the Sea Coast Republican—now suspended, not for want of readers, but because the readers could not or would not pay. I spent about one thousand dollars last year and two hundred and fifty this, besides giving my time to its management; and would have continued to do so if I had had the money to expend. . . . I have carefully computed the cost, and find that I can, upon the salary of the office to which I aspire, publish a Republican paper here, and furnish it to Republicans in every county in the State. The Republicans are poor, and they need papers as much as anything. If I can be placed in a position where I can furnish them the paper they will get it, regardless of the labor it may impose upon me. I hope and believe that in a year or two a Republican paper can be made self-sustaining. . . ."—ALS, DNA, RG 56, Collector of Customs Applications. On Sept. 2, Arthur E. Reynolds, Corinth, Miss., wrote to USG recommending Avery as collector of customs, Pearl River.—ALS, *ibid.* On Dec. 6, USG nominated Isaac N. Osborn to replace the suspended Heiderhoff; on Jan. 24, 1877, USG withdrew Osborn and nominated Harris P. Hurst.

[*1874, May-June*].   B. Bowser and P. C. Dunwoody, Buchanan, Liberia, to USG. "We Your Humble petitioners, take this method of acquainting you, as well as beseeching you, to aid us in our efforts to come to the 'United States:' having heard that, during the latter part, of last year (1873) that there was a letter received from the 'United States Goverment' enquring if any persons wished to return, that provision would be made for the return of such persons if 50 could be found—ready to go, and that the aforementioned letter was reced, and destroyed by 'Henry Dennis' at 'Monrovia' thereby prohibiting the general news coming to our knowledge, with certainty.—Now we the Committee whose names are hereunto attached, do in behalf of 300 hundred persons, who are now in readiness at Grand Bassa, in the Township of Buchanan Republic of Liberia; Humbly petition your 'Goverment' to convey us back to the place of our birth: and we further beg that you may So arrange that we can pay the Amt charged, per head, in Labor after the arrival in the 'United States'   the greater portion of the names attached to this 'petition' are persons that served in the 'Rebellion,' under the northern officers and there are others who have been her[e] 10 and 15 years are now in a state of al[*most*] Starvation.   there is no money in the count[ry] no work, and if any work, no pay. the Country has become Bankrupt, whic[h] is no secret matter any-more We beg also, Should this meet the views, aprobation, of His Excellency 'President Gra[nt]' that a vessel may be dispatched direct [to] Buchanan, Grand Bassa Liberia. on Short notice, and that an agent b[e] appointed here, or there, to conduct th[e] affairs over here, and collect the peopl[e] at one place so as to facilitate the business. if you appoint one here [we] recomend B Bowser the chairma[n] of this committee, and you can also enquire of Capt L. F. Ricerson as Refe[*rence.*] Now although we are strangers in a Foreign land, although we are far from our land of birth: altho[ugh] our harps are hanging on the weeping Willows [of] 'Liberia' nevertheless; 'America' is still prefered a[s] our chiefest 'Joy' and the last wish of our dep[*arted*] *Souls* shall be *her Peace;* her *property;* he[*r*] *liberty forever for which we have bled'*..."—D (docketed June 16, 1874), DNA, RG 59, Miscellaneous Letters. On Aug. 9, Bowser and Dunwoody, *et al.,* wrote to USG and Congress. "your favour dated June 30th 1874 was duly reced. the 1st inst and the reply not Seeming conclusive; We therefore your humble Committee for and in behalf of the petitioners whose names are hereunto attached, do humbly present to you and your Goverment, our present deplorable condition; we are Suffering here in this land from no cause of our own. we have been here Seven years, and have used our best endeavours to live here, and at this late date find it utterly impossible, more than half of those who came with us, are now dead; som died of utter want, and others of starvation. our lands allotted to us by the Colonization Society, is at a distance from the Seaboard and the old Setlement, and surrounded by lawless Savages, the Goverment giving us no protection, and we are at the mercy of the Natives; for our surplus produce there is no market, and all we raise, dont keep us in the necessaries of life. there is no money in the colony. and none able to employ and pay for labor, here a man gets only 50¢ per day, and has to pay $16 dollars per Barrel for flour; 25¢ per lb for bacon; $30 dollars per barrel for Beef; $18 dollars per barrel for Mackrel; $4 dollars per Bushel for Rice; and other things in proportion. unfortunately for us the Post office is under the entire control of the Colonization Agents, and Goverment officials; and our letters are stoped. and those of our friends in america to us are not allowed to pass through the offices unopened; letters containing money, have invariably been Secreted at 'Monrovia;' only by private means of conveyance we can depend upon reciving or sending letters; having thus feebly put before you our condition and feeling assured that after duly considerationing our case keeping in mind we are men, who have served you as bondmen; and claim your kindness as Christians in allowing us to labor for you; and repay back the amt which may be used in conveying us to a christian land; again we are not asking gratuitous means. our labor will support us, and we are ready and willing to labor: Therefore we appeal to you as a christian Nation, to lend a helping hand to the needy; the more keenly, does our situation appear to us when we remember that it was through misrepresentations of the agents of the Colonization Society there that caused us to concent to come to this land, and now as bretheren in arms for one common case of freedom, and equal Rights to all men, in the land of our birth from which we are ignorantly deprived of the blessings which we labored and fought to gain. now in the name of suffering humanity listen to the cries of us poor down ~~trod~~ trodden cast off Servants here in a land of the Grossest Darkness among heathen; may the 'God' who hears the young Ravens when they cry cause you to hear and speedily answer ours. . . . P. S. Be it further known that we Whos[e] Names are attached to this petition, that cam[e] here since the American War, have never taken the oath of alegience, to this Govermen[t] and consider ourselves american Citizens to all intense and purposes."—D, *ibid.*

[*1874, May-June*]. Ann Willoughby, Carthage, Mo., to USG. "as you well know One George D. Orner late Internal Revenue Collector 5th district Missouri and his Deputy Collector Sanders, was defaulters to the Government about $17000, about $6500 00 of which it appears that Sanders was charged with and failed to account for, for all of which Mr. Orner and his bondsmen have been sued for in US District Court at Jefferson City Mo upon which judgement has been rendered and Orner not being worth a cent his bondsmen hav[e] to pay it, and it further appears that on a crimina[l] prosecution Mr Sanders was found guilty of Embezzeling some of said funds and was by the President pardoned, still leaving the bondsmen of Orner to pay the whole thing, and now Mr Pres. our lands are seized and advertised by Geo Smith U. S. Marshal for sale on the 7th day of July 1874, which if sold to the highest bidder for cash will not bring half the amount of the judgement and it will turn my husband John T. Willoughby and our familey of seven little children out of door homeless and with out a dollar to live upon my husband being one of Orners bondsmen will have to pay about $1200.—Now Mr President I ask you to interpose your kind office in this matter for the following reasons   1st The Government would never feel the loss of $1200 00   2nd My Husband is an entire cripple and cannot raise his right hand to his face having had his arm and shoulder broken—3rd Lawyers say that in a case of this kind there is no property Real or personal exempt from execution & sale and if all our property was sold both real and personal it would not bring one thousand dollars   4th Mr Sanders has been prosecuted by Orners bondsmen and he and his securitys discharged—in fact they are said to be insolvent—and while Mr Sanders and his familey are living in their palatial Mansion The President certainly would not be willing to see poor innocent people suffer as that would be licening bad men to steal and commit crime, with impugnity   Mr President I have consulted with some of our best Citzens and they all say that this Orner matter ought to be stricken from the judgement Docket at Jefferson City & Washington and if it was necessary I could send you a Petition with over a thousand good men of this Jasper county, for relief in this matter   Mr Orner is living at Baxter Kans enjoying his Booty. Mr President I see that the Goverment has given aid to the poor sufferers of Louisiana which is commendable and when the high waters leaves their lands they can return home again but with us if the Goverment allow our lands sold we cannot return to them, any more   If the Goverment can grant us any relief in this matter we will be under many obligations and ever feel grateful for the same &c   pleas answer soon . . . Pleas answer"—ALS (docketed June 5, 1874), DNA, RG 60, Letters from the President. On June 11, 1873, USG had pardoned Daniel E. Saunders, convicted of embezzlement, upon the belief of James S. Botsford, U.S. attorney, Western District, Mo., that "there was no intention

on Saunders' part to defraud the Government."—Copy, *ibid.*, RG 59, General
Records. See Joel T. Livingston, *A History of Jasper County Missouri and Its People*
(Chicago, 1912), II, 910.

1874, JUNE 3.   USG endorsement. "Refered [to] the Sec. of State."—AE (initialed), DNA, RG 59, Letters of Application and Recommendation. Written on
the envelope enclosing a letter of May 29 from Charles von Kusserow, Washington, D. C., to USG. "Your Excellency may please to beleive, that only the
greatest distress in personal and family affairs could induce me to the apparent
obtrusion upon you, Mister President, for which I hope to be forgiven.—I was
an Officer in the Army of Prussia, my native Country, when the War of the Rebellion broke out in 1861. Immediately after reading the report of the first active hostilities I resigned my Commission in the Prussian Army, and came to
the United States offering my services to the National Government. . . . Having
contracted some rheumatic affections during the War, and having experienced
several attacks of sunstroke, I was disabled from further service in the Regular
Army of the United States, for which I was well recommended, and I had to
strive for a decent livelyhood with all possible energy, so much more as I had
been married in December 18763 to a Lady from Philadelphia.—From December 5th 1870 to October 7th 1872 I was employed in the Treasury Department
(First Comptrollers Office)—Great misfortune did befall the family of my good
wife. There are two younger sisters who had to be supported by me and their
own elder brother on account of the death of all the elder parties of the family.
Two years ago this unfortunate brother in law became insane and fell also on
my hands. He has been over one year in the Government Asylum in this District on my expenses. . . . My wife, her sisters and brother are entitled to some
real estate of considerable value in Ireland, which was a life-estate of their
mother, sold by her for her lifetime in 1850, when she came to the United States.
She being dead the children would easily recover their right and estate, if we
could have the chance of making the suit for it—And upon this ground, Mister
President, I am daring to apply to you for the appointment as Consul either
in Great Britain or in France—. . ."—ALS, *ibid.* No appointment followed. See
SRC, 49-1-792.

1874, JUNE 3.   Secretary of the Interior Columbus Delano to Orville E. Babcock. "Ascertain from the President & inform me immediately ~~what~~ if convenient at what hour the President will receive an indian delegation of Rhes"
—Telegram received, DNA, RG 107, Telegrams Collected (Bound). On the
same day, Babcock telegraphed to Delano. "The President will receive the Indian delegation between Eleven thirty and twelve to day"—ANS (telegram
sent), *ibid.* Arikara and Mandan chiefs paid respects to USG.—*New York Times,*
June 4, 1874.

1874, JUNE 3.   Caleb C. Norvell to Orville E. Babcock. "Personal. . . . On my return from Washington last week, I requested Mr Jones to relieve me of further
service on the New York Times, and will immediately join Mr Platt & others in
organizing a new first class morning paper. I write this to let you know that I

am out of a paper that systematically attacks the Administration through Gov.
Shepherd and through every other official supposed to enjoy the confidence
of the President."—ALS, USG 3. See *HRC*, 41-2-31, 275–81; *New York Times,*
Feb. 4, 1891.

1874, JUNE 4.   USG endorsement. "Gen. [H.] Biggs in my judgement will make
a most exelent man for any place in the Treas. that he would accept if vacancies
should occur."—AES (bracketed initial in another hand), DNA, RG 56, Applications. Written on a letter of April 21 from Governor John F. Hartranft of Pa.
to USG recommending Herman Biggs, Philadelphia, for appointment.—LS,
ibid. On June 24, U.S. Representative Benjamin F. Butler of Mass. wrote to Secretary of the Treasury Benjamin H. Bristow on the same subject.—ALS, *ibid.*
See *PUSG*, 19, 389.

1874, JUNE 5.   Attorney Gen. George H. Williams to USG. "I have the honor
to return herewith House bill 3169, and to inform you that, in my opinion, there
are no objections to its receiving your approval."—LS, OFH. On June 16 (twice)
and 18, Williams wrote similar letters to USG concerning Senate bills 693 and
881 and House bill 3359.—LS, *ibid.* See *U.S. Statutes at Large,* XVIII, part 3,
pp. 53, 75–76, 78.

1874, JUNE 5.   U.S. Senator John J. Ingalls of Kan. to USG. "If order for removal of land Office from Cawker City to Phillipsburg Kansas has not been issued, I ask that it may be suspended till I can be heard."—Telegram received,
DNA, RG 107, Telegrams Collected (Bound).

1874, JUNE 6.   Robert Campbell & Co., St. Louis, to USG. "We understand that
Mr David P. Ranken of Helena, M. T. is an applicant for the appointment of Su-
perintendant of the Assay office about to be established there. We have known
Mr Ranken since his arrival in this country, over ten years ago. He belongs to
a good old family (some of whom you may have known here—and all of them
distinguished for truth & honesty—Permit us to recommend Mr Ranken to
your very favourable notice.—He has been a resident of Montana for several
years, and doubtless understands the duties of of the office. He is an esteemed
& valued friend of ours."—L, DNA, RG 56, Asst. Treasurers and Mint Officials, Letters Received. No appointment followed. See *St. Louis Post-Dispatch,*
Aug. 18–19, 1910; *St. Louis Globe-Democrat,* Aug. 19, 1910.

1874, JUNE 8.   USG endorsement. "I am personally acquainted with Captain
Sherley, have been for a number of years, and would rely as implicitly upon
his word as that of any person of my acquaintance."—*HRC*, 50-1-730; *SRC*,
50-18-44. Written on an affidavit of Zachary M. Sherley that vouched for Robert S. Goodall's temperate habits and attributed his lung disease to service as
a gunboat pilot (1863–64).—*Ibid.* See *HRC*, 46-2-99; *U.S. Statutes at Large,*
XXV, 1050.

1874, JUNE 8.   Ella Steele Brooks, New Haven, Conn., to USG. "I am not at all
sure but in all these many years since we have met, that you & Mrs Grant have

forgotten me, notwithstanding the memories of all your past kindnesses come to my mind & incline me to hope you have not—At any rate the name of my uncle 'Fred Steele' will be a passport to your memory, if I should have passed from it—I come to you now to ask a great favor in behalf of my aunt Mrs Livingston—She has no means of support & is very unhappy at her dependent condition, Could you not for the sake of 'Auld lang syne' & Uncle Fred give her a place in the Treasury, for of course she, personally, has no claim upon you & I hope you will not think *me* bold in asking for your aid—? It seems a great deal to ask you to send me only a few words in reply, but it would lift a weight of anxiety from my aunt's heart & I should be so glad for her sake—I read all about Miss Nellie's marriage in the papers & while I felt rejoiced at her prospects of happiness, my heart ached for you & Mrs Grant, who will miss her so much—Please give my love to Mrs Grant, I do hope she has not forgotten me, for I love her so much—I still cherish the hope that some day or other, I shall have those shoulder straps you promised me so many years ago—Hoping that you will pardon me if I have taken a liberty in writing to you & that you will feel interested enough in my aunt to give her the position, . . ."—ALS, DNA, RG 56, Applications.

1874, JUNE 9. Secretary of the Interior Columbus Delano to USG. "You will remember that to relieve you of Dr. Burton, I got Mr. Burgess to recommend that he be appointed an Assistant Collector, and, in view of the large collections in that District, there being about four millions, you, in my presence, called the attention of Secretary Richardson to the propriety of making an allowance to pay Dr. Burton as an Assistant Collector. Mr. Richardson directed me to send Dr. Burton to him. I did so. He informed Dr. Burton that the appointment was made and directed him to go to Richmond. Dr. Burton went and was put to work by Mr. Burgess. It now appears from the enclosed letter from Mr. Burgess, that Mr. Richardson failed to make the allowance for Dr. Burton's pay, because Mr. Douglass objected to it. Mr. Douglass tells me, in private conversation, that, when he objected to it, he did not know of the arrangement made in your presence with Mr. Richardson. I think if you will call Mr. Bristow's attention to this matter, provided you deem it of sufficient importance, that he can so inform Mr. Douglass as to the facts that all objections made by him will be withdrawn. I have no interest in the world in this matter except to take care of a poor old man, who seems more meritorious than industrious and prevent him from daily afflicting you."—Copy, Delano Letterbooks, OHi. Rush Burgess was collector of Internal Revenue, Richmond. As of Sept. 30, 1877, Clodimir Burton worked as deputy collector of Internal Revenue, Richmond. See Burton to USG, July 18, 1876, ALS, DNA, RG 56, Collector of Customs Applications.

1874, JUNE 9. 1st Lt. Joseph C. Breckinridge, Fort Monroe, Va., to USG. "Mr *Kelso*, of Baltimore, seemed to consider his enclosed communication especially personal between you and himself. Allow me to say that there can hardly be another lad in Kentucky and but few in the Nation, whose appointment by you to a position in the Navy of the United States would be more significant. I have requested this appointment for my nephew, *Robert J. Breckinridge,* of Danville, Kentucky, feeling assured that it would be consistent with my Father's wishes, and with the interests of the service. There are probably others in the Nation besides the unionists of Kentucky and Maryland who would like to see my Father's grandson receive this appointment from your hands. I would not like any action of mine to meet with your disapproval, and what I have said is in the hope that you will grant my request or at least deem it worthy of kindly consideration. As you know of the lad, his Father, and his Grandfather, I have not spoken more fully of them here. I invite your attention to the enclosed papers which I submit as representative of the feeling of the union men of the country and especially of those of the border States. These papers are from every one approached upon the subject and were given so readily that it seemed that there was hardly a limit to the number that could have been obtained."—Copy, DLC-Breckinridge Family. Robert J. Breckinridge entered the U.S. Naval Academy in 1875 but did not graduate. For Thomas Kelso, see *PUSG,* 16, 347–48.

1874, JUNE 9. Henry T. Crosby, chief clerk, War Dept., to USG concerning a bill to pay Commodore C. Spaids for service as 2nd lt., Co. A, 4th Ill. Cav. ". . . The Adjutant General reports, that he has no record of commission, or of services rendered by Spaids as a commissioned officer, nor has any claim ever been presented by him for pay as such. During a portion of the time for which the bill allows him pay, he was recruiting for the 1st Mississippi Cavalry, of African Descent. Attention is invited to the report of the Committee, that claimant was discharged for disability, February 6th 1864, while the records of the Department show, that he was discharged January 15th 1864, and on same date mustered in as Captain, 3rd U. S. Colored Cavalry. In view of the conflict between the records of the Department, and the report of the Committee, it is believed that the bill should not receive the approval of the President."—Copy, DNA, RG 107, Letters Sent, Military Affairs. This bill became law without USG's signature. See *HRC,* 43-1-55; *U.S. Statutes at Large,* XVIII, part 3, p. 567.

1874, JUNE 9. Thomas D. Day, New York City, to USG, Long Branch. "Excuse me for the liberty I take. I was in business here for seven years past and am a victim of the Panic, being in actual want of the necessaries of life with a family of seven children from three to Thirteen, to care for. I lived many years in St Louis of the firm of Shapleigh Day & Co   lost by the war about $200 000, and my wife about $200 000 more in land & negroes and I have lost $100 000 since the war in business   I have of course no claim, to the contrary having served in the Confederate Army,   I did nothing to bring on the war but took the side I thought was right and accept the consequences—If there was any place I could fill with propriety being but a plain business man, I thought there could be no harm in presenting myself to your consideration,   I could refer you to Col Robert Campbell Mr Wm E Dodge Gov E D Morgan Mr Philo C Calhoun Prest 4th Nat Bnk   I mention these as Gentn well known to you also Col Bogy,   I have no claim as I said before but if there was a place that I could properly fill It would be gratefully accepted"—ALS, DNA, RG 56, Applications. No appointment followed.

1874, JUNE 9. Governor John F. Hartranft of Pa. to USG. "Permit me to earnestly ask your attention to the application of Col. Richard Realf of Pittsburg

Pennsylvania, who desires to be appointed to a consulate in Europe and for whom I would like to bespeak your kind offices   Col. Realf is an accomplished journalist—a gentleman of enlarged views and liberal education whose quali-fications eminently fit him for servic[e] abroad while his services as an editor and soldier entitle him to recognition   Your Excellency will recollect him as the Gentleman who wrote and delivered the Poem at the Army of the Cumber-land Meeting in Pittsburg last fall   Col. Realf's claims will be urgently and influentially for this place and I will be personally under obligations if he can se-cure some appointment   His wishes are modest and a small consulate will sat-isfy him as his purpose in going abroad is for culture and improvement"—ALS, DNA, RG 59, Letters of Application and Recommendation. Related papers are *ibid.* No appointment followed. See *SRC,* 36-1-278, 90–113; *Poems by Richard Realf: Poet, Soldier, Workman, With a Memoir by Richard J. Hinton* (New York, 1898).

1874, JUNE 10.   Mrs. Fannie Clark, Paw Paw, Mich., to USG seeking restora-tion of her widow's pension after separating from her second husband and re-jecting divorce for religious reasons. ". . . I, received my Pension, which was all I needed for my support, until March 25th /69—when I supposed I had mar-ried me a Husband, but a short time fully convinced me, that I had been basely deceived; by one of the meanest *Scoundrells, villians,* or Liar that our Country is infested with,   he reperesented himself as strickly temperate, a Christian, and a man worth consciderable property   I, soon found that I was deceived in all these; and what was far worse, that he then had a living Wife. . . ."—ALS, DNA, RG 48, Miscellaneous Div., Letters Received.

1874, JUNE 11.   Mary Avery, Manlius, N. Y., to USG seeking a position as copyist. ". . . I am the widow of Lieut. A. H. Maynard. My husband was neither wounded or killed in the Service of his Country but army life so lowered the moral standard that he was taken from me as surely as if by ball or shell. So that now no one calls me by his name. . . ."—ALS, DNA, RG 56, Applications. No appointment followed.

1874, JUNE 12.   To Lawrence M. Hazen authorizing extradition from Canada to Ohio of "Henry Lewis, charged with the crime of assault with intent to kill and murder."—Copy, DNA, RG 59, General Records. Lewis allegedly had run a Little Miami Railroad train off its track.—*New York Times,* July 8, 1874.

1874, JUNE 12.   Governor George L. Woods of Utah Territory to USG. "On the 10th Inst a private Soldier belonging to the command at Camp Douglas was arrested for violating a eCity Ordinance and put in the City Prison. On the following morning—the 11th—the military authorities made demand for his surrender to them. The City Authorities refused, peremptorily, telling Lieut. Dinwiddie, who made the demand, that he 'would have to come and take him'. The Post Commander was informed of the refusal, and, forthwith Capt. Gordons Cavalry was sent down to the City with orders to make another demand, and if refused, to use the force necessary to get possession of the man. While the troops were on the way to the City from the Garrison several thousand persons, a ma-jority of whom were 'Gentiles' gathered around the City Prison to witness this, the first exhibition of *force* in Utah. Much excitement prevailed. I was on the ground, in person. Upon the arrival of the Troops, I accompanied Capt Gordon when he made his second demand; and when refusal was made [h]e proceeded knock open the Prison Door, using a large beam, as a battering ram and took the Prisoner out. By this time the excitement was intense, and shout, after shout, went up from the crowed, for more than ten minutes. I have it, from good authority that the 'Mormon Authorities,' now contemplate arresting Capt. Gordon and Lieut Dinwiddie for breaking the Door of the Jail; but better counsel may prevail. Let them take their own course; *we will do our duty.* Threats have, also, been indulged in, that they will 'pound the Soldiers and make it hot for them, here after.' It was for reasons such as these, and for the further reason that at least *one* Co of Cavalry is indispensibly necessary at *all times*, at Camp Douglas, that I telegraphed, yesterday, to the Secty of War, asking that he rescind the Order by which Capt. Gordons Cavalry were to be sent to Camp Stambaugh. If it is possible, I ask, and *urge* that they be kept here. If difficulty should arise here, in this City, 4 miles away from the Garrison, or in any of the adjacent Mining Camps, which would require force to quiet, the necessarily slow movements of Infantry might not be adequate for a momentary emergency   I do hope that they may be kept here. . . . We are awaiting the Senates action upon the Poland Bill with intense anxiety"—ALS, DNA, RG 94, Letters Received, 2684 1874. On June 10, Henry T. Crosby, chief clerk, War Dept., had telegraphed to Secretary of War William W. Belknap, Keokuk, Iowa, concerning this incident. ". . . The action of Colonel Morrow is based on opinion of Judge Holt that no soldier could be arrested under the articles of war by civil authority for civil or criminal offenses without the consent of his commanding officer. This decision I took to White House together with all the dispatches and the President has put the papers in hands of Attorney General. . . ."—LS (press, telegram sent), *ibid.*, 706 1874. Related papers are *ibid.*

On June 16, Jacob S. Boreman, associate justice, Utah Territory, Beaver City, telegraphed and wrote to USG. "Please do not change troops at Camp Beaver see letter" "I to-day sent a teleagram, requesting you not to have any change made in the troops at Camp Beaver, near this City; until you should see my letter. Four companies of the 8th infantry are stationed here, under command of Col. Wilkins. It was rumored on the streets on yesterday, that these troops had been ordered to report at San Francisco. This morning I went out to the Camp to learn the facts. Col. Wilkins informed me that a telagram had been received from the head-quarters of the Regiment at Fort D. A. Russell, to the effect that the Regiment would be required to report at San Francisco sometime this month. Very much regreting this, I immediately sent to you my telegram of this date. Of course, I do not know the military necessity which would seem to demand the removal of these troops; nor would I in the slightest degree desire to interfere with any disposition of troops, deemed best for the army at large as well as the country. But I view this matter entirely from a local standpoint, outside of the army, and in thus viewing it, most earnestly desire that no change be made *at the present time.* And there are several good reasons therefor. I. If any trouble occurs in this Territory, it will take place in the *few months next succeeding* the passage of the Poland bill or some similar one. A more thoroughly organized body, outside of the army, does not exist in the United States, than the Mormon theocracy, and in feeling, teaching and thought it is utterly hostile to the general government. For a quarter of a century the masses of the Mormon people have been taught to believe that the Federal government is an enemy and a tyrannical and unjust enemy. Such teachings for so long, will bear their legitimate fruits immediately upon the enforcement of the laws. When the masses come to see that such teachings are false and that the government is the friend of the law-abiding, all opposition to the enforcement of the laws will in my judgment die out. Enforcing the laws, will break entirely the iron rule of the priesthood; and the masses will become more independent and self-reliant. All that is needed to settle matters in this Territory and to solve the 'Mormon problem', which is no problem but treasonable emnity to the Federal rule, is simply to *make the laws and authority of the general government respected* here as it is elswhere in the United States and Territories. The Poland bill may not entirely do this, but it will go a long way toward it, and at least break the backbone of the priestly rule and do much toward putting out of sight that crime against American civilization, the union of church and State. The priesthood are wiley, cunning and unscrupulous, and they cannot be understood in a day. If military should be needed to enforce the laws, the most efficient command would be such as had become familiar with the sentiments and character of the people and with the system under which they live. Col. Wilkins' command is thoroughly acquanted with these people and their system, and they know the leaders of thought and power in the various localities of southern Utah. These troops are remarkably well disciplined and under excellent control, and provided with officers of sound judgments and prudent. II. The troops here are not only acquainted with the the people, but are also familiar with the *country*, with the mountains, and valleys, the streams and passes. Such familiarity, as your own judgment will tell you, is of vast importance to any force in any country, and cannot be learned in a day. III. These troops have an excellent influence upon the Mormon masses, and by their uniformly prudent course, have done much in this locality to cause the Mormon people to begin to doubt the truthfulness of the oft repeated charge that those in government employ desire to deal unjustly with them. New troops might be under just as good control and be governed by as prudent officers; yet it would take many months for the people to realize that the priesthood had deceived them in respect to such troop as was done in regard to the former. The Mormon authorities, it must be remembered, do not like any Federal troop, and the people are densely ignorant and prejudiced. They are to be dealt with accordingly, and if the faith of the masses be shaken in their leaders, a great step is taken toward restoring a reign of law and order, and in case of trouble, so great enthusiasm would not be displayed in obeying the dictates of the hierarchy. IV. The prudent and firm course of our present command, has strongly attached all gentiles, apostates and other friends of the government, firmly to it. A most excellent feeling and good understanding exists between these troop and the friends of the government. Such entire confidence would be very valuable in case of trouble, and it takes a considerable length of time for such a feeling to grow up. To get information, it is best to have troop in whom all hostile to Mormon rule, have learned to confide. For these reasons, there-

fore, if it be not inconsistent with the best interests of the army at large and of
the country, I would most earnestly urge that Col. Wilkins' command remain
at Camp Beaver. . . ."—Telegram received and ALS, *ibid.*, 2459 1874. See *PUSG*,
24, 35–41.

1874, JUNE 13.   Emily C. Banks, Baltimore, seeking employment for her husband, Charles W. Banks. "The enclosed letter, President Grant, written by yourself, will explain my knowledge of your benevolent nature, & now, as the Wife
of this same Rebel prisoner, & the youngest sister of Col Wm P. Maulsby, with
whome you are well aquainted, I earnestly beg at your hands some one of the
many means of bread winning you have at your disposal; . . . please return the
enclosed letter, as we value it highly"—ALS, DNA, RG 56, Applications. No
appointment followed.

1874, JUNE 15.   To Senate. "I transmit for the consideration of the Senate with
a view to ratification a declaration respecting trade-marks between the United
States and the Emperor of Russia, concluded and signed at St. Petersburg on
the 16/28 day of March last."—Copies, DNA, RG 59, Reports to the President
and Congress; *ibid.*, RG 130, Messages to Congress. On June 22, the Senate
ratified this declaration.

1874, JUNE 15.   Governor John J. Bagley of Mich. to USG. "I have this day forwarded by Express a copy of the Geo. Survey of the Upper Peninsula of this
State for your library—If your duties ever give you an opportunity to look into
it, I am sure its revelations of the mineral wealth of your old home will gratify
and perhaps astonish you."—ALS, OFH.

1874, JUNE 16.   Charles G. Otis, New York City, to USG. "The father and
mother of one of your soldiers, who fell at Cold Harbor while planting his Bat-
talion Flag on the enemies works, are in destitute circumstances old and infirm.
They have applied for a pension but delays & 'Red Tape' is depriving them of
the means of existence   These old people lost two sons, Sergt Mahlon Downing 7th N. Y. H. Artillery, & Orderly Sergt Benjamin Downing Co A. 21st New
York Vol Cavalry, which I had the honor to serve in. Will your Excellency have
the kindness to request the or order the Com of Pensions to make a special investigation of this case and so far as possible remunerate these old people for
their loss. The number of the case I do not know but application was made in the
name of Mrs Clarissa Downing"—ALS, DNA, RG 48, Miscellaneous Div., Letters Received. On Aug. 18, Otis again wrote to USG. "Last June I had the honor
to appeal to you in behalf of Mrs Clarrissa Downing, Applicant for a pension for
sons killed in battle in Virginia. The appeal was referred to the Sec of Interior
by you, and the case was promptly taken up and pension granted   Mrs Downing request me to thank you, and say that money cannot repay her loss, but it
does Supply some wants. While she lives you will have her prayers and a mothers blessing—"—ALS, *ibid.* Otis, former maj., wrote on letterhead of "Otis
Bros. & Co.," elevator manufacturers.

1874, JUNE 18.   To Congress. "I transmit herewith a report from the Secretary of State and its accompanying papers."—Copies, DNA, RG 59, Reports to the President and Congress; *ibid.,* RG 130, Messages to Congress. *HED,* 43-1-289. On the same day, Secretary of State Hamilton Fish wrote to USG. "The Government of the United States having been invited by His Imperial Majesty the Emperor of Russia, to send delegates to attend the Eighth Session of the International Statistical Congress held at St. Petersburg in August, 1872, I have now the honor to transmit, herewith, a transcript, ~~herewith~~, a transcript of the official Report of the delegates selected by this Government to represent it on that occasion."—Copy, DNA, RG 59, Reports to the President and Congress. *HED,* 43-1-289. A printed copy of this report, dated May 29, from Edward Young, William Barnes, and Edwin M. Snow to USG is in DNA, RG 59, Miscellaneous Letters.

1874, JUNE 19.   Secretary of War William W. Belknap to USG. "I have the honor to return the Bill H. R. 2699, 'for the relief of Robert Tillson and Company of Quincy, Illinois,' with remark that Tillson & Co. entered into *formal contract* with the Ordnance Bureau in Sept. 1862, to furnish 3000, sets Horse Equipments at a stipulated price, . . . The point raised in the bill seems to be of much importance. It is whether or not the payments made by the Treasury during the war in Certificates of Indebtedness and other funds, shall be considered as full payments of the amount so paid, or whether or not the parties receiving such Certificates of Indebtedness still have a claim upon the Government for the difference in value, (when sold or put in circulation by the contractor) between such certificates and U. S. Treasury Notes. It is suggested that the bill be referred to the Secretary of the Treasury, for his views."—Copy, DNA, RG 107, Letters Sent, Military Affairs. USG had endorsed a memorandum concerning this claim. "Place will Bill 2699 when returned from War Dept."—AE (undated), IHi. On June 23, USG signed a bill referring this matter to the Court of Claims. See *U.S. Statutes at Large,* XVIII, part 3, p. 614; *HRC,* 43-1-341.

1874, JUNE 19.   U.S. Senator John H. Mitchell of Ore. to Orville E. Babcock. "Henry A. Webster is the name of the gentleman recommended for collector customs Port Townsend."—Telegram received, DNA, RG 107, Telegrams Collected (Bound). On the same day, USG nominated Henry A. Webster as collector of customs, Puget Sound, Washington Territory, in place of Selucius Garfielde.

On April 26, 1873, Marshall Blinn and many others, Olympia, had telegraphed to USG. "We in behalf of the Republicans of this Territory respectfully ask you to withdraw the Commission of Selucius Garfield as Coll'r of Customs & reappoint the present incumbent Fred Drew who commands the respect of the people who know & have repudiated Garfield for while he holds public office in the Territory there can be no unity in the republican party."—Telegram received (at 12:20 A.M.), *ibid.,* RG 56, Collector of Customs Applications. On May 9, John Denny *et al.,* Seattle, petitioned USG. "We earnestly represent as residents and citizens of Puget Sound in Washington Territory, that the Public Good demands the removal of Salucius Garfield as Collector of Customs, and the appointment of Some one capable of faithfully discharging the duties thereof, With credit to the Government and honor to himself. We respectfully recommend the reappointment of Mr Fred Drew whom all honor: and Sincerly trust that our petition will meet your favorable Consideration"—DS (68 signatures), *ibid.* Related papers are *ibid.* On March 18, USG had nominated Garfielde as collector of customs, Puget Sound, following Frederick Drew's resignation.

On March 16, 1875, A. S. Griggs, Washington, D. C., wrote to USG. "I received a letter from Gen. R. H. Milroy of Olympia, Wash. Territory, whom you recently nominated and was confirm[ed] by the U S Senate as U S Atty for that Territory in place of S C Wingar[d] who is now Judge, and he informed Gen. Milroy that the office was not worth last year more than $700, & that this year would not probably be worth ~~but~~ over $500. above expences. You appointed Gen. Milroy Superintendent of Indian Affairs in that Territory, and feeling assured that it was an appointment which would last 4 years he purchased himself a house, on time, and paid a portion of the purchase money: at the close of the past session of the present Congress, his office, with others, was abolishe[d] which left him largely in debt for his house, . . . Gen. Coburn told me he would try and see your Excellency in regard to Gen. M.   I referred him to the position of Collectorship of Customs for Puget Sound. Henry A. Webster now holds that position, and I am informed, had it been known, at the time of his appointment, a universal protest would have been signed by the Republicans; from 18~~76~~0, to 1872 this man was Agen[t] of the Neah Bay Reservation in that Territory & before he was appointed Agent was a thriving Indian Tra[der.] A pretty full record of his acts are on *file in the Indian Department.* This same Webster got to meddling with Indian matters after Gen Milroy took possession of th~~is~~e office of Superintendent and by an examination of that letter written to the *Comnr of Ind. Affrs* (and long before Webster's nomination and confirmation) *dated* FEBY. 1ST 1873 you can learn the character of the man. If your Excellencys' attention & that of the Hon. Secy. of Treasury had been called to this letter & learned the character of this man he never would have received the appointment. This same man Webster got a $20.100 claim brought the *first* ~~of last~~ session of this Congress as to its justness I have nothing to say, it would appear that he is not needy, whilst Gen. Milroy is; . . . N. B. As to who I am, can refer you to Senator O. P. Morton *who is still here*, also Orth, Coburn, Hunter and Tyner. . . ."—ALS, *ibid.* Webster remained as collector of customs. See *HED*, 40-3-1, 558–59, 41-2-1, part 3, pp. 575–76, 589–90; *U.S. Statutes at Large*, XVIII, part 3, p. 555.

On Jan. 16, USG had nominated Robert H. Milroy as U.S. attorney, Washington Territory. On March 2, Milroy, Olympia, wrote to USG declining this office. ". . . I have fully confered with the Hon. S. C. Wingard who has held said office several years, (& who was recently promoted from it to a Judgeship), and he informed me that the net emoluments of said office of U. S. Atty. when he first received it, amounted to about $1.200.00 per annum; but that since then they have been rapidly falling off, for various reasons, until they will not this year exceed $500. . . . Permit me to remark in conclusion that all my pecuniary arrangements & plans having been disarranged and 'knocked into pi' by the unexpected abolition of my late office, which has left me here with my family in painfully embarrassing circumstances, and there being several good paying Govt. offices in this Ter. some of which are in the hands of men totally destitute of deserts, if you will give me one of said offices you would do myself & family an immense favor and throw sunshine upon my now dark and cheerless life path —"—ALS, DNA, RG 60, Letters Received, Washington Territory. In 1874, Milroy had written to USG on financial concerns and the probable loss of his office as Indian superintendent, Washington Territory.—William Evarts Benjamin, Catalogue No. 42, March, 1892, pp. 15–16.

On July 20, 1875, Secretary of the Interior Columbus Delano wrote to USG. "Gibson, Indian Agent at Nisqually Agency in Washington Territory was appointed on the recommendation of Mr Loughridge, late M. C. from Iowa, the Agency never having been assigned to any denomination. We have no place to which he can be transferred. There is no objection to his removal for the benefit of General Milroy, except such as arise from this statement of facts, and if you deem it best thus to provide for Gen M. it is entirely agreeable to the Indian Office and to the Department. I should have made the change without this letter; but for your language on the subject in your former reference, to wit: 'If Gen Milroy can have the ap't applied for without prejudice to the present incumbent, or by his transfer, I will be pleased to give it to him.' I enclose the necessary papers, in the event of your desiring to make the change."—LS, USG 3. Hiram D. Gibson, incumbent agent, Nisqualli and Puyallup Agency, died on Aug. 12. On Aug. 24, four "catholic chiefs of the Puyallup and Nesqualy tribes," Puyallup Reservation, Washington Territory, wrote to USG. ". . . Many years since, we know not how many, the ministers of the Catholic religion have visited our tribes, baptizing us, our children, teaching us religion, trying to civilize and christianize us. Under their care we have grown up and bettered our condition. Every one admits that during many years none but catholic priests worked as missionaries amongst us. Often we ask: why catholic aAgents are not appointed here according to the principles of the Christian policy, inaugurated under your administration. A third of the population, belonging to the Medicine creek Treaty, is infidel; the two other thirds are catholic. The few families, which are not catholic, can hardly be classified under any religious denomination. We, especially Puyallup and Nesqualy Indians, desire ardently to be more efficiently guided by a religion, which does us so much good; therefore we hope that your Excellency will henceforth appoint catholic aAgents for this agency. Trusting that our petition will be favorably received, . . ."—LS (by mark), Marquette University, Milwaukee, Wis. On Dec. 9, USG nominated Milroy as agent; the Senate never voted on this nomination. On April 26, 1876, USG nominated Milroy as collector of Internal Revenue, Washington Territory. On April 27, USG wrote a note. "The Sec. of the Int. Treas to cause to be examined the result of investigations by the Solicitor of the Treas. Int. touching transactions by Gn. Milroy, who has just been named for Collector of Int. Rev. for Washington Ter."—AN, OHi. On May 18, USG withdrew this nomination. On Dec. 11, USG nominated Milroy as agent, Nisqualli and Puyallup Agency. Milroy promoted a Presbyterian missionary. See *HED*, 44-2-1, part 5, I, 543.

1874, June 19.   Gideon J. Pillow, Memphis, to USG. "There is pending before Congress, a bill to create of West Tennessee, a Judicial District—If this bill
should become a law, you will have to appoint a Judge for this District. In anticipation of this necessity, I write you in behalf of Judge Henry G. Smith of this
city. He is in every way well qualified for the place. He is an able lawyer of many
years practice—He has been upon the supreme Bench of this state & discharged
the duties of that responsible position to the satisfaction of the public. He is a
man of great purity of life—& of spotless reputation. No man could be selected
from the Bar of West Tennessee, who would give more general satisfaction than
would the appointment of Judge Smith. He was an union man from the beginning to the end of the war—He was Presidential Elector in the Grant ticket
at your *re-election,* & is a Friend and supporter of your administration. I would
be personally gratified if you could appoint him. I am pleased to Report to you
Mr President that *your acts,* in the past 12 months, have produced upon the public mind in this section of the country, a most favourable impression. I allude to
your action in the Arkansas affair and upon the currency question   If you could
only get a chance to veto, the Civil rights bill, for its *mixed feature,* it would make
you the strongest man, with the southern people, there is in the nation."—ALS,
University of Tennessee, Knoxville, Tenn. No appointment followed.
    On Aug. 11, Henry G. Smith and Ira M. Hill, Memphis, telegraphed to USG,
Long Branch, via Washington, D. C. "Whites and blacks fighting at austin Miss
armed men going from here   if possible order a company from holly springs to
austin immediately"—Telegram received, DLC-USG, IB.

1874, June 19.   Sarah E. Snyder, "a poor widdow with two children," Penns-
ville, Pa., to USG seeking a pension for her husband's service with the 211th Pa.
". . . all other onses around me get a pension and i have a better wright to
one than some of them   if you will please and see that i get it you shall have
one hundred dollars of it . . ."—ALS, DNA, RG 48, Miscellaneous Div., Letters
Received.

1874, June 20.   Secretary of War William W. Belknap to USG. "I have the
honor to return House Bill 3001 'for the relief of Peter J. Knapp,' with remark
that he was captured November 25th., 1863, and enlisted in the rebel army while
a prisoner of war at Andersonville, Ga. It has been the uniform custom of this
Department to decline favorable action upon cases of men who renounced their
allegiance to the U. S. Government while held as prisoners of war, and took up
arms against it. As soon as this man presents satisfactory evidence to this Department that his enlistment in the rebel army was to prevent starvation and to
make his escape, and that his case was more aggravated than that of the thousands of others Union soldiers confined at Andersonville with him, who suffered stavation rather renounce the Government under which they enlisted, his
case will receive favorable consideration, and in that event there is no necessity
for special legislation in his behalf."—Copy, DNA, RG 107, Letters Sent, Military Affairs. On June 22, USG signed a bill authorizing back pay for Peter J.
Knapp, former private, 5th Iowa, with the proviso that Knapp provide evidence
to the Secretary of War that his agreement to join the enemy was made while

"incarcerated in a rebel prison, and for the purpose of escaping from imminent peril of death from exposure and hunger, and with a view of escaping to the Union lines."—*U.S. Statutes at Large*, XVIII, part 3, p. 606. See *SMD*, 40-2-78; *HRC*, 43-1-440.

1874, JUNE 20.   Levi P. Luckey to George C. Gorham, secretary, U.S. Senate. "President is at home & will be at the Capitol at half past two o'clock."—ALS (telegram sent), DNA, RG 107, Telegrams Collected (Bound). On the same day, Gorham had telegraphed to the White House. "Is the President at home,   it was rumored he had gone to West Point"—Telegram received, *ibid.*

1874, JUNE 20.   U.S. Representative John Coburn of Ind. and fourteen others to USG. "The undersigned members of the Military Committees of the Senate & House of Representatives earnestly recommend and request the reinstatement of George A. Armes, late Captain U. S. A. without loss of rank or pay   His case has had a thorough examination and his innocence is proven hence, his reinstatement, the least measure of Justice should be done at once"— DS (facsimile), George A. Armes, *Ups and Downs of an Army Officer* (Washington, 1900), p. 379. On Jan. 29, 1877, George A. Armes, Washington, D. C., wrote to USG. "I am only one of the many who have received disgrace and punishment through the misrepresentations of persons unworthy of confidence, and I respectfully call your attention to the fact that it is still in your power, and will be for a few days longer, to mend a wrong that has caused me to suffer more than I can express. . . ."—*Ibid.*, p. 419. Armes was restored to the army after USG's presidency. See *PUSG*, 16, 567–69; *HMD*, 43-2-100; *HRC*, 44-1-620; *HED*, 45-2-12; *SRC*, 45-2-121.

1874, JUNE 20.   Henry W. Corbett and four others, Portland, Ore., to USG. "The citizens are opposed to any new bill for a bridge over the Williamette river at Portland   the bill passed in Eighteen hundred Seventy is sufficient please sign no new bill"—Telegram received (at midnight), DLC-USG, IB. On June 23, USG signed a bill authorizing a railroad bridge over the Willamette River at Portland.—*U.S. Statutes at Large*, XVIII, part 3, pp. 281–82. See also *ibid.*, XVI, 64.

1874, JUNE 20.   Chief Justice Morrison R. Waite endorsement. "Most respectfully referred to the President, with the hope that he may find it in his power to gratify the young gentleman by making the appointment—I cannot recommend him too highly personally."—AES, DNA, RG 94, Correspondence, USMA. Written on a letter of May 8 from Harry D. Waite, Toledo, to Morrison Waite, seeking aid in securing a cadetship.—ALS, *ibid.* Related papers are *ibid.* Waite graduated USMA in 1879.

1874, JUNE 21.   U.S. Representative Alexander H. Stephens of Ga., Crawfordville, to USG. "These lines are written in behalf of Hon. Henry W. Hilliard of Augusta in this state: and by whom it will be presented to you—Allow me then briefly to say that Mr. Hilliard is desirous of obtaining some suitable position in the Diplomatic Service of the Government: and I wish hereby to say to you that I have known Mr. Hilliard from my college days and believe him to be well qualified for such position as he desires—He is a gentleman of culture and refinement, of high Scholarly attainments—a writer of eminence, as well as a lawyer of great distinction—He has, moreover, had experience in this class of service anterior to the late war—and gave entire satisfaction to his Government —He was also for several years a Member of Congress—In politics Mr. Hilliard was a Clay Whig and strongly attached to the Union—It was only when his State (then Ala) passed her ordinance of Secession against all the power he could exert against its wisdom & policy that he cast his fortunes in the contest that ensued with the people of the South. This much I think it proper to state to you, touching his antecedents—Ever since the war he has been an ardent advocate of the restoration of peace and harmony between all sections of our common country—If any vacancy occurs in the Foreign Service I commend him to your most favourable consideration—"—ALS, DNA, RG 59, Letters of Application and Recommendation. On June 25, Henry W. Hilliard, Atlanta, wrote to USG. "In forwarding the enclosed letter of Mr. Stephens to the President, it is proper to say that my friend comprehends my political views—He knows too my sincere appreciation of Gen: Grant—My self respect would not permit me to forward a recommendation for a political position under an Administration, that I did not intend to support. . . ."—ALS, *ibid.* Related papers are *ibid.* No appointment followed.

On May 2, Hilliard had written to USG. "I respectfully congratulate you on the service rendered to the country, in withholding your name from the Bill to expand the currency. . . ."—ALS, USG 3.

1874, JUNE 22. Levi P. Luckey to James B. Eads, National Hotel, Washington, D. C. "The President directs me to acknowledge the receipt of your letter of yesterday and say that he has not signified his intention of visiting St. Louis at the opening of the bridge on the 4th of July. He has not as yet received his formal invitation though he has been notified by telegraph that it is on the way. When received he will give a formal acknowledgment, but it will, he regrets, have to be in the negative, as he will not be able to go to St. Louis at that time. He wishes me to convey to you his sincere thanks for your cordial invitation."— Copy, DLC-USG, II, 2. On June 20, Saturday, Chauncey I. Filley and George H. Morgan, St. Louis, had telegraphed to Orville E. Babcock. "The members of the Cabinet are cordially invited to be present at the formal opening by the President of U. S. of Illinois and St Louis Bridge on the fourth day of July next Individual invitations will be sent to each and to yourself on Monday next,"—Telegram received, *ibid.,* IB.

On June 29, William S. Harney, St. Louis, telegraphed to USG. "Glad to hear of your Coming here, hope Mrs Grant will accompany you, four spare rooms,"—Telegram received, *ibid.*

1874, JUNE 22. U.S. Representative William Lawrence of Ohio to USG. "If you approve Bailey claim in Southern Claims bill it seems to me it will be a dangerous precedent please examine senate debate"—Telegram received, DNA,

RG 107, Telegrams Collected (Bound). On the same day, USG signed a bill involving hundreds of claims that appropriated $45,161.72 for William Bailey, Rapides Parish, La.—*U.S. Statutes at Large,* XVIII, part 3, pp. 580–601. Controversy centered on the jurisdiction of the Southern Claims Commission and evidence that Bailey had sold cotton voluntarily to a C.S.A. agent, a disloyal act that would have disqualified his claim.—*CR,* 43–1, 4181–84, 5141–52.

1874, JUNE 22.   George W. Mindil, "late Bvt Major Gen'l Vols 20th Corps," Philadelphia, to USG requesting official reports covering "operations in Virginia from May, 1864 to the surrender of Lee" and an autograph letter.—ALS, DNA, RG 94, Letters Received, 2526 1874. On July 1, AG Edward D. Townsend endorsed this letter. "There are no copies of General Grant's reports for distribution on file in this Office. The report of his Virginia Campaigns is published in 'Frank Moore's Rebellion Record' page 326 Vol. XI. No autograph letter from the President can be spared from the files of this Office without manifest injury to the public service—"—AES, *ibid.* See *New York Tribune,* July 21, 1907.

[*1874, June 25*].   To Pedro II, Emperor of Brazil. "I congratulate you upon the telegraphic connection just es[t]ablished between Brazil and the United States. May it prove as close a link in national friendship as in communication."— *New York Times,* June 26, 1874. Earlier, Pedro II had telegraphed to USG. "The inauguration of the electric telegraph between Europe and Brazil, which also unites us to the Republic of the United States, is a cheering sign of improved international relations, as also a bond of friendship and a powerful instrument of civilization. I congratulate my great and good friend, the President of the United States, upon this happy event."—*Ibid.*

1874, JUNE 25.   Brig. Gen. Oliver O. Howard, Washington, D. C., to USG. "I have the honor to recommend for appointment at large Arthur H. Glennan the son of Dr Patrick Glennan, Surgeon—Freedmen's hospital (to a cadetship at the U. S. Military Academy at West Point). The father has been during & since the war in the service in government hospitals. He is a man of the purest integrity and fidelity to duty that never wavers—For many years he has been my family physician and I take great pleasure in recommending his son, whose promise of uprightness & industry is equal to that of his father. I have not examined him but I judge from his conversation & appearance that he has sufficient ability to master the course creditably. He is under twenty two years of age. . . . P. S. Arthur Glennan's residence is the District of Columbia—"—ALS, DNA, RG 94, Correspondence, USMA; (press) Howard Papers, MeB. Related papers are *ibid.* Arthur H. Glennan did not attend USMA. See *New York Times,* Sept. 23, 1926.

1874, JUNE 26.   Maj. Gen. John M. Schofield, San Francisco, to USG. "Please kindly consider the claims of my aid decamp colonel Wherry to the appointment of asst adjutant Genl."—Telegram received (on June 27, at 8:30 A.M.), DLC-USG, IB. James B. Fry, USMA 1847, was promoted to col., asst. AG, as of March 3, 1875.

1874, JUNE 26.   John Baldwin Hay, "Ex-Consul General at Beirut, Syria," Philadelphia, to USG. "*Personal* . . . During a residence of six years in Syria and Palestine, I have met numbers of American travellers who have expressed a wish that an *American* Church should be built at Jerusalem. A Church where the Ministers of all Protestant denominations could conduct the service and freely worship   You are doubtless aware that the Ottoman government has generously given the Russian, the German, the French, the Austrian, and the British Gov'ts large grants of land for building Churches and monasteries. A similar grant can be readily obtained as a suitable site for a Church or one can be purchased—My object in addressing you is to ask your permission to state that you take an interest in this matter, and will be one of the patrons of the Society I am prepared to state that liberal donations are forthcoming. A Committee will be formed to decide upon the plans which a skillful architect is preparing—for me at Jerusalem and also to estimate the cost of building—"—ALS, DNA, RG 59, Miscellaneous Letters.

1874, JUNE 27.   Carron and four others, "menomonee India cheafes, of Keshena Wis," Oconto, to USG. "this is not the first time that we apply to you for assistance, for we have ben bothered by men whom come here stating that they wer sent here by you—(our great father) for the purpos of buying our pinetimber, which we would be very willing to sell could we but know whom we wer selling to. and whether or not we would ever receive any payment for it, but those whom come her to buy our timber, we dare not trust, and in order to settle the question. we ausk you as any Children should ausk a father whether or not you would listen to us providing we should come to washington with our Interpreter.   our young men ar most all or the magoraty of them ar willen to sell our pine (not Land).   our pine has ben stolen frome us from for many years and will be stolen frome us as long as we retain it by those whites which border our reservation, and by moneyed men whome tell some of our young men that they will give them so much money if they will say nothing about it, and thus they crushus down in then mud whar us (cheaves) ar heared not, and unless we secur help frome you we will go to ruin as well as our pine timber.   our object in comeing to washingto is to sell our timber to you for the simple purpos of leading us out of truble, with the whites and father we can not do any thing without your concent, and if you will but hear frome us and help us through ~~and~~ we will still remain with those whom still survive.   you ar the ownley one whom we depend upon as or for assistance.   for we can not make our agent hear any thing that we want him to.   if you will listen to us should we come pleas state whare and when would be the best time to go to washington, d. c.   hopeing to hear frome you at an earley date . . ."—LS (by mark), DNA, RG 75, Green Bay Agency, Letters Received. See *PUSG,* 21, 486–87; *HED,* 43-2-1, part 5, I, 495; Patricia K. Ourada, *The Menominee Indians: A History* (Norman, 1979), pp. 142–49.

1874, JUNE 30.   James W. Paul, Philadelphia, to USG. "I have received a letter from Professor H. S. Osborn L L D., who desires to obtain a letter of introduction to The Vice Roy or Pasha of Egypt to aid him in some scientific explorations East of The Nile—This undertaking is solely for the cause of science

I beg leave to enclose extracts from his letter which fully explain his design.—
Mr Osborn is a sincere Christian and one of the most scientic gentlemen of the
United States—he has recently published a masterly work on Mining Miner-
als and Mines—He is a thorough gentleman and would not abuse any permission that may be granted to him for the object he has in view   Professor Osborn married my niece and from a long acquantance I can speak adviseably on
the Subject—If you can aid him in the subject matter of his letter you will confer a great favor on me as well as promote the cause of science.—Mrs Paul &
Mamie are now at Newport R. I. With kind regards to Mrs Grant . . . Professor Osborn is of The Miami University Ohio."—ALS, DNA, RG 59, Miscellaneous Letters. The enclosure is *ibid.* The docket on this letter is endorsed.
"Send the ordinary letter civilly declining"—E (undated), *ibid.*

[*1874, June*].   Martin Boppel, Deerfield, N. Y., to USG. "The petition of Martin Boppel respectfully shows the following facts towit—That your petitioner
is thirty five years of age and a native of Germany that his residence is in the
town of Deerfield Oneida County N. Y. and is a married man and has a family of
three children and was a soldier in the late rebellion for two years and while so
engaged lost his right arm that your petitioner is a poor man & has no means of
support except keeping a tavern at Deerfield Corners in said County that he has
purchased a small building for that purpose and is anxious to sell to his neigh-
bours and the public generally or such portion of them as are capable of using
the same with discretion & prudence lager bier wine rum gin whiskey brandy
cigars tobacco &c and to keep an Inn Taver and Hotel   And your petitioner
further says that he has in all things complied with the Statute of the State of
New York for the purpose of procuring a licence for such purposes as aforesaid
and that such licence has been refused by the bord of excise   Wherefore your
petitioner prays that you will grant to him a licence for the purposes as aforesaid"—D (docketed June 23, 1874), DNA, RG 56, Letters Received from the
President. A liquor license application is *ibid.* See *HRC,* 50-1-2672; *U.S. Statutes
at Large,* XXV, 1261.

1874, JUNE.   U.S. Senator William Windom of Minn. and three others to USG.
"Understanding that the name of Judge A. B. Norton, of Texas, will be presented for a federal appointment we take pleasure in endorsing him as a staunch
Republican—a man of superior legal and literary attainments and of strict integrity. Judge N. was formerly a resident of Ohio where he occupied a prominent position in the public affairs of that State. He has been a resident of Texas
for twenty years and at the commencement of the rebellion, as a member of the
legislature of that state, was one of the leading opponents to the secession of the
state. He edited the last Union paper in Texas—the 'Intelligencer' at Austin—
and finally was driven from the State on account of his advocacy of the Union
cause. Since his return he has held various positions of prominence and at the
last two elections was a candidate for the national Congress and upon the State
ticket. Believing that his loyalty & devotion to the Republican cause entitle him
to favorable consideration we respectfully recommend his appointment."—LS,
DNA, RG 59, Letters of Application and Recommendation. Related papers are

ibid. On Sept. 19, 1870, U.S. Senator John Sherman of Ohio, Mansfield, had written to USG. "This note will be presented to you by Hon. A. Banning Norton who is now presented for Judge of the U. S. Dist Court of Texas. I have known Norton since his boyhood. We were at school together   He studied law near 30 years ago and prior to 1854 was a very active Whig. . . ."—ALS, *ibid.*, RG 60, Records Relating to Appointments. Related papers are *ibid.* On March 18, 1875, USG nominated Anthony B. Norton as postmaster, Dallas.

On July 21, 1876, Samuel H. Nieman, Dallas, wrote to USG. "I see by the telegram despatches that General (Judge) John W. Bennett late of the Supreme Court of Arkansas has declined the appointment by your Excellency of the Office of Governor of Idaho. I would respectfully suggest and solicit that the Hon (Judge) A. B. Norton late of the Texas Supreme Court and present postmaster at this place (Dallas) be appointed to the vacant Governorship of Idaho. Judge Norton is and has been an efficient government officer and a live republican as Gov R. B. Hayes nominee for the Presidency would attest, they having been raised boys together and classmates and school fellows in the same school and during their College career, in the State of Ohio. Though the republican party of Texas is greatly in the minority, yet it is no-more than justice that they should be recognise in the patronage of the goverment. Col Don Cameron, Secretary of War, will vouch for my honest intentions and republicanism as we to, were residents of the same town in Pennsylvania for years in our early—younger days."—ALS, *ibid.*, RG 48, Appointment Papers, Idaho Territory. No appointment followed.

1874, July 1.   Winborn Lawton, Washington, D. C., to USG. "The Hon: Fred:k A Sawyer presented me to you in Febr'y,   I then had the honor of a short interview, which I can hardly expect you now to call to mind: sufficient to say however, at that time I had not even a remote intention of asking at your hands an appointment, my object in Washington being to secure a charter for a National Railroad from Port Royal S C to Leavenworth City Kansas; as set forth in the accompanying bill, which bill though meeting the approbation of a majority of the House Committee on Railways and Canals, was temporarily delayed by a resolution offered in Committee . . . I am a native South Carolinian, my family settled the seaboard of the state known as Edisto Island more than 150 years ago,   when the war broke out we owned large tracts of land and thousands of slaves,   to day *much* of our land is growing up into woods, and our late slaves occupy the judicial seats and legislative halls for many years filled by my ancestry: . . ."—ALS, DNA, RG 59, Letters of Application and Recommendation. A related letter is *ibid.* No appointment followed. On Sept. 1, 1873, Lawton had written at length to Secretary of State Hamilton Fish concerning the proposed railroad.—ALS, *ibid.*, Miscellaneous Letters.

On [*July*] 15, 1874, Lawton, Charleston, S. C., telegraphed to USG, Saratoga Springs, N. Y. "You will meet the question by giving the Collectorship to Sawyer—"—Telegram received (on July 16), DLC-USG, IB.

1874, July 1.   James L. G. McKown, Chicago, to USG. "In accordance with your request when I left you, to make my application for my sons soon, and *di-*

rectly to you instead of through Logan. or Farwell, or Ogelsby, I do so now. Please appoint my son *Franklin La Grange McKown*, 25 years of age single now of the U. S. Army, at St Louis Barracks to an Assistant Paymastership, in the Navy. He has had about six years *experiance* in the Navy having entered *during the war.* Charles Woodruff McKown, 21 years of age, married, now of U. S. Army, Co B. 3d U. S. Cavalry Fort, McPherson, to a Lieutenantcy. . . ."—ALS, DNA, RG 45, ZB File. On Aug. 1, McKown wrote to USG on the same subject.—ALS, *ibid.* U.S. Senators John A. Logan and Richard J. Oglesby of Ill., Bishop Matthew Simpson, and others favorably endorsed this letter.—AES, *ibid.* On Jan. 9, 1875, McKown again wrote to USG. "The InterOcean of today has an Editorial on The Army in which it is stated an increase of Paymasters must be had at once. Pardon my intrusion, but if you have done nothing when this reaches you for Franklin La Grange McKown my eldest son, can you not name him for an assistant Paymaster in the Army? You are a father and can sympathize with my anxiety. I need not say your course with the South is approved by the people. The *masses* mutter only at tardiness, and leniency which their want of knowledge, causes. . . ."—ALS, *ibid.*, RG 94, Applications for Positions in War Dept. No appointments followed. On Nov. 13, Secretary of War William W. Belknap wrote to McKown. "I would respectfully inform you that, in response to the application presented by Mrs. McKown, the President has ordered the discharge of your son, Franklin or Frank L. McKown, G. M. S. U. S. Army: and that transportation will be furnished him to place of enlistment."—Copy, *ibid.*, RG 107, Letters Sent, Military Affairs.

1874, JULY 3.   To Walter Gussenhoven, Laramie, Wyoming Territory. "I have received, through the Secretary of the Interior, with much pleasure, the beautiful specimen of a deer's head which you were kind enough to send me for a hall ornament. Accept my thanks for the souvenir, and especially for the kind motive which prompted you to send it."—Copy, DLC-USG, II, 2. On June 26, Secretary of the Interior Columbus Delano had written to Orville E. Babcock. "The enclosed letter from Walter Gussenhoven, whom I have never heard of before, came in an Express box with $6.75 charges. I suppose the concern is intended for Mrs. Sartoris, but am unable to quite understand what the author means. Will you be so kind as to send down for the box, or give me directions what to do with it."—Copy, Delano Letterbooks, OHi.

In [*March*], Gussenhoven, Laramie, had written to USG. "I move with my family to the headwaters of the yelowstone next spring to write that country up, & try its waters for the cure of Rheumatisme,   from Haydens party I heard that some appointements would be made for that U. S. Park to prevent depredation as well as for accomodations of Visitors   I pray for such an appointement just to keep us from starving the first two years,   I wrote to that efect to the Land commissioner, But the war Dep't may have it in hand,   in either case I hope & pray for your influence if it is only in consideration of my devotion and the remembrance of that acrostic Eulogium of Last year,   being Surveyor by profession Mountaineer by inclination I would not be out of place there."—ALS (docketed March 7, 1874), DNA, RG 48, Records Relating to Yellowstone National Park. Gussenhoven included an acrostic poem that spelled "U. S. GRANT.

U. S. PRESIDENT. HELP. ME."—*Ibid.* On March 9, Delano wrote to Gussen-hoven. "I acknowledge the receipt, by reference from the President of your let-ter of blank date, requesting an appointment to some office in the Yellowstone National Park, and inform you that no appropriation has been made by Con-gress for the government of said Park, from which compensation could be paid to persons employed therein. I am unable, therefore, to comply with your re-quest."—Copy, *ibid.* On March 20, Gussenhoven wrote to Delano requesting permission to live at Yellowstone and host visitors; on March 30, Benjamin R. Cowen, asst. secretary of the interior, wrote to Gussenhoven denying permis-sion.—ALS and copy, *ibid.* See *PUSG,* 23, 87.

1874, July 4.   Lycurgus Egerton, London, to USG. "*Confidential* . . . On my return to London, Mr. *Gerstenberg,* Chairman of the Council of Foreign Bond-holders has submitted for my perusal (and approval!) a document bearing date of the 2nd inst., addressed to the President of the United States in the form of a memorial, asking your attention and effective cooperation or (moral support) in aid of correcting the financial policy of the States of the Union, Railway Cor-porations and other Associations who may have issued securities, which have been dealt in on the Stock Exchanges of Europe, especially the London Stock Exchange, the members of which are largely represented in the above named Council, whose Chairman and Secretary have signed the memorial in ques-tion. . . . In conclusion, I will state, that the high pretensions of the Council of Foreign Bondholders, finds no Sympathy nor support, from the great and emi-nent banking firms of Europe, among whom I will name the *Rothschilds,* the *Barings, Morgan, Brown Brothers,* and others of London, including those of Similar Standing and affiliations, in the Continental Capitals. My appreciation of your superior sagacity and intelligence, as relates to the matter in question would render this communication, which I now make entirely unnecessary, but prompted by a natural feeling of national pride and indignation, for the imper-tinence which characterizes the effusion—'*recommended to your serious and fa-vorable consideration*'—by the writers of the same, (who are wholly unwarranted in their high sounding assumption of importance)—I could not forbear to ad-dress you on the subject."—LS, DNA, RG 59, Miscellaneous Letters. The me-morial is *ibid.* Egerton had elsewhere signed himself as Edgerton. See *PUSG,* 23, 471–72; Ellis Paxson Oberholtzer, *Jay Cooke: Financier of the Civil War* (Phila-delphia, 1907), II, 350, 523.

1874, July 6.   Joseph P. McDonnell, secretary gen., Association of United Workers of America, Brooklyn, to USG. "The question of a third Presidential term, having created no small excitement throughout this country and given rise to curious rumors in Europe, will you do me the honor of informing me, whether in the event of a nomination by one of the Great Political Parties, you will again undertake to perform the onerous duties of President of these United States? I hope, Sir, that you will not consider this request an intrusion or an im-pertinence. I make it on the first instance as your fellow citizen and on the second, as the *Special Correspondent* of a European Journal of Great eminence, The *Continental Herald and Swiss Times. Geneva.* Your early reply will confer an

honor . . ."—ALS, USG 3. On Aug. 4, McDonnell, New York City, again wrote
to USG. "Will you kindly reply to the following question: If you are nominated
in 1876 for the Presidency of the United States, will you accept the nomination for a third term? If I receive no reply to this Communication I will regard
your answer in the affirmative. I will esteem your reply a high favor"—ALS,
ibid. Testimonials to McDonnell are *ibid.* See Stuart B. Kaufman, ed., *The Samuel
Gompers Papers* (Urbana, 1986–), I, 493–94.

1874, JULY 7.   President Michel Domingue of Haiti to USG announcing his
election and friendly intentions toward the U.S.—LS (in French), DNA, RG 59,
Notes from Foreign Legations, Haiti; translation, *ibid.* On July 23, Secretary of
State Hamilton Fish wrote to USG. "The Haitien Minister (Mr Preston) writes
that he is charged by the newly elected President of that Republic to inform you
of his election &c., and for that purpose to present an Autograph letter. He asks
the naming of a time either here or elsewhere, when you will be pleased to receive him. It is not a matter of emergence, and should you have it in contemplation to visit Washington at any fixed day within a short period, it may be better
to defer the appointment until then, than to receive the Minister at Long Branch.
I will inform Mr Preston of any appointment which you may make."—Copy,
ibid., Domestic Letters. On July 24, Orville E. Babcock, Long Branch, wrote to
Fish that USG "will receive Minister Preston here at any time, next week, that
may be agreeable to him."—ALS, DLC-Hamilton Fish. On July 30, Stephen
Preston, Haitian minister, Seabright, N. J., telegraphed to Babcock to arrange
a meeting.—Telegram received, DLC-USG, IB. See *Foreign Relations, 1874*,
pp. 621–22.

1874, JULY 14.   Attorney Gen. George H. Williams *et al.* to USG. "We the undersigned, members of the Bar and others, respectfully and earnestly recommend the appointment of the Honorable Jno. M. Thompson to fill the existing
vacancy in the Supreme Court of the District of Columbia. Mr. Thompson is
a lawyer of large practice, has held for years a prominent position at the bar
in Pennsylvania; and would bring to the discharge of judicial duties great experience, indomitable energy and unquestioned integrity."—LS (5 signatures),
DLC-USG, IB. No appointment followed.

1874, JULY 14.   Lt. Gen. Philip H. Sheridan, Chicago, to USG, Saratoga
Springs, N. Y. "This City has again Been visited by a wide spread conflagration
commencing at about three thirty 3 30 pm & Burning nearly Everything out
In An area Bounded on the west by Clark st on the south by twelfth 12th street
& the East by the Lake & north by VanBuren   the fire is now north of Van-
Buren on wabash ave & Will probably Reach Jackson st   there is at the present
time Every Indication of a speedy control"—Telegram received (on July 15),
DLC-USG, IB.

1874, JULY 15.   USG note. "The Sec. of State will confer a very great favor on a
most worthy young lady if he gives Miss Owen the Clerkship she asks."—ANS,
DNA, RG 59, Letters of Application and Recommendation. On March 7, Sue H.

Owen, Washington, D. C., had written to Secretary of State Hamilton Fish. "A bill is now before Congress, for the reorganization of the State Department, the passage of which, will give you the power to appoint on the 1st day of July, thirteen copyists, at a salary of nine hundred dollars per annum. I respectfully ask that you will allow me, at this time and in this way, to become an applicant for the position of copyist in your Department; and to beg that when the opportunity presents itself, you will look into the merits of my case, and give it your favorable consideration. With regard to my social position, I beg to say, I am the orphan daughter of Hon. Allen F. Owen of Georgia; a man widely and well known, as an able lawyer, a brilliant scholar, and an accomplished gentleman; and in this connection refer you, to Mr Evarts of New York, Mr Waite, Chief Justice,—both of whom are much interested in me, as the orphan of an old friend and classmate;—and also to Hon. Alexr H. Stephens of Georgia, who has known me well from my childhood. With my most distinguished considerations of esteem, . . ."—ALS, *ibid.* Letters from Chief Justice Morrison Waite, U.S. Representative Alexander H. Stephens of Ga., and William M. Evarts to Fish are *ibid.* Owen received the appointment.

1874, JULY 15.   To Lt. Gen. Philip H. Sheridan, Chicago, from Saratoga Springs, N. Y. "Please find Gen M D Hardin   his Mother is dead   tell him to come immediately"—Telegram received, DNA, RG 393, Military Div. of the Mo., Letters Received. On the same day, Sheridan telegraphed to USG. "I notified General Hardin this morning; cannot start until the evening train."—Copies, *ibid.*, Letters Sent; DLC-Philip H. Sheridan.

1874, JULY 16.   USG pardon of Cyrus Plumer, convicted in Mass. in 1858 "of murder on the high-seas," whose sentence had been commuted to life imprisonment in 1859.—Copy, DNA, RG 59, General Records.

1874, JULY 16.   William H. C. Bartlett, Nantucket, Mass., to USG, Long Branch. ". . . I know Mr. Hubbard well. He may be known to you. I hope he is. I can vouch for all that Mr McCurdy says of him & more too. He has been much in public life, and is particularly conversant with the business that must come before the Genevan International Congress, and I am sure you could not designate a fitter person to represent our interests before that body. . . ."—Copy, DNA, RG 59, Letters of Application and Recommendation. On July 14, Richard A. McCurdy, New York City, had written to Bartlett recommending Gardiner G. Hubbard as delegate to an international postal congress.—Copy, *ibid.* In 1876, USG appointed Hubbard a commissioner to study railway mail transportation. See *HED*, 40-3-35; *SMD*, 45-2-14.

On April 24, 1874, Bartlett, Yonkers, N. Y., had written to congratulate USG on his veto of the financial bill.—ALS, USG 3. On March 3, 1876, Bartlett, New York City, wrote to USG. "I have just finished a work that has cost me much study & labor, being a report of the Mortuary experience of the Mut: Life Insurance Company from its inception to the close of 1873, and have taken the liberty to send you a copy, with no hope however that you can find time to read it, and ask that you will give it a place in your library till you shall have more

leisure than now. It has a decent dress, so that you may not be ashamed of it."—
ALS, *ibid.*

1874, JULY 18.   Secretary of the Navy George M. Robeson to USG. "In compliance with your verbal request, I have the honor to submit herewith copies of
papers on file in this Dept. relative to the Chirique contract, . . ."—Copy, DNA,
RG 45, Letters Sent to the President. On March 24, 1875, William W. Warden,
Washington, D. C., wrote to USG. "In the matter of the CHIRIQUI IMPROVEMENT
contract, I beg, respectfully to suggest, that whilst, on the part of the petitioners, we claim that there is a subsisting contract ~~with~~ between the United States
Government and the Chiriqui Improvement Company for the purchase of the
harbor, coals, lands, etc. of the said company, we are not now seeking the enforcement of that contract. We call your attention to these contracts at the present time ~~fo~~ to enable you to form intelligent judgment, and to enable you to
do equity in the premises, so far as you may have power to act in the matter.
What we specially request now is, that the property in question be leased by the
Government as a coaling station and naval depot, whi[ch] we believe the President has amp[le] power to do without further autho[ri]zation from Congress."
—ALS, *ibid.*, Letters Received from the President.
      On Feb. 22, 1877, Edwin S. Hubbard, "Atty in fact for Chiriqui Improvement
Co," Washington, D. C., wrote to USG. "Some six weeks since, I had the honor
to submit papers relating to the claim of the 'Chiriqui Improvement Company'
with the request that the same be referred to the Attorney Genl for examination and report. As I have not been informed that a report has been made by the
Hon the Atty Genl, *I respectfully request that he may be desired to give early attention
to the subject, for the reason, that but few days remain in which action can be taken
by this Administration*   The claim is briefly this   During the Administrations of
Presidents Bucannan and Lincoln, contracts were made with the Chiriqui Improvement company amounting to $2,300,000, both approved by Congress, and
now amounting with 6% Interest to over $4.220.000—The land and rights of
the company on the Isthmus of Chiriqui, now Panama, was, under the Lincoln
Contract, vested in the Government by an irrevocable Power of Attorney—The
money has not been paid—It is proposed to merge the claim into a lease of
the Harbors of Chiriqui Lagoon on the Atlantic and Golfito on the Pacific, with
a supply of coal for Naval purposes, on such terms as will settle the claim, practically, without cost to the Government—and also secure important Commercial and political advantages to our country, and open the way to the settlement
of that most important question, now demanding the attention of our thoughtful Statesmen, the conflict of races in our country—All of which will more fully
appear from a careful examination of the papers submitted"—ALS, *ibid.*, RG 60,
Letters from the President. Two lengthy earlier communications (one dated
Nov. 27, 1876) from Hubbard to USG are *ibid.* See *HED,* 47-1-46; Lincoln,
Works, IV, 561–62; *ibid.*, V, 370–75; Paul J. Scheips, "Lincoln and the Chiriqui
Colonization Project," *Journal of Negro History,* XXXVII, 4 (Oct., 1952), 418–53.

1874, JULY 24.   Secretary of War William W. Belknap to John C. Vogel,
St. Louis. "Your letter to the President, enclosing designs for a monument to

General N. Lyon to be erected on the arsenal grounds given to the city of St. Louis for a public park upon condition that the monument should be erected thereon within a given time, has been sent by him, to me. The President is absent at Long Branch, but I have no doubt he will approve the designs. I will see him in about ten days, in the meantime the Monument Association can proceed as if the designs have been approved."—Copy, DNA, RG 107, Letters Sent, Military Affairs. On Aug. 4, Belknap wrote to Vogel that USG had "approved the design of Mr. A. Druiding for the monument to General Lyon."—Copy, *ibid.*

1874, JULY 27.   Albert W. Gilchrist, Quincy, Fla., to USG. "Being desirous of an education and not possessing the means of graduating in a private institution, I, accordingly, appeal to you for an appointment to West Point. Mr John T. Dent, if he is in Washington, will probably speak a word in my favor, when he remembers the kindness of my stepfather, Col. Jas. G. Gibbes, to him, when he was a prisoner at Columbia, So. Ca. If you have any doubts, as to my ability, to enter the Academy, I refer you to John P. Thomas, Supt. of the Carolina Military Institute, Charlotte, N. C. I have been to his school for the last six months: and not meaning to brag, I stand head of a class of 40 Cadets. Hoping that you will consider this, my application, . . ."—ALS, DNA, RG 94, Correspondence, USMA. On Jan. 10, 1875, Gilchrist wrote to USG on the same subject.—ALS, *ibid.* Admitted to USMA in 1878, Gilchrist did not graduate.

On May 2, 1875, James G. Gibbes, Quincy, Fla., wrote to USG seeking appointment as collector of customs, Fernandina. ". . . During the war, I advanced to the union officers—prisoners in Columbia over $1,000,000 to provide them with what they needed,—of this, I have never received *one single dollar* in return, in any manner whatever,—Your brother in law John C Dent can give you full infomation on this subject, anything that he obtained while a prisoner was from & through me—. . ."—ALS, *ibid.*, RG 56, Collector of Customs Applications. No appointment followed. See *PUSG*, 19, 335.

1874, JULY 30.   Orville E. Babcock, Long Branch, to Attorney Gen. George H. Williams. "The President directs me to write to you and say that if Judge Noggle of Idaho Ter resigns, that he will be pleased to have John Clark of Idaho Territory appointed to fill the vacancy."—ALS, DNA, RG 60, Letters Received, Idaho. On Dec. 22, USG nominated Madison E. Hollister as chief justice, Idaho Territory, to replace David Noggle. On the same day, USG nominated John Clark to replace Hollister as associate justice. See *PUSG*, 20, 408–9; *ibid.*, 21, 232.

On Feb. 17, 1873, William C. Whitson, associate justice, Idaho Territory, Boise, had written to USG. "We learn with Surprise and regret that certain parties have made charges against Joseph Pinkham Esq. U. S. Marshal for Idaho Territory—. . . In Idaho as well as elsewhere, the overwhelming victory achieved by yourself as the Standard bearer of the Republican party in the late campaign, has caused some very sudden and *remarkable conversions*. And we now frequently hear from lips, which heretofore could never frame to utter the name of the republican party or its noble leader without adding thereto the most vile and opprobrious terms and epithets—most fulsome praise of President Grant—We cannot believe that any thing urged by such a class will be permitted to obtain credence with your Excellency, against one *Known to be* 'a good man and true'— As friends of Marshal Pinkham and in his behalf we invite the most searching Scrutiny in an investigation into every phase and feature of his official conduct, confident that no result prejudicial or injurious to him can result therefrom— We know there are a *few very few*—individuals, here, who, having failed in repeated efforts to make Marshal P. useful to themselves in his official character, are anxious to '*make him feel* their strength and recognize their importance— but too all such the touchstone of truth will be as fatal as the Eye of the basilisk—And we confidently ask of your Excellency, before credence is given to these unfounded tales, of Secret and cowardly malice—that, the person so assailed, may be allowed an opportunity to refute them."—LS, DNA, RG 60, Records Relating to Appointments. Hollister and Joseph W. Huston, U.S. attorney, Idaho Territory, favorably endorsed this letter.—AES (undated), *ibid.* On Jan. 28, 1874, USG renominated Joseph Pinkham as marshal, Idaho Territory.

1874, JULY 31.   To Benjamin R. Cowen, asst. secretary of the interior, asking him to report at Long Branch on the condition of the hospital at Howard University and the proposed removal of the medical director, "as strongly urged by some parties."—Charles Hamilton Auction No. 103, Feb. 24, 1977, no. 96. On Aug. 25, U.S. Senator Hannibal Hamlin and U.S. Representative Eugene Hale of Maine and Speaker of the House James G. Blaine, Augusta, wrote to USG. "At the last session of Congress a law was passed placing the Freedman's Hospital under the charge of the Secretary of the Interior. The design & object was to place it under civil instead of Army control: that was the precise object sought to be accomplished. The institution is purely civil & has no connection with the Army & we can have no doubt that it will be for the best interests of the Hospital that it shall be under a Surgeon not of the Army. The Secretary of the Interior will call your attention to the matter: & knowing Dr. G. S. Palmer personally to be eminently fitted for the position of Surgeon in Charge of said Hospital we earnestly request that he may be appointed to that place."—LS, DNA, RG 48, Appointment Div., Letters Received. Gideon S. Palmer replaced Robert Reyburn as chief surgeon, Freedmen's Hospital and Asylum. See *PUSG*, 21, 92–93; *ibid.*, 24, 479–80; *HED*, 43-2-1, part 5, I, 787–90, 44-1-1, part 5, I, 951–52.

1874, AUG. 1.   Capt. James E. Jouett, U.S.S. *Powhatan,* off Norfolk, Va., to USG "soliciting Your Excellency's approval of an order for my son's examination, and if successful in its passage his subsequent appointment to a Second Lieutenancy." —LS, DNA, RG 94, ACP, 4933 1874. On Dec. 22, USG nominated James S. Jouett as 2nd lt., 10th Inf.

1874, AUG. 3.   USG endorsement concerning Mr. Keefer, a Government Printing Office employee, written on a letter from his wife seeking his reinstatement. —William Evarts Benjamin, Catalogue No. 27, Nov., 1889, p. 11.

1874, AUG. 7.   USG endorsement. "Refered to the Sec. of War. I think it will be well to make enquiries about the writer of this letter, and, if he proves to be a

suitable person, appoint him."—AES, DNA, RG 94, ACP, 3228 1874. Written
on a letter of Aug. 6 from Sgt. Jesse H. Robinson, Fort Whipple, Va., to USG,
Long Branch. "I have the honor to request an appointment as Second Lieutenant
in the Regular Army to fill one of the 21 vacancies now existing. I have no one
to recommend me outside of the Officers I have served with as I have been a Soldier and away from my native place (Pittsburgh Pa) for the past Seven years.
I have grown out of the memory of such men as Genl Negley the present member of Congress from my district consequently I could not ask him to recommend me. I served during the War with the late Genl Thomas as a Telegraph
Operator and Since the war three years in Arizona as a Private in Troop "B" 8th
Cavalry   my company eCommanders were Bvt Maj H P Wade and Capt William McCleave. For the past three years I have been in the Signal Service. . . ."—
ALS, *ibid.* On Sept. 1, Secretary of War William W. Belknap wrote to USG that
Robinson "has shown intelligence, and has been specially useful as a telegrapher,
*but when not under the immediate supervision of a commissioned officer, he has been in
trouble from intemperance.*"—LS, *ibid.* USG endorsed this letter. "Appointment
not approved."—AES (undated), *ibid.*

1874, AUG. 10.   To President José Ellauri of Uruguay. "I send the warmest congratulation on the completion of the telegraphic line that connects your country with not only the United States of North America but most of the civilized
nations of the world. May this new means of communication cement the present
cordial friendship into the most permanent form."—*Washington Evening Star*,
Aug. 12, 1874. A similar telegram to the Argentine president is *ibid.* On Aug. 8,
Ellauri had telegraphed to USG.—Telegram received (in Spanish, at 12:30 P.M.),
DLC-USG, IB.

1874, AUG. 10.   Theodore D. Smith, Morrisville, Va., to USG. "I desire to respectfully make formal application, for an appointment as cadet, at the U. S.
Military Academy at West Point. The services of my father, General Tho's.
Kilby Smith, are the best claim I have to advance in support of my request, and
are too well known, to need comment from me. I have just completed half of my
eighteenth year, and am consequently eligible for appointment. The residence
of my father, at Torresdale, 23rd Ward, Phila. I consider my permanent abode,
as I am sojourning at this point, for a time only. With the request, that my application may receive due attention, . . ."—ALS, DNA, RG 94, Unsuccessful Cadet
Applications. On Sept. 15, Ellen E. Sherman wrote to USG on Smith's behalf.—
ALS, *ibid.*

1874, AUG. 11.   USG endorsement. "Refered to the Sec. of the Int. Williamson
is my Sec. to sign patents. Several such complaints as the within have come to
me. Please notify him that I shall expect his resignation by the 1st of September next."—AES, DNA, RG 48, Appointment Div., Letters Received. On Aug. 3,
R. W. Carter, Washington, D. C., had written to Levi P. Luckey. "Mr Williamson the Presidents Secy to Sign Land Patents owes me about Two hundred and
fifty Dolls for Rent which I find impossible to collect   will you be kind enough to
help me in the matter if within your power—"—L, *ibid.* See *PUSG*, 23, 252–53.

1874, AUG. 11.   To George B. Slatterly, from Long Branch. "A letter addressed to Gen.l Sheridan at Chicago, Ill. would reach him."—ALS, MH.

1874, AUG. 11.   William W. Holden, Raleigh, to USG. "We have lost heavily in the late elections in this State. The Democrats have the State in the popular vote by some ten thousand, with two-thirds in both branches of the Legislature. They have also elected seven of the eight members of Congress. This result is owing largely to the pressure of the Civil Rights bill. Other considerations had their effect, but this was the main cause of the result. But this is no indication of any loss of popularity on your part. You are stronger to-day in North-Carolina than you have ever been before. I believe many of the Democrats are coming to see and to feel that the great interests of the nation are absolutely safe only when the reins are in your hands. Certainly, this verdict of the people here is not against your administration. Maj. J. J. Yeates, who succeeds Mr: Cobb in the 1st District, is an old Union Whig, an ex-Confederate Major, and a man of respectable ability. John A. Hyman, colored, Republican, who succeeds Mr. Thomas in the 2d District, is above the common run of colored men, though much inferior to such as Elliott, Harris and Pinchback. Capt. J. J. Davis, who succeeds Maj. W. A. Smith in this, the 4th District, is an old Union Whig, an ex-Confederate Captain, and a man of respectable ability. Gen. Alfred M. Scales, elected from the Fifth (Settle's) District, is an old secession Democrat, an ex-Confederate General, and a man of fine ability. These are the new members. We were also injured in several Counties by the corruption practiced by the colored race and by the carpet-baggers. This, the metropolitan County, was lost to us on this account. The Civil Rights Bill pressed us sorely in this County, yet we should have carried it for the Legislature by a small majority but for Timothy F. Lee, candidate for Sheriff. He had robbed the people of Wake of sixty thousand dollars in taxes, including fifteen thousand dollars of their School Fund; yet, by a packed Convention of a portion of the party he procured for himself the nomination. On the same day he was thus nominated, a large mass meeting of the better and more honest portion of the party was held. He went before this meeting and was rejected with indignation, Gov. Caldwell, recently deceased, having just denounced him in severe terms as a defaulter, and warned the party against him. He afterwards pledged himself in writing to the State Committee that he would settle by the 15th of July or retire. But he broke his pledge, not settling, but running through; and hence the election of a Democratc Sheriff and the loss of the County. In some other Counties in which the negroes and the carpet-baggers have the control, they acted with equal bad faith, monopolizing all the offices, and thus seriously injuring us in the State by following the bad example in Mississippi and South Carolina. I have thus, Mr. President, taken the liberty of giving you a brief account of the election and of the condition of things in this State, . . ."—ALS, USG 3. On March 8, 1873, USG had nominated Holden as postmaster, Raleigh.

On Jan. 14, 1875, Holden wrote to USG. "I have just read your Message on the Louisiana troubles. It is a triumphant vindication of your whole course in relation to that unhappy State. The country will sustain you. The recent debates in Congress, and the tone of the Democratic press, show that the spirit of the rebellion still exists. The talk and the threats are pretty much what they were in 1859 and '60. It requires a firm hand to hold the helm in this crisis. If *national* men should lose their hold on the government, the worst consequences might be apprehended. The Republicans in all the States which have the power to hold the government, should stand by you to a man. Your friends in these Southern States, that can do but little, will never desert you. The present Congress has but a short time in which to perform most important duties. The Louisiana matters should be settled clearly and thoroughly; and it would be well for the present Congress to make army appropriations for two years. We can not now tell what will happen during the next two or three years. The next House will be exacting, stormy and unreasonable, and may attempt to block the wheels of government. With my best wishes for your happiness, and for your final triumph over all your enemies, . . ."—ALS, *ibid.*

On March 11, Postmaster Gen. Marshall Jewell telegraphed to Orville E. Babcock. "Mr Lee together with member elect Hyman from raleigh, want to see the President in regard to turning out governor Holden, and putting Lee in his place. Will the President see them say at 12. o'clock today? I am against the removal of Holden and told them so."—Telegram received, DNA, RG 107, Telegrams Collected (Bound). On the same day, Babcock wrote to Jewell. "He says he will see them if at leisure when they come but it will be no use as he will not remove Holden—"—ADfS, *ibid.* Jewell replied: "Gen Lee does not want to see the President until tomorrow. Let the decision be what it may. Your first dispatch was premature"—Telegram received, DLC-USG, IB. Holden remained postmaster.

1874, AUG. 12.   St. Clair Dearing, Wilmington, N. C., to USG. "I entered the U. S. Army in 1855 at the age of 20, as Second Lieutenant 4th Infantry, and served until March 1861, when I come South and was a Colonel in Lee and Johnson's armies until the surrender at Greensboro in April 1865 Since that time I have faithfully tried to be a good citizen, and support my aged mother, now 85 years old, by trade or kindred mercantile pursuits, but some how I have no tact for trading and always get worsted at all attempts of that kind, and knowing your ready sympathy for old Officer's, (even if they differed from you, politically, in the Civil War,) I venture to ask you for some appointment under the Government, abroad, even if it offers but *a bare support,* and I will endeavor to faithfully discharge the duties, in such a way as to increase the respect of foreigners for the name of 'American,' and at any rate bring no discredit on your Excellency's selection of a quondam rebel, who ventures thus to appeal to your kindness. For my personal character and social standing, I refer your Excellency to Genl Young, M. C. from Georgia, and Senator J. B. Gordon from the same state: and in the old Army, to Genl W. F. Barry Colonel 2d Artillery, or General Gordon Granger Colonel __ Infantry or Adjutant General Townsend or Lt General Philip Sheridan with whom I served in Oregon and Washington Territory. I speak French and German, and have been classically educated before spending four years at a Military Academy, *and never was drunk in my life.*"
—ALS, DNA, RG 59, Letters of Application and Recommendation. No appointment followed.

1874, AUG. 15.   Walter Gibson, New York City, to USG. "I have the honor to
state that on the 17th ult. I transmitted by mail sworn charges against U. S.
District Attorney Geo. Bliss alleging that he postponed an examination into a
case of the destruction of the United States mail, that he took unlawful measures
to prevent an indictment in the same case by the U. S. Grand Jury of June & was
guilty of other grave misdemeanors which have been seriously commented
on by the newspapers & still are the subject of notice. Please be kind enough
to inform me if those charges have been received & please send me a copy of
Mr. Bliss' answer when it is obtained. . . . P. S. The charges were signed by Walter Gibson, W. H. Pierce & J. Hobart Haws, Grand Juryman."—ALS, DNA,
RG 60, Letters from the President. On Oct. 25, 1875, Attorney Gen. Edwards
Pierrepont wrote to USG. "The papers containing the charges against Mr Bliss
of New York cannot be acted upon by me for the reason that these same charges
were heard by my predecessor Judge Williams who disposed of the case. . . ."—
Copy, *ibid.*, Letters Sent to Executive Officers. On May 18, 1876, Gibson wrote
to USG on the same subject.—ALS, *ibid.*, Letters from the President.

1874, AUG. 17.   Bill Jones, Marion, Ala., to USG. "I will now beseat my Self
Down in prison at this present opportunity To inform you a Few Lines To Let
you know my present state of health that I am here in Jail & keeps very Sickly
& on helplis & bye been a Stranger in this Country I have no here to help me. I
have one Brother in this Country & he is not able to help me   my people is all
in North Carolina & Petersburg Virginia & I Would thank you if you Would
please sir help me   I am here & the have got me Charge of murder againts a
Colored man Which I am not guilty off & I am Satisfied of that & the been had
me here in Jail Every since the 13 off April be fo this Last goen & my Witnes is
goen to Mississippi & one Term the State Witnes did not appear & the yet hold
me here punishing me & Den etspect to give me a Trial & send me to penitentiary If the can & Dear sir I will State to you again that the have been keeping
me here all this Time & Will not Let me have a bond & When the have a White
man Charge of any thing the give him a bond & the had three White men
Charge of the same that the have got me Charge of & the Give them bond & one
Whiteman that brought me to this Country bye the name of Mr John Ross Sent
me Word to see my Lawyer & get him to make out a bond fore me & he Would
come & go on it   that been three monthes ago & my Lawyer told me that the
could not give me a bond because my case was a United State case   Well them
White people case Was the same case & the give them bond   the Will not give
We Colored people bond to keep us From been out so that We cant vote   now
if you ~~sir~~ please sir Look over this & Sympathy With me & Let me have a bond
that I can go on my Self or one that I can get some other man to go on or releft
me from Jail some Way or the other & I am not with good mother Wite bye my
head been once spleit open & my mother & grand mother & my Misstes Write
Word here in a Letter To my Lawyer that I Was a only 17 years old this Last
March & said that the never new of me Doing anything Wrong before & I can
prove my good Character Every Where I Ever been & my poor old mother She
Try to help me What Little She can   She send me some money some times in
a Letter & I hardly Ever get it   the Stealls it from me before it get here from

Petersburg   I am might Sickly & if I Dont be turn out off here I Dont think that I can be a Liveing six months From the Day   I have Learnt to read & Write since I have been here   I Was a Fool before I cam here & I am very sorry that any such thing happen to me as to have me Charge off murder   I did not Run a Way From my mother   I Was tes off bye a White man & he is Willing to help me now but the Will not Let him Do it   now When you Write to me please Write in the care of a c Lady bye the name of Tilday Lockit   please Answer this now"—ALS, DNA, RG 60, Letters from the President.

1874, Aug. 18.   Mrs. John C. Carter, Fort Monroe, Va., to USG. "In January last, I waited upon you in Washington, with a letter from my nephew Ben. O.Fallon of Saint Louis. The object of my visit was an application for my Son, to the appointmt of 2d Lieut in the Army,   you suggested that I make a formal application in writing, & permitted me to make it through you setting forth his claims &c which I did, at the time you kindly saying that when the proper time came, after the Anual Examination at West Point, you would give it your attention, that time has now arrived, & only yesterday I heard the Examining Board was Ordered for the 15th Sept   May I now ask that favourable attention to his claim, & if not through old, & early friendships of both Mrs Grant, & yourself with my connexions in Saint Louis, I would ask it for the long & faithful services of his Father Commodore J. C. Carter, who Born in Virginia, & appointed from Kentucky, in addition to a Command on the Western Lakes, Captured the confederate spy, & broke up the great Beale raid, & recruited about seven thousand men for the Navy, & after serving over forty years, died sharing the fate of retirement of all who have faithfully served the allotted time,   This broken link, has left us limited in means, & makes this step imperative   My Son Charles Edward C. E. Carter of Erie Pa is 26 years of age, he holds an honourable discharge from the Navy, having served during the rebellion, & was among the first to offer his services at the time of the Cuban outrage. I would only add my gratitude should you promote this object & feel assured you would never have cause to regret it"—ALS, DNA, RG 94, Applications for Positions in War Dept. On Feb. 15, Carter had written to USG on the same subject; in 1876 and 1877, Carter wrote to USG renewing her request.—ALS, *ibid.* No appointment followed.

1874, Aug. 21.   George A. Black, secretary, Utah Territory, to USG, transmitting a copy of the territorial laws.—ALS (press), Utah Archives, Salt Lake City.

1874, Aug. 21.   [Gabriel J. Rains], USMA 1827, Charlotte, N. C., to USG. "Permit me to address you upon the ground of our old friendship, on the subject of introducing the study of Torpedoes at WestPoint Mil.y Academy. It is now an arm of service I beleive in all civilized nations, and I feel unwilling that a knowledge of this thing, which has been almost the study of a life time, should go elsewhere out of our country. By examining my book containing some 70 or 80 diagrams with some 150 pages description, you would readily agree with me, & certainly the U. S. Officers should be made thoroughly versed in this subject, which those of higher rank admit as having changed the tactics of the world! As I am playing schoolmaster for a living, I would not object giving my experiance to the advancement of our service enhancing the peace prospects of mankind in rendering wars measureably impossible by such formidable inventions. Please allow me an interview, or refer me to some capable scientific gentlemen of your own selection."—L (incomplete), DNA, RG 94, Correspondence, USMA. On Sept. 24, Secretary of War William W. Belknap endorsed this letter. "If the introduction of this study should be contemplated there is no necessity for securing the services of a Rebel General"—E (initialed), *ibid.* On Oct. 7, Col. Thomas H. Ruger, superintendent, USMA, endorsed this letter to Belknap. "Instruction in the general subject of torpedoes is now given at the Military Academy including general description of the different kinds, method of placing, using, &c., which is I think all that should be attemped. To give special instruction with a view to make entire classes of Cadets competent to practically supervise the manufacture of and use of torpedoes would not at the present time be expedient."—ES, *ibid.* See W. Davis Waters, "'Deception Is the Art of War': Gabriel J. Rains, Torpedo Specialist of the Confederacy," *North Carolina Historical Review,* LXVI, 1 (Jan., 1989), 29–60.

1874, AUG. 22.   John C. Hamilton, Long Branch, to USG. "In the volumes which I had the honor to present to you previous to your Inauguration as President of these United States, I feel that I have shewn, because it has universally been ascribed to me, an independence and disregard of mere popular prejudices, a subservience to which has been the bane and fruitfully pervading evil of all pure, mere democracies. This in no sense means a disregard or wanton violation of PUBLIC OPINION. The former is, to a great extent, *the* vice of these days; the latter has been the vice and pregnant error of other days. My father, whom honest history now shews to have been the Civil Founder of our National government, felt and lamented the folly in the Federal party, of which he was to a certain extent a leader, in not using proper means to conciliate public favor; and in not guarding against errors or acts offensive to public opinion. John Adams, who had little practical sense, if any—thus ruined the Federal party. The Democratic leaders in a similar manner ruined the Democratic party, both governed for a time by ~~the~~ a dogmatic tyranny, the result of political partizan success. In both instances, the large, pervading common sense of the intelligent American people was underestimated. In my opinion, in this respect the present President of the United States has only not erred but has been singularly and most felicitously wise. That he will be so in regard to the matter which is the subject of these remarks, it being in some degree personal, is to be hoped. More than this would be speculatively complimentary; and I do not choose thus to forget my own self respect. The question is—and it is a great question—whether any true soundness of historical teaching—of recorded experience, or of *principle* forbids an election of President for a THIRD term? I mean to be brief. It is a familiar fact, that my father in his plan of a Constitution proposed that the President's term —should be *during good behaviour*; excluding all idea of an hereditary government; and rendering the Executive office amenable to an *effective* duly organized court of Impeachments—not such as that which acquitted Andrew Johnson— guilty as he was, and which thereby practicably as to a President has become a nullity in our Constitution. Nor was my father alone in this opinion. Strong men in the convention agreed with him;—and above all in public confidence was Washington. I can furnish unequivocal evidence that in *this respect* as in

most others, he agreed fully with my father as to a *prolonged term* of office. Nor
is that surprizing. As a Soldier in chief command he felt as a Soldier charged
with high duties and responsibilities would—indeed *must* have felt. As subordination in an army is a necessity to its salvation and success, So, subordination
in a people is also an essentiality to the preservation & welfare of a people and
of their government. Is it not a familiar fact that subordination is ~~inconsistent~~
incompatible with frequent changes of counsels? In an exposition intended to
be brief and simple, bringing forward familiar truths, such as would be accepted
by common minds, it may not be amiss to state another proposition essentially
true and historically proven in our nations short experience. The proposition
has occurred to you, that a period of office ought to be such as will impose and
secure a sense of responsibility. No prudence would give a trust, were it of an
enduring character—if the trustées terms were only of a tomorrow—Surely
as to a nations welfare who would think only of a tomorrow?   the complexity
of our interlacing interests is such as to require time and *much* time. We are too
rapid. Now for the historical fact. Mr Jefferson would not by his timid counsels
and by his subservience to France have prompted the arrogance and aggres-
sions of Great Britain had the term of office of his official life been such as to
compel him to anticipate & FACE the evils and the dangers of which his policy
was a chief cause. Passing on; I ask—Does the history of this country prove that
in their view Washington and Hamilton were incorrect as to a longer term of
office? Washington yielded reluctantly to a *second* term to preserve this nation
from ruin by its becoming a party to the violent quarrels of Europe; and this nation was saved in its infancy by its difficultly maintained neutrality. Had Washington been elected & lived to serve a *third* term he would have saved this country from the supremacy of the doctrines and policy of conflicting State rights,
which eventuated in the recent Civil War! Indeed, it was proposed, because of
John Adam's crazy vagaries and unmanly inconsistencies, that Washington
should be elected for a *third* term. He died. Now 2d—as a matter of principle;
and this is a *statement worthy all attention.* It was forcibly urged in the convention
which framed the Constitution, as my fathers minutes shew, that men ~~pressing
fram~~ framing a constitution had *no right* as a matter of *principle* and could not
warrantably limit the duration of the Executive officer to a specified term, which
might possibly be inconsistent with the public welfare—and this argument *prevailed*—as there is nothing in the Constitution indicating a purpose to establish
such a limitation. If the office of a Judge could be extended to a period of good
behaviour—that same power—and if the motive existed, the same principle
would have warranted the term of the President being during good behaviour
—and as the Constitution now stands, it manifestly warrants a reelection during successive terms of good behaviour. The principle of a Constitution is the
best elucidation of its purpose. If historical experience and principle are against
the theory of a four years or eight years or of any limited term other than good
behaviour, there is another consideration of greatest moment. It is presented in
a recent event in France. One of her late Constitutions limited the term of office
to a few years; and that happened which was predicted as a possibility, and urged
as a cogent objection in the convention which framed our constitution—that a
power so limited in its duration would lead to sudden and violent usurpation.

In France it resulted in a Coup d'Etat!! It is urged, that the precedent of Washington and Jefferson in retiring each at the end of eight years ought to govern. There is *nothing* in this notion. Washington retired after a life of toil exhausted in the service of his country at an *advanced* age, having, as he hoped, accomplished all that could *then* be done for the public good. Jefferson, after enjoying office retired also at an advanced age, shrinking from the consequences of his own system which had exhausted for a time the vitality of our country. Is there, can there be any analogy in your situation with such precedents? Is this government or will it be sufficiently consolidated, after this civil war, to render it safe to entrust it to new and untried hands? The condition of the Southern States, the involvements of our finances—the depressed state of our industrial pursuits—the questions discreetly presented by you in a previous message as to adjacent territories, land and maritime, under *foreign* dominion; and above all the terrible problem of our future as to a vast Empire of mixed populations— All these must have and will present themselves to your thoughts as of such magnitude as almost to appall the formost minds—and which urge and demand the continued action of great *deliberate consistent* counsels. Thus, whatever may seem to be the popular view, for one I would insist upon a *third* term—and perhaps on a *fourth* term—nothing supervening to unjustify them. I do not hesitate in the opinion, that the President ought not to decline a reelection—certainly not until there is time to judge of the position of public affairs—I have omitted here any reference to our foreign relations, as to which I believe, the full scope of comprehensive counsels has not and perhaps can not yet be reached —tho' I think that a basis can be laid which will be of immense and far reaching importance and benefit to this country and to the world."—ALS, USG 3. On Sept. 30, Hamilton, New York City, wrote to USG. "I beg leave to enclose a paper, which I wrote yesterday, for *your* perusal, for the reason, as it is to a great extent a *personal* matter, there is a delicacy in publishing it without your assent. If any modifications occur please insert them; and a new copy will be made by *me.* The blanks I will fill up. There can exist no reason why *this* paper should not appear forthwith; and if it is what I wish it to be, it ought to be extensively circulated. I am inclined to think, that the Essay I propose to write upon the *merits* of the question, had better be delayed until after our State election. It might give some advantage to our adversaries; but if you take a different view, be so good as to state it. No person has seen the enclosed paper, and it is best the authorship should not be known. Be assured, whatever you may write to me will be sacredly confidential. With kind regards to her: please tell Mrs Grant that I called upon Mrs Pope."—ALS, *ibid.* "A Third Term," the lengthy essay enclosed, concluded: "This closing remark may be used—that in studying with due care the character of Washington, as exhibited not only throughout his public life, but especially in regard to the matter before us, how delightful it is to recall the tribute paid to him by Hamilton, who of all men knew him best and best appreciated him,—'the modest and sage Washington—he consulted much, pondered much—resolved slowly—resolved surely.' There are those who know President Grant well, who will not deny the analogy."—ADf, *ibid.*

On Nov. 4, 1868, Hamilton, New York City, had written to USG. "At my time of life this probably is the last Presidential election at which I shall have exercised the invaluable right of suffrage. I rejoice in the hope and in the belief that it has been given to support the most important interests of our great Republic in your hands; & that, by a wise selection of counsellors who have never faltered in their duty, your administration will promote & confirm the happiness of all the American people; & redound to the permanent glory of our country, & thus to your enduring fame. I beg you to present Mrs Hamiltons & my kindest congratulations to Mrs Grant."—ALS, *ibid.*

On Feb. 7, 1869, Hamilton wrote to John Russell Young. "I have just returned from Washington where I have conversed with Gen Grant in relation to two proposed amendments—originating with my father—*after full reflection* I he expressed an *earnest desire* that they should become parts of the Constitution— That as to suffrage was submitted to the *Senate* by Genl Wilson—That as to the electoral vote by Mr Spaulding in the *House.* The enclosed paper was read in part to Gen Grant by me & its publication was sanctioned. It appeared with great haste in the Chronicle & with some errors which I have corrected. If you think proper to insert it stating this fact of his approval you will do so—either giving my name or not as you may think proper. My object is, that you would in tomorrows issue—if you approve the amendm'ts—come forth *decidedly* & *strongly.* Genl Grants view is, that there can be no quiet in the rebellious states without a final settlement of the suffrage right both as to ~~State~~ the election of state & national officers—& this by amendment of the Constitution—not by bill, as Sumner favors. He is also fully of opinion that the division of the States into electoral districts is essential. These are matters, as I before said, to which he gives a very earnest feeling. . . . The Genl is entirely decided against any measures of unkindness to the rebels unless compelled by circumstances; & he would much prefer nothing shall assume the shape of *retrospective* or *prospective* proscription. He is to receive some persons of consideration at my house *tomorrow morning* at *10* oclock. Should you be able to come I will be happy to see you— *precisely* at that hour & not later, as his engagements compel him. I wish you to consider this note *strictly confidential,* except so far as the statements, marked on the *side.* . . . P. S. The amendmt as to Suffrage—'All citizens &c was proposed by my father in his plan of govt in 1788 but is modified so as to embrace *all* elections in the States. The history of the other is in the enclosed Essay—in my fathers words as stated."—ALS, DLC-John Russell Young. See *New York Tribune,* Feb. 9, 1869. U.S. Senator Henry Wilson of Mass. advocated the Fifteenth Amendment. See Richard H. Abbott, *Cobbler in Congress: The Life of Henry Wilson, 1812–1875* (Lexington, Ky., 1972), pp. 204–6. On Feb. 1, U.S. Representative Rufus P. Spalding of Ohio had proposed a constitutional amendment requiring Congress to create electoral districts after each census.—*CG,* 40–3, 768. No action followed.

On Sept. 11, Hamilton wrote to USG a lengthy memorandum concerning the possible resumption of negotiations with Great Britain over the *Alabama* Claims.—ALS, DLC-Hamilton Fish.

1874, Aug. 23.   Hazard Stevens, Olympia, Washington Territory, to USG. "I respectfully apply for the appointment as commissioner to report upon British Claimants on San Juan Island, authorized by Act, of June 20, '74   A resident of this Territory Since boyhood, having come here with my father, the late Gen'l. Isaac I. Stevens, in 1854, with the exception of four years Service in the Army of the Potomac, thoroughly familiar with the islands in question, acquainted with the Settlers thereon, I feel competent to properly perform the duty. Nor do I ask it, provided anyone more competent, or better qualified, can be found to accept the position. But $1000, is appropriated to defray the expenses of the commission."—ALS, DNA, RG 48, Lands and Railroads Div., Letters Received. On Sept. 23, USG appointed Stevens.—DS, *ibid.*

1874, AUG. 24.   Secretary of State Hamilton Fish to USG. "I enclose for your information, a copy of a despatch of the 30th ultimo from Mr E. B. Washburne at Paris, relating to the 'History of the Civil War in America' by the Count de Paris—the first two volumes of which have been forwarded, at the request of the Count, for your acceptance. I shall be pleased to be informed of your wishes in regard to the disposition of these volumes."—LS, Babcock Papers, ICN. The enclosure is *ibid.*

1874, AUG. 27.   Secretary of the Interior Columbus Delano to USG. "All the persons appointed for the new land office at La Mesilla, N. M. have declined. You will remember that we have appointed two for the office of Register. Hon. S. B. Elkins, the Member, writes me that it is, in many respects, important to have the office opened, and he suggests for Register Lawrence La Point, and for Receiver William L. Rynerson, and says that he knows these men will accept. I therefore forward their appointments for your signature. I have letters from Governor Pennington, of Dakota, and from Hon. Wm P. Dewey, the Surveyor General of that Territory, urging strongly that Geo. H. Hand, now Register of the Yankton land office, be appointed Secretary of the Territory, vice Oscar Whitney and that Oscar Whitney be appointed Register of the land office at Yankton, vice Geo. H. Hand. The reasons for this change are assigned at length in a letter addressed to me by Mr. Dewey, which I enclose for your perusal, if you deem it necessary to take the time for reading it. I also enclose Governor Pennington's letter. My knowledge of affairs, in Dakota, induces me to believe that the changes above referred to had better be made. I think it will be especially agreeable to Governor Pennington, and his relations with the Secretary of the Territory are such as to require mutual confidence and esteem. I have, therefore, enclosed the papers necessary to consummate these changes, which you can sign if they meet your approval."—Copy, Delano Letterbooks, OHi. On Dec. 9, USG nominated Laurence La Point as land office register, La Mesilla; on the same day, USG nominated Mariano Barela as land office receiver, La Mesilla, after William L. Rynerson failed to qualify. Also on Dec. 9, USG nominated George H. Hand as secretary, Dakota Territory, and Oscar Whitney as land office register, Yankton.

1874, AUG. 31.   U.S. Senator William B. Washburn of Mass. to USG. "Lt Merrill who is at present assigned to our Agricultural College a most excelle[nt] officer desires to be transferred to the Ordnance Department. If you can grant his request you will aid a worthy officer . . ."—ALS, DNA, RG 156, Letters Received.

On Sept. 12, U.S. Senator George S. Boutwell of Mass., Groton, wrote to USG. "I am not acquainted with Mr. Merrill, but I well acquainted with Mr. Dickinson and upon his statement I respectfully recommend the application to your consideration."—AES, *ibid.* Written on a letter of Sept. 10 from Marquis F. Dickinson, Jr., to Boutwell, concerning 1st Lt. Abner H. Merrill, USMA 1866.

On March 24, 1876, John D. Runkle, president, Massachusetts Institute of Technology, Boston, wrote to USG. "The detail of Lieut. E. L. Zalinski, 5th Arty, U. S. A. as Professor of Military Science & Tactics, at this Institute will expire on July 1st next, and we respectfully ask that Lieut. A. H. Merrill, 1st Arty, U. S. A. be detailed for this duty from July 1st. We earnestly desire that the present efficiency may be maintained in the department, & feel assured that Lieut. M. is well fitted for the duty—"—ALS, *ibid.*, RG 94, ACP, 4841 1873. On the same day, Governor Alexander H. Rice of Mass. wrote to USG on the same subject. —ALS, *ibid.* On April 7, AG Edward D. Townsend endorsed these letters and related papers to Secretary of War Alphonso Taft indicating that Merrill "is under orders to report for a term at the Artillery School at Fort Monroe May 1st next. Besides, he was only a year ago—relieved from College duty—having been on duty at the Mass. Ag. College, Amherst, Mass. from March 15 1872 to March 25, '75. He would seem not to be eligible."—ES, *ibid.*

[*1874, Aug.*].   "R. T. Anthony" to [USG]. *"Personal—For Executive relief. . . .* I have the honor to state that Mr. Boutwell, in mistaken zeal, withheld, during sickness, the salaries of poorly paid clerks stricken down by disease and impoverished by medical expenditures. When carried before the United States Courts the action of the Department was not sustained. The late Secretary of the Treasury issued an order designating two certain doors of the Department for ingress and egress, and requiring the many hundreds of females in the Bureau of Engraving and Printing to observe the most exact obedience to these arbitrary regulations. Sickly and fragile girls escaping from a heavy storm to the nearest door were inhumanly compelled by the watchful doorkeepers to walk in a drenching rain the length of a square to secure admittance. The restraint, inconvenience and a feeling of being classed as sheep naturally produced the greatest dissatisfaction and humiliation—in one word, the order was so oppressive that it was speedily revoked. The above two examples afford an admirable illustration of the unfortunate exercise of power, whereby an error of judgment in a single person, even though a Cabinet Officer, inflicts injury upon hundreds of innocent individuals. The above cases are respectfully submitted to show that even though an order be issued by the Secretary of a Department, it does not follow that it is either right, proper or just. The present Secretary of the Treasury, in a laudable design, perhaps, of establishing reforms, has promulgated an order which, though prompted, possibly by good motives, will most certainly result in afflicting the poor and the weak—the invariable result of sweeping regulations. He has seen fit to abolish the time-honored, humane and judicious semi-monthly payments to all employees of the Department. Think of it!   3000 human beings, most of whom live from 'hand to mouth,' overcome by this great misfortune will be forced to live on expensive credit, or, if unable to borrow, compelled to [*seek*] the tender mercies of the hook-beaked Shylocks! As a rule, female employees receive $1.75 a day, and males $3.00, and a settlement semi-monthly is now denied them. Mr. President, no reasons, be they what they may be, can outweigh the disappointments, the grief and the manifold hardships, nay, resulting and indirect calamities, which will inevitably ensue from the observance of this well-meaning though injudicious and terrible order. As it would be naturally the height of absurdity for an insignificant employe to appeal to the Honorable Secretary—even though he be the very best of men—your humble petitioner has no other recourse but to beseech the intervention of your good offices in securing the revocation of this most disastrous order."—ALS (docketed Aug. 16, 1874), DNA, RG 56, Miscellaneous Letters Received. R. T. Anthony is not listed among Treasury Dept. employees of this period.

1874, SEPT. 2. Mayor Frank A. MacKean of Nashua, N. H., to USG. "GENL. JOHN G. FOSTER DIED LAST NIGHT FUNERAL SATURDAY SEPT. FIFTH AT TEN OCLOCK A. M. CAN YOU BE PRESENT."—Telegram received, DLC-USG, IB. USG did not attend.

1874, SEPT. 3. Angie B. Martin, Kansas City, Mo., to USG. "In reading the History of the War between the North & South I *reviewed* the Great Seige of Vicksburg. I say reviewed, for I remember perfectly well how deeply interrested *I* felt during the great struggle which ended in one of the most glorious conquests of the age. I remember how I wrote and tried in my weak way, to cheer & encourage one 'soldier boy' who, under his 'beloved General Grant,' toiled and labored beneath a scortching June & July sun, to infuse new spirits into his worn and drooping men,—how I told him that 'I felt as sure of the fall of Vicksburg as I did of the existence of a Supreme Being'—This 'soldier boy' to whom I wrote words of cheer—came home on furlough near the close of the war—1864—and we were married—I believe you will remember him—Capt John W. Martin, 30th Regt Ills. Vols? Well in 1865, he received an honorable discharge from the service and engaged in the 'peaceful pursuits of life,' but his health was gone—the seeds of disease were sown—We left of our home—Marshall Ills—a young and happy couple lived in Indianapolis ten months then came to K. City—My husband labored very hard as Contractor & Builder and succeeded in getting a litle home, but his health failing rapidly he was obliged to borrow money until his property was mortgaged to the am't of $1500. Seeing no way to pay this debt and feeling that in case of his death his wife, must inevitably be left penniless, among strangers—he sank rapidly and in March last he died, a broken hearted man. General Grant, that noble soldier who had served in many battles—Belmont, Seige of Vicksburg, Forts Donaldson & Henry, Atlanta and many others, pined and drooped and died from diseases contracted in the Army and hopeless involvement in debt. His grave is unmarked with any stone and as yet I am unable to even give that last mark of respect to his *dear* memory. The 20th of October my beautiful little home built & fashioned by those beloved hands—and which ought to be worth $2500, wil[l] be sold at public auction for the paltry sum of $1500. . . ."—ALS, DNA, RG 48, Miscellaneous Div., Letters Received. Martin received a widow's pension beginning in Nov., 1879.

1874, SEPT. 12. James M. Allen, Matfield, Mass., to USG concerning his need to visit Indians to complete "a *Universal Natural Alphabet*, equally adapted to represent scientifically any and all languages."—ALS, DNA, RG 75, Letters Received, Miscellaneous.

1874, SEPT. 14.   USG pardon for George H. Christian, convicted in Feb. of "removing dead bodies for gain" and sentenced to one year in prison, "strongly recommended by many of the most prominent members of the medical profession in this City, including the faculties of the 'Georgetown' and 'Columbian' Medical Schools, the editors of the leading Washington papers and many other citizens of the District of Columbia, as well as by Senator Sherman, and a large number of the Ohio Representatives in Congress."—Copy, DNA, RG 59, General Records.

1874, SEPT. 14.   USG endorsement. "Refered to the Sec. of the Navy. Let special attention be called to this application when appointments to the Naval Academy, for the class of /76, come to be made."—AES (facsimile), Alexander Autographs, Oct. 18, 2000, no. 1282. Written on a letter from Samuel A. W. Patterson, son of Commodore Thomas H. Patterson, seeking appointment to the U.S. Naval Academy.—*Ibid.* Patterson graduated from the U.S. Naval Academy in 1882.

1874, SEPT. 14.   Speaker of the House James G. Blaine, Augusta, Maine, to USG. "The result of our Election today is in all respects Satisfactory. We have carried Every Congressional district have a majority I think in Every County in the State have chosen twenty nine or thirty Senators to one by the Democrats Have Elected three fourths of the popular branch of the Legislature and have given Gov Dingley a majority according to present appearances of between Eleven & twelve thousand which is a handsome gain on last years Vote"—Telegram received (at 11:55 P.M.), DLC-USG, IB.

1874, SEPT. 17.   To Secretary of War William W. Belknap. "Please present my congratulations to the *Society of the Army of the Cumberland*, and express my regret that circumstances prevent my being with them on this occasion."—*Society of the Army of the Cumberland: Eighth Re-union Columbus 1874* (Cincinnati, 1875), p. 102. On Aug. 14, William Dennison, Washington, D. C., had telegraphed to USG, Long Branch. "You will gratify my wife and myself very much by making our house your home during the reunion of the army of the Cumberland. Can you do so. We hope genl Babcock will be our Guest also and genl sheridan"—Telegram received, DLC-USG, IB. On Sept. 14 and 15, Cincinnati officials invited USG to visit an industrial exposition after the army reunion.—Telegrams received, *ibid.*

1874, SEPT. 18.   Alfred H. Love, Lucretia Mott, *et al.*, Philadelphia, to USG. "The Universal Peace Union, profoundly impressed with the importance of International Arbitration, desires to call your attention to the following resolutions, passed by Congress: . . . The future historian will, doubtless, record the Geneva Arbitration as one of the most sublime and important events of the age, and one which sheds lustre upon your administration   May not the present opportunity of addressing the other nations of the world, on the subject of these resolutions be equal in its results? We trust that you will take this matter into serious consideration, and direct the proper officer to prepare and forward the necessary documents at an early day. It has been a source of gratification to the members of this association, to know that in your administration you have, in so many instances, evinced a desire to carry out your significant declaration made at an early day, 'Let us have Peace', and we sincerely hope that you will continue in this course."—DS (4 signatures), DNA, RG 59, Miscellaneous Letters. *Voice of Peace*, I, 10 (Jan., 1875), 156–57. On June 17, the House of Representatives had passed a resolution authorizing USG to negotiate "an international system whereby matters in dispute between different governments agreeing thereto may be adjusted by arbitration, and if possible without recourse to war."—*CR*, 43–1, 5114. On Sept. 10, the Baltimore Monthly Meeting of Friends addressed USG in support of the resolution.—DS, DNA, RG 59, Miscellaneous Letters. *Voice of Peace*, II, 1 (April, 1875), 15. On May 7, USG had "expressed a very warm interest in the movement, and said, 'The nations are fast becoming so civilized as to feel that there is a better way to settle their difficulties than by fighting.'" —*New York Herald*, May 8, 1874.

On Oct. 13, 1871, Joseph A. Dugdale *et al.*, Iowa Peace Society, Mount Pleasant, had petitioned USG to praise the Treaty of Washington and to suggest "taking the initiatory movement for a World's Parliament."—*Bond of Peace*, I, 10 (Oct., 1871), 151.

On Dec. 6, 1875, U.S. Representative George W. McCrary of Iowa wrote to USG. "At the request of the officers of the Yearly meeting of Friends held at Palatine Illinois in Sept last, I have the honor to present to you the enclosed Memorial on the subject of a *Peace Congress of Nations*."—ALS, DNA, RG 59, Miscellaneous Letters. Quakers meeting at Mount Palatine, Ill., Sept. 13–16, had addressed USG and Congress. "We are constrained in fidility to Our Sovereign Lord, who is *God over all*, to recognize as preeminent among the testimonies of truth that which regards destruction of human life on the battlefield, as essentially barbaric and to exert our influence in the most *Solemn* and Earnest manner to banish it from the Society of Nations—. . . The American Peace Society computed that in 1869 The army and Navy cost our people one hundred times more than for all the Bibles in half a hundred languages. . . . We regard the Treaty of the joint High Commission at Washington, as the Sublimest triumph of the 19th Century—. . . We earnestly entreat the American Congress Our Senators and representatives to give the weight of your influence in favor of a world's Parliament or Congress of Nations, to adjust all ~~all~~ disputations, that may hereafter arise, and not to permit any nation or people to precede us in this Sublimest reform of the age. Our Religious Society has held and Advocated the testimony against war for more than two centuries, and now Submit this memorial to you, with Sentiments of increasing interest in the common welfare of the human race—"—DS, *ibid.*

1874, SEPT. 19.   John L. LeConte, Philadelphia, to USG. "It is perhaps already known to Your Excellency, that the Zoological Society of Philadelphia has successfully established a Garden for the care & exhibition of living animals. This Garden has been made upon a portion of Fairmount Park, which has been granted by the Commissioners of the Park for this purpose. The success of this undertaking, the first of the kind in the United States, has been extraordinary, even in comparison with the Zoological Gardens of Europe: since the

opening on July 1st 1874, up to the present time, more than 130,000 persons
have visited the collection. Should the Society continue to retain the confidence
& patronage of the community, its collection will form a very important & at-
tractive feature in the Centennial Exposition of 1876: besides being at all times
a useful means for encouraging the taste for, & increasing the knowledge of,
Natural History. It is for these reasons that I, in the name of the Society, would
respectfully request Your Excellency to authorize the distribution of a circular,
a copy of which is herewith enclosed, to the officers & employé[s] of the Government, with such additional recommendation from the Departments of State,
War & Navy, as you may be pleased to permit."—ALS, DNA, RG 59, Miscellaneous Letters.

1874, SEPT. 19.   Octavia du Val Radford, Forest Depot, Va., to USG. "Last Summer, I took the liberty of applying to you, through Mrs Grant, for an appointment to West Point, for my son, du Val Radford;   Mrs Grant was kind enough
to reply, that she had mentioned the subject to you, and that you had said, 'That
the appointments for 1874 were made, that my son would come among the
class that you would seek to appoint from, and if application was made, his name
would be brought before you, when the appointments were being made for 1875
—'   Encouraged by Mrs Grants reply, I have concluded to make the application, in the simplest and most direct way, by writing to you; and if it is not in
form, you will excuse it on the plea that I am totally ignorant of the manner, in
which it should be made. You will probably be surprised, that this application
does not come from Mr Radford—You will possibly remember, that his disposition does not bear disappointment, and feeling that you have so many claims
on your kindness, more urgent than his, fears a failure, while I having so great
faith in old friendships, do not hesitate, to ask the favor at your hands."—ALS,
DNA, RG 94, Correspondence, USMA. On Nov. 9, Radford wrote to Julia Dent
Grant on the same subject.—ALS, *ibid.* Richard C. W. Radford, USMA 1845, had
served as C.S.A. col.; his son did not attend USMA.

1874, SEPT. 24.   Emanuel Vanorden, "Presbyt Min. of the U. States," Rio de Janeiro, to USG. "Permit me to bring to your notice that the United States and
Brazil S. S. Co to which the U. S. Government pays an annual subsidy in money
for carrying the mail to and from Brazil, carries almost on every steamer that
enters into this port, a number of slaves who are received in Brazilian sea-ports
North of Rio-de Janeiro to be delivered in Rio de Janeiro or to be sent farther
South, and to be sold there. . . . It has been for a long time a sore grief to American residents in this empire to see announcements of this kind, and I think it
need only to be brought to your notice to have it stopped at once. The Government certainly does not mean to subsidize a Company, which aids slave dealers
to carry on their illegal trade. . . ."—ALS, DNA, RG 59, Miscellaneous Letters.
On March 9, 1876, Vanorden wrote to USG concerning the persistence of this
slave trade in Brazil.—ALS, *ibid.*

1874, SEPT. 25.   To Alvin J. Johnson, New York City. "I find, awaiting my arrival here, a copy of your valuable publication the 'New Universal Cylcopaedia,'
which you were good enough to send to me, through the Secretary of State.

I beg to be allowed to give you my sincere thanks for the work, and for your thoughtful kindness in sending it to me. Should the succeeding volumes prove, as I have no doubt they will, as valuable as this first one, the complete work will supply a want long felt by furnishing a compact Cyclopaedia which will be available for all."—Copy, DLC-USG, II, 2. On Aug. 27, Secretary of State Hamilton Fish had written to USG concerning the work, "edited by President Barnard of Columbia College."—Copy, DNA, RG 59, Reports to the President and Congress.

On May 8, Adam Badeau, consul gen., London, had written to Orville E. Babcock. ". . . I enclose also the proof of my 'article' on 'General Grant' for the Cyclopedia of which I wrote you. Will you please read it to the President, and then send it with my accompanying letter enclosed according to the address. As you perceive I have taken the liberty of asking that the proof for the volume should be sent to you: I felt sure that you would be willing to revise it. I thought better not to go into details of the President's political career lest, the article might be excluded altogether, if I took too strong sides; and I thought it important to get into such a work ~~our~~ the correct view of the events of the last year of the war, and the correct statement of the figures. They are all carefully prepared. Perhaps it will be better to let my name appear. If the President or you should desire to have make any material change, I will thank you to write to the editor, telling him I am preparing the article, and to apprise me at once. . . ."—ALS (press), NjR. On Jan. 21, 1875, Badeau wrote to John Russell Young declining to write an advance obituary for USG.—ALS, DLC-John Russell Young.

1874, SEPT. 26. USG endorsement. "Refered to the Sec. of the Treas. in who department Mr. Ferguson previously served. If the place formerly filled by him in the 6th Auditor's Office can be given, or one equally good, it would seem from the within testimonial, to be worthily bestowed."—AES, DNA, RG 56, Applications. Written on a letter of Aug. 28 from Erasmus D. Hudson, New York City, "To whom this may concern." "The bearer John C. Ferguson a resident at Washington. D. C. the son of a poor widow. refugee from the South, in 1863, then at Alexandria, Va: was ran over by the Rail Road cars, and suffered amputation of both of his legs, when he was nine years old. Surgeon Edwin Bently, U. S. Army —then in charge of the United States Hospital at Alexandria and myself, were interested to furnish the boy prothetic apparatus—which, with his nice faculty and power to balance, have enabled him to walk commendably. . . ."—Copy, *ibid.* On Nov. 10, John C. Ferguson, Washington, D. C., wrote to USG. ". . . I called to see you about two months ago in regard to my being re-instated and you endorsed my papers. I took them to Sect'y Bristow, but he failed to do anything for me. Now Genl please help me if you dont I shall have to suffer. Hoping that you will aid me is my fervant prayer."—ALS, *ibid.* Related papers are *ibid.* As of Sept. 30, 1875, Ferguson worked as laborer, 6th Auditor's office.

1874, SEPT. 26. Fred Parkinson, Black Rock, Conn., to USG. "Will you Please try to get mee a situation in the United staes mint   if you will you will oblige a boy 15 yeares old and can do as mutch in one day as to men can do in one helf a day   i am working on a farm but i dont like farming and dont mean to work at it if i can help it and i gess i can help it   i dont no wetcher you are the man for me to write to or not and excuse me if your not the man   Please answer this letter ass soon ass conveneyant   excuse my writing and miss speled words"—ALS, DNA, RG 56, Letters Received from the President.

1874, SEPT. 29.   Kate Quinn, Harpers Ferry, West Va., to USG. ". . . My husband Matthew Quinn was a Sutler in the Union Army during the War and in a legitimate business transaction with one of the soldiers of the Regt, he came into possession of some Bonds of the Orange and Alexandria R. R. to the amount of ten thousand Dols,   After the War was over we were married, and he built a house and went into business, and we were getting along very happily: when an injunction was levied on his property by a man from Lynchburg Va (Samuel Miller) who said the bonds my husband sold a short time before were taken from his house by some soldiers in a raid made by the Federal Cavalry during the war (I think the raid was made by Gen. Hunter) . . . My husband died three years ago and as the debt has not been paid or any part of it, and I am utterly unable to pay it my Home is to be sold . . ."—ALS, DNA, RG 60, Letters from the President.

1874, SEPT. 30.   Joseph Walker, *Democratic Statesman*, Austin, to USG. "Mr. R. F. Campbell, of this city, makes application for the appointment of Collector of the 3rd Internal Revenue District. Mr. Campbell has been almost raised in Texas, and although he has acted with the Republican Party, he is regarded by Democrats as an honest man, and his appointment would be highly satisfactory to them. He is well known throughout the District; and would meet with no difficulty in giving a bond endorsed by the most wealthy men of this city. If the acquaintance of early, boyhood's years with your Excellency, has weight, I cheerfully recommend Mr. Campbell to your favorable consideration."—ALS, DNA, RG 56, Collector of Customs Applications. Related papers are *ibid.* On Dec. 8, 1875, USG nominated Robert F. Campbell as collector of Internal Revenue, 3rd District, Tex.

On Nov. 19, Bolivar C. Converse, Springfield, Ohio, had written to Secretary of the Treasury Benjamin H. Bristow opposing Campbell's appointment. ". . . I have in my possession a dearly-prized memento left me by my good mother whom General and Mrs Grant will recollect. It is a silver service sent to my mother by them for her kindness and attention to Mrs Fanny Simpkins, Aunt of Mrs Grant's, during her last illness at our house. . . ."—Copy, *ibid.*, Applications.

[*1874, Sept.*].   Mrs. D. H. Lagow, Versailles, Ky., to USG. "I hope you will pardon this intrusion But I think you will when I make known my object. My Stepson W. H. Lagow of Palestine Crawford County Illinois, aged sixteen years is very desirous of obtaining an appointment to enter West Point Military Institute. . . . He is the son of D H Lagow or who you, will perhaps better remember the nephew of and pet of Colonel C B Lagow whose love & admiration for you was unbounded . . ."—ALS (docketed Sept. 18, 1874), DNA, RG 94, Unsuccessful Cadet Applications.

1874, OCT. 1.   Ignatius Hole-in-the-day and six others, "White Earth Indian Reserve," Minn., to USG. "We the undersigned, chiefs on this Reservation salute you, and shake hands with you. We want to tell you openly and frankly, how we are treated here by your servants, our Indian Agents. We do not like it at all. A great deal of money is sent by you to us, but we allways get very little. The reason is, because, Bishop Whipple and Preacher Johnson are always helping the Agent to steal it from us, and to put it in their own pockets. . . . In this way we are trodden down by Bishop Whipple and the present Agent. If we do any work, we are never paid with money, as we ought, but only with old clothes in the socalled Hospital. We have everything to buy from the Agent, clothes, calico and everything what we need, though there are a great many things which we ought to get according to our treaty without paying for them. We have to work very hard, in order to get a little of any thing from him. So also our wifes must work very hard in order to get a little of any thing from him. If we work very hard the whole day, then we are said to have earned one dollar, but we never receive it in money, we only get a little flour for it, which is scarcely enough for half a meal for the whole family. If you our Great Father would know everything exactly, how we are treated here, you would be surely ashamed to have us treated this way. There are Indians on this Reservation that have not received their annual payment for two years. We know it very well that you sent the money for them to be paid to them. But they have not received it, it remained in the pockets of the Agents. A great many Indians even some chiefs, here are living yet in Wigwams of birch-bark because the Agent refuses to make houses for them, and also refuses to give them or to lend them oxen in order to be able to haul the logs and the lumber and to make the houses themselves. . . . This present Agent is Just like a tree. He never speaks a word to us. We want an Agent that will tell us what he was going to do, that we might know whether we want him to do that for us or not; and we do not want to have an Agent of this kind, as this one is, who is doing everything according to his own head and does not want to listen to us at all. Those three chiefs of whom he is taking such a good care, say that he and his clerk are good, but we say it, that they deserve to be very deep in hell. We therefore very respectfully request you, Our Great Father to take away from us this Agent and his clerk, and to send us an Agent that will serve and obey the Great Spirit in the same way and faith as our first Head-Chief, the son of the celebrated Hole-in-the-day Mi-no-gi-shig or Ignatius Hole-in-the-day, is proud to profess, and which is called the French or Catholic Religion. Then we are sure we will not be treated in such a wrong way but we and all our people will be satisfied and pleased, and always very thankful to you, Our Great Father of whom we know that you are always ready and willing to listen to our complaints and to comply with our requests. We will be satisfied only with a Catholic Agent, and we do not want any Agent of any other kind. We have had Agents enough of those other kinds and one was cheating and treating us worse than the other. We have, and always will have our full and entire confidence only in an Agent appointed by the Catholic Bishop of St Paul and we do not want to have any thing to do with the Protestant Bishop Whipple, because we know it for sure that he has been always helping the Agents to steal from us. Please answer us quick. We salute you our Great Father and shake hands with you . . . Number of Indians on this Reservation who give their full consent to the Petition of Ignatius Hole-in-the-day, etal: Heads of Families: 135; Indians: 754."—Copy, Marquette University, Milwaukee, Wis. On April 20,

USG had nominated Lewis Stowe as agent, Chippewa Agency, Minn. See *HED*, 43-2-1, part 5, I, 339–40, 503–4, 44-1-1, part 5, I, 800.

[*1874*], Oct. 2.   Chief Justice Morrison R. Waite to USG. "The bearer of this, Mr. Egbert E. Morse isa son of a friend of mine at Toledo, is anxious to obtain an appointment as second Lieut. in the army, and will call upon you to present himself and ask permission to go before the examining board, with a view to becoming a candidate for such an appointment if found to be competent. I know his father very well and esteem him highly. If it is consistent with the rules you have adopted for your guidance in this matter to grant the young gentleman's request, I shall be much gratified"—ALS (docketed Oct. 6, 1874), DNA, RG 94, Applications for Positions in War Dept. Related papers identifying Egbert E. Morse as a Cleveland police sgt. are *ibid.* No appointment followed.

1874, Oct. 3.   Reuben D. Mussey, Washington, D. C., to USG. "The purpose and object of the 'Labor Exchange' are expressed by the name of the Association. It is an effort to find work for those who are poor because they have no work; and workers for those whose capacity to produce is limited by their inability to secure labor. Our funds are used not in 'Alms' but in this bringing together of employer and employed. We hope in this way, to reduce, somewhat, the surplus of idle and unemployed persons who hang upon the borders of large cities and to augment production, agricultural and mechanical, in the small towns and the rural districts   The scheme contemplates, ultimately, colonization from the overstocked 'centres of population' into the sparsely settled regions of our country now unproductive because of the paucity of laborers. We believe that the judicious developement of this Plan will do very much to relieve the prevalent 'distress' and restore National prosperity. I was sure, before I spoke to you, that you would sympathize with it. And in behalf of my associates I thank you for your promised pecuniary aid. I venture to suggest that upon consideration of this plan you may see possibilities of its adaptation to our National necessities, that will entitle it to your Official recommendation to Legislative attention"—ALS, OFH.

1874, Oct. 7.   Hinton R. Helper, New York City, to USG. "The international matter at issue in this pamphlet, affecting the Government of Bolivia, in its long and gross delinquency toward our fellow-citizen, Joseph H. Colton, was introduced into the Congress of the United States, on the 7th of May, 1874, by Senator Conkling, of New York; and by him, at my request, it was referred to the Senate Committee on Foreign Affairs, by whom it has been considered and discussed several times; but, as yet, no definite conclusion has been reached. The case is still in suspense. In behalf of common justice to an outraged countryman, and in the interest of a more efficient and honorable system of diplomacy, I respectfully solicit your Excellency to invite the attention of Congress to this subject in your next annual message."—ALS, DNA, RG 59, Miscellaneous Letters. A copy of the pamphlet is *ibid.* On Oct. 8, Helper again wrote to USG concerning Joseph H. Colton.—LS, *ibid.* Related papers are *ibid.* On March 3, 1875, USG signed a bill requesting him to call upon the Bolivian government to pay Colton for maps engraved under an 1858 contract.—*U.S. Statutes at Large*, XVIII, part 3, p. 661. See *SRC*, 43-2-531.

On March 24 and Dec. 9, Helper wrote to USG. "In relation to the Act of Congress, approved on the 3d instant, requesting the President of the United States to call on the Government of Bolivia to pay the money so long overdue from itself to Mr. Joseph H. Colton, of this city, both the claimant and I (as his attorney,) have the honor to express the hope that your Excellency's request in the premises may be made so felicitously, and yet so promptly and so firmly, as to induce Bolivia's early compliance with both the letter and the spiri[t] of the said Act of Congress. . . ." ". . . I now deem it both my privilege and my duty to give you information of the favorable action which that Government,—moved by the intervention of our Congress at Washington,—has since taken in the claimant's behalf. . . ."—ALS, DNA, RG 59, Miscellaneous Letters.

1874, OCT. 10.   Matthew H. Kollock, Philadelphia, to USG. "I herewith most respectfully request the position of Consul, or Commercial Agent at Aspinwall New Grenada. I was born in Norfolk Virginia July 10. 1834. and during the War took sides with the Union Army and served as Contract Surgeon, much to my loss, as all my family have 'cut me off,' and hold no communication with me. Hoping to hear favorably from you . . ."—ALS, DNA, RG 59, Letters of Application and Recommendation. Related papers are *ibid.* No appointment followed. See *PUSG*, 15, 252.

1874, OCT. 12.   William P. Rucker, "late Maj 13th W. Va Infty, and Aid to Genl Crook," Lewisburg, West Va., to USG. "Col James W. Davis of Greenbrier county, West Virgina, who was bred, born and educated by a Thomas Jefferson grandmother, and a John C. Calhound mother, is not only a high toned christian gentleman, and first class lawyer of forty years experience, but also a true, active and unflinching republican. If Genl Goff, U. S. District Attorney for West Virginia, should be elected to Congress, for which all good republicans of this State hope and pray, I respectfully recommend Col Davis as his successor."—ALS, PPRF. James W. Davis had served with the C.S. Army. On May 13, 1876, USG renominated Nathan Goff, Jr., as U.S. attorney, West Va.

1874, OCT. 20.   Richard H. Henderson, Washington, D. C., to USG. "*On the 9th of April 1865, at Appomattox C. H.* my only surviving brother and myself, Officers in the Confederate Service, were the witnesses and partakers of your Excellency's magnanimity. We are of a military family. My father the late General Henderson, of Va, for 40 years Commandant of the U. S. Marine Corps, entered the service when war was imminent with Great Britain, . . . Having been unsuccessful in cotton planting, and having a Wife and children to support, I respectfully request that your Excellency will forward my case, for especial attention, to the Honorable Secretary of the Navy, in whose Department my father and brother served for so many years. But like them, I am willing to serve wherever the President may indicate, either at home or abroad, ashore or afloat; and having experienced General Grant's generosity on a momentous occasion, and standing near General Lee when that great Officer indicated to his Army, about to be surrendered, his sense of General Grant's magnanimity, I beg leave now, a second time, to invoke this high quality in behalf of myself and of my children."—ALS, DNA, RG 45, Letters Received from the President. A note from Henderson dated Oct. 26 requesting an interview with USG is *ibid.* No appointment followed.

1874, OCT. 20.   W. D. Pearsall, Kenansville, N. C., to USG. ". . . In your next message to Congress recommend an alteration in the fourteenth amendment to the U. S. Constitution & advocate payment to the South for their emancipated Slaves in the ratio once proposed by ₱President Lincoln—$300 per capita. You are aware that the Southern people were not solely responsible (or blamable if you will have it so) for Slavery. The whole United States stood equally guilty & it would be an act of justice to the Slave owner whose slaves were liberated to make him that much compensation. Let it be born in mind that the amt. is less than one half of their market value at the commencement of the war & that the South in the end would pay one third of the whole. Aside from its justice, it would be good policy; because it would once more unite the North & the South which is certainly very desirable. . . . Last & least (in a National Sense) it will add greatly to your individual fame and personal popularity. If you desire to be a Candidate again for the Presidency it would almost insure your Nomination & election. If the Northern Republicans acquiesce they would win the whole South over to their Party. If they oppose it—the South would approve—Make it a Democratic Measure—take you for their leader & carry with them enough of the North west to elect you. So far as you are concerned let the result be as it may with Parties you would succeed. . . ."—ALS, DNA, RG 60, Letters from the President.

1874, OCT. 21.   2nd Lt. William W. Robinson, Jr., USMA 1869, Chippewa Falls, Wis., to USG. "In the Spring of 1873 while on your western tour, you had the kindness to give me a personal interview on the cars between Denver and Cheyenne in relation to an appointment for my father Col. William W. Robinson for some position under your administration. At this time you advised me to obtain the recommendations of Senator Howe or Carpenter and directed me to place the papers I had submitted to you in Genl Babcock's hands.—I have the honor to transmit herewith letters of recommendation from both of the Senators as also one from Hon A. S. McDill—Col Robinson's local representative and the personal application of the latter for a Consular appointment to some English or Spanish speaking port. . . ."—LS, DNA, RG 59, Letters of Application and Recommendation. The enclosures and related papers are *ibid.* On March 12, 1875, USG nominated William W. Robinson, former col., 7th Wis., as consul, Tamatave, Madagascar.

1874, OCT. 21.   U.S. Representative Alexander Stephens of Ga., Crawfordville, to USG. "Having been informed a few days ago that the Deputy *Marshallship* of this State had become vacant by the resignation of Mr. Chamberlain at Atlanta I took the liberty of telegraphing to Mr. Atty Genl. Williams the name of Mr. David A. Newsom of Union Point in Greene County as a suitable person to fill the place; and I trust you will now excuse me for addressing you these lines upon the same subject. Mr. Newsom is the person in whose behalf I spoke to you specially last winter in case any suitable position for him should occur in the State—I know him well—He has been a Republican ever since the war—In his sentiments in this particular it is well known I did not concur—But I believe him to be an honest and up right man and that he would make a faithful officer —that is what the people of Georgia chiefly want—I know he is a warm & Steadfast friend of yours and of your administration, and I do not believe you could find any man of this class in the State who would make a better Deputy Marshal—"—ALS, DNA, RG 60, Records Relating to Appointments.

1874, OCT. 23.   Robert Tyler, editor, *Morning News,* Montgomery, Ala., to USG. "Will it be agreeable to the President of the U. S. to receive from the Bar of Alabama a recommendation for the Appointment to the Judgeship made vacant by the resignation of Judge Busted"—Telegram received, DNA, RG 60, Letters from the President. On Dec. 18, USG nominated Lewis E. Parsons as judge, Ala.; on Feb. 23, 1875, he withdrew this nomination and nominated instead John Bruce. See *PUSG,* 22, 293, 333–34; *ibid.,* 24, 417.

On Oct. 16, 1874, Milton J. Saffold, Washington, D. C., had written to USG. "I respectfully apply for Appointment to the Vacant United States District Judgeship, for Alabama—*Vice* Hon. Richard Busteed; resigned. My sole hope of appointment is that, Your Excellency will enquire into, and pass upon my merits, upon your own, independant judgement—regardless of the fact that, I seek no recommendations from either party organization, in Alabama. . . . I quit the democratic party in 1859, because of its advocacy of Secession. I believe that, I was the first Native to avow adhesion to the republican party, even before the close of the war. . . . The Enfranchisement of the negro turned the fruits of many years of Effort, in support of 'loyalty', *to ashes on my lips.* It drove from me, and from the republican party, Nearly all of My white political friends, who had acted with me from 1859 to 1866. It made the republican party, in Alabama, a *Negro party.* The Effect of this, Was to place the political Control of the party in the hands of the very worst of both Colors. To understand how, it has this effect, one must be on the ground, observing it, as I have been, for the past five years. In my native County, of Dallas, at the last County Convention of this year, I saw a notorious negro cotton thief, as chairman of the Convention with an equally Notorious white penetentiary convict, as Chairman of the Committee on credentials Controlling twenty five or thirty professional hired negro politicians, the worst men of the Community, on the front seats of the Convention hall *run out of the Convention,* the Hon Alexr White M. C. from the State at large & Hon. B. F. Saffold, my brother, Judge of the Supreme Court of the State, by incessant yelling, and conduct resembling a heathen orgie, kept up for several hours, at a time, to prevent these gentlemen from being heard, in protest against their disgraceful conduct. The Democratic Charge that, the present organization of the Republican Party, in Alabama, supported in power by the Federal Government, places the State in the hands of 'thieves, fools, & criminals' *is, literally true.* There are a few men of ability honesty and high character, still connected with the organization; but; they have no influence with the Masses, Other

than that, they are Needed, and retained in the party, only, to prevent the organization from sinking beneath the weight of its vallanies—and, thus destroying the opportunity of thieves & Criminals to plunder. The Colored Masses Can
only be controlled by Corrupt means. This draws Corrupt white men, into the
party, to control them. The Corruption goes on, under the eye of the honest
& respectable republican; the Moment he protests against it, *he is Cut down.* I
made War on this Evil in 1870 and they *Cut me down.* For five years, I think, I
have seen, & have Maintained, that, it is as unnatural & impossible, to Maintain
the negro element on top, in the former slave States, by federal power, as it is
to keep water on the surface of oil—while the pernicious effect of the effort is
painfully visible daily, in the Anarchical Condition of Alabama, & other States,
South. I believe that,—if the Democratic party succeed, in the pending Election,
in Alabama—And the Federal Government will leave the Matter alone, to local influences,—it will result in a division of the Negro Vote, under the leadership of Whites, about equal in Numbers and Character—and that, this is the
only hopeful solution of a deplorable Condition. If the appointment, to the
Judgeship, is Made, at the dictation of Republican Congressmen, from Alabama,
interested in maintaining the present deplorable condition of the State, in order that, they may be retained in power—I am aware of the fact that, I stand
no chance whatever to get it. . . ."—ALS, DNA, RG 60, Records Relating to
Appointments.

On Nov. 3, Joseph P. Bradley, U.S. Supreme Court, wrote to USG. "I enclose
to you by request, some memorials from members of the Bar of Alabama, recommending *Peter Hamilton* of Mobile for the office of District Judge of the
United States for the District of Alabama. . . . It is due to you, Sir, however, that
I should also add, that I do not mean to depreciate the claims of other candidates. I have placed in the hands of Secretary Robeson, some time since, memorials equally strong, perhaps, in favor of the appointment of Charles Turner
of Selma; who, I believe, would also be a most accomplished and acceptable
judge. . . ."—ALS, *ibid.* On Dec. 9, John Tucker, New York City, wrote to USG.
"You may remember some years ago, I stated to you that in my judgement, one
of the chief difficulties with which the South had to contend was a corrupt or
incompetent Judiciary. I had sad confirmation of this conclusion, when Judge
Busted was U. S. District Judge in Alabama. I was mainly instrumental in obtaining an act of Congress (as you may remember) to deprive him of his Circuit
Court powers, and to remove an important Case I had before him (the foreclosure of the mortgages of the Selma Rome & Dalton RR Co) to Judge Woods.
U. S. Circuit Court, by which tribunal the decisions of Busteed were substantially rescinded. The Case was then transferred to the Chancery Court of the
Middle District of Alabama over which Chancellor Charles Turner presided. In
a most important point in the case he decided against us but sustained his views
with such marked legal ability as to command my great respect. I can confidently state to you that his integrity as well as legal ability, so far as my knowledge extends, and it is quite general, is *universally* conceded by political friends
and foes. As a politician he is as good a Republican as a Judge should be. . . ."—
ALS, *ibid.* Related papers are *ibid.*

On Nov. 12, Henry Cochran, postmaster, Selma, had written to USG. "You have no doubt heard long before this of the defeat of our Party in this State. But our defeat is not so great as in other states—And were it not for the violence and dishonesty used we would have won—But it may be for the best as we were not Careful enough in our selections of good men for office—there was too many dishonest and incompetent we got into our Party; and it weighed it down. The Colored men also, I mean the leading Polittcians denounced too much but the next Two years under a Democratic Government that will Rule with an Iron Sway will Cure all this   until then the great pitty is our Best Men must suffer for the Acts Committed by the bad—And one among them is the Hon B. S. Saffold a true old Union Man during the war and a Stanch Republican Since, . . ."—ALS, *ibid.* On Nov. 17, John H. Henry, Selma, wrote to USG. "The result of our election has stricken down the very best of our Republicans in Alabama   Amongst these is Hon B F Saffold who became one of the justices of the Supreme Court on the restoration of the Union in 1868. He was a candidate for relection on the Republican ticket and shared the fate of our party   The election was unfairly carried in favor of the Democrats, as the unprecedented vote cast for them shows   But we do not see how under existing laws the fraud perpetrated by them can be resisted in another campign   The colored votes in large portions of the State cannot withstand their aggressive bearing, and are neither shrewd nor bold enough to oppose their artifices . . ."—ALS, *ibid.* On Dec. 11, David Davis, U.S. Supreme Court, wrote to USG recommending Benjamin F. Saffold.—ALS, *ibid.* Related papers are *ibid.* On Dec. 15, H. A. McNeill, Rome, N. Y., wrote to USG. "Seeing that you are about to appoint a Judge to fill the vacancy occasioned by the resignation of Judge Busteed Allow me to beg and entreat that you do not appoint Judge Saffold, & for the following reason He is related to a family against whom I have a heavy claim in the U. S. District court. Saffold has already expressed his desire that I loose the claim & if he gets the Judgeship I firmly believe I shall loose it. Had Judge Busteed acted honestly I should have got it long ago   So if you please dont let another dishonest man have the office"—ALS, *ibid.*, Letters from the President.

On Dec. 3, U.S. Representative Alexander Stephens of Ga. had written to USG. "I take this method of urging upon your consideration as I have upon that of the atty Genl, the appointment of Hon. Samuel F. Rice of Montgomery Ala —to fill the vacant Judgeship in that District occasioned by the resignation of Judge Busted—Be assured in my judgment this is the best appointment that can be made in view of all the surroundings—It will give satisfaction where satisfaction is needed—"—ALS, *ibid.*, Records Relating to Appointments. Related papers are *ibid.*

On Feb. 3, 1875, C. F. Moulton, Mobile, wrote to USG. "In the event of the failure of the Senate, to confirm the nomination of Mr. Parsons, may I venture to suggest the name of Judge, Alexander McKinstry, of this place for the position of District Judge? In the past, the Union elements South, have been almost ignored by the Federal Courts. For God-sake gives us a man who will hold the scales of Justice with a firm even hand. That is all I ask,—not a man, who, like the judges of the present and the past, would bend before the assaults of rebel *insolence* and *persecutions*. In the name of common justice, give to us, of this State, this protection. In it, will center our last hope, should the present Congress expire without extending to us protection. We can trust Gov. McKinstry. He is qualified, he has been tried and not found wanting. In the event of the adjournment of *this* Congress, without placing these States under military rule, or placing the *power* in your hands, of extending to the Union element South, protection, as I live, I utter the truth, that the Republicans of the Southern States, will at once pass out of existence; and in the contest of 1876, there will not be a republican journal published South of Masons & Dixons Line—there will not be permitted, in a Single Southern State, a republican presidential ticket to be run and every man, South, who has been at all prominent in opposition to the 'White Leagues', will be murdered or driven from these States. *These are words of warning and words of truth!*"—ALS, *ibid.* Related papers are *ibid.*

Papers recommending Joseph W. Burke, L. C. Coulson, James S. Clarke, David P. Lewis, Adam C. Felder, and David Clopton as judge, Ala., are *ibid.*

1874, OCT. 24.   Robert T. Lincoln, Chicago, to USG. "I am informed that Henry Foster, son of James H. Foster Esq of this city, is very desirous of being appointed a Cadet at the Military Academy at West Point, and that he would have been nominated by our Member of Congress, the Hon John B. Rice, at the last opportunity, if his age had then been sufficient—Inasmuch as Mr Rice was on this account compelled to pass him by, he is now seeking from you an appointment at Large and I take great pleasure in joining the other friends of himself and his family, who will address you, in asking that you should nominate him as I believe that he is a very worthy young man and if selected will do credit to the service—"—ALS, DNA, RG 94, Correspondence, USMA. Related papers are *ibid.* Henry Foster did not attend USMA.

1874, OCT. 26.   John D. Thorne, Littleton, N. C., to USG. ". . . Now how can this unhappy State of affairs in the South be remedied. I suppose only by your forcing a free expression of the Ballot—by a dismissal of all officials who are so ultra or extreme in sentiment as to have a befogged judgment in the discharge of duty and consequently liable to err through prejudice—and to install men who love their *whole* country—cool and deliberate in action and who have patriotism sufficient to immolate themselves if neccessary upon their Countrys Altar for her good—we want no more time servers, greedy Cormorants whose selfish aggrandisement is the goal of ambition. Allow the States to settle their internal dissensions in their own way so long as they respect the general government.   do away with the Elective (judiciary a most corrupt and blighting system) and we will soon be a reunited & happy people, obeying the behests of the *great lawgiver* of the Universe, without which we can in no sense prosper . . ." —ALS, DNA, RG 60, Letters from the President.

1874, OCT. 27.   USG endorsement. "The within request is approved, and the reservations are made accordingly. The Secretary of the Interior will cause the same to be noted in the General Land Office."—Copies, DNA, RG 94, Military Reservation Div.; *ibid.*, RG 107, Letters Sent, Military Affairs; *ibid.*, RG 153, Military Reservation Files, S. C. Written on a letter of Oct. 12 from Secretary of War William W. Belknap to USG recommending military reservations at

Hilton Head and Bay Point, Phillips Island, S. C.—Copies as listed above. Also in 1874, USG ordered land set aside for military reservations in Neb. (Fort Hartsuff and Sidney Barracks) and Nev. (near Carlin), and to enlarge Fort Boise, Idaho Territory.—Copies, *ibid.,* RG 94, Military Reservation Div.; *ibid.,* RG 107, Letters Sent, Military Affairs. On April 14, USG approved land purchases in Tex. for Forts McKavett, Concho, Clark, McIntosh, Brown, and Griffin, and for Ringgold Barracks.—*HED,* 43-1-282, 12, 24, 29, 32, 34, 35, 36; *HMD,* 50-1-419, 127 (Fort Brown).

1874, OCT. 27.   Cheney R. Prouty, collector of customs, Indianola, Tex., to USG. "Telegraphic dispatches say I have been removed as collector of this port and Judge Ogden appointed but declines   My resignation is at your disposal whenever you feel it to public or party interest but as matter of Justice If any charges are against me I hope I may be allowed an opportunity to refute them by investigation"—Telegram received (at 6:35 P.M.), DNA, RG 56, Letters Received from the President. On Oct. 26, Wesley Ogden, San Antonio, had telegraphed to Secretary of the Treasury Benjamin H. Bristow. "Circumstances forbid my acceptance of the honor you propose and I would respectfully suggest the present incumbent is an efficient and honest officer"—Telegram received (at 9:55 P.M.), *ibid.* Prouty remained in office.

1874, OCT. 28.   USG endorsement. "Refered to the Sec. of the Treas."—AES, DNA, RG 56, Appraiser of Customs Applications. Written on a letter of Sept. 16 from Henry H. Goldsborough, Easton, Md., to USG. "I am advised that Mr. Samuel E Dyott of Queen Anne's County in this Congressional District will be the applicant for the post of Appraiser in Baltimore City about to be vacated by the removal of Col. Anderson. I take great pleasure in saying that I have known Mr. Dyott for many years as an active, influential man in the Republican ranks, ready to do us essential and valuable service at all times and upon all occasions, and I am confident this post could be bestowed upon no one who would discharge the duties of the Office with more fidelity to the interest of the Government, and with more acceptibility to the people generally of this State—. . ." —ALS, *ibid.* On March 13, 1873, Charles C. Fulton, *Baltimore American,* had written to USG. "I am informed that Colonel Ephraim F. Anderson, is an applicant for reappointment to his present position of Appraiser of Customs. Colonel Anderson bears many honorable wounds received in the service, is a thorough gentleman, and commands the respect and esteem of the Commercial community. His record at the Treasury Department is understood to be good, and I therefore cheerfully commend his application to your favorable consideration"—ALS, *ibid.* Related papers are *ibid.* On Dec. 19, 1874, USG nominated Augustus W. Bradford as appraiser, Baltimore, in place of Ephraim F. Anderson. On Dec. 22, Bradford, Washington, D. C., wrote to USG. "The morning Papers of today have brought to my notice the fact, that you yesterday did me the honor to nominate me to the Senate for the office of Appraiser general of merchandise in the Baltimore CustomsHouse. Whilst tendering you my cordial thanks for the nomination, I consider it due to you as well as to myself to state why I feel constrained to decline it. The office is one that Seems to me to require the Ser-

vices of some experienced and judicious merchant, and my own past pursuits
have been so entirely outside of such a sphere—without either mercantile education or experience,—that I can not but feel, that for me to undertake to discharge the duties of Such an Office, would make me entirely dependent upon
Deputies or Assistants. To accept any office under Such circumstances would be
altogether repugnant to my notions of Official qualifications and responsibility,
and I beg therefore Sir, that you will withdraw my name from the consideration
of the Senate and Substitute Some other   Whilst I have thus expressed the
chief, if not the only reason that prompts me to this course, I trust I Shall be understood, that in coming to this conclusion, nothing like hostility or opposition
either to yourself or your Administration has mingled with the motives that
have actuated me; On the contrary, I beg leave to assure you, that for the one as
for the other, I cherish nothing but the best wishes and the kindliest feelings."—
Copy, Maryland Historical Society, Baltimore, Md.

On Dec. 23, Vaughan Smith, "Pastor M. E. Church," Centerville, Md., wrote
to USG. "Will you please excuse me for again calling your attention to the application of Mr S. E. Dyott who is an applicant for the position of 1st. Appraiser
in the Custom House at Baltimore   The reasons for the liberty I again presume
to take, arise from the reported declination of that appointment, by Gov. Bradford, which as we have understood again throws the position open. Allow me to
say that in my interview with you—you were pleased to give me to hope, that
if Mr Anderson were removed, the probalities were in favor of my estimable,
friend & brother, Mr Dyott. Gov. Bradford, we understand declines the position
on the ground of his supposed want of qualification, with the idea also that a
merchant ought to have the place. Now Mr Dyott *is* a merchant of twenty years
standing, & fully conversant with the general details of the business of the department toward which he aspires; & particularly, with the articles of Sugars
& molasses. His circumstances too, owing as I believe, to his stern adherence to
his political principles, have been seriously compromised; burdened as he is with
a large family. . . ."—ALS, DNA, RG 56, Appraiser of Customs Applications. Related papers are *ibid.* On Dec. 24, William Thomson, Baltimore, wrote to USG.
"Learning that Gov. Bradford has declined the appointment of Appraiser in the
Baltimore Custom House, and believing that it would be greatly to the advantage of the Republican Party in Maryland that his successor should come from
that branch of the party which has heretofore been entirely ignored under your
administration, until the appointment of Gov B., I take the liberty of making
application for the vacant Appraisership. . . ."—ALS, *ibid.* Papers recommending Robert L. Widdicombe, John R. Fellman, Hooper C. Hicks, Sewell T. Mil-
bourne, William L. W. Seabrook, and Thomas R. Rich are *ibid.*

On Jan. 5, 1875, James W. Clayton, asst. clerk, U.S. House of Representatives,
telegraphed to Orville E. Babcock from the Capitol. "Mr Booth asked me to remind you of the nomination of Henry H. Goldsborough for appraiser at Baltimore. He desires to have it made today if possible"—Telegram received, *ibid.*,
RG 107, Telegrams Collected (Bound). On the same day, USG nominated Goldsborough. On March 15, 1869, Goldsborough had written to USG. "I beg leave
to present an application for the post of Naval Officer in the Custom House

in Baltimore City and refer to the many responsible positions, to which I have been elected by the loyal people of Maryland recited below, as the best evidence of my patriotism and fidelity to the principles of the Republican party, since the Commencement of our National difficulties . . ."—ALS, *ibid.*, Naval Officer Applications. On March 18, Philip T. Tyson, Baltimore, wrote to USG. "when I had the pleasure to be introduced to you recently by Mr Albert, I recollect of remarking that I was not an applicant for office & I am not now. I cannot refrain however from asking that the case of H H Goldsboro of Talbot co be favorable considered. . . . He has been from the first a firm friend of the Union & in favor of abolishing slavery in Md, having in the beginning of the war set free a large number of slaves that belonged to him"—ALS, *ibid.* Related papers are *ibid.*

1874, Oct. 28.   Clement A. Finley, West Philadelphia, to USG. "The youngest of my six sons has expressed a desire to be appointed a Cadet at West Point, & as I consider him well qualified for the situation, mentally, morally, & physically, I very respectfully & earnestly request that he may receive that appointment from you—I inclose the certificate of the Secretary of the Faculty of the University of Pennsylvania, giving his class average, which places him No. 2. in a class of 35.   he is between 17 & 18 years of age, healthy, & I beleive without any bad habit, not using tobacco in any of its forms. Fifty six years on the army register, is my only plea for making this request—"—ALS, DNA, RG 94, Correspondence, USMA. George W. Childs and Anthony J. Drexel favorably endorsed this letter.—ES (undated), *ibid.* Walter L. Finley, whose father had been surgeon gen., graduated USMA in 1879.

1874, Oct. 29.   Levi P. Luckey to Secretary of State Hamilton Fish. "The President directs me to request you to have the papers, on file in your department, in the application for a consulship by B. P. Brasher, of Cin. returned to this office." —ALS, DNA, RG 59, Letters of Application and Recommendation. Papers recommending B. P. Brasher are *ibid.* On Nov. 9, Fish recorded in his diary a conversation with USG. "He said there was a man by name of Brashear whose family are from same town in Ohio in which he was raised, who wanted a Consulate on Mediterranean or some mild climate on account of his health, that he was very highly recommended & he would like to appoint him to Malaga in place of Hancock who was credited to Kentucky & of whom Secy of the Treasury (Bristow) says 'he knows not why he was retained or why he ever was appointed',— that Brashear has been for a long time a clerk in Treasury or Internal Revenue Service & that Secries of Treasury & Interior are anxious for his appointment —I reply that this is the old story of other Departments turning over their incapables & crowding them on State Department—that I know nothing of the man, except that he has on his recommendations some of the worst names that are in the habit of coming to the Department, such as Flanagan of Texas, Conover of Florida, Spencer of Alabama, Kellogg of Louisa, Butler of Tennessee & others—I add that Hancock does not stand particularly high in the Depart', was a friend of Mr Creswell's & had frequently been brought home at request of Republicans of Maryland to aid in their Campaign,—he says he has been in office since 1861—It is not particularly Malaga to which he wishes to send him, but some southern climate as he is threatened with Bright's disease—"—DLC-Hamilton Fish. No appointment followed.

1874, OCT. 29.   Levi P. Luckey to AG Edward D. Townsend. "The President directs me to return to the War Dept: the papers in the case of Capt. Nash, & say that he desires no action to be taken until he and the Secretary of War can have a consultation on the subject."—Copy, DLC-USG, II, 2. On June 9, Townsend had written to Commanding Gen., Div. of the South, Louisville. "The President directs that if there is no further charge against Captain W. H. Nash, Commissary Subsistence than drinking, he may be relieved on the pledge which he has given and the Court Martial in his case be suspended."—Copy, DNA, RG 94, Letters Sent. On July 3, Maj. Thomas M. Vincent, asst. AG, wrote to the same officer. ". . . I am instructed by the Secretary of war to inform you that as it now appears there are further charges against Captain Nash, the President directs that his trial go on."—Copy, *ibid.* Capt. William H. Nash retired as brig. gen. in 1898.

1874, OCT. 30.   USG endorsement. "Refered to the Sec. of the Treas. for consideration."—AES, DNA, RG 56, Applications. Written on papers recommending Emma Childs, a Baltimore native, for a clerical position in the Treasury Dept.—*Ibid.* On Aug. 12, 1875, Childs, Washington, D. C., wrote to Secretary of the Treasury Benjamin H. Bristow that she "never had any particular occupation excepting one month in the Currency Division, on the lapse fund. I was in the army of the Potomac with my husband where I nursed the sick and wounded soldiers. . . ."—ALS, *ibid.*

1874, OCT. 31.   Joseph Henry to USG. "I have the honor to acknowledge the receipt of the supposed gold ore transmitted to you by Messrs. Cleveland and Northrop, of West Camden, N. Y, and submitted by you to this Institution for examination, and beg leave to inform you that due attention will be given to your request on the return of our mineralogist, who is shortly expected home from the Far West."—LS (press), Smithsonian Institution Archives. On Nov. 21, Henry wrote to USG that these ore specimens contained gold traces too small to support profitable mining.—LS (press), *ibid.*

1874, Nov. 2.   Daniel Brock, Fillmore, Mo., to USG. "We deem it necessary (as Congress meets in a month) to remind you of a matter of National importance, we being somewhat connected with it can speak of our own knowledge; some two years ago we organized an Association known as the National Conciliatory Claims Association, for amicable adjustment of a class of claims which we knew must come up for settlement in some way; being mostly Administration men, and believing that the question could be disposed of better under the present Administration than in the event of a change, which is highly probable; we allude to claims for Slaves belonging to Loyal Citizens of the South set free under Lincoln's Proclamation without provision for indemnity.   having traveled extensively in the late Slave States organizing Branch Associations for the

Registry and preservation of such claims as were entitled to indemnity we found the claims generally preserved with age, Sex and their market value, yet would willingly take one half or less.   would it not be well to meet this class of claims by Legislation,   the Association have over a half Milion claims Registered with the necessary vouchers   the object of the organization was to act as a Conservative party to effect a Conciliation   we will send a clipping from the Toledo (Ohio) Blade   it corroborates our statement.   we know the abolition of Slavery under the Proclamation was unconstitutional and can so show it,   why not have all claims against the Government presented and let them stand on their own merits.   it is no longer a question (only a question of time) that unless timely Legislation is had that we will have every slave to pay for and that at market value, as we have the controling interest in this class of claims by virtue of agreement and Registry, and that they can be settled at a very low figure within the next year,   if not settled in that time the Registry will be preserved for future use; please excuse our calling your attention to this matter, but we Americans cannot help thinking that is the privilege of every American Citizen   we concede that to others,   we have been thinking of this matter since the first news of the Proclamation reached us, and we have not been alone thinking   we have the best Counsel in the United States with a good Attorney in every Branch in the South making over fifty Attorney's besides hundreds of wealthy and influential Citizens   all we ask is an investigation of this matter that justice may be meeted out to those to whom it is due"—ALS, USG 3. The enclosure is *ibid.*

1874, Nov. 2.   Sarah A. Rogers, Lockport, N. Y., to USG. "Whilst at the North some seven years ago I adopted a little boy, and took him South with me. We came up from Louisiana last January, and meaning to return again this Fall I let the child who is now only nine years, and a half of age play about much as he pleased. The Police force of this town being somewhat Zealous in the cause of justice arrested this child on a charge of stealing a Watch—the theft of which he was entirely ignorant of being with me at the time the Watch was stolen, at the other end of Lockport in church. They coerced the child into an acknowledgement of the theft frightening him out of his wits—then convicted him —locked him up, and sent for me. The next morning they sent the child to the House of Refuge at Rochester wither I accompanied him. I stated the case to the Managers, and the reply was no earthly power could get the child out   No! not even the President. Now as I am waiting to return to Louisiana, and I cannot leave the little defenceless, innocent boy in his prisonhouse behind me I apply to you knowing that if you will, a word from you—say in the shape of a pardon can release this child. President Grant let me not ask for your interference in vain, . . ."—ALS, DNA, RG 60, Letters from the President. A clipping advertising a twenty dollar reward for information about the theft is *ibid.* No pardon followed.

1874, Nov. 9.   USG endorsement. "Refered to the Sec. of War. This applicant may be placed on the list of alternates for the class of /75 next below those already designated. He may also be placed on the list of alternates—first—for the class of /76."—AES, DNA, RG 94, Correspondence, USMA. Written on a letter of Nov. 1 from U.S. Senator John H. Mitchell of Ore. to USG recommending George W. Upton, "son of Hon. W. W. Upton, late Chief Justice of the Supreme Court of the State of Oregon," for an at large appointment to USMA.— ALS, *ibid.* Related papers are *ibid.* Upton entered USMA in 1876 but did not graduate.

1874, Nov. 9.   Orville E. Babcock to Secretary of the Treasury Benjamin H. Bristow. "The President directs me to inform you that if there is a vacancy in the office of Collector of Customs at Toledo Ohio—that he desires to appoint Mr. John W. Fuller, a gentleman with whom he has been acquainted many years."—LS, DNA, RG 56, Collector of Customs Applications. A related paper is *ibid.* USG also wrote an undated note. "John W. Fuller, Toledo O. recommended for Consul to St. John, N. B. vice D. B. Warner."—AN, Columbia University, New York, N. Y. On Dec. 7, 1874, USG nominated John W. Fuller as collector of customs, Miami District, Ohio, to replace Patrick S. Slevin. See letter to Chester A. Arthur, Sept. 23, 1882.

1874, Nov. 11.   Chester A. Arthur, collector of customs, New York City, to USG. "I have pleasure in informing you that the Champagne about which you spoke to me, consisting of 200 dozen Quarts and 10 dozen pints, has just been received per S. S. 'Swevia,' and is now in store awaiting your instructions. Please advise me what disposition you desire to have made of it."—ALS, USG 3. See *PUSG,* 24, 226–27.

On Nov. 27, Levi P. Luckey wrote to Secretary of the Treasury Benjamin H. Bristow. "The bill for the Champagne has been received and paid by the President. It amounts to $15.37½ per Case. Your share for ten cases is $153.75."— LS, DLC-Benjamin H. Bristow.

On Nov. 28, Lt. Gen. Philip H. Sheridan, Chicago, wrote to USG. "The express brought me yesterday five cases of your wine sent by General Arthur. It is very fine, much drier and better than can be obtained here and I sincerely thank you for remembering me. If Gen. Babcock will at any time send the bill, I will send him check for it. We have excellent sleighing this morning which you would doubtless enjoy if you were out here with some of your St. Louis fast horses that take premiums. Kind regards to Mrs. Grant."—Copy, DLC-Philip H. Sheridan.

1874, Nov. 12.   Levi P. Luckey to T. Con. Morford, cashier, Long Branch Banking Co. "By the President's direction I enclose you his check for $512.75/100 the amount due from him on the increased capital of the 'Long Branch Banking Company,' as shown by the statement in your letter received yesterday; and also the proxy."—Copy, DLC-USG, II, 2. On Nov. 13, Morford's clerk, Long Branch, wrote to USG. "Your favor of 12th inst is received with contents as stated. Enclosed please find Certificate of Stock for Ten shares"—ALS, USG 3.

1874, Nov. 12.   Levi P. Luckey to M. Werk & Co., Cincinnati. "The President directs me to acknowledge the receipt of your letter of the 6th inst. notifying him of the shipment of the wine, and to enclose you his check for eighty dollars

40/100, the amount of the bill. He desires me to convey to you many thanks for the case of 'Golden Eagle' which you were kind enough to send him."—Copy, DLC-USG, II, 2. See Charles Frederic Goss, *Cincinnati: The Queen City 1788– 1912* (Chicago, 1912), IV, 244–49.

1874, Nov. 14.   USG endorsement. "The within recommendations are hereby approved. The authority asked for is conferred, and the order of November 3, 1869, is revoked."—*HRC*, 44-1-440, 283. Written on a letter of Nov. 12 from Secretary of the Interior Columbus Delano to USG, recommending the release of land granted to the Union Pacific and Central Pacific railroads but withheld pending their completion "as first-class railroads."—*Ibid.*

1874, Nov. 16.   Anna F. Smith, Denver, to USG. "As a soldiers widow I apply to you to ascertain if there is a national home for soldiers orphans. I have one son 12 years of age—he is getting beyond my control and I am desireous of getting him into a Government scholl where he will be under strict discipline . . ." —ALS, DNA, RG 94, Letters Received, 4984 1874. The National Soldiers' and Sailors' Orphans' Home was located in Washington, D. C.

1874, Nov. 19.   USG pardon on grounds of insanity for John M. Cooper, who "pleaded guilty to the charge of embezzling letters, while in the Post Office employ."—Copy, DNA, RG 59, General Records. On July 23, Governor Cyrus C. Carpenter of Iowa had written to USG. ". . . Mr. Cooper's family are among the most patriotic, intelligent, and worthy of our citizens. John, himself, at the beginning of the war entered the Army a noble and ambitious young man, and after three years' faithful service, came home with broken health growing out of injuries received in the line of his duty as a Soldier, and subject to turns of mental hallucination rendering him unfit for severe and exacting labor. Under these circumstances his friends hoped that he could perform the duties of a Postal Clerk and that the change of employment and the nature of the duties would be beneficial to his health, and afford his family the means of support. But unfortunately, in one of the intervals of his mental irresponsibility he committed the offense for which he has been indicted. His detection was in his efforts to make restitution when he come to his right mind. . . ."—ALS, *ibid.*, RG 60, Letters Received, Western District, Mo. On July 27, William H. Buis, Kansas City, Mo., wrote to USG. "I was Route agent at the time J. M Cooper, was arrested   Was with him on the Same Route Boarded with his Family for some time and knew him well, and thought him an honest man. From my knowledge of the man and the circumstances in the case, I fully satisfied if a crime was committed he was not concious of it and Should not be held morrally Responsible   he has a wife and four small children without means of support,   the case is certainly one of mercy"—ALS, *ibid.* U.S. Senator George G. Wright and U.S. Representative James W. McDill of Iowa also wrote to USG in support of Cooper.—ALS, *ibid.* Related papers are *ibid.*

1874, Nov. 23.   David R. Lindsay, Tuscumbia, Ala., to USG. "Last night this town was visited by a tornado which destroyed a large portion of its houses.

Ten persons were killed. As a consequence destitution prevails to an extent that no language can express. There is no money in this county, and the sufferings of the destitute cannot be relieved by individuals, and it is therefore this appeal is made to your Excellency for immediate relief by the order of a supply of rations, and I am authorized by a large town meeting to make this appeal. Hoping and believing that your Excellency will respond promptly and plentifully." —*New York Times*, Nov. 25, 1874. Mayor Henry F. Newsom of Tuscumbia favorably endorsed this telegram.—*Ibid.* On Nov. 24, Secretary of War William W. Belknap telegraphed to Lindsay and Newsom. "The President in reply to your telegram of November 23d greatly regrets that he is unable to comply with your request. The limited appropriations for Subsistence for the Army will not permit him to issue the Subsistence stores required."—Copy, DNA, RG 107, Letters Sent, Military Affairs.

1874, Nov. 25. Secretary of State Hamilton Fish to USG. "I enclose a letter which comes to me from one Jerry Rickard, from Beloit, requesting me to transmit to you one enclosed therein. I have no knowledge whatever of the writer, or of the purport of his letter to you."—LS (press), DLC-Hamilton Fish.

1874, Nov. 26. Daniel Gano Ray, Hanover, Germany, to USG. "The undersigned, of Cincinnati, Ohio, at present abroad, begs most respectfully to present the name of his son, John Burt Ray to His Excellency the President of the United States for an appointment at large—to the Military Academy at West Point for the year 1876. When Cincinnati was a village my great grandfather, Major General John S. Gano was in command at Fort Washington; and he had, also, a command in the Ohio Forces in the war of 1812. . . . John Burt Ray was born Sept 28th 1858 in New York during a temporary stay of the family there. I can affirm him to be a boy of good moral character, sound constitution, clear head and of great energy and pluck. . . ."—ALS, DNA, RG 94, Correspondence, USMA. On Dec. 23, Orville E. Babcock wrote to Secretary of War William W. Belknap. "The President desires you to call especial attention to the application of Mr. David L. Kay (meant for *David G. Ray*) for appointment of his son as a Cadet at West Point when appointments are next made."—LS, *ibid.* John B. Ray entered USMA but did not graduate.

1874, Nov. 28. Lucien Adam, Nancy, France, to USG. "I have the honor to inform Your Excellency that the American Society of France and the Academy of Stanislaus have taken the initiative in calling an internation-congress, to be composed of persons interested in the ancient history of America, the interpretation of its written monuments, and the languages the ethnography of the indigenous races. The numerous letters of acceptance which have already been received by the committee of organization already assure the success of this great enterprise, whereby European science gives a further proof of the interest which it takes in the study of American antiquities. It is with a feeling of entire confidence that we beg you, Mr. President, to grant your powerful protection and your high patronage to the first Congress of Americanists. We trust that Your Excellency will deign to recommend a work which directly interests the inhabitants of the new world to the members of your government, and we entertain the hope that the United States will be well represented, at this international congress, by its men of science; also, that the second congress of Americanists will meet in one of the large cities of the United States."—ALS (in French), DNA, RG 59, Miscellaneous Letters; translation, *ibid.* A descriptive brochure is *ibid.* See *New York Times*, June 13, 1875. On March 1, 1876, promoters of a second "Congress of Americanists" in Luxemburg wrote to USG seeking U.S. support.—LS (in French), DNA, RG 59, Miscellaneous Letters; translation, *ibid.* A brochure is *ibid.*

[*1874, Nov.*].   USG endorsement. "Refered to the Sec. of the Treas. I understand Miss Clarke was discharged when the number of employees was reduced. Can she be reinstated now?"—AE (initialed, docketed Nov. 14), DNA, RG 56, Applications. Written on an undated letter from Susie C. Clarke, "Neice Gov Shepherd," Washington, D. C., to USG. "Several weeks ago you promised me to speak to Genl Spinner in my behalf. As he was absent at the time I fear it has escaped your memory, and therefore take the liberty of reminding you of it. If you can spare as much time, I would like to see you for a few minutes."—ALS, *ibid.* No appointment followed.

1874, Nov.   John D. Ruff, Philadelphia, to USG. "When I had the honor, in August last, to make an application to you in person, at your cottage at Long Branch, for the appointment of 'Cadet, to the U. S. Military Academy at West Point,' for June 1875, you were kind enough to direct me to remind you of myself, and make to you, a *written* application after your return to Washington, in October. I take the liberty of doing so now, and to repeat here, that I am the son of Genl C. F. Ruff, U. S. Army, who has served his country, actively in the field for more than a quarter of a century. That I was born, at a Frontier Military Post, in New Mexico; am without Congressional representation, or influence, and must therefore rely entirely, on your kindness, for the success of this application—I have been for the past two years, a pupil of the 'Philadelphia High School;' am in the 17th year of my age; can furnish testimonials of good, & moral conduct; studious habits, & fair scholarship—I am very earnest in my desire to be appointed a Cadet, at the Military Academy, & will always endeavor to merit, the great favor I now ask of you."—ALS, DNA, RG 94, Correspondence, USMA. A related letter is *ibid.* Ruff entered USMA in 1876 but did not graduate.

On Dec. 11, 1866, Charles F. Ruff, USMA 1838, Washington, D. C., had written to Brig. Gen. John A. Rawlins requesting assignment in Philadelphia. ". . . I have been on the retired list of the Army for nearly three years & am perhaps the only retired officer who is not now, or has not been during any part of that period placed 'on duty—' my necessities compel me now to ask this—"—ALS, *ibid.*, Letters Received, 501R 1866. On the same day, USG endorsed this letter. "Refered to the Adj. Gn. to make the assignment if the duty can be given either for the recruiting service, or as member of the Retiring Board or other duty required to be done by a Commissioned Officer."—AES, *ibid.*

1874, DEC. 2.   Sarah F. McBurney, Okawville, Ill., to USG. "Please pardon this intrusion upon your fully occupied time   Hope and trust is my apology. As I am making one more effort in behalf of the children of my half brother David

Bayles, and wish to leave nothing undone on my part. . . . I thus address you, knowing of your personal acquaintance with Mr Bayles therefore I think you will be cognizant of the case, when it is presented to your mind afresh. I believe, that you remarked, at the Soldiers' Orphans Home when visiting that place, that the greatest trouble in this case, originated in the fact that one Col. had been paid for the 11th Regt. and you thought it could only be remedied by an act of Congress. How that may be I cannot tell, but I do know, that Col. Bayles was reinstated to the command of the 11th Regt. Mo. Vols. but was never able to take command of it in person   After a severe and painful illness of fourteen months, during which time I was his constant watcher, he died without ever realizing, his abitious hopes, either for himself or his country. And his children have never been comforted in any way by the Government, for the loss of their sacrificed father   Will you, Honored Sir, Plase kindly, give this case a moment of your attention, and inform me what measures may be taken, if indeed any can, in order to obtain the back pay of Col. Bayles, and a pension for his children, as p[er]haps his only son might be entitled to a Soldiers' Land Warrent, if all else fails . . ."—ALS, DNA, RG 48, Miscellaneous Div., Letters Received.

1874, DEC. 8.   To Congress transmitting a State Dept. report on consular fees collected in 1873.—Copies, DNA, RG 59, Reports to the President and Congress; *ibid.*, RG 130, Messages to Congress. *HED*, 43-2-8.

1874, DEC. 8.   To Senate. "I transmit to the Senate for consideration, with a view to ratification, a Convention concluded between the United States of America and the Mexican Republic on the 20th of November last, for extending the time for the duration of the Joint Commission respecting claims originally fixed by the Convention between the United States and Mexico signed on the 4th of July, 1868, and extended by those of the 19th April, 1871, and 27th November, 1872 between the same parties."—Copies, DNA, RG 59, Reports to the President and Congress; *ibid.*, RG 130, Messages to Congress. On Nov. 19, USG had authorized Secretary of State Hamilton Fish to negotiate this convention.—DS, DLC-Hamilton Fish. On Jan. 20, 1875, the Senate ratified the agreement. See *PUSG*, 21, 356–57.

On Dec. 11, Philip B. Fouke, Washington, D. C., wrote to USG concerning payments awarded to Americans for Mexican claims.—LS, DNA, RG 59, Miscellaneous Letters.

1874, DEC. 8.   To Senate. "In answer to the Resolution of the Senate of the 3rd of February 1873, I transmit, herewith, a report from the Secretary of State, together with the papers which accompanied it."—Copies, DNA, RG 59, Reports to the President and Congress; *ibid.*, RG 130, Messages to Congress. *SED*, 43-2-3. On the same day, Secretary of State Hamilton Fish had written to USG concerning Mexican records and documents relating to land in Arizona and New Mexico Territories.—*Ibid.*; copy, DNA, RG 59, Reports of the President and Congress.

1874, DEC. 8.   To Senate. "I transmit to the Senate for consideration, with a view to ratification, a Convention between the United States of America and the

Ottoman Empire, relative to the naturalization of citizens and subjects of the two countries, signed by their respective plenipotentiaries at Constantinople on the 11th of August last. A copy of the correspondence which accompanied the Convention on the subject is herewith transmitted."—Copies, DNA, RG 59, Reports to the President and Congress; *ibid.*, RG 130, Messages to Congress. On Jan. 22, 1875, the Senate amended and ratified this convention. See *Senate Executive Journal,* XIX, 490–91.

On Dec. 8, 1874, USG had written to the Senate. "I transmit to the Senate for consideration, with a view to ratification, a Convention between the United States of America and the Ottoman Empire, relative to the extradition of criminals, fugitives from justice, signed by their respective plenipotentiaries at Constantinople on the 11th of August last."—Copies, DNA, RG 59, Reports to the President and Congress; *ibid.*, RG 130, Messages to Congress. On Jan. 20, 1875, the Senate ratified this convention.

1874, DEC. 9. Secretary of the Interior Columbus Delano to Orville E. Babcock concerning arrangements for USG to meet a Navajo delegation.—Telegram received, DNA, RG 107, Telegrams Collected (Bound). On the same day, Babcock telegraphed to Delano. "Twelve o'clock to-morrow will be agreeable to the President"—LS (telegram sent), *ibid.* A newspaper reported on Dec. 10. "Secretary Delano, Commissioner Smith and Governor Arny, accompanied by a delegation of Navajo Indians and interpreters, visited the Executive mansion to-day and had a long conference with the President. The Indians laid before the President a series of complaints relative to their lands, their children held in captivity by their enemies in New Mexico, and depredations committed by Mormons and miners prospecting for gold. The President listened very patiently, and in reply referred the delegation to the Secretary of the Interior and the Commissioner of Indian Affairs, whom he said would take the necessary steps to right their wrongs. The President also gave the Indians some good advice relative to their own conduct. Among other things he advised them to stay upon their reservations, cultivate their lands, and fit themselves and their descendants to be come citizens of the United States."—*Washington Evening Star,* Dec. 10, 1874.

1874, DEC. 9. Isaac Errett, editor, *Christian Standard* (Cincinnati), Chicago, to USG. "I take pleasure in stating that Rev. G. G. Mullins is a regularly ordained minister in the Church of Disciples, commonly known as the Christian Church, and is in good standing and acceptable alike as a Christian gentleman and a minister. He is a Kentuckian, a graduate and an A. M. of Kentucky University, and has been an acceptable and popular minister in Philadelphia, Pa., Syracuse, N. Y., Covington & Louisville, Ky. As a cultivated, generous and earnest Christian man, he is entitled to confidence, and as a chaplain would win his way to the hearts of the soldiers. It ought not, perhaps, to be, that *political* considerations should enter into such an appointment, but I regard it as a high *moral* consideration that during the war, and before it, when it cost something in Ky. to be true to our common country & to humanity, Mr. Mullins was thus true & faithfully."—ALS, DNA, RG 94, ACP, 5053 1874. On Dec. 22, USG nominated George G. Mullins as chaplain, 25th Inf.

1874, DEC. 11.   To N. Newlin Stokes, Cinnaminson, N. J. "I am in receipt of your very kind note of the 3d inst. I am obliged to you for the support extended and for the kindness that prompted you to write the letter."—Copy, DLC-USG, II, 2. See *New York Times*, April 20, 1905.

1874, DEC. 11.   Mary J. Rittenhouse, Newfield, N. Y., to USG concerning a widow's pension. ". . . In the name of humanity will my little ones have to suffer another long long winter for the comforts of life & the government abundantly able to pay them what belongs to them & still it is withheld from them & why because it is a little matter with them. . . . I never aske the goverment for one cent untill the last dollar was gone   I had no friends to take me in   I have no one to look to for help . . . if you have the least sympathy left for the widow & orphans that have been made so by this cruel war May the Lord or some other good spirit help you to manifest it. 10 moments of your time spent would se-cure to me what lawfully belongs to me & make me & my children comfortable for life: . . ."—ALS, DNA, RG 48, Miscellaneous Div., Letters Received. As of Jan. 1875, Rittenhouse received twelve dollars per month.

1874, DEC. 15.   U.S. Senator Oliver P. Morton of Ind. to USG recommending Thomas J. Brady, "now Consul at St. Thomas," as minister to Ecuador.—LS, DNA, RG 59, Applications and Recommendations. On Jan. 19, 1875, Morton again wrote to USG. "The name of Mr Maney of Tennessee nominated as Min-ister to Ecuador having been withdrawn I beg leave to call your attention to the recommendations for Col T. J. Brady to that position"—ALS, *ibid.* Related pa-pers are *ibid.* On Dec. 8, USG nominated Brady as supervisor of Internal Reve-nue. See *PUSG*, 22, 400.

1874, DEC. 15.   Palmer Tilton, Washington, D. C., to USG. "I have the honor to make application, for appointment in the Army as Second Lieutenant of In-fantry. I was born in Massachusetts, I am twenty-two years old, and am very desirous of serving in the Army. Praying that my request may receive your kind consideration and approval, . . ."—ALS, DNA, RG 94, ACP, 4527 1875. On Dec. 17, the docket was endorsed. "Filed by Hon B. F. Butler . . . Mark 'Special' on list—"—E, *ibid.* On Sept. 20, 1875, Secretary of War William W. Belknap wrote a note. "The President directs that Palmer Tilton (whose name is on list) be examined for appt as 2d Lieutenant. His name is, I believe, on the list—"— ANS, *ibid.* On Dec. 6, USG nominated Tilton as 2nd lt., 20th Inf., as of Oct. 15.

1874, DEC. 15.   Martha Custis Williams, Georgetown, D. C., to USG. "The object of my visit to you is to present the claims and plead the cause of my Brother Maj. Lawrence A Williams formerly of the 6th Cavalry U S Army who was as he believes most unjustly dropped from the Army during the reign of Mr Staunton. He was not officially notefied of his dismissal and no reason for it was given either to himself or others. He demanded a court of inquiry and a court martial and both were refused. . . . My Brother was aid to Gen McClellan during the War and I have a letter from the Gen. at that time, expressing the highest appreciation of his character as an officer and a gentleman. I have there-fore come to you Gen. Grant as an old army officer and as I believe one of my

Brother's regiment, to plead his cause with you and to ask that this record against his name which he feels to be so unjust may be blotted out, and that for his Fathers' sake who so gallantly gave his life for his Country in Mexico, he may be restored, for the few years that he will probably have to live, to the retired list of the Army."—ALS, DNA, RG 94, ACP, 4606 1871. On Jan. 12, 1875, Secretary of War William W. Belknap wrote to Williams "that the President has considered your application, but it is not within his power to grant your request —the only way your brother can be restored is by an Act of Congress."—LS (press), *ibid.* Lawrence A. Williams, USMA 1852, failed to secure favorable congressional action. See *HRC*, 44-1-482; *SRC*, 45-2-466.

1874, DEC. 16.   USG pardon. "Whereas, on the 29th day of July, 1874, in the United States District Court for the first Judicial District of the Territory of New Mexico, one Andres Sanchez was convicted of selling liquor to Indians, and was sentenced to be imprisoned for three months, and to pay a fine of one hundred dollars;—And whereas, he has served out his term of imprisonment; —And whereas, his pardon is recommended by the Hon: S. B. Elkins, M. C., United States Attorney Catron and the Hon: William Breeden, Attorney General of New Mexico:—Now, therefore, be it known, that I, . . . grant to the said Andres Sanchez, a full and unconditional pardon. . . ."—Copy, DNA, RG 59, General Records.

1874, DEC. 17.   Esther S. Collard, Thornton, Mich., to USG. "I take my Pen in hand to right to you to see if thair cant be somthn Don in be half of myself my husban Drinks up Evey sent he git from the goverment   he gits 24 dols a month   he dont drow a Sober Breth as long as it last . . ."—ALS, DNA, RG 48, Miscellaneous Div., Letters Received.

1874, DEC. 21.   Levi P. Luckey to William Borden, New York City. "The President directs me to acknowledge the receipt of your polite invitation to be present on the occasion of the 69th anniversary of the New-England Society, in the city of New-York, on to-morrow evening, and convey to you and the members of the Society his sincere thanks, and his regrets that his public duties just at this time prevent his attendance. He desires me to say that it would have given him great pleasure to be able to comply with the invitation, and he was in hopes he might be able to do so, but it is impossible."—*Sixty-Ninth Anniversary Celebration of the New-England Society* . . . (New York, 1874), p. 85. Borden had written to USG inviting him to the anniversary dinner.—William Evarts Benjamin, Catalogue No. 27, Nov., 1889, p. 5. See *New York Times*, Dec. 23, 1874.

1874, DEC. 26.   Attorney Gen. George H. Williams to USG. "I have the honor to return herewith Senate Bill, No 974, and to inform you that in my opinion there are no objections to its receiving your approval."—LS, OFH. For the bill concerning jurors in D. C., see *U.S. Statutes at Large*, XVIII, part 3, p. 293.

1874, DEC. 26.   Orville E. Babcock to Brewster & Co., New York City. "The President will be pleased if you will make for him, to be ready when he goes to Long Branch for the summer a top buggy, suitable in width and strength to carry two heavy persons (say 200 pounds each.) He wants it secure for the above weight, and no heavier than necessary for security. Make it for pole only. He drives with breast plates, same as single harness, the beast yoke to use with breast plate harnesses."—Copy, DLC-USG, II, 2. On Dec. 29, 1874, and March 23, 1875, Babcock again wrote to Brewster & Co. "The President says his harness has plain black trimmings, and he will leave the trimmings and color to you to select." "I have to acknowledge the receipt of your favor of the 22d instant and beg to call your attention to the enclosed copy of my letter of 26th Dec. last. By yours of yesterday there would appear to be a misunderstanding as to whether the President wished pole or shafts, for you say that you have reduced the price &c &c 'with shafts' to $460. You will see by the enclosed copied letter that his order was 'for pole only.'. . . P. S The President is pleased to know the buggy is completed, and will send word when to send it to the Branch."—Copies, *ibid.*

1874, DEC. 29. USG endorsement. "Refered to the Sec. of War. The Rev. Mr. Reese may be ordered to his home to report as required by regulations from month to month his condition."—AES, DNA, RG 94, ACP, 2405 1871. Written on a letter of Dec. 26 from Aquila A. Reese, Philadelphia, to USG. "Having reached the age (62) at which the President may, 'at his discretion,' retire an army officer, I very respectfully present this my application to be placed on the retired list of the Army. I have been a Minister of the Gospel for more than forty (40) years, and the last thirteen (13) years I have served as Post Chaplain in the Army; the greater portion of that time I have spent on the frontier. I am getting old, and besides I am suffering from heart disease, which incapacitates me for duty. I have been absent from my post, on Surgeon's certificate of disability, since Oct. 19 last, and medical officers give it as their opinion that I will never be fit for duty again. In view of these facts, I hope the President will grant my request to be placed on the retired list, provided a vacancy Exists—or if there be none at present, then I most respectfully request that I be ordered to my home to await the occurrence of a vacancy."—LS, *ibid.* Bishops Matthew Simpson and Edward R. Ames favorably endorsed this letter.—ES, *ibid.* On Jan. 26, 1866, Reese, post chaplain, Fort McHenry, Md., had written to USG urging more prominent rank and emoluments for army chaplains.—ALS, *ibid.*, RG 108, Letters Received. On March 24, 1876, Secretary of War Alphonso Taft wrote to AG Edward D. Townsend. "The President directs the retirement from active service of Chaplain A. A. Reese, U. S. A., provided he cannot be assigned to duty at Fort McHenry. If he cannot be so assigned, the Adjutant General will notify me of the fact & issue the order of retirement"—LS, *ibid.*, RG 94, ACP, 2405 1871. Papers reflecting uncertainty about Reese's age and eligibility for retirement are *ibid.* Reese retired as of March 2, 1877, and died on March 7, 1878.

1874, DEC. 29. Culver C. Sniffen to A. S. Barnes & Co., New York City. "Enclosed please find Draft on N. Y. to your order for $5. amount of the subscription of the President to the International Review. Please send me receipted bill." —Copy, DLC-USG, II, 2.

1874, DEC. 30.   Levi P. Luckey to Lewis Wallace, Boston. "The President directs me to say that he has read your letter of the 19th instant together with the copy, which you had prepared, of what you proposed using in your speech on the 5th of January in relation to your trip to Mexico in 1865. The President desires me first to express his regret that your letter did not receive his earlier attention so that a reply could have been sent to you at Crawfordsville. He authorizes me to say that he perceives no statement of fact in your copy which he would change at all, and that as for the portion relating to your visit in Mexico and your return you of course are the best judge. The President gave the suject of the French occupation of Mexico much study, and thought and sympathized most warmly with the cause of the Republicans, as he could not but look upon the war upon them as being also directed against ourselves."—Copy, DLC-USG, II, 2. Wallace delivered "Mexico and the Mexicans" during a speaking tour. A copy of the speech sent to USG is in InHi. See Robert E. and Katharine M. Morsberger, *Lew Wallace: Militant Romantic* (New York, 1980), p. 241.

1874, DEC. 31.   To Maj. George H. Elliot (USMA 1855). "I am in receipt of the Copy of your Report on Light Houses, and am obliged to you for sending it. I shall read it with much pleasure."—Copy, DLC-USG, II, 2. See *SED*, 43-1-54; *European Light-House Systems; Being a Report of a Tour of Inspection Made in 1873* (New York, 1875).

[*1874?*].   USG note. "Returned to the Postmaster, Washington D. C. with request that these letters, which are coming from one to five daily, be no longer forwarded."—ANS (undated), Historical Society of Washington, Washington, D. C.

Index

All letters written by USG of which the text was available for use in this volume are indexed under the names of the recipients. The dates of these letters are included in the index as an indication of the existence of text. Abbreviations used in the index are explained on pp. xvii–xxi. Individual regts. are indexed under the names of the states in which they originated.

Grant, Ellen (Nellie). *See* Sartoris, Ellen Grant

Grant, Frederick Dent (son of USG), 50, 174*n*, 258*n*, 260–61, 261*n*, 265, 367, 386

Grant, Ida H. (daughter-in-law of USG), 258*n*, 260–61, 261*n*

Grant, Jesse Root (father of USG), 79*n*

Grant, Jesse Root, Jr. (son of USG), 148, 148*n*–49*n*, 167, 261, 313

Grant, Julia Dent (wife of USG): brother dies, 50*n*; Philadelphia friends, 54, 55, 81*n*; children marry, 104, 105*n*–6*n*, 260; misses children, 135*n*; travels with USG, 136, 139*n*, 144, 145, 175, 187*n*, 209, 233; monitors son's friend, 148*n*–49*n*; at Long Branch, 166–67; childhood, 203*n*, 422; receives threatening letters, 234*n*; note to, [*Sept. 28, 1874*], 245; questions William T. Sherman, 258*n*; greets King Kalakaua, 297*n*; as hostess, 313, 314, 315; fondly remembered, 394–95; facilitates USMA application, 432; acknowledged kind act, 434; mentioned, 143*n*, 146*n*, 168, 170*n*, 207, 261, 265, 291*n*, 302, 303, 335, 349, 400, 406, 409, 425, 448

Grant, Orvil L. (brother of USG), 364

Grant, Ulysses S.: during *Virginius* affair, 3–5, 5*n*–7*n*; fulfills special requests, 8–9, 9*n*, 351; administers Reconstruction, 9, 9*n*–11*n*, 51–52, 52*n*–53*n*, 61, 61*n*–65*n*, 83–84, 84*n*–87*n*, 87, 87*n*–88*n*, 93, 93*n*–95*n*, 98, 98*n*–99*n*, 99, 99*n*–101*n*, 106–8, 108*n*–10*n*, 156, 157*n*–59*n*, 187–88, 188*n*, 196*n*, 198*n*, 213–14, 214*n*–15*n*, 222*n*–26*n*, 228*n*, 228–29, 234 and *n*, 240*n*, 280–81, 295, 295*n*–96*n*, 304–6, 306*n*–7*n*, 426; impeachment advocated, 14*n*; personal finances, 19, 265 and *n*, 266*n*–67*n*, 270, 324, 448; seeks chief justice, 20, 20*n*–23*n*, 29 and *n*; administers Indian policy, 23, 23*n*–24*n*, 104, 254*n*–57*n*, 257 and *n*, 336, 337, 342–43, 344–47, 353, 355, 356–58, 359–60, 362–63, 375–78, 403, 408, 434–36, 453; owns farm, 31, 56–57, 126–27, 155, 156*n*, 207–8, 262, 265, 266, 268–69, 269*n*, 312, 313*n*, 330; owns horses, 31, 44–45, 56–57, 126–27, 155–56, 156*n*, 232–33, 244, 245*n*, 262, 266, 268, 312, 312*n*–13*n*; advocates currency reform, 32–33, 34, 37–41, 41*n*, 65–67, 68*n*–73*n*, 73–75, 75*n*–76*n*, 114–17, 117*n*, 118*n*–19*n*, 122*n*–23*n*, 272–75; oversees centennial, 34–35, 207, 332; in New York City, 41*n*; issues pardons, 43, 319–20, 328, 341, 350, 356, 386, 392–93, 414, 430, 449, 455; appoints Boston

collector, 45, 45*n*–50*n*; brother-in-law dies, 50 and *n*; during Civil War, 51 and *n*, 181*n*, 193*n*, 219*n*, 269, 335, 369; meddles at USMA, 57–58, 58*n*, 202, 202*n*–3*n*, 209*n*; authorizes emergency relief, 58–59, 450; promotes Civil Service reform, 59–60, 60*n*, 112, 112*n*–13*n*, 283–84; vetoes bills, 73–75, 75*n*–81*n*, 173*n*, 174*n*, 349, 368, 380, 386, 406, 414; annual message, 74, 252*n*–53*n*, 268, 269*n*, 269–70, 271–87, 287*n*, 288*n*, 292–94, 347, 436, 438; mediates Ark. political dispute, 83–84, 84*n*–87*n*, 87, 87*n*–88*n*, 93, 93*n*–95*n*, 98, 98*n*–99*n*, 99, 99*n*–101*n*, 106–8, 108*n*–10*n*; encourages western exploration, 88–89; reviews Fitz John Porter case, 91–92, 92*n*; children marry, 104–5, 105*n*–6*n*, 260–61; third term for, 110*n*, 193*n*, 250*n*, 251*n*, 310*n*, 339, 380, 381, 412–13, 423–25, 438; favors friends, 111, 138*n*–39*n*, 204–5, 205*n*, 206 and *n*, 321, 394; protects Tex. frontier, 113, 114*n*; promotes interoceanic canals, 123, 123*n*–24*n*; praised, 126*n*, 404; implements Treaty of Washington, 128–29, 129*n*, 160–61, 161*n*, 388; administers D.C., 132–33, 134*n*–35*n*, 286; attached to family, 135*n*, 148, 202 and *n*, 203*n*, 260–61; travels to West Va., 136, 137*n*, 138, 139*n*; manages cabinet, 136–37, 137*n*, 140, 140*n*–41*n*, 171*n*–75*n*, 246, 246*n*–48*n*; receives railroad passes, 139*n*; early life, 139*n*, 178*n*, 232–33, 267–68, 328, 338, 358, 394–95, 400, 422, 434, 445; appoints river survey boards, 141, 141*n*–42*n*; invites friends, 144, 166–67, 168, 168–69, 175, 302, 313, 314*n*, 314, 335; at Long Branch, 144, 145*n*, 148, 149, 150, 152*n*, 155, 156, 157*n*, 158*n*, 159*n*, 160*n*, 164, 166, 167, 168, 169, 170, 171*n*, 175, 177*n*, 180, 181 and *n*, 184, 254, 387, 389, 396, 404, 414, 416, 418, 419, 430, 451; replaces minister to Russia, 144–45, 145*n*–47*n*, 151–52, 152*n*–53*n*, 154*n*–55*n*; at Saratoga Springs, N.Y., 145 and *n*, 146*n*, 410, 413, 414; administers Rawlins fund, 149, 149*n*–50*n*; shields Western Union Telegraph Co., 150–51, 151*n*, 164–65, 165*n*–66*n*; confronts Miss. civil unrest, 156, 157*n*–59*n*, 304–6, 306*n*–7*n*; attends army reunions, 159–60, 160*n*, 257–58, 311–12, 430; at Paterson, N.J., 159–60, 160*n*; encourages domestic manufactures, 162, 251, 284–85; dedicates Abraham Lincoln monument, 163, 258–59, 259*n*–60*n*; selects financial agent, 170, 170*n*–71*n*,